MW00450242

FIRST STEPS

The hardest part of writing this book has been figuring out what to say to start it. There is so much to write about. So many thoughts and ideas have relevance, and I had an overwhelming desire to try and say all of it up front. The trail narrative has been relatively easy by comparison. Like the trail, in the narrative the thoughts come in progression, day by day, I just follow the white blazes north.

Ultimately I let the trail narrative speak for itself. It says everything I feel I need to say about the thru-hiking experience. I will have lists and indexes and congealing thoughts in a few chapters at the end, mostly to provide future thru-hikers with some tools to prepare them for their own hikes. Everything is there in the narrative though, the trail will provide.

On the trail you become a new person, one closely related to, but not quite the same as the person you were before you committed yourself to the undertaking. Adopting a trail name is a rite of thru-hiking. Having a new name is a way to recognize your new identity. You will not become an entirely new person on the trail, but within the transitional aspect you can create a separation from the person you have lived inside for your whole life. You have no history with the people on the trail, and your actions and words are going to shape both how they see you and how that reflects upon your view of yourself.

Some people resist the practice, and wish to keep using the names they came on the trail with. I suspect they are the people who are already the happiest with who they are when they come onto the trail. Not every through hiker has a trail name, although most eventually adopt one, if for no other reason than to keep other hikers from constantly trying to pin a new name on them. Many section hikers also adopt trail names, embracing the idea of having a separate identity in the woods.

My trail name is Possible. I had a trail name discussion with my 12 year old daughter who sometimes accompanied me as I was practice hiking in preparation for the trail. She knew I was thinking about trail names; I wanted to have one before I set out so I wouldn't be given something I didn't like. I wanted a trail name that was a positive expression of my hope.

My daughter would ask me on our walks together if I was really going to hike the whole trail. "It's possible" I replied. After one of these exchanges she stopped, and said, 'That's it, that's your trail name. You are Possible."

And so I became Possible.

1

Once I had been hiking for a while and people started to recognize me when I came into camp, I came up with a catch phrase answer.

"Hey, it's Possible"

"Hellz Yeah it's Possible!"

It was both a response and recognition of the greeting, and a statement about the trail itself. In the early days many of us were questioning our ability to complete the entire journey, and my refrain was a statement of intent, a positive comment on achieving the goal.

Hiking the Appalachian Trail is simple. It is as easy as putting your head down and taking one step at a time, five million times. Every climb, every ford, every granite face and rock scramble, one step at a time.

The difficulty is in the repetition, the five million part, not the individual steps themselves. That is where the ordinary becomes epic. There is a cumulative effect, a weariness that becomes a part of you, dull aches and pains that infuse your being. The weariness is offset by a sense of purpose, and punctuated by moments of intense joy. The joy came frequently enough for me that I kept going until all of the miles were behind me.

Every day there was something to make me appreciate what I was doing. Some days it was as simple as listening to a chorus of frogs in a pool or watching how the light moved through the leaves of trees in a breeze. There were constantly places where I stepped out onto a high place and the world lay at my feet. There were fascinating, inspiring people I met, and conversations I treasured.

Some days I had experiences that made me rise into a greater awareness of myself and the world around me. I knew I was having a moment other people would rarely, if ever, come close to. Civilization has removed us from the more basic parts of our natures in some ways, and these are brought back to you during an extended stay in the woods.

You would think that over the course of five million steps great changes would occur in a person, that a greater, improved person would emerge, a person stronger and more capable than the one who started the trail. A common thread among thru-hikers is that they are universally people in transition

The truth for me was that the issues I left behind me when I started the hike were still there when I finished the hike. The act of completing the Appalachian Trail did not provide any answers, and it didn't fix my problems. In fact, they plagued me while I hiked, I couldn't leave them behind, and they still were waiting for me unresolved when I stepped back into the world.

What the hike gave me as a person was a greater belief in myself. I conquered distance, mountains, weather, and myself to walk five million steps through the forest. The accomplishment is real, and it can't be taken away from me. I thru-hiked the Appalachian Trail.

Hellz Yeah it's Possible.

WHY I HIKED

Thru-hikers are a varied group of people, but they are all engaged individually in a common endeavor. As such, there are certain shared ideals and attitudes towards the world. The number one shared characteristic of a thru-hiker is that thru-hikers are individuals at a transitional point in their life. Something is occurring that has made them carve out a significant block of time to challenge themselves against nature.

In my case it was a several events, which is not uncommon. I had the dream of thru-hiking the trail since I was 12 years old, when a thru-hiker came and talked about his experience at a Scout meeting. In the intervening 40 years I hiked small sections of the trail and read books about the topic.

The events that pushed me out onto the trail were not positive ones. I was tired of my civilian job, and had gotten laid off. I was also an Army Reservist, and after 25 years of military service, 21 of it one weekend every month, 2 weeks every summer, countless extra training obligations, and 3 year long deployments into combat zones, I was burned out.

I wasn't the only one who was burned out with my life. The hard work schedules and the weeks, months, and years away had taken a toll on my family life. My wife and I had become combative, and a divorce was very much on the horizon. I was still very much attached to a toxic relationship. The kind of determination that allowed me to complete my thru-hike, that made it an imperative to finish, also made it difficult to walk away from the investment of life and commitment I hade made in my marriage. My hike would give me separation, time to think, and I hoped clear my head and allow me accept failure and follow through on a divorce. And even while I was thinking this, in the back of my head there was still a faint hope that the marriage could somehow be saved.

Taking personal time and space to make the hike was an investment in myself. To some extent, rage was a factor in my decision to go, and kept me moving down the trail It is not an emotion I wanted to embrace, but I was desperately unhappy with how life was turning out. Hiking the trail was a statement, a positive act for myself in a world that felt like it had turned against me. I was cognizant of my anger, and thought the trail was a place I could choose something else emotionally to face the world with. I was minimizing outside influences, and might find a new, better self by immersing myself in a different world. I sought inner peace and a clear head, a chance to be just me, without other people's expectations shaping my perceptions. Paring life back to the basics was going to be my

3

approach to coming to grips with who I was and perhaps find the better person I could be.

THE TRAIL AS AN ENVIRONMENT

One of the things the trail teaches you, and something you don't fully realize until you are home again and readjusting to normal life, is just how disconnected from nature normal life is. To disconnect from normal life for 6 months is a cultural immersion in nature.

You become aware of seasonal, daily, hourly, and momentary changes that are unscripted and often are unexpected, some great, and some small. Your experience changes with the environment. You are no longer are protected. Weather changes in instant; winds, rain, hail, and sunshine can all be a part of your life within a single hour. Light changes slowly through the day as the sun rises, moves across the sky shrinking then lengthening shadows, until dusk eases into darkness. Temperature changes, and ice turns to water turns to humidity.

The world becomes a big place again. Instead of zipping from one locality to another in an automobile, you walk. Walking is slow; you truly experience distance and the time it takes to get places. From a mountaintop you can see the ridges you have spent days crossing behind you, and days more of hills ahead. The landscape becomes real, not a scene flowing effortlessly by the car window but solid ground you have to move across in a long sweating exertion, five million real steps in the real world.

Unfortunately, even on the Appalachian Trail we are still just visitors to the natural world. We are no longer an integral part of that world, living within and as part of the environment. We are outsiders in someone else's house. We are not direct players in the game, just watchers. Our support comes from without, requiring frequent periodic returns to our own land for resources. Food at a minimum, along with other expendables like cooking fuel, lighters, toothpaste, Dr. Bonners soap, toilet paper, hand sanitizer etc, require a trip into town and away from the trail even if it is for an afternoon. The land does not directly sustain us.

Sometimes the trail is a dangerous place. People die on the trail, sometimes through mishap, being in the wrong place at the wrong time, or ignorance. There is wildlife, weather, and terrain that all can fell you, injuring you or even killing you. It may seem scary, but it really is not any different than living in the city, where there are plenty of ways to die as well. We are just more familiar with the manmade landscape, recognize the dangers and are adapted to them. We have to learn the same things about the Appalachian Trail when we enter the woods,

THRU-HIKERS

There have been a number of demographic studies conducted on the thru-hiker community. There are all kinds of statistical data on the population. Thru-hikers may be limited in numbers, but regenerate each year anew, providing a discrete population every year within a particular time frame and event. I suppose we are an interesting group to study.

Because it is a moving population, and some of the members eschew attention, the numbers will never be entirely correct. Even the number of hikers completing a thru-hike in any given year is debatable, a rough estimate. Some people avoid being recorded. They don't want their highly personal experience to be reduced to a statistic. Some hikers just don't want to be known, and follow one of the tenants of the trail and they Leave No Trace.

I myself had to work to get counted. I didn't start at Amicalola Falls, and didn't sign in at the Springer Mountain register. I didn't announce myself by writing in a register until two days into the hike. I was too busy hiking, camping, and adapting to take the time.

Some things are known. The thru-hiking population is mostly white and middle class. It was for years predominantly male, but that has been changing, and a much greater proportion is now female. Perhaps as many as 4 in 10 thrus are now women. It is difficult for people to take six months off in the middle of life and work obligations, so most thru-hikers are young and searching out the world, or have retired.

OTHER PEOPLE

I think I am nicer to strangers now. I noticed it when I got home.

Thru-hikers are hard to separate from homeless people, really. We are dirty, smelly and unshaven, in ripped and tattered clothes, carrying our house on our back. Occasionally I was made very aware that I was a not entirely welcome outsider when I re-entered civilization. Many of the people we had to interact with off of the trail were in positions where they had to be polite, but it was obvious it was forced. Store and postal clerks, taxi and bus drivers, hotel clerks, and waiters and waitresses were correct rather than friendly. Some people didn't even make an effort to be polite and showed their disdain openly.

I understand some of the homeless person's plight. To be treated as awkward and unwanted, to be shuffled off out of sight at the earliest opportunity, was a new thing for me. To be treated as a problem rather than a person, something we are all familiar with when we are confronted by bureaucracy, is diminishing. When it is not just systems, but people who treat you as a problem, it eats at your identity.

Fortunately, I had an identity that was strong enough to counteract the reaction. I was a thru-hiker, a person having an adventure that most of the people I was offending would never even think of attempting. I could bear their discomfort and antipathy by reminding myself why I was receiving their scorn. I was striving for personal greatness, and some dirt and odor was part of my struggle.

Some thru-hikers responded to the negative reactions by throwing their otherness in the face of those displaying their distaste. The hikers were loud and rude, demanding the attention the townspeople did not want to give them by pushing their dirtiness and funk forward as a badge of pride.

My own reaction to antipathy was to be extremely polite. I tried to present myself as an example of a thru-hiker that was understanding and patient with those who had to serve me. Sometimes the effort was rewarded by a more patient friendliness.

There is another side, a more positive discovery that goes along with being a smelly vagabond. You learn that the kindness of people is genuine. There are an amazing number of people who will reach out and help people, who are friendly and helpful to hikers without any thought of reward. I had people go far out of their way to help me in one way or another. When it was juxtaposed against a background of suspicion and hostility, it was surprising. Random acts of kindness were frequent, and actually more the norm than scorn.

Some kindness was not random. People, communities, and organizations set up planned food events along the trail, provided shuttle services, and opened the doors of their homes, churches, and business to support hikers. Many of them had some connection with the trail, but some of them just wanted to help, to be a small part of our experience.

It is easy to fall back and exclude strangers, it may be safer, but it limits your life experiences. I was more closed to others when I came onto the trail. I was taught acceptance by receiving it all along the way.

THE BEGINNING

LEAVE NO TRACE (LNT)
Leave only footprints, take only pictures.

The following guidance is from a USFS Wilderness Area trailhead sign:

You are one of many who use and enjoy this trail. Follow these simple tips to leave no trace of your visit.

Stay On The Trail

Pack Out All Of Your Trash: including food scraps, aluminum and cigarette butts.

Bury Human Waste: Dig a small cat hole about six inches deep and at least 200 feet away from a water source, then bury everything, including toilet paper.

Respect Wildlife and Plants While You Visit Their Home.

Control Pets at All Times: or leave them at home. Clean up after your pet and pack it out.

Protect The Soundscape: by allowing natures sounds to prevail, Respect others primitive experience.

Preserve Your Heritage. Do not remove artifacts from the forest.

Selecting A Campsite: Camp on durable surfaces; select a site where people have camped before.

Cooking And Campfires: If you are cooking use a backpackers stove to minimize your impact. If you must have a campfire, keep it small and safe. Make sure it is dead out before leaving.

Care, Share and Protect; Your actions make a difference

GETTING STARTED

There is some moment in time when a thru-hiker chooses to hike the Appalachian Trail. It is a great undertaking for an individual and there has to be a point when a person makes a decision to make a dream become a reality.

The common theme I saw in thru-hikers, who are a very varied lot in personalities, was their transitory situation. They were moving from one stage of life to another, and somewhere in the moment they decided to hike the Appalachian Trail. Many people had planned it for a while, but there were a few who just decided to go on a whim, throwing a pack together overnight and heading for Georgia. Most of us had nowhere better to be.

My own moment came in the summer of 2014. I dreamed of thru-hiking for almost as long as I can remember, I hiked sections of the Appalachian Trail while I was a young man living on the East Coast, and there were occasional reminders as I grew older. I read books on the subject, I went on smaller backpacking trips all around the country, and always the great hike was out there, waiting.

I had a bad summer in 2014. I actually had some bad years. The culmination of unhappiness in my careers, and the decline of my home life were overwhelming me. My wife was becoming a stranger to me, and in some ways I was becoming a stranger to myself. I wanted to make a great change in my life, to have some special time that was just mine.

I met a hiker over the summer, another Army officer, who was planning a thru-hike of the Long Trail in Vermont. My own long held dream of thru-hiking the Appalachian Trail started to surface.

Sometime during the summer my dream coalesced. I talked to my wife and got her acceptance, if not her understanding. My ROTC job was laying off contractors, and I let myself be put on the list, letting go of my seniority. I also processed the paperwork to go to inactive status in the Army Reserve.

I was free, and I had enough money saved to go. I got myself ready.

I bought several packs, and tried out all sorts of outdoor equipment trying to decide on my gear. I built spreadsheets comparing equipment loads, costs, and weights. I read every book on the Appalachian Trail and backpacking I could get my hands on. I planned, and I planned.

And I went.

FORMAT:

The book is written in two sections. The first and largest is the trail narrative describing my journey day by day. I took notes each night I was on the trail, and sometimes my notes were incomplete, or a little inaccurate. I have done my very best to keep it true.

I wrote the trail narrative so as to provide as much information as possible about the Appalachian Trail while still keeping it an entertaining adventure. I have recorded every day I was on the trail, and there can be a certain monotony to the daily log. There are plenty of days with interesting happenings, and every day was an adventure, but from a readers standpoint some of the days will have a deja vu quality.

I start each day with a header dividing the hike by the number of days thus far on the trail, the actual date, the location, the total overall miles on the Appalachian Trail, and mileage hiked on the trail for that day. I periodically sum up the same information along with mileage averages, so anyone considering the hike themselves will have the progress of a slow but successful hiker as a measure for their own planning. I only track actual miles on the Appalachian Trail, and do not include trail mileage to and from shelters and water sources and other side trips, or miles to and from trailheads for resupply

Actual mileages are approximate, for a number of other reasons. The trail is a walking trail with any number of obstacles and small deviations that make it hard to get exact mileages. The two primary guides, AWOL and ATC, differ from point to point on trail mileage. On occasion I stopped for the night at unmarked locations, and have had to estimate mileage.

I am including definitions of commonly used trail terms and abbreviations under the heading TRAILTALK the first time they appear in the narrative. All of the terms are listed again in a glossary following the trail narrative at the back of the book.

At the back of the book I have a section called "If You Go". It is meant to provide information specific to backpacking and thru-hiking the AT, for people seeking help with their own preparations for outdoor adventure. I include my gear list, item by item, a typical food pack out, and other useful information for prospective thru-hikers.

If you have been thinking about going on a thru-hike or other adventure, stop thinking about it and go.

GEORGIA

Day 1 to Day 8, April 6th to April 13th
Springer Mountain to Hiawassee GA,
TRAIL MILES 0.0 to 69.6 miles, AVG 8.7 Daily Miles

Day 0-4, April 6th to April 9th
Springer Mountain Summit to Neel's Gap, Trail Mile 0.0 to 31.7
31.7 miles, AVG 7.9 miles per day

0 DAY, April 5th, Easter Sunday
Dahlonega, GA

TRAILTALK:

SPRINGER: Springer Mountain, the southern terminus and start of the Appalachian Trail for North Bound hikers.
TRAIL TOWN: A town on or near the Appalachian Trail that supports backpacking and trail activities. Some receive an official designation by the ATC by meeting certain requirements.

I flew into Atlanta Airport on Easter Sunday. I had very little with me. I was already wearing my hiking clothes and everything else was in my pack, which was checked. I picked it up at the baggage claim and went outside.

My mother, dressed in the black clericals and white collar of an Episcopal Priest, was waiting at the curbside pick up in her little red Subaru. She came all the way from coastal North Carolina to pick me up at the airport in Atlanta and see me off at the first trailhead of the Appalachian Trail.

She tells me the story of how she knew how long I had held an Appalachian Trail thru-hike as a dream in my heart as we drive north from the airport. She reminded me of a day when I was still a Cub Scout. Our pack had brought in a thru-hiker as a speaker, and I came home then, at all of 10 years of age, and announced I was going to hike the Appalachian Trail. Here I am, 41 years later, with my mother driving me up to Dahlonega and Springer Mountain. It is really happening.

Dahlonega itself is a little tourist town, where people can leave Atlanta for a weekend getaway. It has a charming downtown, an eclectic mix of old buildings and shops, and has some awareness of the Appalachian Trail and other hiking areas nearby. There are a couple of outfitters, which are closed for Easter Sunday. I couldn't bring alcohol for my stove on the aircraft flying in, and I find a bottle of isopropyl (rubbing) alcohol at the Dollar General. I can't resist adding just one or two more Snickers Bars to my already over laden backpack.

We have dinner together at a country style restaurant and sleep at a Holiday Inn Express. I attack the bagels and cereal at the free breakfast bar the following morning like it is my last meal. My mother feeds my excitement about the trail on this last day, asking me questions about my preparations and what I am expecting. She is a great morale boost.

Day 1, April 6th
Springer Summit to Stover Creek Shelter, Trail Mile 2.8
Daily Distance 2.8 miles

TRAILTALK:

AT (Appalachian Trail): The 2189.2 mile continuous hiking trail stretching from Springer Mountain in Georgia to Mount Katahdin in Maine.
THRU-HIKER: A hiker attempting to hike the entire distance of the Appalachian Trail. They are going all the way through. This can be done in a single season, or as a series of sections.
SECTION HIKER: A hiker doing a section of the Appalachian Trail.
NoBo: North bounder, a thru-hiker starting at Springer heading to Maine.
SoBo: South bounder, a thru-hiker starting on Maine and heading towards Springer Mountain in Georgia.
ATC (Appalachian Trail Conservancy): The organization which maintains oversight of the Appalachian Trail.
AWOL Guide: David Miller's mile by mile guide to the trail mapped by elevation profile and distance on the trail
TRAIL REGISTER: A book and a pen are kept in each shelter, and many hostels, along the Appalachian Trail. Hikers will provide information about trail conditions and write their thoughts and reflections down. By making entries a hiker also establishes a last known point if they disappear. Also called a trail log.

Most people start the Appalachian Trail in Georgia in the early spring, and head north in one continuous journey to Maine. The Appalachian Trail Conservancy (ATC), the organization that has overall oversight of the trail, and maintains records, says 87 percent of thru-hikers start in Georgia, These people are known as NoBos, trail language for north bounder.

There are a couple of major advantages to starting the Appalachian Trail as a NoBo. Time is a critical factor, it is a long hike through mountains, and best not done in winter. An earlier start is possible in Georgia. Even though the weather is bad in early spring in the south, it is survivable, and the trail is open.

In Maine, Mount Katahdin will not officially open until June 1st, two or three months after most people want to start their thru-hikes, and even fast SOBOs (South Bounders) can find themselves unable to complete their hikes until November or December. I passed by two SOBOs still trying to finish their thru-hike during my first month of the trail.

The terrain in Maine and New Hampshire is the most difficult on the trail, and in some of the most inaccessible sections. Facing it in late summer or early fall after hiking 1800 miles is a challenge. Starting the trail there is a whole new level of difficulty. Most SOBOs are aware of the additional challenge of a SOBO hike, at least intellectually. I think the initial drop out rate for SOBOs is even higher than that of NoBos.

Amicalola Falls State Park is where most NoBos begin their hike. The actual beginning of the trail on Springer Mountain has no road to it. You must hike in. There are some unimproved forest roads that will get you closer, but the Amicalola Falls State Park approach trail is the most common start point. There is a visitor center and bunkroom lodge at the base parking lot, a pack scale, and a register. It is another 8.9 miles from the visitor center parking lot to reach the summit of Springer. The approach trail from Amicalola is fairly challenging for an out of shape aspiring thru-hiker, and includes a 600 step stairway next to the water falls, followed by a more gradual but continual incline up to the official start at the Springer Mountain summit. The approach trail is enough of a challenge that it deters a significant percentage of hikers from continuing further. Aspiring thru-hikers turn around and stagger back down to the Amicalola Falls visitor center, defeated by the initial experience, before setting a foot on the actual Appalachian Trail.

Statistics on the trail are voluntary, based on trail log sign-ins, and a certain amount of guessing is involved. Of the 6500 or so thru-hike attempts estimated in my year 2015, a quarter, or 1600 people, quit in the first 4 days. Some turned around on day one. Most of the early bailouts get to Neel's Gap, a point 32 miles down trail and the first real opportunity to use a well traveled, paved road to return back to civilization. In four days they get a good taste of what lies ahead.

There are several shelters and campsites near the summit, including Black Gap Shelter on the approach trail, Springer Mountain Shelter at the summit, and another at Stover Creek. Hawk Mountain Shelter, 7 miles in and nearly 16 miles from Amicalola, is a common goal for most hiker's first day, and a few actually get that far. Most end up at, or camped near one of the sites closer to the summit.

Personally, I missed Amicalola Falls State Park. I thought I would skip the dubious pleasures of climbing 600 stairs and come in from United States Forest Service FS Road 42 at Big Stamp Gap, a mile to the north of Springer, and backtrack to the summit. I would add a mile to my start, but skip most of the approach trail, and get a little jump start on my thru-hike.

Skipping Amicalola Falls turned out to be one of the biggest regrets of my entire thru-hike. I hoped to save a few miles, but I missed the start off experience. You sign in at a register there, and weigh your pack. There is lodging, a bunkroom, and a restaurant. It is a good place to begin, and is a shared initial experience for most NoBos.

In the event, I got lost trying to follow the rather vague map in the AWOL guide of the forest roads leading into the woods from the paved highway. My mother and I plowed down some rough miles of unimproved roads, me driving her little red Subaru along a muddy road barely wider than the car as she served as copilot. She had a rather pale face, and I think her fingers left permanent indentations in the armrest of her car, but she didn't say much. She gasped occasionally at moments when the wheels spun in place or the car slid sideways towards one potential catastrophe or another. We went through big puddles, and washed out sections of road, eyeing the rather sharp and steep drop-off at the road's edge as we slipped and slid our way forward.

We finally came to a small clearing where there was room for several cars to park. We stopped there to assess the situation, and two backpackers came out of the woods on a blue blazed trail. I meet my first fellow thru-hiker, Yeti. He is a tall, cheerful Viking of a man and is moving along easily under his pack.

I had managed to get us pretty thoroughly lost, and I asked Yeti if he knew where we were. It turned out we were on the approach trail at Nimblewill Gap, rather than where I planned to be, several miles further along the trail. The AWOL Guide sketch of the forest roads didn't show this intersection at all. Nimblewill Gap is on the AT approach trail 2.8 miles south of the summit. From this point I could get to Springer Mountain and the AT start point in an hour of two of hiking.

I decide to forgo further exploration of Georgia's forest service roads and get going. It is already close to noon. I put on my pack, pick up my poles, take a selfie with my mother and receive her priestly blessing. We had a discussion about how she was going to extricate herself from the fine mess I had gotten her into. She urged me onto the trail despite both our misgivings about the roads leading out. I set off down the path following where Yeti had already vanished into the woods. I was on the trail.

The first days on the trail can be pretty awful. You are not in condition yet for the ordeal you are undertaking. Being fit helps. If you run or play an aerobic sport it helps a lot, but nothing really prepares you for the trail like the trail itself.

I had taken steps to prepare myself. I went on daily short hikes with my loaded pack getting myself comfortable with the weight and testing my equipment. There is a mile and a half loop near my house I hiked nearly every day for a month. I occasionally went farther, up to 4 or 5 miles. This was over nice running paths in a neighborhood open space park, or walking on streets and sidewalks. The week before starting I went out hiking with a group in the nearby Ohito Wilderness area, which was more rugged.

While my preparations were far, far better than nothing I was not as ready as I thought I was. Hiking on roads and running trails is not the same as hiking on trails. I ventured forth for an hour or two and then returned to my warm and comfortable house.

My body had to adjust to a new reality. I suffered during the process. I was exhausted at the end of most days of hiking from the beginning to the end of the trail, and in the beginning I wasn't ready for it. My legs, in particular, were in continual pain. Carrying an overloaded, poorly adjusted and fitted pack made my back and shoulders ache, all day long. I was sleeping either on hard shelter floors or on the ground, with a thin sleeping pad beneath me, and it did not fully compensate for the unyielding nature of the surface beneath me. Rest was hard to come by.

In northern Georgia, in the spring, it rains. At higher elevations it can be sleet, hail, or even snow. Part of the area I hiked through during my first month NoBo was the Catawba rain forest, the only rainforest in the eastern United States. Unsurprisingly, it rains a lot in a rain forest. It rained twelve days out of the first fourteen I was on the trail. Water flowing downhill follows the path of least resistance seeking channels down from the heights, and one of the best channels is the trail.

Wet and uncomfortable feet in continual motion generate blisters. Blisters will be a central fact of life in the first month, and initially appear during first few days of hiking. New shoes are being broken in, and feet are toughening up. Some people battled blisters for months, and developed elaborate rituals for foot care. For a few the blisters were bad enough that, with all the other difficulties, it eventually drove them off the trail. I had a few blisters, not bad ones, but they became a part of my daily pain until I was well into New England. I had a blister bad enough to take me off the trail for a day just once, the rest of the time I endured.

All of the suffering starts right away, as I get onto Springer Mountain. The weather is rain and cold fog. It is beautiful, and cool weather is preferable when I am sweating my way ahead, but wet and squishy are not comfortable day long sensations. My first 2.8 miles are on the approach trail to get onto Springer Mountain, not even a part of the Appalachian Trail proper. It is a climb, but not a hard slope by any comparison to what lies ahead.

On day one it seems endless.

I am buoyed by an emotional high despite the dismal weather. I am finally making a dream happen. A little cold, wet, and suffering are background noise to the joy of actually being on my way. The forest is a wonderful place in the rain. Grey skies and mist have an ethereal quality, softening the edges of the world.

The sounds of water are mesmerizing, the water dripping off of trees, falling into larger pools where it gathers and runs in trickles and gurgles. It is a soft symphony of wet, and I added to nature's composition with my own rhythm section, splashing through puddles and rivulets. There is an undeniable childhood pleasure in announcing my presence to the world at large as I march along.

I pass my first shelter on the approach trail at Black Gap, and look in. There are hikers about, but there are also a couple of soldiers camped out in the shelter. I assume they are support troops for the U.S. Army's Ranger school, which uses the area for training. As a (now inactive) Army officer, I know they are not supposed to be in there, using resources built for a different purpose, with other people's money, and briefly considered having a word, but I am beginning what I hope is a detachment from the world I leave behind to thru-hike. I consciously let it go.

I worry about my mother extricating herself from the maze of rough forest roads in her little car. I check my phone every few hundred yards to see if I have gotten a text or message telling me she is safe again on a blacktop road.

Detaching myself from the smartphone is going to be a process on the trail. The trail itself helps wean me away from the technological need for constant electronic input, signal is touch and go at best. Leaving my phone on quickly drains the battery life as the phone hunts for cell towers.

On arriving at Springer Summit I find a small crowd of hikers waiting in line to take a picture at the Appalachian Trial start plaque imbedded in a stone at the summit. There are seven or eight hikers up here besides me. As slow as I am moving, I still manage to pass a couple of people on the approach trail, and I know more people are coming up behind me.

I get a text through to my mother, and find she had own little adventure making it out to a paved road after dropping me off, but she is back, safe, on civilized infrastructure, a relief.

I am concerned with my late start. Some books I read suggested Hawk Mountain Shelter as a good first day's hike. It is still 7 miles ahead. Looking back I see it was an unrealistic goal for an average hiker on day one. It is 15 miles from Amicalola Falls State Park, a good day for me a couple of months later into the hike.

I am moving now though, and I want to maintain momentum. I do not want to have a long delay on the summit.

The crowd of hikers at the summit keeps growing, milling around getting selfies by the plaque for the southern terminus of the Appalachian Trail. I wait in the line and get my picture at the summit, but when everyone else troops off to the Springer Mountain Shelter to fill in the register with their starting thoughts, I shake the accumulated water off of myself, shoulder my pack, and forge on ahead.

The summit has a lot of foot traffic, and there are a number of paths worn into the ground. I push off the summit down what I think is the main trail. I choose poorly, and my path peters out after a couple of hundred yards. I stop and look around at the dripping shrubbery trying to figure out where I am.

I am reluctantly coming to the conclusion that I will have to backtrack to the summit and begin again when I hear voices somewhere out ahead of me in the underbrush. I figure voices have to be hikers, and I plow forward through the bushes and trees, and soon find myself on a trail again.

15

It is not a good trail. Still, I keep heading in the direction where I heard the voices. I started my hike without a watch. I have a philosophy that I want to be unbound from the confining structures of everyday life, and I think a watch is the ultimate symbol of created artificial restriction.

My philosophy is already biting me in the butt. I have no real idea of how long I have been hiking, no sense of how long I have been following this game trail through the bushes. I do know that as a general rule, when people think they missed a turn and are uncertain of where they are, they usually haven't yet gone far enough. I keep pushing forward. Eventually, with a feeling of relief, I come to a definite hiking trail. It is four feet wide and well trodden, an obvious hiker highway through the forest.

I take out my compass and it points north, right down the trail. I set out confident I am back on the AT. I hike along through tunnels of rhododendron and make three different stream crossings. Unfortunately, nothing I pass is noted in the AWOL Guide. After the forest road debacle, I am rapidly losing faith in the guide. It is what I have, though, and I keep looking at it hoping landmarks will start matching up.

My misgivings are an experience that will become all too common on the trail, nearly a daily experience on some sections. Here there are occasional trail markers, but they aren't the trail markers I remember from my youth up in the Mid-Atlantic sections of the AT. These are white diamonds rather than the white rectangular blaze I am expecting. My doubts are compounded by the fact that I don't see any other hikers, either in passing or being passed, where on the approach trail there was considerable traffic.

I keep checking my compass and it continues to indicate I am traveling north. I follow the trail for a good 3 hours. I am walking far more slowly than I thought I would. My pack presses down on my back and shoulders, the weight slowly going from manageable to a nearly unbearable pressure working against my every step. I trudge onward through mist and drizzle until I find a monument for Benton MacKaye.

Benton MacKaye is one of the two great visionaries recognized for the original concept of the Appalachian Trail (the other is Myron Avery), and he devoted a lifetime to seeing it come into existence. Reading the brass plate at the monument, I gather that this part of the trail was dedicated to him. I have a moment of happiness. I am on the trail!

My happy moment is short lived. I walk past the monument and find I am on a T trail intersection, and the cross trail is marked with the white blazes I had expected but not seen thus far. With a sinking feeling I follow them, still traveling north by my compass. I hike another 10 minutes and I find myself back at the Springer Summit.

I sag in dismay. I just hiked the better part of the afternoon and I am right back where I started. I take out my compass again and look at it. I look ahead, and the compass needle wavers a bit, and then settles on north. I turn around and look back down the trail, and the compass needle bounces around and then settles back again on north. Whichever way I turn, the compass obligingly settles on north. I put the compass back into my pack and leave it there.

Standing on the trail, it is obvious that it is *the* trail. It is a well worn path, no eeling through undergrowth and squeezing through saplings. There are familiar looking blazes in view, painted marks roughly 2 inches wide and 6 inches long.

I have spent the last 3 hours hiking on the Benton MacKaye Trail, a parallel trail system that also begins at Springer Mountain, crisscrossing the Appalachian Trail, and I followed it in a loop all the way around Springer Mountain to arrive back on the AT.

I sit for a few moments, taking my pack weight off of my aching shoulders, sigh, and begin again. Now the AWOL Guide makes sense. Landmarks come in the order I expect, but much, much more slowly than anticipated. I planned on getting to Hawk Mountain Shelter on day one. I only make it as far as Stover Creek Shelter, hiking just 2.8 miles of actual Appalachian Trail on my first day. I figure I hiked 8 miles in total distance between the Benton MacKaye trail loop (which continues to crisscross the AT for the next 50 miles), the approach trail, and the actual trail mileage to Stover Creek Shelter. By my reckoning it is a poor start, but a start it is.

There is a Chinese saying, I think it originated with Confucius, or a fortune cookie factory somewhere, that states, "The longest journey starts with a single step." I have taken my step.

My meanderings around Springer Summit mean I am late getting to the shelter at Stover Creek. I have just an hour of daylight left to settle into my first night of camp life. The weather deteriorates as the sun drops down in the sky. It gets colder, and even wetter, so I am counting on the shelter for a protected night of rest.

Stover Creek Shelter is a big two story structure, with room for 16 hikers. It is a three sided rectangular shed, like the majority of Appalachian Trail shelters, with one of the long sides left open to the elements. The roof overhangs the open side, and there is a picnic table and fire ring out front. In Georgia the shelters come with a bear cable pole set up nearby, so I can hook my food bag onto a clip on the cable and haul it up on the pole for the night. There is no need to make my own bear hang.

The top floor of Stover Creek Shelter has a group of college boys who have come out for the weekend, and they are passing around a bottle. I am focused on eating and sleeping, and want to avoid that kind of group. There are several raised sleeping platforms on the ground floor that are already occupied, but not full. The people on the lower level are two thru-hiking couples on their first night out, just like me. I introduced myself by my new trail name, as Possible, and meet Swayze and Cosby, Cosby is still settling on her trail name, and will later become Star Stuff. She is from Albuquerque, the first and only other New Mexican I will meet hiking the trail.

The couples consolidate on the platforms so I get a little one all to myself. There is some quiet conversation, a self-consciousness about identifying ourselves as thru-hikers, but also a general sense of self-congratulation for actually being out here, committed, on the Appalachian Trail, confronting Mother Nature. We are here, finally, living a dream.

I cook dinner on my little alcohol stove and settle in, taking off my soaked socks and hanging them on a peg to air dry, and stripping down to my base layer before crawling into my sleeping bag.

Nobody builds a fire on the first night. It is raining and it might have been a futile attempt. We all have stoves, and fire really isn't needed.

Sleeping on a shelter platform is rather uncomfortable. The hard wooden floor has no give, and for a person with aching muscles, a continual state of being for thru-hikers, that soreness can keep someone awake all night.

I have an inflatable air mattress, and it provides some cushioning. I soon find mine has a leak in it. I must have punctured it with a splinter from the shelter, because I inflated it and tested it at home before packing it, to make sure it worked. It loses all of its air in about half an hour, leaving me on the hard platform without any insulation from the cold seeping up from the floor. Periodic downfalls of hard rain and hail rattling against the roof also keep me awake.

At some time close to midnight, when the night is darkest, another group of hikers comes in. Late arrivals to a shelter do not get a warm reception. No one wants to wake up and battle a personal fog of exhaustion to rearrange a shelter while new people settle in.

The newcomers are a family group; a man, a woman, and a small child. The man shines his headlamp around the lower level of the shelter and takes in all of our sleeping bodies filling the platforms, then climbs up the ladder and shines his headlamp around up there. There is a muffled conversation between the man and woman. I think now the woman was spent, the child was sleepwalking, and the man must have been going on willpower alone, trying to take care of his family. At the time, I am more annoyed with the intensity of his headlamp as he shines it around the shelter, waking me from my uncomfortable half doze. I just want them to go away and set up their tent

Set up their tent the man does, with help from the woman. I don't get to sleep yet; they set the tent up inside the shelter overhang directly in front of my platform to gain protection from the worst of the weather. It takes them another hour or so to get their tent up and settle in, with the man doing most of the work. He sweeps his headlamp back and forth across the inside of the shelter while he performs his chores, and it is impossible for me to sleep.

There probably was room enough in the shelter to accommodate the family if they had separated and slept in available individual spaces on the platforms, or if another shuffle of all the people already sleeping was performed, but no one is willing to get up and start making rearrangements after it has gotten so late and everyone is trying to sleep. Everyone was surely exhausted, and I am sure few of them were sleeping soundly, but they were definitely trying. It is midnight.

I know I have a miserable night that night, but that family had a harder time of it. In the morning they get up and moving pretty quickly, so I never speak to them. I also never see them again. I don't know if they were thru-hikers who rather quickly changed their minds, or if they were just out for a short backpacking trip.

It is a rather dismal end to the first day. Physical misery will be a persistent theme of thru-hiking. Through the suffering the world is still a beautiful place, and I am in a wonderful forest, in direct contact with that world in its raw elemental form.

Day 2, April 7th
Justus Creek, Trail Mile 14.3
Daily Distance 11.5 miles

TRAILTALK:

SOLO: A solitary hiker not associated with the trail families, groups and couples that formed and hiked together on the trail

The second day on the Appalachian Trail, my first full day, is another wet, cold one. A series of weather patterns develop that leave the trail wet and muddy for my first month on the trail. It is spring, and the wet season in a very wet part of the country.

I mention my irritation over the late arrival and light show of the previous night to Starstuff as we are preparing our breakfasts. She politely points out to me just how hard they had to have had it last night. It brings on a moment of self-reflection and something for me to chew on as I hike today. I recognize I am naturally irritable, and I very much need to develop a perspective on how other people are struggling, on trail and off, instead of letting things get to me

I get out of camp and onto the trail. Between the ups and downs, the muddy conditions, and my pack weight, I do not move well today, especially on the uphill stretches. The weight of my pack is staggering. Each individual step is a conscious effort. It is akin to going up and down an endless muddy set of stairs. I look for a landmark 50 yards ahead, be it a tree, a bend, a cutback, a rock, or a fallen log, and plod forward to it. I take a quick breather, and set my sights on the next small conquest. It is agonizingly slow progress, but it is progress.

Several hikers pass me, and I speak briefly with them as they pass me by, but find that today is mostly a lonely effort. I will be a solo hiker for most of the journey, and this is my first real plunge into what it will mean to spend hours in my own company with only the trail for distraction.

I stop at Hawk Mountain Shelter, yesterday's goal, at lunchtime. There are several other hikers also using the limited facilities for a break. I meet

Magician, a large man who appears even more out of shape and unprepared than I am. He is sitting atop the single picnic table with his gear spread out around him, considering what he can leave behind at the shelter to lighten his load. He apologizes and quickly consolidates when he sees other people want to use the table. He leaves Hawk Mountain before I do, and he will be the only NoBo hiker I actually pass, rather than being passed by, during my hike today. I am making judgments on hikers during these early days, trying to figure out who will make it all the way. Magician looked like a long shot. In retrospect, so do I.

Hawk Mountain looks well used. There is garbage and abandoned equipment strewn about. I learn from the other hikers that there is a significant crowd of people who started the trail right on Easter weekend, and the shelter areas are jam packed with backpackers at night. After I talk with Psych, StarStuff and Swayze at Hawk Mountain I plan to aim for campsites rather than shelters, and try to avoid the bigger crowds.

Everyone I speak to is also facing the reality of how much they can actually accomplish in a day of hiking against their plans, and ratcheting down expectations. The younger crowd is looking at 10 mile days now, getting started. My original thoughts of knocking out 15 miles a day are also tempered and I am looking at even 10 miles with trepidation.

I am already thinking like Magician. My pack weight is a good five to ten pounds heavier than that of many of the other hikers who are passing me by. I start reviewing my load in my head as I hike, assessing all of it and considering what is really necessary. A shakedown at the outfitter at Neel's Gap a couple days ahead is a traditional part of a NoBo thru-hike, and I look forward to it,

At Hawk Mountain I have my first encounter with a king snake. I wander down a game trail thinking it leads to a water source, and as it slowly peters out I slowly realize I am off the mark, again. (I found the proper, well used trail back near the shelter, under a sign in a tree I overlooked). I decide I should look a little farther, just in case.

I come to a log that has fallen across the path and I step out over it without really paying attention. Midstep a large black vine running along the top of the log moves. I levitate backwards six feet without any effort at all. After a couple of seconds to let my heart rate slow down, I take a closer look. A big, black snake, six feet long, is stretched out across the top of the log.

In general, I find snakes fascinating animals, at least when I am not taken by surprise. I spend some time watching this creature. There is a pattern woven into his black scales, an intricate weaving of a slightly lighter color, creating a texture to his appearance. He must find my inspection a little disturbing, and slowly eases himself down from the log and slides out of sight into the bushes

I think most of the snakes I see in the cooler month or two starting out are sluggish; they are just coming out of hibernation. This is my first snake encounter; I will see many more on the trail ahead.

I camp with a few other hikers near Justus Creek. I pitch my tent for the first time on trail, and put up my first bear bag. The process of hanging my bag takes time. Selecting the right tree, with the right branch, at the right height is challenging. A number of hikers keep their food bags in their tents with them, from exhaustion or laziness. I worry about bears, and want to develop good routines and practices for my hike.

Conversation with other thru-hikers is sprinkled with the use of trail slang. The terminology is familiar through trail literature. Other hikers read the same books I did, but we are all a little self conscious using the new lingo. People are slow to call themselves thru-hikers in these early days, and identify themselves as a "thru-hiker, I hope" or with some other qualification. I expect we will get more comfortable with our new persona as we go along.

The use of trail lingo is part of the tradition that fosters our identity with the trail, our purpose, and the community of hikers. Two days in, and I am beginning to become a thru-hiker.

My sleeping pad still leaks. I have an uncomfortable night on the cold, hard ground. Also a part of becoming a thru-hiker.

Day 3, April 8th
Lance Creek Tent Area near Trail Mile 24
Daily Distance 10 miles

TRAILTALK:

SHAKEDOWN: Going through a pack and assessing each piece of equipment and getting rid of all excess items, to reduce weight.

TRAIL FAMILY: A group of hikers that form a lasting social bond on the trail, usually hiking and or camping together.

TRAIL LEGS A level of fitness developed on the trail where every step is not a struggle, ideally a state where striding along the trail seems effortless.

My third long, damp, day of hiking on the Appalachian Trail is ten comparatively easy miles, not quite as hilly as yesterday's. My mantra is "one step at a time".

Lance Creek tent site, where I stop for the evening, is very crowded. There are a hundred hikers or more crowded into the shelter, camped on the established tent sites, and overflowing onto every flat space along the fire road that parallels the creek.

I am approaching Blood Mountain, the highest peak in Georgia at 4,461 feet, and it looms large in my mind. The mountain has a five mile approach of a gradually steepening grade over 1500 foot of elevation gain. It is the first big climb since Springer. It is begins to take on epic proportions in the mind, like the Lonely Mountain in the Hobbit. Compared to what lies ahead it really isn't much of a muchness, but it is my first serious terrain challenge.

Blood Mountain's forbidding name is not encouraging. It is named after a terrible battle fought in the vicinity between the Creek and Cherokee Indian tribes. Hikers like to attribute the blood to our own struggles climbing it.

Blood Mountain is a popular overnight destination and campsite. It is, in fact, the most popular destination on the Appalachian Trail south of Clingman's Dome in the Smokies, and gets 40,000 visitors a year. There is a 3.3 mile exclusion zone around Blood Mountain Shelter where hikers are required to have a hard shell bear canister to store food in if they camp overnight. Too many hikers were leaving garbage and food around the shelter atop Blood Mountain, and bears came looking for the easy pickings.

Thru-hikers do not carry bear canisters on the AT. It is a heavy and awkward piece of equipment to put into a backpack. The nearest water source is .3 miles away from Blood Mountain Shelter, and no fires are permitted. Apparently, the food that has been left out also attracts rats. These unfavorable factors make Blood Mountain Shelter an unappealing site for thru-hiker to stay the night, despite the views. The climb up and over the mountain through to Neel's Gap is daunting enough that everyone is laying up at Lance Creek, hence the crowded campsite.

When I arrive at Lance Creek it is late afternoon, and most of the hikers who are going to camp there are already present. The four tent pads at the site are woefully inadequate to handle the number of hikers present. I look around and set up my tent in a gap between two of the tent pads.

One of the campers on the pads I am setting up between comes out of his tent, and is unhappy I am setting up so close to him. He grumbles a bit at me. I really don't see any other viable options for a camping spot. It is already getting dark, and I am just too tired to care much. I wave my hands helplessly at the overcrowded camping area. He is not placated.

He is a thru-hiker. I make a point of inviting him into a conversation I am in at a campfire later. I think it best to mend fences, I am already seeing the same faces over and over, and developing an animosity with someone this early along would be foolish. He seems a little more accepting of me afterwards.

I am proud of myself that night for resolving this little social friction, but my self-congratulations are premature. First impressions are lasting ones, and this one haunts me for much of my hike. We run into each other time and again all along the trail. He is aloof and cool towards me every time we meet. He quickly becomes associated with a trail family, people I might have been friends with, and I will get the same reaction from its members.

Discussions between hikers inevitably come around to pack weight, load plans, and equipment, especially this early during the hike. Most hikers are struggling under the weight of their packs and dealing with gear problems. Neel's Gap is on the other side of Blood Mountain, and everyone at Lance Creek is planning on reaching it tomorrow. Mountain Crossings, the outfitter and hostel there, is a major trail landmark. The hostel has bunks and a shower, there are food options that are not coming out of our pack, and it is a full backpacking outfitter. One of the services provided is a pack 'shakedown'. The outfitter staff members are all successful Appalachian Trail thru-hikers, and they empty out your backpack and go through it and assess each item. There is a mail service at the outfitter, so all unneeded items can be sent home.

Mountain Crossings also supplies, for a price, needed or replacement items. After 4 days of suffering have shown the real value of new gear to a hiker, the extra cost for having the items right there to hand is bearable. I have shopping to do myself. I am desperate to replace my leaking air mattress; I have not yet had a good night of sleep on the trail.

I am eager to go through the shakedown. I have seen people carrying all kinds of equipment, including several other fools like myself toting guitars. I worried while preparing for the trail and I constantly added in additional 'back up' of critical items, enough so that someone has tried to stick a new trail name on me; 'Redundant'. I am sticking with Possible. I am more than willing at this point to let go of some security and drop weight. There are so many people on the trail I think I can borrow any item for a one time use if at need.

Sticking trail names on people is a popular conversational past time on the trail. So many hikers are not yet set on a name, and are holding out for names that define them. Later on it will devolve to what they can live with, but at the moment some are still waiting for that crazy special name to come.

I have met a lot of through hikers already. Psych, Crosby (StarStuff) and Swayze, Lost, Filmmaker, Kamikaze, Foxfire, Magician, The Breeze, Spudz, and Trolley, to add names to the record. There are around twenty thru-hikers I have been seeing regularly during my first days of hiking,

Kamikaze is a big blonde girl who is determined to lose weight by completing a thru-hike. She says, "It was the Appalachian Trail or fat camp". She is one of the most experienced backpackers in the group; she section hiked a significant portion of the Mid-Atlantic States last year. Still, she is carrying over 20 pounds of food in her pack, separated out into portion sized bags each labeled with the nutritional and caloric content. She is a very determined person and will ultimately finish the trail the day before I summit Katahdin. I will see a lot of her in the future.

Psych is a psychology student. He won high-end gear on an Appalachian Trials (not trails) website video contest.

Foxfire's struggles on the trail include a loss of appetite. Something about the trail is throwing off her desire to eat. She is a small, lean woman already, and intellectually she knows she needs the food. She is still meeting the daily challenge of hiking, and going very hard, but at some point she is going to run out of gas.

Filmmaker is videoing his entire hike on a selfie stick. He constantly takes hiking breaks to editorialize, and is walking with a camera held out in front of him. It is slowing his pace, allowing me to pace him even though he is strong hiker. Most hikers are keeping some kind of record of their experience. Psych has a blog, Kamikaze posts constantly to Instagram, and I have my nightly journal.

There are some hikers from outside the U.S. with us, including a Quebecois, who may now be named Spudz. He ate an entire economy sized instant potato pack last night for dinner. He thought it was the regular size and felt obligated to eat it all once he cooked it. It was a lot of potatoes.

The Breeze has already cut out for a town stop. He is taking a leisurely approach to thru-hiking and I wonder how far he will get; he is a strong hiker, but I don't know about his focus. Strong hikers have an advantage, knowing they can power out a few days and get back into the groove for Katahdin. Many of the rest of us are already looking at the daily mileages and averages needed to finish the thru-hike on time with concern

Hikers set up camps in small groups centered around campfires here at Justus Creek. I wander around and meet the neighbors. I meet Redlocks, Bubbles, Snack Time and Thor for the first time. I will see them many times during the miles ahead.

I play my guitar at their campsite. They are a part of a group of thru-hikers who later will be dubbed the 'High Flyers' by another hiker, Rikki Tikki. The High Flyers are a younger group whose membership isn't fixed but is more of a type, essentially the type who like to have a little smoke now and again. I do not partake at any time on the trail (although I am invited almost every day I see other hikers) I have too many years in the Army, and I feel like it would be a lapse of personal discipline to use recreational substances on the trail.

I spend time with the High Flyers all along the trail. I like many of them despite their vice. As a group they are able to relax and have fun on the trail because they are also quite energetic when they get around to it, and are able to pick up and hike 20 miles a day when they want to make progress.

Redlocks is a young man with red hair in dreadlocks. He is the first hammocker I see. He sleeps strung up between two trees, and is quite comfortable at night. I envy his restful nights. Bubbles is a bright, perpetually cheerful young woman. Snack Time seems to be a bit of a philosopher, and Thor is a tall, broad shouldered, blonde, bearded trail warrior, with a stride that eats up the miles.

I sleep well this night despite my lack of a sleeping pad, probably due to my overall state of exhaustion. The night is warm enough to be comfortable, so I don't have any bouts of the shivers.

Day 4, April 9th
Neel's Gap, (Mountain Crossing Outfitters) Trail Mile 31.7

Daily Distance 6.4 miles

TRAILTALK:

LEDGES: Long flat stones on a ridge, generally alongside a steep drop or on a summit, the exposed rock underlying a mountain.

CCC (CIVILIAN CONSERVATION CORPS): During the 1930s Great Depression one of Franklin Delano Roosevelt's back to work programs that employed people and taught them marketable work skills doing construction projects in National Forests and Parks.

HIKER HUNGER: Thru-hikers cannot carry enough food to sustain themselves with the 4000-5000 calories or more they burn each day. Thus, thru-hikers are always hungry, and eat massive quantities of food whenever they get the opportunity. Most hikers loose a lot of weight even with the binge eating.

I wake up early, just before dawn. A full moon is lighting up the sky, reflecting off of patchy cloud cover. Many people are already up breaking camp.

I am yearning for the day when my fitness level is truly up to the challenges of the Appalachian Trail. In Georgia the hills get progressively higher and steeper as we move north, and will continue to do so as we move towards North Carolina and the Smoky Mountains. Developing the physical speed, strength and stamina to hike easily is called getting your trail legs.

The climb up Blood Mountain does not prove as bad as I feared. I hike with Kamikaze, following her lead for speed and pacing. I abandon my technique of hurling myself at the uphills in short spurts and then stopping to catch my breath. Instead we take one easy step at a time, making slow but steady progress. The four mile approach gradually gets steeper, and the last mile of the ascent is the steepest of all, climbing through 1000 feet of switchbacks to the top. I show some patience following Kami's lead and I am rewarded with a faster and less tiring overall climb. Slow is smooth, smooth is fast.

The view from the top of the mountain makes it obvious why it is such a popular destination for day hikers. The fieldstone Blood Mountain Shelter is right next to the summit, and there are rock ledges on the summit itself to sit on and admire the view. Despite the general wetness the weather takes a break, and the views are mighty fine, allowing us to look back at the rolling hills we have already conquered. It is still wintry in the mountains, and there are no leaves as of yet to block the sights. I can see trees down in the valleys showing a ghost of green as buds appear on the branches. Psych is up on top and takes a great panoramic photo he shares with me.

The descent on the far side is quick, and ends at Neel's Gap. The little outfitter and hostel is packed full of thru-hikers, and there are plenty of day hikers visiting, up for the excursion to Blood Mountain or a scenic drive.

Neel's Gap is an old CCC (Civilian Conservation Corps) building, a typical work, solidly constructed of local fieldstone and timber. There is a breezeway splitting the hostel, the Walsiya-yi Inn, on one side from the Mountain Crossings outfitters on the other. The Appalachian Trail passes through the breezeway, the only place on the trail where the AT passes through a building. Another noted landmark at the outfitter is the 'shoe tree'. Many hikers change out their footgear at Neel's, and the unwanted shoes are thrown up into a tree out front. Hundreds of pairs of boots and shoes dangle from the branches.

The first order of business for me at Neel's Gap is food, as it is for most thru-hikers returning to civilization. The next is getting clean. For some hikers, myself included, priority could go either way, but usually food wins out. Four days into the trail and hiker hunger is beginning to show.

Mountain Crossings sells frozen pizzas, as would just about every hostel along the trail. They charge about ten bucks a piece. You pick a pizza, pay, and they pop it into a small oven. Ten minutes later you have a nice, hot pizza. I probably wouldn't eat many of these at home, but on the trail it is a hot, cheesy, tomatoey bit of paradise, every time. At Neel's there is a long wait as they cycled pizzas through their little oven for the many hungry hikers coming in. They also sell a variety of snacks, sodas, and trail food.

I buy and down a cold 16oz Coke as soon as I arrive. I don't normally drink soda, and the sugar and caffeine hit me like a hammer after being on the trail. I am running around acting like an excited five year old asking questions, and I may have irritated the staff just a little.

The staff at Mountain Crossings loves what they do. They are all successful Appalachian Trail thru-hikers, and you can feel their joy at being a part of the next generation of thru-hiker's experience. They want to help and share their knowledge. Unfortunately, there is also a sense of superiority, a little bit of condescension displayed by a couple of these people who have completed their thru-hike towards the crowd of inexperienced hikers at the outfitter that is a little hard to take. My amped up condition from the soda makes made me talkative and goofy, and I may have felt the attitude more, but other hikers comment about it. I tell myself I need to remember this feeling and adjust my own attitude if I am successful myself. I still remember it now.

It takes a great amount of courage to get out onto the Appalachian Trail and attempt a thru-hike. Most of the hikers now at Neel's Gap know the odds are against them, and have already gotten their first taste of why. The poor weather and the physical pain of backpacking are making themselves evident. Still, all of these people made a choice to come here, to face the odds, to leave the comforts of warm homes and loving companions and put themselves to the test. They are all worthy of respect, however far they may get up the trail.

The hostel fills quickly, and there is a wait for all hostel services. An overnight in the bunkroom is $17.00; laundry with soap was another $3.00, a total of $20.00. The cost is on the low end of typical for a hostel bunkroom stay on the AT. The coin operated washer and dryer and the showers have long waits, both for hostel users and nearby tenters who pay for these services separately. There is also a wait for a gear shakedown from the staff at the outfitters. I arrived at Neel's in the late afternoon, and I want to push out early tomorrow. The outfitter closes soon so I wait for the gear shakedown before waiting to get clean.

Prices are high for purchases at Mountain Crossings. Everything is at full retail price; expensive, but not quite at the level of gouging. You just are not going to get Amazon.com prices for purchases at a bricks and mortar establishment. When I consider the free service of the shakedown, having a staff tell you how of to lighten my pack, along with any number of bits of advice, tips and tricks to make what I have work, full retail prices are a reasonable exchange.

Watching other hikers go through their shakedowns is a form of educational entertainment. The Mountain Crossings staff member empties out an entire pack and goes through each piece of equipment, sorting everything into keep and discard piles. Everyone's load is a little preposterous, looking at expectations versus real need, and mine will be no exception.

I am an argumentative type of person, and having this little bit of self-knowledge, I tell myself I will rid myself of everything the staff member tells me to lose, except for my tablet and my guitar. If I find I really need something I discard I can buy another one up the trail.

The staff member who shakes down my pack is named Sqaurl. He is thorough and unrelenting. I manage to keep my mouth shut despite misgivings about what is going into my discard pile. Squarl points out that what most beginning thru-hikers have tried to do is pack for a long expedition, when what we are really doing is a series of 3 to 5 day long sections, with frequent opportunities for resupply.

Squarl removes items from my pack. My clothes are trimmed down to seven main articles; a set of long underwear, a t-shirt, one pair of shorts, a rain coat, a long sleeved Smartwool top, and my down coat. I also keep a pair of gloves and three of the four pairs of socks I packed. Squarl convinces me to get rid of my long pants, which is primarily what I have been wearing, in favor of hiking in shorts. Long pants with a belt weigh over a pound.

My fancy solar panel for charging my phone and tablet is the biggest item to go into the discard pile. I haven't yet used it; it has been grey and wet for the first four days and the sullen light is not enough to power up the panel. Squarl tells me once the leaves sprout on the trees over the next month the canopy will block the sun. I will have no real opportunities to generate power.

Most of my redundant items go into the discard pile. Overall, Squarl strips six pounds of weight from my pack. He advises but doesn't push me to discard some of the items I am still too insecure not have a back up for, such as an extra lighter and a spare knife.

The aspect of my pack that gives experienced thru-hikers pause is my waterproof integrity. I place every item in my pack into separate, protective Ziploc bags, and then have the Ziplocs inside dry bags. I have a garbage bag lining the inside of my pack, and a pack cover on the outside. It doesn't seem like much to me, but I am the marvel of Mountain Crossings for a little while. Squarl consolidates my items into just a few bags, and weighs the stack of plastic bags being discarded. The pile weighs seven ounces, or nearly a half a pound of pack weight just in Ziploc bags. I am almost tagged with Ziploc as a new trail name.

Into my ship home box goes my leaky air mattress. Mountain Crossings has a tub filled with water where you can submerge your air mattress to find and patch a leak. I could try a fix, but I have a vision of constantly developing slow leaks and sleepless nights on the trail. I opt for a new 3/4 sized Thermarest replacement, The Thermarest is a durable product, and it is honeycombed to retain some of its cushioning and insulation even if it develops a leak. The smaller size will save a little weight.

I look at new sleeping bags. I want to get warmer and lighter, but to upgrade my existing synthetic bag to a down bag with the same insulating qualities will cost me $600.00. I would save a pound, and might be a little warmer, but synthetic has some advantages, and at that price I decide to save my money.

My cook pot and stove receive scrutiny from the staff. My cooking equipment is covered with nasty black soot that is coming off on the storage bag and on my hands. The soot easily transfers onto everything it touches, but perversely resists all attempts at being washed away. Isopropyl alcohol is the correct fuel, and it has been cooking my food, but the rubbing alcohol I bought at the Dollar General in Dahlonega has an additive that leaves a terrible residue. What I should be using is Heet, an automotive product that is usually available at stores and gas stations along the trail, or Coleman camp fuel. Both products burn cleanly without producing soot.

When the outfitter closes, hikers are still sitting around tables and benches on the surrounding decks eating pizza and drinking beer. There is a group of partiers who are drinking and smoking, but they are low key group and aren't a bother to anyone else. I hoist a beer or two of my own.

I am the last person to get through the washer and dryer, and as I wait for my clothes to dry I take out my guitar for the first time on the trail. I am trying to justify my guitar weight as much as I really want to play.

I am playing my first song when a caretaker comes out of an apartment above the hostel, yelling and actually cursing at me, dropping F-bombs for playing. He is rude, aggressive, and insulting enough that I almost go up the stairs after him. I just shut up instead, but it is a moment of self-restraint.

I am apparently violating quiet hours, things are supposed to settle down at 10:00 PM, and it was a few minutes after. Baltimore Jack, a long time hiker and fixture on the trail, calms me down, explaining it to me in far more polite terms than the explosive personality caretaker.

I do not get the rest I so long for after my nights of semi-sleep on the trail. The bunks in the hostel are stacked and packed to get the largest number of people into a small space. There are more than 20 hikers stuffed into an area not much larger than a big living room. Gear is hanging everywhere as people try to dry and fix their tents, sleeping bags, clothes and other equipment in the tight quarters. It is a hot and smelly room. Even after quiet hours it is noisy, people are moving about restlessly, and the drone and buzz of snores and low conversation resonate in the cramped quarters. I cannot get myself to drift off. I end up leaving the bunkroom, and I sleep a little on the dayroom sofa. I am still agitated from my encounter with the caretaker, and the constant movement of people in and out wakes me up each time I start to drift off.

Days 5-8; April 10th to 13th
From Neel's Gap to Dicks Creek Gap (Hiawassee), Trail mile 31.t to 69.3
36.9 miles, AVG 9.25 miles per day

Day 5, April 10th
Low Gap Shelter, Trail Mile 43.2
Daily Distance 11.5 miles

TRAILTALK:

GAP: A common term in Southern Appalachia for the terrain feature consisting of a saddle or low spot between two hills or mountains.
HIKER BOX: Hostels and other places hikers stay usually have a box or two filled with of food and equipment left behind by hikers who ended up with more than they wanted to carry. Because many hikers set up mail drops far in advance of starting the trail their boxes are usually overloaded with more than they want to use. Many hikers also purchase boxes of items rather than individual sets, take what they need for their next leg, and leave the rest in the hiker box. The hiker boxes in the South are usually so full you can do a full resupply out of one if you are not too particular about what you eat.
MAIL DROP: A box filled with supplies and goodies mailed forward or from home to a predetermined point along the trail to provide logistical support during the hike.

It is a very tired thru-hiker waking early from my night of half sleep in the hostel. I only slept two hours intermittently through the night. Kamikaze is also up, and plans on leaving soon. Kami is a slow hiker; she is carrying a lot of weight. She makes her miles by starting early and finishing late, with almost no breaks. She is working harder than most of the other hikers I see on the trail. She has a wedding she has to go off-trail for and intends to reach a specific location before taking that week off. She is an insane planner.

It is pouring down rain, and I still have not done food resupply, but I don't want to wait for Mountain Crossings outfitters to open its doors at 9:00 AM. My meal planning is a little haphazard. I generally know what I want, but actual purchases are dictated by what is available. Outfitters have backpacker specific food, but it a convenience store sized selection, and I can never rely on what might be on the shelves at any given outfitter.

I come up with an alternate plan, deciding to get motivated and push out with Kamikaze, getting an early start despite the weather. I do my resupply out of the hiker box.

I have two resupply options going forward. There are road crossings on the trail 20 and 37 miles ahead, so at my hiking pace I am looking at two or four days. I really don't want to waste a whole day going into town, as would have to happen at the 20 mile road, and there is a hostel right near the road crossing at Hiawassee 37 miles away. I can go in and out of there quickly overnight, much like Neel's. So I plan for four days.

The hiker box at Neel's is overflowing, but there is a crazy randomness to what is available. This was very common in hiker boxes all the way up the trail, although certain staples are usually present. At Neel's there are a number of hand labeled Ziploc bags with strange concoctions in them, and bits and bites of different kinds of snacks. I still have not eaten all of the food I brought for the first four days. Like everything else, I packed way too much. I still have enough for two or three days, and I just filled in from the hiker box.

It rains steadily and thunder grumbles until about noon. It is a wet start to the day. I start hiking with a lot of energy and leave Kamikaze in my wake. Two hours later I slow. My overall exhaustion catches up with me and so does Kamikaze. She passes me at her steady mile eating pace while I take a break. The last miles of the day are slow and painful. I slog along, head down, waiting for the camp at Low Gap to appear. There will be many times along the trail where the end never seems to come into sight, and this is the first of them.

I finally limp into camp at 6:00 PM. It is another large encampment, with a full shelter and circles of tents set up in half a dozen or more separate little communities in the vicinity.

I set up my tent a little aside from the other groups, and cook up a concoction of Ramen noodles and some kind of potato mix from the hiker box in a mixture called a ramen bomb. I am tired and feeling kind of nauseous, but still force myself to eat. I am only able to eat half of my dinner, leaving me with a dilemma.

There is no kitchen garbage can in the woods. I don't want to toss my leftovers on a fire (and none are lit yet in the wet anyway). Burying it seems like a bad idea. I don't want to attract and feed bears or any other wildlife. I decide to toss my leftovers into the latrine.

On my way to the privy carrying my pot an older woman meets me. Under interrogation, she discovers my intention; I endure a lecture from her on not wasting food. She is some kind of Girl Scout leader out on a section hike, and doesn't seem able to rein in her need to direct and manage when confronted with adult hikers.

One of the drawbacks of large encampments (this is the first logical camping area hiking out of Neel's, and very crowded) is that a number of disparate groups are crowded together. Conflict appears to follow me wherever large groups gather, and so I am finding I don't much care for shelter area camping. There are groups that are very festive, but I seem to be mostly on my own in the crowds. I am also doing some self-contemplation, and wondering how much my sense of being an outsider is self inflicted.

Day 6, April 11th
Rocky Mountain Peak, Trail Mile 54.3
Daily Distance 11.1 miles

TRAILTALK

TRAIL MAGIC: Assistance or comforts provided free along the trail. Trail magic takes many forms. Sometimes it is just serendipitous, like a ride into town on a rainy night, but it also takes the form of organized events supporting the hike.

TRAIL ANGEL: A provider of trail magic; a person who provides assistance to a needy hiker.

PCT (Pacific Crest Trail): A trail similar to the AT on the west coast running from Mexico to Canada through the Sierra Nevada and Cascades of California, Oregon and Washington.

BEAR BAG: A bag in which food and scented items are placed and hung from a branch high in a tree to keep bears and other creatures from getting into them during the night.

My new Thermarest sleeping pad is working, and I am sleeping! My good night of rest may be due to the cumulative exhaustion, but I slept long and sound last night in my tent. There is a big difference in my energy level and my attitude. The sun is out, and not just figuratively. It is the first day since starting the trail it is not cloudy and raining. I am not walking fast, but I am not trudging along either. Today I enjoy the most basic backpacking task of putting one foot in front of the other.

I hike with Kamikaze and Older Dog after meeting them a little before Unicoi Gap. Older Dog is an early retiree who spends his time visiting

31

National Forests and Parks all over the United States. I am identifying more with the older hikers than most of the young ones.

The trail isn't getting any easier. NoBos are gradually conditioned as they move north. Georgia prepares me for the rest of the trail, providing sufficient challenges in effort and logistics to make a competent backpacker out of me without killing me in the process. The terrain is varied, and the mountains slowly grow larger and steeper. The shelters and campsites are spaced further apart as I move north, a testament both to my improving abilities and the early dropout rate.

The Smokies are my new Lonely Mountain. The elevation profiles in the AWOL guide are scary. Huge ups and downs lie a couple of hundred miles ahead; just a couple of weeks of hiking. I feel dread in the pit of my stomach wondering how well I will cope

In Unicoi Gap I get my first taste of trail magic. Older Dog, Kamikaze and I run into a day hiker coming south, and she tells us there is organized trail magic set up ahead in the gap. We pick up our pace to get down to it. I heard of trail magic being set up earlier along the trail, but my timing was off, and I missed it. I am pumped; I am not going to miss this one!

As we descend into the gap we can hear it, a buzz of activity on the road below, hidden from our view by the branches of trees. I start singing on the way down, belting out a little Janis Joplin "Lord, won't you buy me a night on the town". I think my companions are both a little amused and annoyed.

The trail magic is spectacular, among the best organized I encounter anywhere along the trail. A full resupply and feast is waiting for us at the trailhead, set up by a little non-profit called the Todd Taylor Foundation. The foundation sets up on the trail for a few days each year in remembrance of hiking veterans. The trail magic is a living memorial to friends who have passed on.

The magic is set up on two rows of long folding tables. There is a small grill, and all kinds of food laid out along the tables in a buffet of ready to eat items and trail foods. There is a section of other sundry, expendable items such as batteries and hygiene items that hikers need. They have a charging station for electronics, and stationery and stamped envelopes for hikers wanting to write home. The foundation pushed food and goodwill on us until I am ashamed to find I am helping myself to a third hotdog. I fill my pack with food, and only concerns about the weight put limits on what I take. I also use the opportunity provided to write quick letters home to my daughter and wife.

Kamikaze, Older Dog and I spend more than an hour feeding, talking, and relaxing at the Todd Taylor Foundation trail magic. Eventually we have to pack up, leave the little cornucopia of comfort behind, and hike on. With groaning stomachs and fully loaded packs, the mile and a half climb 1000 feet up out of Unicoi Gap is more effort than expected, and we don't get much further. We end up camping for the night near the top of the next summit, Rocky Mountain.

Names of terrain features on the trail can get repetitive. Many of the names were applied locally for reference, and so every region has its own Rocky Mountain, Low Gap, Sassafras Gap, and so forth. The repetition of names is a bit of a joke to thru-hikers. Were our ancestors so lacking in creativity? Did none of them travel to the next county and see that the place names they bestowed on their landmarks were already in use fifty miles away?

This Rocky Mountain has nothing specific to distinguish it from other similarly named rocky peaks along the trail, but it will be our home for the night. We loaded up with water at the trail magic, enough to camp with, and find a lot of other thru-hikers have also decided that Rocky Mountain is far enough for the day after stuffing their stomachs and packs full at Unicola Gap.

We stop early, and there is time to relax with our fellow hikers. Many of the people in this particular group of hikers are older, and it is a pleasant night spent with a more mature group. I talk for a while with two of them, Runs With Beer and Giardia, who have an interesting story to share.

According to them, there is a girl named Slow and Steady a day or two behind us, who brought a bivy sack for her shelter. A bivy sack is a waterproof sack that goes around your sleeping bag to keep it dry and provide a little more insulation while you sleep at night. It is used in lieu of a tent. It is very convenient. Roll it out on a sleeping mat, stuff in your sleeping bag, crawl in, and go to sleep.

There are some disadvantages, practical and psychological, in using a bivy sack. The thin walls of a tent or hammock may not be much more than fabric, but they at least create an illusion of separation and protection from the great outdoors.

On the second day out of Springer Mountain Slow and Steady put down her bivy near Gooch Gap on a little side path that went down to a stream. The path she chose turned out to be a game trail animals used to get to the water at night, and she did not have an uninterrupted night of sleep.

First, a herd of hogs came through. Wild hogs are no joke. They are not the cute domesticated pink animal from Charlotte's Web. Wild hogs are large, sometimes up to 600 pounds. They are hairy. They are tusked. They are territorial, and they are aggressive. They are also omnivores, eaters of opportunity, and not opposed to eating meat if it presents itself. Slow and Steady would have a few scary minutes as they passed around her.

The hogs are not the only users of the game trail. Slow and Steady's visitors that night included a black bear that stopped to sniff at her in her bivy. Imagine yourself lying in a cocoon on the ground as a wild bear comes and investigates you, jaws and claws right there above you while you are wrapped and trapped in a sack on the ground. I think I would lie still for a very long time during and afterwards, eyes wide open, listening to every little creak and footfall in the darkness.

The next day, following the sleepless night, Slow and Steady's arm started swelling up and turned purple. It is serious enough Highlighter calls

911. Emergency services respond with a helicopter, which lowers a sling and a medic to assist her. She refused the ride. Nobody wants to give up trail miles, and helicopters rides are expensive. The medic stayed with her and walked her out the couple of miles to the next road crossing, where she was brought in to a clinic.

Slow and Steady was bitten by a brown recluse spider. Whether the bite occurred while she was on the ground that night, or elsewhere is unknown, but she had a hell of a 24 hours interacting with wildlife. Trail news is she got right back on the trail again, this time with a tent.

Older Dog teaches me the PCT (Pacific Crest Trail) method for hanging a bear bag. The bears out west are a little smarter than the bears in the east, and have learned to pull on bear bag cords tied off on branches so the bags fall down into their paws. The PCT method is a neat way of removing the tie off down low so bears can't get a free meal at a hiker's expense.

It is a good day on the trail.

Day 7, April 12th
Deep Gap Shelter, Trail Mile 66.0
Daily Distance 11.7 miles

TRAILTALK:

NEARO: A day with very little hiking, nearly a zero, hiking a couple of miles down the trail for the day. These are often days where a hiker runs into and out of town on a same day resupply, but a particularly fine relaxation spot on trail such as a waterfall or a view might also inspire a short day of hiking.

ZERO DAY: A day without any hiking, usually a full rest day in town.

There are a lot of short climbs today, and a couple of thousand foot ascents grow into a long day of hiking. I am assessing why I am ending my hiking day later than other hikers going close to the same distance, and I think I have an answer.

I have been making a hot breakfast of oatmeal and coffee each morning, while other hikers just eat a cold packaged item and go. I use an alcohol burning stove; it is basically a tuna can with denatured alcohol in it that sits inside a little stand that holds my pot over the flame. It is very simple, but it works. It is also very slow, and it takes 10 to 15 minutes to set it up and boil water. Using the Heet recommended at Neel's Gap instead of isopropyl rubbing alcohol is working much better and burning clean. It has burned away most of the soot left behind by the rubbing alcohol after a couple of uses. It is still slow.

In an effort to get ahead, I wake earlier this morning and start sooner, but I am soon passed by the rest of the people I camped near. I am turning into the back door sweeper for our little cohort, enough so that someone tried to tag me with Sweeper as a trail name. I am still Possible.

It is a hard day physically, and emotionally as well. I hike alone. There is turmoil about goings on at home. I end up talking to myself, conducting imaginary arguments with my wife. I am aware I am on the road to madness. Usually it doesn't matter; the rocks and trees bear my insanity without flinching, but when another hiker comes across me expostulating to the trees they quickly move along.

I meet another damned fool thru-hiker carrying a guitar, a Martin Backpacker. We meet when I take a lunch break at Tray Peak Shelter. We trade instruments and play for a while. I still like my Washburn better, although I have not played it very much. The rainy weather makes it hard to protect, and I find I don't have much time for music.

I hike a mile with a mom and her 14 year old son. Mom is going along to support her son's dream of hiking the Appalachian Trail, and she looks as worn and tired as I am, especially next to her energetic son. I think she is close to the end of her rope. They are very nice and very positive, but mom talks continually without much opportunity for me to respond. Even after feeling lonely and isolated an hour earlier, I find the one way conversation irritating, and I long for a quiet forest again.

I really want my trail legs to come on, every day something else new aches, a fresh and insistent addition to the familiar aches from before. I can count myself lucky; some people are developing major blisters, while I only have a couple of little ones. Other hikers are developing serious physical issues, muscular and skeletal protests, but they are still going, and are in fact still hiking faster than I am. I am trying not to use ibuprofen every day, every few hours, but may have to just to keep pain at bay. I arrive at camp last and very tired, again, at 6:00 PM.

Camp food is getting crazier. People are throwing everything together in their pots. Hunger tells of course, and trail food is getting boring. Hikers are experimenting with what they throw in their pots. Oatmeal, ramen, cheese and sausage tossed together in one pot are looking pretty good to me.

I look forward to a hostel stay and a nearo day tomorrow. There was cell phone reception on top of a mountain, and I called ahead to make arrangements. I tried to get a hotel room in Hiawassee to avoid another hostel experience like Neel's, and hoped to find another hiker to split the cost. I called the Mull Motel listed in the AWOL guide and spoke to an apathetic and unhelpful motel desk clerk. She has no rooms available, but when pressed directed me to the local Hilton. It is listed in AWOL as a hundred dollar a night hotel, more than I want to pay. I end up calling the Top of Georgia hostel instead. I have heard it is a better hostel than Neel's Gap. The front desk is cheerful answering, and I have hopes it will be a good night.

The one pair of shorts I have left after Squarl's shakedown at Neel's is not enough for me. I don't like having my legs exposed, and I miss my cargo pockets. I also have nothing to wear when I do laundry. I intend to buy a new pair of long pants in Hiawassee.

Day 8, April 13th
Dicks Creek Gap, Top of Georgia Hiker Hostel, Trail Mile 69.6,
Daily Distance 4.6 miles

TRAILTALK:

NOC: The Nantahala Outdoor Center, A tourist destination along the Nantahala River in North Carolina in the Smoky Mountains, with river rafting, kayaking, bike touring, mountain biking, and hiking all supported. There are restaurants, an outfitter, a resupply grocery shop, lodging, and a hiker hostel there.

It is a nice, short hike today to Dicks Creek Gap and the Top of Georgia hostel. I make it to the road by noon, hiking with Kamikaze and Older Dog. It is raining, again, and the trail is flooded, again. Rain really slows hiking. I adjust my hiking poles, and they help me keep my stride and balance better at a longer length. The mud is very slippery and poses a real hazard, especially on descents. I take one spill, but my poles let me control my fall once I start to slide, and I keep to falling on my butt instead of on my pack, my knees, or worse, a face plant.

Inevitably, my tent and Tyvek ground cloth get wet during the night, and there is never a real opportunity to dry them out. My tent has become a damp refuge. It keeps the rain off of me, but the wet is pervasive wet, and I slept uncomfortably. I am really looking forward to the possibility of a good, dry night of sleep at the hostel.

The Top of Georgia hostel is a short half mile up from the U.S. Route 76 Appalachian Trail crossing. They have a shuttle van running back and forth to the hostel from the trailhead, and it arrives in the parking area at the same time we do. The town of Hiawassee is 12 miles up the road, and the hostel offers a shuttle service into town for resupply and dinner.

The Top of Georgia is a contemporary style house converted into a hostel, and it is comfortable. There is an open, airy common room with high ceilings and lots of glass to let in natural light. The common room includes the kitchen, dining area, and living room. The walls have inspirational writing on them, and trail art is everywhere. There are decks built all around the house, and currently there are tents, clothing, and other gear hanging from the railings as hikers attempt to dry out their equipment. The air is still saturated and it appears to be a futile effort.

Wireless internet is available, and there is a small computer station hikers can sign up to use. The connection is slow and spotty, since the three dozen hikers staying here tonight immediately overload the bandwidth trying to get online with their phones and tablets when they come in. I learn that waiting until late in the evening, or first thing in the morning, gives me much better service, something that will be true at hostels all the way up the trail.

My wife is looking at possible medical issues and I want to build contingency plans online on the chance I may have to go off the trail. If I leave I want to come back, but I need to get the finances and travel arrangements to work.

Veteran thru-hikers staff the hostel, and they seem a friendlier lot than the staff beset at Neel's Gap. Volunteers like Buttercup and Renaissance believe in the thru-hike as a life changing event, and are eager to share their own experiences and love of the trail with the next generation. They volunteer for the season, working hard for free, and the occasional tip. One of their primary roles is encouraging those whose motivation is starting to flag. While we haven't yet covered 5 percent of trail distance, the dropout rate at this point is over a quarter of those people who started at Springer Mountain. I hear that of the 6500 hikers that have already started a thru this year, perhaps 4000 are left.

There are a couple of bunkrooms, each one filled with a dozen people. I end up in a bunkroom converted from a garage. It has concrete floors, is crowded, a bit damp, and hikers' wet gear is everywhere. The bunks are small and packed tightly into the space available. It is better than Neel's Gap, but I won't spend much time lounging about there.

The hostel's operation is a smooth machine. When I arrive, I am directed to the showers. My dirty clothes go into a mesh bag for laundry, which the staff does for me. I am given a set of hospital scrubs to wear while I am waiting. Many loads of laundry are awaiting attention, so it will be a while before my old duds come back. The scrubs are comfortable and clean.

I take the shuttle into Hiawassee to resupply at a supermarket and get a hot meal. The van is full of familiar faces taking the ride into town, and there is a lot of chatter and laughter. We are wearing our varicolored scrubs, and we look like a bunch of mental patients on the loose as we pile out of the vehicle and wander about town. A big group of us eat together at a southern buffet, the Georgia Mountain Restaurant. The staff sits us at a single big table and treats us like royalty.

In various stores in town I pick up a pair of long pants, a cheap web belt, a micro towel, and a tiny pair of medical scissors. I am adding more things to my pack rather than losing them, which is not successful thru-hiker behavior. I ditch my multi tool in the hiker box as a sop to my conscience. I still have a small knife, and it is the only tool I have used.

Kamikaze, Older Dog, and I make a plan to go four days and then see if we want to push three more and get to the NOC (Nantahala Outdoor Center) without taking a day off the trail. We carry a lot of food to go the distance. Hostels commonly have big hanging scales for checking pack weight. I am at 46 pounds, and 14 pounds of that is in my food bag.

I came into the hostel with two days worth of food still in my pack, so I know I am over packing. I am also overeating; I have actually gained a couple of pounds since starting the trail, while most other hikers are seeing a five or ten pound weight loss. Figuring out the right balance of food to carry will be a challenge I don't really sort out until I am in the Mid-Atlantic States. At this point I am just shoveling in fuel.

Tomorrow we look forward to a long gradual climb to the North Carolina border in the rain. I am worried about it, concerned about keeping up with the others and dreading the effort itself. I feel rested today; the break is doing me good. I take Tylenol PM to help ease my aches and help me sleep through the night in the noisy bunkroom. I really don't like how much I am using aspirin and ibuprofen to keep me going, but I hate pain and sleeplessness more.

NORTH CAROLINA

Day 9 to 27, April 14th to May 2nd
Hiawassee GA to Green Mountain Road, Trail Miles 69.9 to 241.0
171.1 miles, AVG 9.0 miles per day

Day 9-12 April 14th to April 17th,
Dicks Creek Gap to Winding Stair Gap (Franklin), Trail Mile 69.6 to
109.8
39 Miles, AVG 9.9 miles per day

Day 9, April 14th
Near Courthouse Bald / Sassafras Gap, Trail Mile 80.5,
Daily Distance 10.9 Miles

TRAILTALK:

BALD: An open pasture or meadow on the top of a mountain. This term and terrain feature is particular to the southern Appalachians. The balds provide a critical ecological niche as well as spectacular views.

I am up early, unable to sleep comfortably in the hostel bunkroom. I am the first person into the common room, and use the predawn quiet time to get business done at the computer work station. The sun rises and people start filtering in, beginning with the staff. They prepare a breakfast for the guests, and I and some others pitch in to help.

After breakfast the hostel owner, Sir Packs A Lot, has a question and answer session with us novice thru-hikers, sharing his knowledge and philosophies on the journey ahead. He has a list of 10 'rules' for successful thru-hikers painted on one of the common room walls he uses as a guideline for his talk. As you might guess from his trail name, Sir Packs A Lot was not an ultralight backpacker, but even he talks about the need to get rid of unneeded weight.

One of his emphases is on enjoying the trail experience. He recommends taking some of the blue blazed side trails and seeing the places they lead to, taking a break at beautiful spots along the trail. A thru-hike is a once in a lifetime event, and we should make the most of it.

The trail is definitely making me stronger. Backpacking is like learning to walk all over again. I use stride changes and coordinate with pole use to help me power up the ascents, and switch to slow, steady, and above all, careful movement on the downhills. I can step out on the few level stretches.

The wet weather continues, and I have invented my own trail word, 'churn', for the soup of mud and sodden leaves in the middle of the trail that is mixed together by the action of hiker's feet. Churn is slippery and quite dangerous, especially on the steeps. It only takes a single misstep to put you off the trail with a sprained ankle, broken bone, or torn ACL.

We enter North Carolina, Pisgah National Forest, and the Catawba rainforest all at one step today. The Catawba rain forest is a temperate rain forest, the only one in the United States east of the Olympic peninsula in Washington State. It is caused by orographic precipitation (try and work that phrase into a conversation). It is a three way collision, weather systems coming from the Gulf of Mexico meet with the Atlantic weather systems in the east and those coming down across the prairies from the North. The clouds collide over this section of the Appalachians. During the past few years the Southeast has been in a drought, and hikers had a drier time of it. Normal weather patterns are re-establishing themselves this year. The constant rain will be a fact of life for weeks yet to come.

I am worried setting out that I will suffer from the lack of rest after another poor night of sleep in a hostel. Some of it is due to emotional turmoil caused by learning of events out of my control at home, some by sleeping arrangements. I have a harder time of it mentally getting back onto the trail after the comforts of civilization.

I should not have worried. On an eleven mile hike slowly climbing higher and higher I keep up with the group, which now consists of McGyver as well as Kamikaze and Older Dog. We also see a lot of Spudz.

McGyver is a man in his sixties and one of the more renowned trail personalities in our year. He resisted his trail name for a while. He is an engineer, and did not want his profession to stereotype him on the trail. His mental processes betray him. He showed up on the trail with clever equipment adaptations, introduced many hikers to the PCT bear bag hang method, and helped a lot of people straighten out their equipment during the first days of hiking, and the McGyver name came and stuck. He gradually accepts it, introducing himself for a while as "McGyver, I guess". He spells his name a little differently to distinguish himself from the television character who built Rube Goldberg machines to defeat evil using only his pocketknife.

We cross over our first state line into North Carolina. Groups tend to spread out while hiking, and consolidate at rest points. I am sweeping the rear, as usual, and would have passed the NC border sign if I hadn't seen the rest of the hikers standing by it. The sign is an unexceptional little six inch by four inch board nailed to a tree with the initials GA/NC carved into it. We have a celebratory moment.

When hikers start the thru-hike they are still daunted by the immensity of the task they are undertaking. Most have the intention of thru-hiking, but aren't really believers. When asked if they are going all the way in Georgia, they answer with "I hope so", or "I guess". You don't quite own your identity. I think the North Carolina line is where the identity of thru-hiker begins to feel real. You have faced a challenging portion of the trail, met Mother Nature head on, and overcome it. You begin to feel worthy.

Less than a mile past the North Carolina border there is a twisted tree directly on the trail. It has several trunks and many oddly angled branches reaching up towards the sky. It is noted in the AWOL guide as a "much photographed tree" We feel obligated to stop and admire it, and of course take pictures. There will be several trees that have individual distinction ahead of us on the trail. This one has a creepy quality appropriate to a rain forest.

Our party splits up after hiking eleven miles, just after we pass the tree. Kamikaze, Spudz and Older Dog push on, intending to reach the NOC in six days. It is wet, and getting dark, and McGyver and I decide that eleven miles is enough for us. Kamikaze is so determined to meet her mileage goals that she just doesn't quit. McGyver calls it the Kamikaze Death March. We peel off from the rest of our group at an open area that already has a tent set up in it.

Our new neighbor is SuperFeet. She is an Australian girl, a little out of shape, who has come all the way from Down Under to hike the AT. She was something of a local news sensation back home, and is making periodic updates on her adventures to followers in Australia.

SuperFeet's trail name comes not from her progress, but the cause of her lack of it. She is struggling hard at this point, and barely managing six miles a day. Her feet have swollen. Many hikers' feet do under the punishment they take day after day, but hers have swollen to extraordinary dimensions, going up three full shoe sizes. She is purchasing new, ever larger pairs of footgear in each successive trail town to cope.

The constant rain aggravates her situation, and she has pulled up lame and taken a zero here in the middle of the woods. She sits on a log next to a fire she built, reading a book while it drizzles down on McGyver and me as we set up our campsite. She is still determined to go north.

It is nice setting up camp a little earlier and chilling in camp before total darkness falls.

Day 10, April 15th
Beech Gap, Trail Mile 90.7
Daily Distance 10.2 miles

It rains, and rains some more. SuperFeet doesn't even come out of her tent as McGyver and I break camp in the morning.

McGyver has a little swim towel, a synthetic chamois leather, which he uses to sweep up the moisture from his rain fly before rolling it up. It helps dry it, and water is weight, so the more of it shed from our gear the lighter our loads. I have a micro fleece towel, but it is larger, heavier, and just doesn't seem as effective as McGyver's little wipe. I am envious.

Despite the rain, hiking with McGyver is a boost to the spirits. He is a very positive man, and hiking with such a companion helps eat up the miles. I push myself harder to stay up with him; my pride is kicking in. The trail stays churned; sometimes we are wading through a trench 6 inches deep filled with mud, leaves, rocks, and water.

Rhododendrons crowd close to the trail in many places. They are evergreens, with big, long, tough leaves, something between a bush and a tree. They are tall enough that they often create a tunnel the path passes through. It is beautiful, but very wet; any contact with the branches brings down a shower of water.

I want to get a plant guide loaded onto my tablet for reference. These woods are now the world I live in, and I would like to know what I am looking at. When I am home I know the purpose and significance of just about every object I see in the urban landscape. My ignorance of plant life is profound. It comes to me as I walk that I am looking at the woods and seeing nothing much more than green and brown shapes, and worse, I am accepting it. I know little about my environment, and I think becoming a part of the woods rather than just a visitor requires me to gain an understanding of what I am walking through.

We cross Standing Indian Mountain, a significant climb at this stage of the thru-hike. McGyver and I separate as we work our way up the mountain, each of us in our own groove toiling up the trail. The mountain has a lot of unofficial campsites around the top. It is well used by overnight hikers, and they have left some things behind.

McGyver picks up trash as he hikes along, a habit I also adopt. It is very hard to stop for a break, even a momentary breather, see a small piece of trash lying on the ground before me, and ignore it. McGyver is more diligent about it than I ever will be, and he proves it this day. When we meet up again after Standing Indian he is carrying a small beer keg in addition to his pack. He found the keg on the mountain, and couldn't stand to leave it there. It is half full, with a couple of gallons of beer in it, and it weighs upwards of fifteen pounds. McGyver carries it the next three miles until we make camp for the night, refusing any assistance. It is a heroic effort.

We are both wet and when we stop hiking our bodies rapidly begin to cool. I am shivering uncontrollably, even wearing all of my clothes. I set up my tent, cook and eat as quickly as I can, and I share McGyver's bear hang for the night to save the time of getting my own separate one established.

We make some half hearted attempts to break into the beer keg and maybe have a drink. We have no tap, and it is just too cold to fool around with it for very long

I crawl into my damp tent and sleeping bag, and slowly warm up enough to stop shivering. I finally fall asleep. My last thoughts are a contemplation of animals in the rain. Do deer, bears, raccoons, birds and other creatures have to struggle with hypothermia? Can they die of exposure, or are they so well adapted to their environment that hypothermia is not a concern? I am certainly feeling the frailty of my human body tonight.

Day 11, April 16th
Long Branch Shelter Trail Mile 102.5
Daily Distance 11.8 miles

TRAILTALK:

PURIST: A thru-hiker determined to follow the trail past every single white blaze on the trail, avoiding any shortcuts.

BLUE BLAZE: Trails marked with 2 inch by 6 inch blue blazes (as opposed to the white blazes of the main Appalachian Trail) are side trails, bypasses, cut offs, and short cuts that avoid some of the more difficult sections of trail, or lead to points of interest off the main trail.

BLUE BLAZER: A person who habitually uses bypasses and shortcuts rather than facing every challenge of the trail is called a 'blue blazer'. Sometimes this practice is a response to physical limitations, or weather, but sometimes it is attributed to laziness and used as a derogatory term.

FIRE TOWER: The United States Forest Service used to have observers who sat up in little cabins mounted on top of steel framework towers on mountain tops, where they would scan the forest for the smoke of forest fires. Detecting fires is now mostly done by aircraft, but the old towers remain scattered throughout the National Forests.

USFS: The United States Forest Service is the primary federal organization on the Appalachian Trail. The USFS is a separate entity from ATC, the National Park Service, and the various state lands that create the land mosaic the AT crosses.

Rain still comes down. It is not consistent, except in its presence. Sometimes it is short heavy downpours, and sometimes the downpour is sustained. Most often it is a drizzle, or a misty air. Water drips from the trees soaking my clothes, and every time I pass a bush it dumps water on me. The trail is still a trough to wade through, and my shoes, socks and feet are wet and squishy.

Rain gear helps, but less than I would have thought. My raincoat is effective in keeping the rain off, but the waterproofing also keeps sweat in, and I sweat a lot working hard all day. My raincoat is keeping my body heat in along with my perspiration, so it is still well worth wearing.

Staying warm while hiking is not much of a problem, in fact, I look forward to the first climb of the day knowing it will heat me up. It is in camp, in the evenings, when I stop moving and have exhausted myself that I feel the cold.

I have five layers of clothing I can wear on my upper body. I have my T-shirt, long underwear, long sleeved Smartwool shirt, my rain jacket, and the down jacket I call my "puffy coat" I usually wear only the t-shirt and raincoat while I am hiking. I am working hard enough that it is enough to keep me warm, most of the time. If I get cold enough I add the Smartwool top. On cold mornings I begin hiking with the extra Smartwool layer and take it off a half hour later as exertion warms me.

I only wear the down coat in camp, and I am very careful with it, wearing it under my raincoat when it is raining (all the time, presently). Down does not dry quickly when it gets wet, and can clump up, killing its insulating qualities.

I wear long underwear as sleeping clothes. It is nice to have something comfortable and a little cleaner and less stinky to sleep in. It also keeps my sleeping bag from getting foul.

The zipper on my Teton sleeping bag has failed badly, and I am losing body heat from the resulting gap in my bag as I sleep. I wake up cold, sometimes in the early hours of the morning, and it is very hard to recover body heat once it is lost. Sometimes I lie there a long time shivering, adding layers and rearranging my clothing until the shivering stops, and I try to sleep again. On a few nights the shivering never quite goes away, contributing to my overall lack of rest.

North Carolina is kicking my butt. My original plan of a seven day push to get straight to the NOC is abandoned, and I will zero in the town of Franklin for recovery. It will be my first zero day on the trail, a whole planned day of rest. I want to recover from the relentless rain and try and dry out, repair, or replace equipment.

I still hike with McGyver. He feels he has done his duty by the beer keg he carried yesterday, and writes a note that he puts in a baggie and attaches to the keg, asking other NoBo hikers to carry it a mile or so further along, until by relays it gets to the road out at Mooney Gap, eight miles ahead. He leaves the keg by the trail.

McGyver's plan succeeds. When we take our first break for the day we hear clanking coming up the trail behind us. It is Piston, and he has the beer keg hanging from a shoulder strap on his pack. He managed to drain the 10 pounds of beer out of the keg by the simple expedient of repeatedly smashing it against a rock until it made a hole. He is intent on carrying the keg all the way to the road; he is another hero of the Appalachian Trail.

Our goal for today is the fire tower at Albert Mountain. The mountain in the AWOL Guide profile is a very steep little climb following a long gradual rise. It is a well known and talked about terrain feature by thru-hikers. It was a topic of interest in Bill Bryson's book, 'A Walk in the Woods'; Bryson had bad weather, and used the bypass trail to go around the last, difficult, steep section.

I have already determined at this point that I am a purist, a thru-hiker determined to pass every white blaze on the Appalachian Trail. I am not going to use the blue blaze marked bypasses if I can possibly avoid it. No weather detours for a purist.

We meet a mother and daughter, with the trail names of Hakuna Matata and Bluebird, thru-hiking on the approach to Albert Mountain. Hakuna looks to be in her forties, and her mother, Bluebird, is seventy years old. The thru-hike is a love gift to them from Hakuna's husband, who is helping support them financially and emotionally on their journey. They are quite chipper despite the weather.

Albert Mountain is a challenge. The initial approach trail is flat, and the trail well drained, so it is more of a hike and less of a wade. As the trail gets closer to the peak it runs along the edge of a steep mountainside with a considerable drop-off on one side. At places the trail is no longer carved into the mountain's side, but travels over the tops of rhododendron and tree roots clinging to the side of rocks. I have a fear of heights, and this stretch presents a psychological obstacle for me.

As I traverse the drop-off, I can see across the deep valley to another steep mountain face opposite a half mile away, and a mist shrouded forest far down in the gap below. Halfway around the approach trail, I see clouds coming up the valley behind me. They slowly fill the gap between the mountains, eating up the landscape in an opaque white shroud chasing me around the mountain. I pick up my pace, knowing that whatever is in the approaching white cloud isn't going to improve my hike, but the mist and rain slowly overtake me.

The fog has its fortunate aspects. The mist closes down visibility to a few yards, and while I can actually see air in the gaps between the roots I am walking on, I can only see 20 feet of granite cliff face falling away below me in the gaps between the roots before the abyss is swallowed in the cloud. My agoraphobia is diminished, except when I stumble once or twice walking on the slippery bark. These are moments of stark terror, since there is nothing but the fog to my right and beneath me to arrest a fall.

I meet up with McGyver just before the final ascent, at the blue blaze bypass forest road used by Bill Bryson. There is a sign advising its use in bad weather, but even with the rain we are determined to go straight up the mountain.

The last few hundred yards up Albert Peak are the steepest we have faced on the trail up to this point. It is an ascending scramble over rocks and boulders ad we use hands as well as feet to get to the top. It is hard work, with not a few backwards slides and quick moments of fear, but we finally get to the peak. It is foggy enough we can barely see the cabin on the fire tower above us.

McGyver climbs up the tower to check it out. He heard a rumor that it was unlocked and could be used as a shelter at need, and we definitely are in need. To our chagrin, the cabin is locked. The exposure and weather on the peak rule it out to us as any kind of place to camp unprotected for the night, and we decide to go on, even though it is getting late.

The descent is a little easier than the ascent, but just. We are coming down from the steepest part of the north side when we run into a large group of men backpacking in the other direction. They are a men's church group heading up to Albert Peak with the intention of camping up there, like we had considered. We are in no way eager to share a camp with 20 men doing a kumbaya circle, but we still try to dissuade them from undertaking the climb ahead, if with small enthusiasm. We know it is unsuitable, and it will be several miles down the other side before they find another flat spot to camp. They hike on, heedless of our warning.

It is another mile to Long Branch Shelter and we arrive as darkness is falling. The shelter is empty. It is the first time I have slept inside a shelter since my first night. We are pleased to see Hakuna Matata and Bluebird show up a little after dark, finishing their day's hike using headlamps to pick the way along the trail. McGyver and I had both discussed concerns about Bluebird's age and apparent frailty, and the difficulty of Albert Mountain. We assumed they took the bypass, if they came this far at all.

Bluebird surprises us. They went right up and over Albert Peak, the same as we did. Hakuna looked like an athlete, but Bluebird showed us she was a tough and determined bird with that climb. They passed the church group, still in good spirits at the top, trying to set up camp.

Day 12, April 17th
Winding Stair Gap, U.S. Route 64 (Franklin), Trail Mile 109.8
Daily Distance 7.6 miles

TRAILTALK:

HYOH (Hike Your Own Hike): a trail philosophy that recognizes and embraces the many different ways and reasons to hike the Appalachian Trail. Sometimes it is used as an admonishment, as in 'mind your own business'.

AYCE (All You Can Eat): A buffet. Hikers love AYCE. AYCE establishments do not generally love hikers. Besides eating them out of a profit, hikers sometimes eat first when they get to town, bringing their unwashed trail funk into the restaurant with them.

I wake up to a chorus of birdsong. I can hear at least four discreet calls going back and forth. There is also a sound like a Harley Davidson starting up. I thought it was a machine off at a worksite in the woods at first, but it is organic. It is a loud, rhythmic, thumping noise. I don't know if it is a frog, a woodpecker, or maybe a grouse.

Later, after hearing this sound countless times, I find out it is a grouse. Grouse are basically wild chickens, smaller, smarter and wilier than the domesticated fowl. Their mating call is not a song; instead they call out to each other by flapping their wings together. They create a vacuum with the rapid wing movement, and the thudding; engine-like sound is the noise of air rushing in to fill the void. It is similar to how thunder is produced by air rushing in to fill the vacuum created by lightning, on a much diminished scale.

I feel strong moving out today, like my hiker legs are finally coming on. I have two climbs and both are easily surmounted. The relatively lighter weight of my pack on the days I head into town makes for easier hiking. I have eaten two pounds of food a day for the last four days, and my pack has progressively gotten eight pounds lighter.

McGyver is an early riser, and I am slower and more sluggish getting up and going. He has gone on ahead. I see Piston, another of the Quebecois I keep meeting along the trail. He does Eco Challenge races and has some serious knowledge from his endurance racing. He slows down and paces me for a while so we can talk.

We talk about food as fuel for the trail. Piston believes that fitness level is actually less important for endurance on the trail than fuel. He constantly stokes the fire driving him, eating very small amounts of food every half hour while he walks. He chews everything thoroughly, down into liquid, so his stomach doesn't have to break food down before digesting it. It provides a steady flow of fuel so his body doesn't have work at robbing fat, muscle, and even bone to provide the right biochemical nutritional mix to keep moving forward. I have already been snacking more frequently, but I am going to be more methodical after listening to Piston's advice. Go, go, gadget legs!

I pass other hikers, as well as being passed. Some of them are hikers who started fifteen, twenty, even as many as thirty days ago. They are all still slowly moving forward, much like Super Feet. They are content with low daily mileage, enjoying being in the woods rather than focusing on summiting Katahdin in some distant future. Hike your own hike; it is their journey and not my destination. I am one of those who are determined to complete every mile, and sometimes I have to remember it is not always a shared goal.

I pass a woman with a big cabin tent set up along the trail. Her pack and gear look like it weighs eighty pounds. She doesn't appear to be very focused on making miles, and may be homeless, living along the trail.

I stop and talk to her for few minutes. She is very religious, and speaks to Jesus as a third party during our conversation, as though he is sitting on a log next to us in the camp, sharing beliefs and insights with us as we talk.

Atop the unnamed mountain of today's second climb I start calling places in Franklin looking for a ride into town. The Budget Inn has a shuttle that makes a circuit from Franklin, the nearest town, to two different Appalachian trailheads, each one about fifteen miles from town. When I get to the trailhead I only have to wait a few minutes at the parking area for a van to appear. Several other thru-hikers have gathered and all take advantage of the ride into town.

The shuttle services two motels owned by the same man, Ron Haven. I get off at the Budget Inn, where I made my arrangements by phone. It is already full, and the overflow of hikers who have not called in ahead are taken off by the shuttle to the nearby Sapphire Motel.

The Budget Inn is an old, run down, one story motor lodge, and currently is festooned with tents, ground cloths, sleeping bags and jackets hanging from every railing and strung up on lines under the breezeway in front of the rooms. In the gravel parking lot there is a garden hose for washing down gear, and there is a coin operated laundry room. The rooms are decorated in 1970s chic, and have well used, battered, stained, but functional furnishings. There are a couple of restaurants nearby, and Ron Haven runs a shuttle to Wal-Mart and an outfitter for resupply. Everything about the Budget Inn is worn, but clean. There are little touches, like a rock garden, that show care and pride of ownership in the operation. The staff is tolerant of grungy, loud, obnoxious hikers and their wants and needs. It is thru-hiker paradise, for $40.00 a night.

In the evening I take the resupply shuttle into the Three Eagles Outfitter and Wal-Mart. The outfitter doesn't have a sleeping bag I really like at a price I am willing to pay. There is a second outfitter in town, but I don't have time to visit it. I barely make the shuttle after getting showered, doing laundry, washing down my gear, and making my own additions of wet equipment to decorate the breezeway railings.

I go on to Wal-Mart and hit the local Chinese AYCE (All You Can Eat) buffet, sitting with a crowd of other hikers. I am taking a zero day, staying in Franklin tomorrow. I justify it with the need to get my sleeping bag situation resolved, but really, I want a day off. I have hiked continually for 12 days.

Day 13, April 18th
Ron Haven's Budget Inn, Franklin NC, Trail Mile 109.8
Daily Distance 0.0, ZERO DAY

I have a lot of thoughts to process on this zero day. Zero days are full recovery days, no hiking. I am awake at 7:00 AM and I a feel an impatience to get on the trail. The rhythm of hiking has gotten into me, and the need to get back in the action gnaws at me.

I desperately need that new sleeping bag though, and I need the recovery time. I paid for two nights in cash for my room yesterday. Normally, if you come into town in early afternoon it is possible to do all of your chores, shop, rest, feast, and still be out on the trail the next morning. Staying in the comforts of town leaves me with a vague sense of guilt.

I spend part of my zero day cleaning and doing make and mend. Boredom comes quickly, and the Katahdin closure date of October 15th already looks like a challenge as I calculate my daily mileage.

Ron Haven owns two motels in Franklin, NC; the Budget Inn and the Sapphire Motel, and a third motel in Hiawassee, back down in Georgia. Every hiker coming into town meets Ron. He drives the shuttle as often as not, and is a presence around his places. He is a true character, with a Carolina country mountain accent so thick you could cut off a slice and eat it like smoky bacon. He is opinionated, a result of a direct way of looking at things, but is charming. He works to support the needs of hikers staying at his establishments. He is a most entertaining booster and ambassador for the city of Franklin. Ron is a businessman, and a politician, literally, having been an elected official in the county. He wants hikers to come to his town and happily spend their money.

I go to the town's second outfitter, Outdoor 76, after I didn't quite find what I wanted yesterday at Three Eagles. Outdoor 76 is located in the small, old downtown area, a short walk in the rain from the Budget Inn. It has the distinction of serving hikers making purchases mugs of micro brewed beer at a small bar inside of the store. Selection is larger than at Three Eagles, and I find a sleeping bag that suits me both in weight, cost, and in warmth rating. It is a Marmot bag weighing less than three pounds, and costs under $200.00.

I have been spending money faster than I expected, mostly on equipment purchases. These are repurchases really, since I am replacing gear I already bought with lighter, better items. I was a little too cost conscious when buying my gear initially, and now I am getting to buy it again as my initial cut rate gear shows itself to be inadequate.

I walk through the old downtown of Franklin to eat at a 1950s styled burger joint for dinner. On my walk back to the Budget Inn there is a little bluegrass trio playing with their back to the front window in a coffee shop. I stop and listen for a while. Inside looked crowded, but I was only a pane of glass away from being able to touch the musicians. Letting a little bit of rain fall on me is a small price to pay to feel like I am right up on the stage with them.

Forecasts of up to four inches of rain in thunderstorms possibly accompanied by tornados are predicted in the news for tomorrow's weather, and I am debating staying for yet one more zero. I have two options; I can stay, or I can go head back out to the trail. I can hole up at the first shelter four miles from the trailhead, if the weather turns out to be as bad as it is predicted. I am favoring the second option, but if I wake and the rain is coming down in buckets I may change my mind.

Day 14, April 19th
Ron Haven's Budget Inn, Franklin NC, Trail Mile 109.8
Daily Distance 0.0, ZERO DAY

TRAILTALK:

BOUNCE BOX: A supply mail drop sent ahead from one point to another further along the trail. If you do not open the box you can continue to keep forwarding it through the postal system for free. Hikers who have things like prescription medicines that are cheaper to buy in bulk, but that they do not want to carry in bulk, will often keep a bounce box going.

The rain is coming down in buckets. After twelve days straight of hiking I have stalled out for two. It is weather driven, it rains with extreme prejudice, and the tornado warnings are scary. I enjoy being safe, warm and dry.

I have a second reason for taking another zero. Ron Haven is warning us that resupply at Fontana Dam ahead of us is poor. There is a fancy lodge there, and a small store that he says is not geared towards thru-hiker resupply needs. Fontana is also the gateway to Great Smoky Mountain National Park, which is one of the more difficult places to get in and out of, with Gatlinburg as the only resupply point about 40 miles in.

Ron presents the thru-hikers hiding from the rain at the motel a solution. We can purchase our resupply in Franklin, and ship a bounce box forward to the Fontana Lodge. I am not particularly interested in visiting the tourist trap in Gatlinburg, so I buy eight days worth of food, enough to get me all the way through Great Smoky Mountains National Park, and I put it in a priority mailbox to ship from Three Eagles Outfitter.

The Budget Inn is still full of the same hikers who came in when I did, waiting out the weather. I meet most of them on the shuttle. There are Pebbles and Bam Bam, a pair of younger women hiking together. Bam Bam is one of the few people of color I see on the trail. She is thru-hiking, and Pebbles, her companion, is keeping her company for a while.

Grip is splitting cost on a room with Highlighter. They are about my age. Grip is an ex-military man and contractor, Highlighter is a female nurse. They are splitting the cost of a room, but I don't think hanky panky is going on.

Jumanji and Crusty Goat are also here. They are a couple of what Rikki Tikki will later coin as High Flyers, people who are smoking a lot of marijuana on their way up the trail. Jumanji has a frequent, loud, gurgling laugh, not unpleasant, that I will hear many times going up the trail. Watching them reminds me of the days when the Grateful Dead were touring. They would have been exactly the people to follow a tour, and are part of a very merry band.

There is not much to do once resupply is set up except watch the rain, and I go around the motel and bang on doors. I am carrying a mini set of Farkle, and I set up a tournament, Farkle being a dice game similar to Yahtzee. I post a note on my motel door as well. I bill it as the 'World Championship Tour' and I make a big, phony, million dollar check as a prize. Grip, Highlighter, and Pebbles show up and we play away part of the afternoon.

Discussions about shoes are an ongoing topic for hikers at the motel, and everywhere else we gather. Footgear is highly individualized to the person hiking. Many of the hikers in Franklin have foot problems they are trying to resolve, and are looking for shoe solutions.

Our poor dogs are taking a pounding, walking every day over rough ground, constantly wet, and under a heavy load. Getting the right shoes is critical. Unfortunately, the only way to know if a particular type of shoe or boot is going to work for you is try them out backpacking for a couple of weeks. Day hikes or weekends help, but can fall short, because feet begin to swell as you hike over time. Super Feet was an extreme example, her feet swelling three shoe sizes.

The wrong shoes wreak havoc on your feet. Some people show up on trail with brand new shoes they have only tried on in the store (like a lot of their other gear) setting them up for disaster. Trying them out a few times under load won't ensure a great fit, but will let someone know about some serious problems right away. Any small friction or discomfort will be magnified once a hiker gets on the trail.

Hikers with ill fitting shoes get blisters, and blisters on their blisters, and then the blisters crack the skin so they cannot hike any longer without taking a day or two for recovery. Tendon issues like Plantar Fasciitis are becoming common. In the wet, trench foot is also appearing. Trench foot is when the feet get overly soft from being soaked all the time and the skin starts sloughing off. It is also called immersion foot. None of it is pleasant, it is a morale killer, and can potentially be hike ending.

People hike in everything from the old school, high rise, stiff leather mountain boots to sneakers, sandals, and Crocs.

Gore-Tex shoes are a popular starting choice. Gore-Tex can keep your feet drier most of the time when you are hiking, but if you continually submerge your feet in heavy rains and trail churn the water will come in over the top, and through the holes for the laces, and in through the seams. Gore-Tex's disadvantage is that once it is wet it takes longer for the shoes to dry back out, the waterproofing holds the moisture in once it gets in. Gore-Tex shoes also cost $20.00 or $30.00 more than the same shoes without Gore-Tex.

Most people will go through three to five pairs of shoes while hiking the trail. People confident in their shoe choice will have them already waiting for them in mail drops at 500-800 mile intervals. Local outfitters usually only carry a couple of brands, and perhaps not a preferred one.

The shoes I begin with are Merrill low cut hiking shoes. They are Gore-Tex, and because of the continual rains, are perpetually wet. I picked them based on fit, not materials. I am cursed with wide feet and I needed the bigger toe box. My feet are not blistering much, except for a little on my toes.

Socks are as important and individual a choice as shoes. I wear a single pair of Smartwool socks, a merino wool blend. The socks are expensive but prove their worth to me by keeping my feet warm even when wet. Cotton is a poor material choice. It loses its insulating quality when it is wet, and is slow to dry. You won't see many cotton garments of any type on hikers for this reason.

I consider a pair of camp shoes a must to rest my feet after hiking. Most people have Crocs or flip flops, lightweight, comfortable, loose shoes they can wear around camp. I went with garish neon green and pink Crocs I got on clearance. They are easy to spot in the shelter or campsite.

Days 15-19 April 20-24
Winding Stair Gap to Fontana Dam Hilton, Trail Mile 109.8 to 165.9
56.1 miles, AVG 11.22 miles per day

Day 15, April 20th
Wayah Shelter Trail Mile 120.8
Daily Distance 11.0 Miles

I have come to expect to fail to meet my expectations reaching my daily distance goals. The 11 miles I hiked today really is not a bad day at this point in the hike. It isn't good, mind you, but it isn't bad either. We are getting bigger ascents as we enter the Smoky Mountains. I set up my tent near Wayah Shelter.

It was raining when I left Franklin on the shuttle, but I pushed out anyway. Two days off the trail was too many. The shuttle is full of hikers making the same decision. It is not a great day for hiking. It rains, then it hails, and finally it clears up a bit, although it stays very windy. It is still better than a third day chafing from inactivity in a motel.

I cross over Siler Bald during today's travels. While many area peaks are named as balds, they don't fit the description. The mountain and hill tops are grown over with second story growth. Balds are manmade high country grazing areas, rather than naturally occurring features, and require maintenance. Siler Bald was the first bald on the trail that is actually bald. The mountain top is a meadow covered with grass and spring wildflowers in bloom.

McGyver and Spudz are here at Wayah Shelter. I also meet Yeti, and it takes a little discussion to establish that he was the very first thru-hiker I met on trail, passing through Nimblewill Gap on the Springer approach trail. Yeti is a big, tall, powerful, hiker, and is thoroughly enjoying himself on his hike.

The wind is constant, and can really be felt on the exposed bald and on the ridgelines the trail follows during the climb. I set up my tent in a slightly sheltered spot getting out of the main thrust of the wind. It is still quite cold. I employ a trick I was told about to help keep body heat inside the tent. I kick dried leaves up in mounds to cover the gap between my rain fly and the ground. It works pretty well.

I see a lot of trees I am trying to identify. The white flowering trees are dogwoods, the trees showing the first buds of green are poplar. Maples are showing some red leaves now, and locust trees have hanging clusters of lavender flowers. While we don't have real leaf canopy growing in yet, the forest is starting to bloom. Spring is here.

Campfire discussion tonight centers around the establishments at the NOC, Fontana Dam, and Great Smoky Mountains National Park. The word is that thru-hikers are barely tolerated and considered a nuisance at these places. The real focus by the people who run the shops and lodges is on the day tourists who have money to spend, and leave at the end of the day or weekend.

I will learn this is a little true, but if you treat others with respect you are generally well treated in return. It is thru-hikers who expect special services or who think the establishment rules shouldn't apply who will have the most difficulties.

Day 16, April 21st
Wesser Bald Shelter Trail Mile 131.4
Daily Distance 10.5 miles

I make 10 miles today. The last climb exhausts me.

Thru-hikers who are crunching the numbers say you have to average 11 miles a day, including town days and zeros, in order to finish the trail by October 15th, based on where we are today. I do the math on my own and find I need to average 12.16 miles per day to finish the entire Appalachian Trail in 180 days. Based on my current progress I fall a little further behind each day. Even this early in the hike there is pressure to make miles.

The tribal wisdom of thru-hikers is that in Virginia you make big miles. The trail is supposed to get easy and flat to a point where you can regularly hike 20 miles a day (don't believe it). I will make better miles in Virginia, but they will be neither easy nor flat,

I wake up cold despite my leaf barrier around the base of my tent. It helps some, but the wind was determined and persistent, and it blew away all my heat last night. I add to my woes by waking up in a big puddle of water. I did not close the top of my water bladder properly last night, and it leaked out in the tent while I slept.

The best way to get warm is to get active. I get busy fast once I leave the cocoon of my tent and I am back hiking on the trail quickly. The climbs are getting bigger, and I continue to go up, and up more often than I go down as I gain altitude.

The highlight of this day is the observation tower on Wesser Bald. It is at the top of the day's climbing, where there is a platform with broad views of the surrounding mountains.

It is somewhere in this stretch of trail that I meet a woman backpacking on the trail, doing sections heading south. She is suffering from Leukemia, and some days she only gets a mile or two. She is trying to see as much of the trail as she can. I very much get the sense that she is also out here avoiding a hospital bed, and may very well go to sleep in her tent and not reawaken, that she even welcomes the prospect. It strikes me as a better way to go, myself.

I am cold and tired starting out, and the day devolved into a wet blur. I crawl into my tent tonight without really paying attention to anything or anyone. I take the sketchiest of notes and fall asleep.

Day 17, April 22nd

Grassy Gap Trail Mile 140.2
Daily Distance 8.4 miles

Today I pass through the Nantahala Outdoor Center (NOC). The trail drops into a gap, crosses a road, and then a bridge over the Nantahala River, traveling through a small commercial village that supports outdoor activities in the area. It is directly on the trail and there are no logistical issues with getting a ride into and out of town.

The sun is out and the sky is blue, I think it is only the second day on my hike it has not rained. My sense of smell goes into overdrive as I make the four mile descent down from the mountains into the Nantahala River gap. As I lose elevation I move from late winter into spring time, and bare tree branches sprout leaves and flowers bloom. I hike past a spring where two immense trees have fallen and I pause to look at how the trees rearranged the landscape as they fell.

When I step past the spring, my nose opens. I become aware of the most wonderful, powerful smell of wildflowers. There are four or five different types of flowers visible growing up out of leaves and bushes, and they are perfuming the air with a complexity of competing fragrances.

I breathe through my nose the rest of the way down to the NOC, reveling in my awakening sense of smell. From here forward on the trail, I stop from time to time just to smell the world, as well as see it. The overall green, earthy smell of the forest changes with the environment. Springs, streams and rivers each have their own living odors. Wood smoke lets me know when people are about and camping. The fragrances are most powerful during the next couple of weeks, while the forest blooms.

As I hike I have made a habit of stopping for a minute or two every half hour. Initially I stopped to catch my breath, and then pushed on with a single focus on taking more steps on down the trail. Now, as I get into better condition, it is a pause to take in the world around me.

On the descent I pass by a point called the Jump Off, a really nice view from a rock ledge with a very steep rocky descent just after it. The switchback under the ledge reveals a big cave tucked underneath Jump Off. The Appalachians have numerous stories of hermits who haunted certain areas along the trail, and I think this little cave looks like the very type of cave a hermit would live in. Later I find that no one else hiking by today even noticed it. It is very easy to get focused on the trail in front of you and miss the most amazing things just a few feet off to either side.

It is extremely tempting to stay the night in the hostel at the NOC. Besides the promise of a warm, dry bed and a hot shower, there are several restaurants, outfitters, and a beach by the river. The greatest temptation of them all is a free 8 mile raft trip down the river offered to thru-hikers by one of the outfitters working out of the center. Redlocks and Bubbles got to the NOC early enough today to go rafting. They say it was a hoot.

I am still hiking close to McGyver, and we do our resupply at the small convenience store, browse the outfitters, and have a nice lunch together at a restaurant overlooking the village. When we hit the trail again, hikers are relaxing on the deck of the hostel overlooking the trail, and it is not without considerable regret that I pass it by. In Franklin one of the rumors we heard was that there were bedbugs at the NOC hostel, but no one who stays the night there reports any problems.

McGyver and I start the long hike out of the NOC towards Cheoh Bald, the biggest sustained climb of the trail so far. We get about two and half miles further up the trail before calling it a day. We camp at a spot that has obviously been much used by previous hikers. There are reports of bear sightings in this area, although no real problem incidents. Still, McGyver and I are choosy about where and how we hang our bear bags.

I prepare my dinner and I realize I forgot to get hot chocolate and coffee at the NOC. I usually add a chocolate packet to my coffee each morning, and have a cup or two with my first boil of water at night, as the rest of my meal cooks. I will have to ration myself to one cup of either each day. I am a big fan of the restorative effect of warming caffeinated beverages, and this is a small blow to my morale.

I am trying another backpacking trick of the trade tonight. I will be bringing my pack into my little tent and sleeping with my feet propped up on it, rather than leaving it leaning up against a tree outside. Putting my feet on my pack serves several purposes. It gets my feet and lower legs off the ground creating a layer to preserve my lower body heat, and it keeps me from rolling around and sliding about inside my tent. On slightly sloping ground it is not uncommon to wake up wedged against the side of my tent wall. It is uncomfortable and presses the interior wall of my tent against the rain fly, letting water seep in. Putting my feet on my pack also helps protect it from mice and other creatures that might chew a few exploratory holes in it if it is left outside.

I kick leaves up against the outside of the rain fly again tonight. I am trying anything that will let me have a better, warmer night of sleep. I am convinced I can develop techniques that will allow me a proper rest at night.

Day 18, April 23rd
Between Stecoah and Sweetwater Gaps, Trail Mile 151.2
Daily Distance 11.0 miles.

This is one of the hardest days of hiking, both physically and mentally, I experience on the trail. The total elevation gain from the NOC to the top of Cheoah Bald is 3,000 feet over seven miles. It is not a steady, easy elevation gain; there are additional ups and downs. The climb entails going over a series of false summits, each successive crest a little higher than the last. The summit at Cheoah Bald is surrendering to the advances of the surrounding forest, but there is still enough open ground to have a view of mountains shrouded in mists and rain.

We heard a report of another bear sighting, the third in as many days. The black bear population is definitely coming out of hibernation and moving around. I saw another big black snake; McGyver thinks it was probably a king snake.

I put Piston's nutrition ideas into creating my snack plan. I carry fewer snacks, but have concentrated ones. I keep small pieces of jerky, candy bar miniatures and other small items in a Ziploc bag I carry in my cargo pocket. I eat a single bite of something once an hour. I am still trying to assess what the minimum amounts of food and water I need to consume during the day are, without robbing my body of the nutrients it needs

I made some pack load and strap changes at the NOC, and my burden is riding more comfortably. The hip belt on my backpack is giving me a lot of trouble; it slides down my hips as I hike, and my shoulders end up bearing most of my pack's weight. Where my pack rides on my waist it has created an uncomfortable heat rash. It feels better after my adjustments, but is still heavy. My hips are not as sore, but my Achilles tendon perversely cramps up instead, and I have an awkward limping gait for the day.

The amazing smells that buoyed my spirits descending into the NOC vanish as we climb out of the valley and back up into elevations where winter still holds a grip. The green is gone, and the trees are lifeless brown poles reaching into a grey, windy sky.

Just before Cheoah Bald I pass a big, colorful, cabin style tent set up in a thick growth of rhododendron on top of one of the false peaks. Cabin tents are not often seen on the trail; they are far too heavy for backpacking. This one is 8 or 10 feet square and would house six people comfortably. There is no one near the tent. I look inside to ensure there isn't someone in trouble lying inside, but it is empty, and there is an abandoned feeling to the set up.

Finding gear left behind isn't terribly uncommon. At the beginning of the trail in Georgia I saw it frequently, where people just gave up and walked off the trail. I can see why someone didn't want to carry a fifteen pound tent through the woods, but leaving it in the middle of the wilderness seems like a crime. It wasn't in me to try and pack it out myself. I was struggling just to carry my own load. I thought about it pretty hard though. It was possible campers were using it as a base who had hiked off for a little sightseeing and were planning on returning tonight. Or so I tell myself.

The ups continue endlessly today, even after getting atop and over Cheoah Bald. I am hiking with McGyver, more or less. We separate during the day due to differing hiking paces, but meet up during breaks along the way, and camp together. We aim for Stecoah Gap tonight. There is a succession of little un-named peaks after the Cheoah Bald summit. I am exhausted summiting the last little unrecognized peak, and after I finally get up there I dub it Mount-Possible, for my own self and my achievements.

At Locust Grove Gap McGyver and I hike down to get water, there being none on the trail for some distance. It is a half mile excursion, up and down to the spring, that adds another mile to our day. The little extra distances down side trails do not figure in my daily trail mileage, but are hiked nonetheless.

We finally get down to Stecoah Gap and find a double disappointment. We heard there might be trail magic at the parking area picnic table. We arrive near dark, and the area is empty, no trail magic. We were also planning to camp in the gap, but there are 'Bird Sanctuary, No Camping' signs prominently displayed in the area. I am tired enough to consider going a little ways into the woods, out of sight, and pitching camp anyway, but hiking with McGyver is hiking with a conscience; he will not break rules for his own convenience.

There is nothing for it but to climb up the ridgeline on the far side. We are hiking with headlamps to see into the gloom as we near the top of the ridgeline. It seems an eternity, but it is only a half mile climb away from the gap before we find a flat spot large enough for our two tents.

We set up camp. I cook a pot of Knorr noodle sides (A hiker dinner staple), and I bend down to pick it up. In my exhaustion I stagger and kick my meal into the dirt. I nearly cry. I scoop up what I can back into the pot. I eat around the dirtiest bits, and take the rest fifty yards down the trail and bury it. I am done with the night. I am at the end of my rope.

McGyver pulls out a surprise for me when I come back to our little campsite He purchased two 25 ounce cans of Budweiser at the NOC, and carried the four extra pounds of weight all the way through two day's struggles. With a great big smile, he offers me one.

I am so dejected, and so wiped out all I want is to crawl into my tent and sleep. I turn down the proffered gift of beer.

McGyver can't believe it. Carrying beer in its heavy cans is a major undertaking on the trail, and he thought he would cheer me up with this extravagant treat. He is just a little angry at my rejection. The can of beer represents a sacrifice of his pain and suffering, but I don't have it in me in my own sphere of personal misery tonight to sit and enjoy a beer with him.

I still get texts from him now and again teasing me about turning down that can of Budweiser.

Day 19, April 24th
The Fontana Hilton, Trial Mile 165.9
Daily Distance 14.7 Miles

The profile for today's hike shows a steep climb out of Sweetwater Gap called Jacob's Ladder starting out, followed by a long ridgeline walk and a short descent down and a pop up of about 500 feet out of Yellow Creek and Cable Gap. After that there is a long, steep three mile, 2500 foot descent ending at Fontana Dam. It is fifteen miles, my longest day yet, but the profile makes it look fairly easy. My initial plan was to cover it in two days; I would stop short and do a nearo the next day finishing short miles in the morning and spending the afternoon at Fontana Village.

McGyver wants to get into Fontana tonight. The profile looks like it can be done, and I need to up my miles, so we both go for it. Once mentally committed it is hard to back down. The elevation profile of the long ridge showed three small knobs. I look back at it the next day from Fontana and I count nine separate, distinct knobs on that same ridgeline. It is an endless journey of ups and downs, thinking each new knob is the third and final one.

Descents are just as hard as ascents in a different way, jarring the bones and muscles rather than as an aerobic exercise. The constant braking is hard on knees and ankles, and the urge to quit resisting and let gravity pull me down the slope is strong. It won't do though; there are treacherous rocks, roots and slippery leaves to give me a nasty fall if I let go of control. Most of the non-repetitive injuries I see or hear about on the trail occur on downhills.

McGyver and I separate on the way. He moves a lot quicker than I do, but we meet at the bottom of the hill in Fontana. There is a parking lot with a bathroom that has running water and electricity at the trailhead, a wonderful outpost of civilization. There is a pay phone with a shuttle number posted on it. I am ready to be done for the day, and call in to the Fontana Lodge, but there is one single room left and it $100.00. It is too much for either of us. We hike one more endless mile in the dark to the shelter, our headlamps bobbing pools of light hugging the side of Fontana Lake.

The Fontana Hilton is one of the biggest shelters on the trail, providing room for 24 hikers on two shelves. There is a camping area with pads, a big fire pit with logs around it, and a key luxury that helped give it the name 'The Hilton'; a separate outbuilding with showers, sinks and running water. I am so tired I don't bother with the tent and head into the shelter. McGyver sets up on one of the tent pads.

The Hilton is packed; there are 26 hikers and two dogs crammed into a space rated for 24 very friendly hikers. The friendliness is helped by someone handing me a beer when I approach the campfire. Tonight I have a little more moxie left than last night, and the cold beer right off the trail is bliss.

There is a single shower on the men's side of the bathroom building. It dribbles hot water in fits and starts, and it is a heavenly trickle. The relaxation of hot water and being clean, along with another beer or two, help me get what sleep I can in the shelter tonight.

I am tired and sore and find sleep elusive. The constant comings and goings of hikers in the shelter wake me up when I start to drift off. Jumanji is present, and his frequent, happy laugh drives me crazy. I miss the peace of the woods.

Day 20, April 25th
Fontana Hilton, Trail Mile 165.9
Daily Distance 0.0, ZERO DAY

TRAILTALK:

GREAT SMOKY MOUNTAINS NATIONAL PARK (GSMNP): A stretch of the Appalachian Mountains in Western North Carolina and Eastern Tennessee. It is the heart of the southern Appalachians, and has the highest mountain peaks east of the Mississippi River.

BUBBLE: A group of people hiking in rough proximity to each other as they move north up the trail. As the hike progresses hikers maintaining the same rate of progress see each other a lot.

TRAIL DAYS: Various towns along the Appalachian Trail in the south celebrate the flood of hikers coming through with festivals called Trail Days. There are often gear representatives and people marketing other things to hikers present, and there is usually some kind of free food and camping involved. The largest of these events, the original Trail Days, is a 4 day event in Damascus, Virginia.

WORK-FOR-STAY (WFS): Trading work for a space in a bunkroom and a meal at a hostel.

Today I am doing a zero instead of the nearo I intended. I did fifteen hard miles yesterday rather than doing a regular day of ten or eleven miles and finishing with a short hike today. My net progress is the same. I am already here, and worn out.

Tomorrow I will enter the Great Smoky Mountains National Park (GSMNP), beginning with the most intimidating climb yet seen in the profile. I am starting the biggest, toughest section of the Appalachian Trail until I get into the White Mountains of New Hampshire. I have 7 days of food, most of it from the bounce box I sent forward from Franklin. It is 14 pounds of weight in my food bag, and I already dread how it will tell on the climb.

I hope to make it through the Smokies in a single sustained push. It is difficult getting off the trail in GSMNP. There are no easy roads into town except for the one road into Gatlinburg, an expensive tourist destination.

I am thinking about money on the trail, and the haves and have nots among thru-hikers. It is possible to hike the trail on very little money, even on a few hundred dollars. It is not easy, and I suspect budget hikers go hungry or suffer extra discomfort at times.

There are a few thru-hikers who just take a pack, empty out their bank accounts and run up their credit cards to finance their trip. More have carefully budgeted and planned their journey. As one of the planners, I have found I have spent more than expected, mostly on gear changes. Expenditures will even out as I head north.

Budget hikers employ a number of strategies to sustain themselves. Preparing boxes of food and supplies and sending them to strategic locations along the AT in mail drops allows them to have much of their costs already accounted for before they even set out. Budget hikers rarely stay in motels, unless there are 4 or 6 or even 8 people sharing a single room and splitting costs.

Hiker boxes are gold mines for budget hikers, if they are not too particular. I am not very budget constrained; I am a 'have' on the trail. I always end up throwing extra items into the hiker boxes. I won't carry the extra packages from a bulk buy because of weight and space. People like to switch out fuel canisters before they go empty, and put canisters that have a few burns left in them into the hiker box. There is usually enough fuel to make it to the next town stop and hiker box for someone looking to get free fuel. Clothing, shoes and gear that doesn't suit also ends up on the hiker boxes. It is easier to leave the items for someone who might use them than it is to ship items home.

The cornucopia of the hiker box is not endless. As the bubbles of thru-hikers start thinning out and the survivors become more experienced food shoppers there are fewer extras. Hikers have also settled on their gear, and are no longer discarding equipment to lighten their packs at each town. The boxes get pretty lean in the Mid-Atlantic States. In Vermont and Maine, where there are a lot of section hikers, the boxes fill up again, and can have nice surprises in them.

Trail magic can help budget hikers along. At organized trail magic there is free food, and some resupply needs for hikers. It isn't enough on its own, and certainly cannot be planned on, but it helps enormously. Organized trail magic is more common in the south than in the north.

Some trail towns provide various kinds of support for thru-hikers, namely free camping in town and free shower sites. Organizations along the Appalachian Trail such as churches and hiking clubs put on spaghetti dinners and other feeds, and sometimes open their doors or yards for a place to stay.

A budget hiker can also ask for Work-for-stay (WFS) at hostels along the way. The hostels are businesses and not charitable operations, but they often have a work list and a bunk for one or two people a night, to get needed work done while giving something back to the trail.

Many of the low budget hikers don't appear to suffer greatly from their want on the trail. In fact, many of them thrive. There may be an added dimension to their trail experience because they are letting fate influence a large part of their journey, and are in a situation where they are only driven by the most basic material needs. "The trail will provide" is a mantra you hear all along the trail. It speaks to spiritual and emotional wants and needs as well as the material.

There is a girl named Jessica, barely out of her teens, (Trail names 'Rocks that Shit', and 'Miles', for more appropriate occasions) who is not just ultra cheap but ultra light. Fontana is the second time I see her. She is already hiking a heroic 20 miles and more each day, and I will only see her one more time, when she comes back to Damascus for Trail Days. She has dreadlocks, and a charming, laid back sweetness. She speaks with a thick Virginia country accent, so when she is asked why she is hiking the Appalachian Trail her response is "Ah jes laak to wok". (I just like to walk)" She is working with a budget considerably south of a thousand dollars to complete the thru-hike.

Jessica did extensive research on inexpensively equipping and supplying herself. She made her own pack and shelter, using plans from the internet, and utilized the newest wonder fabrics to custom build exactly what she wanted. She called or emailed equipment designers, authors, and other thru-hikers to get advice.

She is a vegan, and has food drops meeting her dietary requirements waiting for her all the way up the trail to Maine. She doesn't cook, living mostly on home made energy bars. She field tested her equipment and food on the Colorado Trail before tackling the AT. Her pack weight, loaded, is less than 15 pounds.

Jessica is an extreme example of a budget hiker. She rarely goes into town except to pick up her mail drops. She is entirely focused on walking each and every day, and she is foregoing some of the social aspects of the trail to do so. She is an experienced ultralight backpacker. I imagine she is cold sometimes at night, and her diet must be repetitive, but she is in the woods, walking, doing what she wants, and the sacrifices don't seem to bother her.

I head into Fontana village looking for food and entertainment. At the road a German thru-hiker is attempting to get a ride. There are people around, even a shuttle, but he speaks just a few words of English. He is using hand signals and his very limited vocabulary to make his needs understood. I can't imagine how difficult it is for him to backpack. I expect he thought backpacking in the woods wouldn't require language, but logistics must be very hard for him.

The word about Fontana Dam resort being overpriced, poorly supplied and hostile is all wrong. The store at Fontana Village is basic, and does cater to people staying at the resort, but carries a nice range of hiker foods. Prices are high, but not so much as to outweigh the shipping costs added on to the bounce box I sent here.

The lodge is tolerant of the hikers staying there or just using some of the facilities. I eat at the AYCE breakfast buffet while I am here. There are eggs, meats, grits, biscuits and gravy, fruit, rolls, juice and coffee for only $10.00. It is a very fine morning of eating.

The Lodge at Fontana is a resort, and its big attraction is not hiking but motor sports. The Tail of the Dragon is an 11 mile stretch of U.S. Route 129 that has 318 curves in it. It is touted as 'America's number one sports car and motorcycle road' and Fontana Lodge is close to the end point by motor vehicle. Two groups of motor sport enthusiasts are in Fontana Village today, a BMW motorcycle club, and a Volvo C30 enthusiast's organization. I mix with them at the breakfast buffet and at the general store. I like cars and motorcycles, and these people are well heeled adventurers in their own right, so conversation is spirited. A couple of thru-hikers actually get to drive a few of the souped up Volvos, at the owners' insistence. It might well have been another once in a lifetime experience for the hikers.

In addition to motor sports there are mountain trails for day hiking, horseback and mountain bike rides. (No horses, pack animals, bicycles or motor vehicles are permitted anywhere on the Appalachian Trail) Fontana Lake has houseboats for rent, and fishing, and all of the other recreational uses a big lake in the mountains offers. It is a place I wanted to bring my family back to, an alternative to a Disney vacation or a cruise.

There is a historical cabin on display at Fontana Village. In the 1930s the Appalachian "mountain people' were living hand to mouth on what they could hunt, raise and gather in the Appalachians. As a population they were very poor, I think hardscrabble was coined to describe them, and their suffering was poignant enough to draw particular national attention even while the country was in the throes of the Great Depression. The Gunter Cabin has a tragic story.

The Gunter Cabin was built in 1875 by Jesse Gunter, a man who came up from Stecoh Gap to visit a family member and fell in love with the Fontana area. He packed up his wife, moved out to Fontana and built his house. The cabin is two and a half rooms. Judging from pictures of other historical cabins in the area posted in a gallery in the lodge, it was a mansion by the standards of the area. It is all hand built, and while it is small and rough by today's standards, for a hand built structure where the builder had to pick and shape each log into a piece of his house, it is a masterpiece.

The tragic tale is presented on historical plaques on site. Ten years after moving into his new house, Jesse's two young children caught a sickness and died. Heartbroken, Jesse declared he would not allow his children to be buried in plain pine boxes, and he tore up the tulipwood floors laid in his cabin to build coffins for them. A year later his wife, weakened by her own grief, also succumbed to a passing illness, and died. Jesse tore up his remaining flooring to provide a coffin for his wife, buried her, packed up his belongings, and left his valley of tears forever.

The cabin floors have been replaced, and period furniture and tool displays are on show in the cabin. It is a reminder of the far harder life that was the lot of many people not too terribly far back in our past.

A party is underway around the fire pit at the Fontana Hilton Shelter when I return. The Hilton has a reputation for hiker parties, and some people stay a couple of zeros to play. It isn't all hikers; there are people at the shelter no one has ever seen on the trail. There is a man who is playing in a poker tournament in nearby Cherokee who didn't want to spend money on an expensive room at the casino and knew of this place from section hiking. He is in late and out early.

There is at least one person present who appears to be homeless, and squatting in the questionable luxury of the shelter. He fits right into the thru-hiker community.

Joker had a couple of friends meet him here to hike part of the trail with him. This isn't uncommon, and the Smokies are special enough that friends and family who want to hike a section with their thru-hiker choose GSMNP. One of Joker's friends is out of shape, apparently some sort of computer wizard who doesn't get out of his cubicle much.

He has been drinking (a lot), and gets up to go to the bathroom in the wee hours of the morning. He is on the second sleeping shelf, seven feet off of the floor. He turns on his headlamp to scan and plan his descent from the shelf, sweeping his light beam across the faces of all the sleepers on the lower deck as he tries to figure out the best way down. It wakes up most of us, and sets up a public performance. I am restless already from the sounds of the crowded shelter, and wake up early on during his shenanigans.

I watch his light beam going to and fro. At one point he turns around and dangles his feet over the edge of the upper shelf, probing around looking for a foot hold. His feet retract and a minute or so later reappear facing forward. They peddle about in the air, and then he must have tried teetering too close to the edge while giving himself a bit of a boost, and he dives from the seven foot high deck into the middle of the hard shelter floor below. He lands hard, with a thud and a shriek that wakes everyone in the shelter not already watching his antics.

There are five seconds of stunned silence, then everyone's headlights come on and people start asking what is going on and offering help. The diver rolls around, and then staggers up, mumbling something about being OK. He goes off to the bathroom and everyone goes back to their rests.

The following morning I see the diver again, as I prepare to head out to the trail. Both of his arms are bandaged, and one is splinted. He went to a nearby clinic early in the morning to get patched up. He is in pretty good spirits considering, and laughing at himself. I don't think he ends up doing any hiking, but he is a trail angel shuttling hikers around the area in his car.

GREAT SMOKY MOUNTAINS NATIONAL PARK

Days 21-24, April 26-29
Fontana Dam Shelter to Newfound Gap, Trail Mile 165.9 - 207.3
41.4 Miles, AVG 10.35 miles per day

Day 21, April 26th
Mollie's Ridge Shelter, Trail Mile 177.0
Daily Distance 11.1 Miles

TRAILTALK:

RIDGE RUNNER: A person hired by the USFS (or in some cases a hiking club) to hike and watch over the trail, seeing to the safety and welfare of hikers, cleaning up sites and informally watching for adherence to local and federal rules. They are not usually law enforcement personnel but do carry radios to call in enforcement when needed.

GO OFF-TRAIL: Leave the trail, either for an extended period of time or permanently.

LEAVE NO TRACE (LNT): A philosophy, and often a policy, wherein hikers endeavor to make the smallest possible impact on the wilderness, ideally as if man had never been there. "Take only pictures, leave only footsteps".

PRIVY: A trail outhouse, without running water.

I enter the Great Smoky Mountains National Park this morning. Fontana is the last place to organize logistics before entering GSMNP. A backcountry permit is required to stay nights in the park. It is purchased online and printed out to carry through the park. I completed mine earlier at a computer station at Three Eagles Outfitter in Franklin. There is a much resented $20.00 fee for the thru-hiker permit.

There are a many things thru-hikers resent about Great Smoky Mountains National Park. It and Baxter State Park up in Maine have the most restrictive regulations, some specifically aimed at thru-hikers, and when thru-hikers flaunt those rules, the parks are serious about enforcing them. It creates tension between the two groups, as groups.

In GSMNP backpackers are required to stay at shelters. They have to actually stay inside the shelter, unless the shelter is full, in which case a hiker can camp in close proximity to the shelter. For people who, like me, don't like shelters, this is an unpleasantry. To hikers who don't even like camping near shelters, preferring to pick their own isolated places to camp; it feels like a great imposition.

The requirement for people to stay at shelters means the shelters are always crowded in GSMNP. The shelters are not especially nice ones. At one time they had chain link fence cages covering the fronts to keep bears out, caging the hikers within in a weird sort of reverse zoo. It not only made the shelters less enjoyable, but it backfired in its intended purpose.

There were (jackass) campers who, feeling safe behind the protective barrier, wanted to interact with the bears. They fed the bears through the openings in the mesh, attracting even more bears to the shelter sites and conditioning them to associate people with food. Thru-hikers like to point to day hikers and section hikers as the culprits for many of the issues on the trail, arguing that thru-hikers, as a population, are far too respectful of the Appalachian Trail and all it represents as an experience to act to endanger it in any overt way. I still saw the occasional jackass thru-hiker. I may have even been one myself once depending on whom and how jackass is defined.

Thru-hikers are required to stay in a shelter, but if the shelter is full they can camp next to it; it is a first come, first served arrangement. Some hikers dawdle intentionally, showing up at the shelter later in hopes it will be full so they can set up their tents instead. Thru-hikers also delay because they have second priority in the shelters. Backpackers on short trips into GSMNP buy a different permit than thru-hikers, and have first priority to stay in shelters. A thru-hiker can get settled in, laying out all of their gear for the night, and then be kicked out by any arriving section hiker, even at midnight, in the rain. The thru-hiker has to get up, pack everything and set up a tent site in the dark, cold, and rain.

The park has a Leave No Trace (LNT) policy, as is common practice along the trail. LNT means different thing to different people in execution. In GSMNP, the interpretation of Leave No Trace often includes not having privies at the shelters. While thru-hikers all learn how to poop in the woods, most people are on a biological schedule, and do their business before leaving camp in the morning. Some people have to go at night. Generally, the urge does not come while a body is in motion, but occurs when the body takes a rest in camp.

In GSMNP, instead of privies there are designated waste fields near the shelters, separated by a small distance from the shelter area. In practice, there are poop piles all around each shelter, each marked by a little flower of toilet paper sitting on top. Besides being unsightly and making you watch your step very carefully, especially at night, it is pretty unsanitary. I am not sure it really reduces the impact of humans on the forest by spreading rather than concentrating the waste.

No dogs are allowed in the park. Thru-hikers with dogs must arrange to kennel their pets while they hike through GSMNP, an expensive undertaking. It costs around $300.00 to have a dog picked up, kenneled, and returned to the hiker when they leave the park. The NoBo pick up is usually at Fontana Lake.

Ridge runners are the main personnel enforcing the rules. I had not seen a ridge runner before entering GSMNP, but there are greater numbers of them here, especially during the main thru-hiker season, than anywhere else on the trail. Having police, however informal, is also resented by some thru-hikers, who interpret the 'wild' aspect of their thru-hike as being an absence of law and rules.

It is a long, long climb out of Fontana. The beginning is a mile of gently sloped road walk to the actual GSMNP entrance. The best part of the road walk is crossing the top of Fontana Dam, the largest concrete dam east of the Mississippi River. It is a tourist attraction and has a visitor center on the south side of the dam. It is under construction and closed for the season, so I work my way through a maze of fences and detours to get on the dam and on my way.

The walk across Fontana Dam is enjoyable, and on my morning there is a reflection on the still waters of the lake lapping against the inner wall, a double image of lake, forest, and mountains in the mist is mirrored on the lake's surface. It almost draws the eye away from the 480 foot drop of the dam and spillway on the other side. It is an enormous manmade structure, a great concave, concrete wall holding back the lake. Far below a river emerges, looking tiny in the distance. It is a breathtaking start to Great Smokey Mountain National Park.

I am hiking alone. McGyver still has not left Fontana. His family has met him and supplied him with treats for an army, and he is passing around bags of home made granola to thru-hikers at the shelter. I will see him again in the miles ahead, but his walking pace and mine don't really match. He likes to get up very early, before dawn in fact, and be on the trail at first light. I like to linger in my sleeping bag and don't usually get on trail before 7:30.

There is a little kiosk at the GSMNP entrance, a hundred yards back from the road after the trail re-enters the woods. I tear my preprinted permit in two, drop one half into the box, and put the other half in my pack. Backpackers are required to carry the permit while hiking through the park, and show it to authorities on request.

Once I pass the kiosk the climbing begins. It is three and a half miles up to Shuckstack Fire Tower, rising from 1700 feet at the dam, to 3900 feet at the tower. From there I will continue to climb in fits and starts until ultimately reaching Clingman's Dome at 6,643 feet. The first day is a punishing day, the hike up to the shelter going up and down until finishing the day at about 4500 feet, following more than 3000 feet in elevation gains.

A section hiker on his way down from Shuckstack tells me there is trail magic left in the fire tower. The tower is a tenth of a mile off-trail on a blue blaze. I don't take many of the side trails, but the promise of trail magic along with a view prompts me to make the detour. After three continuous hours of climbing I need a break.

There are a couple of packs at the trail junction. Other hikers decided to drop their packs, make the walk out to the tower and climb up the staircase without their backpacks throwing off their center of balance. It is tempting, walking for just a little while without forty some odd pounds on my back, and I leave mine there as well.

Shuckstack Fire Tower is like many of the fire towers along the trail, a tiny cabin mounted a hundred feet high atop a spindly metal frame. A steep metal stairway rises up to the cabin, an 8 foot square box, just big enough to offer a little protection for an observer with binoculars scanning the forest for fires.

I do not like heights, so climbing up the ladder is a challenge for me. Inside the tower, the wooden floor is half rotted away. Someone left cookies and fruit inside. It is the trail magic. The cookies are chocolate covered graham crackers, one of my favorites. I take two, enjoy the panoramic view of Fontana Lake below, then work my way slowly back down the stairs.

I was lucky. I don't usually leave my pack unattended for a lot of reasons. One of them is that untended packs attract wildlife. Shuckstack is a popular place for hikers to climb up and take in the view, and many of them, like me, want to make the climb unencumbered by a backpack.

A black bear cottons on to the presence of a new food source. The trail magic may have had just enough odor to alert Mr. Bear that there was food in the tower. Further down the trail I hear two different stories about the bear.

The first tale is of a group of hikers who went up into the tower looking for the trail magic. They left their packs at the base of the tower. One look at the narrow, rickety staircase would convince most hikers they didn't want to be unbalanced by their packs. This group made it up to the tower, and was eating cookies and fruit when the bear arrived. It circled the base of the tower, trapping them up on the top for an hour while he smelled the snacks, looked at the stairs, looked at the hikers, and, debated his courses of action. He didn't attempt the ladder, but he found their packs on the ground. He pawed through their packs, but wasn't able to get at the food inside. The bear was probably a little distracted by the crowd of hikers yelling at him from above. The bear finally got tired, bored, or annoyed, and left.

The second story I hear involves Spudz, the Quebecois potato eater. Spudz was one of the great characters of the trail. He hiked in bright red gym shorts with a yellow flower print and an electric blue top. He told wonderful stories with quirky turns of phrase and a charming French accent.

Spudz scoffed at the potential threats posed by black bears on the trail. He said "We have bears in Quebec. They are nothing to be afraid of. You see a bear in a tree; you say 'Boo!', and the bear? He falls out of the tree and runs away."

Like so many thru-hikers coming up from Fontana Dam, Spudz took the detour to Shuckstack Fire Tower. He climbed up the long, narrow staircase, and was on the last couple of risers before reaching the cabin, when Mr. Bear stuck his head out of the cabin entrance. The bear figured out how to climb up to the top to get to the trail magic, and Spudz met him face to face on the rickety staircase.

Now Spudz was struggling to stay on the trail. His finances were in disarray, his Canadian credit card would not work in the U.S, and he had to go through a complicated shuffling of money and wire orders each time he needed funds. He also had a girlfriend in Quebec who wanted him back home. Shortly after the incident at Shuckstack, Spudz went off the trail. I know there were lots of reasons for him to go home, but I think it was the bear.

I keep going up mountains after Shuckstack, but the hardest part of the climb out of Fontana Dam is over. I have my first GSMNP shelter experience at Mollie's Ridge Shelter.

There is a ridge runner present. I don't realize who he is until after he greets me and asks to see my permit. There is no uniform for ridge runners, and he looked like any other hiker. My expectation after hearing stories about ridge runners is that I am meeting some sort of National Park storm trooper. I heard wrong.

The ridge runner turns out to be a great person. One of the qualifications to become a ridge runner is completing a thru-hike. He is not a storm trooper, he is one of us. The runner is full of helpful advice and information about the trail ahead. His presence keeps the shelter from becoming too crowded, despite it being the first shelter on the way out of Fontana. There is another shelter just 1.3 miles further up the trail, and thru-hikers who don't want to camp with John Law watching are moving on to the next shelter. It makes for a peaceful night, the hikers passing by are generally the more disruptive and inconsiderate ones

The ridge runner puts many of my concerns about the policing of rules in GSMNP at rest. He is mostly here to help and is reasonable about enforcing park rules. He stops enforcing the priority rule forcing thru-hikers to give up their spaces to section hikers at 8:00 PM. As the last thru-hiker to arrive I worried about settling in and then being displaced, but after our conversation I am able to relax.

His attitude is typical of the ridge runners I will meet along the trail. They are positive and helpful, facilitating the trail experience, enforcing the spirit of the rules governing the sections they are responsible for rather than making a burden of them. I would like to see more of them on the trail.

There is an assigned section for each ridge runner. In the Smokies more than one ridge runner shares a section, staggered so ridge runners a day or two apart move south against the flow of NoBo thru-hikers. Most trail areas can't afford to provide that level of trail over watch, but I was always pleased to meet a ridge runner, and felt safer for their presence on the Appalachian Trail.

Day 22, April 27th
Derrick Knob Shelter, Trail Mile 189.0
Daily Distance 12 Miles

I wake to a cold morning, and a biting wind drives a chill throughout the day. It is a beautiful section of the trail. I hike through the remnants of an old apple orchard, where the randomness of the forest gives way to order and open space. The AT passes though many areas that were once cultivated but have since been abandoned. The mountain soil is too poor and rocky to sustain more than a subsistence farming economy, and the slopes and rocks defeat the mechanization that makes modern farming profitable. The forest has reclaimed these areas, but reminders remain.

The AWOL Guide notes a section called 'The Devil's Tater Patch". I am really looking forward to seeing it, expecting a rock garden wonderland, but isn't all that much rockier than other points on the trail. It must have been some farmer's heartbreak though. I amuse myself for the next hour of hiking adapting the lyrics of the Charlie Daniel's song 'The Devil Went Down To Georgia' to incorporate a middle aged man named Possible, and a shiny tater made of gold.

The wind lets up for a minute when I get on Rocky Top, on the Tennessee boundary. The Appalachian Trail roughly follows the state boundary between North Carolina and Tennessee through the Smokies, so I am never really sure which state I am in at any given moment. A trail runner passes me going up, and again as he is returning while I am still ascending the mountain. It is a little demoralizing seeing the speed with which he bounds past me in both directions.

There are many mountains named Rocky Top along the way, but this is *the* Rocky Top, famous in the old Tennessee song. It has another fabulous vista, and the wind has swept away the clouds that often obscure the view in this wet season. While I am sitting on the peak admiring both the vista and a small brass plaque mounted in a stone memorializing the scattering of a deceased Tennessee loyalist's ashes from the peak, the trail runner appears again. He has his girlfriend running along with him this time. They both seen unwholesomely energetic and unwinded by their exertions. We exchange pleasantries and I move up the trail.

The trail is difficult during the next six miles. The most challenging obstacle is a ravine the Appalachian Trail follows up a mountain side. It is so rough I start to wonder if I missed a branching and have wandered off-trail again. I claw my way up the rocks looking for the next white blaze, with no small amount if anxiety. I finally see one painted on a rock after a long hundred yards of working my way up the cleft in the mountainside.

Twelve miles is a good distance for the day. I am tuckered out when I reach Derrick Knob Shelter after a hard day of hiking.

I am trying to set myself on a goal for tomorrow. The requirement to stay in shelters in Great Smoky Mountains National Park regulates the distances a hiker can hike each day. Sometimes the shelters are at awkwardly placed distances, either too far apart or too close for my current hiking ability. Tomorrow is going to be one of those occasions. The next two shelters tomorrow are 7.5 miles and 13.8 miles from Derrick Knob. 7.5 miles is a short distance for a full hiking day, and 13.8 miles is a stretch for me. The trail has been difficult, and 14 miles would be one of my longest days so far. The stretch between the two shelters includes Clingman's Dome, the highest point on the Appalachian Trail. I am feeling pretty good emotionally, if physically tired, and I am inclined to go for it.

It gets colder as I gain elevation. It is spring down in the valleys, but still the tail end of winter up here above 5000 feet. The rule of thumb is that there is a 3.5 degree Fahrenheit drop in temperature for every 1000 feet of elevation gain. We are 10 or 15 degrees cooler than temperatures in the gaps, and colder still than the areas surrounding the mountains. In April, a warm 60 degree day in Dahlonega or Franklin is 45 degrees up on the

Appalachian Trail, and a cool day below is below freezing on the ridgelines.

There is another ridge runner at Derrick Knob Shelter tonight. There is also a fully equipped backpack left in the shelter without an owner.

Day 23, April 28th
Double Spring Shelter, Trail Mile 196.5
Daily Distance 7.5 Miles

TRAILTALK:

FLIP-FLOP: An alternative to the standard NoBo or SOBO hike, The thru-hiker starts out somewhere in the middle of the trail, hikes either north or south to either Springer or Katahdin, then go back to your start point and go the other way to complete your hike. It avoids crowds and can work better with the seasons if you cannot start at one of the traditional times.

One of a ridge runner's tasks is packing out the garbage they find along the trail. This morning our ridge runner is faced with carrying two complete backpacks down the trail. No one has claimed the backpack found in Derrick Knob Shelter last night. Another person has found carrying a load not to their taste and walked off the trail, leaving their belongings to litter the wilderness.

The ridge runner goes through the pack piece by piece showing off its contents. It is filled with a lot of cheaper, heavier, department store equipment. The ridge runner gives away the equipment anyone interested in them, and then figures out how to strap the extra pack onto his own pack for his next leg south.

Despite my hopes, I find I am unable to make the push over Clingman's Dome today. It is still tough trail, and my dietary plan utterly fails me. I pull up short at Double Spring Shelter, a scant 7.5 miles from my day's start at Derrick Knob Shelter, physically, mentally and emotionally spent. There is no go left in my tank, and at the time I don't know why. What I do know is that it is still mid-afternoon, and I just can't go any further.

I am frustrated by it. Initially I think my exhaustion is the cumulative effects of the climbs up along the ridgeline. I settle into the shelter and cook an early dinner. After eating I feel a revival of energy and spirit.

My snack plan is very skimpy, trying to keep down both weight and costs. I am eating frequently, but only a small bite at a time. At Fontana Dam I parsed out my snacks for each day in the Smokies. A day's snacks consisted couple pieces of jerky, a couple of Hershey's miniatures, and a little trail mix in a Ziploc sandwich baggie. I took a snack baggie out of my bear bag each morning and munched out of it as I walked along.

I wasn't getting enough calories for the amount of effort I was expending, even with the constant inflow of small bits of food. I am only getting 500-600 calories a day in snacks. Even with another 400 calories at breakfast and 600 more calories at dinner, I eat less than 2000 calories a day.

I burn a good 4000 to 5000 calories a day, perhaps even more. Estimates on what a thru-hiker uses each day vary, but everyone agrees it is very hard to keep up with how much energy is expended every day. Almost every hiker on the trail loses weight (women can be an exception as they build muscle mass). There is a balance between what is provided for fuel by eating, and what a body needs to take from itself to keep going.

I have gone too far.

I spend the better part of the afternoon sitting around in recovery. I go over my gear and do another assessment of needs and wants, and perform maintenance. My backpack is starting to come apart. The little pocket on the waist pouch is tearing open, and the shoulder straps are coming loose, requiring constant adjustments as I hike. The waist belt has a hole worn in it caused by the friction of it endlessly shifting against my body. No matter how I adjust the straps and buckles the belt just won't ride on my hips properly. It slowly slides down my waist onto my hips as I walk. My pack weight ends up riding low on my back, and my shoulders bear most of the weight. I have a perpetual heat rash on my flanks from the belt.

My alcohol burner stove is a little haphazard. It is a simple device. I pour alcohol in a canister the size of a tuna can. It has holes perforated along the sides. I light the alcohol on fire. My pot sits on a little stand above the fire. Sometimes the fuel is a little reluctant to burn, and I have found it is best to slop a little fuel over the top of it so it catches easier. Unfortunately the slop sets other things on fire as well, including picnic tables, leaves, and pieces of gear. I have burned a hole in the sleeve of my raincoat. It is in just the right place to serve as a thumbhole. I also had a little mesh bag that held my pot together with my little stove and stand inside it, but I torched that into uselessness early on in the hike.

I conduct make and mend with my gear until evening. The awkward spacing of the shelters means very few people stay at Double Spring Shelter, and there are only 3 other hikers in the shelter with me tonight. It is nice having a roomy, quiet shelter for the night. One of my fellow shelter mates is The Lone Hiker, who is hiking south. He started at Harpers Ferry, close to the center of the trail in West Virginia, doing a flip-flop hike. He began in February, and is now a veteran hiker. I talk to him about the development of trail legs. He said his took a good 500 miles of hiking for his to come on.

It is a restful afternoon and evening, and I am restored.

Day 24, April 29th
Newfound Gap, U.S. Route 441 (Gatlinburg), Trail Mile 207.3
Daily Distance 10.8 Miles

TRAILTALK:

SUPPORTED HIKE: Hiking sections of the trail while someone else provides logistical support. Usually this involves a person with a vehicle waiting at road crossings and other vantage points to provide either camping support or trips to town each night. It is hiking the trail without the need to carry all of your camping gear with you on your back.

As I breakfast at Double Spring Shelter a mother and her teenaged daughter appear. They are trying to set a record for the fastest supported thru-hike of the Appalachian Trail for a mother and daughter team. There are various unofficial records for thru-hikes, but ATC refuses to maintain official records in an attempt to discourage competitive hiking on the Appalachian Trail.

A man named Dan is supporting them, by setting up camps at road crossings. In the Smokies he is bringing in equipment and setting up camp for them. The Smokies are difficult because there is so little access to roads. Today they are carrying their camping gear out with them from the shelter to the road at Clingman's Dome. Their equipment is camping gear, rather than backpacking gear, and they are struggling to carry it all down the trail. They still pass me.

It is another cold and wet day within the clouds. Clingman's Dome is anticlimactic. It is the highest point on the Appalachian Trail at 6,643 feet of elevation. A standing thru-hiker joke after summiting the Dome is 'It's all downhill from here'.

The hike up from Double Spring Shelter to the Dome is not a difficult one. It is a gradual 1000 feet of elevation gain over 3 miles. There are no little forays up ravines or creek beds today.

I still manage to get lost just before the summit of Clingman's. There are several trails wandering around the top of the mountain, it is a popular day hiking destination. Near the top I take a trail that leads down to the day tourist parking lot rather than up to the peak.

Since I am already down there, I go into the little tourist information center and store to get additional calories. All they sell are pricey chocolate bars and brownies. I spend $10.00 to buy two, and enjoy both immensely.

I follow the main road back up to the peak itself. There is a structure here, an odd, space age looking observation tower with a spiral ramp leading up to the top. I first back track my hike and pick up the quarter mile of trail I missed taking the wrong fork. I am a purist and wouldn't want to be haunted by the missing distance.

The observation tower is a significant trail landmark and I feel obligated to go up the ramp and look around the top. Despite the bad weather there is a sprinkling of day tourists here with me, looking at fog and getting pictures of each other. It is a miserable view; the clouds have completely closed in around the peak. This is not unusual at the Dome; it is the rainy season in a temperate rain forest.

The hike down from Clingman's Dome to Newfound Gap is an easy, slow decent. There is not one, but three different 200 mile markers designated on the trail, the number spelled out with rocks. The overall trail distance changes a little each year, and the guides are all a little off, so I expect people were relying on different guides when they placed the markers. It is a good moment, passing the 200 mile mark. I am making progress.

I run into McGyver at the turnoff for Mt Collin's Shelter. We have lunch together. He wants to push on past Gatlinburg and try and do the Great Smoky Mountains National Park in a single leg, while I have abandoned that plan and intend to go into town at the road crossing at Newfound Gap. I want to do a resupply and fix my food plan. I have some surplus food; it is just the wrong food. McGyver was not planning a stop at Gatlinburg, but now he doesn't think he has enough food to make the distance. It is an easy solution. I lighten my load and McGyver takes my additional food so he can keep moving.

It is not entirely without regret that I give up my food, I don't miss the additional weight. I will float down to the gap with a pack that is four pounds lighter. I am wondering when I will see McGyver again. Trail partings are iffy things, you can increase separation, and only see each other as notes in trail registers, or sometimes you keep running into each other over and over again. I think McGyver is going to get ahead of me and slowly get further and further ahead, he is a better hiker than I am. This will probably be our last parting, and McGyver is a great trail companion.

Newfound Gap trailhead has a big parking lot for the tourists coming and looking at the woods from picnic benches. Sometimes they venture a mile or two down the trail. There is a fair amount of traffic despite the cold and the rain.

I make my first venture into hitchhiking on the trail. I stand next to the road and stick out my thumb, acutely aware of my wet, dirty, and generally disreputable appearance. I have a ride in less than 20 minutes.

A couple, a traveling salesman and his wife are just passing through, and pick me up on a whim. I am a little adventure story for them. I tell them tales of the Appalachian Trail to entertain them on the drive into Gatlinburg. They drop me off right in a motel parking lot.

I stay at a Motel 6. I am met with suspicion by the desk clerk and have to haggle over my room price, which is $50.00 for a basic room, reflecting the seedy quality of the motel. It is listed in the AWOL guide at a lower price. The desk clerk is unmoved when I show him the guide, and I am too tired to put much effort into negotiations, or find somewhere else. I pay.

Disgruntled, I go see what my $50.00 has bought me. The interior of the motel is better than the exterior. The room is basic but clean, the floors are linoleum rather than carpet, and the other fixtures are cheap but functional. The popularity of Gatlinburg as a tourist destination drives the cost of everything here higher than most places along the Appalachian Trail south of the Mason-Dixon Line,

Gatlinburg's attractions are constantly updating themselves. There are a lot of shops and restaurants, little museums, activities, and a tram to nearby Dollywood. I take a long, hot shower and get myself clean. There is no coin laundry at the motel, and it is a considerable walk to the Laundromat, so I run my hiking clothes through the tub to wash them off. My washing does not amount to much. I have one extra t-shirt and pair of shorts for 'town clothes' and I wear these when I go out and find a little brew pub for dinner. The town is upscale touristy, nice, but lacking an essence of reality. There is no real working population beyond providing for tourists. I take another long, hot shower before turning in. I sleep well.

Days 25-27, April 30-May 2
Newfound Gap to Green Corner Road (Standing Bear Hostel),
Trail Mile 207.3 to 241.0, 33.7 Miles,
AVG 11.26 miles per day

Day 25, April 30th
Peck's Corner Shelter, Trail Mile 217.7
Daily Distance 10.5 miles

There are a couple of options for resupply in Gatlinburg. The local outdoor outfitter is an extension of the NOC. It has dehydrated meals, Cliff bars, beef jerky, and other snacks, but not enough for my new meal plan, A touristy 'Ye Olde' styled country store is on the other side of the street. Between the country store and the outfitter I spend $60.00 on candy, energy bars and a couple of Mountain House dehydrated meals. I am usually able to complete a better 4-5 day resupply for under $50.00. Prices are high, and selection is limited

I finally make the decision to give up on hot breakfasts. Cooking in the morning takes time I can spend more productively hiking. It has taken a half hour every morning boiling water, waiting for my oatmeal to cool enough to eat, eating it, and cleaning up. I will eat energy bars for breakfast, and get a move on a little earlier.

There is an older married couple, a pair of retired professors from Brooklyn, New York, at the outfitter, trying to work out a transportation plan to the Wal-Mart a few miles outside of town. They are thru-hikers, but have no previous outdoor experience whatsoever. There are stories spreading about the couple, even the simplest of camping tasks are a puzzle for them, yet here they are, where I am, in the Smokies, so they must have game.

I see why they struggle as they organize their ride. They analyze, discuss, and debate every option with each other before taking action, and it takes them half an hour just to get a shuttle.

It is hard going through any outdoor outfitter. I look at the equipment and think about what I could upgrade, or what new gadget is going to make my trail life easier. I end up buying a new pair of hiking gloves for $25.00. The thin Smartwool pair I have been using let my hands chill when the winds blow.

I pool resources with four other hikers doing resupply at the outfitter to get a shuttle out to the AT trailhead. We discuss and debate the plan as much as the professors did. Everyone has different plans and different ideas on when to leave. I am eager to get on the trail, but some people still want to eat or shop still. We finally get a shuttle together after an hour. The Wings of Angels shuttle service has a comfortable minivan and a $30.00 fare, and we split the fee five ways. I add a couple of dollars for a tip, but it is still a small cost for the fifteen mile ride.

I see Patches, the ultimate budget hiker, standing at the last stoplight out of town with his thumb out as we go by. Patches is an entertaining hiker, he came to the trail from a situation of near homelessness. He was a Carnival huckster, the kind who calls out to men on dates and challenges them to win a prize for their girlfriends and prove their worth. He is extremely resourceful, and his antics and stories can leave everyone around a campfire laughing until the tears come. His trail name comes from Patches O'Houlihan, the crazy coach in the movie 'Dodgeball'.

My night in Gatlinburg runs me over $200.00 between the motel, my dinner, resupply and the cab fare. It is an expensive overnight, especially by hiker standards. McGyver was wise to pass it by.

While it is a delightful warm and sunny spring day in Gatlinburg, the weather up in Great Smoky Mountains National Park is not. The trailhead is foggy and wet. Climbing up to Charlie's Bunion is not difficult; my legs are definitely getting stronger, a little at a time. Newfound Gap is a high pass for a road at an elevation of 5045 feet, and the climb back onto the high ridge is not as hard as from most town gaps.

I take a detour down a blue blaze trail to Charlie's Bunion, a little spire of rock sitting above a precipitous drop that gives a wide panorama of the mountains. The bottom drops out of my stomach as I look at the drop-off at the edge of the trail hiking to the Bunion. I still force myself to inch my way out to the very edge at the Bunion to see everything. I get there just in time to watch a patchwork of clouds turn into a solid blanket obscuring the valleys below

The weather turns ugly. The trail follows a knife edge ridge across a very small flat patch with slopes falling away 400-800 feet from either side. The ridgeline traverse is several miles long. Thankfully, the clouds hide most of the daunting empty space below on either side of me.

The clouds bring rain, then sleet, then snow, in rapid succession. The winds gust, the occasional eddies giving me glimpses of the land far below me on either side. I eat my way through my day's supply of snacks. Even my improved, beefed up food plan proves inadequate to my hunger and most of my snacks for the day are gone. I save my last half of a Snickers bar for the possibility of an uphill climb. The extra dollop of energy from the sugar is always welcome before an effort and I fear today it will be much needed.

I am lost in the fog. I know I am on the trail, but I have no idea how far I have hiked. The light is failing and I still have not seen the shelter. The

AWOL Guide says is it is off on a little side trail. I am exhausted, wet, and cold and I may have missed the turn off in the mist. It is miles to the next shelter.

I am ready to ignore the GSMNP rules for a night in favor of survival. I sit down next to the trail where a tree has blown down and exposed its root ball. There is a small hollow there, and I contemplate setting up my rain fly to make an overnight shelter. The trail is off of the knife edge, but it is still on a steep slope, and there is nowhere flat to set a up tent. I am shivering in the cold.

I sit on my log, mired in a fear I may have passed the turn off for the shelter. I grow more and more convinced that head down, trudging along in misery, I missed the marker. I have not seen another hiker in four hours, and I am alone in a forest gone creepy and hostile in semi-darkness and mist. I eat my hoarded last half of a Snicker's bar, and decide I can make myself go on a little further, either until I see the shelter or a better campsite presents itself.

I summon will, and lever myself and my pack up off the log and start putting one foot in front of the other. I walk a scant 50 yards and I see the double white blazes marking an upcoming side trail on a tree looming up out of the mist beside the trail. I found the shelter trail!

I hike down the side trail a couple of hundred yards to the shelter. It is rated as a 12 person shelter, but 16 people are crowded onto the stacked double row of sleeping shelves. I am shaking uncontrollably from the cold. Other hikers jump to my aid. Ice (still called Beth at this point, her trail name is still miles ahead of her), makes me a hot cup of tea. In that moment she becomes one of my heroes of the trail. The other hikers on the shelves start squeezing themselves together just a little tighter to accommodate one more hiker. I am urged to crawl into a space 18 inches wide.

I look around as I slowly warm up and become sensible. This shelter has an overhang, and a tarp is hung over the front so the normally open side is closed off from the elements. In addition to keeping out the wet, the tarp helps trap collective body heat inside the shelter, and while it is cool in here, it is not bitter. I slowly stop shivering as I drink my hot cup of tea.

There is an open space between the edge of the sleeping platform and the wall made by the tarp, four or five feet wide of hard packed dirt floor. There is a small fireplace with a chimney and there is a small fire going, I have no idea how anyone found dry wood. I sit on the floor by the hearth listening to the wind howl and the hailstones rattle off the roof, and I realize there is enough room on the floor for me to lay out my sleeping bag. I ask and no one minds me at their feet. I am set for the night.

I am not the only person coming in late tonight. Two more hikers show up and fill the rest of the floor space, crowding the floor as well as the sleeping platform. It makes me think of historical stories about the old slave ships; how men, women and children were chained together on small shelves in the holds of ships crossing from Africa to the Caribbean and

America. It is tight but manageable for a night on the boards, but I can't imagine how bad it was for weeks on end in a tossing ship. I have an inkling now.

The hikers inside the shelter are all cheerful in the face of adversity, many are contributing what they can in aid and comfort to each new arrival. It is bad outside, but no one will die of hypothermia tonight.

Thor and Squirt arrive. Squirt is a little over five feet tall, and she is dwarfed standing next to the mighty Thor. This is the first of the female companions I see Thor with. His Nordic good looks are paired with a laid back, generous, philosophical personality that makes him very attractive in many women's eyes.

Thor and Squirt are much as I was when I arrived, shivering and cold. Tea and goodwill are administered, but there really isn't anywhere left inside for them to sleep, even if Thor wasn't 6 and half feet tall. Thor sets up his tent out under the tiny outside porch to get some protection from the main force of the weather. Both of them are traveling lightweight, and already have on all of their clothes, even less than what I carry. People dig into their packs to help them out. They get a Mylar emergency blanket, and I pass on my extra pair of gloves. They are not the best, but they are better than no gloves, and I am happy to ditch the weight while making my own contribution to hiker aid. I am lucky I have big hands, for my gloves are still stretched to protect Thor.

Well after dark one last hiker comes in. It is Redlocks. He gets his tea, and people start crowding together on the shelves again to try and give him a space. He defies all persuasion and logic, and goes back out into the storm to set up his hammock nearby. I don't think I will see him in a shelter the entire hike, although he camps near me fairly often.

The night is filled with snores and the sounds of people crowded into too small a space. Every time someone gets up to go the bathroom I get stepped on, and I sleep poorly. I thank God and the trail I am inside every time the wind shrieks and rain or hail strikes the roof. I worry about Thor, Squirt and Redlocks outside.

Day 26, May 1st
Cosby Knob Shelter, Trail Mile 230.6
Daily Distance 12.9 miles

I wake to a very cold morning in Pecks Corner Shelter. Everyone is alive.

I, as usual, am one of the later hikers to leave. During the morning shuffle of everyone making breakfast, eating, packing, and leaving, Redlocks comes into the shelter, shivering. I think it is from sleeping in his hammock out in the elements, but he insists he slept well and snug wrapped in his hammock sleeping quilts. He makes himself cup after cup of hot, warming coffee to drink, and he is still drinking when I leave.

It is an easy day of hiking. There are a few small climbs; the Appalachian Trail goes up and down even on the 'flat' stretches. The trail follows a slight downhill ridgeline. It is a rocky stretch, and there are many of the small stones that can turn or break an ankle and end a hike, and I pay attention to my footing.

The cold (and oh, is it cold!) coats a frozen rime of ice onto the branches of the trees on either side of the trail, and I hike beneath a crystal canopy. As I slowly descend from 6000 feet to 4000 feet the sun shows itself and the temperature warms. It is not to anything like comfortable, but it is not a killer cold anymore.

McGyver passes me. He stopped at Mount Collins Shelter the day I went ahead into Gatlinburg. He did a 15 mile day yesterday, and was in the same shelter I was in last night, but I missed seeing him in the crowded sleeping shelves. (It was McGyver who provided Thor and Squirt the Mylar blanket to keep them alive last night). He is slowing his pace to enjoy the Smokies, and is only going to hike five miles to Tricorner Knob Shelter today. I plan on going further, to Cosby Knob, so we are out of synch again.

I come across a backpacker sitting on a log in a small clearing off to the side of the trail, staring off into space.

He is a section hiker doing a month long hike. He is very much a budget hiker, his gear looks pretty cheap and ill suited for the trail. He has come a fair distance with it, but he has run out of money, has run out of food, and has run out of energy. He is sitting on a log without the will to continue.

He asks me for food. I am hoarding my own supply, but give him a couple of Cliff Bars. He is only ten miles from a road where he could hitch out, and I suggest he do so. He scarfs down the Cliff Bars, but doesn't seem very interested in my advice. I move on.

I slowly descend down the ridges to reach Cosby Knob Shelter. I am happy to see the shelter is full, but not overflowing like last night. The requirement to stay in shelters, and the spacing between them, means I see many of the same people who were in the icebox last night, and a good deal of the fellowship remains.

Tonight is my last night in Great Smoky Mountains National Park, and I look forward to sleeping on my own in my tent again. Tomorrow I will hike out of the park, leaving behind the coldest, steepest, hardest stretches of trail so far, and all of the rules governing it. Getting this far is reason for all thru-hikers to feel proud of ourselves.

Day 27, May 2nd
Green Mountain Road (Standing Bear Farm Hostel), Trail Mile 241.0
Daily Distance 10.4 miles

The rain finally lets up and it is a glorious spring day, in sharp contrast to yesterday's frozen wonderland. The first couple of miles are a climb up to Mount Cammerer. There is a blue blaze side trail up to a fire tower that is .6 miles. I don't hike the extra mile there and back, I resented the extra half mile I had to walk last night to Cosby Knob Shelter and the return to the AT again in the morning, and I miss a fine view with few regrets.

I still lose time. The ridgeline is open meadow, and blooming with wildflowers. I stop and take pictures of each different type of flower I see. I wanted to take at least one picture a day while on the trail. I resisted taking photos during the first days because I didn't want to view the trail through my cell phone, but I found looking for and taking pictures makes me spend more time looking around and appreciating what I am experiencing, rather than less.

There is a work crew of volunteers from the Smoky Mountains Hiking Club performing trail maintenance along one of the oldest sections of the trail. It is next to a trail bend originally built up with fieldstone by the CCC that is a featured photograph in 'Walking With Spring', Earl Shaffer's book on his experience as the first Appalachian Trail thru-hiker.

Earl Shaffer was the first person to hike the entire trail south to north (NoBo) in 1948, and then again was the first to hike it north to south (SOBO) in 1965, and for a while he was the oldest person to complete an Appalachian Trail thru-hike after completing a third hike in 1998 at the age of 79. His original intent completing his first thru-hike was to "walk off the war" (Shaffer was a WW II Veteran); a tradition now continued by several veteran's hiking groups. Earl's trail name was Crazy One.

While Earl was completing his pioneer thru-hike the Appalachian Trail Council (ATC) was still debating the nature and purpose of the Appalachian Trail, including arguments about whether it would even be a single, continuous trail, and whether anyone would ever try to hike the whole thing. Earl Shaffer showed up and announced his deed while the ATC was in deliberations. The ATC as a body initially doubted Shaffer had in fact completed the entire trail, but Shaffer had documented his trip in a journal and taken pictures, the foundations of his book.

The trail crew is on a break when I come by, and they dig through their lunches to provide a little trail magic, in this case some fruit. Fresh fruit and vegetable snacks are prized by thru-hikers, who out of necessity eat a lot of processed foods.

I drop into lower elevations and the world warms. I am acutely aware of my sense of smell again and I revel in the smells of the forest. On the lower slopes water comes off the heights in babbling brooks, rather than the seeps and springs higher up, providing a merry background sound to go along with songs and mating calls of birds. The leaf canopy is coming in down in the valleys.

I am staying at Standing Bear Farm Hostel tonight. It is a short hike up from the second Green Mountain Road crossing, a mile past where the trail passes under Interstate 40. I feel a weird kinship with I-40, since 1800 miles away it passes through my home town of Albuquerque, New Mexico. It is a long way, but I feel a momentary, distant connection to my desert home so far away.

Standing Bear Farm is best described as rustic. Even by hostel standards it is very basic accommodations. The bunkroom is in a barn, the bunks themselves are home carpentry projects, the toilets are an overflowing port-o-potty and a privy. There is a common area that is supposed to be cleaned by users, which means poorly. There is a resupply shed stocked with hiker food for sale. The proprietors buy in bulk at some kind of budget food thrift store, so much of the food is near (or past) its expiration dates, and the flavor varieties are those already rejected by the general population.

Despite its many flaws, Standing Bear Farm is a charming place to spend a quick night off of the trail. It has a hot shower, there is a cooking area in the common room, and a table with assorted chairs around it as a place for hikers to gather and relax. The bunks in the barn are twin sized and are spaced a comfortable distance apart, with a big wood stove to provide copious amounts of heat. The ubiquitous frozen pizzas are for sale, and a small oven is available to bake them. The hostel goes through the pizza in such quantities they do not sit on the shelf long enough to expire. Compared to shelters it is luxurious accommodations.

There is a bathroom scale in the common room, and I find I lost 20 pounds during my first month of hiking. There is a full size guitar in the common room I enjoy playing for a while. I still carry my own guitar on my pack.

I am very happy staying at the hostel my first night out of Great Smoky Mountains National Park, and Standing Bear Farm is woodsy enough, and isolated enough, that it didn't feel like I left the Appalachian Trail at all.

Standing Bear Farm is full up on this night. I am there with McGyver, Jumanji, Crusty Goat, Redlocks, and Chief. Springy Turtle (His name later morphs into Spring Eternal, signed as Spring-E in the logs), trades three hours of work-for-stay (WFS) for lodging. Springy may have gotten the worst of the bargain. To meet his three hours of WFS, they have him clean the waste (a nice sterile term) out of the privy and move it to a compost pile the following morning, a task he pitches into with vigor and a smile.

McGyver is unable to look at the kitchen and common room in the disorder it is in, and I help him clean up. It is a pleasant moment, doing small domestic tasks with a friend, spending time in relaxed conversation while washing dishes, sweeping up, and putting things away.

The laundry set up is two metal washbasins with a hose, an old fashioned washboard, and a wringer. I give it a try, but I think it rearranges a lot of the dirt rather than removing it from my clothing. The dryer is electric, and free, so I have cleaner, if not entirely clean, dry clothes for the next leg of hiking, and a new appreciation for how my great grandparents had to do laundry.

I look forward to a night of rest in a bunk. My left shin has tightened up as I am hiking, so I am limping just a bit. I think it is a repetitive use problem, and I believe a proper sleep will ease it.

As an endnote, GSMNP does not permit dogs, and Standing Bear Farm provides a kennel service while thru-hikers complete the section. There is a trail rumor that a dog kenneled at the hostel got loose and was killed on the road. The management at Standing Bear is in transition. The original proprietor died last season and the family seems diffident about keeping it going.

Most of the day to day operations are entrusted to a former thru-hiker named Lumpy. There is another trail rumor floating around about Lumpy. According to shelter gossip, Lumpy managed to offend a number of the female thru-hikers with not quite appropriate comments and advances. We are all men the night I am here, and Lumpy seems all right to me, if a little less than entirely efficient. I think it may be there is a cultural collision occurring, back country Tennessee doesn't speak modern American political correctness well when showing an interest in romance. Since I do not have to fend off advances from Lumpy I am in no position to judge. I understand from the thru-hiker community that the family at Standing Bear has recently taken the management back in hand, and it is a better run hostel now.

Whatever the issues, the strategic placement of this hostel at the northern exit and entrance to GSMNP makes it a welcome end point for hiking through GSMNP. My own stay was very enjoyable, and I have fond memories of my stay there.

NORTH CAROLINA AND TENNESSEE BORDER AREA

On the stretch of the Appalachian Trail exiting Great Smoky Mountains National Park, the trail runs along the North Carolina and Tennessee state line. When they made the state line they followed the highest ridgeline, which is also the path of the Appalachian Trail. The trail crosses back and forth between the two states and it is often difficult to know exactly which state you are in. The occasional state marker sign only adds to the boundary confusion.

This area has more hostels along it than anywhere else on the trail, in some places they are only a day apart. It is a popular jumping off area for day and short section hikers.

Days 28-30, May 3rd to May 5th
Green Corner Road (Davenport Gap) to Hot Springs, NC,
Trail Mile 241.0 to 274.4, 33.4 Miles, AVG 11.13 miles per day

Day 28, May 3rd
Groundhog Creek Shelter, Trail Mile 248.2
Daily Distance 7.2 Miles

I linger until nearly noon at Standing Bear Farm. As I start my hike out and up from the gap, Redlocks, who left the hostel a lot nearer to dawn, comes hiking back the in the opposite direction.

At first I think he may be turned around. It happens to most hikers a time or two. You take a break at a spot along the trail, and hike back the wrong way when you get started again. The trail can look much the same in either direction, a green tunnel through the woods, and you don't realize you are going backwards until you either meet another hiker or recognize a landmark you have already passed.

Redlocks has not accidentally turned around. He left a critical piece of gear back at the hostel. It is the second time in a week he has backtracked, repeating miles after forgetting something. He left his wallet up at Clingman's Dome, and didn't discover it was missing until he was in Gatlinburg. It cost him an entire day of hiking.

Redlocks is a natural athlete, and is easily able to make big miles. I see him a lot. While I grind out the miles with my slow pace, he surges ahead, then stops at a nice lake or mountain top and relaxes. I see him again as I come plodding up from behind. I am a tortoise to his hare. Most of the thru-hikers I see regularly will take his approach to thru-hiking. I am envious of others' ability to enjoy more of the trail while still making miles, but since I could be home working in a cubicle, I also count my blessings, frequently.

Climbing out of Davenport Gap to Snowbird Mountain Bald and back down to Deep Gap makes for a slow day's hike. Standing Bear Hostel had a pack scale, a big hanging hook with a dial, and my pack weighs just a hair under 40 pounds loaded with my resupply to get to Hot Springs, 33 miles, 2 big climbs, and 3 days away. My pack weight is dropping and I am carrying less food and water on this leg. I suspect the scale at Standing Bear is as efficient as the laundry set up. I am probably carrying a couple more pounds than the scale indicates. It is a fine, sunny day, and I enjoy the trail even with the extra weight on my back.

The shelter at Groundhog Creek is a disappointment, and even more so its occupants. The Tennessee shelters are old and small, often built of concrete blocks covered with graffiti. They have all the charm of sleeping under a highway bridge. There are two men and their pit-bull already in the shelter. Thru-hikers can recognize their own pretty quickly, and can differentiate between thru-hikers and section hikers, people out for a night or two, and others.

The two men and their dog are others, definitely locals, and more than a little threatening. Their gear is haphazard and heavy, and could not be carried far. They are wearing tough guy muscle shirts, and are putting out waves of hostility. One of them suggests to me that there are plenty of tent sites available.

I was planning on tenting anyway, but I react poorly to intimidation. I consider making this event into a confrontation. I can climb right into the shelter and tell them to get their dog out, and see how they react. I can't imagine it going well, but I could make them uncomfortable enough to leave; I can do obnoxious really well. I was Army, and have some training if things get physical. I am in pretty good shape after backpacking for a month, and almost look forward to a scuffle. It isn't a wise course of action though, and one of my personal improvement goals of the thru-hike is to let things go more. I let them have the shelter and go set up my tent.

McGyver shows up about an hour later. He looked in the shelter and gets the same impression of its occupants. He was already planning to put up his tent; he rarely sleeps in a shelter. Tents can become home. The same space, arranged in the same way, the same little rituals for setting up, sleeping arrangement, and breaking camp become a comfortable routine.

McGyver is from the Southeast, and has spent time over the years hiking on the balds. He is particularly eager to see Max Patch, one of the best known balds in the Appalachians. We observe how the balds in this region are getting covered over with saplings and blackberries.

The United States Forest Service (USFS) has taken a hands off policy in its forest management policies after too many ecological disasters occurred during years of taking a more involved approach. The balds, however, are most likely the result of man's actions acting in a positive way. The mountain tops were burned off and used for summer grazing by local farmers, going all the way back to the original Native American inhabitants. Without human action, the balds are turning back to forest. It is threatening a lot of plant and animals that have adapted to the sunlight and open space of the mountain top meadows. USFS is has recognized the need to keep these ecological niches, and is experimenting with different ways to maintain the balds as pasture.

Day 29, May 4th
Walnut Mountain Shelter, Trail Mile 261.3
Daily Distance 13.1 miles

TRAILTALK:

COWBOY CAMP: Sleeping in the open without erecting a tent or having a fire, just roll out the sleeping bag and look at the stars above. Romantic but risky, since the weather can change rapidly.

HIKER HOBBLE: The cramped, limping gait backpackers develop at the end of the day, brought on by stiffening muscles and small injuries. Hiker Hobble can also set in immediately after a break before the legs have warmed back up.

It is another day of fine spring weather. The ice, snow and biting cold of a couple of days ago are nothing but a memory. Max Patch is ahead, a large bald, and a favorite thru-hiker location.

Near the base of Max Patch, just before the climb, two of last year's thru-hikers have set up trail magic. Scout and Gadget are cooking hot dogs on a grill, and have fixings, home baked goods, snacks, and drinks laid out on folding tables. They provide folding chairs, and Scout has a little guitar with him he carried during his thru-hike. I take mine off of my pack and we play a little together, and in between I stuff myself with hotdogs, baked goods and drinks.

There are frequently times when I feel I am all alone on the trail. Trail magic shows me just how many hikers are close ahead and behind me when I hike. Hikers keep coming out of the woods in ones and twos. A friendly group gathers and chats, mining Scout and Gadget for information about the trail. I am always looking for insights on what lies ahead, and enjoy hearing Scout and Gadget's trail stories.

Max Patch is a memorable place. The walk up is under open sky, breaking cover from the usual canopy. USFS mows it to maintain it, and there are several square miles of mountaintop meadow. It is great sweep of mountain grassland, and every few steps the vistas change and broaden. Up close there are many varieties of wildflowers in bloom, and birds of all sorts flit about. It is little more than a mile of trail, but I am so absorbed in the surroundings, and pause so often to look around, it takes me an hour to walk over the bald.

Max Patch has some history to it. There was a hermit who haunted the area a century or more ago, a jilted recluse, not an uncommon story in the Appalachians. This hermit was killed by the local blacksmith with a shotgun. How the hermit offended the blacksmith is unclear to me, although there are several stories. It may be the blacksmith just wanted to shoot someone. Hermits were the equivalent of today's homeless, at a time where you could get away with murder if there was no one to stand up for the lost soul. Other versions of the story say the hermit's unrequited love was either the blacksmith's wife or daughter, and the blacksmith grew tired of being a part of his tragedy.

A more recent story is about a marriage proposal. Max Patch's natural beauty makes it a fine place for a proposal. It is also a high, exposed point in an area with frequent thunderstorms. The tale is the young beau's paramour was struck by lightning and killed when they were caught on the top by a storm. He watched her die with the engagement ring still in his pocket.

How much truth is in the stories, and how much is embellishment, or even outright fabrications by generations of thru-hikers passing through is a matter of belief. I am sure there are written records somewhere, but hunting them down would steal some of the magic of Max Patch.

Roaring Fork Shelter is close to the bald, and so are some camping areas. Many people choose to stay in the vicinity of Max Patch so they can take in the sunset on the top. Some hikers cowboy camp, rolling out their sleeping bags on the bald and sleeping under the stars. No actual tent camping is allowed on top of Max Patch.

Later on down the trail, Kamikaze tells me about her experience here. She camped nearby in a wood line, wanting to see the sunrise. She woke up to the ethereal sounds of a traditional Indian flute playing as the sun came up over the mountains. Rikki Tikki carried the flute during his journey, and welcomed the day to Max Patch with his music.

I am carrying two cans of beer I picked up at the trail magic, and already regretting the extra weight. The trail passes within 50 yards of Roaring Fork Shelter, and I hear Jumanji's distinct laugh rising from the structure as I pass. I shout down to him and Crusty Goat and tell them I am leaving them a present. I put the two beers down at the side trail intersection. I am lighter, and they get a little trail magic.

Spider webs are crisscrossing the trail and I walk into a succession of webs. Certain spiders like to construct webs across the open spaces to catch insect traffic. Usually they are swept clean by the first hikers down the trail in the morning. I have not had to break trail through webs before, since I am so rarely the first person on the trail in the morning. It is not a pleasant experience.

The webs give rise to two thoughts, (after waving my arms around a bit and running my hands through my hair repeatedly to remove displaced spiders). My first thought is why no one else has already come through and cleared the webs. Is it possible these spiders are so determined and resilient the trail was cleared several times and the little creepers have rebuilt their traps already?

My second web ponderation is on the nature of web construction itself. How do spiders get the first traverse across the trail? I am pretty certain that they do not anchor one end, climb down one tree, cross the trail to other, and carry the far end up to an attachment. Either they are floating web filaments across in the faint movements of air, reeling out a gossamer cable and hoping it catches on the other side, or they are making some kind of mighty spider leap across the gap.

I walk over 13 miles today before coming into Walnut Mountain Shelter, a very satisfactory distance. I would like to make 13 miles my new regular daily distance, increasing from my current 10 or 12 mile a day pace.

I am tired and sore coming in, but it is manageable. Hiker hobble is now a constant companion. Whenever a thru-hiker takes a break muscles stiffen, and it takes a few minutes of walking to warm them back up again. Many thru-hikers walk through the pain of blisters and minor muscle issues, which smooth out while you are hiking, but come back on with a vengeance if you take a rest. Hiker feet and legs take a pounding, and at the end of a day of beating them against trail they just ache. Sometimes I limp on both legs at the same time.

I am still keeping pace with McGyver, and I also meet Chef and Bluto for the first time at Walnut Mountain. Chef carries an array of cooking implements and prepares his food with actual fruits and vegetables, using flour and spices to make real meals. His pack is very heavy, but he is young and strong, and doesn't seem to mind. Much.

May 5, Day 30th
Hot Springs, North Carolina, Trail Mile 274.4
Daily Distance 13.1 miles

It is another good day of sunshine and miles both. The descent into Hot Springs is a knee and ankle pounding trial, but the gravity assist makes it aerobically easy.

On the very last stretch of trail descending into town I am attacked by a dog. I am a couple of hundred yards from the trailhead, and there are two dogs loose on the trail. One is a puppy, and the other a German Shepherd. The puppy comes running up, tail wagging, all eager curiosity, but when I lean down to pet it the Shepherd growls, and lunges. I back up quickly. The Shepherd blocks the trail, and growls and bares it teeth when I try to go around. I use my poles as a shield and try work my way past, but the dog gets my pants between its teeth and worries at my leg. I shake it off and use the brief struggle to get around it.

The Shepherd is trying to protect the puppy, I think. I can hear a voice somewhere off in the distant calling names, I assume the dogs. It is an unsettling encounter.

Hot Springs is one of a very few towns the trail passes through directly. The white blazes are painted on the pavement as I follow the road through town. There is a big river and a bridge crossing, a regular feature in most of the places where the trail follows a road through town.

Most access to resupply requires thru-hikers to leave the trail, and visit one of the nearby towns that are accessible by road crossings that occur, on average, every four miles along the trail. Averages don't tell a full tale, of course, in the densely populated Mid-Atlantic States roads are common, and there are stretches where roads are separated by considerable distances. Getting from an AT trailhead to a resupply point and back is a logistical challenge, and occasions where resupply is right to hand are welcome.

Hiker friendly towns actively supporting hikers receive recognition by the ATC as 'official' trail towns, and get included in the ATC Thru-hiker's Companion guide book.

Some of the resupply towns are little more than a convenience store at a road junction. There is an old joke about small towns with a sign that says 'Welcome to' on both sides of the same sign, and these hamlets qualify.

Hot Springs is a wonderful trail town, a real hikers' paradise. There is an old downtown and the trail passes through it on the main street. There are several great hostels, good places to eat, and a Dollar General and an outfitter for resupply. There is a Christian outreach ministry catering to hikers providing computers and snacks, with little pressure to convert now, just good fellowship. The public library also has computers, internet, and printing capability that can be used by hikers.

The town is named for the hot springs emerging along the bank of the French Broad River. The springs are channeled into tubs and soaking pools in a little resort and spa. Tubs are expensive to rent, but there is a discount rate for thru-hikers. Dividing the cost of a tub can reduce it to less than $10.00 apiece, if you don't mind soaking close together. Other services include massages, one of my favorite trail luxuries.

Hot Springs lives on tourism. First and foremost, the hot springs are an ongoing attraction. In the spring the town gets the thru-hiker surge as the bubbles come through. The town sponsors events to bring crowds in on the weekends. I just missed a bluegrass festival that filled all of the rooms in town and had people camping along both sides of the French Broad River. I am sorry I missed it. I don't particularly like crowds and was happy to get a room instead of being forced to pitch my tent in town, but I like bluegrass music, and I am enjoying it more here at the source.

Thru-hikers can get stuck in town, finding it hard to leave the comforts of civilization. Hot Springs is more appealing to hikers than most places. There is quite a crowd when I am there. McGyver, Redlocks, Swayze, StarStuff, Chef, Squirt, Bubbles, Thor, and Snoopy are all hanging out on the deck of a pub overlooking a small stream that feeds into the river. I see Kamikaze and Scribe, Older Dog and Rikki Tikki on their way out of town; they have formed a trail family, hiking together up the Appalachian Trail.

Laughing Heart Hostel sits at the point where the AT exits the woods and enters Hot Springs. The hostel is adjacent to the park like grounds of a fancy lodge. There are hikers sitting outside, and Baltimore Jack has followed my hiker bubble to this point. It. looks nice and is fairly priced; an individual room is $28.00. Without further exploration of the town I put down my pack and have a home for the next two days.

My wife calls while I am checking in, and we have another argument. She believes I am hiking with another woman as a companion. She doesn't really grasp why I am out here on the trail.

Our conversation will impact my emotional state over the next several days. The cell phone is a curse in some ways; the negative aspects of life outside the trail intrude into the mountains and create a background noise making anger and frustration an aspect of my journey, rather than the serenity I seek.

Day 31, May 6
Hot Springs, NC, Trail Mile 274.4
Daily Distance 0.0 miles, Zero Day

I spend a zero day wandering around Hot Springs. There isn't a terrible amount of town to the place; the main drag is only a quarter mile long. There are a couple of pubs, a Mexican restaurant, Bluff Mountain Outfitters, a Dollar General, the Hot Springs Spa, and a lodge.

I tend to my town chores. I do my laundry, I go to the outfitter, and I go to Dollar General to do my resupply. I splurge on a massage at the lodge, and it is wonderful. But mostly I just wander around and eat.

Laughing Heart Hostel is in a modern building, and it is the nicest hostel I have been to thus far on the Appalachian Trail. Quarters are twin beds with personal space for each person, more like a college dorm than the stack 'em and pack 'em bunks I saw further south.

McGyver is staying at another hostel, Elmer's Sunnybank Inn. I visit him and find it is in a charming old Victorian building. It has a common room with a lot of loaner library books to read and musical instruments to play. They serve organic breakfasts and dinners to their guests

Dollar General is a basic resupply point. I pick up ramen and Knorr's Sides, Little Debbie's snack cakes, granola bars, Pop Tarts and Vienna Sausages. It is not all of my favorites, and it is a heavier four day load than usual, but it will keep me going.

I find I stop in every outfitter I come to along the trail. They are expensive, but they generally cater to hikers. I pick up a few more food items at Bluff Mountain Outfitter, some little luxuries and variety items. The prices are fair, especially for an outfitter. There is a resupply point in 18 miles so I can round out there if I like, but I have enough food to stay on the trail longer.

I twisted my left ankle a number of times during the past few days of hiking, and there were a couple of particularly violent turns on the descent yesterday. It is swollen and tender, which isn't all that rare a condition for me as I hike. I twist my ankle on a regular basis, one of the background pains that are a part of everyday living on the trail. I am very happy to give it a day of rest.

Many of the people who were here last night left this morning, and I am a little behind the bubble. Everyone wants to get ahead, the big Trail Days event in Damascus is in a week, and hikers want to get as close as they can. Most thru-hikers will shuttle or hitch hike into Damascus from wherever they are for the big weekend, and proximity makes travel arrangements easier. I am on the fence about attending myself, it is 3 to 5 days off-trail at a huge party, and I am a little reluctant to lose the time. The idea of a prolonged camp in a mob of drunken and stoned hikers has little appeal to me.

There are many reasons to go to Trail Days. Hiking organizations show up at the event and there are speakers of note. Many gear manufacturers and other commercial enterprises involving hiking will be there as well, displaying and selling the newest in backpacking equipment. I am rethinking the gear I am using, and Trail Days would give me a great opportunity to look at swapping some of it out.

Day 32-37, May 7th to May 12th
Hot Springs, NC, to Erwin, TN, Trail Miles 274.4 to 343.0, 68.6 Miles
AVG 11.43 miles a day

Day 32, May 7th
Near Round Top Ridge, Trail Mile 279.9,
Daily Distance 5.4 miles

I dawdle about town, and don't leave Hot Springs until after noon. I have a nice breakfast and then visit the Hikers Ridge Ministry building. Besides snacks and fellowship they have Wi-Fi and computers so I can get some needed real life work done.

When I leave town I see a number of other thru-hikers still loitering in town, including Spring-E, Mainer, and McGyver. The weather is fine as I leave town, and I wonder about the others wasting time in town on such a fine hiking day. McGyver in particular is not one to let the moss grow under his feet. It turns out there is a thunderstorm advisory for the afternoon that I have not heard about, and the other hikers are waiting it out.

I see an opossum that is lying in the middle of the road on the way out of town. It is not quite dead, and it twitches and writhes in pain. Its entrails are stretched out on the road, and it will not live for very long.

Watching the animal suffer while cars and people pass by is a little more than I can bear. I wait for cars to pass, and then step into the center of the road. I steel myself, and push my hiking pole tip down into the possum's eye socket intent on putting the creature out of its misery.

The pole tip penetrates with a sickening little crunch, and the possum twitches even more. I wiggle my tip around, and the possum continues to shake, with even greater intensity. I pull my pole tip out, and I back towards the sidewalk, somewhat appalled at what I have done. I walk away slowly, looking back once at the possum still quivering on the road. I hope it is just dead nerves firing.

The climb out of town runs up a series of switchbacks on the bluffs facing the far side of the French Broad River. I stop at Lover's Leap, which has an old story about a rejected suitor's jump from its height. There is a wonderful view of the river and town below.

I take a break, eating a snack and ponder love, the withdrawal of it, and reflect on my own marital woes. I can understand the pull of that one big step out into nothingness, wiping the emotional slate clean; eventually I leave tragedy behind and continue my climb back up onto the high ridge. I am carrying a lot of weight, and the trail is steep.

In mid-afternoon the predicted thunderstorms arrive. The skies open up and it pours on and off until dusk. The climb, the rain, and my stops to take in the scenery make a slow afternoon of hiking. As I get up towards the top of the hills and start following the ridgeline I find a small, abandoned, moss covered dam in the final ravine of my ascent. It is holding back an acre of stagnant pond. The mossy face of the dam presenting itself to people climbing the trail looks ageless and eternal, but I wonder what kind of rainstorm it would take for it to fail. Perhaps one like the one I am in now?

I would not want to be immediately downstream if it gave way; it looks large enough to sweep out the ravine and carry along any hapless hiker caught within its confines.

After the rain come the bugs, so many bugs. I walk in a cloud of no-see-ums, a type of little biting fly. They have been in wet boggy areas before, but not in the swarms that appear today. I am already wearing my raincoat with the hood up, and add a small mesh head net to protect my face and neck. The screen works, but I heat up quickly in the raincoat and the mesh impairs my vision enough to be a bother. It is far less a bother than giving the bugs free access.

I pick the first flat area following the ascent out of town to set up camp. I wear my raincoat and bug screen while I put up my tent and cook dinner. I try to stay ahead of the bug swarm when I take the net off to eat, and I pace rapidly up and down the trail while gulping down my meal.

I am camping alone. The only people I saw on the trail today were day hikers at Lover's Leap. Everyone else knew about the weather. I prefer camping near others, if for no other reason than to have a united front in case a bear takes an interest in my food.

My food bag is very heavy. I am overloaded, and pay a price when I set up my food bag bear hang for the night. I toss my line over a promising branch of a tree about 30 feet tall, attach my bag, and I try to pull the heavy bag up. The bag doesn't want to rise, and I tug harder. The tree's roots give way in the wet soil, and the whole thing topples down instead. It falls directly onto my tent.

Locating a suitable tree for a bear hang can be a chore, and sometimes the lack of a good tree or two with a sturdy branch at the right height can make an otherwise perfect campsite undesirable. Trees are stunted by poor soils and exposure along certain areas and ridgelines on the trail, leaving the trees too short to get the needed height. Areas with pine trees and fir can also be difficult, as they rarely have big branches down at the 12 to 15 foot mark. Getting a line up for a bear bag is a trial and error affair. I have been attaching my personal hygiene dry bag to a carabiner on paracord to get a line over first, and then attaching my bag to raise it into the air.

I go find a stouter tree, well away from my camp, and try again. After a few attempts I get my line over, and my food bag goes up and it stays up.

I go back and wrestle my tent out from under the fallen tree and relocate it a few yards away. I discover my tent's bug screen now has holes torn in it by the tree's branches. I patch the larger holes with duct tape, but no-see-ums still get in, and I sleep with my head net on. It is an uncomfortable night.

I write my notes while lying in my sleeping bag. Somewhere in the darkness I hear a barred owl's cry, "Who cooks for you? Who cooks for you?" Other birds are sounding off in the near dark. I hope they all feast well on bugs.

Day 33, May 8th
Hemlock Holly's Hostel, Trail Mile 290.7
Daily Distance 9.8 miles

TRAILTALK:

SLACKPACK: Hiking a section of the trail as a supported hiker, with just some basics needs for a day in your pack. You are slacking off, and also carrying a nearly empty, or 'slack' pack

It is less than a ten mile day of hiking, a disappointing distance. I stop at Hemlock Holly's for the night, I tell myself I would have passed the hostel by except I discover, to my mixed pleasure and regret, that I forgot to buy more fuel for my stove in Hot Springs. I don't think I have enough cooking alcohol to get all the way to my next planned resupply in Erwin, so Hemlock Holly's, here I come.

While I was in Hot Springs I had a long discussion with Mama Skillet, who was getting ready to go off the trail, always a hard moment for a thru-hiker. It is giving up a dream.

Mama Skillet is a watercolor artist, and she imagined a trail experience where she stopped every day during her hike and took an hour or so to capture an image in watercolors. What Mama Skillet discovered was that trying to pursue a creative endeavor while on the trail is almost impossible. The consistent rain was an issue, more so were the demands of the trail.

In order to make Katahdin before the weather turns a hiker has to make miles every day. Hiking becomes an all day task, between breaking camp, making miles, and setting up camp, there isn't a lot of time left in the day to pursue other interests. Mama Skillet was not making the art she wanted, and also felt she wasn't making enough progress on the trail (she started in March). Her new plan was to follow the bubble, but only day hike selected sections of it as she moved north, giving her an entire trail experience without it being wholly consuming.

Her situation gave me pause for thought. I am carrying four and a half pounds of guitar and accessories on my back. I planned on playing at night while lazing about camp, and am carrying music and exercises with me. The reality is I have only played my guitar five times since starting the trail. I am too busy, and it is too wet. I

The guitar is adding to my burden, and it is an awkward addition. I am perpetually ducking and weaving to avoid having my guitar catch on branches. The guitar is strapped to the outside of my pack, and it likes to move around. As it shifts about it slowly pulls my center of gravity from one side to the other, inducing strange gaits and shoulder pains.

The climb out of Hot Springs has not been a pleasant one, and after a night of thinking over what Mama Skillet said, I decide it is time to for me to lighten my own load. My guitar is holding me back.

Most hostels have a house guitar sitting around for hikers passing through to play. I have played some of them. The hostel guitars will give me a chance to put my fingers on strings at least once a week, and once a week will do. I will donate my instrument to the next hostel I come to.

In the meantime, I have the weight to bear down the trail. Once I make the decision to give up my instrument, it is dead weight on my back. Today a church group out on a backpacking retreat is traveling south on the trail, passing me by in small, cheerful parties of eight or ten hikers. One of the groups offers me some snacks as trail magic, and I stop to talk.

My guitar comes up as a discussion point, being very obvious and visible on my back, and of course it is very much on my own mind. One of the hikers is a player, and has been looking for a good backpacking guitar, and here I have one I want off of my back. I give him the guitar.

He rifles through his own pack and gives me a bar of organic chocolate. He feels he should give me something in exchange, and this is all he has to offer. I want to get the weight off my back, and happy to see a player gets my instrument. The exchange is complete.

Now, I shouldn't say I am entirely happy to get the guitar off my back. It has been my companion for a goodly piece of the trail, and I have invested it with a certain amount of emotional value. When I hike away from the exchange, I hike away quickly, before I can change my mind. In the long run, it is the right decision for me, but whenever I come across someone else toting an instrument I will feel a sense of loss. My pack is noticeably lighter, if not my heart, and I have better balance with the odd shifting gone from my load.

Hemlock Holly's is listed as being eight tenths of a mile away from the Appalachian Trail, following a forest road down to a residential area. I come to the forest road and realize I am going to have to walk down a mile that is not an on the trail mile, never an idea to gladden a thru-hiker's heart.

A pickup truck is sitting on the road, with a man waiting in it. We exchange hellos. He is supporting his wife, Smoking Toes, as she thru-hikes the trail. She slackpacks each day and they sleep in the bed of the truck at night. He still bears himself like a soldier, so I ask him about his background. He is a retired Army vet, like me. I call him Ma Deuce, since he was a M-2 .50 Caliber machine gun range operator and trainer.

He offers me a ride down to the hostel if I will wait a few minutes for Smoking Toes to come in, which is awesome. I meet Toes when she comes in, and she is definitely smoking down the trail. They exchange hugs and he has food and a drink for her. He drives me up to the hostel soon afterward. He likes what he sees, and he and Toes come back to the hostel cafe later for dinner.

Hemlock Holly's is a house and some outbuildings along a little stream. The house has been largely converted over to a hiker resupply point and a cafe, and has a deck with picnic tables on it overlooking the stream and road. The bunkroom is a rustic cabin set a small distance away from the house. The resupply is adequate, standard hiker fare, and Holly's has the fuel I need.

Some familiar faces are at Hemlock Holly's when I arrive. Chief is here, and Kamikaze. Kamikaze has twisted an ankle and is taking a day off of her death march for it to heal. She pushes herself very hard, but it isn't always that productive. I catch her a couple more times during the hike because of injuries she sustains from driving herself so hard, and I will summit Katahdin the day after she does.

Holly's cafe is quite homey. Hattie, the owner, (also known as Hemlock Holly), is an older woman and has a thru-hiker doing a week of Work-for-stay and collecting tips as a helper. The food is unexpectedly good for a hostel café in the middle of nowhere. There are a couple of selections each night, and Hattie brags they are made from scratch. I believe her after eating a couple of entrees. It is a welcome break from frozen pizzas and Ben and Jerry's ice cream, the standard fare at hostels. The food is good enough that Hattie is not wholly dependent on thru-hikers; her cafe does business with the neighbors as well.

The bunkroom is rough, but there is a lot of space with a communal table and chairs, and a small, basic kitchen area. There are some troubles with the showers housed in a separate building. The water pressure is going in and out. I took my hot shower as soon as I arrived, before the problem developed. The other thru-hikers waited to eat first, and are now a little miffed the showers are not fully operational.

Finishing early means I can relax this evening, and I finish my day eating ice cream on the deck. It is drizzling rain, but the deck is covered. I sit looking at raindrops dimpling the surface of the stream in the dusk until the ice cream and dusk start to chill me more than is comfortable, and I turn in.

Day 34, May 9th
Bald Ridge, about Trail Mile 301.8
Daily Distance 11.1 miles

There is a lot of vehicle traffic on the little road going by Hemlock Holly's in the morning. USFS is sponsoring a young hunter's day and gun safety program half a mile up the road, and pickup trucks and SUVs full of kids pass by as we have an early breakfast. Hattie shuttles us back to the Appalachian Trail afterwards, a free and very welcome hostel service.

My hiking day begins with a mild climb up to Little Laurel Shelter, and then the trail gets steep. There is an exposed rocky ridgeline trail that has a bad weather bypass. The weather looks ok, and I am now determined to see all of the white blazes, so I pass the blue blazed Firescald Bypass.

The trail is difficult along the ridgeline. The trail section is dedicated to a man named Howard MacDonald, a master trail builder in the area. The route on the ridgeline is his piece de resistance, an obstacle course up, over, and under boulders on the ridge. When I discuss this section with McGyver later, he is a little angry about this section. He doesn't like that someone went out of their way to make a trail section a difficult traverse, difficult enough to require a bypass. I don't know if I agree or not, I like a little variety, and some different challenges, even after my adventure along MacDonald's ridgeline trail.

A large rock named after Howard perches on the ridgeline two thirds of the way across the traverse. It provides a fine overlook to the west. I sit here for a minute, the view shows me the valley below, and dark, anvil shaped thunderheads reaching in from the west. I need to get off of the open heights before the storm reaches me.

It becomes a race between me and the oncoming storm, and I lose. As I work my way through the obstacle course I am confronted by wind, then rain, then gale force winds accompanied by pouring rain and thunder. The thunder cracks loud, so loud and violent it must be directly overhead. I don't see lightning, visibility is limited to just a few feet in the downpour, but I keep waiting for it as I scramble across and down the ridgeline as fast as I can go. One of my REI hiking poles collapses under protest as I thrust my way through rocks.

I get back down to a more sheltered section of trail and the rain subsides. I take a short step off the trail to examine my collapsed hiker pole. I hear a noise behind me, look around, and nearly jump out of my skin. There is a female hiker directly behind me, and she gives me a strange glare as she goes by.

"Whoa, you scared the tar out of me there" I say to her (tar is not the word I actually used), but she keeps on hiking without a word or backwards glance. I am a little spooked, by her sudden appearance, her hostile glare, and her silent passing. If I had needed help, which was a possibility after a ridgeline crossing like Howard's, I feared she might have left me there.

I jam duct tape into the joint of my hiker pole as a temporary stop to replace the failed lock. A hiker named Freestyle comes by while I am finishing the repair and he stops for a moment. We talk about the MacDonald ridgeline, where he caught the whole force of the storm. I bring up the hiker who blew past me afterwards. He asks me to describe her. "Oh, that's Hummingbird" he says.

Hummingbird is becoming notorious along the trail. She has issues, especially with men. She carries a large canister air horn and a big camera slung around her neck. When she passed Freestyle, she didn't like how he looked at her. She snapped his picture, brandished her air horn at him, and told him she was watching him and reporting him to the rangers. Freestyle wasn't too sure what to make of it.

Another hiker comes up behind us as we are stopped on the trail talking, and he has his own Hummingbird story to tell. Back at the forest road crossing by Hemlock Holly's, Hummingbird heard the far off gunfire coming from the USFS young hunter's program, and went absolutely wild eyed insane. She started sounding off her air horn and shouting into the woods, demanding the far distant and uncaring shooters cease, and of the report she would make to the rangers.

I hiked with the other two men for a while, talking as we went, but our paces separated us. I, of course, fell behind. We are all a little worried Hummingbird might be at the next shelter, Jerry Cabin. The other two guys are going to push past, but it is my intended goal for the day.

I am thirsty, and contemplating a dubious looking seep as a water source when a woman named Cheerio comes hiking by. It is the first time we meet.

The bugs have come out in force after the rain, and I am slapping at them without much effect, debating wearing a head net while I filter my water. Cheerio stops and looks at the seep, and decides she can push on to the next, hopefully better looking water source.

I notice the no-see-ums are ignoring her and I ask her what her secret is. She is wearing a citronella essential oil, and it seems to be working. It also makes her smell nice, a rarity for thru-hikers. I resolve to get some myself, I have been trying to avoid DEET based insecticides, and essential oils may be a viable alternative.

I continue to slap away at the bugs as I operate my Sawyer squeeze bag filter. They are really getting to me, and follow me when I start hiking again. I go just a little crazy for a minute, and try to outdistance the persistent pests, running down the trail as best I can with my pack and hiking poles, waving away at the bugs as I go. I may have screamed just a little.

Running actually works; I get past the wetter, low area of the seep where the bugs are concentrated, and I am only occasionally bothered afterwards. The no-see-ums find a moving target hard to keep up with.

Hummingbird is in Jerry Cabin Shelter when I arrive, along with Cheerio and The Fonz. I hesitate, and then I try to talk to her. I ask her why she walked by me, since thru-hikers usually watch out for each. We are each other's lifelines in the woods, we can't count on anyone else coming by. I think it is important to instill awareness and a sense of community. I try to explain my thoughts to her.

"I can fucking take care of myself" she snarls at me, the first full sentence I have heard out of her. She retreats to the back wall of the shelter, clutching the camera strapped around her neck firmly in her hands before her and aims it at me. I imagine there is now a photo of me on a bulletin board, looking slightly annoyed and bewildered, at a ranger station along the trail.

I decide right then I will not share the shelter or the nearby camping area with Hummingbird and her personal demons. I load up on water at the spring to take with me to a more peaceful spot further up the trail. There is a weird trail conversation when I get back from the spring. One is between me, The Fonz and Cheerio, and the other between Cheerio, The Fonz, and through Cheerio, Hummingbird. Hummingbird appears extremely unwilling to speak to men. I have no idea what has happened to her, but I would not want to live inside her head.

I have been struggling with my own inner demons along the trail. My wife and I are coming apart, and the trail is part of my own processing of the emotional distress. She calls, and when she does it often turns out badly. I have become the person who mutters to himself on the trail as a result. I am not sure how this relates to Hummingbird. It was a conscious decision to confront her about the pass by on the trail earlier. Maybe I handled it poorly; I could have let a little more conversation flow before bringing it up. Then again, maybe not. She wasn't speaking directly to The Fonz either, and he didn't seem to have anything offensive about him.

I find out Kamikaze has already hiked on by from Cheerio. Kami's ankle must be better, or else she is gutting it out. I follow along in her footsteps for another mile. The trail opens up onto a long bald; a beautiful, giant, mile long meadow. In the center, just by the trail, in the center of all that open space, there are four large trees growing close together. There is a fire ring between them, and lots of flat space. I have a found my place for the night.

I set up the tent wearing my head net and raincoat. Stationary, I am a bug magnet for the no-see-um swarm that rises with the dusk. I cook and eat quickly, and crawl into my tent for the night.

Day 35, May 10th
Between Big Flat and Rice Gap, about Trail Mile 314.8
Daily Distance 12.5 miles

Hummingbird passes me as I am breaking camp in the morning. I am singing a lullaby as I break camp. I enjoy the sound of my own voice and there is rarely anyone but the flora and fauna to disturb along the trail. She greets me and compliments my singing as she passes. I give her a 'good morning!' and a 'thank you' back. I am struck for a moment. It is like I am talking to a different person. How much of last night's social and emotional friction was my creation?

It is Mother's Day, and spring is flowering all along the Appalachian Trail. I take a picture of a Flame Azalea cluster in bloom and send it to my mother as an e-bouquet. I sent money and some ideas on how to spend it in a letter to my twelve year old daughter back in Hot Springs, so she can take her mother out.

I am still pretty upset from my last phone call home with my wife. Anger makes powerful hiker fuel, driving me forward. It does have its deleterious effects on my psyche and relationships with other thru-hikers. I am the man who raves and mutters to himself.

I have a snake count, and I see my tenth snake since beginning the trail today, a ribbon snake. McGyver comes hiking up behind me, and he saw a big king snake climbing up the side of a tree, a long, black, moving vine. He shows me his pictures. I walked past the same tree just a minute or two before he did and noticed nothing. It was on an uphill climb, and I was more focused on the trail, and on muttering to myself. I probably walked right by the same sight live as I went by in my funk.

My climbs can be ugly things, I drive myself forward, head down, sweat pouring out of my body and dripping off of my face, soaking my shirt, heart racing. I have to pause every so often to let my heart rate drop a little, which is when I take a look around. Sometimes I see some pretty amazing things, but I missed the snake. McGyver's photograph of the snake is impressive; it is at least six feet long and is gripping the tree bark with his scales. King snakes climb trees looking for bird's nests and eggs.

After the first 1800 foot climb the trail is easy enough, and I make good miles. I am gunning for Erwin in two days. To make it I will need to finish two 14 mile days. The days are getting longer as we get closer to summer solstice, and I think I can do it. I only have two dinners left, and about two days of snacks, so I am committed to the timeline.

Someone discarded a pair of swim goggles at the Flint Mountain Shelter where McGyver stop for a break. I can't imagine what use someone had for them. The shelter is otherwise clean, and I throw the goggles in my pack to carry out. I am emulating McGyver and others now, picking up garbage along the trail.

I set a goal for myself, to pick up two pieces of trash a day. It doesn't seem like much, but if I do this for the 180 days I think I will be on the trail, I will have packed out a cumulative 360 pieces of trash, a neat accomplishment.

Someone also left behind a Sawyer mini filter and a full flask of whiskey at the shelter. I am tempted to take the whiskey, but the shelter trail register has a warning. Sickness is showing up along the trail, and it is hard to pinpoint the sources. The owner had uncontrollable vomiting and diarrhea at the shelter last night. It sounds like Giardia.

The victim blamed either their filter or their whiskey in an explanation they wrote on the shelter log. I left both for the next person to come along. If they wanted to trade risk for whiskey and a filter they were welcome to them. I don't think either was responsible, but I will do just fine without the extra items.

I pass a plaque noting an Eagle Scout project along the trail. Boy Scouts are a very active organization on the AT. Many parts of the trail benefit from Eagle Scout projects. In order to attain Eagle, the highest scouting rank, a Boy Scout has to conceive, drum up support for, and execute a community service project.

The plaque is for an Eagle Scout prospect out of Raleigh, NC, who completed a community service project based on ecological preservation. Many species in the Appalachians have suffered and even been exterminated by exotic diseases and parasites introduced from overseas. The Elm trees and American Chestnuts that once had prominence in the Appalachian Mountains are gone. Now Hemlock trees, the Sequoia of the Eastern forests, are under attack by a parasite introduced from China, the Woolly Adelgid.

There is no cure yet, but it is possible to treat the soil around Hemlocks to hold off the attack of the Wooly Adelgid. A treatment lasts about 10 years. USFS, which is poorly funded to face its many responsibilities, cannot devote many resources to saving the species. The Scout raised money to buy this treatment and apply it, protecting this one great grove of Hemlocks, giving this one majestic place some time for scientists to find a cure.

It is an impressive achievement for a young man, one I would expect a team of graduate students in Forestry or Environmental Science to tackle as a thesis project, not a boy on the cusp of graduating high school. I was a Boy Scout myself, and I never made it to the exalted rank of Eagle, but seeing scouting's presence all along the trail makes me proud I was a Scout at any level.

One of the reasons I was aware of the Appalachian Trail and its significance, and had a desire to thru-hike, was because of the high esteem my old Scoutmaster, Mr. Peters, held for the AT. Our Boy Scout troop, Troop 152, Watchung Area Council, did small weekend backpacking trips along the AT in New York, New Jersey and Pennsylvania when I was a teenager. Mr. Peters heightened my own awareness of the trail as a resource and a community, and the possibilities it offered.

McGyver and I share a campsite tonight. When I cook dinner I find that I no longer have my spork. The spork is a universal hiker eating implement, it is concave like a spoon, but it has small tines in the ends like a fork, and mine was serrated on one edge. I was tossing things into my bear bag camping the night before Hemlock Holly's, and the last items left out of my bag before I closed it and hung it up were my Ziploc trash bag, and my spork. I tossed my spork into the Ziploc to keep the critters away from it that night, telling myself to remember to retrieve it before emptying the trash out. I did not remember.

I whittle the bark off of a forked stick as my eating implement. It is not great, but I eat.

Day 36, May 11th
Bald Mountain Shelter, Trail Mile 326.1
Daily Distance 11.3 miles

Note left with a short piece of rope on a tree at Sam's Gap, where the trail crossed a gravel road, mile 317.6 (verbatim):

HICKERS

This is the Bloody rope that was tied to the Collar of a Ten Year old Boys Dog at Dan's Fork Gap, where he lived. and led to Sams Gap where he got loose and run over in the road. if a dog comes to you Please run it off. they live here. don't let them follow you.
4-27-15
Sad to live next to the trail

I come up short on my miles today. It is a crazy day. There are a lot of short ups and downs, and then there is Bald Mountain. I go over any number of mountains and ridges named 'bald' on the Appalachian Trail, but this is *the* Bald Mountain. It is 5516 feet high, and dominates the surrounding area.

I pass day hikers coming down from one of the little hills in the morning, and one of them is carrying trail magic. The angel has little bags of home made chocolate chip cookies she is handing to thru-hikers as they pass. I sit on a rock along the trail to eat mine, and they are little bites of bliss melting in my mouth.

I reach the approach to Bald Mountain at mid-afternoon. The weather has developed a new pattern. At the beginning of my thru-hike it rained all day. As I progress north, spring is following and overtaking me. I see more sunshine. The mornings are nice, but thunderstorms develop in the afternoon, passing by and leaving wet evenings.

McGyver and I hike together on and off in the morning, at our own paces. At a water stop I have cell signal, turn on my phone, and immediately get a call from my wife. McGyver goes on while I talk to her for an hour. The conversation does not go well, demands and accusations cross the airwaves, and I am in a particularly bad frame of mind, torn and tangled when I get to the base of Bald Mountain.

The first spatters of rain and wind of the afternoon's thunderstorm are coming in, and I pause at a trail junction with a warning sign indicating a blue blazed bad weather bypass trail around Bald Mountain. I already determined that I will not miss any parts of the trail to follow blue blazes, although this is noted as a very dangerous bald to cross. The mountain has a history of deaths caused by lightning. In my agitated state of mind I am bent on self-destruction, and I welcome the storm and whatever it may bring.

I rise through the forest working my way up the switchbacks to the mountain top, and the weather worsens. Ahead of me there is the bald itself, the open space atop Bald Mountain that gives it its name. The bald is visible for miles on the approach from the hilltops preceding it. I pause at the treeline on the edge of the bald. The rain is fierce, the wind is howling, thunder is rumbling, and lightning is flashing.

I could go back down the trail a mile and follow the bypass around, but I am mad at the world. During the brief moments when the rain thins I can see a ridge 200 yards ahead, and I assume that the little rise hides a treeline on the other side of the exposed ground. If I make a determined rush I can get across, and if this is meant to be my last day, so be it.

I launch out onto the bald in a staggering half run, the best I can do with a pack weighing down my back and the wind and rain in my face. My hiking poles, two lightning rods in my hands, go clickety-clack across the ground. I am pushing with my arms and driving with my legs for all I am worth. I get up to the little ridge, and find a false crest.

Ahead of me is not a treeline, but an enormous open space, bigger even than Max Patch. It looks like at least a mile of open ground on a mountain top in a lightning storm. I have already committed myself, and I forge ahead after the slightest hesitation.

The rain comes and goes, and the wind circles around, coming from a different direction every minute. Thunder makes a continuous rumble, and lightning is sheeting overhead. It is terrifying, and yet I am alive. I am going forward.

It is beautiful, one of the most memorable visual, physical and spiritual experiences I will have on the Appalachian Trail.

You can smell a storm, I don't know why, but the air is cleaner, and the freshness fills me up with wild energy. I can see a vast circular panorama of the other mountains around and below Bald Mountain. I am running beneath a dark, solid patch of cloud cover. It seems close enough I can almost reach up and touch it above me. I can see separate storm systems in the broken skies gathering around some of the mountain tops in the sweeping view, and in other places there is light coming through small patches of blue sky, rays of sun spotlighting this ridgeline or that hill. In the blue and black thunderheads I see other jagged lines of lightning flashing down towards peaks, and in calmer spots the clouds towering over a mountain are fluffy white. Along storm edges the clouds are purple and pink where the sun catches them. It is awe inspiring.

I have to keep moving while I stare at the beauty around me. There is no time to sit and take it in. The lightning erupting all around on my mountain is scaring the hell out of me. The trail goes over the summit and drops onto a tree lined road that slices into the bald halfway across. The road offers some kind of shelter, but I keep going, down between the two rows of trees, and back out into the open.

I think to myself, in this moment, if God wants me, he can have me now. My rage is gone, in the beauty of the event, in the sheer feeling of life at its greatest. There is also an acceptance. It will be painless; I will never know what hit me. One minute I will be rushing across Bald Mountain, the next I will be a smoking cinder. Still, I duck and cringe each time lightning strikes too close and the thunder cracks too loud. There is an insane joy, a defiance of the world filling me as I surge across the open ground.

I make it across. Bald Mountain Shelter is on the reverse slope of the summit, not too far from where the trail enters back into the treeline. I am not even trying to set up my tent today, I will use the shelter.

I am still filled with adrenaline, vastly energized and happy from my experience. There is a SoBo stalled out in the shelter as the rain comes down around it. He is a young man calling himself Big Country, who lives up near the trail in Virginia. He put together a pack one day, got on the trail, and started walking south with no specific goal in mind.

The view at Bald Mountain is notable, and Big Country wanted to see it in good weather. He is camped out in the shelter waiting for a scenic opportunity, which apparently will not be until tomorrow.

McGyver is also at the shelter, having crossed the bald ahead of the storm. I, however, am not the only fool who took a chance and crossed the bald in the storm. Three more hikers come in.

Castaway is a solo, and he ran across the bald half an hour after I did. He is as pumped up as I am. He tells of lightning striking around him, and how he threw himself to the ground every time the storm reached a crescendo signaling an incoming strike.

The other two hikers got out as far as the tree lined road crossing the center of the bald, and decided it was enough, following the protection of the sunken lane down the mountain to the bypass trail and avoiding the second half of the bald crossing in the storm.

Everyone is pretty excited and talking about their experiences, but eventually we calm down. We settle in. There is soaking wet gear hanging up all over the inside of the shelter. Outside it still rains. I eat my dinner with another whittled stick.

McGyver and Castaway have a common bond. Castaway is carrying a small volleyball painted and shredded to look like the icon Wilson in the Castaway movie, which he calls Mini Wilson. McGyver has a hiking staff he has a long history with, having acquired it as a Boy Scout on his first hike on the Appalachian Trail nearly fifty years ago. It is a capped with a Wilson tennis ball. He calls his pole Wilson. They take a picture together with their Wilsons.

My crossing of Big Bald in a terrific storm is a reaffirmation of the sheer joy of living life. The one experience, if it was my only incredible moment on my thru-hike, makes the entire effort worthwhile. I have never felt quite as alive as when I was running across the mountain against the wind and rain, with the thunder rumbling and the lightning striking. It is one of my finest memories, among many remarkable experiences of the trail.

I am still hoping to make Erwin tomorrow. It will be a big day, 16 miles, but they are mostly downhill miles and I think I can make it. I am still eating with a stick, and I would like to eat tomorrow's dinner with a proper utensil.

Day 37, May 12th
Chestoa Bridge, River Road, Erwin TN, Trail Mile 343.0
Daily Distance 16.9 miles

It is a long day of hiking, and I am incredibly proud of myself. I complete nearly 17 trail miles, with yet another added road mile in town. I am beginning to see where I might bring in bigger daily miles in Virginia. I am pretty tore up, and have a pronounced hiker hobble as I stagger my last mile along the road into town, my thumb out to the few cars that pass.

I dropped a little cash on Big Country on my way out of the Bald Mountain Shelter. I do a little trail magic myself here and there along the way, trying to help out hikers needing a boost to get a little further down the trail. Big Country qualifies; he is obviously operating on a shoestring, packing marginal gear, but has already made it quite a way south from his start point. His family is helping him out where it can, and he didn't ask, but it is apparent he can use a little help. I give it to him just as I leave, sticking it in his hand, telling him to pay it forward and immediately set out on the trail. I usually try to help anonymously where I can; it avoids awkwardness. It is easier knowing Big Country is heading south, and I will not see him again, and he won't see me. There won't be a vague, awkward sense of debt hanging over us.

I get underway on the trail, starting with three medium sized hills, and an elevation profile like the teeth of a crosscut saw in between, then easing up and rolling down through the last miles approaching Erwin, Tennessee, and the Nolichucky River.

There is a small stream crossing at Spivey Gap. It is only a few feet across, a couple of hops across rocks. In the stream I count four small native brook trout holding their places in the flow, as well as crayfish, snails and water dancers. One of the trout might be regulation, the minimum size for a legal catch. The others are small fry. Each is in a little hole or riffle of its own.

I fill my water bottles from a small hole that has a trout in it. The fish doesn't move, even with my water bottle dipping in 18 inches away. It is National Forest, and the stream is protected; the little trout may grow to be big trout without fishermen chasing them.

I am constantly amazed how streams in the East teem with life. Western rivers and streams are barren in comparison. I do not know what accounts for the difference. Forests in the East seem more alive as well; tree branches are shaking and twitching with squirrels and chipmunks, many bird species fill the forest with the sound of their songs, and there is a lot more variety than a section of forest the same size in Oregon or New Mexico, my last two home states. I see two more snakes bringing my count to twelve, and a raccoon sighting adds a little spice to the day.

Uncle Johnny's hostel in Erwin is strategically positioned right next to the Appalachian Trail where it crosses the Chestoa Bridge over the Nolichucky River. The hostel looks tempting, a big banner outside offers Snickers Bars for 40 cents, and it is right there. I look in briefly, but I want a private room and internet tonight rather than a bunk, so I trudge on down the road, away from the Appalachian Trail towards town.

I get out to a main road, a mile on a country lane upstream along the river, and a little pickup truck with 3 teenagers in the cab pulls over and gives me a ride right to the Super 8 Motel doorstep. I ride in the truck bed, and we have a shouted conversation through the slider window at the back of the cab. They are lively, friendly, and curious trail angels, asking the usual questions about the trail, and I provide the usual answers.

The Super 8 is nice and located near the restaurants and stores of Erwin. It is a bit pricey for hikers, but there are still a fair number of my fellow thru-hikers present. The Scribe, Rikki Tikki, Older Dog and Kamikaze trail family is here. Trail Days starts in Damascus in a couple of days, and for the thru-hikers now in Erwin the primary preoccupation is figuring out transportation plans to get up there for the big event.

Day 38-41, May 13th to May 16th
Erwin TN and Trail Days at Damascus VA, Trail Mile 343.0 Zero Days,
AVG 0.0 miles per day

Day 38 and 39, May 13th and 14th
Uncle Johnny's Hostel, Erwin TN, Trail Mile 343.0,
Daily Distance 0.0 miles, Zero Days

TRAILTALK:

HIKER MIDNIGHT: A reference to how early thru-hikers go to bed. When the sun goes down, thru-hikers go to sleep. Hiker midnight is around 9 PM.

I zero in Erwin and think about attending Trail Days. The Super 8 Motel empties out as hikers figure out their transportation schemes to get to Damascus, a couple of hours by road away. There are various shuttles, trail angels, and family members employed giving people rides.

Erwin is a friendly town. Kamikaze is skipping Trail Days, but is taking one zero day. She has twisted her ankle, again, and is giving it one day of rest to let the swelling go down. As I wrote earlier, downhills are treacherous.

Kamikaze is trying to get miles under her belt; she has to go off-trail for a friend's wedding in Seattle, and is a bridesmaid. She has dress shopping and preliminary festivities to attend to as well as the wedding. She will be gone at least a week, and her hope is that she will get ahead of her trail family while they are at Trail Days, go off-trail, and return in time to rejoin them as they pass.

I walk with her about half a mile to the Laundromat and grocery store in the morning. She is limping noticeably, but will only give it this one day of rest. We do our laundry and get our resupply complete. Someone sees Kamikaze walking in obvious pain, pulls over and offers us a ride, which we take; just one more friendly, helpful person in Tennessee.

I check out of the Super 8 and go over to Uncle Johnny's Hiker Hostel. I have had the luxury of my own room for a night, but I want a jump off point by the trail tonight, one that isn't going to cost me an arm and a leg.

At Uncle Johnny's there are cabins, a bunkroom, and an area where you can pitch your tent for a lesser cost and still use the shower and internet. Uncle Johnny's main office is also a resupply shop.

A huge banner hung outside of the hostel advertises Snickers bars for 40 cents each, a bargain price. I load up, only to find there is a limit of 2 at the 40 cents price advertised on the banner outside, and the rest are considerably more expensive. I unload all but two Snickers bars. I look at hiker poles but the hiker box at Johnny's only has genuine junk in it. From the 'used' equipment sale area I think I may see where the good stuff is going.

Everyone around me is making arrangements to get to Trail Days. I have been on the fence about going, and after spending some time at Uncle Johnny's I decide that rather than heading out on the trail I will follow the crowd and go on to Trail Days. It is a part of the thru-hiker experience, and I really do not want to miss it. I justify the lost time and expense by committing myself to a gear change out.

A lot of my equipment needs attention. My REI hiker poles are held together with duct tape and need replacement. I would like a lighter tent and a better backpack. My Eureka tent has worked well, but it weighs 4 pounds even using a Tyvek footprint and replacing the original steel stakes with aluminum ones. My tent also has holes in the bug net from dropping a tree onto it back near Hot Springs, and is patched with duct tape.

My backpack is the six pound REI expedition pack. It has developed holes in the waist belt, the straps are sliding, and the waist belt just won't stay in place. In addition to putting most of the pack weight up on my shoulders rather than carrying it on my hips, the pack belt is giving me a big, permanent heat rash on my hips and butt. I hope I can find replacement gear that will drop my total weight by 3 or 4 pounds. I might just be able to get my pack and tent repaired instead.

There will be so many equipment companies at Trail Days that I should have a large selection of options, instead of being limited by the brands any given little trail outfitter carries. You see so much equipment on trail, and have so many conversations about it, that I think I am about as knowledgeable as I can be about gear, and will make better purchasing decisions.

Uncle Johnny's has a shuttle to Hiker Days, and I sign up for the next morning's ride. It costs $40.00, and includes a return trip (which turns into a 'space available after new paying riders are on' when I make the return; Uncle Johnny works hard at turning a profit).

Uncle Johnny's is bustling with business. It is a little haphazard in its operations. McGyver is here and has rented a cabin room. He had to switch cabins after they found a dead or dying dog in the first one he was offered. I didn't quite get the whole story, but some thru-hiker wore their dog out on the trail, couldn't afford the vet bills, and wouldn't take it home or take time to care for it, abandoning the poor animal to be Uncle Johnny's problem.

It is good to see McGyver again, and we swap experiences. He shares a Hummingbird story of his own with me. McGyver camped on a ridgeline near a water source, not a shelter or designated campsite, but a good, known, and commonly used spot. There were a couple of other tents sharing the site with him.

Hummingbird came into the little campsite around dusk and set up her tent a little apart from the others. Many hikers try to find a little separation for privacy and peace when they set up camp where other hikers are present, and this was not cause for comment.

Later in the evening a thru-hiker named Mainer came in, at about 10:00 pm. He was night hiking. Ten o'clock is late by thru-hiker standards; hiker midnight is about 9:00 PM. When the sun goes down, thru-hikers go to sleep, and they don't like to be disturbed. We are all very, very tired.

Mainer set up fairly close to Hummingbird, and was a little noisy. Mainer was a known quantity on the trail, a good natured if boisterous companion. No one knows exactly what happened in the camp, or whether Mainer may have said something to Hummingbird to set her off, but sometime in the early morning hours she woke up and blasted the night with the canister air horn she carried, while shouting out strange accusations. She packed up her camp and stormed off into the night, continuing to shout and blow discordantly on a harmonica as she left.

The now wide awake hikers Hummingbird left behind were flabbergasted. Mainer disclaimed any wrongdoing, said he was as shocked as anyone else present. No one knows what actually happened, but I think several hikers are resolved to bring her situation to the rangers when they get an opportunity. There is an ongoing ATC blog about this year's hike, and Hummingbird has her own thread. I don't see her or hear about her presence after Trail Days, so maybe the rangers had a conversation with her, or she found a new place to be.

Along the trail Uncle Johnny has a reputation for being mercenary. A hostel is a business and ultimately needs to make money. Thru-hikers are watching their dimes and some are looking for a lot of free or very inexpensive services. There is a balance in there somewhere and hostel owners try to live on the sweet spot. Uncle Johnny seems reasonably priced, but there are a number of little issues where it seems he is squeezing a little too hard, and he will take financial advantage of a situation if he can find a way.

One of the free services he provides with a night's lodging is an evening shuttle into town for shopping and food. I go out just for the change of scenery and a good meal.

Day 40, May 15th
Trail Days, Damascus VA
Daily Distance 0.0 miles, Zero Day

TRAILTALK:

BnB (Bed and Breakfast): A lodging option providing a bedroom and a meal for about the same price as a decent hotel. It is an expensive option compared to a hostel, and like a hostel you can never be quite sure what you are going to get making reservations in advance.

Damascus is jumping. Uncle Johnny's shuttle van drops a full load of hikers off at the outfitters downtown, and we join the throng. The town is small, with an old main street surrounded by a few blocks of businesses. The town lives off of hiking and biking. Not only does the Appalachian Trail go right down the main street, but the Virginia Creeper Trail is also here, a network of bicycle trails that follow the old Virginia Creeper railroad lines.

I walk through town getting myself oriented. There are several hostels and BnBs, and they are packed to capacity. There is a community center with a full schedule of seminars and talks about the AT, and a free cold lunch hiker feed. I carry my pack out to the campgrounds a half mile outside of the town proper. There are thousands of thru-hikers, hiker alumni, and people just looking for a good party present. The camping area fills the Damascus athletic fields and spills deep into the surrounding woods. Some of the gear companies are set up here, most notably Osprey, which has huge tents full of workers and sewing machines making repairs or replacing broken equipment. Osprey has a huge presence on trail, their packs are solid, comfortable, lightweight, and they have an amazing guarantee that they actively support.

There is a fee to use the campground, $10.00 for the weekend. I have to hunt around to find the permit sellers and buy one. The camping area is fenced off, and there are a number of uniformed law enforcement agency officers around the perimeter. John Law does not venture inside unless there is an incident or a call; they keep a low key presence. McGyver and I have both come in at the same time, but find widely separated tent sites. I am aiming for close to the edge, things are supposed to get pretty wild deeper into the center of the camping areas near the nightly bonfires. McGyver wants closer in to the action.

Tents are packed in close enough so stake lines are overlapping. I find a cluster of tents with a little bit of separation, drop my pack, set up my tent, and go exploring. My objective is better, lighter gear. I find the main set up area for the equipment and services companies near downtown in a park running parallel to the bank of a small river. I look at tents, backpacks and poles, as well as some other smaller pieces of gear.

I see several lightweight tents I like, weighing less than two pounds for a tent that is nominally for two very friendly sleepers, but they are more than I want to pay, at $400.00 to $600.00. Some companies only have tents as displays, not available for immediate sale. There has been some sort of disruption in the production of Cuben fiber, the latest lightweight, waterproof, super durable wonder fabric the best ultralight gear is being made from these days, and as a result, tents are back ordered.

I am looking for a ULA (Ultra Light Adventures) pack specifically, and also for REI for potential replacement or repairs of my existing gear, but neither company is present.

I check out Gregory, another pack that is popular along the trail, and I look at other stands and displays. Most of the companies present have free equipment raffles a couple of times a day and I sign up for a few. I look at a bewildering assortment of equipment. It is Friday, and I have to make decisions. The post office is only open for a few hours in the morning tomorrow, and I need to ship my discarded gear home, where hopefully REI will accept returns. REI has a one year customer satisfaction guarantee, and besides my equipment falling apart, it also is not best suited for a thru-hike. They had much of the same gear I saw on display in Damascus at the Albuquerque store, but neither of my local store clerks understood thru-hiking and I was steered to equipment less suited to my adventure.

I see many hikers I know, both in town and out at the camping area, including people that I haven't seen since the very early days on the trail. I can't walk more than 20 feet without another meet and greet with an old companion, catching up and exchanging stories. I attend the North Face and Gregory raffles and watch some really nice items given away. I don't get drawn, but I get a nifty little lightweight folding bowl from Gregory just for stopping by.

Several hammock companies are represented. I have considered switching to a hammock. They have some advantages over tents, and some drawbacks. I am thinking ahead to New England. The Appalachian Trail through the White Mountains is mostly above treeline, and lacking in supports for a hammock, which is problematic. On the other hand, the possibility of being in snow up north is very real. Hanging above the snow seems better than sleeping in it.

Hennessey Hammocks is having a half price sale, and I can get a full hammock set up with the hammock, tree straps and rainfly, for $160.00. No other hammock company is even close to that bargain price. I dither a bit, looking back at the tents, but eventually walk away with a Hennessey

Ultra Light Asymmetrical Hammock that weighs in a little less than 3 pounds.

I look at a lot of packs. All of them, even the mainstream styles like Gregory, Osprey and North Face, are a pound to a pound and a half lighter than my REI monster. I keep looking until I find a little one man operation called Elemental Horizons making backpacks similar to the ULA products. The Elemental Horizons backpack weighs in at 42 ounces, a little less than 3 pounds, and is less than half the weight of my current bag. The thought that the designer, Matthew, puts into the details of construction and ergonomics is impressive. He usually makes his packs as custom orders, but he has a couple of finished packs as samples, and one is the right size for me. Again I walk around looking at other packs, mulling things over. I have to make decisions quickly, and they are decisions that are going to shape my camp life for the next 1900 miles of trail.

A disadvantage of ultralight packs is their necessarily flimsier construction. More to the point, as a small operation Matthew may not be able to support his equipment like a larger manufacturer can. I like the idea of supporting a start up and a craftsman though, and I end up coming back to him and buying the pack. It sets me back $330.00, a little more than a comparable ULA, but I have shaken the hand that designed and built this particular pack.

I end up buying a pair of Kelty hiker poles from an outfitter in town for just $22.00, a bargain price, and I also buy a new alcohol burning stove. My old Traeger is going home and I am saving a couple of ounces with a titanium stove built by Vargo, a company that specializes in titanium, ultralight, super durable hiking equipment. Titanium is expensive, but I get a deal for Hiker Days. The stove still sets me back more than the hiking poles.

Shopping completed, I hunt around for a dinner place that doesn't serve bar food and isn't jam packed with thru-hikers. Most of the pubs have long lines of hikers waiting for tables. I wander over to the far side of town and find a little restaurant called In The Country that isn't particularly crowded, and it has a shrimp and grits special. I order the special and it is one of the few times I have a truly memorable meal on the trail. I get a good sized bowl of big, perfectly cooked shrimp swimming in a salty, cheesy mass of grits. There is an ice cream parlor nearby, and I round out my feast with a banana split of locally made ice cream. Afterwards I return to the camping area with all my new goods and prepare for a last night in my trusty Eureka tent.

The party in the camping area is an ongoing affair, but it has its ebbs and flows. The bonfires are lit, and as the exhibits, booths, and seminars wind down the camp fills and the party builds. Many new people have arrived in camp, and while I thought I was fairly close to my neighbors before, new tents are wedged in on either side of me when I get back to camp. There is little space left anywhere I see, except right on the trails or right next to campfires.

I have a couple of beers and wander over to the bonfires. There is a drum circle going and people milling about, some are dancing. I had enough of drinking and partying for its own sake when I was closer in age to most of these hikers, and I head back to my tent. Different camp areas have their own little social scenes and I pause to watch a few. There is a group running around with foam swords and speaking in fake British accents, and another playing with fire. The fire group has twirling, flaming batons, and some kind of fire lit weights on a cord they swing about in mesmerizing patterns.

Somewhere on my wandering I lose the cash I am carrying with me. I have everything for the first half of my trip with me, wrapped in a Wal-Mart bag. I did not want to leave it in my tent unattended, just in case. Instead, I have dropped it in the camp somewhere. I have some anxious moments as I backtrack looking for it, and luckily find it lying unmolested near the fire group's camp. I decide that it is enough excitement for one evening and turn in.

I may be done with the night, but the night is not done with me. Tent walls create an illusion of privacy, but they are no barrier to any sounds of activity without. I hear conversations and shouts, and a couple makes love in a nearby tent. The crowning moment occurs at about 3:00 AM; it seems every camp circle has been given its very own loud, drunk guy. Ours gets into some kind of a shouting match with the neighboring circles loud, drunk guy, and they carry on until half a dozen people are shouting at them to quiet down, (expletives deleted). I do not sleep long or hard.

Day 41, May 16th
Uncle Johnny's Hostel, Erwin, TN, Trail Mile 343.0
Daily Distance 0.0 miles, Zero Day

There is a pancake breakfast being served at a Christian church and outreach center right next to the campground in Damascus. I am looking for a shipping box to mail my stuff home, and I figure a pancake breakfast would have some large, strong boxes from the economy sized foods they are bringing in. They would also have pancakes! I am right on both accounts.

I eat hearty, go back to my little villa of the woods, take it down one last time and pack it in the box I acquired, along with my old pack, hiker poles, stove, and other odds and ends I have collected. I load up my new pack and head into town.

Somewhere in the cut grass near the ball fields there is a hole hidden by the evenly cut grass, and while I am overbalanced with a full pack on my back, and a boxed pack in my hands, I stick my foot into the hole, stumble, and fall. Something gives way in my foot, and I get a blast of pain and nausea. I sit up and wait for the pain and feeling of sickness to subside, and it does, somewhat. My foot continues to throb, and I take off my shoe and have a look. Everything looks fairly normal, it just hurts. I put on my shoe, shoulder my pack, pick up my box, and limp into town.

At the post office a line of thru-hikers waits, mostly doing the same thing I am doing, mailing excess gear home. The clerks are friendly and efficient, despite the long line of hung over and grumpy customers. It costs me a little less than $20.00 to ship my box home to New Mexico at the cheapest rate. I am counting on REI accepting the pack and poles as returns. It will help defray the $500.00 I have dropped on replacement equipment.

My chores are done by 10:00 AM, and I am free now. Uncle Johnny's shuttle is due in the afternoon, and I wander about Trail Days aimlessly, or more exactly, I limp about aimlessly. My big toe seems to be the pain center.

There are a number of Trail Days events laid on; the Hiker Parade in the morning, the Hiker Talent Show, and in the evening there is the Hiker Prom. The local thrift stores are filled with hikers rummaging through the racks looking for inventive trail prom outfits.

I go from store to store and booth to booth. I am specifically looking for a harmonica. I gave up carrying my guitar, but I would like some kind of musical instrument with me to play. A lot of other thru-hikers seem to have had the same idea ahead of me and bought every harmonica in town. I participate in a few more raffles, again winning nothing. Watching a raffle happen is a lot of fun. The winners are cheered, especially when a known needy hiker gets a particularly useful item.

One of the wonderful things about the Appalachian Trail is that it has its own legends and heroes. The heroes are not out of reach and untouchable, they are people actually out walking around in the flesh, and you may very well end up meeting them on the trail, or at Trail Days. I meet one, David AWOL Miller, the writer of the trail guide I am using to find my way down the trail. McGyver has a lively discussion with him and asks detailed questions on sections of the guide that seem a little sketchy to him. AWOL relies heavily on input from hikers to keep the book honest, and McGyver's queries are treated with respect.

The Hiker Parade is a late morning event, and all the hikers slowly drift over to the start point before it begins. Thru-hikers are broken up by year group 'classes' each bearing a banner. 2015 is the largest, of course, but previous years have fair representation. Trail Days in Damascus serves as a thru-hiker reunion, and trail families with strong bonds meet there year after year. The parade is a riot, the hikers move in a mob down the main street, and the townspeople and other onlookers line the sidewalks armed water pistols, water balloons, hoses and buckets of water to give the dirty hikers 'showers'. Many thru-hikers are wearing the wild ensembles they have put together for the Hiker Prom tonight, adding to the chaos.

I follow Yeti in the parade. He is tall enough to stand out in the crowd and draw the attention of water wielding townspeople. I think he will shield me from being a direct target. I don't count on Yeti's natural enthusiasm. He makes himself an even bigger target by taunting the townspeople along the way, and our section of the parade gets more than an equal distribution of water. We are all soaked and laughing at the end point, where the parade just kind of peters out and hikers wander away to whatever activities draw them in.

I watch the Hiker Talent Show, set up on a little stage by the food truck court near the exhibits. I eat and watch an array of questionably talented hikers who jump on to the stage and show off random specialties in front of a small crowd. It is very entertaining. It starts to rain, the electric to the stage is cut off, the microphones are silenced, and the crowd disperses.

Among the booths is a stand for the Hiker Yearbook, a publication that looks a lot like a high school yearbook. I stand for a picture and get on the mailing list. The yearbook representatives are working to gather as many hiker photos as they can. They gather photos at Amicalola, here at Trail Days, and have representatives with cameras working on the trail itself. Hikers also send in their own photos, including Katahdin summit photos. I have a copy on my bookshelf; it is a nice memory and a resource for remembering people and trail names, and provides email contact information.

There is a graduate student with a little booth doing a survey on Appalachian Trail conditions for his Master's thesis in Recreation Management. I take the survey with Grip, and we both stop about halfway through. The questions are all focused on how 'challenging' the trail should be, and there is an obvious bias in the questions for trying to make the trail a more difficult physical endeavor. We ask the student what he is trying to achieve.

The grad student thinks the trail would be better if it was more challenging, and thinks this is an attitude shared by thru-hikers. I think about the many grueling days already finished, and the greater stretch of trail yet ahead. I remember Albert's Mountain, Howard's Rock, Big Bald, and many other long hard climbs. Grip asks him where he got this idea in his head and the grad student says he read another article suggesting this was what hikers wanted. We ask him if he has thru-hiked the Appalachian Trail. He has not; he has just done some day hiking. It is kind of scary how an academic perspective can be so divorced from reality. I wonder if the researcher who wrote the article that inspired our grad student's thesis had done any significant backpacking along the trail either.

I know many thru-hikers, like Grip and I, think the trail is challenging enough as it is. I wonder what the survey results showed. Even with the questions skewed towards a particular result, I don't think that the looked for result is going to come out of it. What happens to the graduate student's thesis when his survey doesn't support his idea, based on someone else's article of their opinion of the trail? Did he truthfully report what he has found and start a meaningful dialogue there, or did he adjust his survey to represent what he wants? The bias in the questions makes me believe the result is already preordained.

The shuttle back to Uncle Johnny's is full, even with Trail Days still going strong for at least another day or two. I sit between two thru-hikers who have conceived a slackpacking scheme to get some long, quick, supported miles at a reasonable cost. I listen to them talk, and then join in the conversation.

The trail between Erwin and Damascus has an unusual density of hostels right on the trail. The plan is to slackpack the trail jumping from hostel to hostel, using shuttle services to carry backpacks forward to the next hostel, and try to knock out 24, 27, and 24 miles over the next 3 days of hiking. Without the burden of a backpack the mileages should be possible.

The more people who are in the mix, the more ways the shuttle costs are divided. I agree to give it a try, and when we arrive back at Uncle Johnny's we arrange for the pack shuttle. We are to leave our packs with the shuttle driver first thing in the morning before moving out. Sadly, no where in my notes do I track the names of my fellow slackpack schemers during the three days I am in contact with them. I believe one of them was named Priest.

I need a small pack to carry my slackpack items forward. I want to carry snacks, a raincoat, water bottles a water filter, and a headlamp in case I can't finish in daylight. The hiker box has nothing useful, but the used items Uncle Johnny's is selling include a string bag with a small tear in it that I buy for two dollars.

Almost every hiker box along the trail has neckties. This is due to Miss Janet the Trail Angel, who found some hikers were denied entry to a restaurant because they didn't have ties, and decided to fix the problem. She went to thrift stores and bought and distributed ties all along the trail in hiker boxes. Because they are so available, there are hikers wearing ties over their t-shirts as a flamboyant piece of regular trail attire. The scheme works for me; I find a nice, wide, colorful silk tie and use it to make a comfortable shoulder strap for my string bag. I am set for the following day's slackpack

I use the bunkroom to sleep in, rather than camping in the yard. There is nowhere to hang my new hammock. I am packed and ready to go for the following morning.

The bunkroom is on the seedy side, and there is a huge hostel dog named Jerry Garcia that sleeps on a sofa inside. The door to the outside has no latch, and the dog comes in and out all night, pushing open the door. It slams shut behind him every time he goes through it, waking me each time. Although the dog himself is a friendly enough animal I build an animosity towards him through the night as my sleep is interrupted over and over again.

Day 42-46, May 17th to May 21st
Erwin, TN, to Roan Mountain TN, Trail Miles 343.0 to 393.6, 50.6 Miles
AVG 10.12 miles a day

Day 42, May 17th
Clyde Smith Shelter, Trail Mile 369.1
Daily Distance 26.1 miles

The great slackpack marathon is a failure.

Our slackpacking trio doesn't get started until after 9:00 AM. We have to wait for the hostel shuttle to take possession of our packs before we can get going. It is 8 o'clock before anyone representing the hostel is available, and then the worker has a whole host of little chores and other people to help before we can check in our packs and go.

The other two hikers are faster than I am, and soon I am hiking alone. The walk starts out fairly pleasantly, and I move quickly with just the slack sack over my shoulder, limping slightly from my damaged toe. There is a climb out of the Nolichucky River valley, going from 1700 feet of elevation up to the top of Unaka Mountain at 5180 feet, but it takes the trail a long 14 miles to make the ascent. There are ups and downs and it gets harder as it goes. There are a lot of water sources along the way, and I am letting my water supply get down to half a bottle before stopping to filter water and refill the two bottles I carry with me

While I am making good time, I realize in the late afternoon it is not fast enough. The toe I injured in Damascus is hurting now, a lot, and it is slowing me down. It begins to rain, and the day cools considerably. I am going to be night hiking, a prospect I really don't relish, especially hiking alone. I don't have any choice in the matter; slackpacking is a commitment to finish. I have to get to the planned endpoint to get back to my food and gear.

Dusk turns to night, and I find myself in the dark following the narrow beam of light produced by my headlamp. The misty rain closes around the beam so I am peering into a shadowy tunnel centered on the trail. I worry I am going to get lost. I think myself lucky when I come across Redlocks, Snack Time and Bubbles sitting around a campfire.

They tell me Greasy Creek, my goal, is just ahead. I am cheered and press hard to get there. What I expect is a gravel or forest road leading down to the hostel. The reality is a small sign tacked up on a tree about 20 feet off to the side of the trail. The forest road to the hostel runs parallel and slightly apart from the Appalachian Trail. I plod right on by the sign, unseen in the rain and dark.

I hike on for 10 or 15 minutes and I begin to wonder if I have missed the expected road. I know the hikers I passed gathered around their fire are very strong, very fast hikers, and I think maybe their definition of 'just ahead' may be something farther than I would reckon as 'just ahead'. I keep walking.

It is cold and wet, and I am wearing all the clothes I have with me, nothing more than a raincoat over a t-shirt. I have eaten all my snacks, and

I am down to a few swallows of water, I hoard what is left. If there is a spring, I won't see it in the dark.

Night hiking can be spooky in the best of circumstances. There is a reason our ancestors feared the forests, and there are so many fairy tales of woe for those who were trapped out in the woods at night. These are not the best of circumstances.

It is cold and foggy, and I am physically, mentally, and emotionally exhausted after more than 20 miles on the trail. The minor injury of my toe drains me, and I feel every step forward as I peer ahead into the small light of my headlamp in the darkness

The night closes in around me. The forest is noisy; I hear strange noises from creatures unseen outside the edges of my little beam of light. There are whistles, grunts, snarls and howls. The shadows cast in the mist by trees and rocks from my tunnel of light take on threatening shapes. Sometimes a shape seen just on the border of darkness in the mist seems to move, as though alive.

I tell myself over and over as I walk peering into the darkness there is nothing to be afraid of. The movements I see are probably only the effect of my bobbing headlamp. As I approach shapes the resolve into trees or a rocks rather than nightmares, but there is always another shadow to threaten me just ahead. At a very basic emotional level I feel the ancient fears.

The night seems endless. I stumble forward, on and on in the dark forest. I know there is a shelter somewhere on ahead past Greasy Creek, and if I miss the one, and I keep going, there will eventually be one after that. Or dawn. There are roads and towns somewhere out there in the darkness as well. Finally I see a sign up in a tree along the trail, with no small amount of relief. I am at Clyde Smith Shelter, more than 2 miles past my intended turn off.

I have two options, now I know where I am. I can turn around and try and find Greasy Creek again, or I can use the shelter. I have nothing in the way of food, warm clothing, or bedding, and I really want the hostel.

I think about all the tales of hikers who have vanished after trying to push just a little further, only to be found dead after an extensive search a few days later. Their last words are always something along the lines of, "I am fine. I can go just a little further...."

Cold and exhaustion does things to the human mind. People who die of exposure are often found far from their intended tracks. Sometimes they are found naked, the brain interpreting cold as heat for some reason, and victims feel so hot they strip off all of their clothes trying to get relief. I am feeling far from fine, and I weigh the possibility of death against a cold and uncomfortable night. I have already hiked 26 miles. I head to the shelter.

Clyde Smith Shelter has a number of people in it, and they have spread out to take advantage of all the available space. Everyone is asleep. I lean against the front frame and my headlamp is waking a few people, who try to ignore me. I am absolutely at the end of my tether, cold, hungry, wet, and exhausted. I am numb, and I am barely able to process thought. I flash my light around the sleepers again, and I can see some are awake. I ask for space. Finally a couple of people edge over and I crawl into the gap between them.

I am still miserable. I am shivering with cold, lying on a hard wooden floor. It is wet outside, and not particularly cold, but cold enough; it is around 50 degrees. I try to edge in closer to the person, the absolute total stranger, next to me, feeling heat. They edge away. I am a little angry and resentful inside. Can't these people see I need help? I am freezing, hungry, cold, and wet, lying against the hard wood floor.

Of course they cannot, I am just another hiker who has come in during the night, and none can really see my situation. I understand this later, but at the time I waffle between anger and self pity.

It is a very long night. I imagine my comfortably sleeping neighbors waking in the morning to find a rigid, frozen corpse in their midst, a thought that keeps me from falling asleep lest it actually happen. I lie there shivering and awake, and I wait for dawn.

Day 43, May 18th
Greasy Creek Friendly, Trail Mile 367.2
Daily Distance -1.9 miles

Today, I do I not make miles, I go backwards.

I rise as soon as there is a little light, in the predawn. Moving generates some warmth, so I am just deeply chilled instead of shivering uncontrollably. I go to the spring and get water. I can't drink much even though I need it; the coldness of the water is repellent. I see Spring-E, he is tented out, and he is a bit desperate himself, asking me if I have any food to spare. I mumble something negative. Had I my pack I would have gladly dug in and found some extra, I always carried more than I really needed and was happy to drop a little weight, but Spring-E's luck is out with me. I am as destitute in the moment as he is. It is the last time I see him on the Appalachian Trail.

I stumble back down the trail towards the way I came last night. It is only two miles, but it seems nearly as long in the morning as it did in the night. I find the sign on the tree I missed last night in the dark indicating the trail down to Greasy Creek. The sign is obvious in daylight.

The way down to the hostel is little over a half mile, and is a little confusing. There are a few trails that crisscross each other heading down from the ridge, but there is no signage, I am stupid with weariness, and it takes me a half hour to find the right forest road to bring me down to the hostel.

Greasy Creek Friendly is its own unique cultural experience. It is a small house on the edge of the woods. There is a small barn with a bunkroom, and a more expensive room with a couple of beds in the house.

A woman named Cici is the proprietor. Her Friendly is quirkier than most hostels, which is saying something about a very eclectic ensemble of habitations. Every hostel operator is a distinct character in one way or another, but Cici is in her own category. Greasy Creek is not just a hostel, it is her home. Cici shuns the word 'hostel' and its homonym 'hostile', and labels herself the Friendly instead.

Cici has a lot of rules. Many of them have to do with cleanliness. Incoming hikers must sit in a small vestibule at the back of the house, or on the front porch, until they read all three pages of rules and have a shower. There is a single hiker bathroom, so the vestibule can get backed up with waiting hikers. One of the rules is to wash your hands before you touch anything in the Friendly. A lot of the rules are basic common courtesy and personal hygiene, but some hikers ignore them, and Cici fusses about it, in a kindly way.

Thru-hikers get used to living in dirt and close quarters, and illnesses and parasites can wreak havoc if they get a hold. There was a run of a sickness on the trail where people vomited and had diarrhea; Giardia like symptoms, but contagious. Many people attribute it to Norovirus.

A thru-hiker was stricken by Norovirus while at the Friendly, and spent three days fouling the bunkroom. No one else could stay there during that time, of course, and Cici got stuck with both the loss of income, tending to the sick hiker, and the clean up. There is hard, unpleasant personal experience driving her rules.

Cici belongs to a religion that follows both Christian and Jewish traditions, and she keeps a kosher kitchen. It creates another layer of rules. No one but her is allowed in the kitchen. If you order non-kosher food from the take-out place in town, it can come into the house, but not into the kitchen.

Cici is fussy about her rules, but shows an unfailing good humor in enforcing them. It felt like staying at grandma's house, an impression reinforced by the breakfasts she is cooking for everyone.

I came in early, at about 7:00 AM, and the past night's guests are preparing to depart. As I sit in the vestibule waiting my turn in the bathroom, the other two thru-hikers on my slackpack adventure plan appear. They both are also snookered from the preceding day's adventure. They made it to the hostel before nightfall at least, but one was worn out enough he was looking into buying a plane ticket home. The other is younger, fitter, and wants to continue. Despite my own misadventure I contemplate pushing on with the plan and slacking for miles again this day, but the little voice inside of me knows I am going nowhere. I am spent.

Greasy Creek Friendly is inexpensive, even for a hostel, and comfortable. The common room is Cici's living room, and I doze and nap away the day on the sofa and in the bedroom. I have some lazy philosophical conversations with Country Gold. He has a dog kenneled outside, and makes frequent trips out to the front porch to provide his canine company, and I go out with him to listen to his stories.

Country Gold completed a thru-hike last year, and is back going over his favorite parts of the trail, taking his time and enjoying those parts instead of being driven past by the need to make miles. His dog is a happy, brindle, Carolina Coon Dog brimming with adolescent puppy joy greeting the world

Dinner is a treat from a local restaurant down in the area's little town center of 3 or 4 buildings. Cici shuttles us down, and Country Gold surprises us and buys the other three hikers in residence that evening dinner, an exceptionally generous act since he waited to tell us it was paid for until after we had all ordered hiker hunger driven double entrees and appetizers. It was a way for him to put something back into the trail experience, and much appreciated.

It brews up a nice storm during the afternoon, quite enjoyable when viewed from a sofa on a covered porch, but hard on the hikers out on the trail. A number of wet hikers come in after dinner.

Across the road from Greasy Creek Friendly is a neighbor who has retreated into the woods to avoid human contact. He has tarps draped over the fences surrounding his home to screen him from view, and there are lots of 'no trespassing' and 'hikers not welcome' signs posted. He dislikes the stream of thru-hikers passing by and intruding on his solitude. His dislike is not passive. He puts his own signage up on the trail trying to discourage hikers. Some are lies with overpriced resupply and stay prices, some say the hostel is closed; some are deliberate misdirection's to get hikers lost in the woods. Thru-hikers coming back up from the Friendly act to remove these efforts, but it is still a problem for Cici.

I sleep well.

Day 44, May 19th
Ash Gap, Roan Mountain approach, Trail Mile 375.4
Daily Distance 8.2 miles

The day is kind to me. It is sunny, and I can tell the difference my new Elemental Horizons pack and lighter load from Trail Days is making on my hiking. Roan Mountain is a significant climb, associated with a couple of different trail landmarks. I move well, with a slow but steady pace taking me up the mountain.

On reflection, I am glad I did not succeed in powering through the next 50 miles in two more days of slackpacking, The trail has wonders I would have missed if I were hell bent on making distances.

When I pick up my brand new pack to take it on the trail for the very first time I discover the buckle for the sternum strap is missing. Since I wore it around Damascus I know it was there when I left it for Uncle Johnny's shuttle to carry forward. The staff at Uncle Johnny's must have closed a door on it, or someone stepped on it. I tie a knot in the two ends of the strap. The discovery of the lost piece of pack and the subsequent fruitless search for it take some time and make a dent in my miles for the day.

A type of eft called the Red Spotted Newt is all over the trail today. The recent rains have them out and moving (very slowly) around. They are a couple of inches long and are burnt orange color, with faint yellow spots. I count them as I go, as something to pass the time. I lose track and give up when the count gets up and over 30. The Red Spotted Newt is a trail icon, and I am glad to see so many of them.

I am passed by a couple who are pushing road bikes up the trail, something I haven't seen before. No bikes are allowed to be ridden on the trail, along with motorized vehicles and pack animals. The couple is not riding, but are alternately pushing and carrying their bikes up the mountain. They rode out on the road from the parking lot at Carver's Gap up past Roan Mountain ahead, and thought to cut short their ride by completing their loop with a 5 mile walk on the trail. Like many parts of the Appalachian Trail, it proves to be more difficult than they were expecting. They are both young and fit, obvious athletes, and will be fine. They have run out of water however, and I share a liter with them. I am sympathetic to their situation and I am loaded down with hydration, overloaded after running short on my Greasy Creek marathon slackpack.

I stop short of the summit at Ash Gap to make camp for the night. Roan Mountain's last 1000 feet have a steep profile, and Ash Gap is in a saddle just before the final push. There is a shelter up past Roan Mountain, the highest and coldest shelter on the trail sitting at 6,285 feet. It is a popular stop just for that reason, but I am not going to make it that far today.

Ash Gap is the last point in the two miles before Roan Mountain Shelter with water, so it is a natural stopping place, and there are a lot of campsites scattered in the area. Four other hikers are camped in the general area, but I am alone at my site.

I hang up my hammock for the very first time. I still have to learn the tricks of getting it up quickly and efficiently, and understand the angles I want in the hang ropes to sleep comfortably. It is like learning to hang a bear bag, and I will have to develop the knack for it.

Ash Gap is at 5,350 feet of elevation, high enough up so it is still chilly even in the middle of May. I feel the cold underneath the hammock. There is no insulation beneath me, or trapping of body heat by the thin material. I pull out my air mattress and stuff it under me inside the hammock to provide a layer of insulation. I hear a lot of sound around me in the darkness, but my rain fly hides the night from me. I think my elevation off of the forest floor lets me hear more sounds carry further to people hanging up a few feet in the air rather than sleeping in a tent on the ground.

Day 45, May 20th
Overmountain Shelter, Trail Mile 384.6
Daily Distance 9.2 miles

TRAILTALK:

RAMEN BOMB: A meal made by mixing ramen, instant mashed potatoes and meat or vegetables in a single pot, It makes a gelatinous but filling carbohydrate mass for dinner.

I have my typical slow start to the day, this morning taking time to fool around with my hammock, trying to find the right combination to get the most comfortable hang, and tinkering with the assembly. It was a cold sleep, but not the most uncomfortable I have had by far. The hammock as a bed is very comfortable, even for a side sleeper like me. It is getting just the right tension that is the trick, and compensating for the chill.

I don't make a lot of miles today. I now consider anything fewer than 10 miles of hiking a substandard day. Back in Georgia it was a good, hard day.

The terrain is a lot tougher. There are four climbs, none of them especially long, but all together they make for a lot of work. The first climb, up to the top of Roan Mountain, is the hardest. It is the last peak over 6,000 feet high until I get into New Hampshire, over a thousand miles to the north.

The trail maintainers have been working on the trail again, and have put in a whole lot of little switchbacks. They cross and recross the original trail that went straight up the mountain. It must have been a truly awful climb before, because even with the switchbacks it is hard graft. Roan Mountain narrows into a ridge as I get higher, until I am making little cuts back and forth that are just 20 yards per leg. The views on either side are wonderful, slowing my ascent further. It is hard not to pause and stare out across the world at each successive turn.

It is a perfect spring day, warm but not hot, sunny, and fresh. The top of Roan Mountain is a sub-alpine fir forest. It is a micro ecosystem unique to the area, created by the altitude and the mountaintops isolation from the surrounding geography. The next sub-alpine forests are up in northern New England and Canada. The summit smells of balsam and pine, like Christmas on steroids. The smell is what air fresheners strive to replicate, and fail, falling far from the mark.

Roan Mountain is a popular hiking area, and the day is so fine I see many day hikers despite it being a weekday. I see a number of other thru-hikers as well, I have caught McGyver, Thor, Squirrel, and Chief, and we pose for a group photo at Roan High Knob Shelter. It is the highest, coldest shelter on the AT. The structure is an old one room log cabin with a loft, converted from a ranger station. It has four walls, helpful in protecting occupants from the wind and weather outside.

The next three climbs are a succession of balds. After stepping down from the fir forest on Roan Mountain we enter a different world. We are in Pisgah National Forest, and the balds are true balds, not just in name but the actual article. USFS grazes the big meadows with goats to maintain their character. Each bald is a distinct area apart from the others, and they are all covered with wildflowers in bloom, creating waves of delicious olfactory sweetness and a visual treat.

Overmountain Shelter is another celebrated landmark on the trail. It is an old barn that has been turned into a shelter, and it looks out and down across a meadow. There is an outer sleeping platform built under an overhang where hikers can watch the sun rise up over the mountains from their sleeping bags in the morning.

I stop early to take advantage of Overmountain. There are about twenty thru and section hikers who have made this a destination, and because it is a barn there are a lot of places to sleep. It does not feel particularly crowded even with the large number of people here. Some hikers, including McGyver, elect to pitch their tents in the meadow and get some separation even so. The meadow has no trees, of course, so I will not hang in my hammock tonight. I secure a spot on the large sleeping platform outside, which I share with six or seven other hikers wanting to watch the sunrise.

Thor leads a foraging party finding wild spring onions in the meadow, to add flavor to our ramen bombs. Overmountain Shelter was once a farm, and the meadow was its grazing area. A family once lived a hard but beautiful life here on top of the mountain.

Day 46, May 21st
Roan Mountain, NC (Roan Mountain BnB) Trail Mile 393.8
Daily Distance 9.2 miles

TRAILTALK:

STILE: A small set of steps or a ladder over a livestock fence. They are common on the trail since hikers can't be trusted to close gates behind them.

YOGI: Begging for food or other services, after Yogi the Bear; "Hey Boo Boo, I think I smell a Pic-a-nic!"

After yesterday's glories, I wake up this morning to a cold rain. There will be no observing the sunrise from my sleeping bag, just a sky lightening from black to grey. It is hard to get out of the barn with the rain coming down, but I, for one time, am out earlier than most of the crowd.

From Overmountain Shelter the trail climbs a long series of meadows, one enormous two and half mile long bald, up to Little Hump Mountain. The AWOL Guide puts in a specific warning, "many false crests".

The rain, which was an annoying drizzle when I left the shelter, builds up into a storm. Winds whip water horizontally across the unprotected fields. I have my head down staring at the trail beneath my feet as I push myself up the hill against the winds, one step at a time. The trail itself is a gentle rise, but it seems never ending.

I start counting the false crests. The hilltop rolls a little as it rises, creating a slow upward undulation, and at each little height you can see the next rise, but not beyond it. In total I count seven false crests before gaining the true top.

There is a hiker wrestling with his tent out on the bald. Several hikers wanted isolation and space in which to watch the spectacular sunrise that did not occur, and chose to camp out on the bald instead of near Overmountain Shelter. It is Rhino, and as he struggles to take his tent down the wind seems just as determined to tear it away off into the grey. The tent is moving around like a living thing trying to escape his grasp. He has an older cabin style tent. Rhino is a budget thru-hiker, and he has last generation's heavy gear, but he is young and strong and makes the miles with a certain élan under his heavy load.

I hurry over to help, and a section hiker named Snakebite comes running up behind me. Between the three of us we tame Rhino's tent and he is able to break camp. I get back to my climb, and at the summit of Little Hump I find Peppermint Patty, Buzzkill, and Tumbleweed, a mother and her two daughters thru-hiking together, hunkered down in a big three person tent. I call in to see if they are ok or need any help, but they are snug within, and are content to sit out the storm.

Little Hump Mountain, is followed, inevitably, by Hump mountain. I know I am finally off of Little Hump when I come down over a couple of stiles to a treeline. I enter the forest as the rain eases. The weather has prevented me from seeing one of the most renowned series of views on the Appalachian Trail, the vistas from the balds of Little Hump. I still had a great adventure.

Another trail name is suggested to me to go along with the previous offerings of Redundant, Ziploc, and Sweeper after this particular episode, Storm Magnet. Oddly enough, I am starting to take a perverse enjoyment from the series of storms I am encountering on nearly every bald I cross. I pass on the new moniker however. I will be Possible all the way up the trail, but it is fun to hear suggestions for new trail names. Some thru-hikers names evolve as they journey north, occasionally creating identity confusion.

Hump Mountain is forested, a goodly climb up, followed by a long and steep climb down. On the descent clusters of little flags are planted along the trail marking where trail maintenance is under way. The trail definitely needs it. It is rough and uneven, with granite and rock patches, and the soil is a slippery clay, especially dangerous when wet. I slowly work my may down to U.S. Highway 19, and I cross the North Carolina border back into Tennessee for the last time. It is another short mileage day, but the town of Roan Mountain has a special, can't miss attraction for thru-hikers, and I am stopping to take advantage of it.

Mountain Harbour resort is in town, not far from the AT trailheads, and has a bunkhouse for hikers. It is reputed to have the best breakfast on the trail, and many hikers are looking to enjoy it. It is less than a mile down the highway from the trail, an easy walk along the road. Between the breakfast and the weather, the place is packed. They can only offer me the sofa in the bunkroom common room, and do so for full price. I think about it, but waiting in the night for everyone to clear out of the common room before I can sleep is a nuisance. There is a tenting area, but I have a hammock now, and cannot set up in a treeless yard.

I break out the AWOL Guide and look at my options. I make some calls, and there is a little bed and breakfast on the other side of town that has a room for $65.00 a night. It is an expensive thru-hiker night, but cheap for a BnB, and the host, Anne, will come pick me up. I tell her to come and get me.

The room at Roan Mountain BnB is very nice, a master suite with a large comfortable bed and a private bathroom. Snakebite is also at the hostel, as well as a fast moving thru-hiking expatriate doctor from Romania, trail named Evi, who is doing 20 miles a day. We split laundry costs, and the hiker box is full of food. There is enough that I complete most of my resupply right out of the box. I get ramen, hot chocolate, half a bottle of hand sanitizer, Heet for stove fuel, and even a bag of dried apple rings. I take just what I need, leaving plenty for the next set of thru-hikers.

Evi is a hoot. Evi's trail name was bestowed on him by his Romanian wife. It is the beginning word of an apology, "I am very sorry", in Romanian. He said his enthusiasm sometimes led him into social awkwardness, and he had a habit of sticking his foot into his mouth. He has a great story to support it.

Evi stopped at a mountaintop view to take it in. While he was there a family group of day hikers appeared. They were carrying a cardboard container that they started tinkering with once they caught their breath on the summit. Evi thought they had ice cream, and being a typical thru-hiker he was hoping to yogi some trail magic, and he asked if they were going to share.

There was a moment of shock. It turned out the container was not filled with ice cream. Instead it held the family's beloved grandfather's ashes they brought up to the summit to scatter in the mountains he loved.

I am very sorry, indeed.

Anne provides a shuttle back a mile into town, I eat a fantastic, fresh baked pizza at a little local artisan place called Smoky Mountains Pizza Bakery. I hoped to get some bagels for the trail; there was a sign posted announcing Thursday as their bagels special day. I am disappointed in this, they sold out early. I get a six pack of brownies instead, some for myself and some to give away on the trail. I hit up the Dollar General to finish out my resupply.

There is an old burger and ice cream place called Bob's Dairyland where we wait to be picked up and brought back to the bed and breakfast at 7:00 pm. The restaurant has been frequented by a lot of heavy smokers, and there is sheen of grease from the grill and old smoke on the walls and ceiling. It may be the surroundings, but the ice cream is not enjoyable. It is the worst part of a pretty decent day of trail experiences. I think that when a banana split is the low point of a day, it is a fine day indeed.

Day 47-51, May 22nd to May 26th
Roan Mountain TN, to Damascus VA, Trail Miles 393.8 to 469.1, 76.7 Miles
AVG 15.34 miles a day

Day 47, May 22nd
Upper Laurel Fork (Vango Hostel), Trail Mile 406.4
Daily Distance 13.6 miles

I meet the other half of the bed and breakfast team at the Roan Mountain Bed and Breakfast in the morning, Anne's husband Steve. The breakfast part of Roan Mountain Bed and Breakfast is provided at Happy's Cafe in town, and a ride is then provided from the cafe to the trailhead after eating. It is a typical southern breakfast, good, filling, and loaded with fat and protein. I have a very good night overall in Roan Mountain, even missing the "best breakfast on trail" at Mountain Harbour resort. Steve and Anne are gracious hosts, and Evi and Snakebite made good company.

My day of hiking begins with the inevitable climb out of town. It is a mild ascent, followed by rolling ups and downs. The trail follows the Elk River, a beautiful little passage. There are two waterfalls enroute, one of which is supposed to be down a side trail. I explore a bit looking for it but I must have mistaken a game trail for the side trail, and after blundering along into thickets I finally turn around and return to the AT without seeing the first waterfall.

Mountaineer Shelter is next to the second falls (Mountaineer Falls), and looks like a very nice place to stay the night. I am less than 9 miles into the day's hike and it is still only mid-afternoon. I want to make more distance. I take a short break, but keep moving on. I share my bakery brownies with hikers at the shelter, and then I set my feet on the path for a hostel up the trail.

Scottie's Place, the Vango Hostel, is on a side trail on the far side of Upper Laurel Creek, a pretty, slow moving stream. The side trail follows the creek up to the hostel from a bridge on the trail. The creek is not large and the bridge is a luxury, a good jump would see a hiker across the water. A short distance before the bridge there is a bench placed where it has a view overlooking a valley. The bench is a memorial dedicated to Vango, and is part of the trail maintained by Scottie.

The main house sits ten feet away from the National Forest. The USFS boundary signs stare me in the face from the edge of Scottie's front porch. Scottie lives in the house, and while no hikers stay inside (besides Scottie, of course), the big wrap around front porch serves as the hostel's gathering place. The bunkhouse is a separate structure. Quarters in the bunkhouse are pretty rough, but it is a bed under cover, and it is only $10.00.

A number of other hikers are here, mostly tenting out, but one or two are sharing quarters with me in the bunkhouse. There is a separate, private, upstairs room in the bunkhouse, and a married couple is up there now, shunning the crowd. Ice, Lego, Rambler and Penthouse are all on the porch and we buy and eat frozen pizzas and Ben and Jerry's Ice Cream. There are musical instruments and we sit, relax, play, and watch the sunset.

Scottie is an engineer, and trail named after the Star Trek character. There is something a little sad about Scottie and this place. There is another memorial for Vango on the grounds, but I do not know who Vango is, and I feel a little awkward asking the obvious questions, so he remains a mystery. Obviously he was someone important to Scottie. There are pictures of Scottie on his own thru-hike years ago inside the bunkroom. He appears with a woman, and they both look happy and filled with positive energy.

Scottie is by himself tonight, and he seems detached and alone. He is friendly enough baking our pizzas, and he sits down for a while to play on an upright piano that is on the porch, but still I feel a sadness.

Temperatures are cool in the evening, and weather reports on iPhones say it will get down to 45 degrees. I had the energy to go another mile or two, but I am quite happy not to have another trial with my hammock in the cold tonight.

Day 48, May 23rd
Dennis Cove, Black Bear Resort, Trail Mile 418.5
Daily Distance 12.1 miles

Today should not have been the long hard day it felt like. The trail is flat and stays at relatively low elevations between 2000 and 3000 feet. The weather is good and there were no particularly difficult sections. It must just be me. Maybe I ate too much frozen pizza and ice cream last night.

Leaving Scotties I take a picture of one of the privies that has a sign painted on it labeling it the Shiter X-2. Something about an outhouse that has a name like an experimental rocket ship tickles my fancy, but no one else seems to get the joke.

I struggle to hike down to the Route 50 road crossing and the hamlet of Dennis Cove. There are two lodging options here, each one famous in its own way. One is Bob Peoples Hostel in Kincora, run by the legendary thru-hiker and trail maintainer. There are jokes written about Bob Peoples legendary toughness in nearby registers, and graffitied on shelter walls.

"Did you hear Bob Peoples was bitten by a rattlesnake? They rushed him to a clinic and performed emergency CPR, but the snake still died!"

Unfortunately Bob Peoples Kincora Hiking Hostel also has something of a reputation, and it is as infamous as Bob Peoples is legendary. The word is Bob likes cats. There are a lot of semi-feral cats running about, all of them beloved by Bob. They have done what cats do, marking their territory, and the hostel is reputed to have a distinct aroma.

Bob Peoples is the favored stop for budget hikers and the party crowd. I decided to forgo the cats and the party, and choose to go to Black Bear Resort, a half mile away in the other direction down Route 50. Black Bear Resort is more expensive than Kincora, but it is still very reasonable. There are plenty of thru-hikers here, and the bunkroom and cabins are full. I get one of the last available bunks.

The owners live in a separate house on site, and are actively pursuing different marketing strategies to fill the place in the season. It is well kept, the amenities and bedding are nearly new, and the resort sits along a nice little river. I watch some children fishing in one of the pools as I walk in.

There is a game of Scattergories played in the common room that evening hosted by one of the female thru-hikers. I play in the game and enjoy a couple of cans a beer to go with the standard frozen pizza and Ben and Jerry's Ice Cream. The bunkroom is a crowded space but it is an experienced and conscientious group of thru-hikers in occupancy, making for a decent, mannerly night.

For some reason my notes for this day are a little confused. I have written the phrase 'Electric Bagpipes' as an isolated phrase, with no recollection as to why. It can't possibly be anything good.

Day 49, May 24th
Past Wilbur Dam Road, Trail Mile 432.5
Daily Distance 14 miles

I am getting longer miles in with more hours of daylight to hike and better physical conditioning. I hope to make 15 miles a day my new standard. I may have done it today; I am not quite sure where exactly I have stopped. I had to hike the half mile of road back to the trail from Black Bear Resort, some of the extra distance not counted as trail mileage, but walked nonetheless. There is an 1800 foot climb up to Pond Flats, quickly followed by an 1800 foot descent back down to Lake Watauga. Pond Flats is a mountain with a small flat area on top that catches and holds rainwater, creating a small body of water on the summit.

Bear activity has created a camping exclusion zone around the Watauga Lake Shelter to past the Wilbur Dam Road. There is a rumor going around that a teenager sleeping in his hammock was attacked here by a bear, but thankfully was shaken up by the event rather than hurt. Whatever the reason, signs announcing the closure have been posted at every trailhead for the last 50 miles, so the need to hike past the lake is no surprise.

There is a public beach on the lake, and it is crowded with locals out for Memorial Day weekend. A group of thru-hikers lounges about trying to yogi some beers and hotdogs without a whole lot of success. The lake's crowded beach has restrooms, but no snack bar for treats. I hang out for an hour and a half, just sitting and enjoying the sun and water with other hikers. A couple of them are trail families and have an easy fellowship I envy. I still haven't found that group I can blend with, even if I could keep the pace.

A fair population of beer drinking, motor boating; short-short, muscle shirt, and bikini wearing locals have turned out in America's finest tradition of the Memorial Day summer kick off at the lake. Souped up cars and pickup trucks prowl the parking lot revving their motors to compete with the roar of jet skis offshore. I find of particular interest a teenaged boy walking around shirtless with "Death Before Dishonor" tattooed in four inch high Gothic lettering on his chest. I wonder what his parents thought about it, and if this boy were actually faced with a little shame could he swallow it or would he just die? I am thinking it is a lot of principle for a sixteen year old kid to have to carry forward for the rest of his possibly short life.

I ruck up and go around mid-afternoon. I hike around the lower end of the lake and cross Wilbur Dam, which is beautiful. I see Thor and Squirrel atop the dam as I hike down the approach road. It is hot enough that our clothes are continually soaked with sweat from our hiking exertions. The notch between the two mountains where the dam is built generates a strong wind, and Thor has his shirt off. He is holding it over his head; it flies in the wind as a makeshift drying method. He looks like a conquering hero, proudly flying his banner in the pass.

I pause to talk with them for a couple of minutes, then Thor and Squirrel move on out ahead as I take in the expanse of sun washed lake on one side of the dam, and the darkening drop below on the other.

As I cross a hawk is riding the winds, and soars just a few feet above me. The raptor is held stationary for several long seconds by the force of the wind. The last golden light of the day defines his feathers, and I stand transfixed until he swoops away.

The climb up from the Dam is quite steep, and I labor my way up. As soon as I pass a sign denoting the end of the camping exclusion zone I hunt for a good pair of trees as a hammock campsite. I find one fairly close to a dirt road. I set up in the darkness wearing my headlamp. It is my second hammock hanging experience. It seems good, and I fall asleep hoping it doesn't turn cold in the night.

Day 50, May 25th, Memorial Day
Past the Nick Grindstaff Monument, Trail Mile 444.4
Daily Distance 11.9 miles

Nicholas Grindstaff: He lived Alone, He suffered Alone, He died Alone

As a solo hiker I am feeling Nick when I look at his grave and marker. I have been spending a lot of time by myself

Nick Grindstaff is another Appalachian hermit, gone but not forgotten. I talk about this monument in Damascus later, and there are a couple of hikers there who say they met his great nieces. They told them this story.

Nick was a local boy who went West in the 1800s chasing his fortune, and he managed to find it, He brought his fortune and a much loved young bride home to Tennessee to settle down.

Now, back then money was actual, physical coinage you kept around in the house, not an electronic number in a bank, and Nick's fortune was a tangible item that could be picked up and carried away. So was his young bride, and he came home one day after spending time in the mountains to find out they both were gone.

Heartbroken, Nick went into the woods and built a little cabin on a mountain crest right along what is now the Appalachian Trail. He went into town once a year to buy staples, and otherwise lived off the land, shunning people. He had occasional visitors, who reported he kept a pet timber rattlesnake that slept on the warm stones of his cabin's hearth.

When Nick died his body was taken back down into town and given a pauper's burial. Some distant relatives found out, and came to his rescue in death, if not in life. They had him disinterred and reburied by his old cabin, and built the monument that is now a trail landmark. The family still checks up on it from time to time.

It takes me a long time to get twelve miles today. The long climb up from Lake Watauga exhausted me yesterday, and I move slowly today. I hike from 8:00 AM to 8:30 PM and do not achieve a mile an hour of forward progress. I take a lot of breaks along the way. The trail rides a ridge that follows along the considerable length of Lake Watauga, and the views are ever changing and wonderful.

Many of the hikers who were at the Watauga Lake beach yesterday pass me today, maybe never to be seen again except as register entries. Everybody but me seems to have fresh wind in their sails. Penthouse is trying a 44 mile single day push into Damascus, and he may have the youth, legs and will to do it. I wish him luck. Many people take the last 26 miles into Damascus from Iron Mountain Shelter in one fell swoop, making the Damascathon a single day marathon event. It is more than what I think I have in me, and I am planning two more thirteen mile days to finish this leg.

Water stops in particular seem to take a long time. The pure gushing springs of Georgia are behind me. I am now in a land of slow seeps, requiring a long time to channel their dribbling flows through a rhododendron leaf spile into my squeeze bag and filter. I have a Sawyer Mini, and the flow rate of the smaller filter is a lot slower than that of the larger version. It didn't matter when water was everywhere and it was nice and cool. Now it is hotter. I am sweating buckets and need more water, and the smaller filter slows my roll.

There are a lot of slower moments today besides the big views and the frustrating water stops. I sit on a log for half an hour watching a swarm of a dozen iridescent purple and black butterflies engaged in an aerobatic swirl at a spot where distinct rays of sun filter down through the leaves. Two smaller black and gold butterflies dart in and out of their larger cousins doing their own aerial dance.

I think of my daughter as I watch them flit about. Her name, Vanessa, means butterfly in Greek. I try to capture a picture to share with her, but the fluttering wings darting in and out of the sun are too swift for my phone camera to capture.

I also look at salamanders, birds, and toads, usually while waiting for my water squeeze bag to fill. The seeps have a lot of wildlife around them.

The rhododendrons and azaleas are flowering, and there are stretches of a hundred yards at a time along the ridge where the trail is walled in by blooms. I also see many of what I was calling parachute plants, a small plant maybe a foot high that has a single large flower that blooms beneath a small canopy of leaves. I have found the actual name of these flowers is Mayapples.

I pass Iron Mountain Shelter. It has a crowd of hikers staging for the Damascathon and I hike just a little further to the Nick Grindstaff monument seeking solitude for the night. I think deep thoughts about Nick and move on. There is enough space to camp here, but a woman section hiking is already setting up a tent. She had also come past the shelter to avoid people, something she not too subtly pointed out as I looked at the surrounding trees for two the right distance apart.

I take the hint and move yet a touch further down the trail. I wait a touch too long to make a decision to camp, and set up in near darkness again. This time I have my hammock slung in the narrow space between the trail and a drop-off along the ridge a few feet away. I get it set up faster, so practice is making it less of a nit picking detail. I eat my dinner by headlamp, and settle in with unidentified and sometimes creepy forest sounds around me.

Day 51, May 26th
Damascus, VA, Trail Mile 469.1
Daily Distance 24.7miles

DAMASCATHON!

I wake to rain. It comes in fits and starts blowing across the ridgeline. It takes me longer to break camp in the wet. I am trying to keep things dry as I pack, and the rain fly is the last item I take down, to leave a shelter to work under. I have a Lightload towel about the size of a washcloth they gave away to hikers at Trail Days. It is proving very useful. I use it to wipe moisture off of everything, ending with the fly, wringing out the towel every few swipes. Things don't end up really dry, but water is weight, and the more I wipe away the less weight I have to carry.

The Appalachian Trail from Iron Mountain Shelter to Damascus is 26 miles of steady, fairly level downslope. I am already nearly a mile past the shelter, and I am toying with the idea of going all the way in a day, doing the Damascathon. Even with the late start I might be able to pull it off. I feel rested, and I will take a zero tomorrow in town if I punish myself today. It is after 8:00 AM by the time I am packed up and moving.

I see some forked branches fifteen feet up in the air at a perfect distance apart to hang a hammock, and I try to figure out just how I would manage hanging my bed for the night from such a lofty perch. Besides the engineering feat of setting up that high while clinging to branches, the troubles lie in getting into, and especially out of the hammock at such a height. I will not try this, but it gives me something to think about as I hike.

I settle into a good hiking pace. I am going at least two miles an hour, even taking occasional short breaks. I get lucky along the way, and I hit trail magic not once, not twice, but three times, at successive road crossings. A Baptist Church is providing support at the first, former 2012 thru-hiker Skunkape is at the second with his mother. There is a cooler with snacks and sodas left by Rabbit at the third. Water is scarce on this stretch, and the free drinks and snacks provide fuel to speed my journey.

At 6:00 PM I am at Abingdon Gap Shelter, still 10 miles from Damascus. It will be dark between 8:30 and 9:00 o'clock. I will need to finish the hike on a headlamp if I want to go the full distance to Damascus.

Abingdon Gap has a Boy Scout troop using the area. They are friendly, but are not who I want to camp with for the night. I can feel the pull of Damascus down the trail, and the challenge of pushing myself hard for the plain old glory of doing a crazy distance is calling to me. A hiker named Dale is also at the shelter, and going through the same thought process as I am.

Dale and I talk. If we stick together, night hiking will be a lot less painful, and if something happens there will be someone there to provide assistance. Two is safer than one. Dale is a stronger hiker than I am, but I think I can keep a decent pace for this one push. We go. Damascus or bust!

Many of the hikers who were trying to push the Damascathon back at Iron Mountain Shelter have run out of steam, and are camping along the trail. A large cluster of campers are in sites around the Virginia state line. Many of them are members of the Easter Pod. I have caught and passed some of the crews I started the Appalachian Trail with.

Dale and I continue on. As night falls we put on our headlamps and keep heading down the trail. The last five miles are a moderately steep descent with some switchbacks, and Dale is moving fast, and I am just hanging on. There are stumbles and curses in the dark.

We come off the trail into a little residential neighborhood in Damascus at 10:30 pm. We have covered a little more than 10 miles in just over four hours, two hours of it night hiking. I am exhausted, but proud.

Dale already has town plans and we separate. I stagger part of another mile into town. I end up at 'The Place', a hostel run by the United Methodist Church.

The Place has a caretaker but he is not in residence, a 'gone hiking' note is posted on the door. The building is an old 19th century house and it has 40 bunks scattered in rooms upstairs and down. There is a kitchen and a large common room. A dozen hikers already occupy bunks, and I pick a bed and settle in.

I have made it to Virginia.

VIRGINIA, PART I

Day 52 to 74, May 27th to June 18th
Damascus to Pearisburg, VA, Trail Mile 469.1 to 727.8, 258.7 miles
AVG 11.75 Miles a Day

Day 52 - 57, May 27th to June 1st
Damascus VA to Marion VA, Trail Miles 469.1 to 531.5, 62.5 Miles
AVG 10.41 Miles a Day

Day 52, May 27th
Damascus VA, Trail Mile 469.1
0.0 Miles, Zero Day

I planned on taking a zero day in Damascus all the way back at Trail Days. The town of Damascus supports hiking, and without the Trail Days crowds it would be an excellent and restful place to take a day off. Completing two days of hiking miles in a single day yesterday doing the Damascathon leaves my conscience easy about resting my aching feet, legs and back.

Damascus is a much more enjoyable place without the Trail Days crowds. There are a couple of good inexpensive pubs and other restaurants. My hostel, The Place, is remarkably inexpensive. A $7.00 donation gets you in out of the rain for a night. It is basic quarters with a twin bed in a bunkroom, a shared single shower, and a kitchen, and it suits a thru-hiker's basic needs admirably.

There are a few people who are on prolonged stays at The Place, and in a couple of other hostels around town, They have to get special permission to stay in residence for more than one or two nights, but the hikers are so obviously injured the hostel caretakers are lenient. There is a free clinic in town providing rudimentary medical services for thru-hikers. The clinic is telling the really broken ones to go home and heal; they are not going any further this year.

There has been some weeping. It is a difficult to give up on the dream. Giving up something your mind and will are focused on completing when your body simply can't comply is hard. It is even worse when you have already committed a couple of months and substantial financial resources to the effort. It is difficult having conversations with hikers who are still trying to give up on the trail even after the doctor tells them they could ruin themselves for life if they continue.

I see more women with trail ending injuries than men. Women carry proportionally more weight and are pushing themselves harder with smaller bodies, trying to keep up with the men. There is something about the female thru-hiker psyche that is willing to push past the point of sense tying to achieve their goals.

There are people who are half broken as well, or who are going to ignore the clinic's medical professionals and keep on going as soon as swelling and pain start going down. Some of these hikers will hold on for many more miles, but most will eventually come to terms with having a body they are driving to ruin with their determination to get to Katahdin, and will go off the trail. Some of the ones who have already resigned themselves to leaving are already talking about next year.

Sickness is also moving on the trail, whether it is the Norovirus, basic dysentery or Giardia, or all three, no one is too sure. Whatever it is, it puts people on their backs. People who catch it while in the woods suffer badly. It takes a day or two to ride it out, while leaking and occasionally spewing uncontrollably from both ends. The practice when stricken out on the trail is to rig a rain fly, dig a cat hole next to it, and lie under the fly on your air mattress. Victims keep the side of their sleeping bags unzipped so they can roll over and go when the need is urgent. When the cat hole is full, the hiker has to summon energy, shift the set up over a few feet, cover the old cat hole and dig a new one. It makes for a very bad day or two. Some sick people are laid up in town, but not at The Place.

Whatever the cause is, thru-hiker numbers are starting to dwindle. A number of familiar faces have disappeared. Damascus is a decision making point where a number of people who are struggling finally say enough.

Damascus has three outfitters, and I am, as always, looking for better, lighter, replacement equipment. The outfitters have very little of the equipment favored by thru-hikers still in stock. Trail Days emptied the shelves. I move slowly on tired legs from shop to shop searching for the items I want.

I need a new Sawyer water bladder for my mini filter. The bladders are prone to going out at the seams after a couple of weeks of use, and it is a must have item. You can get by with using the filter on certain types of threaded bottles, but the bladders are the way I am working. I carry two, one to use, and one spare, but blew through both during this last stretch.

I find one replacement bladder in the hiker box at Mount Rodgers Outfitters, but it is a small one and I preferred the larger sizes. The big ones are easier to squeeze and take less time to refill. It was what was available though, and it was free. Small bladders are sold in packs of three, and two backups are just extra weight so somebody donated one.

Mount Rodgers Outfitters has a small shrine to a thru-hiking pioneer, Grandma Gatewood, the first woman to successfully thru-hike the Appalachian Trail. She hiked the trail with a shower curtain as a shelter, and wore Converse All Star sneakers as her hiking shoes, when she wore shoes at all. A pair of her worn out sneakers is on display, with an informational plaque about her adventures.

What I am looking for today is not new gizmos, but replacing equipment I already possess with lighter or more efficient equivalents. I am only interested in basics. I switched out my headlamp for a brighter, lighter one, after finding the one I got for free with a coupon at Harbor Freight in Albuquerque was less powerful than I wanted. I sorted out some clothes as well. I sent home my hat and Adidas running shirt, replacing them with ultra light items that weighed less than half as much. Lightweight is expensive, and my two new t-shirts that weigh 3 ounces each replaced a 16 ounce shirt, but cost $40.00 apiece. I bought both of the shirts left in my size, one fluorescent orange and the other neon green. Everyone will see me coming, and hunters should know I am not a game animal.

I considered different sleeping mats and sleeping bags, but keep what I have. My systems are working, but are a little cold, and it would take a significant improvement at a reasonable cost to tempt me into changing out a major piece of equipment. The lighter outdoor gear is, the more expensive it is, and the absolute lightest items can cost you hundreds of dollars to lose a few ounces. My best find of the day utterly contradicts this; I find a sleeping system improvement at the Dollar General. The reflective window shades for automobiles make a fine under layer of insulation in a hammock, weigh little and costs even less.

I have mail drops waiting for me at the post office. My stepmother, Twirp, and my wife have both sent packages. Twirp sent Anzac cookies she home bakes for me, continuing a tradition she started when I was deployed overseas with the Army. She separates the cookies into little packets of four or five each. I eat some, stash a couple of packets, and give the rest to hungry hikers at the hostel.

My wife is experimenting with dehydrating food. I am particularly seeking proteins, and she has turned 10 pounds of ground bison into 2 pounds of dehydrated 'gravel'. There are also packets of dried peas and pineapple. These will all become trail staples, the gravel will be different ground meats, and are perfect for adding to my nightly ramen bombs and Knorr Sides.

My fully loaded food bag, with the additions from home, weighs 10 pounds, or about 2.5 pounds a day. It is heavy, 2 pounds a day is the common formula. Most of my extra weight is from carrying supplies of bulk dehydrated foods intended for longer periods of time.

I spent some time hanging around Rambler, an older man, a Navy Vet, with great, curly hair and beard. He wears unusual shoes, Z coils, that have a big spring built into the heel. They help him with his Plantar Fasciitis, a very common and painful foot ligament trail ailment.

Damascus is a dry town; I can get beer but no liquor. I wanted to fill a flask with a little sleep and pain aid, but Tennessee has some strange, puritanical blue laws that seem to change every half mile or so. I could try and get a ride out to a nearby area that sells booze, but it isn't worth the investment of time and effort, not for a flask.

. I want to get out of town and get moving tomorrow, but I still have to send a package of replaced items home from the post office, and I want a nice breakfast to begin my hiking day.

Day 53, May 28th
Saunders Shelter, Trail Mile 478.6
Daily Distance 9.5 miles

TRAILTALK:

PUDS: Pointless ups and downs. The trail often seems to take the most difficult route for no other reason than it is there. Sometimes there are geographic or engineering reasons, but sometimes it appears to be just plain orneriness. Each little section of the Appalachian Trail is built and maintained by another club or individual trying to put a memorable stamp on the section. Many thru-hikers wish they wouldn't indulge themselves.

I start back on the trail at noon, after getting my package mailed and waiting out some rain. It rains hard, which is enough of an excuse to keep many hikers enjoying the comforts of the Damascus hostels and pubs for another day. I make good time, despite my late start, hiking a little less than 10 miles in a little more than 6 hours. The initial walk is along the Virginia Creeper Trail, a bike route, and Damascus' other major outdoor tourism draw. There is a continual flow of bicyclists along the VCT, some out for a day, some pedaling from town to town on a mini holiday. Leaving Damascus the old Creeper railroad bed follows a small river along a flat stretch. The Appalachian Trail moves off of the VCT, but parallels it, staying some 20 to 50 feet away. Instead of enjoying the flat rail bed, the trail makes lots of little PUDs, pointless ups and downs following the nice level bike trail beside it

Saunders Shelter is very nice after the concrete bunkers of Tennessee. Virginia shelters are generally well maintained. This one is built of wood, it is roomy, and there is a privy. Tennessee disability law required each privy to be handicap accessible, which in general created enough issues that many sites just did without privies altogether. There are rare shelters deep in the woods and high in the hills of Tennessee, along rough sections of trail, that have privies with wheel chair ramps and handholds built into them. Usually I dug a hole in the woods.

There are six or seven people at Saunders Shelter. A couple are pitching tents, but with sporadic rain falling I decide to keep my hammock dry tonight, and sleep in a shelter for the first time in several days.

I meet Stirling, right out of Georgia. He woke up one morning and said, 'I think I will hike that trail over there', and here he is. He is wearing combat boots because they happened to be the pair he picked up on his way out the door.

Stirling is a budget hiker, his hike is entirely unplanned, and he has been foraging to supplement his diet. He and Wander caught a snapping turtle down by the river and decided to cook it. Chef came along as they were determining how to prepare the turtle, Chef got his name (one of two with the name this year) from his openness to new culinary experiences, and he makes an effort to prepare real meals on the trail. He carries spices and cookware in his pack.

Together they figure out how to get the turtle out of its shell and cooked up a calabash. The rest of us are watching them after they relate their tale to see if they start to exhibit any ill effects. So far, they seem good, but there is a faint fishy odor lingering about the shelter tonight.

Ice tells a black bear story. I am one of the few hikers who has not yet met a bear on the trail. Ice and Lego have seen a couple, and in this particular encounter the bear was very close to the trail. A small group of thru-hikers, not wanting to challenge it directly for passage, gathered and waited for it to move away. They tried shouting and singing to encourage the bear to move along, but the bear was a little confused. It tried to hide from the hikers by sticking its head behind a tree, where it couldn't see the hikers anymore. Of course the bear's entire rear end was still sticking out visible in the open. The hikers were yelling "We can still see you" until the bear finally wised up and moved away, yielding the trail to the loud and annoying humans.

I hear another tale of food foraging while we are swapping stories. Thor ran low on food during a trail section. It was a rainy period, and a lot of earthworms were on the surface. Thor heard worms had a lot of protein, and decided to give them a go, He came up with a technique for squeezing out all the dirt inside them, and then gobbling down the raw worms as he walked. There was too little meat on a worm for Thor, they did little to assuage his hunger, and he gave up on them as a snack choice.

Day 54, May 29th
Elk Garden, VA Route 600, Trail Mile 493.1
Daily Distance 14.5 miles

I am disappointed with my progress, again. I really shouldn't be, today is a respectable day's hike, but I keep thinking I should be knocking out 20 miles a day now I am in Virginia. We have been told by the veteran Appalachian Trail thru-hikers we meet at hostels, doing trail magic, or revisiting sections of the trail approaching the state, that when we get to Virginia it will be flat and easy, and we will start making big miles. It becomes a joke, a very painful joke.

Today's hike includes a long steep climb up Whitetop Mountain. The crest has a nice bald, a great view, and a spring for a water source. I sit for a while talking to an older man thru-hiking who has completed 62 marathons, including one in every state. He is named Marathon Man, of course.

I am drinking a lot at the break near the water source. My latest hydrating strategy is to camel; I drink my fill, up to the point of discomfort, at good water sources, so as to help carry me the distance to the next one. I am trying to carry less water; it is 2.2 pounds a liter. There are several sources marked in the guide, but they are dirty, little, unappealing, slow flowing seeps. I am continuing along some stretches of trail thirsty rather than slowing down for water resupply.

Whitetop Mountain would make a good campsite, but it lacks hammock trees and it is early when I get there, so I keep going. I end up camping next to a road with a trailhead parking area. There are good sites all around. Initially, I have a single other hiker as a neighbor, a ridge runner named Storyteller who sets up 30 yards away. I settle in with an hour of daylight left. Storyteller walks about the area picking up trash. One of the duties of a ridge runner is to clean up the trail, campsites, and shelters in their duty sections and pack out the trash. I have continued to pick up a couple of pieces of trash every day, and maybe I am easing his load.

I am finishing my camp chores when a bus stops along the road and disgorges a crowd of teenagers bearing backpacks. They are quite noisy in a cheerful, clueless way, and thankfully they set off up the trail on the far side of the road towards Grayson Highlands, a celebrated section of Appalachian Trail a couple of miles ahead.

No sooner does the teen group depart when a car pulls into the trailhead parking lot and a family of five starts pulling camping gear out of their car trunk and setting up their tent near the parking area. They are a good 75 yards way from me, but they have brought an infant with them into the woods. The baby does what babies do, crying throughout the night. It is not restful.

Day 55, May 30th
Old Orchard Shelter, Trail Mile 508.5
Daily Distance 15.4 miles

Today I cross the Grayson Highlands. The terrain and land by themselves are as beautiful as a movie set. The trail comes up from the road crossing where I camped last night and goes through a conifer forest before it opens up onto balds on the ridgeline. The trail passes but does not summit Mount Rodgers, the highest mountain in Virginia. The ridgeline has a number of rock formations the trail goes up, over and around, with names like The Fatman Squeeze. The views are impressive.

The Grayson Highlands would be wonderful all by themselves, but there is an added attraction. USFS is experimenting with grazing animals to maintain the open character of the balds, and at Grayson they have built herds of small ponies. These are descendants of the herd from Assateague Island, one the barrier islands off the Atlantic coast of the Delmarva Peninsula. The ponies there are themselves descendants of horses that escaped the wreck of a Spanish Galleon offshore in a great storm 400 years ago. The ponies are small and hardy, and appear to be thriving in the Highlands.

Veteran hikers have told us how wonderful the Grayson Highland experience will be. Stopping to eat at Thomas Knob Shelter has been recommended over and over, The ponies often come to visit and can actually be a nuisance. They have been turned into equine beggars by too many handouts. It is a rather gentle looking profile, so it looks like I can get a lot of miles for the day. The profile proves deceptive because the rocky obstacles on the ridge take time to navigate, and of course it takes some time just to take in the spectacle and enjoy the Highlands.

There are a lot of day hikers out on this first weekend in June and the trail is crowded. At Thomas Knob Shelter it looks like USFS has taken steps to keep the ponies away from the camping area with fencing. So, no ponies.

I do find one of the most unpleasant privies I have seen anywhere on the Appalachian Trail. There are hundreds of hikers up on the highlands, and this is the only privy. It is very, very full. It has attracted a dense population of flies and I hear the buzzing of the fly festival from several yards away as I approach. Opening the privy door it is a scene out of a horror movie. A mounded pile of feces and toilet paper rises up out of the throne, and coating the fecal mountain, the seat, and every wall is an ever shifting carpet of flies. The smell is massive and dense. I dig a cat hole in the woods instead.

Pooping in the woods is a backpacking chore that takes a little getting used to. I used to look for a fallen log out of sight from the trail where I could sit and hang over the edge. Fallen logs can become suddenly scarce when the need strikes and I developed a new technique, where I dig my cat hole with my hiking pole next to a sapling I can hold onto. I use the sapling for support, clean myself with a paper towel I wet from a water bottle, and cover over my business with the hiking pole, I use a lot of hand sanitizer. Paper towels are sturdier than toilet paper and more environmentally friendly than wet wipes.

I see my first ponies a little further on up the bald. There are several small herds on the Highlands. The ponies have no fear of humans. I approach a small herd with a new born foal to take pictures. While I focus my phone I am startled by a horse that comes up from behind me and starts licking my arm. Thru-hikers are nothing more than giant mobile salt licks to the ponies. The rest of the herd crowds in and mobs me to get their licks. It is a little disturbing.

There are other people hanging around the herds, and this one herd in particular, since it has the new foal. One of the other onlookers, a frequent visitor who knows all of the ponies, tells me it was born yesterday. It hides behind its mother who remains apart from the rest of the licking crowd. There are notices posted everywhere that it is forbidden to feed the ponies, and everywhere I see people feeding the ponies, feeding them candy bars and other trash.

I still have a few of my dried apple rings, hoarded and eaten a couple at a time for my own enjoyment. A ridge runner told me earlier that if you absolutely must feed the horses, or any wildlife for that matter, it should only be foods natural to their environment, and apples are ok as a food. There are old abandoned orchards all along the trail dropping apples everywhere come late summer. I offer my rings to mama, and she nibbles them out of my hands. Mama stays between me and the foal, and the unsteady colt looks around her flank at me as her mother eats my little treat.

I am still, even now 6 months later, eaten by guilt for having fed that horse. I may have provided a natural snack, sure, but I am still a perpetrator in making these animals beggars for human food. I am reminded of Crater Lake in Oregon, where one of the views of Wizard Island has a parking turnout where there is always a crowd of people. There is also a crowd of chipmunks that stand at the edge of the parking area and beg. They become so dependent on human food, and junk food at that, that come winter, after the visitors leave, the chipmunks will be ill prepared and ill nourished for sleeping through the season. Caches of Cheetos and Cheese Nips may not carry them through the cold months.

My guilt doesn't stop me from dropping a few nuts and raisins most times I stop and eat trail mix on the trail. I feel I am making a small offering to the wildlife I have disturbed with my presence. In these places where I am passing through, I don't think I do much damage. The ponies were almost a petting zoo though, and I wonder how they would truly fare as a wild herd. Their Assateague progenitors are as bad or worse. I went camping there for a weekend when I was in college, and the ponies walked right into camp and started rooting around on our picnic table, and I had to push them away. The horses survived for centuries as wild herds on some of the most desolate, wind swept stretches of beach in America, and now they are camp robbers.

A lot of hikers have unleashed dogs with them, and one big group of day hikers has some sort of small breed with them; a dog hiking club. I pass them in at an area constricted by rocks. One of the dogs takes offense to me and lunges at me snarling and barking. I block it with my poles, and the owner gives me a nasty look before getting a hold of the dog's collar and dragging it off. Perhaps he could see how tempted I was to give the dog a wallop with one of my poles. It is my second dog confrontation on the trail.

I am very much a dog person, but there are owners out there who have either no awareness, or no consideration of how their dog is going to respond to strangers on a trail.

I pass from USFS land to a Virginia state park, also part of the Grayson Highlands. I am low on water; there are no sources on the ridgeline and it is a long stretch of hiking on a warm day. Between the two parks there is a wooded area, and Wise Shelter. I go to the shelter for water. Every shelter on the Appalachian Trail is near an identified water source. I find it is more than a half mile on and off the trail to the stream here. I load up, a full 3 liters, nearly 7 pounds of water, because water is also supposed to be scarce ahead. Several hundred yards later I walk over Wilson Creek on a bridge. It is an iffy water source, anything that has run through pasture is a little questionable, but it is right there under the trail, after I just hiked a good mile to water and back at Wise Shelter. That is how it goes sometimes.

I leave Grayson Highlands and its wonderful ponies behind, and climb over Stone Mountain. It has a herd of cattle grazing it, and there are bulls with giant horns standing and watching me hike through their domain. I like Stone Mountain almost as much as Grayson Highlands; it has much of the charm and none of the crowds.

I am feeling the pain today, and I resort to taking ibuprofen in the afternoon for some relief. I try to avoid taking medications too often, I worry about my liver, and it would be easy to build a dependence on a little unnatural relief. I am feeling knees and feet and back especially today. I take three tablets, the aches go away, and I enjoy my hike.

I dip down to The Scales, a place between two hills harboring a big horse corral. Guided horse tours into Grayson Highlands are operated from here on regular riding horses, not the dwarf ponies of the Highlands. There is a separate trail network in the area for horseback riders; the Appalachian Trail is restricted to foot sloggers. The trails cross at The Scales, and a horseback tour is coming in as I hike through. A man and a woman are having a terrific row shouting at each other from the backs of their horses. The other riders are giving them some space. It must have been an unpleasant tour for everyone involved.

Old Orchard Shelter is a tiny structure that only sleeps six people. There are several people here tonight, but they are tenting, and only the mice and I sleep inside. The only thru-hiker here tonight is Marathon Man. I am either falling behind, or possibly I am a little ahead of my bubble.

Water isn't really as scarce as I feared it would be from reading the AWOL Guide, but there is a lot less of it in this stretch than in Georgia and the Smokies. It is also getting hotter, and I am often as not soaked through with my own sweat as I hike. I am drinking a lot more water. I will have to figure out what I really need to carry over distances, with a little extra for safety, and calculate it against use and distance. I came into camp full, ready to camp away from water if need be, and I can definitely feel the extra pounds.

I have been hiking without a watch. Watchless, time seems to pass irregularly, going faster or slower, keyed to my emotions and physical state. I thought it would be more relaxing, hiking with only the sun to mark the passage of time.

I was wrong.

A watch doesn't just measure time but also allows me to measure distance. When I hike long sections without a landmark I can lose track of where I am. I roughly know my pace on different kinds of terrain, and a watch will allow me to keep a better sense of my location. I also want to rise earlier and start hiking sooner, my chronic late beginnings are costing me a couple of miles a day. I want a watch, and one with an alarm.

I have an iPhone, which can serve the same functions, but I keep it put away in a waterproof bag most of the time, either switched off or in airplane mode. When the phone is fully on it eats through battery life and I get a day and half of power before it goes dark. I usually only turn it on when I am somewhere I think I will get reception and there is something I want to know. Having it off also disconnects me from home, which, considering the state of my marriage is a good thing.

Day 56, May 31st
Trimpi Shelter, Trail mile 521.4
Daily Distance 13.4 miles

This day is missing from notes. I must have been pushing myself. I also may have let the battery run out on my tablet. I am camped near Thor and Rabbit.

Day 57, June 1st
Partnership Shelter, Trail Mile 531.5
Daily Distance 10.1 miles

A month ago this would have been a good day of hiking. Now I consider it a short day, both in miles and in time spent hiking. My goal today is the Partnership Shelter, another trail landmark. I know I write about a landmark shelter every day or so, but I usually pass two or three shelters a day, and only a few are noteworthy. Virginia has active trail cubs and maintainers and has the best shelters on the trail.

Partnership Shelter is notable for several reasons. It is a large shelter with two levels, and it is at a trailhead that has a visitor center. There is an outdoor shower at the shelter, and the visitors' center has bathrooms with running water. There is a payphone at the visitor center, and posted at the phone there are numbers to call for rides into the town of Marion. There is also what makes this shelter specifically looked forward to as a night's stay, a phone number for pizza delivery.

I follow Thor starting out of Old Orchard Shelter in the morning. He is traveling with a new woman, Rabbit. They hike apart but rest together and stop together at night. Thor is closer to 7 feet than 6 feet tall, and is strong as well. Like many thru-hikers this particular year, he worked in the oil industry, in his case as a roughneck. There are a lot of petroleum engineers and oil field workers being laid off due to the glut in oil supply, and a number of them on the trail.

Keeping up with Thor's hiking pace is a challenge for me, and I am breathing heavily as he chats away. He isn't very old yet, still on the young side of thirty, but he has definitely lived in his years, and he has stories to tell. He is also, obviously, slowing down so I can keep up, and I am still struggling to maintain the pace. I finally wave him on ahead and slow my steps and heart.

Rabbit comes up behind me when I stop to photograph a box turtle parked in the middle of the trail. She is slower than Thor, but is still going better than my usual pace. I fall in behind her, and we talk and walk. I end up completing the 10 miles into Partnership Shelter in 4 hours, a quick pace for me.

At Partnership Shelter a couple of people from a farming co-op are recruiting hikers to do work-for-stay. They run a children's summer camp and need work parties to get the place ready for the arrival of their campers next week. The co-op is offering a bunkroom and organic meals in exchange for a day's work. Goodfeet is coming back, and says the experience is well worth the stay. I am tempted, but it is a loss of a day of hiking, and I am finally starting to make progress. I would like to get another day or two further along the trail before taking a zero. Rabbit and Thor take advantage of the offer, and load up into the co-op's truck.

I head down to the visitor center. It is a nature interpretive center and gift shop, as well as having bathroom facilities. There are a couple of thru-hikers outside making decisions on whether to go into town or stay at the shelter for the night. There is a regular shuttle into the town of Marion, about 10 miles away, and I decide to ride it in. While waiting for the shuttle a thunderstorm lets loose and I retreat inside and walk around the visitor center. There are displays on wildlife in the area, and also displays on the Appalachian Trail and thru-hiking. I have become an exhibit!

A little pickup truck pulls into the parking lot with a bed full of soaked thru-hikers riding in from town, and a relatively quiet wait fills with noise as the hikers come running into the visitor center through the downpour. They are filled with energy, and are all talking and laughing at the same time.

Five or six hikers were crowded into the bed of the truck, including Shine On, Grip, Whiz Bang, and Figgy. The hitchhikers found a small pile of burlap sacks in the bed of the truck and tried to arrange it as padding. They were talking to the driver and passenger through the slider window and the passenger warned them to be careful, as he had a snake in a sack back there with them.

Now, there is only so much panic you can fit into the crowded bed of a moving pickup truck in a thunderstorm. Announcing that there is a snake in sack with the passengers would get all of it. There was a crazy scramble to find the snake and move away from it. It turned out Shine On was sitting on it. Fortunately it was a black snake, and not a copperhead or timber rattler. The hikers shifted around with their packs in a complicated game of Twister trying to leave the area with the snake open without actually jumping out of the moving truck. They were all very happy to be out of the truck, in from the rain, and free of the snake.

In the headlong rush to get out of the truck, one of the hikers, Whiz Bang I believe, left her hiker poles in the truck, which has vanished into the rain with its snake in a sack, never to be seen again. Hiking poles are not critical, you can hike without them, but they are a big help in retaining balance and building a hiking rhythm. They are also going to be a bit of a challenge to replace right away; there is no outfitter at hand. Hiking poles can represent a significant financial expenditure. Poles run from about

$40.00 for a pair for cheapies, to upwards of $200.00 for the latest super light, high tech wonders. There is group commiseration at the loss.

A friendly older couple comes onto the parking lot and offers rides into Marion to the thru-hikers hanging about, and I hop in. They take me right to the Traveler's Inn. It is a Christian couple, not trying to convert anyone, but not hiding their faith, and doing a Christian deed. I have mixed feelings about the Southern Baptists, but they do reach out to hikers, and I assume others in need of a bit of help. Christian is as Christian does.

The Traveler's Inn is another seedy hiker dive. It is a motor hotel that started out as basic lodging to begin with, and has deteriorated significantly. It is still cleanish, has all the necessities, and it is well priced for what it is. The motel is on a four lane wide stretch of state highway in an area populated with gas stations and strip malls.

I walk over to a nearby strip mall looking for food and find an AYCE Chinese place. It is not particularly good, the place is a little run down like the rest of the area, and the food selection is small. Some of it looks like it has been sitting out under the heat lamps for a while. I worry a little about food poisoning, but I still fill my plate three times.

It is still raining when I wander back to the motel across the busy road margins and turn in for the night.

Day 58, June 2nd
Marion, VA, Trail Mile 531.5
Daily Distance 0.0 miles, Zero day

I am taking a zero in Marion. I have work to do on the internet, and the weather today is an intermittent combination of rain and hail. Rambler is staying at the same motel and there is another crowd of thru-hikers sharing a room a couple of doors down from me. I can't tell how many hikers are actually inside. I am guessing somewhere between 4 and 8. You can identify a motel room occupied by thru-hikers by the battered boots and shoes left outside to dry and air out.

I get my resupply at the local grocery store. I buy many of the same items over and over, and a thru-hiker becomes an expert on the comparative costs for the same item from location to location. Usually gas stations and convenience stores are the priciest, and Wal-Mart is the best when one is nearby. Local groceries vary widely. The store in Marion proves to be one of the most expensive stops on the entire trip. I spend $86.00 on four days of food. It is a smaller store, and the selection is limited. I have to choose lesser alternatives to replace some of my favorite items.

I walk down to the old downtown area of Marion and spend an enjoyable afternoon. I find a wristwatch, a Timex Ironman, with a few functions like a stop watch and an interior light that I hope will prove useful. The Ironman will be an excellent choice. It survives the hike, and I am still wearing it after I finish the hike.

I am with Rambler for part of the day. He steers me to a massage therapist, and I have some pain worked out of my back, legs and feet. There are pubs, a nice coffee shop, and some antique malls.

Rambler is interested in antiques, as I am, and we go through the shops. He has more knowledge than I do, and a collector's acquisitiveness. He finds an irresistible deal, a genuine crystal ball the size of a basketball, buys it, and arranges to ship it home.

Rambler and I seem to get along, and we are going to try hiking together tomorrow. He wants to slow his pace down, and I want to speed mine up, so maybe we can find a comfort zone for both of us. Rambler is of indeterminate age, although I would say in his late 40s. He has an enormous explosion of curly hair on his head and beard. He laughs easily and often, and I think he will make a good companion.

Day 59-62, June 3 to June 6
Marion to Bland, VA, Trail Miles 531.6 to 589.2, 57.6 Miles
AVG 14.4 miles a day

Day 59, June 3rd
Davis Branch Campground, Trail Mile 545.5
Daily Distance 13.9 miles

TRAILTALK:

TRIPLE CROWN: The triple crown of Thru-Hiking is completing the three trails that span the United States from South to North, the Pacific Crest Trail (PCT), the Continental Divide Trail (CDT), and the Appalachian Trail. The AT is the shortest but also the most physically demanding of the trails. Each trail has its own particular challenges.

Today is a good hiking day. It is a wet day after all the rain of the last two days, so the trail is soaked and the streams are swollen. Having a companion is improving my morale. Rambler is an interesting companion, his life philosophies are kind of out there, he is far more spiritual than I am and finds meanings where I see only what I see. I am hoping this works out.

We are camped out at Davis Campground, a couple of fire rings scattered about near a spring. Thunderfuck, her friend Saint, and Shaggy are camped nearby. There is also a man finishing out the triple crown of long distance hiking named Burglar. Burglar's experiences on the PCT and CDT have given him a lot of insights he shares with us through the night. He travels very light. He emphasizes that what we are on is not a camping trip, it is a hiking trip.

What Burglar is getting at is that the camping aspect of thru-hiking is a big focus of preparation. We are obsessed with the gear we will carry and what we will do when we are stopped. Burglar minimizes everything. He carries very little equipment, and just enough food to get to his next resupply point, sometimes maybe not quite enough. He does not cook and saves the weight of stove, fuel and cook set. He is carrying less than 20 pounds in his pack. Hunger and cold are a price he is willing to pay for a light load and quick movement. He is an obsessed, incredibly funny, and positive person. Neither Rambler nor I are ready to strip down to Burglar's level, but he definitely is giving us some food for thought.

Rambler is pushing for earlier wake ups so we can make more miles each day. I am with this plan in the evening.

Day 60, June 4th
Lynn Creek, Trail Mile 558.2
Daily Distance 12.3 miles

Rambler and I do not get off to the anticipated early start. I am to blame; I am just slow to get going in the morning. It is raining, which makes it even harder for me to get out of my hammock cocoon. I am still cooking oatmeal for breakfast on my alcohol burner stove, also slowing our departure. We leave camp at 8:15 AM, more than two hours after the sun rises.

It is still a long day of hiking, although we do not make long miles. The trail is tough, medium sized hills come one after another. I am tracking distance and pace using my new watch and it makes me feel a little more secure. We are hiking about 2 miles an hour, a reasonable if not a particularly fast pace. The power hikers typically are moving at about 3 miles an hour, even over terrain such as this.

We stop at a rural road crossing with a fence line because Rambler wants to dry out his tent and other gear after last night's rain. He has a Six Moons ultralight Cuben fiber tent. It is extremely light, breathable, and waterproof, but it is only a single wall tent. The outside gets wet, and eventually the inside ends up wet too. It isn't just a comfort issue, water adds weight.

The road crossing is between two fields, a pleasant spot, and I hang out some of my own gear on the fence to dry as well. Cows occupy one of the pastures and walk by looking at us with either interest or suspicion. Who knows what really happens inside a cow's mind.

The tread on my shoes appears to be wearing out. The rule of thumb is that a pair of shoes lasts anywhere from 300 to 800 miles on the trail. My soles are as slick as racing tires. I take a crazy fall along a wet and muddy section of the trail.

We are traversing a steep hillside, and the trail shows scars from the slips and slides of previous hikers. I try to take the section slowly, carefully placing my feet and poles, but still I fall. I lose traction slowly, my shoes refuse to grip the slick mud, and I windmill my arms before going off the trail and falling down the slope on my back. I slide down 20 feet, grabbing at plants to arrest my fall, until I slow, then stop.

I take a deep breath and realize, once my plunge is fully halted and I regain awareness of my surroundings and the messages my body is sending me, that the plants I was grabbing to brake my ride down the slope are stinging nettles.

Rambler watched all of the action, and has time to whip out his camera and take pictures of the end of my fall. He enjoyed it very much, and his laughter doesn't help my humor at all as I scramble back up the muddy slope.

I try rubbing jewelweed sap on the nettle stings; it is a plant that grows paired with nettles. Jewelweed sap is supposed to ease the stings, but either I have the plant incorrectly identified, or it just doesn't work. My hands and arms burn for the next 10 or 15 minutes, and are red and itchy for the next couple of hours.

We hike to a bridge over a considerable stream, the North Branch of the Holston River. Rambler likes to soak his feet in cool water when he gets a chance, to ease some pains. I soak my own feet as well, and enjoy being by the water.

Kamikaze appears from the trail behind us. I have not seen her for weeks. She hiked ahead, went to her wedding in Seattle, and is back on the trail. She has already caught up with me. She is pushing hard to regain her trail family. There is a new addition to her family, a woman named Bookie, and she and Kami haven't quite settled out how the new social dynamic works. Seeing it in action could be a bit like watching Wild Kingdom.

It is really nice hiking with company. Rambler's interest and knowledge of antiques and auctions make great trail conversation, as does his existential philosophizing. I am wearing on his patience with my late starts though. He and Kamikaze are going to wake me at 6:00 AM tomorrow and see if I can't start building a pattern of earlier rises and more trail miles.

Virginia is proving lovely. There is a wonderful mix of forested hills and ridgelines that dip down into farmland and pastures. There is plenty of water along the trail again, so I can count on it being available without a lot of forward planning and carrying extra weight.

Day 61, June 5th
Garden Mountain Ridgeline, Trail Mile 572
Daily Distance 13.8 miles

The easier miles are going away. Whoever told me that Virginia was flat and smooth didn't hike this part. It is seven miles up to the top of Chestnut Knob, and we don't get there until 2:00 PM. We started at 8:15 AM, me being laggard getting out of camp again.

We have a long rest stop at an unnamed stream crossing so Rambler can soak his feet. He has Fasciitis, and the cold water provides relief. We also stop simply because it is a really nice place to be in the woods. Enjoying nature is one of the reasons why we are out here, after all.

The area has a lot of iridescent blue butterflies, and one keeps settling on me. Rambler gets some pictures for me. I am seeing a lot of salamanders, both orange and black types. I haven't seen much in the way of larger animals, but the woods are alive with smaller life whenever I pause to look around.

The elevation profile in the AWOL Guide gives no hint as to the difficulty of this section of trail. There is a stretch of nearly 10 miles without water, and the source just before this stretch is described as 'iffy'. We have to load up on water, and carry our heavily laden packs up and down a series of little climbs along a rocky ridgeline. There is a shelter at Chestnut Knob, but thunderstorms are moving in and it is crowded. We pass on by.

We find a place to camp out, and I have just gotten my hammock and rain fly up when a fierce thunderstorm cuts loose. I huddle beneath my hammock to cook. The rain is blowing in sideways but I manage to protect a small dry space. I do not like my Vargo stove as much as the Trangia it replaced. It uses less fuel, but it takes longer to boil water in the same pot, and it has some issues getting and staying lit. Working under the asymmetrical 4 foot by 6 foot hammock rain fly is very cramped, and I manage to spill quite a bit of my fuel in the process.

Other thru-hikers pass us during the height of the rain. They are heading for Jenkins Shelter, four more miles ahead. They are using headlamps to finish the distance and I can see their passing by the bobbing of their lights. They are already soaked and I expect they are planning on getting dried out at the shelter, rather than trying to set up in wet. I can't really see who they all are, but I am sure that one of them is Bubbles. I have a small bag of hard candies I bought in bulk back in Marion, and I pass them out to the passing night hikers.

A number of thru-hikers take a chance and drink their water raw, not treating or filtering it. Water resupply takes time; the process of squeezing water through the filter is slow. I have the mini Sawyer, and it has a slower flow rate than the full sized version, a trade I made to save a couple of ounces. I myself am starting to take a couple of risks. Where water comes right out of the earth I am filling and drinking without filtering. Anywhere it has been on the surface for a while I am filtering, as I did before the long waterless stretch today.

I am having muscle cramps tonight. I don't know if it is from the high level of exertion, whether I am dehydrated, not getting enough salt, or if it is from my experimentation with drinking water directly from the sources

Virginia is not living up to my expectations; it is far more difficult than anticipated. Every day brings new and varied terrain. It is a wonderful state, but it is not an easy state. The longer days are still making bigger miles possible as we approach the Solstice. Tomorrow we are going to try for Bland, 18 miles away, hoping to make it a nearo stop rather than a zero.

Day 62, June 6th

Bland, VA, US Route 52, Trail Mile 589.2
Daily Distance 17.2 miles

I get my groove on and Rambler and I finally get started early, early enough that there are still hikers in their tents when we pass Jenkins Shelter. It is a slow go initially as we navigate over some rocky areas of trail. Our pace is troubling, and we doubt our original plan to aim for Bland. Then the trail smoothes out, and we start moving. The lure of a night in town helps us go, and we cruise over the miles. I will sleep in a motel tonight.

Tomorrow's plan is a quick resupply in Bland, then get back on trail and try to get in another day of good miles. I am proud of my personal efforts on this stretch. I also like the bubble of hikers we are moving with, I smile when I see the faces we pass or are passed by each day as we leapfrog forward.

Bland lives up to its name, and there is nothing notable about the place. I make little in the way of notes, and as I write this 6 months later, when most towns and experiences are still vivid in my memory, I cannot remember much about the motel we stayed in, except that it had a big old steam driven tractor out front and an exhibit of old farming equipment and memorabilia in the front office There is a Dairy Queen, and a gas station convenience store for resupply, and not a whole lot else.

Day 63- 66, June 7 to June 10
Bland, VA, to Pearisburg VA, Trail Miles 589.2 to 634.9, 45.7 Miles
AVG 11.42 miles a day

Day 63, June 7th
Brushy Mountain, US Route 52, Trail Mile 600.0
Daily Distance 10.8 miles

Rambler and I pool funds together with some other hikers and pay for a local taxi to take us the 10 miles from Bland back to the trailhead. The taxi driver tells us a 600 pound black bear has been seen roaming around the trailhead. Usually animals are smaller than actually reported, size seems to increase in the telling and locals like to put it on for hikers, but you never know. We did not see the monster bear. I would love to see a big Ursus Americanus, preferably from a safe distance. I still have not seen a bear on this hike.

I don't leave town till after 1:00 PM. A number of thru-hikers, including Thor, Cookie, Wookie, Peacock, and Grape are loading up on water at the last easy water source for the next 9.7 miles. The water from Kimberling Creek tastes bad, even after filtering it. I had hopes of making it to the next shelter and getting better water, but I filled up anyway, just in case it turned out we needed it.

Rambler and I make pretty good time hopping on to the back of the train of hikers leaving the creek, but trying to match the pace of the younger hikers eventually is too much for me and for Rambler as well, and we fall away from the back of the pack.

We run out of daylight before making it to Jenny Knob Shelter, and camp atop Brushy Mountain. The mountain is of no particular eminence or elevation, and we just pick a likely spot after passing the 600 mile marker, spelled out in stones on the trail.

600 miles! It feels like real progress, and gives us both a boost. I am feeling cranky and socially awkward in general; my knees, hips and feet have reached a constant state of pain in varying intensities. Rambler is still sticking with me though, and I am very glad for his company.

This section of trail looks pretty easy, three 10 mile sections of pine needle softened trail until the next resupply, and there is a hostel and a restaurant on the way. In general my daily mileage is up, and although I am no power hiker I feel like I am building myself up physically to endure the thru-hiker to the end.

Day 64, June 8th
Stream past Ribble Trail (Dismal Creek), Trail Mile 614.8
Daily Distance 14.8 miles

TRAILTALK:

PINK BLAZING: Thru-hikers engaging in romance on the trail.

There is dissention between Rambler and I today, and we hike separately to the same three points. I start slow, Ramblers particular sore point, but once I get going I make good time. The trail is relatively smooth and the small ups and downs provide variety rather than challenges. I meet my goals for the day.

There is a grocery a half mile down from the trail crossing at VA RTE 606. Trent's Grocery is a convenience and hardware store with a grill. I eat a nice hot lunch, and buy a big can of beer I schlep up to the next landmark, Dismal Creek Falls. The falls are a .6 of a mile down a blue blazed side trail. There is a crowd of hikers here, bathing and sunning. I spend an hour and half just chilling. I add an extra mile and a half to two miles of hiking beyond the Appalachian Trail miles going to the store for lunch and taking the blue blaze to the waterfall and back.

Rambler and I part company. Personality differences, probably helped by my crankiness, and my inability to get moving in the morning, have made him decide to go back to walking solo. I am going to miss having a hiking buddy. When you hike together you live in one another's pockets, and I am afraid I have not proven an especially compatible person. I am sorry to see Rambler go on without me.

Thor is sick. He has not been filtering any of his water, and it may have gotten to him. It may also be the Norovirus. He is hiking on, but slowly. I see Bubbles. She and Redlocks seemed to have some kind of a thing going, but she had an ear infection and he moved on. Seeing that I am still in the bubble with these people I consider strong hikers is encouraging, even if I only keep up because they are sick.

The crowd at Dismal Falls is coed, and females outnumber the men today. Trail wisdom from past years was that there was a big difference in numbers between men and women hikers, with many men and few women, but it appears that this year women are a more significant proportion of the hikers, maybe as high as 4 in 10. There is some pink blazing drama among the younger hikers.

I get to the campsite, which has very limited space, as a storm moves in. I have my rain fly and hammock half up when it hits, and I work from beneath my scant shelter rescuing my gear with one hand while holding one side of the rain fly out over everything with the other trying to keep the rain off. I am mostly successful, and I sit and wait until the storm moves on.

The stream next to the campsite changes from a clear and babbling brook before the storm into a muddy torrent twice the size afterwards, and filtering the water takes a little more effort. The sound of the rushing water drowns out any other sounds tonight, and serves as white noise carrying me into sleep.

Day 65, June 9th
Woods Hole Hostel, Sugar Run Gap, Trail Mile 623.8
Daily Distance 9.0 miles

It is a short day of hiking. There is a significant climb involved, and the trail has rocky sections. I start at 8:15 AM and I am at the hostel at 2:15 PM.

I stop for a half hour at Wapiti Shelter, also known as the Murder Shelter by thru-hikers. Two women were killed here a few years back, by a local nut job who took exception to their romantic choice to be with each other.

The shelter is one of only a very few places where a murder is known to have taken place on the trail, and it is one of the most documented trail events. People have disappeared off the trail, if rarely, and in the wilder stretches there is no telling what actually occurred.

Some people disappear on the trail by their own will, for sure, and getting lost and hurt with no rescue claims some more, but there are probably cases of foul play as well. The Appalachian Trail thru-hiker community is similar to a homeless population; no one knows where someone went unless there is a body. The trail is generally a peaceful, non-violent place, but humans are unpredictable, especially outside the overwatch of normal societal convention. Wapiti Shelter gives me a reason to stop, to think about these things, and of course to get water and use the privy.

I tear out pages from my AWOL Guide to use for quick reference as I make progress down the trail, keeping the current page in a plastic baggie in my pocket. I throw the page away when I am past a section, so my guide gets ever, slightlier lighter the further I go along. Occasionally I look at a page, set it down, and forget it at a break, leaving me ignorant of the next 20 miles of trail, and feeling frustrated and lost.

I did so for the third time on the thru-hiker somewhere in the miles before Wapiti, and I copy information down from another hiker's guide at the shelter. I will use the handwritten notes until I get to the next printed page in my guide.

Woods Hole Hostel is highly recommended by everyone on the trail, and AWOL calls it "a slice of heaven, not to be missed", and I don't plan to. It is just over 20 miles to Pearisburg, the next logical stop along the trail, which is too far for one day of hiking unless I am feeling heroic, but definitely is a short two days. Woods Hole Hostel is my destination and I will have time to enjoy it. The hostel is an organic farm as well as a hostel, and serves a dinner right off of the farm with a night's stay. The proprietors are Licensed Massage Technicians as well, so it may be paradise on the trail.

There are thru-hikers everywhere about the hostel's main house, bunkroom, and bathing areas when I arrive. The bunkroom is a two story barn like structure with bunks crammed into every corner, like most hostels. There is a single private room, which I might have treated myself to, but Rambler arrived ahead of me and claimed it. I get a bunk instead, for $36.00, which includes the organic dinner and breakfast.

I sit on the main house's big front porch after checking in. Rambler has good things to say about the massage, and I get on the schedule. I spend a little more money and I revel in a smoothie made with newly picked strawberries and Amish homemade ice cream as I wait. There is also fresh baked bread and butter right from the farm available, and I stuff myself.

Massage time comes. The owners are a married couple named Neville and Michael, operating both the hostel and the farm. Neither is making them rich, but I expect they value their life more than most. The hostel was run by Neville's grandmother Tillie, and Neville is carrying on the tradition, and expanding on it.

Neville is a tiny little person and I think perhaps the massage will be a weak, fluffy one, but hard work has made her strong. Neville has magical, knowledgeable fingers and hands, and it is a memorable experience.

Before dinner there is a group yoga session, led by Prana, a female thru-hiker doing work-for-stay at the hostel. It is a gentle session, since everyone has hiked today. It is a restoration session, not a workout. Everyone who wants to participate forms a circle on the lawn and gets a good meditative stretch.

Dinner is wonderful, and plentiful enough some is left even after feeding hungry hikers all they can eat. Guests are encouraged to help out with making meals, serving, and other chores about Woods Hole. It isn't required, but pitching in makes it feel like family. I especially enjoy a carrot ginger soup, a food I normally wouldn't eat, and it definitely is now added to my food choices. I am thinking hard about what I might change about my diet and lifestyle when I get back to civilization.

Some people don't quite understand the concept of an organic farm. A thru-hiker gets stopped while laying out her clothes and sleeping bag to treat them with Permethrin, an insecticide. The bugs are getting to be a nuisance, and ticks are a constant concern. Ticks carry Lyme disease, which is a life long disability, and it is a souvenir no thru-hiker wants but many get.

Having any kind of chemical let loose on the farm can cause Woods Hole to lose their organic certification. It takes a couple of years of letting farmland lie dormant to get rid of lingering traces of chemical fertilizer and pesticide treatments. Stopping the hiker before she gets her insecticide out saves the farm's certification. The hiker is upset they stopped her and made such a fuss. Ignorance, not malice, is at fault.

There is no cell phone service in Sugar Run Gap, where Woods Hole is located. It is an isolated valley, on a dirt road, far away from infrastructure. There is a single landline computer station for hikers to share and there are a number of hikers waiting to use it. Some of them are responding to various emergencies. Thor is here, and is sick enough to be looking for a way to get to a medical clinic. I will wait until Pearisburg to get my online business done. I have to stop there regardless to pick up the new buckles Elemental Horizons is sending to the post office to fix my pack after the mishap at Uncle Johnny's.

I hear the co-op farm and camp near Partnership Shelter that was offering work-for-stay to hikers in exchange for getting the camp ready for the summer had its main building burn down. The camp will not open this summer or possibly ever again. It is the loss of a unique trail experience. (I find out later they rebuild, and are back in business.)

Day 66, June 10th
Pearisburg, VA, Lane Street Crossing, Trail Mile 634.9
Distance 11.1 miles

Today's hike is easy. I am moving well. It is a short mile day following a short mile day, with a massage, yoga, a good hostel rest, and organic meals as part of the journey. I am also enjoying the motivational luxury of listening to music on my iPhone. I charged it up at the hostel and will have electric again tonight, so I feel free to squander battery life.

Most of the day's hiking is on the high ridgeline. I am hiking through a green tunnel, and trees obscure most of the views, although there are a few looks. There is some climbing, and a big descent of more than 2000 feet down into town. Water is scarce.

I may have cut my continual gaming of my water supply to reduce weight a little fine. I carried a single liter out of Woods Hole, and it is 9 miles to the next spring. The spring is close to town, within a couple of miles, and I continue past it with just a little bit of water left. I carefully hoard what I have left taking single small sips to keep myself going. When I find my way onto the road into town I drink the last meager swallow wetting the bottom of my bottle. I am thirsty.

Hitching produces no ride, one of the very few times I don't get a ride quickly from the trailhead, and I walk the better part of a mile uphill on hot asphalt. I can see at the top of the hill there is a collection of businesses and restaurants, and I trudge up the hill with water on my mind. I stop at the first gas station and I fill up with a giant can of ice tea, so cold condensation forms a mist on the top of the can. I guzzle half the can down in a couple of seconds before slowing to savor the rest. It is wonderful.

Pearisburg is a rural, run down, roadside stop, a town where economic progress ground to a halt sometime in the 1970s. The Holiday Motor Lodge is one of three lodging choices, and I commit to it by calling in a reservation while I am up on the ridgeline. It may have been a mistake.

The town of Narrows, further down the road in the opposite direction, has a shuttle to the Macarthur Inn and looked pretty good. I went to Pearisburg because I have pack parts waiting at the post office and I wanted to make getting them easy. In some towns it is hard to get rooms and I made the reservation as a precaution, but there is little competition in Pearisburg.

My room is cheap and seedy. I have spent $45.00 on my own private economy room, with a few decades of accumulated smoke and dirt on the cheap, aged, scratched, and chipped furniture. The bedcover has cigarette burn holes in it. The room is rough, even by thru-hiker standards. There is a large swimming pool in the center of the U-shaped building's parking lot, and it at least looks inviting. There are already thru-hikers out there sitting on plastic lounge chairs drinking cheap beer under the shade of big beach umbrellas.

I find that there is a bunkroom at the motel, and it is nicer than my room. It has a big TV, a computer station, books, hiker boxes, and a kitchen. There are only a couple of hikers resident on the twin size beds. The front office won't switch my room to the cheaper, nicer option, and I reserved with a credit card, so I am stuck.

Pearisburg has a little strip mall with a supermarket and an AYCE Chinese restaurant. I get my resupply and dinner. The supermarket has limited options, and I find I am light on protein for my next leg. Protein is heavy, and in this town it is expensive in its various forms, so I minimize it. I have a five day resupply; I am aiming for a town 67 miles away as my next resupply stop. I hope I can get it done in four days by pushing my pace.

Day 67-73, June 11 to June 17
Pearisburg to Daleville, Trail Mile 634.8 to 727.8, 93 miles
AVG 13.27 Daily Miles

Day 67, June 11th
Rice Field Shelter, Trail Mile 641.8
Daily Distance 7.1 miles

TRAILTALK:

MOLDERING PRIVY: A type of outside outhouse that relies on the addition of compost and slow heat to break down and sterilize human waste. Most privies along the trail have gone to this type. You are not supposed to urinate in these privies, just defecate, since too much liquid kills the microbiotic agents that break down the solid waste. Good luck.

The hike out of Pearisburg is not pleasant, but it ends in a wonderful place. I eat lunch at an AYCE pizza buffet, it is bready but filling. I feel the weight in my stuffed stomach weighing me down. I walk it off during the first couple of miles. It is almost a mile back down to the trailhead, and again, hitchhiking produces no ride. The pizza gurgles away in my stomach trying to settle as I trudge down the road in the heat and humidity.

I pick up the trail where I left off yesterday. The AT continues to follow the road across a four lane highway bridge over the New River. It is a long bridge, the better part of a mile across. On one side of me there are semis and cars thundering by, below lies a large brown river. I can feel the roadbed flex under the weight of passing semis, a rather unsettling sensation. The hot day is soaked up the hard concrete and asphalt and rises back up to meet me. I am walking on an oven.

At the end of the bridge the trail comes down from the bridge approach and I follow an access road for a large chemical plant, pass under the highway, and head back up into the woods at Hemlock Ridge. It is a little cooler, and a little softer underfoot.

It is a big climb out of Pearisburg, and in addition to carrying 5 days worth of food and 3 liters of water I also have two 25 ounce cans of beer, Budweiser, in honor of McGyver. The walk is cooler under the canopy, but the trail skirts a dump of some sort on the hillside. "Do not Drink" signs are posted prominently along a stream paralleling the trail. It is all very much less than inviting. Past the dump the tranquility and cleanliness of the forest returns and the work of climbing out of town begins in earnest. I feel my food and beverages trying to cooperate with gravity while I make every effort to oppose it, step by step.

It turns into a social climb. Thor and a woman named Cookie are now a hiking pair. I see Bubbles and Caesar, Socrates, Zera, and Shadow Monk. A couple of sisters are thru-hiking together, Nettles and Briar. One of them is trying to hike the entire trail barefoot, and seems to be doing all right with it. These are two young women, tall and lean in tip top shape. They just look fast, and they are cranking out miles.

I wonder about the wisdom of barefoot hiking. Grandma Gatewood, the first recorded woman to thru-hiker (with multiple repeats thereafter) hiked much of the trail barefoot, and there are published books on barefoot hiking. Nettles and Briar have made it this far, so I suspect they know what they are doing.

I lighten my load of its two cans of beer on my way up the hill, drinking one and sharing one with Cesar. It is over 3 pounds of weight gone, and beer is a good hiker fuel. The liquid carbs produce energy, and a bit of alcohol both improves my morale and eases aches and pains.

Just about everyone stops at Rice Field Shelter even though it is only 7 miles from town. It is not the climb, which while vigorous is not overwhelming, but the beauty of the site that makes hikers pull up short for the day. The shelter sits inside a treeline on a ridge. The ridge opens up into a bald and there is a wide panoramic view of the surrounding countryside.

Many hikers choose to set up camp out on the open ridge to get a view of the stars. My hammock confines me inside the trees, unless I want to cowboy camp, and I do not. There are hints of impending rain. The shelter is fairly crowded, and I set up my little hammock campsite a little apart.

The center ridgeline of my Hennessey hammock sets the distance of the hang and suspends my bug net. It snaps as I climb into my hammock. As it parts under pressure from my 200 pounds (probably a bit less by now) its whip like release also tears a small hole in my bug net. I spend an hour trying to make an effective repair. As dusk falls and my vision goes, I just settle for what I have. Duct tape is over the hole in the mesh, and the hang from the spliced ridgeline is a little off balance.

I have replaced the buckles on my pack. I can't fault the quick response from Elemental Horizons, but now a waist belt seam is starting to come apart. I wrap duct tape around the belt. The trail is very hard on equipment, and gear that would stand several years of occasional use just can't hold up to the relentless ongoing stress of thru-hiking. I intend to try and get more permanent repairs on all of my equipment at an outfitter before hitting the Shenandoah, probably at Waynesboro.

Rice Field Shelter has one of the most awkward privy arrangements anywhere on the trail. The moldering privy stands atop of its waste box six feet in the air, without any surrounding walls. It is truly a throne, set up 10 feet off of and overlooking the main trail. It does not just lack privacy, it is an unavoidable sight.

There are signs the trail has been recently rerouted to pass by the privy and the maintainers have not yet moved the privy to a more secluded area. Hikers try to respect each others' modesty, but for people hiking along the trail it can provide quite a surprise to come upon this particular seat of ease unsuspecting when it is in use.

Day 68, June 12th
The Captains (Dismal Creek), Trail Mile 655.8
Daily Distance 14 miles

TRAILTALK:

ROCKSTACKING: Placing rocks on top of each other in aesthetically pleasing stacks. It is an art form that conforms to 'leave no trace' concepts, since the rocks are picked up from the ground and the stacks eventually fall and redistribute the rocks. There is a popular book on the subject.
VIRGINIA BLUES: Virginia is the longest single state on the trail, over 500 miles long. Virginia is often where the novelty of backpacking and camp life can fade away into a tiresome repetitive blur, and a number of hikers get burned out on the trail experience and quit.

There are eye-catching views this morning as the trail follows the ridgeline away from Rice Field Shelter. It is a perfect June day, sunny and warm. The distance and the terrain are not particularly arduous; it is an easy ridgeline hike with small ups and down. Despite the wonderful day I find myself running out of energy. Thor gives me a powdered energy drink mix with something called taurine in it that restores me somewhat, enough so that I plan to add it to my regular load out
There is a large king snake, almost 6 feet long, just off of the trail near a water point. It is the 15th snake I have seen since starting my hike. Thor comes up from the water point and he plays with the snake, picking it up by its tail and laying it out for a better look, much to its annoyance. Thor seriously contemplates eating it. I convince him not to; such a magnificent specimen of a reptile deserves to live.
We go back to the water point to do our water resupply and are busy filling our bottles when we are startled by a great shriek from the vicinity of the snake. We go running back up the trail and find Bubbles standing there. She is courageous without measure against the normal rigors of the trail, but has a terrific personal fear of snakes. Once she is past the snake it is a moment of humor, at least to me, Thor, and Cookie; Bubbles, not so much.
Bubbles is now a Gregory Trail Ambassador. Gregory is one of the leading names in backpacking equipment, and they had a booth at Trail Days in Damascus providing services, fixing equipment and making sales from their booth. Bubbles impressed them with her outgoing personality and was sporting a lot of their gear. They offered her some trail support, free gear, and resupply mail drops if she would represent them on the trail. They couldn't have found a better person to be their ambassador. I own some Gregory gear I now use regularly at home, particularly the lightweight Z Pack for day hikes in the Sandia Mountains.

There is another long stretch of trail without water after the snake encounter. I come across a thru-hiker, of sorts, sitting on a log beside the trail, looking exhausted. He is on the chubby side, something rare for thru-hikers at this point in the hike. He is toting an enormous pack, bulging at the seams, with various odds and ends dangling from it.

He asks me for water. I loaded up at the snake, and have more than I really want to carry forward at this point. I give him one of my bottles to finish, leaving me with a liter to get a few more miles to Dismal Creek. All hikers start gaming food and water, balancing need against weight, but I find out later this hiker also ran out of water the day before, and this is the second day he has resorted to begging for help along the trail. He does not seem like an efficient hiker.

I end my hike early, about 2 hours and 2.5 miles short of my original objective, Bailey Gap Shelter. On Dismal Creek, the Appalachian Trail runs parallel to the creek for half of a mile, and there are a few houses built on a dirt road backing up on the far side of the creek. A man called The Captain has built a zip line across the creek, and lets hikers camp on his spacious lawn. He built a fire ring, put in picnic benches, and allows hikers the use of his water spigot. He also has a refrigerator stocked with free sodas on his porch.

The zip line is a small adventure, and a free cold soda is hard to pass up. Thor crosses before me, and so I know it will bear my weight. I cross. The angle on the line is flat and traffic crosses the river both ways, so there is no real zip. It is hand over hand pulling myself across in a sling with my pack hanging awkwardly before me.

Once across Dismal Creek, surveying the peaceful lawn with the little river rumbling merrily past, cold soda in hand, it is too good a place to leave just to get in a couple more trail miles. Today, a lazy evening suits me just fine.

The river has an amazing collection of rock stackings on and around a large pool right by the house. Some hikers swim in the pool, which is at a refreshing temperature, carefully avoiding the carefully placed towers of rocks. The combination of moving water and stone towers is mesmerizing, and I spend a half hour on the bank just watching the water pass the creative constructions.

I sling my hammock between two trees that lean out over the stream, thinking I will be comforted by the sound of water running below me. I am sleeping without a rain fly tonight. One of my anchors would have been in the water, so I take a gamble that it will not be a wet night. My plan is if it does rain is to grab my stuff and flee onto the Captain's porch.

The Captain has a big friendly dog patrolling the grounds, and he sits and begs while I eat my dinner. I sometimes give in to my own dogs, but do not want to upset an unknown dog or his owner, so his efforts get him nothing but pets. The Captain himself remains unseen.

The heavyset, waterless hiker I helped earlier along the trail arrives, and he guzzles several sodas in a row out of the Captain's fridge. It looks like taking unfair advantage of hospitality to me, but I don't say anything, nor does anyone else around the place. It bugs me a little, and it bugs me that it bugs me.

The act of walking on the trail is starting to get monotonous. There is an affliction called the Virginia blues, where hikers just get tired of the day after day tedium of backpacking and quit the Appalachian Trail. I see how it happens; the trail can be a pain filled routine: wake up, climb hills, get rained on, stop and make camp. The novelty is gone, and it can be a grim endurance contest. I am personally determined to finish the entire hike.

I am still looking for my trail legs

Day 69, June 13th
Near VA Route 632, Trail Mile 668.0
Daily Distance 12.2 Miles

TRAILTALK:

LASHER: A Long Assed Section Hiker. Some hikers are knocking the AT off in long sections over a couple of years, or are just out on an extended hike and are going hundreds of miles. Many of them are experienced hikers with a broad background of experience, and are generally held in high regard by thru-hikers.

BASHER: Bad Assed Section Hiker. See Above

CLASHER: Completing Long Assed Section Hiker. A lasher who is on his last section, and is now completing the AT.

EYE BOMBER: A pesky sort of gnat that looks for moisture. They make suicidal dives into your eyes when you are walking.

TRAIL MAINTAINER: A person who works on building and repairing the trail. Most of the maintainers are part of trail organizations, and are volunteers. Many of them receive support from USFS.

I do not sleep well at the Captain's. My hammock hang over Dismal Creek, rather than providing the peaceful gurgle of water gently easing me into sleep I expected, instead creates a strange anxiety. I worry through the night that if for some unknown reason the tree straps holding up my hammock let go and I fall, I will drop down against the rocks into the stream below, wrapped up and helpless inside my zipped up cocoon, and I will drown in six inches of water.

I know it is a ridiculous fear. My tree straps are sturdy, and I have never fallen, or heard of anyone falling. For whatever reason I cannot get the vision out of my mind. I understand it is irrational, but it haunts me, a video replaying over and over in my head.

I also have bugs getting inside my bug mesh. I am going to have to find and duct tape a couple more holes. Tonight I will endure the nuisance.

I think the real cause of my restless night is the caffeine and sugar that were in the free can of soda I drank in the evening are keeping me from a sound sleep.

I am disappointed with my hiking today. My mileage isn't good. There is a steep, leg draining climb to start, then a rocky ridge, followed by a steep descent. I stop short of the next climb, my legs and back are rubbery from exhaustion. I think it should be easier at this point.

I am adjusting my goals again. There is a hostel 34 miles north, 2 hard or 3 easy days of miles ahead, and I can resupply there. Several trail landmarks are in this section, notably the second largest oak tree on the trail, and the Audie Murphy monument. I may take a zero soon, perhaps in Daleville. I can feel just how tired my body is, and I am still relentlessly driving it forward each and every day. I am struggling with my morale as well as a tired body, and the two are no doubt connected.

I spend a good part of this day worrying about water. The springs providing water move around under the earth over time, and they find new paths to the surface. It is rare, but occasionally nature makes a liar out of the AWOL Guide. I face a six mile stretch with almost no water when an expected spring does not materialize. I can see where the spring used to flow, but it is now a dry course. I go thirsty.

The bugs are out in force. The no-see-ums hang in small clouds above wet spots on the trail, and they tag on as you pass. A couple hang about my ears buzzing away, looking for an opportunity to land and take a bite. The no-see-ums are attracted to moisture, and they often try suicide dive runs into my eyes, ears, and mouth. Some people call them eye bombers.

I am trying a DEET based spray, and one of the citronella insect repellent wrist bracelets. Neither is discouraging the little pests. A passing hiker told me that mosquitoes can only fly 3.2 miles an hour, so I put on little bursts of speed to lose my followers. It works briefly, until I walk into the next cloud of pests another hundred yards up the trail.

I see two does from the trail today. I have not seen all that many deer on the hike, or large mammals generally. The deer have their own personal clouds of biting insects in a halo about their heads. On this misery we achieve empathy.

I meet a lasher today named Ghost. He is connected to the ATC in some capacity, and he is out backpacking a stretch of several hundred miles. Most of the mountains we are traversing are gently sloped on one side, while on the other erosion and natural forces have cut the mountain down to a steeper, rockier angle.

Ghost tells me the reason why the trail is so often on the rocky side of the mountain is a trail maintainer choice. It is easier to stabilize a trail over rocks, whereas the softer side of the mountain gives way over the relentless pounding of thousands of feet each year. Maintainers are volunteers, and can only give so much attention to their stretch of trail each year, so they route the trails where the trail will last the longest.

Unfortunately, it is also much harder hiking. The rocky trails are dangerous; the rocks stick out at all angles, are slippery, and often turn your feet and ankles in different, unexpected, and painful directions. It is one of the factors slowing my pace, as I have to pay attention to each foot placement as I move along.

I set up camp at a likely looking spot, too exhausted to try the next big climb. I am getting used to hiking and camping solo. I reflect on the Nick Grindstaff monument back before Damascus; "He lived alone, he suffered alone, he died alone."

I hike on, alone.

Day 70, June 14th
Sarver Hollow Shelter, Trail Mile 679.3
Daily Distance 11.3 Miles

Another day of high mileage expectations are dashed against the rocks of Virginia's Blue Ridge Mountains. I make two steep climbs, with an equal descent in between, of around 2000 feet. My hike is plagued by periodic downpours. The weather convinces me to stop at a shelter instead of pushing on to a solo campsite. At mile 702 ahead there is a hostel and a grocery, and I think I can make it in 2 more days if I can just get my daily mileage up a little more. I would like to go in and out to the grocery, and pass the hostel by, to gain a couple more miles rather than staying the night.

Today's hike passes the largest, or second largest oak tree on the Appalachian Trail, depending on who is doing the measuring and what criteria they use. It is definitely the largest oak along the Appalachian Trail in the south, but it has a competitor in the north. The southern tree is called the Keffer Oak. It is in a wood line windbreak between two pastures on a farm, in the valley between the two climbs of the day. It is awe inspiring; a thick, towering, many branched living structure. It is hundreds of years old, and how it survived in a populated area is a mystery. It will survive now; it has become a special landmark. It is also a good place to stop for a snack beneath the enormous branches, each of which would make a fair sized tree on their ownsome.

Approaching Sarver Hollow Shelter I climb up and follow a ridgeline past Bruiser Knob. There are strange rock piles all along the ridge, each one 10 or 12 feet high. They aren't natural piles, but obviously some sort of man made structure, shaped like collapsed, walled, circular chimneys. I cannot fathom what they were built for, and it will nag at me for a few days. The AWOL Guide, usually informative about the small landmarks along the way, has no mention of the structures. I ask about them up the trail, but never get a satisfactory answer.

My own musings include the possibility of Indian burial mounds, or some sort of colonial or industrial age furnace structures. Why, if they are ovens of some sort, are there so many clustered atop this particular ridge?

Whatever they burned would have to be hauled up to the top of the climb I just labored up. Most remains of previous human activity are in the gaps and near watercourses, easier to get to than up atop the ridgelines.

I am already dreading the shelter as I come near. I am becoming more sensitive to people crowded into small spaces. There is the expected crowd of hikers in Sarver Hollow Shelter, many there to get out of the night's rain, just like me.

There is wet clothing and equipment spread and hung everywhere inside. The hikers already present shuffle their stuff around to make room for one more person. It is crowded and messy, but it is still a dry place to sleep on a wet night.

Day 71, June 15th
Pickle Branch Shelter mile 695.4
Daily Distance 16.1 miles

I meet Warren Doyle and his supported hike group today. The group is eight older hikers, and Warren Doyle has put together a high speed supported hike that will allow them to complete the Appalachian Trail in 140 days.

Warren Doyle is a trail legend. He has completed the trail more times than any person alive, and isn't shy about announcing it either. He was a speaker of note at Trail Days in Damascus. He is also very opinionated and outspoken, and it has alienated a number of thru-hikers. His hiking group seems very happy with him though, and they are progressing right up the trail. They call themselves the Doylies.

They are NoBos; Doyle himself starts each day at the end point and hikes SoBo seeing his group in passing. He has one other person helping him out, Bob, soon to be trail named Just Bob, who follows the group. They have a van, and do a key exchange at the middle of each day's hike.

The trail follows a ridgeline on the rocky side of the mountain, making for difficult walking, and then drops down into Craig Creek Valley. Brushy Mountain is a tough, rocky, switchbacked climb back out. Once on Brushy Mountain there are a couple of miles of graveled forest road. It is a day hiking area, and there are benches at the summit to sit on and rest.

Brushy Mountain is the site of the Audie Murphy monument. Audie Murphy has a place in every soldier's heart. He was the most decorated American soldier of World War II, celebrated for his toughness. Obstacle courses are named after him.

The remarkable thing about Murphy is he almost didn't get to fight at all. Murphy was turned down at enlistment offices for being too small and weak by all the other services before the Army finally accepted him. He became a hero many times over, ultimately gaining a battlefield commission and earning the Medal of Honor. Murphy became a film actor, mostly in westerns, after the war. He was killed in a small plane crash near the memorial spot in the 1970s.

People place small rocks in cairns along the trail to show respect to memorials, and the Audie Murphy monument is dwarfed by the pile of stones beside it. Many of the rocks and stones have writing on them, passing veterans of all of our wars since World War II acknowledging this courageous soldier. I spend more than a few minutes here, and add my own rock to the pile.

The rest of the day's hike follows the rocky side of the mountain back down to Trout Creek. Warren Doyle's group met their support van and set up a camp near the road. They have a fire with a Dutch oven on it, and it is filled with chili and cornbread. I am hiking along with Phyzzy, and the Doylies invite us to stop and eat. It is delicious, filling, and hot. I eat my fill, and I am urged to eat more by the hospitable Doylies. We don't stay long. Bugs are attracted to the fire, and to us, and the best way to defeat them is to get moving again. Phyzzy and I leave the Doylies to their feast, and their bugs.

I have to hike down off the ridge to Pickle Creek Shelter, adding another half mile of blue blazed trail distance to my daily trek. I had to do the same thing at Sarver Creek Shelter last night. The shelters are built near water sources and there is little available water on the ridgelines. The next water past Pickle Creek is 6 miles away, so I am committing to this extra half mile on the side instead. I hate non-trail miles. I walk over 17 miles today, but only 16.1 are on the Appalachian Trail. I set up my hammock near the shelter, and sleep.

Day 72, June 16th
Catawba, VA, Four Pines Hostel, Trail Mile 708.0
Daily Distance 12.6 Miles

TRAILTALK:

WIDOWMAKER: A dead tree branch caught up high in a tree, a deadly gravity powered missile awaiting a gust of wind to release it.

There are spatters of rain throughout the day, and at one point there is a tremendous blast of wind. A huge branch, a log sized piece of deadfall, crashes down from out of the treetops not 10 feet from me, and scares me half out of my wits.

Branches frequently fall down from the trees. There is a rain of twigs, nuts and leaves that come down on the trail with every big gust of wind. Sometimes I hear an entire tree coming down in a storm, usually pretty far away. People are occasionally killed by falling branches in the forest, but somehow it seems a distant statistic until a big one comes down next to you. Just a few feet over and this one would have been a widowmaker.

I manage to get stung by a bee, not for the first time, on this section of trail. I catch my arm in a trailside bush as I am passing, and disturb a resident bee. The bee demonstrates his upset by putting a stinger in my arm. I am not allergic to bees, a bee sting is just a nuisance; but for anyone allergic I would expect them to carry appropriate counter measures when they hike. There is a certain inevitability to getting the occasional sting on the trail.

I hike past the Dragon's Tooth, a prominent spire of rock that sticks up out of Cove Mountain. It is a 1/10th of a mile off of the main trail, and is a regular diversion for thru-hikers. Climbing the tooth itself is a rated technical climb. The tooth is a thin tower of stone rising 80 feet up from the top of the mountain. I pass on the climb and enjoy the views from the base. Warren Doyle's group is there, and will pass me on my way down at Lost Spectacles Gap.

The hike up to the Dragon's Tooth is on a knife edge ridge and rocky, but it is the descent on the northern side of Cove Mountain where the fun truly begins. The hike changes from hiking over rocks to mountain climbing. It is a steep jumble of boulders and rock faces. There are pieces of rebar sunk into the rock to provide handholds. It is the only such section rated as a technical climb on the Appalachian Trail south of the Mason Dixon Line.

I have to throw my poles down to the bottom of each section of rocks to free my hands for grabbing handholds, climb down to my poles, then throw them down past the next technical section. It is not a particularly well marked section of trail, so I had to backtrack here and there to make sure I was going the right way. Going up is far easier than going down a technical section. I ran into Ghost later on and talked to him about this section.

Ghost got lost a lot. It didn't seem to trouble him much; it was part of his adventure. At Dragon's Tooth he missed a switchback on the descent and just forged straight on down the mountain. He knew he was lost after a little while, but had no desire to climb back up the steep hill to regain the trail. As a lasher he felt no obligation to see every white blaze like a purist. He continued down the mountain until he came to a power line trace, and followed that to a housing development. A man mowing his backyard saw him looking around and quit his chore to give Ghost a ride back to the trailhead. People's friendliness to thru-hikers is still a wonder to me. It restores my faith in humanity.

I hike in to a little convenience store in Catawba, a half mile off the trail. It is a general store, and there is a grill where they cook burgers and other foods. Hikers sit at tables outside, charging their phones on outside outlets and gorging themselves,

There is a minivan with a dragon painted curling up on its side driven by a retired Philadelphia firefighter in the parking lot. The vehicle is the Dragonwagon, and it supports operations by the nearby Four Pines Hostel, This afternoon it is collecting hikers to stay at the hostel. I am still bent on making miles and pass on the offer.

The trail drops off the ridges into a gap at VA Route 624 where the grocery is located, then climbs up a little hill and drops back down to VA Route 785 a couple of miles later. I run into Wisconsin and High Life, a young married couple, coming southbound on the hill towards me. I saw them at Sarver Creek Shelter the night before, and I am a little confused seeing them coming back the other way today.

Wisconsin and High Life are working a slackpacking scheme to make a couple of big mile days. Today they are coming backward between the two roads to get a couple of extra miles. They met up with the Dragonwagon as I did, but accepted the offer of a ride, and are staying at Four Pines Hostel. They stored their equipment in the Dragonwagon and are picking up this extra couple of miles of trail without their backpacks on.

Tomorrow they plan to have their equipment shuttled all the way forward to Daleville, twenty miles ahead, and then slackpack the distance between Four Pines and Daleville across the Tinker Cliffs. The van cost is fixed at 40 dollars for the shuttle, so the more people who buy into the scheme, the less each individual has to pay. It looks like eight hikers are interested, so it is a really low cost option. I am able to make fifteen miles in a day fully loaded now, and the slack looks pretty appealing. I could make big miles.

I pass Wisconsin and High Life and consider the slack option as I finish crossing the little mountain. By the time I come down to Route 785 I am decided. It looks like a great opportunity. I call the hostel and arrange to get picked up by the Dragonwagon at the trailhead.

Waiting for the van at the trailhead I meet a renowned trail angel, Miss Janet, for the first time. I used one of her neckties back in Erwin. Miss Janet drives up and down the trail helping hikers, providing rides, shelter, information, and the occasional bit of motivation. She has a full sized Dodge Tradesman van covered with hiking stickers, and the van is emblazoned with a set of wings surrounding an AT symbol painted across the hood. She also has an old style Aah Ooh Gah horn, so I always know when she is around.

I walk over and introduce myself, and receive a cold non-caffeinated soda for my trouble. I usually avoid soda, especially caffeinated ones, but after the day's long hot miles a shot of cold sugar is a blessing, and Miss Janet digs around in her cooler to find me a drink without the caffeine.

The Dragonwagon eventually shows up and transports me to Four Pines Hostel. It is a rather haphazard place, in a comfortable way. I have heard that some big parties sometimes happen on the grounds, but I am here with some of the more sedate members of the bubble I am currently traveling in. Wisconsin and High Life, Rhino, and Phyzzy are here, and others whose names I didn't record.

The hostel at Four Pines occupies a huge multi-bay garage. It feels ever so much like a buddy's high school hippie hangout. There is an odd assortment of beds, and a collection of mismatched couches and chairs is scattered about. A counter along one wall has basic appliances for cooking, and there is a pool table and some loaner guitars for entertainment. The owner holds court at a long communal table. Payment is donation based, and I had to ask to even find the donation box hidden in a corner. A number of hikers are camped around outside on the grounds, and there are cornhole boards set up. The master of the property is also a master of the game, and makes money and beer in challenges.

Baltimore Jack is here, still following the thru-hikers. It is a good sign I am still firmly imbedded in my bubble. He has a question and answer session with the guests tonight, based on his multiple thru-hikers, and gives out a lot of good information as well as moral support.

I prepare for tomorrow's slackpack by making a hobo bag, which Phyzzy defines it as a 'bindle', using items I find in the hiker box. I tie off the sleeves of a t-shirt and tie another one of Miss Janet's neckties onto them as a strap. I knot the bottom, and leave the neck as an opening. I fill the bag with snacks, my raincoat, water, my headlamp, water filter, paper towel wipes, my phone, and this time, remembering my Greasy Creek experience, I bring a Mylar blanket, just in case.

Day 73, June 17th
Daleville, Trail Mile 727.8
Daily Distance 19.8 Miles

Baltimore Jack told us how easy this section would be. It has been a while since he hiked, and he must have been a power hiker in his day. Compared to Maine or the White Mountains it may have been easier, but it wasn't easy. It is a typical Virginia rocky ridgeline walk with a lot of little ups and downs, work all the way.

The first climb, up to McAfee Knob, is nice. McAfee Knob is the single most photographed point on the Appalachian Trail. A big ledge projects out into space, and it is traditional to get a photo sitting with your legs dangling over the edge. It is not nearly as daunting as it appears in photos, but if you don't particularly like heights, and I do not, getting out onto to the edge and sitting so close to unsupported space is a challenge. In my photo Chef is sitting up on the ledge behind me playing his ukulele. A clot of hikers all started out together from the trailhead coming out of the Four Pines shuttle, and it is a picnic at the knob.

While McAfee Knob gets all the tourist attention, I find the real attraction up here is the Tinker Cliffs, five miles further along the AT. The path travels along a precipitous cliff edge, and there are sweeping views of the surrounding countryside all the way. There are a lot of idyllic little spots to take a break and look out over the world.

When I am past the Tinker Cliffs the rain begins. The uphill and downhill traces become streams, and low spots become long troughs of water to splash my way through

I see many box turtles today. Maybe the rainfall is bringing them out. I know little of turtle motivations and behaviors. I rescue a few from the center of the trail where they are struggling against the flow of water, looking like orange and black rocks with water gushing around them. I pick them up and place them on whichever side of the trail stream it appears they were fighting to attain. Not one of them thanks me.

My hike gets dicey after the Tinker's Cliffs. Thunderstorms tee up one after another to drench the trail and the thru-hikers upon it. I photographed my maps onto my phone to try and simplify my load, instead of carrying my AWOL guide page in its baggie. I have my phone out looking at a map when one of the downpours strikes. My phone is immediately soaked, and goes dark, despite its Otterbox case.

My maps are gone. Years of telephone contacts and email addresses are gone. Two years of photos, including the ones documenting the last 700 miles of the trail, are gone. My ability to access the internet on the trail is gone.

I am in a panic for the rest of today's hike. I throw myself at the trail trying to hurry into town, where I can try and dry out my phone in rice. I want to stabilize it, and find a technician to save it as fast as I possibly can.

The trail is not cooperative. It is rocky and slippery in the places where there isn't flowing or standing water I to have to wade through. The ridgeline seems endless. I pass Wisconsin and High Life, Ghost, Rhino, and others. I fall, hard, twice in my haste, twisting my ankles and bruising and bloodying my shins against the rocks. What was represented as easy three mile an hour terrain takes me four and a half hours to travel 9 miles. I take no breaks, eat my snacks on the move, and keep pushing, cursing Baltimore Jack's trail description all the while. When I finally come down off the ridge going into to Daleville, the trail passes below a series of huge power line towers, and they crackle and pop ominously above me in the falling rain.

I surprise a pair of deer in the valley, coming upon them suddenly in a thicket. They freeze, and I freeze. I stop rushing for a couple of minutes to watch them ease away from me. My orange and green clothing must confuse them; they come to within ten feet of me before moving away. Even in my worry over the phone, seeing the deer is a welcome stop, and watching them makes me smile.

I finally make it into Daleville, and I stop in at a gas station convenience store near the trail and buy a box of instant rice. I tear the box open and plop my phone inside. It has been wet ever since that first rainfall. It was raining so hard that water has even gotten inside my protective Ziploc bag, and in that kind of downpour there was no drying anything off until I had shelter.

The Appalachian Trail crosses a major four lane road in Daleville; the town's main commercial strip. I check into a Howard Johnson's just a quarter mile from the trailhead. It is a big motel, several two story buildings with rooms and a separate building for the main office and dining area. It is a little run down, but compared to other thru-hiker priced motels it is pretty nice. There is a big outdoor pool, and they offer a free breakfast.

There are thru-hikers all around and about, staying here and at a Super 8 Motel across the road. I see Rabbit, Olaf, and Shine On taking zeros.

Rabbit tells me Spring-E is laid up with Norovirus across the way at the Super 8 Motel. Sickness is following us up the trail.

I am heartened by the familiar faces I am seeing. I am still in the bubble!

Everything a thru-hiker could want is nearby. There is a Kroger's supermarket, a brewpub, a Goodwill, an outdoor outfitter, and a number of restaurants within half a mile of the trailhead and my motel. There is also a Verizon store, which is now high priority for me.

Getting to the stores can be a little hazardous. Everything is built up in strip malls, and cars and trucks are racing by me when I walk the shoulders of the four lane road.

I have a mail drop at the post office to pick up. My wife has sent another package of dehydrated foods. Tomorrow will be busy. I hope to get all my business done and get back out of town in one day.

Day 74, June 18th
Daleville, Trail Mile 727.8
0.0 Miles (Zero Day)

I spend the entire day in Daleville. I am undecided about what to do about my washed out cell phone. I can get the battery light to come on, and that is all. I am reluctant to spend $700.00 on a new phone, but it is an important piece of equipment. I am still conducting a job search while I hike, looking to land regular employment when I finish the trail. The phone is my link to potential. I am even more concerned about the loss of my photographic record of the trail. The Verizon store is not very helpful; a full diagnostic will take a couple of days I don't want to lose. I have to think about my options.

I hitch a ride to the post office and I am picked up almost immediately. The driver says she and her husband are on a list of trail angels that will provide overnight stays for thru-hikers in town. I haven't heard anything about it, and I am already set at HoJo's. I get her card to pass along in case I run into a less set hiker. The generosity of the residents in trail towns is a never ending source of amazement.

A number of hikers are in town recovering from Norovirus besides Spring-E. I think my tendency to hike and camp by myself may be helping me to avoid exposure to trail sickness. Norovirus makes for an unpleasant couple of days. It is better to face it in town, with facilities, but however it happens is a bad way.

I tend to all of my chores. The HoJo's is set up well for hikers. I eat the free Continental breakfast, do laundry in the motel's coin operated laundry room, and get local information from a friendly staff.

I see Finch in the lobby. There is a story circulating about her that she camped up by McAfee Knob, at the Pig Farm Campsite, and had her bear bag taken by a bear, leaving her begging for enough food from passing hikers to get her down to Daleville. I ask Finch about it and there is truth in the story.

Finch tells me she didn't want to go through the time consuming trial and error task of hanging her food, and was camping with a group. She felt safe leaving her bear bag next to her tent. She slept late, and the people camped around her left early, leaving her alone and unaware. Finch awoke to the sounds of a bear right next to her tent. It tore open her bear bag and ate the contents nearby. Afterwards the bear circled her camp while she sat terrified waiting for it to move on. It finally went away, leaving her without food, and with a harrowing tale.

I resupply at Kroger's, and I stop in at the Outdoor Trail outfitters. I replace my bear bag, which I have torn. I am ripping the closure handle off of the bags. I use my smaller bags as weights, flinging them into the trees with a line clipped on by carabiner trying to get them across a high branch to put my bear bag up. The torn handles are not a big surprise really, I went cheap on dry bags, and I step up the quality (and cost) here. I also switch from my alcohol burner stove to a canister type, a Snow Peak. Cooking with the alcohol stove is taking too long, and I keep setting things on fire. I have melted a new thumbhole into my rain jacket. I really envy people with the Jetboil system but there are none available for sale here. There are a lot of empty shelves in outfitters after the main waves of thru-hikers have passed for the year,

I eat lunch at the Mexican restaurant across from the HoJo's. As a New Mexican I am used to a high quality in Mexican food, and in the South they have removed most of the good spice and heat from the dishes. They prefer a blander meal here, and I miss my green chili. I eat dinner at Three Lil' Pigs Barbeque with Ghost, Rhino, and Boston. Rhino followed Ghost coming down from the Tinker Cliffs and they both managed to get lost (again). They had to bushwhack a way back to the Appalachian Trail. I am sensing a pattern in Ghost's hiking.

Tomorrow I have to make a decision about the phone, get out of town, and get back onto the Appalachian Trail where I belong.

VIRGINIA PART II, NORTHERN VIRGINIA

Day 75 to 95, June 19th to July 10th
Daleville VA to Harpers Ferry WV, Trail Miles 727.8 to 1022.8, 295.0 miles
AVG 14.75 Miles a Day

Day 75 to 83, June 19 - 27
Daleville to Waynesboro VA, Trail Miles 727.8 to 861.5, 9 days 133.7 miles
AVG 14.85 Daily Miles

Day 75, June 19th
Wilson Creek Shelter, Trail Mile 739.0
Daily Distance 11.2 miles

I have the usual delay leaving the comforts of town. I buy a burner phone at Kroger's, a cheap smartphone that has most of the main functions of my iPhone, but less reach, less photo clarity, and fewer applications. I pay for a month of service. It gives me time to figure out my iPhone issue and still have something for communication.

I don't get onto the trail until 12:30 PM, but I still rack up decent mileage. I am conserving food, even though my urge is to eat down some of the extra weight I carry out of town. I believe it is possible for me to make Waynesboro in a single 5 or 6 day push. I will need to stretch my food supply to do so, and crank out 16 miles a day. I am always ambitious on these plans, and have usually fallen short. On the other hand I am a thru-hiker who finished the Damascathon, so who knows what I can accomplish?

I am still losing my personal battle against the bugs. DEET is a tasty topping to them, not a repellent.

Nose Blind is hiking in my vicinity, and says he saw a bear as he hiked just ahead of me. I still have not seen a bear, yet every other thru-hiker has a bear story or two. I feel I am losing out on a part of my trail experience. High Life points out a deer to me as I come even with him, and we watch it walk away through the woods.

It feels like easy hiking. It is getting summer hot, but summer hot in the Appalachians isn't a patch on the heat in Iraq and Kuwait; it actually feels pretty good to me. It is starting to slow some hikers down. The water situation can be tricky; there is no water on the high ridges, just down in the gaps, requiring hikers to load up in each gap. At each water source most thru-hikers are playing camel now, forcing hydration by drinking as much water as they can in the hopes it means they can carry less on their backs.

My new Snow Peak stove works much better than my alcohol burner. I bought two fuel canisters but it is far more than I will need for the next leg of the trail. Scent Blind is almost out and doesn't want to go into town for a new canister, so I lighten my load by trading one of my full ones for his mostly empty one. I will have the security of a back up for a couple of burns if I need it with his used can, and I unload a few ounces of extra weight with the full one. Everything is heavier on the day you leave town.

I fall asleep in my hammock, listening to a whippoorwill. There are two barred owls in the vicinity as well. When one owl calls it sets the other one off and they hoot and call to a crescendo, fall off, and then there is relative quiet until one or the other sets to it again.

Day 76, June 20th
Past Jennings Creek, Trail Mile 756.1
Daily Distance 17.1 Miles

It is a long day of hiking. Not an especially challenging day, just a lot of miles, putting one foot in front of the other. We are paralleling the Blue Ridge Parkway, and Slowmo has a friend who came out to see her hike. He has brought loaves of home made banana bread with peanut butter baked into it for protein, baked just for the trail, and they share two big slices with me. He told me to take what I wanted, and I restrained myself from grabbing the whole loaf and running off into the woods with it, just barely. It was awesome banana bread.

I come up with some extravagant food ideas while I hike. Food is never far off from a thru-hikers mind, and thinking of new items whiles away the time. I am thinking of a reverse truffle Oreo, an artisan cookie with chocolate truffle filling and strawberry or vanilla bean biscuits sandwiching it. Mmmmmm.

There is no water over the last ten miles. My destination, Jennings Creek, is supposed to have campsites, but there are 'no camping' signs posted. It is at a road crossing, and there is a pay-to-stay campsite down the road with a little camp store listed in the AWOL Guide. I really don't like the idea of paying to set up camp when the woods are right here, and campgrounds don't often have trees or posts for hammocks. I decide to keep moving and see what I can find ahead.

Jennings Creek looks dirty; it has been raining off and on through the day. The silt in the creek clogs my water filter up when I try to squeeze it through. Some trail angel has left some 16 oz. water bottles at the base of a tree by the trailhead. I limit myself to two; I will make them do me for the night. I climb away from the dirty creek and its no camping signs, and I find a flat spot between two trees to hang my hammock for the night.

Camping alone heightens my awareness of bears, and my vulnerability to them. After hearing Finch's story in Daleville, and seeing bear poop all along the trail, there is no way I am not hanging my bear bag. I try several trees before getting my bag up in a hang. It is only ten feet up, rather than the recommended twelve feet. It is a lot closer to my hammock than I would like as well, but I am too tired to keep trying trees, so I let it go, then worry about it all night.

I have been making good miles, but tomorrow's profile has a booger of a climb on it. I hope I am truly developing hiker legs. I will find out in the morning. I am still hoping to make Waynesboro in a single push. Batteries, food, fuel, and my own endurance are the constraints. The Snow Peak hasn't made a real dent in my canister of fuel yet.

Day 77, June 21st (Summer Solstice)
Thunder Hill Shelter, Trail Mile 770.0
Daily Distance 13.9 Miles

It is five thousand feet of climbing today, rising in fits and starts from Jennings Creek at 800 feet of elevation, up to 4200 feet at the top of the ridgeline, and there are a lot of 400-500 foot ups and downs preceding and following. I am taking the climbs in stride; I think my trail legs have arrived!

I would have made more miles but for a late start. I had a thirty five minute phone call from my wife, and our conversation is not a good one, another, pointless unwinnable argument, Long phone calls take the wind right out of my sails; this one alone cost me a mile. Time is distance.

I see a dead raccoon next to the stream below Bryant Creek Shelter. I considered taking water from Bryant Creek, but I smelled something a little repellent in the air. Holding off I found the raccoon's body in the stream a hundred yards further up. Fortunately there is a nice clean water source right at the shelter upstream from the corruption. Bryant Creek is a really nice shelter, large, well situated and well designed. I am on a roll though, and push on past to Thunder Hill Shelter.

I pass two landmarks along the trail. There is a blue blazed side trail down to Apple Orchard Falls. The falls are supposed to be impressive, and there is the possibility I might yogi some food, but it is a 3 mile round trip, a mile and a half down from the Appalachian Trail intersection. It is not just the distance but the 'down', and the inevitable return 'up', that dissuades me.

Sir Packs A Lot, the proprietor back at the Top of Georgia Hostel near the start of the trail, talked about scenic bypasses along the way during one of his informal information sessions. He said hiking the trail was a once in a lifetime experience, as it was unlikely you would ever come this way again. Hikers should not be so distance driven that they miss the scenic wonders just a little way off the main trail.

I have passed many great spots up because I am distance driven, just as he warned against. I still make the occasional detour, but I won't go far off-trail. I find at the end of the trail, as I write this, that I have few regrets. The trail has enough variety and splendor, each and every day, that one waterfall, more or less, doesn't figure.

The second landmark is a feature of the trail itself. The Guillotine is the first of several guillotine rocks on the trail. It is a place where the trail channels into an alley between two very large rocks, and a knife edge slab of rock is caught hanging above. I take a couple of pictures, but it doesn't hold my interest long.

Thunder Hill Shelter has bear activity warning signs posted all around it. They started to appear at trailheads a couple of days further back. There has been a lot of bear activity at the shelter, and there is a story circulating about a group of hikers spending a night besieged in the shelter while hungry bears circled around outside. I approach the shelter with mixed feelings. I really want to see a bear, but not necessarily have a bear confrontation.

There are passing storms and showers during the day's hike, and I have some trepidation about the 'Thunder Hill' name. I have a reputation as a storm magnet, and I would prefer a dry night tonight. The shelter is not great, but it is not terrible, and there is water here.

Ryan, from Boston, who is resisting being called 'Boston' (he gives in, eventually) is here, and the Lone Ranger, a Pennsylvania Dutch thru-hiker. He needed to get a dispensation from his religious elders to be allowed to come on the hike. Phyzzy has also set up his hammock nearby.

Today is summer solstice, and there is a hiker tradition of it being celebrated as 'hike naked' day. Most of the hikers I see today are too abashed to participate in the tradition, myself included. The only person I actually see naked is Phyzzy, and he has a t-shirt strategically draped over his waist belt. He said it was a little uncomfortable, but he wanted to have the full trail experience, and 'hike naked' day was part of that experience. He wants no regrets.

Ryan is an outspoken and opinionated man, usually friendly enough, but tonight he comes off as loud and abrasive. Phyzzy's strategic nudity gets him some derogatory observations. Phyzzy then upsets the leaf used as a spile in the water catchment basin for the spring, and Ryan is merciless, giving him even more of a hard time over it. The spile is a way of directing a trickle of water so it can be collected in a water bottle.

I get tired of the commentary about the spile, go to the spring, and reset a new leaf in a couple of minutes.

Day 78, June 22nd
US Route 501, Glasgow, VA, Trail Mile 784.6
Daily Distance 14.6 miles

Thunder Hill Shelter was bear free last night. I don't know if I am disappointed or relieved.

Today the hike is an easy, well graded trail coming down off the ridge to the James River, except for one ascent onto Highcock Knob. On a trail with many unusual names, this one elicits more discussion than most.

Water is plentiful, there are sources every 3 miles, and I only carry a liter with me, refilling it as needed and cameling at the sources.

A sign posted in a grove allows me to positively identify hickory trees by leaf shape. I am still trying to increase my knowledge of flora as I go along, where I can. I can identify a car's make and model at a glance, ditto computers, but I am struggling in the natural world. I have replaced the survival ability of species identification with brand identification. It gives me something to ponder as I walk; how separated man has become from the natural environment and how we have substituted a constructed environment to take its place. There is a cultural anthropologist's dissertation in there, I think.

The trail levels out on the James River flood plain and follows a stream to the river. Along the stream I see my first copperhead snake coiled up on a rock in the middle of the stream. I don't know it is a copperhead at this time, just that it has a nice and different color pattern that I haven't seen before. I look it up later.

Copperheads and timber rattlers are the only two types of venomous snakes found on the Appalachian Trail. Copperheads have the more dangerous reputation; they are silent, territorial, and aggressive. Fortunately they are a lot rarer than the rattlesnakes, which will become common further north. A lot of snake stories are starting to circulate on trail from encounters with both types of viper.

The longest footbridge on the Appalachian Trail crosses the James River, which is several hundred yards wide at this point. I manage to pass the footbridge entry and come onto a railroad bridge about a quarter mile further downstream instead. I start across, but I realize something is wrong, there are rails and railroad ties filling the width of the bridge I am about to traverse. I can see the footbridge clearly, upstream from the bridge I am on, and hike back to it.

While I am on the true footbridge a freight train crosses the bridge I left. Getting caught on the bridge with a train coming the other way would have been ugly; I probably would have had to take my chances jumping over the side into the river.

The footbridge has 'No Jumping' signs posted all along it. I look down at the murky brown water flowing by underneath and I wonder why they even bother putting those signs up. It seems common sense to me that no one would risk a jump into unknown waters from these heights unless there was, say, a freight train coming across the bridge in the opposite direction. What I don't know as a solo hiker, and I find out in Glasgow, is jumping off the James River footbridge is an AT thru-hiker tradition. I miss out on that one.

On the far side of the bridge there is a parking lot, and the trail crosses a paved road, US highway 501. It leads to one of the two resupply points between Daleville and Waynesville. It is my fourth day of hiking, and I have come almost 60 miles since my last town stop in Daleville. I talk myself into going into town for a quick overnight. I do not have enough food to make it into Waynesboro in a single push; it still lies another 80 miles ahead, so a single night in and out to resupply is going to have to happen either here or at Buena Vista, 20 miles ahead. I have one day's supply of food left, so I can make Buena Vista.

I am ready for a break, and there is supposed to be a good Italian place in Glasgow. I decide to let my thumb determine my fate. I will stick my thumb out on the road, and if I get a ride in less than a half hour I will go to Glasgow. Otherwise, I will keep going to Buena Vista.

The third car passing by on Route 501 slows, stops, and gives me a ride all the way into town.

Glasgow is a disappointment. For a budget hiker it would be a boost. The town has a free hiker camping pavilion, basically a glorified shelter built in an open park. The pavilion has a screened cold water shower, a grill, a fire pit, and a set of hiker boxes filled with discarded hiker equipment and an ample supply of donated canned goods. A local Eagle Scout had a hand in the building and operation of the place as his community service project, and has worked to keep it going. There are several hikers occupying the area, and a couple of them look like homeless people who have taken up residence rather than thru-hikers.

It is Monday, and as it so happens the Italian place is closed on Mondays. Small businesses being closed on Sundays and Mondays is common in the small Southern towns we pass through, but I am still incredibly let down. I don't keep very good track of the calendar as I hike, and the restaurant closure is unexpected. The only choices for resupply are a Dollar General, a Grocery Express, and a gas station convenience store. They are all much of a muchness. I buy hot dogs and eggs for dinner, as the only readily available proteins for sale I can cook with my camp stove, and do a basic resupply.

I can't eat all of my eggs and hotdogs, despite hiker hunger. I am hungry all of the time now, but I am eating smaller meals on trail and sometimes I don't have quite as much capacity at a single sitting as I think I have. Some of that may be heat. Of course a dozen hot dogs and a dozen eggs is a massive meal, so I shouldn't feel shame for not eating all of it.

It has been getting hotter. It is true summer now, and temperatures are up in the 90s. The clothes I am wearing day in and day out are soaked with sweat within the first hour of hiking every day. Some rash issues developed early on during the hike, and I gave up on underwear. I welcome the rainstorms that roll in most afternoons as they help wash off the accumulated salt on my body, as do immersions in any likely stream I pass. In Glasgow there is a coin operated laundry down the road, but I just take my meager clothing into the cold shower with me and let it rinse. It will be slimy and salty with sweat very soon again tomorrow.

My Merrill trail hiking shoes are starting to disintegrate. They have numerous holes in them, and the bottoms are peeling back from the uppers, flopping about as I walk. The soles have lost most of their tread and are slick and slippery. I will buy new shoes in Waynesboro. My Merrills have lasted 800 miles of the Appalachian Trail, where shoes normally are good for 300-600 miles. They probably haven't really been good since about 600 miles, but I am pleased with them. I am not looking forward to breaking in a new pair of shoes. There will be blisters, and pain.

Day 79, June 23rd
Robinson Gap, Trail Mile 795.8
Daily Distance 11.2 miles

I am going to try hiking with Phyzzy today. When I first heard Phyzzy's trail name I thought he was Fizzy, like a soft drink, but it is actually a reference to his background as a physicist. The people who thru-hike the trail have varied backgrounds, but all of them, even the ones just out of school, are the kind of people who have done things with their lives. When people reveal their backgrounds to me on the trail I often end up feeling like I am a booger eating moron by comparison.

We have to hitch out of Glasgow; the trailhead is a good 10 or 15 miles away and Glasgow itself is on the side road to nowhere. We hike out to the T-intersection with the US Highway 501, a grandiose title for a two lane country road. There are a couple of hikers already out here hitchhiking. We go over and talk to them. They are out here first and we don't want to take away the prime spot. They are happy on the far side of the intersection, so Phyzzy and I go back to the other side and stick out our thumbs. The other couple moves away from us, and further away from the intersection. A few cars pass them, and us by. A pickup truck comes out to the T intersection between us, turns towards me and Phyzzy, and stops. We hop in back, not without feeling a little guilt, and away we go, waving to the other couple two hundred yards up the road.

We get to the trailhead at 11:00 AM. We have a big climb out of the James River valley and back onto the ridgeline. On top of Brush Mountain we pass the Ottie Cline Powell monument. It is a trail landmark, a sad one, and one of the mysteries of the trail. Back in 1891, a teacher in a one room schoolhouse sent her children out on a recess to gather firewood for the schoolhouse stove. Four year old Ottie Powell was among them when they went out, but when the rest of the children returned with their armloads of sticks for the stove, Ottie did not.

A massive search was called, hundreds of people searched the woods, but no trace of little Ottie was found. Four months later a hunter and his dog found the boy's remains atop Brush Mountain, some seven miles away from his start point. He completed the same climb, more or less, that Phyzzy and I had just labored up, but as four year old boy, alone, in an ice storm. He is believed to have fallen asleep and died from exposure.

An entire book has been written about the subject, and sales benefit the memorial, which has been renewed a few times over the years. It is under the care of the Natural Bridge Appalachian Trail Club. There are stories about the area around the memorial regarding Ottie Powell ghost sightings. It is probably not a good place to camp.

174

Phyzzy and I make it as far as Robinson Gap. My goal is 15 miles a day if I want to get to Waynesboro in 4 days. I am behind. I might have pushed a little farther on my own, but I would like to find a suitable hiking partner, and compromise is part of that process. I am faster than Phyzzy on climbs, but he is faster on the flats and down hills, so we are both trying to adjust our paces and accommodate each other.

We camp near a forest road. A couple drives by in a pickup truck, stop, and give us a couple of cold beers. We talk to them for a while, trading trail stories for local news.

Phyzzy and I are both hammockers, and we are in a dense growth of pine right next to the trail. The trees are small and grow close together, and it is hard to find trees the right distance apart. I just can't get a comfortable distance or droop to my hang tonight and I spend considerable time adjusting and readjusting trying to get it right.

When we boil up our dinners, Phyzzy ponders the necessity of boiling water for five minutes to purify it. We filter our water, but USFS also recommends boiling raw water in addition to filtering or chemical treatment. Phyzzy questions the need. What is magical about boiling water? Can harmful bacteria survive 180 degrees? 200 degrees? What makes 212 degrees lethal? The temperature is significant to water as the point it turns into gas, but does that apply to life as well? And why five minutes?

Phyzzy tends to question the why of things, and how they relate to the how. I guess that is why he is a physicist.

It was a hot day, and the night is hot and muggy as well. There are signs of rain to come; the wind is picking up and clouds are building. I am hoping my hang and rain fly spread are good enough to keep me suspended and dry tonight.

Day 80, June 24th
Cow Camp Gap Shelter, Trail Mile 810.2
Daily Distance 14.4 miles

Phyzzy and I drop down to into a gap of less than 1000 feet of elevation to the Pedlar River Bridge, and then have an endless, long, uphill slog 10 miles up to Bald Knob at 4000 feet. There is no water on the climb, and we arrive on top with empty water bottles and bladder.

I don't use a water bladder at this point, but Phyzzy still relies on one. It is a personal choice. Bladders are very popular with thru-hikers. I switched away from a bladder to bottles for several reasons. I cannot see how much water I am using with a bladder hidden inside my backpack. The one I started with leaked a few times in my tent and in my backpack. It is not the bladder itself, but the hose connections when they get pretzeled up inside the pack that leak. Unseen leaks in the pack make a mess I can do without.

I see a lot of Nalgene bottles in use on the trail, but I favor 1 liter PowerAde bottles, being of sturdy construction and half the weight of a

Nalgene. When a PowerAde bottle gets manky I just toss it in the garbage and buy myself another PowerAde. I also carry a big squeezable Lipton Ice Tea bottle that holds a liter and a half of fluid. I rarely carry all of my bottles filled unless I have a big waterless stretch ahead, or I am coming into a dry camp for the night.

We pass the US Route 60 crossing leading into the town of Buena Vista, the second option for resupply on this stretch of the Appalachian Trail. I spurned it in favor of Glasgow. I hear later that while Buena Vista isn't very big, it is a whole lot bigger than Glasgow. It does not have a free camper pavilion, but there is a five dollar a night pay-to-stay camp with a pool, and a couple of motor lodges. It sounds like a much nicer place than Glasgow. There is a Food Lion supermarket, an Italian restaurant and pizza place, and of most particular interest, the Amish Cupboard.

The Cupboard sells Amish baked goods and other products. There is a fair sized Amish population in the Blue Ridge Mountains and the Cupboard serves as a community grocery as well as an outlet for Amish farm products. I did not know about Buena Vista's charms when I choose Glasgow. It just seems like a nicer place. It is not a grass is greener assessment. It would be hard not to improve on Glasgow.

Many plants are starting to put forth fruit, and berries are becoming common. I don't know my berry types, and some are poisonous. For those who know, it is free snacking on the trail. According to Phyzzy compound berries, those with lots of little bumps, are universally safe. It is the simple round berries that can either be blueberries or painful slow death berries.

The lack of water on the trail forces a decision on us late in the day. Do we hike into darkness, with a short hard climb ahead and a thirst on, and get another 3 miles of trail completed, or do we go to the next shelter, which is a half a mile descent down a blue blaze side trail? We hem and haw, but it has been a hard day, and trail ahead is always uncertain. We head down the blue blaze.

Neither of us likes staying in shelters, and we start looking for hammock sites on our way down. The ground is a sloped mountainside, but we find an area with suitable trees and set up our hangs with the ground slanting away beneath us. There is good water at the shelter a few hundred yards away, and a couple of thru-hikers inside, including Boston.

I like Phyzzy but we are rethinking each other as hiking partners. Our paces just aren't meshing, and we just look at some aspects of hiking differently. Tomorrow I am hoping to make up the miles lost today. There is a big climb followed by a long ridgeline stretch, and I am hoping to get a 17, or even 20 mile day out if it. Phyzzy has his own goals, and is expecting a diversion off-trail when he gets to Shenandoah National Park.

We pass the 800 mile marker today, and the hundred mile markers are always a sign of progress and a boost to the spirit. AT tribal wisdom is that if you can make it to Harpers Ferry by the 15th of July, you are making sufficient miles to finish the whole trail by October 15th, Katahdin's semi official closure date. I only need to average 10 miles a day to make the

Harpers Ferry date. Of course, tribal wisdom also pronounced Virginia as flat, easy, and boring, and that is three strikes right there. Virginia is hard, hard work, and lovely for it.

Day 81, June 25th
The Priest, Trail Mile 827.5
Daily Distance 17.3 miles

My morning begins with an unforgettable moment. I get out of my hammock at first light, half awake, with a pressing need to relieve myself, and I forget that I am suspended over a steep slope. I step out of my hammock and gravity immediately takes control, sweeping me off down the hill. My legs are unresponsive and stiff from the night's stasis, and I lurch uncontrollably down the slope for 15 or 20 yards. I come to an abrupt stop by running face first into a tree.

Ouch.

The adrenal surge catches up with the event. I am shaken, and shaking. Phyzzy has observed my launch from the hammock, and is also shaking, but with laughter.

There is no single big climb today, but a wearying succession of smaller ones going higher and higher. There are plenty of low spots and water sources along the way. Somewhere during this day, and I don't note exactly when, Phyzzy and I part ways.

The Priest has a shelter, and I stop in to get water. There are a number of thru-hikers settling in, but I am trying to get just a bit further today, and I am impatient with crowded shelters.

Hiking solo has separated me from some casual knowledge in my social isolation. Trail traditions, such as jumping off the James River footbridge, are communal knowledge, and I am not picking it up. I don't know that there is a thru-hiker tradition associated with The Priest, and it is why so many are gathered at this particular point for the night.

The Priest Shelter register has become the Appalachian Trail confessional. Hikers divulge their trail secrets in the shelter's log book, to cleanse themselves, or air things out. I find out about it later, when people share insights they gain about others from the confessional in trail conversations. Most of it is associated with pink blazing on the trail, so it is kind of a melodrama. I don't know from first hand experience, having watered up and gone.

I hike another half mile to the Priest's summit. The Priest is shaped as a long ridgeline to the south, the one I just walked up, and on the north side there is a pretty sharp drop. I think the name is derived from the mountain's resemblance to a pulpit looking over the gap below. The summit sticks out as a prominence where it can catch the weather.

There are a lot of open spaces suitable for camping, and I find a good location to set up my hammock. Wisconsin and High Life show up and set up camp 50 yards away. The couple usually camps away from shelters, seeking their own privacy. I run into them a lot on the trail, and hike some short stretches with them.

High Life's boots gave out on him on one stretch. He did what so many other thru-hikers do with their first pair of trail shoes and hiked in them until they fell apart on the trail. His boot failure was catastrophic, and he ended up hiking in Crocs, his (and mine, like many hikers) camp shoes until he could get new trail shoes. It looked awkward, but he still made time.

High Life's trail name comes from a can of Miller beer he hauled up the mountain as a treat. He is not one of the high flyers. He and Wisconsin are a quiet, young, married couple, respectful of others, and of the trail. I have watched Wisconsin fill up her pack with the garbage she collects at campsites, cleaning up every area where they stop. It made me and my strategy of picking up two extra pieces of garbage a day seem like a piker by comparison.

Repeated storms roll over the Priest this night. Rain hammers down on my rain fly and the wind tears at it at while thunder and lightning flail the peak. Water is blowing in under my rain fly and I am getting wet. My pack is sitting on the covered ground directly beneath my hammock hang, and has a rain cover over it, but there is an inch of water on the ground. I am concerned that it will soak through, but there is little I can do about it except worry.

Tomorrow is the last climb of over 4000 feet until the Appalachian Trail gets up into the Green Mountains of Vermont. The Mid-Atlantic States are a low saddle between the heights of the Smokies in the south and the White Mountains of the north. Phyzzy pointed out that there could be long succession of 3,999 foot peaks yet ahead. Still, we are gradually coming down.

I think I am looking at the big descent off the Priest, followed by four or five hours of climbing Three Ridges. Beyond that, if I can make the miles, there is a road crossing with a brewpub a few miles away that welcomes thru-hikers and allows camping on the grounds. A burger and a beer are a great motivation to make it a day's end goal.

Day 82, June 26th
Reeds Gap (Devils Backbone Brewery), Trail Mile 842.5
Daily Distance 15 miles

TRAILTALK:

AQUA BLAZE: The Shenandoah River parallels the AT as it passes through Shenandoah National Park, and it is a common adventure for thru-hikers to raft down from Waynesboro to Harpers Ferry, taking a bit of a break on their feet and missing this section of trail. Riding the river is called aqua blazing.

YELLOW BLAZE: To skip sections of trail by hitching rides on the road. To purists, people who make a habit of yellow blazing the difficult or boring sections are cheating.

Today is a trial, a long day of hard hiking in bad weather finishing in near darkness. The descent down the Priest is steep enough to be dangerous, and my knees and ankles take a pounding, braking on every step. It is followed by the hard climb back up to Three Ridges, and then back down again. It rains without let up; drizzles punctuated by periodic downpours throughout the day.

At the beginning of the Three Ridges climb I stop into Harpers Creek Shelter. I get water, have a snack, and just get out of the rain for a minute. There are four people in the shelter, two women and two men. One pair is a mother and son team, the other couple is undefined. Their gear is spread out all over the shelter and it looks like they have been here for a while. They make room for me, but don't appear friendly about it, and make no efforts to include me in their conversations. They are smoking pot inside the shelter, which I consider a breach of courtesy. Usually I am at least asked if I mind (I do, but generally not enough to object) or I am even invited to join in, which I see as generous offer of sharing of resources, even though I don't smoke. This quartet ignores me.

They have a conversation about the evils of GMOs (Genetically Modified Organisms, usually referring to food products) and how they avoid them, even as they snack on Pop Tarts. I know both the Pop Tarts and the weed are genetically modified products, and marvel at their hypocrisy, but keep my mouth shut.

The quartet begins discussing how to best aqua blaze the Shenandoah. As a purist I am intent on seeing every white blaze, but a younger me might have wanted to experience the river as part of my lifetime adventure. I have some small boat experience, and volunteer an observation. They continue to completely ignore me, as though I never even spoke, continuing to talk as though I am not sitting right there with them. I get the message, pack up my snacks, and head back out into the rain.

I am not in a positive frame of mind. I was riding my inner monologue about my marriage, which is in the final stages of another disintegration via text and telephone, on the way into the shelter. Perhaps I was sending out my own vibes, although I was trying hard to put my woes behind me. Maybe my mental state warned the occupants to ignore me. I don't know. What I do remember from this day is that anger fueled the next climb.

It is a hellish, rainy, endurance contest climbing the Three Ridges. I pass a blue blaze bypass, which I ignore, intent as I am on seeing the entire trail. I follow the white blazes as they march up the steep, rock strewn trail. At times the trail is flowing deep in water following the easiest path down the mountain. I make it to the top, the sights invisible in the clouds, and keep marching through the rains back down the other side (sounds like a song, doesn't it? if I were an ant....). Something about the transition from up to down, the expenditure of energy, the change in rhythm, also changes my mood, and I become defiant in the face of the unceasing rain, and perversely quite cheerful.

Maupin Field Shelter lies on the far side of the Three Ridges descent. It is late and moving towards darkness and the rain still comes down in buckets. I stop into the shelter for another breather from the rain before completing the couple of miles over a last hill to the road crossing where the comforts of a brewpub await.

The shelter is full. I recognize Olaf, a German girl, and here also are the four hikers from the last shelter. In a larger group they are less exclusive. Apparently they took the easier bypass around the mountain and beat me here. Room is made for me without dirty looks. I sit and eat my snack, and step back out into the rain to finish my day's hike, the thought of a burger and a beer buoying my spirits.

It is dusk when I arrive at the VA Route 664 road crossing. It is 100 yards down from a T-intersection with the Blue Ridge Parkway. There is a gravel parking lot, and Rhino is in a meadow across the road, setting up his camp. I wave and we shout unintelligible greetings to each other. I stick out my thumb.

Few cars make the turn and come past where I stand in the rain hitchhiking. Their lights are on, and I must present as the worst, most bedraggled, hopeless sort of drowned rat as they go by. After fifteen minutes only four cars have come down the road. In the rain and gloom I am not sure the passing cars even see me until they are past. My dreams of a burger and beer are slowly flowing away down the road with the rain, and I am thinking about camping at the next treeline. I am resigning myself to a wet camp when a car that has already passed comes back up the road, turns around, and pulls over. Joy and gratitude overwhelm me.

I have to wait to get in the car. It is a late model sedan, and there is already a family of five people inside. They rearrange themselves and give me the front passenger seat against my protests. I am not even sure I should take this ride; I am obviously putting them out of their way. It is an African-American family dressed up very nicely, coming from some kind of an event.

My saviors felt a Christian duty to turn around and pick up a miserable hiker in the rain. When they tell me this I brace myself for a missionary effort, but no proselytizing comes. It hasn't anywhere I meet church based support on the trail, or from people like these who say they are performing a Christian act. Collectively they are common in the South, and present a strong argument by example for their faith.

The family asks me the normal trail questions as I fog up the passenger side of the car sitting in my self-created patch of dense humidity. They are not even aware of the existence of the Appalachian Trail; I was just a random hitchhiker they picked up. I always feel obliged to trot out exciting tales of the trail to pay for my passage, and I offer up some gas money at the end of the ride, which is politely declined.

Devils Backbone Brewery is making a transition from a brewpub restaurant into a full on resort, and construction areas surround the main building. They are building an outdoor bar and amphitheater, and already have a parking lot for RV hook ups. They are well on their way to being a Destination, not just a beer and burger joint.

I enter. I am a contrast to all of the well dressed, well groomed, and, especially, dry customers in the pub. I get a seat at one of the bars, and order beer and food. I sit dripping, awkward, and out of place. I am the only thru-hiker to venture down here this evening. I am still wearing my rain jacket with its burn holes and faint reek of mildew, because the air conditioning is giving me chills.

The U.S, Women's Soccer Team World Cup semifinal is on the TV, and I am sitting among soccer fans. I am swept into cheering the game, and join the celebration as a closely played game is won. I eat more food, drink another beer. It turns into a good time among strangers. Eventually, though, I have to go back outside into the rain and darkness.

The property has an area where thru-hikers are allowed to camp, on the far side of the construction projects. There is a small grove of trees, and I struggle to set up my hammock and keep it dry. I get the tree straps up and as I am looking around on the ground for a place to stake in the rain fly I realize I am standing in a nice patch of poison ivy. Everything comes down and I try again in a less vine covered patch.

It is warm out, and despite being wet, in a damp hammock and sleep system, I am not cold. I stopped shivering the moment I walked out of the climate controlled brewery. It is an uncomfortable night, and the constant traffic of cars beaming their headlights across my hammock as they pass by to the resort exit make it difficult, but I sleep.

Day 83, June 27th
Waynesboro, Trail Mile 861.5
Daily Distance 19.0 miles

I wake up early. It is already turning into a hot muggy day. It stopped raining, but it is a very wet world outside my hammock, and none too dry on the inside either. Devils Backbone doesn't serve breakfast, but occasionally they will do something for a party of hikers. I walk back to the brewpub with some small hope, but it is deserted. I get water from a hose at the construction site, dump my small bits of collected trash into the dumpster, use the construction site port o' potty, pack up and go. I hitch from the road back up to the trailhead.

I had 4 days of food laid out setting out from Glasgow. It is now day 5, and I am still 19 miles from Waynesboro. I usually carry too much food for each day, and I ate a big meal at the pub last night that didn't come out of my pack, and I am left with a small assortment of snacks to get through today. My pack is very light, ten to fourteen pounds lighter than when I am laden with a full load of food and water.

There are no steep climbs ahead; the ridgeline slowly works down from 3500 feet to 2000 over the 19 miles ahead. It is not flat as a board, but it is as close to the mythical flat and easy Virginia as I have seen on a profile. I am tired, but I move, eating up the miles one by one.

I come to Paul C. Wolfe Shelter in the late afternoon, with 5 miles yet ahead of me. Olaf is sitting there, and as I take a break I describe the legendary Ming's AYCE Chinese Buffet ahead in Waynesboro to her, reputed to be the finest on the trail.

I have seen Olaf off and on along the trail since somewhere in the Smokies. She is from Germany, and somewhere in her varied educational pursuits studied English and started going abroad on periodic adventures throughout the English speaking world. She looks like a cute baker's daughter, round faced and perpetually cheerful. She resisted a number of trail names before accepting Olaf.

I tried sticking Mouthful on her, since for an entire night in a shelter in the Smokies I managed to catch her right in the middle of taking a bite of food whenever I asked her a question. There was no way she was going to let that one stick. She has a perverse love of cold weather, and she allowed the trail name Olaf, after the Disney character from Frozen, to stick.

Olaf is a good hiker, but has never completed a 20 mile day. The temptation of Ming's, and town, are enough to motivate her to join me in my final run for town, and we set off. Despite being just over five feet tall, her pace is faster than mine. I work harder, and she slows a little to achieve unity.

It is just about dark when we reach the road into Waynesboro at Rockfish Gap. There is a list of 30 local trail angels posted on the back of a steel highway guard rail at the road crossing, and I start calling them one by one on my cheap contract cell phone looking for a ride into town. None of them answer. It is Saturday evening, and I expect they are otherwise engaged. We stick out our thumbs and in five minutes we have a ride. Our driver drops us right in Ming's parking lot.

There are several thru-hikers at Ming's this evening and the staff puts us all in a corner, away from the main flow of customers. It is the end of the night and they are not renewing dishes, but what they have is plenty. There are many choices, variations of a standard Chinese buffet. While we eat I start dialing hotels and hostels looking for a place to stay. They are all booked, every single room in every single venue. The town is hosting a state championship swim meet this weekend and lodging is full up.

The AWOL Guide lists a free camping spot in a town park for hikers, managed by the town through the YMCA. There is also supposed to be a church hostel in the same area of town, but they may already have closed for the season, since we are at the back of the bubble.

Olaf and I have already hiked 20, and 19 miles today respectively. The prospect of even a little more walking on our worn out feet and legs is daunting, but we have no choice. We shoulder our packs and hike a little more, first to the church hostel, which is indeed closed, and then to the free park.

The park looks bad. There are piles of trash everywhere. There are many tents up, and a number of them are big cabin tents, not the sort thru-hikers carry. There is a pavilion filled with garbage and people have sleeping areas laid out inside between small piles of refuse. There is screened area with a hose where I clean myself off, although the past days' constant rain has provided a natural shower of sorts.

There are posts set up for hammockers, but there are tents using them as anchor points and clotheslines. I clear off one set of clotheslines and hang my hammock. Olaf sets up her tent nearby. Our neighbors in the cabin tents are noisily enjoying themselves.

It is late, after 11:00 PM and I am trying to drift off to sleep when a set of headlights sweeps across the park and I peer out from under the rain fly of my hammock. A rattletrap Chevy Suburban comes rolling right across the lawn kicking up rooster tails of dirt from its tires. Music is blasting out the windows. There is a man and a woman inside and they start shouting.

"Woo Hoo! The party is here! Who wants eighths? Who wants quarters?" I can hear some responses. Great. A drug dealer and a party, and I just want to sleep.

The camping area is a small public park in the middle of an old, well kept neighborhood. Houses face the park on three sides of a square. I can't imagine what they think of this community that has sprung up in front of their doorsteps. I shout at the truck from within my hammock. It is twenty feet away from me, stopped with the engine running and the lights on, in front of a little encampment of cabin tents and tarp structures, conducting business.

I yell, "Hey, people are trying to sleep over here, pipe down!" or something close to that. I have not recorded the exact words, so I am trying to capture the spirit of the incident. Stay with me.

The driver of the truck starts yelling back at me. There are a lot of expletives and the tone is definitely confrontational. I am tired, and cranky, and I get out of my hammock to go talk to this guy.

I walk up to the Suburban. The driver is a young white man, dressed like some redneck parody of a gang banger looking a lot the worse for wear. He has a girl with him, just along for the ride I expect. I try to talk to him. I point out to him that while I don't enjoy having drug deals going down on my threshold, all I really want is a little respect and quiet so I can sleep.

He is belligerent. "I don't see anybody else around here sleeping." Expletives deleted.

I know Olaf, among others, is probably trying to sleep in her tent. I am keeping a lid on anger. I may even be too tired for anger. I just want to sleep. I suggest to him that law enforcement is but a phone call away, and discretion should be a part of his business model.

I have maintained my short haircut, and I shave on days I am coming into town. I do not look much like the typical male thru-hiker. Some of it is habit from 25 years in the military; some of it is a belief that maintaining hygiene and appearance will help me hitchhike and yogi (which ultimately matters very little at all). The drug dealer makes some kind of cognitive leap based on my appearance.

He starts yelling out "It's a narc, everyone, look at the narc." and so on. I guess he is trying to disrupt my covert sleeping operation. There are a lot of people in the vicinity, all of them are ducking back inside their tents and going silent. I give up and walk away, but I overtly take a picture of his back bumper and plate with my phone as I walk away.

Mr. Drug Dealer finally realizes he is doing himself no good, or his girlfriend does, and he finally leaves. He spins his tires and rips up some more grass on his way out. I think about calling the police for real, but he is gone, and really, all I want is sleep.

I am a little worried about him coming back to make trouble in some way, coming back with buddies or a gun. I am full of 'I don't give a damn' at this point in my hike, mostly because of events at home, and the worry isn't enough to keep me from drifting off. I am in that zone just before sleep when I hear someone approaching my hammock.

"Hey man, you in there?" A voice asks me from outside my hammock.

Ok, what now, I ask myself. "Yeah?"

My invisible pesterer is an emissary from the cabin tents, apologizing for the scene. I tell him it's OK. I just want to sleep. He keeps apologizing, and I keep telling him to leave me alone. I think he is worried I have called the police. I just want to sleep. He finally gets the message and leaves me alone.

I get to sleep, finally.

Day 84, June 28th
Waynesboro, Trail Mile 861.5
Daily Distance 0.0 Miles

I break down my camp in the Waynesboro city park immediately when I wake up, and Olaf is also packing up. The swim meet has ended, and there are hotel rooms available now, but they are pricey. Olaf agrees to split a room with me, on a no hanky panky deal. I am taking a zero day to hit the outfitter and take a needed break.

Olaf is waiting for Kamikaze, who is a day or two behind us. Olaf wants to set up an aqua blaze to Harpers Ferry from here, but is looking to get together with a group. Kamikaze has a plan.

A lot of other people are emerging from tents around the park, including Sam I Am and his dog, Rambler, and some other thru-hikers. A bright Tonka yellow pickup truck pulls into the park, operated by a local trail angel as a charitable public service. He picks up a load of hikers to take to the trailhead, and we get his number to take us out to the Best Western afterwards.

Waynesboro is at a critical point on the trail. It is the Southern gateway to Shenandoah National Park, and also the start point for the aqua blaze rafting trips down the Shenandoah River to Harpers Ferry. It is a fair sized town, and boasts a number of supermarkets and a good outfitter at Rockfish Gap. Olaf has her own special knowledge about the town.

There are a lot of German thru-hikers; Germany is right behind Canada as far as nationalities of people hiking the trail from outside the United States. This is in large part due to a documentary circulating in Germany about the Appalachian Trail. No American I have met has ever seen this film, but it is popular in Germany. The documentary features a scene at a Waynesboro cafe called Weasie's showing an 'American Breakfast'. As a result it has become a must visit landmark on the trail for German thru-hikers. So we go to breakfast.

Olaf has been in the States for a while now, and is at least familiar with the part that is the Appalachian Trail. She still marvels at American breakfasts, which are huge affairs compared to a typical German breakfast. Her idea of a proper breakfast is a hot drink and a roll, a good roll mind you, but a roll. Weasie's is crowded with a Sunday lunch crowd, and she revels in the whole American big breakfast experience.

We half walk half hitch our way out to Rockfish Gap outfitters after our meal. I spend a lot of time looking at gear. I need shoes, badly, and as always, I am contemplating a few other gear swap outs. I spend some time checking out shoes. There are other thru-hikers in the store, and they are almost all looking at shoes as well. Many hikers have held out, as I have, to the beginning of the Shenandoah to buy new shoes.

The trials and tribulations of Pennsylvania usually referred to by thru-hikers as Rocksylvania, lie ahead. I change from my lightweight Merrills to a sturdier pair of extra wide Keen boots. I want more support and protection for the rocks ahead. I also want new tips for my Kelty hiking poles. The salesman gets me going on a new pair of Lekis instead. He sells me on Leki's lifetime warranty, and points out the cost isn't too much more than tip replacements on my bent and battered Keltys.

The salesman is an experienced hiker and backpacker, and a hammocker. I am always looking for ways and ideas to improve my hiking and camping processes and equipment. He ties trucker hitches in his hammock hang line, and he then just hooks onto his tree straps using mountain climbing carabiners. It looks simpler than tying new knots on the tree strap each time I set up, and picking them apart every morning can be a trying experience. I buy the carabiners and plan to try his methods. I walk out of Rockfish Gap Outfitters with new shoes, new poles, carabiners, and I am lighter by a couple of hundred bucks.

The Tonka truck trail angel comes and takes us over to the Best Western. It is a hundred dollars for a room. There are other hikers about, and it looks like a small group is camped out in a wooded lot nearby and hanging out in the parking lot, probably to latch on to the hotel's free Wifi.

Olaf and I eat at the Waynesboro Golden Corral buffet, one of the nicest of the type I have ever been in. It is immediately Olaf's favorite place to eat. I get resupply at Wal-Mart. I am ready to head back out.

Olaf is still working on organizing her canoe trip down to Harpers Ferry. The water is low in the river, which is odd considering the constant rainfall we have been hiking under, and it is complicating her plans.

Aqua blazing is an expensive undertaking. You cannot rent a canoe; you buy it from an outfitter and they buy it back for a greatly reduced price in Harpers Ferry. The outfitter doesn't carry have any liability then, or any interest in the boat during your trip. The canoes are not in great shape, and you are paying new prices for them. You also have to pay for three truck portages in advance along the way. I hope it works out for her; word is it is an adventure worth the expense.

I have gotten used to the same questions from passing day hikers as I hike. The most common question is "How far are you going" In a moment of bored insanity in the motel room I take out a Sharpie and write 'All the way', and 'It's Possible' in 3 inch high letters on the front of the orange t-shirt I wear as my hiking shirt.

I thought it would identify me as a thru-hiker and save the first question from the curious, but for the next 500 miles, until the Sharpied letters start to fade and blend in with trail dirt on my shirt, the first question will now be "What does 'all the way' mean?'.

Tomorrow I enter Shenandoah National Park.

SHENANDOAH NATIONAL PARK
Days 85-96 June 29 to July 11
Waynesboro VA to Harpers Ferry WV, TRAIL MILES 861.5 to 1022.8
61.3 Miles, AVG 13.44 Miles A Day

Day 85 to Day 91, June 29 to June 97
Waynesboro to Front Royal VA, Trail Mile 861.5 to 969.4, 107.9 miles
AVG 15.41 Daily Miles

Day 85, June 29
Past Sawmill Run Overlook, Trail Mile 872.3
Daily Distance 10.8 Miles

TRAILTALK:

NPS (National Park Service): The National Park Service is an organization distinct from the United States Forest Service, and operates with different rules, regulations and practices,

PATC (Potomac Appalachian Trail Club): One of 22 non-profit trail organizations that maintain the Appalachian Trail. PATC has a long stretch reaching from the middle of Virginia up into Pennsylvania, and has a large and active membership. Myron Avery, the great Appalachian Trail architect, was its founding President.

TICK CHECK: Examining every inch of your body for ticks, paying special attention to the cracks, crevices and hot spots they prefer. Deer ticks are very small, and can easily be overlooked, especially on a dirty body.

I am in Shenandoah National Park (SNP), one of the most anticipated sections of the Appalachian Trail. The park is supposed to be (cough, cough) flat and easy hiking. It is a haven for all sorts of wildlife, and is reputed to be overrun with black bears. Personally, I am beginning to believe Ursus Americanus are mythological creatures, although every other thru-hiker I have spoken to has seen at least one on the journey thus far.

It is not a bad day of hiking, and the trail is well graded and maintained. I see Potomac Appalachian Trail Club (PATC) trail maintainers hard at work improving a section, and stop and talk.

PATC is my favorite trail club. The section they maintain includes SNP, and stretches north into Pennsylvania. It is a numerous and well funded organization, and they put those resources to work. They have the most engaged trail and shelter maintainers I see along the trail. It is a non-profit organization, and is dependent on donations for operating funds. Their resources are greater than that of most other trail clubs, but they still have a small amount of money to accomplish some very great tasks.

I am breaking in the new boots I purchased in Waynesboro. They are a looser fit, and I have lost some of my feel for the trail. I also feel a few hot spots coming on. I hope starting with a shorter day of hiking will give my feet a chance to adapt to their new protective units.

I cross paths with Older Dog, and I talk to him for a moment. I end up finishing the last few miles of the day with The Machine. The Machine is another older hiker, a capable man who just keeps going, the origin of his trail name. I have passed Calf Mountain Shelter wanting to make a few more miles. I am worried about the mythological bear presence and want the security of another hiker camping nearby, and so does The Machine.

We spot a small dark snake with a single bright band of red around its neck. The Machine tells me it is an uncommon species called a Ringneck.

We fill up with water at the spring at the base of Sawmill Run Overlook, and the last couple of miles are heavy lifting. I am carrying a full load out of food from town and four liters of water for making camp. We settle in at the top of a hill. There are open areas of former campsites, but they are overgrown with blueberry bushes. Bushes are beneath where I hang my hammock, and I can reach out from my recline and pluck berries to nibble.

Bugs are not bad until dusk, and then they are an irritation, but not the madness inducing clouds experienced further south. I am trying new things against the bugs, especially since the tick threat is getting real.

I saw a rabbit at close range. The wildlife in the park are definitely aware of their protected status and have no fear of humans. I was near enough I could see big, fat, blood filled ticks hanging all over this poor rabbit, a sight that gave me the creepy crawlies. I nearly sat down and did a full tick check right there in the middle of the trail.

I do a tick check every night at the time when I do a little body wipe down with a wet cloth. I found a single tick so far, embedded behind my knee while at the campgrounds at Waynesboro. Sam I Am maintains a sketchbook of tick types and I brought mine over to him for examination. The biggest differentiation on the deer ticks that I can see is the number of white dots on their back. Mine is nothing special. I check the bit spot regularly, and thus far, two days later, there is no sign of the telltale bull's-eye mark indicating a Lyme disease infection.

Lyme disease is no joke. It affects your joints, and can cripple you. If the signs are spotted early and treated quickly with antibiotics it can be beaten, but if it gets a chance to get a hold in your body, it can take you off the trail, and affect you for life. It troubles a fair number of thru-hikers, during and after their hikes.

DEET doesn't seem to be working as a bug repellent. My new anti bug defenses include garlic pills and a dog's flea collar I am wearing around my ankle. I am still wearing long pants as well, protecting my legs against many things, sunburn, thorns, and poison ivy as well as bugs. I am a rarity, by now just about every other thru-hiker is wearing shorts.

The profile for tomorrow looks promising, and I am hoping to rack up one of the big mile days Virginia is famous for.

Day 86, June 30th
Near Loft Mountain Camp Store, Trail Mile 889.7
Daily Distance 17.4 Miles

TRAILTALK:

SNP (Shenandoah National Park): National Park in Northern Virginia. Much of the infrastructure was built by the Civilian Conservation Corps (CCC) during the Great Depression.

BRP (Blue Ridge Parkway): A two lane highway that runs up the spine of the Blue Ridge Mountains of Virginia. The Appalachian Trail parallels it for much of Virginia.

WAYSIDE: A roadside restraint along the Blue Ridge Parkway in the Shenandoah National Park. Famous for their blackberry milkshakes.

I have a great day of hiking today. I am in love with Shenandoah National Park (SNP). I see my first bear on the trail!

The Machine departs our camp before I do. I still get moving early, and I start out in a bit of a funk. I am in a closed loop inner monologue, muttering to myself resentfully about the mythical black bears, and how I have hiked nearly 900 miles and haven't seen one yet, and I am starting to think I never will. I am so wrapped up I almost miss a big black shadow rustling around just off the side of the trail.

But I don't.

I stop and peer at the shadow in the bushes ahead. Light filters in through the canopy making the trail a little brighter than the surrounding forest. My eyes adjust to the darker woods along the trail's edge, and I realize, there, peering back at me, is one of the black bears I am grumbling about.

I back up a few steps and fumble about getting out my phone. The bear has turned back to his business, which is turning over logs along the edge of the trail, presumably to get at the tasty bugs and grubs he reveals beneath. I advance a bit with my camera out trying to get a picture. He blends in with the shadows so well the camera on my cheap phone can't focus on him, and my attempts at pictures are just showing him as a dark area. My short contract burner phone is sold as a smartphone but I am quickly coming to the understanding it is only of average intelligence at its best.

I am trying to figure out how to get a picture when the bear solves my problems for me. I am bothering him a bit with my presence and have interrupted his foraging. He nonchalantly steps out onto the trail not 20 feet ahead of me. I have my camera snapping away as he stares at me, turns away, gives me a saucy look over his shoulder, and saunters up the trail. He is a good sized bear, 250 or 300 pounds.

I take more pictures as he moves away, and then I get my phone put back away. I start hiking up the trail again, positively elated by the encounter. I don't get far. Mr. Bear is still on the trail and heading back my way. He stops and I stop, face to face on the trail. I start singing and banging my hiking poles together. He doesn't quite get the message. He turns and slowly heads back up the trail. I follow him, poles clacking and singing away, and he keeps ambling up the trail, with more annoyed looks back in my direction. I edge up behind him, and finally he gets bothered enough to step off the trail and let me by.

Subsequent bear encounters let me know I was ignorant and lucky with this bear. He could have as easily charged me as let me pester him off the trail. Bears are dangerous, and I treated him like a giant dog, not my smartest action ever.

Regardless, my spirits are soaring as I climb up Black Rock Mountain. It is an interesting topography above, the views are great, and there is a huge open space; a boulder field of huge black rocks tumbling down the mountain. It is covered with day hikers coming up from the other side. I am splitting open with the need to tell my bear story, and I get some listeners.

The trail in the Shenandoah is everything promised. It is almost like a Disney movie. There is still more up and down than flat and easy, but the trail is so well graded and maintained that the miles just flow away under my feet. I see another Ringnecked snake, this time with a bright yellow necklace instead of red. When I pause to look at my AWOL guide and orient myself a little later, a rabbit hops out of the shrubbery and sits not three feet away from me, chewing on grass and cocking an eye and an ear my way.

The miles add up, and at the end of the day I am footsore and tired, but I have made a good distance. I am camped out near a wayside camp store. In SNP the trail closely parallels the Blue Ridge Parkway (BRP). In years past, the BRP was the trail. A footpath has been built paralleling the road now, wandering along 100 to 500 yards away. On the BRP there are periodic waysides, camps, and restaurants that serve thru-hikers just as well as they do car tourists. This is my first roadside attraction, but they will be regularly spaced after this.

I hit the store for dinner, and eat refrigerator sandwiches and Good Humor ice cream, a thru-hiker feast. The Forest Service worker in the store is a little leery of thru-hikers. I talk to her, and she has had issues with thrus who hang around outside the door, smoking pot, and generally being nuisances, especially to the white bread car tourists who are the main trade. Hikers' unleashed dogs have caused her a number of problems. I buy some beers and drink those out in front after checking to see if it is OK. Rhino is also hanging out here, and is working his way through a liquid dinner. I pack up a little before it gets dark, staggering a little farther down the trail until I find a good place to put up my hammock and I set in. The new trucker's hitch and carabiner rig I learned about at Rockfish Gap Outfitters works better than my old knots.

I spend more time locating a good place to hang my bear bag and getting it set up than I do putting up my hammock. I hang my bag way up in a tree about 100 yards away, giving myself a good distance from any inquisitive bears. I am feeling more confident in my bear handling skills after today's encounter, but I still feel the need to take precautions. The hang is directly over the trail, and my bag advertises my presence. It is bright yellow, and has 'Possible' written on it in three inch high letters.

Based on the profile in the AWOL Guide the trail tomorrow is no more difficult than today's hike, and if I can stretch myself there is a wayside in 26 miles. It seems doable, the only barriers being my own conditioning and mental endurance. Even if I only get 18 or 20 miles, the next wayside will be positioned just right for a late breakfast the next morning.

Day 87, July 1st
Hightop Hut, Trail Mile 903.7
Daily Distance 14 Miles

By any other measure today's distance would have been a great day. It is still a good day; it just didn't meet my overly optimistic expectations.

I don't sleep very well. A thunderstorm blows through and I have some anxious moments waiting to see how my new hang holds up against Mother Nature in a bad mood. It all works out, but I lose sleep. It is chilly after the rain, and I try to ignore the cold, but after an hour or so of pretending I can sleep, I finally break down, dig out my sleeping mat and stick it in under me for some underside insulation and I can finally make some fitful Zs.

In the morning I don't get far down the trail to start. There is a restaurant just a mile ahead. I have to go down a steep blue blaze a half mile to get there. I stay there for a good 2 hours enjoying a cooked breakfast. The Machine and Older Dog are there too, and we eat together, sharing stories. Older Dog had a run in with 'my' bear. He was behind me, and came upon Mr. Bear on the trail, still trying to get back to the logs he was tumbling when I disturbed him. There were a couple of day hikers with children there too, and Older Dog took the point position to get everyone past the by now thoroughly bothered bear.

It is 11 o'clock before I really start moving again. I have some kind of ankle pain. It is locking up in the arc of each step, and giving a little stabbing pain before it lets go. It takes a few miles to get it worked out.

I cruise along until I get to Hightop Hut Shelter and decide to call it a day. I haven't made 20 miles, but I am no slacker either, and I am tired. I leave the hammock aside and sleep in the shelter. Setting up camp and taking it down takes time. I am feeling lazy, and rain is expected tonight.

The mice are active in the night, and wake me a few times when they skitter across my body in their search for food. My food bag is all up and away, safe in my bear hang. Some thru-hikers who are regular shelter users actually carry the extra weight of a couple of mousetraps to discourage the little pests.

Day 88, July 2nd
Near Big Meadows Wayside, Trail Mile 923.2
Daily Distance 19.5 Miles

I make big miles today, big, big miles. I get an early start. The other hikers in the shelter rise early for a dawn exodus, and I am not far behind.

I get up to the Lewis Mountain Campground camp store at 3:00 PM, and find out the Big Meadows Wayside is only another 7.5 miles ahead, and it stays open until 8:00 PM. I have snacks at the store and leave at 3:30 PM, turning and burning. I am keeping an eye on my watch and push myself hard the whole way. I clock a 17 minute mile hiking, my fastest I track anywhere along the trail. I arrive at the wayside at 7:10 PM, and have a burger and my first blackberry shake to celebrate.

The blackberry shakes of the SNP waysides are legendary, and this is my first chance to taste one. I expect an overpowering high fructose berry blast, but this is not what the SNP blackberry shake is. It is fairly subtle, with a nice, sweet, tart flavor riding in the blended vanilla ice cream. Yum.

I am invited to sit with some car tourists while I eat my meal. They have all kinds of questions about thru-hiking. I am on exhibit, and don't mind a bit. They leave, and I find out afterwards, when I try to pay my bill, they have already taken care of it. Trail angels, Trail Magic!

It is a relatively cool day of hiking. It clouded over but never rained and stayed in the 70s, just about perfect hiking weather. I see many deer along the way, utterly unconcerned about my presence. I stop to watch them, even seeing how they graze has a kind of magic to it.

I pass The Machine and Older Dog during my speed run. We are aiming for the same area tonight in order to have breakfast at the next wayside tomorrow morning. Figgy and Whiz Bang are camping near where I hang my hammock for the night. They are still following the old trail walking on the BRP. They have had a bad bear encounter and are shaken. They are still doing the miles, following the trail route, but trying to stay away from the bears.

I get a cell phone signal tonight, take a chance, and call my wife. We get along, and I have hope. It is a good day.

Day 89, July 3rd
Byrd's Nest Shelter, Trail Mile 938.5
Daily Distance 15.3 Miles

I see my second bear today while hiking with Older Dog. It stares at us from behind a log 50 feet from the trail. Another hiker coming south warned us about this one as he passed, and he had seen a cub with her. We saw no cub, but we are very careful passing by, making lots of noise. The mamas with the young cubs are the most protective, and most dangerous.

Older Dog has had more bear run ins and is more cautious around them than I was with my first one. He likes hiking with company just to provide a little security in this area where there are so many. Shenandoah bears have little fear of man due to their protected status within the park.

I leapfrog with Older Dog and The Machine. I am making an effort to stay with them, and it helps push my pace. I do not make huge miles, but I make good miles, even stopping to sit down and eat in two different wayside restaurants. I also spend a good half hour at Shenandoah Skyland Resort stables with Older Dog talking to the manager as she works. She seems very content, trading poor pay for a great life.

The food in the restaurants is pricey, but quality and portion sizes are good. I eat my breakfast at the main lodge at Big Meadows. It is an old NPS lodge built of fieldstone and timbers, and the lounge where I wait with Older Dog and The Machine for a breakfast table is a big open space fronted by huge picture windows looking out over the mountains. It is furnished with comfy sofas and tables, games, books and puzzles.

I hang on to Older Dog for the last six and a half miles of the day, and we really move. We are racking up 3 miles an hour, a power hiker pace.

I stay in another shelter, Byrd's Nest. The ones in the park are not crowded, and one of the reasons I make good time is I am not taking time to cook or set up camp. I am throwing down my sleeping mat and bag in a shelter, going to sleep, getting up, putting them away and going again. I am relying on the waysides for my main meals. My pack is lighter without the need to carry several days' worth of food.

For some reason beer is really inexpensive in SNP. Prices are set by the government, and a burger and a beer costs ten dollars, pretty reasonable, except the burger is nine dollars, and the beer just one.

Day 90, July 4th (Independence Day)
Gravel Springs Hut, Trail Mile 956.2
Daily Distance 17.7 Miles

Byrd's Nest Shelter is disturbing. There are large piles of some kind of insect eggs covering one half of the shelter floor, and more periodically rain down out of the ceiling. No one sees the actual insects, so whether there is a massive ant or termite infestation above our heads, or it is something else is a guess. Obviously, only the other half the shelter is occupied. I end up on the edge of the sleepers, in the center of the shelter, near the pile of eggs. When I wake up I have a light sprinkling of them on my sleeping bag.

The infestation seems to be centered on a big 12" by 12" wooden roof beam, rough hewn, and 20 feet long. Many of the structures in SNP are historic CCC structures, built of fieldstone and timbers of a size and quality not seen anymore. The camp store before Big Meadows had a 10" X 10" pine beam that had to be 80 feet long, a thick, straight beam from a single tree. SNP had it insured. It would be very hard to replace now. The big, old, straight trees are rare, and generally protected.

I am back to hiking solo again as The Machine and Older Dog rise earlier and are pushing harder than I am today. The first twelve miles are easy trail and it is wet without rain. There are a lot of low hanging clouds that often manifest as banks of fog at the higher altitudes of the trail. A lot of tourist groups are out this holiday weekend, and there are many day hikers within a mile of the trailheads.

I see a lot of thru-hikers at the waysides. Some are making plans for viewing fireworks, picking campsites near overlooks, or hitching into town for the night. I am a little put off by fireworks now. I saw enough of the real item in Iraq and Afghanistan.

Figgy is wearing the best Independence Day t-shirt I have ever seen. It is pink and it has a kitten licking a red, white and blue Popsicle set against an American flag with fireworks in the background. The fireworks are reflected in the kitten's eyes. She found it in a thrift store, and promises to give it to me to mail home when the 4th is over. It is in my closet now, waiting for the next Independence Day.

The last five and half miles of hiking today are a wildlife safari. I see deer, and then I surprise another momma bear and her cub. The trail runs through a thicket of blackberry bushes, and I walk up on the bears while they are snacking. They run parallel to the trail to the nearest tree, just a few yards away from me and the trail, and shimmy up the trunk of a tree, the cub above Momma.

I try to get my camera out, but Momma starts chuffing, a kind of a strong panting noise, which is a warning. I back away when both bears slide off the trunk and out of sight in the berry bramble, and I drop my phone on the ground, get my hiking poles up, and start shouting, watching the bushes trying to locate momma. I am expecting a charge.

The bears finally pop back up into view on another tree trunk about 20 yards away from the trail, and I breathe a sigh of relief. Momma bear is dangerous.

Further along there is an old site that was used as a launch point for hang gliders. The ramp is closed. Around the edge of the trail a warning tape runs along the trees and a sign is posted. It protects a Peregrine falcon breeding site, and I see several of them. One falcon is perched out by the drop-off on the launch ramp. I see more of the Peregrines zooming in and out of the mists directly above my head, like fighter planes appearing and disappearing into the clouds.

Last night in the shelter there was a lot of pot smoking. I am debating whether it is worth a confrontation when it happens again. I don't know why it is bugging me today, but it is. I don't like having other's vices pressed upon me. A confrontation would mark me for the rest of the trail, and I have no desire to be a pariah. In general I really don't care about the pot smoking, but when it is right next to me in a shelter it comes across as disrespectful of the other people in the shelter. I let it go.

I come across the only Park Ranger I will meet on the trail at any place other than a trailhead. When I was younger and hiked in National Forest land you saw rangers all the time. They were always on the trail, and there was a comfort in seeing these friendly, competent guardians of the woods. This is no longer true.

I bring up the lack of ranger presence on the trail to the ranger I meet, and he tells me they are just overloaded. The amount of National Park and Forest Service lands has doubled since the 1980s, the amount of use has quadrupled, and no new rangers have been added in this time. There are just 2000 Park Rangers for the entire National Park system. They are sticking to the roads and driving around in SUVs, which is where most of the problems are located and their presence needs to be felt. I still miss them on the trail.

Day 91, July 5th
U.S. Route 522 Front Royal, VA, Trail Mile 969.4

194

Daily Distance 13.2 Miles

Shenandoah National Park is done, and it was everything I heard it was going to be. The easy miles were there and I rocked 15 miles a day without great difficulty. The restaurants and wayside stores made resupply ridiculously easy and provided a great amount of comfort. The blackberry shakes were awesome, and I don't even much care for berries. Wildlife was everywhere, and I saw my bears.

My last day in the park is short miles. I am hoping for one last blackberry shake and burger for lunch on my way out of SNP, but the Tom Floyd Wayside is not a wayside restaurant at all, it is a shelter. I am enormously disappointed.

Tom Floyd is a very nice shelter; something I am beginning to realize is standard for the Potomac Appalachian Trail Club (PATC). It has a big deck built in front, with benches and a picnic table. There are a couple of section hikers here camping out for the day, just trying to dry out. They have their gear hanging everywhere, and get up to start moving it aside, but there really is plenty of room and I tell them not to bother.

Immediately upon leaving SNP the quality of the trail falls off. It isn't a bad trail, but it just isn't the nice, graded, rock free, clearly defined walking path that they have in the Park. There are rocks again, iffy spots, and sections that are less well marked.

I have a nasty fall on some wet rocks. I start sliding, try to stop, but I build up momentum until I finally smack down on the ground. It hurts, and I spend a minute lying there on the ground doing a check for broken bits before getting up, fixing my pack, and moving forward again.

The last stretch into town follows a fence line. On one side there is a pasture overgrown with berries, and on the other there is a treeline backing on a sub-division's back yards. There are big piles of bear poop. A bench is placed along the trail, with an advertisement for an upcoming hostel on a nearby signboard, The Cabbin, (not a misspelling).

The Cabbin is built in the old slave quarters of an antebellum manor house now under restoration. The owners plan to turn the larger historic structure into a bigger bed and breakfast operation. I like history, and I want to see this place. It is only 200 yards off of the trail. Unfortunately, when I get there the 6-8 bunks they have are all full.

I join an informal tour of the historically correct manor restoration, and it is fascinating. The building was used as a field hospital during the Civil War, and Robert E. Lee himself camped on the grounds during the Confederate retreat from the battle of Gettysburg. The owners found a journal kept by a young girl who lived here during the Civil War period, and share her story of how day to day life unfolded at the house. They are painstakingly restoring the building. It is on the National Register of Historic Places, and their challenge is providing modern conveniences and making the structure handicap accessible without destroying the building's historic construction.

I really want to stay here at this place, and I want a zero day to get a new phone. I have finally accepted that my old iPhone that was washed out on the Tinker Cliffs is done for. It is time for me to bite the bullet and buy a new iPhone. There is a Verizon store in Front Royal.

I make reservations at the Cabbin for tomorrow night. I call around Front Royal on my temporary phone to find a place for tonight, and find the cheapest option is not cheap. It is a Comfort Inn at $62.00 a night. I have been on-trail seven days, need resupply, and I make the reservation. One of the guests at the Cabbin is a section hiker down from Canada, and he gives me a ride the 10 miles into the town of Front Royal proper.

The Comfort Inn is a nice place, a lot better than the usual seedy hiker dive. It includes a free breakfast, and is worth the extra money. I eat that night at a foodie brewpub place across the street and have a gourmet version of cornbread and chili that has a nice heat to it.

Day 92, July 6th
Front Royal, VA, (The Cabbin), Trail Mile 969.4
Daily Distance 0.0 Miles (Zero Day)

I wake up early, eat a lot of the complimentary motel breakfast, and use the hotel's free computer station. The desk people at the motel are talkative, and we end up discussing the old 1960s Western TV shows that they are showing on the lobby TV. I relax there until 8:00 AM when I think businesses are starting to open up for the day.

Front Royal is an ATC designated trail town (they get a special sign), which means it offers support to thru-hikers and other Appalachian Trail users. The town is a little mixed in practice of its actual reception of hikers. I walk through most of town to get to the Verizon store a mile away. I throw out a thumb but get no rides. Walking on pavement in the hot Virginia sun for an hour is draining, which is a surprise. I thought I was better conditioned. On the trail you are under the canopy, and on nice soft(ish) rocks. I find I would rather hike two miles on the trail than walk one mile in town.

Walking through the town is a pain in the butt. Besides the heat, towns are designed around cars and not pedestrians. Sidewalks come and go, and switch back and forth on sides of the street. I end up walking on the shoulder a lot. This is not particular to Front Royal, but is all of America.

The Verizon store has a good iPhone and a new waterproof, shockproof Lifeproof case, lightening my load by a mere $800.00, my single most expensive gear purchase on the trail. I make my purchase and walk back to the motel. I get a delayed checkout time so I can look around town. I want to get a haircut, and buy new Sawyer squeeze bags for my water filter. The bags are plastic bladders that I fill with raw the water to squeeze through the Sawyer filter into drinking bottles. My latest set of squeeze bags have burst, again, a chronic problem with the Sawyer Mini.

I get a cold reception in town. I look like a thru-hiker in my ragged hiking clothes, or a bum. I clearly don't belong to this town, nor am I a visitor from the city. I stop at the Front Royal visitor center to find out where I can find a barber, which turns out to be nowhere in downtown on a Monday, in a tourist town on a holiday. The information desk person is rather aloof, and answers questions reluctantly. I try going to the barbers I am directed to without success. The small town tradition in the South is that mom and pop business are closed Sunday and Monday. There are barbers in town, but none are open today. I am told there is one that might be open up by a supermarket strip mall a half mile away.

I go to the post office to mail my old phone home, with hopes that the phone tech savants at home can rescue the data and photos on it. The postal clerk is another person who appears reluctant to speak to and serve a thru-hiker. I try the outfitter next.

The outfitter is geared towards local hunters and fisherman, not backpackers. I get more cold looks and no attention from the people working at the store. When I ask about Sawyer bags I get a brusque answer; they don't carry them. I poke around and the store and workers eye me like I am a potential shoplifter. My pants have a lot of rips and tears in them, and I am looking for replacements. I find a suitable pair and bring them to the counter. The staff lightens up a little when I produce money and make a purchase, but overall it is an unpleasant experience. Again I get a sense of how the homeless are treated when they enter public places and businesses.

I check out of the hotel and walk up the road to the supermarket, stopping at the other (closed) barbershop on the way. I eat at a local diner, again being treated with barely civil politeness. At the intersection a man in a pickup truck offers me a ride out to the trail, but I still have shopping to do. It illustrates the split in town between the friendly and the unfriendly, reminding me there are plenty of good people in town too.

The supermarket is a big one, and I find all of my favorite trail treats. I get a cab for $10.00 back out to the Cabbin hostel.

The Cabbin, the old slave quarters to the antebellum manor, has its own individual history. It predates the manor, originally built as a courthouse in the 1700s, and became the slave quarters later in its history. It is a small building, but surprisingly airy and beautiful on the inside.

The hikers in residence are a mix of section and thru-hikers, including a SoBo lasher calling she Flamethrower. We have a talk session with the couple who own the property in the evening. The husband half of the hostel owners was a thru-hiker himself, and we share our trail name. He was also Possible, and also named by his daughter. As much as I am a disappointed to share what I thought was a unique name, there is a kinship there. I bring up the barely concealed hostility I was feeling from people in the town, thinking it might just be me.

It is not me. The Cabbin is actually a Bed and Breakfast because the town fought against having a hiker hostel. The owners are trying to bring the town around, showing the economic benefit that comes from being trail friendly. Some people are receptive, and some are not. There is a segment of the town population that has an old, isolated mountain town distrust of outsiders, and the highly mobile and free living thru-hiker population represents everything they fear.

There is a really big black bear in the area and it has come onto the grounds. The other Possible has a small office set up in the manor being restored, and has had run-ins with the bear. He tells a tale of working late one night and hearing something outside. The sound was really loud, a crazy kind of moaning and groaning. The Manor didn't have electric outside at the time due to the construction, so he went outside to check wearing his hiking headlamp.

Possible advanced slowly into the yard, and the groaning ceased. He took a few more exploratory paces into the yard and he found a pair of widely spaced red eyes reflecting his headlamp light back at him. He had immediate second thoughts about being outside, alone, at that moment, and slowly retreated back into the house. A few minutes later the moaning and groaning started again. After a half hour or so it ceased. In the morning, Possible went out to check the ground in daylight, and found some large bear tracks, and a great mountain of bear fecal matter. The moaning was a constipated bear!

Tonight I sleep with History.

Day 93 to Day 96, July 7 to July 10
Front Royal VA to Harpers Ferry, WV, Trail Mile 969.4 to 1022.8, 53.4 miles
AVG 13.35 Daily Miles

Day 93, July 7th
Dicks Dome Shelter, Trail Mile 984.6
Daily Distance 15.2 Miles

The Cabbin serves breakfast to stay within the rules and function of a bed and breakfast. It is a good, hot breakfast, served early. I have French toast and yogurt, a perfect hiker meal, light enough to roll on, with substantial nutrition and protein.

I heard from Baltimore Jack that there was a copperhead snake nest beneath Manassas Gap Shelter, and it is a common belief. The shelter is on the next trail leg, and a subject of conversation among the hikers eating breakfast. Scott, the Cabbin Possible, told us he knew the trail maintainer who was responsible for that section of trail and assured us there was no nest of vipers beneath the floorboards. I still think I will skip that shelter if I can.

Leaving the Cabbin is a little slow, as such things usually are, and I don't get hiking until 10:00 AM. Flamethrower is taking a zero day here and is stretched out on a chaise lounge outside with a good book to read. I envy her; it seems a fine way to spend a day.

The hike into the woods travels through a couple of large stands of old growth tulipwood trees. They have tall, straight trunks rising up a hundred feet or more before the branches spread into a canopy. The trees have a wide, distinctive leaf that is easy to recognize, and produce a tulip-like flower.

It is Virginia summer; hot, humid, damp, muggy, and buggy. The ascents are not difficult, rather gentle, but there are wet, slippery rocks so I watch each step. There is a stream crossing close to the trailhead, and I find Sublime naked and soaking in a pool close by the trail.

Sublime is an older French-Canadian hiker. He thru-hiked the Appalachian Trail back in the 1970s, and has also thru-hiked the PCT. Now he is back. Second time thru-hikers seem to have a better time if it. They know when and where to relax and enjoy themselves, and since they have already done the whole hike, if they miss a bit here and there, it is of no concern to them. It is a no-pressure hike.

On the hike out of Front Royal the trail runs alongside the fence for the Smithsonian's rare animal enclave, where they give animals a break from the zoo, and attempt to breed the rarer species. After some encounters with tourists on the trail I can imagine just how stressful being stared at through bars each day might be, and how it might put a creature off of romance.

Looking at the fencing I wonder exactly what kind of breeding is going on inside. There are places where sections of fence have been breeched by falling tree limbs and I speculate on the possibility of running into an escaped Giraffodile, Hippopotorat or Chimpanaconda. I keep myself amused coming up with unlikely animal pairings as I walk. The only mammal I actually see is a deer, which bolts into the woods as soon as it realizes I am near. The transition from the protected, nearly tame animals of the Shenandoah National Park and the hunted animals outside is immediate. I also see a red bird with black flashes on its wings and a finch type beak. Highlighter tells me later it is probably a tanager.

The section of trail from Front Royal to north of Harpers Ferry was contested bitterly during the Civil War. I will pass near the Antietam and Gettysburg battlefields, and come across many smaller battle and skirmish sites from Stonewall Jackson's Valley Campaign. Today includes passing by Mosby's Camp, where a Confederate raider had his hideout and rally point. The next 30 miles or so of trail are the eastern border of an area called Mosby's Confederacy, so much did he plague United States forces in the area.

I come into camp at Dicks Dome Shelter and find Highlighter, Grip and Redlocks camped nearby. I am pleased to see people from my bubble. Besides letting me know I am keeping pace, it is nice to have familiar faces about.

Day 94, July 8th
Atop Buzzard Hill, Trail Mile 998.4
Daily Distance 13.8 Miles

Today I enter the Roller Coaster, a section of steep hills following one another closely in succession. It is one last taste of 'flat and easy' Virginia to kick me in the butt as I exit the state.

I pass through Sky Meadows State Park. The meadows are wonderful, large, open spaces, and are a nice escape from the damp forest. There are berries growing in profusion in the open spaces, and groups of pickers with buckets are collecting them. My berry knowledge has increased as I hike, and I pick a few choice raspberries and wine berries to snack on as I stroll along.

Highlighter took a fall and bumped her head. I find her sitting on a log, recovering. I follow along behind her until she gets to shelter for a lunch break, just to be sure there is no lasting effect. I enjoy hiking with someone for a while. She seems OK, but it is better not to take chances with a knock on the noggin.

The Roller Coaster proves a real challenge. It has steep, rocky ascents and descents, and it is raining, hard. My pace slows.

I see clothing draped on bushes and hanging on tree branches for a mile-long section. I don't know if someone was lightening their load, or maybe they just went crazy and were running through the woods buck naked. I have already picked up quite a bit of trash on this leg, including a set of broken hiker poles, and I leave the wardrobe for someone else to collect. Who knows, maybe somebody needs a change of clothes or two.

Between two large hills I come to a stream crossing that is normally a couple of hops across on rocks, but the heavy rain has swollen the stream and it is a raging, frothy, muddy torrent. I almost stop there for the day, but I decide I am not going to let a little flash flooding keep me from making miles today. I search upstream and downstream until I find a place where a tree has fallen across the water at a narrow point, and I shimmy across. It takes me close to an hour to overcome the obstacle, but I am very proud of myself in the moment. Go me!

On top of Buzzard Hill, the second big up of the Roller Coaster, I find a cleared space that has been used previously as a campsite. I am concerned about the height of the hill and the potential for lightning strikes, but the biggest part of the day's storms seem to have passed. I set up my little camp, and have gear hanging up in a vain attempt to dry it out, or at least air it out a little. There is still mist and drizzle fogging the mountain.

I didn't seen a spring described in AWOL on the climb, but big streams of rain runoff are crossing the trail everywhere, and I fill and filter some bottles from the readily available water flooding the trail. The rain seems to bring out box turtles and frogs. I see many along the way, especially by these runoff sites.

No one comes up behind me. I am a little worried about Highlighter, but only a nut job (ahem) would cross the flash-flooding stream, so I am pretty sure people are stopping there and camping for the night, waiting for the water to subside. I text McGyver and find out he, Kamikaze, and Thunderfuck are only two days behind me.

The word is out along the trail that Scott Jurek is nearing Katahdin. He is an ultra marathoner trying to break the unofficial speed record for a supported hike. The current record is held by Jennifer Pharr-Davis, who completed her supported thru-hike in 46 days, 11 hours and 20 minutes, heading SoBo, arguably a more difficult feat.

Scott Jurek is headed NoBo, and he is 42 days into his hike. He is being cheered on by many thru-hikers. He passed through most of the NoBo bubble a couple of weeks ago. He was very approachable and friendly, stopping to talk to and take pictures with thru-hikers along the way. Rhino, who is exceptionally fit, ran with him for 8 miles while carrying his heavy pack. He says he thinks Scott slowed a bit so he could keep pace. People also saw Jennifer Pharr Davis section hiking down south, and at Trail Days. Real life legends of the trail walk among us.

It is 30 miles to Harpers Ferry, an important waypoint on the trail. It is the spiritual, but not the actual physical halfway point on the Appalachian Trail. It is also in West Virginia, the first new state in over 500 miles.

Day 95, July 9th
Blackburn AT Center, Trail Mile 1010.9
Daily Distance 12.5 Miles

TRAILTALK:

FOUR STATE CHALLENGE: From the border of Virginia it is 42 miles through West Virginia and Maryland to the Pennsylvania border. Hikers can attempt to hike the distance in a single 24 hour period in an unofficial personal endurance event called the Four State Challenge.

The Roller Coaster continues to put the hurt on me. It is another rainy day. It also rained in the night atop Buzzards Hill, and I had a scary night listening to the thunder rumble hoping I wouldn't catch a mountaintop lightening bolt. I spend time in the morning trying to get the majority of water out of my gear by wiping it down with my little Lightload towel and wringing it out, repeatedly.

I go up and down the rocky hills, at a bare one mile an hour pace. Near the Roller Coaster's end there is a hostel right off of the trail called the Bear's Den. It is operated by the PATC. The hostel was a rich man's summer home in the mountains from back around the turn of the last century. It is built to look like a castle. I stop in hoping to find some food, but I am out of luck. I settle for a Coke, a trash drop, and a phone charge up, and enjoy just being inside out of the wet weather for an hour. It is still mid afternoon, too early for me to stop for the night.

I pass the 1000 mile mark. I have walked 1000 miles, an odyssey in its own right, and I am still less than halfway to Mount Katahdin. I am making serious progress though, and I also, finally, get out of Virginia.

The Appalachian Trail is only in West Virginia for a few miles, and there is an unofficial hiker event called the Four State Challenge. The goal is to hike from the Virginia state line across the narrow bits of West Virginia and Maryland into Pennsylvania in a single 24 hour period, a distance of 42 miles. It is an easy piece of trail, generally level and smooth, but it is still a big undertaking. I already know it is outside of how hard I am willing to push myself.

The wildlife is out. I see a black snake and a really big, ugly beetle, as big as a crabapple. I have been under assault by flies, gnats and mosquitoes all day. I have hosed down my hair with insect repellent, as well as spraying it on a chili pepper bandana my daughter gave me that I wear around my neck, and sometimes pull up over my ears. None of it works, and I feel especially merciful when I spare the big beetle's life, since its kin show me none.

I am struggling to make progress today. I crash from hunger at one point after pushing for three hours without stopping. I can feel the difference in my performance after I eat a snack. I was really dragging and out of energy.

I stay at the Blackburn AT Center for the night. It is another PATC site. There is a main house they use for meetings and community events, and a caretaker lives in it. A small, separate bunkhouse serves as a shelter for backpackers coming through, and there is a solar shower and tap water. You can chill out on the screened-in porch of the main house, which has comfortable furniture and some games and books. It is a free site.

I get in after 8:00 PM, so having everything set up is very welcome. There are several section hikers present. The little cabin is almost full, and Redlocks has his hammock strung up nearby. I just throw down my sleeping bag on a bunk, cook dinner, and go to sleep, blessedly dry.

Day 96, July 10th
Harpers Ferry WV, Trail Mile 1022.8
Daily Distance 11.9 Miles

It is another late morning start hiking out of the PATC Blackburn Center. I meet the caretaker, a pleasant man in his 70s, and find out he is the famous, or infamous, Trailboss. He leads the crew of trail maintainers who built the Roller Coaster. I suspected him of going out at night to secretly add more rocks and hazards to the trail.

I ask Trailboss why he chose to build such a difficult route. It turns out that in the 1980s this section of the trail was still following a road. In fact, back in the 1970s, over 600 miles of the Appalachian Trail was still on roads, and it was a sustained effort by the USFS and the various trail clubs to get it all into the woods. Now there are only a few road miles where the trail passes through a town or goes on a bridge over a major river. The Roller Coaster was one of the last sections to be brought off the road. The ATC and USFS got a federally recognized continuous right of way for the AT four years earlier, but still have to be respectful of the various state, federal and private lands the trail passes through.

The patch of forest leading into Harpers Ferry is rough, and the Roller Coaster makes the best of it. Because it is a hilly, rocky section it is difficult to maintain. Trailboss is still out there with his crews doing a lot of work, not adding rocks to the trail.

I am eager to get into Harpers Ferry today, and I push myself hard. The profile is level, but it is rocky and I am not able to make fast miles. Water is also scarce, but I get lucky. A trail angel left water jugs at a road crossing six miles away from town. I am so incredibly happy to see those jugs; I was trying to figure out how to ration my last few sips of water over the intervening distance, and was preparing myself for suffering. Some unknown angel made my day.

The trail makes switchbacks on the descent into Harpers Ferry, crossing over the siege lines and defensive works for one of the many Civil War battles fought over the town. The switchback trail is rocky and cants slightly downhill, making it treacherous; I have a nasty fall and roll my ankle.

I limp into Harpers Ferry at 3:50 PM. The Appalachian Trail Conservancy headquarters is in town, and most hikers will register and get a photo here, as well as picking up information about Harpers Ferry and the trail ahead. I feared it would close at 4:00 PM, and it was a good half mile from the trail itself. I pick up my pace into a shambling jog through town, but still arrive just a little after the four 4:00 PM deadline I have on my head.

The ATC is open until 5:00 PM; I have plenty of time. There are tourists everywhere and a good crowd of thru-hikers as well. I register as NoBo Thru-hiker number 1200 for the year 2015, and have my picture taken in front of the building to put in the journal the ATC keeps.

Harpers Ferry is the symbolic halfway point of the Appalachian Trail. The true halfway point has migrated over the years as the trail has been rerouted and extended and it now lies a hundred miles to the north. Harpers Ferry is still where most people choose to flip-flop if they feel they need it. Baxter State Park in Maine closes to overnight camping on October 15th. Katahdin can be day hiked, depending on weather conditions, which are generally pretty bad by then. The rule of thumb is that the average thru-hiker needs to be in Harpers Ferry by July 15th in order to make Katahdin by October 15th. If you are in doubt, you can work out rides north from Harpers Ferry to Katahdin, and start hiking south, doing a flip-flop hike.

The ATC HQ is a nice place. Harpers Ferry, despite its significance to the thru-hiker community, barely seems to recognize our presence. It is a huge tourist destination, especially for weekend visits. There are rafting and float trips on the two rivers that join here (including the take-out for the aqua blazers from Waynesboro on the Shenandoah River), bike paths along old canals, and a large number of Civil War and Civil Rights historical sites within the town. Its popularity as a tourist destination makes it a very expensive place.

Rabbit and Coyote are sitting out in front of the ATC Center with me when the place closes. We are trying to come up with our plans for the night. I am calling hostels, which are all both high priced and booked full. There is a hostel outside of town, but taxi costs are extortionate, and we are all trying to figure out options. I finally decide to break down and pay $100.00 to stay at the Econolodge for the night.

Highlighter is at the Econolodge as well, sharing a room. She is worried about her feet. She has bad blisters, as well as recovering from a few bad sprains and turns. She has a hostel stay set up for tomorrow over the Potomac River in Maryland, where prices are much lower, but this was a far as she could get today on her damaged feet.

We share a delivery order from a pizza place. The Econolodge is expensive, but it is a modern motel with all the conveniences, and the management and staff treat the dirty groups of thru-hikers in their establishment like valued customers.

WEST VIRGINIA, MARYLAND, and PENNSYLVANIA

Days 97 to 116, July 11th to July 30th
Harpers Ferry WV to Delaware Water Gap, PA, Trail Miles 1022.8 to 1293.4 270.6 Miles, 20 Days,
AVG 13.52 Daily Miles

Day 97 to105, July 11 to July 17th
Harpers Ferry, WV to Boiling Springs PA, Trail Mile 1022.8 to1121.3, 98.5miles, AVG 14.07 Daily Miles

Day 97, July 11th
Crampton Gap Shelter, Trail Mile 1033.8
Daily Distance 11.0 Miles

TRAILTALK

ATKO: The Appalachian Trail Kick Off, a preparatory event for thru-hiking the AT held at Amicalola Falls every year at the beginning of hiking season. It is a seminar, a gear exhibition, and all things Appalachian Trail

I leave Harpers Ferry at 2:00 PM. I spend an hour in the morning wandering around the town trying to get a haircut, and find only high end, expensive, hair salons requiring appointments. I return to the Econolodge still shaggy, pack up, and head back to the trail.

In Harpers Ferry the Appalachian Trail goes through the historical district. I am one of those people who cannot pass by an historical marker, and I get bogged down reading plaques, looking at buildings, and going into little museums about the Civil War and Black History.

Resupply is from a little store catering to bicycle riders and day hikers, and very expensive. It is insufficient, and I end up going to two more places to get enough food and fuel for four more days on the trail, going to a hostel with a resupply area and a general store outfitter. Going from place to place I lose track of what I need, and I forget to pick up new batteries for my headlamp.

I meet Highlighter at the bridge crossing the Potomac River, heading for her hostel in Maryland. She wants to give her feet a chance to heal, and then decide if she is going to continue NoBo, jump to Katahdin and flip-flop, or put off her finish for another year.

Highlighter has tough choices. Once you make the emotional commitment to hike the Appalachian Trail the inclination is to keep going. There is a sense of defeat switching to a flip-flop, as though you didn't have the mustard to get it done going one way. If you are worried about the Katahdin closure date and are struggling it is the wise choice, as the time pressure is removed from your hike. I have considered the flip-flop myself, but I am determined to make this an all the way, one direction, continuous hike.

Highlighter studied and prepared for her hike with great intensity. She is an obsessive planner. Every year there is a thru-hiking seminar at Amicalola Falls prior to the beginning of thru-hiking season in March, called the Appalachian Trail Kick Off and many people planning on making the hike for the year attend. Highlighter went, and showed up with her AWOL Guide already highlighted, annotated and color coded. David Miller, the AWOL Guide man himself, bestowed her trail name on her.

The trail leaving Harpers Ferry crosses the Potomac River and passes into Maryland. The entire West Virginia portion of the trail is only about 5 miles long. The trail follows a canal towpath paralleling the Potomac River away from the bridge for 3 miles, and Highlighter and I hike together.

Where the trail leaves the towpath to head back up into the hills it crosses a road. A motorcycle accident occurred on the road a few minutes before we arrive and we are pulled into the scene.

The rider misjudged a turn and went down at a slow speed. He is older and is having trouble getting up. A woman with a medical background has called 911 and is giving assistance. We offer help, but the rider isn't seriously injured as far as anyone can tell. He is stunned and maybe has a broken rib or two. The responder keeps him from moving about until an ambulance arrives. The paramedics slide him onto a litter and take him away.

Highlighter gets a ride to the hostel from the Good Samaritan at the scene, two good deeds in one day for that woman. I follow the trail away and climb out of the river valley. It is very hot, and I drink too much of my water climbing up the first hills. A day hiker coming the other way tells me water is scarce for the next 7 miles ahead. He turns trail angel on me, and refills my water bottles from his own supply, allowing me to skip the water at the Ed Garvey Shelter and make it to Crampton Gap Shelter without a delay.

In the distance between the two shelters there is a small state park with open fields and an enormous, and somewhat overstated monument to War Correspondents. It is a big, garish castle looking thing with statues of horses heads and a naked boy Mercury on it, looking very out if place sitting in a meadow surrounded by trees.

I walk through another Civil War battle site, and again I wander around reading the signs and looking at the little monuments, slowing my progress up the trail.

I arrive at Crampton Gap Shelter near dusk. I am committed to the shelter because I need the water source. I set up camp using the light of my tablet, since I neglected to pick up batteries in Harpers Ferry. The mosquitoes find the tablet light extremely attractive, and convince me to set up my hammock with its bug net rather than sleeping unprotected in the shelter. Before I finally go to sleep I chase down and dispatch a couple of stray mosquitoes that manage to get inside the bug net.

It was them or me.

Day 98, July 12th
Annapolis Rocks, Trail Mile 1047.9
Daily Distance 14.1 Miles

Today Scott Jurek set the men's (supported) Appalachian Trail speed record, 46 days, 8 hours, and 7 minutes, from May 27 to July 12, 2015 (Georgia to Maine).

Jennifer Pharr-Davis the former record holder, still retains the women's AT speed record, 46 days, 11hours, and 20 minutes (supported), from June 15 to July 31, 2011 (Maine to Georgia).

I wanted to crank through Maryland. This is part of the Four State Challenge some thru-hikers complete in a single 24 hour period. I am thinking it should be easy enough to knock off the challenge section in three, or even two days. The trail is accommodating; it follows a low ridgeline with small ups and downs. It is wide and smooth, and there are few rocky patches.

I slow my roll in order to have a fabulous brunch at the South Mountain Inn, just 500 yards off of the trail. It is fairly quiet here, just me and mounds of eggs, biscuits, bacon, fruit, French toast, pancakes, and other good things. It is a very nice restaurant in an old colonial style building. The buffet is more expensive than a thru-hiker's normal budget allows, but the quality of the food, and of course the quantity, are well worth it.

It is an elegant establishment, and I am slightly uncomfortable sitting there in my smelly, dirty hiker clothes, but I end up in a couple of conversations about thru-hiking with some of the other patrons, and I relax.

There are more battle sites to explore along the way, and I visit the 'original' Washington Monument. In 1827, long before they built the obelisk on the Mall in Washington DC, a local community here in Maryland celebrated Independence Day by gathering together and erecting a stone tower on a nearby mountain. It ultimately took several months to construct; the townspeople started it on the holiday and then made a continual, cooperative effort to complete it in the fall, after harvest.

The monument is a squat tower 4 stories tall. It is closed when I view it. A thunderstorm caught several thru-hikers on the mountain about a month prior, and they took refuge within the monument. Their refuge turned into a trap when the Washington Monument was itself struck by lightning with the hikers inside, and one of them was injured. The monument is now closed for repairs, and one expects new lightning rods and grounding will be installed. It is going to go on a long list of needs for recreational funding, and it may be a while before anyone gets up on top again. It looks like there was quite a view from up there.

I see a dead Luna moth lying on the trail. Luna moths are huge, and this one is 6 inches across, a luminescent silvery blue in color, and it has a graceful, exotic appearance, with curling wings and antenna. I have seen some creepy alien looking beetles and such, from places dark and unpleasant, but the Luna moth looks like it is from a magical fairy world rather than Earth. Night hikers sometimes see them on the wing.

This is still PATC country, and the shelters are well built and nicely maintained. You are required to stay in the shelters or at official campsites over the short stretch of trail in Maryland. Since these sites also coincide with the only water sources along this stretch, I find it no hardship.

I swapped out my Sawyer Mini for a full sized Sawyer filter in Harpers Ferry. I ordered it in Front Royal from Amazon and had it shipped as a mail drop to the ATC HQ. It has significantly cut down on the time it takes for me to filter water, now my water stops are taking 15 minutes now instead of half an hour. That is time for another mile of trail each day.

Annapolis Rocks has both a shelter and a camping area. The rocks themselves are a big west facing ledge atop the ridgeline affording sweeping views of the surrounding countryside. The Antietam battlefield is out there somewhere close and the rocks are an excellent sunset and star viewing point. I am opting to hang my hammock again to get the inside the bug net and away from the relentless mosquitoes and gnats. I stop earlier than usual today because I forgot to buy headlamp batteries in Harpers Ferry, and I don't like trying to set up in the dark.

Based on techniques used by other thru-hikers I thought about making my one hot meal each day at lunch. I prefer a hot supper, having my hot meal at the end of the day allows me to hydrate and restore salts before sleeping, and I think this is important,

My early stop today allows me to go about my camp chores in a leisurely manner. I soak my feet in the ice cold spring and it numbs the pain of the daily twists, turns and rock pounding.

There is a maze of tape blocking some areas of the campsite, protecting them for reforestation, and somehow on the way back from the spring to my hammock I get lost on the wrong side of the tape. There is a ridge runner named Bob minding the site and he is walking the trail I am looking for, and redirects me back onto the proper path. The path is obvious when you are standing on it, but nearly invisible from ten feet away. I feel pretty embarrassed, I am stomping about in a fragile area just a few paces from the approved corridor. Bob is pretty understanding.

Everyone staying at the site gathers on the rocks to watch the sunset. There are some overnighters, section hikers, and thru-hikers. Some of the thru-hikers are in the middle of the Four State Challenge and took a nap during the heat of the day. They will night hike the rest of the way into Pennsylvania. Overall it is a very nice setting, sitting and watching the sun go down. I make my dinner and eat it on the rocks. Redlocks is here with a little ukulele backpacker bass, and he is picking out tunes.

Day 99, July 13th
Falls Creek Footbridge, PA, Trail Mile 1064.9
Daily Distance 17.0 Miles

Today is one of the rare days I succeed in meeting my daily distance ambitions. I get all the way to Pennsylvania, hiking across four states in three days. It is a hard day, and I hike late into the evening. The last miles of Maryland to the Mason-Dixon Line include a long three mile section of rocky ground, and there is a scramble across High Rocks.

My plan is to get to the Mason-Dixon Line and then hitchhike at a road crossing to get to a nearby Wal-Mart listed in the AWOL Guide for a resupply. I need food, and batteries for my headlamp. I find the road is remote, and there is no traffic at all. There will be no ride in to get resupply. I stay on the trail. If I stretch what I have I can last another two days.

I may go a little hungry.

I don't see many other hikers while I am on the trail today, just a father and son section hiking together. The father is struggling, and offered me some of his food to cut down on his weight. I should have taken him up on it, but I was counting on the Wal-Mart.

I hike alone all day, but when I get to the campsite there are a number of hikers here and more come in behind me. It is one of the curiosities of the trail. There are always people on it, but everyone is moving at similar paces, and don't overlap. I can feel very isolated.

Flying insects of every kind are ever present. The mosquitoes, gnats, flies and bees are a constant nuisance, and can induce craziness. I have run down sections of the trail wind milling my hands about trying to break free of persistent patches.

The bugs aren't quite bad enough to hike with the head net on, but I am covered in insect repellent. I try to apply it to my bandana and clothes rather than directly to my skin, but when I get annoyed enough I hose everything down. I don't think any of it is working particularly well.

The campsite here is unofficial, but well used. It is at the end of the Four State Challenge, on the edge of Pennsylvania, and people finishing the challenge drop here after completing the forty-two miles. As the hikers come in they are greeted with cheers and applause by the small group accumulating here for the night.

My feet and legs are in pain. The high mileage days hurt more. It is hard to describe how legs stop functioning properly when they stop moving on a little rest, or how aches and pains travel around my feet as I walk. There is a constant overall ache punctuated with feelings like someone is randomly sticking a knife blade onto parts of my arch and heel. Some parts of my toes and feet have gone totally numb, nothing there but pins and needles. It will take several months after completing the thru-hike before I will feel my feet fully again.

I soak my feet in the icy water of springs and the cool water of streams each time I stop to fill my bottles, and it helps for a little while. All of the older hikers talk about the foot pain, but I don't hear it from the younger hikers. I wonder if it is a function of age, or are the young ones just better at sucking it up?

I pass a momma turkey and her brood on the trail today, the first gobblers I have seen since the very first day driving up to Nimblewill Gap on Springer's approach. They are skittish and flee into the underbrush before I can get a picture.

Day 100, July 14th
Near Hermitage Cabin, Trail Mile 1072.6
Daily Distance 6.7 Miles

I am beset by thunder and lightning storms throughout the night. My hammock hang isn't great, and water collects in a sag in my rain fly. The additional weight and wet ropes let my hammock to droop low enough for my rear to end up in a giant puddle that forms beneath my hammock. I have to get out of my hammock in the rain and tighten up the ropes. I set my shoes directly under the lowest sag of my hammock in an attempt to support my fundament and keep it out of the water. The rain passes, and my body heat helps dry my bag out so it is merely damp when I put it away in the morning.

The storm defeats rest and I rise early. I hike two miles before coming to a crossroad and hitching into the town of South Mountain, Pennsylvania. My thumb gets me a ride in 10 minutes from a man in a car filled with Franciscan tracts. I am not particularly religious, and I am always a little cautious when a car pulls over covered with religious bumper stickers. I suspect that someone is going to spend the ride hard selling me on their particular flavor of faith, but not a word is said about religion on my ride. It doesn't happen any time I am on the trail, and I am picked up by overt Christians many times.

My Christian drops me at the town's Wal-Mart center and I stop in at the attached Subway sandwich shop. I get 'the look' when I come in, and I am treated with disdain. Again, I gain a far better understanding of some of the day to day logistical and emotional issues homeless people have to face as a result of my experiences thru-hiking.

There is a bumper sticker out there for 'Hiker Trash', long distance hikers self-identifying themselves and how we appear, and are sometimes treated in towns. Some hikers will go out of their way to be obnoxious about it, and force their stinky, dirty selves into situations where they have to be acknowledged.

I ask the manager if I can plug in my phone while I eat by one of the wall outlets, and I am refused. The manager sits at a nearby table and I watch her conduct job interviews during my meal. I don't think she would have offered me a position.

I complete my resupply and catch another quick ride back out to the trailhead. I hike another four and a half miles and pick a camping spot near the Hermitage Cabin and its ready water supply for the night. Kamikaze shows up, and her hammock hangs near mine.

Day 101, July 15th
Past a Woods Road, Trail Mile 1087.6
Daily Distance 15.0 Miles

Kamikaze and I are hiking together today. She is hiking a little slower than I remembered, or perhaps I am faster. She bought new shoes and there is a question as to whether she is breaking them in, or are they just breaking her. She took a side trip into Baltimore to visit friends, and they filled her pack with little food luxuries that have increased her pack weight to upwards of 45 pounds. I slow my pace a little to stay with her, and the miles go by faster with company.

Kamikaze still is a driven hiker, continuing the McGyver dubbed 'Death March', and she is making good miles. I am only paced with her because she went off-trail for a week to a wedding and now also her side trip into Baltimore. Hiking with her is a guarantee of making miles, since she pushes so hard. Kamikaze is determined to regain her trail family, still a week ahead of us. I learn all the trail gossip from her. McGyver and Olaf are a day behind us.

We pass by a couple of shelters. We are still in PATC territory, and their shelter maintainers are inspired. There is an informal contest between the various shelter 'owners' to see who can make their shelter the best. The maintainers visit regularly, the shelters are exceptionally clean, and have all kinds of thoughtful little touches. I have seen hanging plants, weather stations, clotheslines, eating pavilions, graveled paths, and sculpture gardens. Care extends to the privies, which are cleaner, decorated, and have the good toilet paper provided.

We start seeing some of the rocks Pennsylvania is famous for on a small scale, and there are some steeps, so it is work, but our biggest up today is only 1000 feet, and the trails are well maintained. There are a few stretches where it is a stroll rather than a hike.

A lot of people live nearby. It isn't the city, or even the suburbs, but it is a heavily populated rural area. There are roads, cars and buildings close to the Appalachian Trail, and we cross several old rail beds. I haven't seen a lot of wildlife besides a large paper wasp nest hanging from a tree branch just off of the trail. We take advantage of the frequent brushes with civilization to get burgers and ice cream for a late lunch at the Caledonia State Park snack bar.

Water sources are fairly regular along this stretch, and we are well fed. We hike until close to dark, and camp near a woods road crossing. The woods roads crisscross the forest the whole length of the trail. They are old logging and forest roads. Some exist as traces from when the area was still farmland a hundred years ago. The roads provide vehicle, horse and bicycle access into the Appalachian forest, and many of them are marked in the AWOL Guide. Many of them also are not marked, creating difficulties when I cross two or three and I am trying to determine my location using the roads as landmarks.

Day 102, July 16th
Past Pine Grove Furnace, Trail Mile 1104.0
Daily Distance 16.4 Miles

The cold gets me out of the hammock this morning. The night is chilly for mid July in Pennsylvania. Temperatures are in the 60s or low 70s. We have a really nice campsite. It is spacious, clean, bug free, and there were logs scattered around perfect for sitting on. I am still hiking with Kamikaze and enjoying the company. She is one of the many petroleum engineers, geologists, seismologists, and roughnecks laid off from the exploration side of the oil industry that are on the trail right now.

It is easy hiking today, small climbs with some dirt and rock patches mixed in for variety. We don't get to Pine Grove Furnace State Park (PGFSP) until late afternoon. The state park was once the official physical half way point for the Appalachian Trail, but the trail has shifted so many times the real halfway point is approaching notional. There are three or four different small monuments and markers at nearby locations along the trail based on where different halfway points were established over the years.

PGFSP is a small place, but it has three major items of interest. The first is the Appalachian Trail museum, which is already closed when we arrive. The museum has all sorts of trail memorabilia, including an old Katahdin summit sign. It is supposed to be worth seeing, but I miss it. Someday…

Pine Grove Furnace has a wonderful hostel that serves thru-hikers. It is an old historic building that once belonged to the local owner of the furnace called the Ironmaster's Mansion. Unfortunately when Kamikaze and I arrive it is booked for a PATC conference, we have hit upon the only night of the season it is not open to thru-hikers. Today we will have to push on.

First we have to honor another thru-hiker tradition. There is a general store and grill next to the hostel that is famous for the Half-Gallon Ice Cream Challenge. The half-gallon challenge celebrates the halfway point on the trail by a tribute to thru-hiker's ravenous appetites. We are close to Hershey, PA, and the challenge is to eat a half-gallon of ice cream in one hour. It is a marketing ploy that sells a lot of Hershey's ice cream. The prize is a little wooden ice cream spoon stamped 'Pine Grove Furnace Half-Gallon Ice Cream Challenge'. Mine is one of my proudest possessions.

A couple of thru-hikers are indulging in the challenge when we arrive. Rhino is on his way out, after finishing his half-gallon in 40 minutes. His advice to me is to let the ice cream melt a little to ease spooning it up and digesting it, as well as avoiding brain freeze. Rocking Ronnie and Pippin are also here. Ronnie has finished all of his ice cream and is stealing more from Pippin, who is struggling to eat her first quart and a half.

Kamikaze gets a small bowl of ice cream and a burger. The burger looks and smells marvelous. I go for the whole half-gallon challenge, which is a quart and a half container of ice cream, and an additional pint. Ice cream doesn't sell in real half-gallon cartons anymore. It takes me 30 minutes to earn my spoon, and I get two of the delicious burgers afterwards, one for immediate consumption and one to eat at camp.

The burgers are a third of pound hand pressed patties on Cibatta bread, and they are a better treat than the ice cream. We are entering the Mid-Atlantic States, where they take food seriously, and even out here in the boonies food is made to individual order, and to a high standard.

On the way out of PGFSP we pass a pond with a beach and swimming area, with a public changing room that includes showers. Kamikaze and I take the opportunity for long showers. I wear my clothes right into the shower. They are already soaked through with sweat, and I strip down and rinse the clothes as I clean myself. I have to put wet clothes on after, but they are cleaner wet clothes, and the hiker miracle fibers that everything is made out of dry quickly in the heat.

We are entering a section of the AT known as Rattlesnake Alley. The alley runs up to the Delaware Water Gap from PGFSP. We have been warned about this section and its big population of vipers. Many people have already had venomous snake encounters, since there are rattlesnakes and copperheads inhabiting every state on trail except Maine. In Rattlesnake Alley, seeing a rattler changes from a possibility to a probability. We see another black snake today, but no vipers. Eyes and ears are open, and I am leading with my poles, just in case.

Kami and I push up a hill a mile coming out of PGFSP before picking an open patch of woods as a campsite near the top of the hill. The trail follows a woods road and is well graded, but the half-gallon of ice cream is now challenging my digestive system, and the hike is a bit rougher than it should have been. The campsite we pick has plenty of room, and the brothers Chef and Waldo come in and pitch tents near our hammock hangs. (There are two other hikers, unrelated, named Chef and Waldo on the trail this year, and I will spend time with them as well).

When we set up our bear bags I find that I have carried a rock in my pack all day. When I put up my bear bag for the night, I put a rock in a small dry bag, clip my hang line onto it with a carabiner, toss the weight over a branch, then take off the bag and clip on my food bag to hoist it up into the air. I forgot to take the rock out of the small bag last night after making my toss, put it in my pack and carried it forward. Talk about useless weight, an extra pound of rock in my pack. Kami gets a laugh.

The bugs are relatively quiet, and except for the ice cream churning away in my digestive tract it is a peaceful night. I finish my second delicious burger for dinner.

Day 103, July 17th
Boiling Springs, PA (The Allenberry Resort), Trail Mile 1121.3
Daily Distance 17.3 Miles

Kamikaze is pushing me along. Her pace is steadier than mine. She keeps moving, starting early and ending late, and I am making miles staying up with her. She likes to pick up speed during the last couple of hours of daylight, a time when I am typically flagging, so she really is making me hike harder.

Today our goal is Boiling Springs PA. We have a series of five hills to conquer, a mini roller coaster that puts work into the day. The last miles are across a valley floor, through flat cornfields. You would think cornfields are easy, but it is so much hotter out in the open than it is under the canopy that we may be going slower over the flatter ground. There is very little water along the way, and we plan the day's hike and breaks around available water sources. This will be a repeated pattern all the way through the Mid-Atlantic States. The low hills retain less water.

Both of us are suffering and in pain from the higher mileage days. Kami's shoes, especially, are giving her a lot of trouble. It has been seven days since I last overnighted in a town.

Boiling Springs is an old resort town, dating back to the old iron making days of the 18th and 19th Centuries in Pennsylvania. Its heyday has passed and it is a quiet place now. The lake containing the boiling springs that the town is named for are in a nice grassy town park, Springs beneath the ponds make the water bubble.

The ATC's Mid-Atlantic office is in town. I have heard they are not especially friendly to thru-hikers, but then many thru-hikers are not especially respectful of town etiquette. The ATC center is closed when we pass by, but there is a water spigot, and the open, furnished, big porch and bulletin board seem friendly enough.

We hike down a road past the Appalachian Trail turn off, a half mile in the heat to reach the Allenberry Resort. Kami and I hobble along the hard, hot asphalt on our broken, aching feet. I imagine I know what walking several miles on live coals feels like.

The Allenberry is a great little resort, with many lodging options, a restaurant and bar, and a live performance theater. They have rooms they offer to thru-hikers at discounted rates even a thru-hiker can afford. Kami and I are told initially no rooms are available, but while we are sitting dejected, contemplating our next move, a double opens up, and we split it. I prefer my own room, but Kami and I have been hiking together long enough we can respect one another's boundaries. And it is the only room.

The Allenberry has a dinner buffet, also discounted for thru-hikers. It is still around $20.00, which is thru-hiker expensive, but it is a fancy buffet with delicacies like prime rib and salmon, well worth the price. We hear about its excellence from other thru-hikers already coming out of the dining hall with swollen bellies, but we have arrived too late to join in. We eat a far more expensive, but wonderful meal in the main restaurant.

Day 104, July 18th
Boiling Springs PA (Allenberry Resort), Trail Mile 1121.3
Daily Distance 0.0 Miles, ZERO DAY

Kamikaze and I have our breakfast as other thru-hikers filter into the main hall of the Allenberry Resort, and we all group together in the big room, sitting at adjacent tables as we eat.

One of the thru-hikers joining us is Olaf. She is making plans to use mass transportation to jump forward past the main rock zone of Pennsylvania. She is on a travel visa from Germany and on a deadline. She is going to have to bounce forward to ensure she gets to see the best of the trail and make Katahdin before her travel visa expires.

The bus system in rural Pennsylvania requires considerable planning for Olaf to find all the connections she needs to get off the Appalachian Trail here and back onto the trail up north.

Kami and I decide to take a zero day at the Allenberry for several reasons. We want to spend some time with Olaf, since this is likely the last time we will see her. Our bodies and feet are throbbing with pain, and need the rest. And we just want to relax and enjoy this fine place.

We enjoy feasting at the buffets, and the other amenities of the resort. We do our laundry, and I check out a fly fishing museum they have in the basement of our lodging building. Some of the exhibits are home fly tying and fly rod building workshops that have been transplanted in their entirety to spaces in the exhibit. There are many famous local tiers and builders, and their contributions to the art of trout fishing are on display.

Some of the exhibits work hard injecting excitement into the sport. Books by local writers are part of the show, and I am particularly interested in a book called "The Ring of the Rise" described as "A Startling and Interesting Look at Trout Behavior" It may not quite be startling, but it is interesting.

"The Ring of the Rise" cites studies on native trout populations and the deleterious effect of introducing hatchery fish to native waters. The native trout have evolved social hierarchies and feeding patterns in the stream environment that are destroyed by the socially backward and inept hatchery fish. Native trout are forced out of existence by flooding the waters with large numbers of ignorant, stocked fish. The hatchery fish are then either caught or die in short order, leaving the entire ecosystem without a permanent trout population. The book presents strong arguments for Catch and Release programs on major streams and rivers.

We catch the matinee showing at the Allenberry's live theater, a professional production of "Damn Yankees". It is an entertaining afternoon. I had not realized until the opening curtain that the show is a musical production, which is not my favorite form of theater. I do learn why Lola always shows up as a seductress in New York Times crossword puzzles. Whatever Lola wants, Lola gets.

It is a very pleasant day and afternoon. There are no more available rooms for thru-hikers and Rhino shows up at the resort. He ends up sharing our room for the night. I also see Pippin, Rocking Ronnie, and Joker.

Day 105 to 111, July 19th to July 25th
Boiling Springs PA to Port Clinton, PA, Trail Mile 1121.3 to1218.8
97.5 miles, AVG 13.92 Daily Miles

Day 105, July 19th
Darlington Shelter, Trail Mile 1135.6
Daily Distance 14.3 Miles

It is a smoking hot day of hiking. Kamikaze and I leave Boiling Springs and travel across a valley floor through 10 miles of cornfields. There are very few water sources and the natural water is carrying the fertilizer and pesticides from the farmland. All the water in this valley, both natural and from spigots, has an unpleasant metallic taste.

The valley has to be crossed in a single hard push from Boiling Springs, as the trail is mostly on private lands and there is no camping allowed anywhere until Darlington Shelter.

We leave Allenberry resort under the threat of rain. Other thru-hikers set out ahead of us, and one of them helped himself to an umbrella from the loaner rack at the resort. The clouds clear up quickly, and Kamikaze and I find the 'borrowed' umbrella left on the side of the trail. Kami is furious, and I am not especially amused, for a couple of reasons. The disrespect for the Allenberry after the fine care it took of us, and then leaving the borrowed item on the trail as trash are both kinds of behaviors I don't want thru-hikers associated with. I pack the umbrella out a few miles to a trailhead and leave it at the registration station, hoping someone will pick it up.

The ATC has a Cumberland Valley office at Conodoguinet Bridge. It provides a much needed spigot, and a privy. The water scarcity crossing the valley in the high summer heat and humidity makes it a must stop point. There are a dozen thru-hikers gathered outside the ATC barn. Some of them are chronic yellow blazers, and they are drinking beer and getting high. I am hoping someone will offer me a cold beer in fellowship, but I am ignored. The yellow blazers have their own fellowship, and I am not included. We have caught the heart of the partying group that follows the last big bubble up the trail, and have stumbled into one of the parties.

The party bubble is going to be a source of trouble. Some of them are just out having a good time, which is all well and good, but a couple of them show little respect for the towns and trail they are passing through, and it creates ill will towards thru-hikers in general. Being behind this group as they hitchhike their way north means I am going to feel the wrath

216

they leave in their wake. They are either better hikers, or hitchhikers, than I am, and I end up stuck behind them for many weeks ahead.

Today I ponder daddy longlegs as we hike. They are everywhere on the trail. They pose no threat, but I wonder what it is they eat, and where they live, and pretty much their whole place in the ecosystem. I hear that they are super venomous, but their fangs are too short and weak to pierce human flesh.

We finally rise out of the baking pan of the Cumberland Valley and onto the next ridgeline. It is only an 800 foot climb up to the shelter, and water, but the heat has drained us. It is not a particularly long distance into Duncannon tomorrow, a famous trail town, but it is rocky, and we are too tuckered to make any extra miles today. We are trying to get to Duncannon before the post office closes. I have a mail drop from home waiting, and Kami and I both need resupply. Boiling Springs didn't have much to offer for shopping opportunities.

Day 106, July 20th
Duncannon, PA Trail Mile 1146.9
Daily Distance 11.3 Miles

Up, fed, packed, and hiking before 8:00 AM, Kamikaze and I arrive in the trail town of Duncannon by 3:00 pm, and I get my package at the post office before it closes at 4:00 PM. The day's hardest section of hiking is the short steep descent into town, which is in the Susquehanna River Valley. The dreaded Pennsylvania rocks begin to appear on the trail. It is manageable, but slowing.

The Appalachian Trail runs right through Duncannon before taking a pedestrian walkway on a long highway bridge crossing the Susquehanna River. The centerpiece of Duncannon for thru-hikers is the Doyle Hotel.

Like the rest of Duncannon, the Doyle has seen better days. It is a 19th Century structure, an old hotel that catered to miners and railroad workers. As the iron mines closed up, so did much of Duncannon, and there are a lot of structures with cheap facades and barely surviving businesses in the old downtown. The Doyle does not appear to have been updated since it was built, except for the addition of a TV in the bar. When it was built it was a model of Victorian elegance. More recently it might have been considered a flophouse, and now it caters to thru-hikers. There are rooms upstairs with worn out beds, high ceilings, and no air conditioning, TVs, or other amenities. There is a rumor that they have a problem with bed bugs, and thru-hikers have been posting pictures of bitten skin on AT blog sites. Kamikaze and I take a look at the rooms and decide to get a shuttle to a motor lodge outside of town.

We need resupply before heading out to the motel. There is a van operated by the local supermarket running between the Doyle and the supermarket in the evening. We have a meal at the Doyle's bar, and a beer, and enjoy the atmosphere while we wait. The hotel has two entrances, formerly one for Men through the bar, and an entrance to a public room for Ladies. The public room now has a pool table, and the bar is coed. It is an old bar, with a lot of character.

The bartender has control of the remote and a fondness for cheesy horror movies. Currently she has us watching 'Two Headed Shark', a movie that requires a serious suspension of belief in reality to accept the mutated shark and the bad judgment calls of the bikini clad women who are its prey. The next two movies on the agenda are 'Three Headed Shark', which is the exact same movie with a more mutated shark, and 'Sharknado', a movie about a tornado filled with sharks that terrorizes a city. It could happen.

The supermarket van comes and fills up with hikers. We do our shopping and are transported back to the Doyle. We are picked up by the Red Carpet Inn shuttle, and taken out of town. It is $70.00 for a double room in a basic motor lodge, but compared to the Doyle it is a good deal. The price is high, but it includes the shuttle to and from the Doyle. There is air conditioning, and no bed bugs.

I have the contents of my mail drop, dehydrated meats, veggies, and fruits as add-ins and snacks for my meals, and six days of food from the supermarket. My pack is feeling very heavy. I hope to get some real distances without having to stop for another resupply. I have been making good miles hiking with Kami.

Day 107, July 21st
Peters Mountain, Trail Mile 1157.6
Daily Distance 10.7 Miles

Kamikaze and I take the shuttle in the morning from the Red Carpet Inn back to Duncannon and the Doyle to resume our hiking. Across the street from the Doyle there is a small breakfast place called Goodies. It has a mix of locals and thru-hikers eating breakfast, and there is a general good fellowship. Like a number of eateries in trail towns along the way, they offer a food challenge for thru-hikers to test our enormous appetites. At Goodies it is a pancake challenge.

Usually when there is a food challenge the contest it is eat to a specified, large amount of food, and if you are successful you eat for free. The pancake challenge at Goodies followed this example but it required you to break the current record for pancakes eaten by the previous single sitting champion. The record stands currently at seven pancakes, so a person taking on the challenge would have to eat eight. There was a whole wall of pictures of thru-hikers sitting in front of stacks of enormous half eaten, plate sized pancakes.

Wonderland came in looking a little hung over. She is a petite woman, with a bit of attitude. She looked, saw the pancake challenge, thought "Free breakfast!" and ordered up, without having seen what the eight pancakes looked like, or the wall of failure. The other thru-hikers quickly clued her in, to her dismay and our delight. Challenge eating is a spectator sport.

Each of the pancakes individually weighs at least a pound. They are an inch thick, and overlap the edges of a big platter. Apparently they are made special, and are not particularly tasty, probably by design since everything else Goodies makes is quite good. Wonderland manages to eat three or maybe four of the eight monster flapjacks in an hour. The pancakes were three dollars apiece, so Wonderland is out twenty-four dollars, and worse, some pride.

I wash my clothes at the Laundromat during breakfast, running up to check on my clothes, and then back to observe Wonderland's progress. There is something sad about the whole town. It makes me think of the evil version of the hometown in "It's a Wonderful Life". The town is rundown with a lingering air of hopelessness. Everyone smokes, and I watch a girl standing with a lit cigarette dangling from her hand as she pumps her gas. No explosion, thank God.

The trail out of town avoids the main street, paralleling it a block over in a working class neighborhood that has a nice variety of old architecture and some well cared for properties. It looked prosperous enough that I wonder what happened to the downtown. It is two miles along roads to the bridge over the Susquehanna River. Just before the trail crosses the river there is a place where two four lane highways meet, and Kami and I veer off the trail markers to get a sandwich for up the trail at a Pilot truck stop.

It is apparently Duncannon's Red Light District, and it lives off of the flow of trucks on the busy four lane roads. We walk through a gauntlet of awful looking strip clubs, a massage parlor, adult bookstores, and porn shops before we get to the Pilot. A thru-hiker named Yahtzee tells me he was solicited for ten dollars in the parking lot. He passed up the opportunity. I can only imagine the desperation of an actual ten dollar whore offering herself to a dirty thru-hiker.

We buy our sandwiches for up the trail, and I buy a portable power supply so I can have more life in my iPhone. We walk back through the red light district as fast as we can.

The Susquehanna is a great river, the bridge nearly a mile across. There are messages along the walkway for thru-hikers, asking us to report to a phone number if we spotted one of the Peregrine falcons they suspect are living on the bridge structure. Kami and I see no falcons. We do see ducks, a heron, and there are many spiders and webs in the bridge walkway. It is a relief to get away from the bridge, the roads, and the traffic and get back into the woods again.

Climbing out of town with an overloaded pack is the expected struggle. It is a rocky, steep ascent out of the river valley and back onto the ridgeline, but once we are on top there are flat stretches; flat, but rocky.

Water is scarce again, and we add a lot of water to our overloaded packs at Clark's Ferry Shelter, based on reports that it will be another 13 miles to the next reliable water source.

We see Rhino, and he shares a video with us he has on his phone of his first timber rattler encounter here in rattlesnake alley. The snake looks mad, his tail shaking the rattle hard enough it is a buzzing blur,

Day 108, July 22nd
Rausch Gap, Trail Mile 1175.9
Daily Distance 18.3 Miles

It is Rocksylvania indeed. With Kamikaze driving us forward, the rocky stretches slow us but we make miles anyway. There is a single climb today; the rest is a fairly flat ridgeline. We are passing the Indian Gap military reservation and are treated to A-10s flying overhead and the sounds of a military range in the distance.

We are carrying so much water we pass up the first couple of springs. When we need water the widely spaced springs and little streams have changed from clear, drinkable looking water to a strange, bright orange fluid, influenced by the high levels of iron in the water. It is still hot and humid, and the water I am carrying dwindles.

I end up taking a chance at Rattlesnake Run. It has manky looking yellow water, and even after filtering it an unwholesome tint remains. I add a flavoring packet to try and hide the strong metallic taste and I drink of it sparingly. Luckily, we come to a clear spring that is not marked in the AWOL Guide a couple of miles later and I am able to dump out my strange water and refill with the cleaner stuff. The water sources afterwards vary between the orange flows and clear ones. The AWOL Guide does not distinguish between the two, and we carry more water weight than usual in our uncertainty.

Darkness and water shortages put us into Raush Gap Shelter for the night. The shelter is a good third of a wasted mile down a blue blaze off the main Appalachian Trail. There is a mother doe and her fawn at the trail split, and they are not terribly skittish, so we watch them for a minute before hiking the last short distance. The shelter is nicely built on an old foundation of some historic use, and it includes a small stone enclosure with a clear, cool spring running not ten feet away from the structure.

Shepherd, a thru-hiker, and her friend, who is section hiking this part of the trail with her, are also at the shelter. They debate how far they can push on without going back into town. They are short on food. I gladly give up the additional weight of an extra day's food to them, helping them and myself out.

Kamikaze had planned on jumping forward from the Delaware Water Gap. She completed a big section hike of the Mid-Atlantic states a couple of years ago and was looking at skipping those sections already hiked and rejoining her old trail family which has leapfrogged ahead as well. She is now reconsidering, which gladdens my heart. It is really helping me having her push my distances, and I enjoy having someone to talk with as I hike.

Day 109, July 23rd
PA 501 Shelter, Trail Mile 1193.4
Daily Distance 17.5 Miles

TRAILTALK:

MAYFLIES: Hikers who start in May, generally when college gets out of session. They must hike quickly as they have 4 and a half months or less to get to Katahdin before Baxter State Park closes for overnight camping.

TARP TENT: A small lightweight tent that is erected on hiker poles. It is essentially just a waterproof cover. They provide a level of protection from the weather but since they are not fully enclosed, there is no protection from insects.

Kamikaze and I see a lot of old artifacts from this area's mining and transportation past today. We cross two old, iron trestle railroad bridges, pass an old canal lock, and peek into an abandoned mine shaft.

We have two climbs to start the day, and a nine mile stretch without water. It is rocky, of course, and there are some buggy areas to contend with, but overall it is not a particularly taxing day.

We met Benjamin yesterday, a thru-hiker without a trail name, and see him again today. He is a fast mover, hiking over twenty miles a day. He started in May and is racing his way up to Katahdin. May is when college gets out, and a number of young, college students and graduates start late on the trail and try to finish early, before the new school year begins. They are called the Mayflies.

Benjamin camped out last night, and we pass him as he is breaking down his camp in the morning. He is an ultra light backpacker, and sleeps in a tarp tent with his feet up on his pack. Tenters often get a 3/4 length air mattress and put their feet up on their packs to get them off the ground. The ground robs you of body heat in the night.

Benjamin woke late in the night, disturbed by the sensation of his pack moving under his feet. A raccoon was after it, and trying to drag it out of the tent from beneath Benjamin's feet. As soon as Benjamin woke enough to realize what was happening, he grabbed his pack back from the thief.

The raccoon was determined to make something of the encounter, and obviously had no fear of man. Deprived of the pack, it made a grab for Benjamin's clothing bag. Benjamin drove the critter away from his tent, and got it to release his clothes.

The raccoon then ran up a tree. It picked well, it was the same tree where Benjamin hung his food bag. Benjamin had to throw rocks at the persistent creature to get it back out of the tree, away from his food, and finally drive it away from his camp.

Raccoons can be dangerous animals. They get to a good size, up over 30 pounds, and have teeth, claws, agility, and aggression working for them. They are a match for most dogs, and since many of them are trashcan raiders, they have lost their fear of mankind. People will sometimes feed them in their yards, or at campsites, because they are cute, furry creatures. They are also wild animals. They don't attack, but you don't want to tangle with one that is cornered, or disputing territory or food.

We stay at the 501 Shelter for the night. It is a recognized trail oasis close to a road crossing. It is a roomy, fully enclosed building and has access to clean water from a hose running from a nearby cabin. There is a makeshift shower set up. There are twin beds on bunks, and a large common area and table inside the building.

The 501 is also one of the three shelters on the Appalachian Trail where you can order a pizza delivery. Kamikaze and I are obviously stopping here for the night. There are a couple of other section hikers in residence, and everyone cleans up and feasts on good Italian food tonight.

Day 110, July 24th
Eagles Nest Shelter, Trail Mile 1208.2
Daily Distance 15.8 Miles

It is strange to consider 16 miles as a short day, but if you are hiking with Kamikaze it is. Today we are on the ridgeline so there are no real climbs. Plenty of rocks of course, and there is an unexpected boulder field not marked in the AWOL Guide requiring the use of the hands as well as the feet to cross it, for almost a mile. It is the most significant feature in this stretch. There is a lot of water in this section, much of it not in the AWOL Guide. AWOL seems a little weak in Pennsylvania, I don't know if he has had someone reliable hike it and update it recently.

I have my first rattlesnake encounter in the alley. We see a big black snake, which gives Kamikaze the shivers; she does not much care for serpents. We hike another 200 yards and Kami almost steps on a big rattler in the middle of the trail. To her credit, she does not shriek.

It coils up next to the trail and almost wears out its rattle as I hover nearby taking pictures. I like rattlesnakes; I think they are the gentleman and ladies of the viper family. They have an etiquette; if you get too obnoxious they warn you before they strike, which I think is very respectful. Some of it is an instinctual self-preservation I am sure. Venom is a resource, a viper only has so much on hand and so much they can produce each day. Anything they use in defense can not be used for the hunt.

Rattlesnakes are common enough in Pennsylvania to be considered a nuisance. There is an annual hunt to thin out the population. Snake meat is supposed to be OK, their skins can be made into leather and used for things like boots, and the rattles make souvenirs. Practical uses aside, the hunt is really an attempt to keep the population down. Seeing one rattlesnake means there are others about. They are family creatures, hard to imagine, social snakes, but they live in colonies with particular territories.

My snake count for the trail is now at 22.

My miles are increasing, but at a cost; my feet and body do not stop aching. I am still not making the easy twenty mile days forecast for us back in Georgia. Some of the younger hikers seem to be achieving this feat, but not me. I was really hoping for a greater fitness improvement as I made distance on the trail, but perhaps this is the best I can expect from my body. I hope it is enough to finish.

Older Dog is back on the trail and coming up behind us. He is in communication with Kamikaze. He wants to catch up with us. If McGyver and Highlighter are coming too, we could manage a group summit at Katahdin.

Day 111, July 25th
Port Clinton, PA, Trail Mile 1218.8
Daily Distance 10.6 Miles

Lots of rocks and some boulder fields make for slow going today. Kamikaze and I get into Port Clinton around mid-afternoon. The AT passes right through the trail town. Walking into the little village there is a small railroad museum, and we pass by the old engines and railcars on our way into town proper.

Port Clinton is a small, 19th century village that at one time was an important rail station, but has faded away into obscurity in the 20th and 21st Century. It has a few old Victorian houses, a couple of bed and breakfasts with restaurants and bars, and a candy shop. There is a camping gazebo that is free for backpackers, but when I am in town I want a bed and a hot shower with all of the amenities. There is another event going on in the area and the Microtel, the cheap, clean motel option over in Hamburg, is full. I call them a couple of times in hopes that something will open up, without success.

I am planning to meet Meg, an old friend, here in town. I grew up in New Jersey and hiked a number of small sections of the trail in my youth, starting when I was a Boy Scout and lasting through college, until I moved out West. Meg is out hiking with her godchild Armando and her friend Steve. Kamikaze and I hitch a ride a mile over the Schuylkill River to Hamburg, the nearest real resupply point. It has a set of strip malls including a Wal-Mart, and the world's largest Cabela's outfitter is here.

Cabela's is our first stop; we expect a great array of backpacking goods. Security intercepts us at the door. We are not allowed to bring our packs into the store; we have to leave them outside. Security also will not keep an eye on them, and this is a store with a lot of traffic coming in and out, so it is a risk. Kami and I take the risk, eager to see what the world's largest outfitter has to offer us.

The store is vast, two stories high with its own little restaurant complex, and a pool filled with live trout. To our disappointment Cabela's really isn't a very good outfitter for people doing active outdoor sports like backpacking, or climbing. The backpacking equipment is Coleman gear, good enough for car camping, but hopeless for thru-hikers. Their shoe selection isn't geared for hikers either. The store is set up for fishing, hunting, car campers, and people who want to buy sporty clothes. In our unwashed state right off the trail we get some nasty looks and expressions from the staff. Kami found a replacement Sawyer, but it is fifty dollars, twice what it costs elsewhere. After an hour or so of hunting around looking for our gear needs we both leave empty handed.

Wal-Mart is next. It is a big one, and here we find everything our hearts desire. They have a better selection of backpacking equipment than the Cabela's across the way.

Meg is waiting when we come out. She and Steve played trail angel shuttling thru-hikers back to Port Clinton from Hamburg while they waited for us. A personal visit to the Microtel still does not yield a room, and there is a waiting list of thru-hikers looking for a room on the list ahead of us. Meg and Steve take us back to Port Clinton.

Port Clinton is the first of the places I remember from my old section hikes of the Appalachian Trail in my youth. I have a picture of me and my old college roommate Joh, with a couple of girlfriends, from back around 1990, sitting in front of the Union House bed and breakfast with a Grand Opening banner hanging from the porch.

I have the picture on my Facebook account on my phone, and I show it to the manager hoping for some kind of recognition, or maybe a better room rate, but I get no empathy. There are available rooms though, and Kamikaze and I are charged $67.00 apiece for small, antique furnished rooms with single beds. We have to leave our packs downstairs. There are fragile and delicate decorative items in the rooms that can be soiled and broken by packs being swung about. Laundry is in the basement.

Hakuna Matata and Bluebird, the mother and daughter thru-hikers, are also at Union House, and we have a little reunion sharing our trail experiences since the last time we saw each other. I have caught up with them. For a 70 year old woman Bluebird really is moving.

We eat dinner with Meg and her gang at a restaurant a few doors up. Meg is a champion long distance runner, coach, and fitness guru. I am worried about protein since I know I am losing muscle mass. She did some calculations and found I needed 73 grams of protein a day based on my weight and activity level. I have been eating about 45 grams, so now I am sure of what I suspected, I am losing muscle mass. I am going to be a lot more focused on nutrition labels, and eat a lot more peanut butter and tuna fish going forward.

Day 112 to 116, July 26th to July 30th,
Port Clinton to Delaware Water Gap, Trail Miles 1218.8 to 1293.4, 74.6 miles
AVG 14.92 Daily Miles

Day 112, July 26th

Windsor Furnace Shelter, Trail Mile 1223.2
Daily Distance 4.4 Miles

Kamikaze and I are in no hurry to get out of town today. We walk a mile down to a local cafe, eat a big breakfast, walk back to the Union House, take a nap, visit an old fashioned candy store called the Peanut Shop and buy hard candy to eat and give away on the trail. Then we eat a big lunch. We finally get moving after 2:00 PM.

The Appalachian Trail follows along through Port Clinton, crosses a highway, and travels through an area where the locals like to come to use a beach on the Schuylkill River. There is a bit of up and down hiking, including the steep climb out of the river valley. I remember a lot of this hike from my old section hiking days.

The shorter hikes of yesterday and today should help us with our physical recovery. I feel the need to get a move on. Kamikaze is usually chomping at the bit, but seems willing to slow roll these two days. She is suffering from the accumulated aches and pains of our drive north.

Windsor Furnace Shelter is less than a mile from a road, and there is a group of men here who have come in just for the night. They are pleasant enough, but drinking, and one of them is showing it more than the others. They have their portable party strewn all over the shelter. I hide my irritation, or think I do. People hiking in a short distance from the road to have parties in the woods are a major reason to avoid shelters near roads. Pennsylvania is so populated there are not too many shelters that aren't near roads. I sleep in my hammock tonight.

Day 113, July 27th
Allentown Hiking Club Shelter, Trail Mile 1239.7
Daily Distance 16.5 Miles

Today is a grueling day of hiking. There are many rocks, and a couple of 1000 foot climbs. The 1234.5 mile point is spelled out with rocks on the trail.

While Kamikaze and I hike along we come across a set of rosary beads left on a rock along the trail. It is not the first set we have passed. There are often bibles in shelters, and other offerings left beside the trail. There is a section hiker who is a carver and he makes wonderful, decorative wooden spoons, often with a touch of color added to them. He leaves them along the trail. They are much sought after souvenirs. I have not found one myself, but have seen a few that other thru-hikers have picked up.

The Allentown Hiking Club Shelter is the first water source after our final seven mile stretch, and the rocks and climbs are slowing everyone. There is a crowd of thru-hikers in for the night, some familiar to me, and some new. Rhino, South Pole, Wonderland, Mismatch, and Socrates I have met before. Rashie, Mayo, and Dixie are new to me.

I am again reminded how accomplished a group thru-hikers are. South Pole is an Ivy Leaguer, and has 5 different college majors wrapped into a special program just for him. He has been doing research with the National Oceanic and Atmospheric Administration.

Dixie is an Alabama girl, blonde and pretty, with a strong southern accent, who initially comes off as a little ditzy. When she really starts talking I find out she is another petroleum exploration engineer and has a discussion I can only begin to understand with Kamikaze.

The thru-hiking women this far along the trail all appear strong and confident compared to the women back in civilization. And of course they would be, as they have all successfully faced down the terrain, weather, and bias and advances from men, for over a thousand miles. One of the subjects of conversation tonight in the shelter is from the four women, comparing unwanted advances and sexual weirdness they have experienced on the trail. Nothing is a rape or violence, but certainly uncomfortable situations.

Rhino has a story about finding a man masturbating right in the middle of the trail. Dixie had another hiker in a shelter starting to do the same thing, except he was noisy and people turned their lights on him. He rolled over to cover himself and started shouting "leg cramp, leg cramp!"

I find it hard to credit, because on the trail we are all so sweaty, smelly, dirty, and generally disgusting. Sex seems repulsive in these conditions, but I am older, and the young folks stay active, from what I hear, both from stories and from the noises coming out of tents at night. A thin wall of nylon does not provide real privacy, just the illusion of it.

We came in late, and the crowded shelter means Kamikaze and I will need to hang our hammocks, get our water, cook our meals, and hang our bear bags in the dark. The mosquitoes are out, and the work of setting up the hammocks is worth it to get inside the protection of a bug net for the night.

We want to make 16 miles of the same terrain tomorrow. Kami and I are meeting Older Dog at a shelter ahead where he will join us, and hopefully finish the entire hike with us.

Day 114, July 28th
George Outerbridge Shelter, Trail Mile 1256.5
Daily Distance 16.8 Miles

I hear a thru-hiker say 'Ten before Ten' this morning. It means getting up early and hiking 10 miles before 10:00 AM. If you get up, packed, and on the trail by 5:00 AM, and you have the legs to do a consistent 2 miles an hour, it is a realistic goal. For those with the ability to do this, they have already knocked off a substantial hike before noon, and if they want to chill for a bit during the rest of the day the pressure to make miles is off. I seem unable to get up and out early, and the Shenandoah was the only place along the trail I could pull that pace.

Pennsylvania's rocks are taking their toll. The trail doesn't have big climbs or difficult terrain, and it is flat, so it should be quick, but the rocks, oh, the rocks. They jut out of the trail this way and that at odd angles, ranging in sizes from baseballs to bread baskets, in a solid carpet of ankle twisting, toe jamming pain.

The ridgeline here isn't an upthrust of tectonic plates or from volcanic activity; the hills are actual piles of rocks. Pennsylvania is the place where the glaciers made their furthest advance during the last ice age. The glaciers pushed huge mounds of rocks forward, and left them behind after they melted. It is this very mound of rocks we are now hiking on, called a glacial moraine. The biggest difference between the Northern and Southern Appalachians, from a geological standpoint, is that the landscape from here north has been shaped by glaciation, while the landscape behind us has only felt the normal erosion of the last 50 million years. The mountains ahead have been carved by ice, and are steeper for it. Some of this information is revealed by another exceptional person on the trail, a woman named Mayo, who is a geologist. Any mistakes written here are in my translation and poor late night note taking, not in her knowledge

My hiker hobble began to let up because of the shorter miles we hiked for a couple of days. The relief is short lived. We don't do ten before ten, but still manage a quite respectable 6.2 miles before noon. Kamikaze and I amuse ourselves with a mosquito killing contest. The creatures are so aggressive we can sometimes kill two or three with a single swat.

We pass another timber rattler coiled up next to the trail. We give it space, and it stays quiet.

Older Dog joins us at a road junction, and now we are three. The trail gets harder and rockier as we progress, until our actual rate of progress falls to a mile an hour. The midday heat and lack of water drains us physically. We stop at Bake Oven Knob, a shelter I stayed at 23 years ago. It is a small cinder block shelter, and it was dirty, cramped, and uncomfortable back then. It now has another two decades of graffiti layered onto it.

Water is a good half mile away, and I have to climb down from the ridge to get to it. Water is just hard to find in Pennsylvania, and I have to spend the time to go off-trail and fetch it where it is available.

We push on to the George Outerbridge Shelter, a small wooden shelter that is as dirty and graffiti covered as Bake Oven Knob, except this one has been burned down, just a bit, charred mostly. Some thru-hikers are setting up inside: Dixie, Wonderland, Mayo, and Rhino. We set up our hammocks outside by headlamp.

It is very hot; so hot everyone carrying chocolate is now carrying brown goo. I need to change what I am buying for snacks, both for protein and for transportability reasons. My Snickers bars have to be licked out of their wrappers. I am going to have to give them up until the weather cools again. They have been my special treat and I mourn the necessity of taking them out of my food selections.

Day 115, July 29th
Leroy Smith Shelter, Trail Mile 1273.2
Daily Distance 16.7 Miles

Kamikaze, Older Dog and I have to plan on an entirely waterless hike going from shelter to shelter today. We rise early and load up with all the water we can carry. We have a wonderful start, the steep, challenging, and surprisingly fun climb out of Lehigh Gap. The climb requires some technical attention as we surmount big boulders and rocks jutting out from a nearly vertical overlook of the Lehigh Valley. As we climb we can see the world dropping away behind us. Considering how little actual climbing there is in Pennsylvania, this mile or so of upward trail is a nice change, and worth the slowdown of an hour to complete it.

The top of the climb puts us onto a ridgeline that passes through a Superfund site. Superfund sites are industrial areas that were identified back in the 1980s as places so polluted and hazardous that the federal government stepped in and created a special fund to clean them up, or at least prevent the toxins from spreading. There were about a thousand of these sites identified as highest priority scattered about the country. Some of the cleanup money came from the still existing companies that created the pollution in the first place, but many of the companies are gone, passed onto the ash heap of commerce, and we taxpayers bear the cost of the ongoing clean up. Many of the sites are so toxic it will take generations to make them entirely safe again.

The Appalachian Trail passes directly through the Superfund site after the climb out of Lehigh Gap. It was a zinc mine and the tailings spread out over the mountain contain high levels of heavy metals. At one time the site was so toxic that it was denuded of plants, but now there are shrubs and grasses sprouting up. It is quite pretty, almost like hiking on a bald down south, an open stroll of four miles. There is a spring along the way, but there are warning signs posted about the presence of heavy metals in it.

The ridge overlooks an even greater old industrial site, the enormous zinc smelter. The furnace is a huge rusty dome. It looks like the landing of an invading alien ship, and there are conveyor belts and buildings stretching for a couple of miles along the valley floor. There are massive piles of coal in huge open lots past the furnace. There is some slight activity going on, I watch a single dump truck, a tiny speck below us, come in, fill up with coal, and leave.

It becomes a very hot day, and I am thankful we started and completed the climb early. Hikers coming up later behind us say it was pretty awful on the rocks and open space in the sun; they cooked like bugs beneath a magnifying glass.

After passing the Superfund site we find trail magic. Veteran thru-hikers Pound Puppy and Mountain Momma set up a little picnic, and they know exactly what we need. They have doughnuts and fruit, cold water and

Gatorade, as well as little amenities like batteries and toilet paper. We stay an hour, relaxing and enjoying their hospitality. They brought a guitar, so I can play a little. Thru-hikers continue showing up as we sit there, and it turns into a nice little trail party.

I am still counting kills; my mosquito toll for the day is 21. I don't think I really made a dent in the population, but it gives me a small measure of satisfaction. For some reason Older Dog doesn't seem amused by the mosquito killing contest.

Leroy Smith Shelter is better than the last two shelters we have camped beside. It is cleaner, has a privy, and appears to be looked after. If we make our miles tomorrow it will be the last shelter we stay at in Pennsylvania. We aim for a big 20 mile day tomorrow, to get into Delaware Water Gap. The Gap is both a terrain feature and the name of a town at the Delaware River crossing into New Jersey.

I fear Older Dog and Kamikaze are not enjoying my company. There seems to be little distance developing. It is little things, like not being invited over to eat dinner with them when we set up camp near Leroy Smith Shelter. They had their own trail family before, and are hoping to regain contact with it. Maybe I am imagining it, but I will see if they seem like they want to include me tomorrow or whether I should let them hike on ahead.

Day 116, July 30th
Delaware Water Gap, Trail Mile 1293.4
Daily Distance 20.2 Miles

Today Kamikaze, Older Dog and I have a long twenty mile trek. There is only one climb significant enough to show on the AWOL profile, but the rocks are relentless. I am reminded of an old Flintstones episode, where Fred and Barney are impressed when Rock Rockson, the movie star, comes into their local watering hole and orders "Rocks, on the rocks, in a dirty glass".

We carry a lot of water, and drink it. I go through all 3 liters in my bottles on a 13 mile stretch between water sources, and come in dry. At Kirkridge Shelter there is a water spigot at a nearby cabin that allows hikers access. I guzzle two liters in between refilling my bottles.

The rocks get big enough to turn into a scramble at Bear Rocks. I am careful where I place my hands in the rocks as I climb over them. Rattlesnakes hide in the nooks and crannies, and might not take kindly to an intruding limb.

The three of us are covered in bug bites. DEET is only so much of a deterrent for mosquitoes, and I find that I am working hard enough in the heat that the repellent is sweated away within a half hour of applying it.

Sweat itself is a problem, not just the wet, and the smell, and feeling nasty. There is a salt buildup that creates rashes anywhere there is friction, and a hiker in constant motion makes a lot of friction. There are products that can help, roll on application friction reducers, but they, like bug dope, only last so long before they sweat away. I wash in the water sources I come to, but in Pennsylvania they are few and far between. There really isn't time to take repeated long breaks to clean up the way I want to anyway, not if I am going to make miles.

The last six or eight miles today are especially hard on the feet. It is level, easy hiking, except for the rocks. Some hikers refer to the challenge of foot placement in the stones as 'Foot Tetris'. In addition, we have both high heat and a few periods of rain, so we are hiking wet. Enough turns, twists and bruises, and all three of us are doing the hiker hobble on our blistered, abused feet and limbs as we come into town. It is hard to limp on both feet at the same time, but we manage.

There are some choices on where to stay in Delaware Water Gap, but there is a big bubble of hikers in town, perhaps as many as forty people. The party bubble is here, and they and many budget hikers are taking advantage of a donation based (which means free, to some) hostel run by The Church of The Mountain that puts on a free hiker feed on Thursdays. The hostel is crowded.

There are expensive bed and breakfasts in town; Delaware Water Gap is a tourist destination for river float trips and bicycling. There are also a couple of old run down motels out by the end of town. We opt for run down and cheap(er), and go to the Pocono Inn. It is ten dollars more than the rate they post in the current AWOL Guide, a source of discontent with no recourse, and is pay or leave. The seventy-five dollar hiker rooms are in one hall. Another hall looks to have some very sketchy semi-permanent residents. I believe this is a meth-cooker motel. It is kind of sad since it appeared to be a much nicer establishment at one time, with a big pool and conference rooms.

I inspect myself in a mirror in my room tonight. I am still losing body mass on my arms and legs. On my upper body especially I have lost a lot of muscle. I am unhappy to see that even with my weight loss I still have a little jelly roll of fat around my midsection. I am 30 pounds lighter than when I started in Georgia three and a half months ago.

NEW JERSEY, NEW YORK, CONNETICUT, AND MASSACHUSETTS

Days 117 to 139 July 31st to August 22nd
Delaware Water Gap, PA, to Mt. Greylock, MA
TRAIL MILES 1293.4 to 1508.1, 292.9 Miles, 23 Days
AVG 12.73 Daily Miles

Day 117 to 121, July 31st to August 4th
Delaware Water Gap, PA to Vernon, NJ, Trail Mile 1293.4 to 1356.7 miles
63.3 miles, AVG 12.66 Daily Miles

Day 117, July 31st
Sunfish Pond, NJ, Trail Mile 1299.5
Daily Distance 6.1 Miles

TRAILTALK:

AT PASSPORT: A booklet produced by the ATC that can be bought at many locations along the Appalachian Trail. The passport gets stamped at various places along the hike route as a memento of the trip. Collecting the stamps becomes a scavenger hunt along the way for those who participate.

I am still with Kamikaze and Older Dog. We haven't been taking any zeros, so our days getting out of town are leisurely while we take shorter breaks. There are several highly recommended diners, bakeries, and eateries in town. We go to a diner for breakfast and it is Mid-Atlantic good, the kind of breakfasts I remembered from my youth, a plate groaning full with greasy, delicious food. They have pork roll, which I was never fond of but order anyway, for tradition's sake.

There are no supermarkets for resupply within walking distance of town. We have a choice of two gas station convenience stores. The stores know what hikers like, and are stocked up. It is an expensive resupply, and it isn't exactly what I wanted, but it is sufficient for my needs for the next four or five days hiking through New Jersey.

We stop at Edge of the Woods Outfitters on our way out of town. I am still looking for a Jetboil stove, and Older Dog wants different shoes. The store is out of Jetboils, but they have an acceptable pair of hiking shoes for Older Dog. Hopefully his feet will be a little better. Mine are aching from the battering from the rocks.

We eat a sit down lunch at the Village Farmer Bakery, which is wonderful. I have a chicken pot pie, and pick up some treats for further down the trail. We start hiking out of town and don't make it but a few hundred yards before we stop for food again, this time for ice cream.

We cross the Delaware River on the Interstate 80 highway bridge walkway. All of the big bridges we cross on the hike have suicide hotline phone numbers posted on them at the ends and in the middle. I wonder how much they are used.

The bridge also has the NJ/PA state line marked on it, and I sing the Rutgers school song in celebration of entering my birth state, to the visible irritation of my companions.

A big USFS ranger station and visitor center awaits us on the New Jersey side of the river. The rangers are eager to talk with us, and we have a prolonged conversation.

Older Dog has to beg a ride back and forth across the river; he left his AT Passport back at the ice cream shop. The AT Passport is a souvenir book. Many different places along the trail have stamps for the book if a hiker stops in for a visit, and the book becomes a physical reminder of the places visited. Losing the passport halfway up the trail is losing a memento the owner has invested work into. A couple of day hiking visitors are willing to help Older Dog out and drive him back and forth.

Kamikaze charms one of the rangers while we are waiting, so he is in storytelling mode. We end up with free patches and junior ranger badges, as well as a lot of trail information and gossip by the time Older Dog returns.

Some of the trail information from the ranger is not good. There was a female backpacking with a couple of men, ostensibly thru-hikers, who reported they tried to order her to have sex with them. It didn't quite turn into a rape, but it is an ugly story nonetheless,

I can't figure out who it might have been, whether it was regular thru-hikers, party bubble hikers, or section hikers. I can't imagine it being anyone in the bubble that I know, but men can act poorly where women are involved. Kamikaze has a story from her section hike a few years ago about a male hiker who started following her, and she pulled the Four State Challenge just to hike away from him.

The trail seems safer than most places to me. There are not a lot of helpless people out here for a predator to stalk. Hikers are a fit and self-confident group, and don't ignore situations when someone else is in trouble. It is more civilized here away from civilization. As a thru-hiker who spends much of his time alone, and as a man, I may be missing some of the group dynamic, and it may be tougher on single female hikers.

Older Dog returns with his AT Passport and we are on our way again. The short section of the trail through New Jersey is one of the most pleasant and beautiful parts of the Appalachian Trail, belying the state's general industrial reputation. It has the greatest density of black bears per square mile of any section of the trail, and other wildlife abounds.

We hike up the ridgeline away from the Delaware River on the Jersey side five miles to Sunfish Pond. Sunfish Pond is a unique body of water, an actual glacial melt remnant. The water has a curious acidic balance that limits what kinds of animals can live in it. Sunfish survive, and even thrive, but not trout. It is forbidden to swim in the pond, and camping is also managed very tightly, USFS is trying to preserve the special quality of the pond.

Sunfish Pond and its surrounding area are beautiful, and we are camped at a site nearby. No fires are permitted; it is low impact camping area, but I am always low impact camping by choice anyway. It is just easier.

It is difficult to sleep at night. The frogs and whippoorwills are loud and continuous, and sound off without any sort of rhyme or reason, making it hard to ease into sleep.

An astronomical event brought a party of young hikers up to a nearby camping area for an overnight star gazing trip. At midnight the group comes up with flashlights, and with a certain amount of exuberant shouting they circumnavigate the pond. I am able to track their progress by sound listening from within my hammock. The frogs are keeping me awake anyway.

Day 118, August 1st
Buttermilk Falls Trail Divide, Trail Mile 1314.3
Daily Distance 14.8 Miles

Kamikaze, Older Dog and I are moving slower than we thought we would. Our hard hiking in Pennsylvania has worn us out, and we are all feeling it. In addition, we may have caught a sickness in Delaware Water Gap. It could be the water along this stretch; it has a suspicious yellow color. We stop at 6:30 PM. There is still daylight left.

The trail itself isn't particularly challenging. There are some rocky parts and small ups and downs, but the views are wonderful, especially looking down into the Delaware River valley.

We are seeing a lot of day hikers and weekenders on the trail today. We thru-hikers are a trail attraction. A young woman who is hoping to thru-hike herself stayed with us for several miles mining Older Dog for knowledge.

New Jersey is filled with wildlife, a contrast to the last, barren stretch of Pennsylvania. Today we see snakes at our watering point, a herd of deer, frogs and toads, hawks flying above us, and lots of bear poop on the trail. The wildlife includes mosquitoes that become ferocious at dusk.

We pass the Mohican Outdoor Center (MOC). It is listed in the AWOL Guide as being .4 miles from a forest road crossing, and we pass it by. Later we hear from Boston Ryan it is closer, and they have a snack bar.

The MOC is expensive. It is an outpost of the Appalachian Mountain Club (AMC), the big trail club up North in the White Mountains. AMC is frequently called the Appalachian Money Club by thrus for their high prices and practice of catering to affluent hikers. The MOC charges thirteen dollars to pitch a tent at their site, and five dollars for a shower. I am sorry to miss the snack bar, but I can camp in the woods and bathe in a stream, free.

Wonderland is sprawled out in her tent near a road crossing. Her shelter is half erected; the poles stick up haphazardly, with only a couple of stakes set before she crawled in. She is feeling very sick, and is stopping mid-day to take a recovery break. There is little we can do for her misery, and her character is such that she resists help. We leave her a couple of bottles of clean water. She is near enough to the road to get out if she needs it, and is able to take care of herself. She is a thru-hiker.

The weekend fills the woods with hikers, backpackers and campers. Three different groups of hikers camp around the Buttermilk Falls Trail junction where we stop for the night. Besides our little encampment there is a small cluster of section hikers in another small camp, and a large, loud, youth group in another set up within a hundred yards of the junction. The youth group finds the idea of finding peace in the woods alien and are quite boisterous. The other group of backpackers is barely noticeable. It takes a while for the young campers to settle down enough so it is possible to sleep.

Real sleep proves elusive. Sometime around midnight we are awoken by the sounds of cracking branches, and we find a bear is trying to get at Kamikaze's and Older Dog's food bags. They hung them together on the same branch of a tree thirty yards from our camping area.

My own bag is hanging both higher up, and closer to my hammock, but I join in the common defense of our encampment. I cannot find my headlamp in the dark, so I follow Older Dog to the food bags looking ahead by his light, but I see nothing but a large moving black shadow in the tree. Older Dog is yelling and beating his poles, and Kamikaze is banging pots and pans together behind us, and the bear leaves us.

Our bear is persistent, and it has three camps to scavenge food from. We hear the other two camps exploding into their own shenanigans to drive the unwanted visitor away from their camps. There is a brief period of quiet, and I start to fall asleep again, and the bear tries us out, again. Again we drive it off, and it makes the circuit of the other camps with the same results.

There is another pause, a few minutes of silence, not enough to sleep, before the bear comes back for a third time. Older Dog loses his patience, and his mind, and charges the animal yelling and cursing. The bear decides it wants no part of his brand of crazy, and finally flees into the night without returning.

Day 119, August 2nd
A few miles past Sunrise Mountain, Trail Mile 1329
Daily Distance 14.7 Miles

This day begins a period that is one of my emotional lows of the trail. I am hiking solo again.

I start the day with Kamikaze and Older Dog. We pass Thor and Cookie, who camped alone a mile further up the trail from us last night. They also had a bear visitation. Their food was inside their tent and Thor had to drive a bear away. It was sniffing around right outside of their tent when Thor emerged to do battle. I wonder if it was the same bear that plagued our encampment. The animal still has some fear of man, and can be driven away.

The trail crosses Route 206 near Branchville, where a hoagie sandwich shop, a lakeside bar, and a beach on Kittatinny Lake are all within easy walking distance. It is an irresistible attraction, and we have already made miles today. We go into town for a break. There is a crowd of thru-hikers sitting around outside at the sandwich shop, including the recovered Wonderland. We go down to the lakeside restaurant and have lunch. My day goes to pieces pretty quickly after that.

There has been a little repressed social anxiety on my part wondering if I am suddenly a third wheel in our party. At the restaurant I get a call from my wife. We have been having some real difficulties. She is calling to tell me she has been dating other men, and is bringing our daughter to meet someone she has been out with a few times. I am crushed. I say something about it to Kamikaze and Older Dog, but I am self absorbed in the moment.

Older Dog is offended by me, and I am not quite sure about what. I said something about getting going after we had eaten and had been sitting for a while, and he thinks I am trying to give him orders. I don't think I have, but I really am not quite sure what is going on, and my thoughts are deep in my own internal issues.

We go to the sandwich shop, and Older Dog has something bothering him there too, and starts telling me he can order a sandwich if he wants to. I haven't told him he can't. I don't understand what is going on. It seems he is deliberately seeking to create reasons to take offense.

Kamikaze is silent during our exchange. I can't put up with additional drama after my wife's emo-bomb, and I am not up to figuring out what is going on with Older Dog at that moment. I think he is trying to use my distress to drive me away. If so, it is working. I get my sandwich and tell them I am going. I take off up the road and back onto the trail without them.

I hike fast, letting my angst drive me forward. I want to be alone. I am initially aiming for the Gren Anderson Shelter, and I hike down a blue blazed trail to the shelter for water. There are other hikers there, and I don't want to be around anyone. I head back out to the AT. I see Kamikaze and Older Dog heading in as I am heading out, and barely acknowledge them as I pass. They do not appear like they want to talk, nor do I.

I find my solitude, and camp further down the trail. Getting my bear bag up seems to take forever, a manifestation of the frustration I am feeling with life in general. The mosquitoes seem especially intense as well. They swarm around me all night, buzzing and trying to get in through my hammock and bug net. Some of them are able to get to me through the bottom of my hammock, getting their proboscis into my skin through the thin fabric.

I have to use the bathroom at one point, and when I turn on my headlamp I can see the underside of my rain fly has a coating of mosquitoes. It is thick enough to hide the rain fly itself, a fuzzy, buzzy coating of bloodsuckers, all waiting for me. I unzip my bug mesh, jump out of the hammock, and take a few steps aside to do my business. The mosquitoes follow. I jump back inside my mesh as soon as I can and spend the next half hour hunting down and swatting the pests that managed to come in with me. It is a long, long night.

Day 120, August 3rd
Near Quarry road, Trail Mile 1344.2
Daily Distance 15.2 Miles

A long day as a solo hiker unfolds. I get up early, as soon as it is light. I don't think I really slept all that much last night. My emotional state is poor. My notes from this day are filled with upset and self-pity.

The trail itself is as easy as it gets anywhere outside of the Shenandoah. I look at High Point, a veteran's monument erected by the State of New Jersey at the highest point of elevation in the state.

Lake Marcia has a beach with a concession stand and showers .7 off the trail, and I hike down and spend a couple of hours getting clean and eating. Boston Ryan comes in as I am leaving and we exchange greetings.

I plan on camping at the Jim Murray Property, a private piece of property a half mile off of the trail. The owner has set up a little oasis for thru-hikers. There is a shelter, and an outdoor spigot rigged as a shower and water source, all on a beautiful large lawn.

There are other hikers here, including Older Dog and Kamikaze. Kami doesn't have a word for me; she utterly ignores me. Older Dog politely asks for a headlamp back he loaned to me on the night of the bear attack. I give it back to him, but that seems the end of our conversation.

I feel very much an outsider and change my mind about staying here. I head back out onto the Appalachian Trail and hike on up the trail another mile to get separation before setting up for the night.

I camp a quarter mile up a hill on the first flat spot that offers itself after I cross Quarry Road. I feel like I am not making miles, but I have added 2.5 miles to my hiking for the day by my side trips, and have hiked nearly eighteen miles in total. I am physically and emotionally spent.

My hiker hobble is very pronounced; I have a perpetual cramp in the ball of one of my feet. I am worried it might be a form of Plantar Fasciitis coming on. I continue to hike with the foot pain, hoping it will work itself out. It is a poor strategy, but while I am in pain, I am not crippled, and I am in no mood to stop moving.

I set up for the night in a stand of small pine trees, with thin lateral branches. I make multiple attempts to get my bear bag up, and I just can't get it up onto a branch that doesn't droop back down to the ground with the weight of my food bag on it. I end up hanging it from a branch 8 feet away from my hammock. I am so wound up emotionally I welcome the thought of tangling with a bear, if one comes looking to trouble me or my food during the night.

Day 121, August 4th
NJ Route 94, Vernon NJ, Trail Mile 1356.7
Daily Distance 12.5 Miles

This is a very easy and fun section of the Appalachian Trail. I would enjoy it more it if my feet were not in such bad shape. I am staggering rather than hiking. Pain and stiffness is common at the start of any day, but the pains normally work themselves out. Today the pain stays with me.

The trail has a section of four miles that is entirely boardwalked as it crosses a wetland, and there are bridges along the way crossing watercourses. It would be a beautiful stroll but for the continuous pain in my foot.

There are a lot of mosquitoes. I can't say I am quite getting used to them, or don't notice them, but I am becoming more accustomed to their presence. There are a lot of locals out in the area on day hikes.

I hitchhike into the town of Vernon from the trail. It takes me a little while to get a ride, and standing there with my thumb out it is a misery. My mental and emotional state is aching, and my feet throb. I get a ride into Vernon to a local church within a half hour.

The Episcopal Church in Vernon has divided its carpeted basement so a section is available for thru-hikers to stay the night sleeping on the floor or on a sofa. They provide a shower, laundry, and a kitchen for hiker's use for a suggested donation of $10.00 a night No alcohol is allowed. AA meetings are held in the other half of the basement.

A thru-hiker comes in and has obviously been drinking. He gets a shower, but gets eased back out by the caretaker because of his condition. There is an alternative place for him to stay. Near the Appalachian Trail road crossing there is an open space, a former farm, and the owner allows thru-hikers to camp. The space is used for outdoor concerts, and it is gearing up for a local folk festival. The owner is giving some thru-hikers a chance to work and earn a little cash during the festival. Thru-hikers can be a part of the festival experience in addition to camping.

At the church I inspect my feet. I find the expected blisters. What I thought might be Plantar Faciitis from the debilitating, stabbing pain in the bottom of my foot every step is not. I discover a big, deep blister in the ball of my foot. The how and why of its formation are beyond me, but I have been hiking hard on rough terrain for a while.

The hostel discourages hikers form staying more than one night, but I show the caretaker my foot and he allows me a zero there for the next day.

I heat a needle and pierce the blister to drain it. A large quantity of blood and pus come out along with the clear fluid usually found in blisters.

I am worried about miles. I am already at the back of the bubble expected to make Katahdin by October 15th. I have to leave the trail for the first week of September to go to my sister's wedding, and it will set me back seven days. I am running the numbers in my head, trying to calculate times and distances. I need tomorrow's zero to physically heal, and to get a mental grip on myself. I also want to allow Older Dog and Kamikaze to get some distance ahead of me, since I don't want repeated, uncomfortable meetings.

I am going to take the zero, but I am determined it will be my last one for a while

Day 122, August 5th
Vernon. NJ, (St.Thomas Episcopal Church Hostel), Trail Mile 1356.7
Daily Distance 0.0 Miles, ZERO DAY

I am taking my zero day to rest my injured foot. Hakuna Matata and Bluebird are in, and a young man has teamed up with them as well, named Ramblur. He is spelling his name with a 'U' to distinguish himself from the Rambler I hiked with back in Virginia. Certain trail names, like Rambler, come up regularly, once or twice every season.

I go to a local breakfast cafe and have a feast in the morning. I slowly limp to the grocery store and do my resupply. I get my dinner from a little Italian place. I eat my fill, and more than once.

I spend the best part of the day resting. I try to stay off my feet as much as I can. I nap and read through the day. I have started a Tom Clancy novel, a poor choice; it is so big I will never finish it. I picked it up from a shelf at the hostel since it is relatively mindless, but I get stuck in it. I end up tearing off the half I have read and plan to carry the unread remainder to finish on the trail. It is probably the better part of a pound of paper, a big brick of unnecessary weight in my backpack.

Day 122 to Day 129, August 6to August 14
Vernon NJ, to East Cornwall Bridge, CN
Trail Mile 1356.7 to 1478.2
121.5 miles, AVG 13.5 Daily Miles

Day 123, August 6th,
Greenwood Lake NY (Anton's on the Lake Hotel), Trail Mile 1371.7
Daily Distance 15.0 Miles

Hitchhiking is uncertain in New Jersey. Some of the other thru-hikers at St. Thomas Episcopal Church spent over an hour getting a ride in from the trail. One even walked the extra miles from the trailhead into town. I hire a cab as a precaution to pick me up at the church hostel in Vernon and take me back out to the trail in the morning.

A folk festival is setting up on the property adjacent to the Appalachian Trail trailhead, and I see thru-hikers who are working the event hanging about as I get started back on the trail. They give me a wave and yell greetings and encouragement as I go by.

My feet are still hurting. They are better than before, but I can feel them complaining about the blisters and soreness down there at the bottom of my legs. I can manage it.

There is a short climb out of Vernon. Wawayanda Mountain called the Stairway to Heaven that has a reputation with local hikers, but doesn't feel like much compared to what I have already experienced. It is less than a 1000 foot ascent. Water is still scarce along this stretch of the Appalachian Trail, and some of what is available is pretty dubious looking. I find a spigot at a New Jersey State Parks building, and fill every bottle I have. I end up giving some of my water away to a group of thirsty hikers, including the second Castaway I have met. They are sitting looking forlornly at a dry creek bed where a good spring is listed in the AWOL Guide, but the streambed is bone dry.

I cross the border into New York State. The trail follows six miles of knife edge ridge. There is no up and down climbing, but it is a horizontal rock scramble nonetheless. I meet and hike with Hakuna Matata and Bluebird. They are both amazing women, a mother daughter thru-hiking pair. Bluebird is seventy years old, and I still find it hard work keeping up with her.

State lines often follow natural lines of change in terrain and vegetation. Passing into New York from New Jersey the rocks change from grey granite to a darker purplish color, and the trees devolve from big hardwoods to smaller pines and scrub oak.

The end of the day finds us at Bellvale Farms Creamery, an ice cream parlor a quarter of a mile off of the AT at the NY 17A road crossing in Bellvale. They make ice cream farm fresh from local cream, I can see the dairy cows from the picnic benches scattered about outside. It is a popular place locally for dates and family outings, and crowded. The ice cream is very good, and reasonably priced. Portions are generous, I get a banana split that I can barely finish, even with hiker hunger aiding and abetting my appetite. While I eat I talk to Hakuna and Bluebird about their plans.

They are staying at a motel in the nearby town of Greenwood Lake called Anton's on the Lake. It is a higher end motel, and expensive by thru-hiker standards. They offer a hiker rate of $80.00 a night, which is a big cut from their ordinary prices. I am hesitant about joining them, Ramblur has already begged off of the stay because of the expense, and plans to meet back up with Hakuna and Bluebird further up the AT.

Anton's has a particular hook for thru-hikers besides offering a reduced price. They offer free shuttles for slackpacking. Most places charge by the mile and a shuttle can run upwards of forty dollars. The free shuttle makes the overall price of Anton's a much more attractive proposition. It is a way to make some long miles easier, and I will get to hike for a while with Bluebird and Hakuna, whose company I have very much enjoyed.

I am in.

Anton's on the Lake is a wonderful little motel with big clean rooms. Not quite five star luxury, but far better in atmosphere and comforts than a chain motel. My room has a Jacuzzi in it. Anton's is on the lake, of course, and sits on a small peninsula. There is a view of lake activity all around the motel, and I can sit in a chair on the lawn in front and watch geese and ducks swimming by.

Trisha and Robert are the owners, an older couple who are quite friendly and accommodating. The town of Greenwood Lake is a little touristy, but has a number of good restaurants and a big drugstore for resupply.

I eat dinner at an Italian restaurant, and I brought my half of a Tom Clancy novel with me to read as I wait to be served. I see a skunk wandering around town, the only one I actually see while on my thru-hike. It is one of the few animals I don't want to see on the trail.

Skunks can be dangerous, they are scrappy fighters, and have no fear of humans. Their ability to spray musk makes them the ruler of any camp they invade, and thru-hikers pretty much let them do whatever they want to do. Some dogs get into it with them, and invariably end up as unwelcome hiking companions for days afterwards.

Day 124, August 7th
Harriman Garden Road, NY (Anton's on the Lake Hotel), Trail Mile 1389.2
Daily Distance 17.5 Miles

Today's trail profile is mostly flat, a long ridgeline run with an occasional dip in it. It looks easy on the profile, but proves to be hard trail to hike. The Appalachian Trail zigzags back and forth across the top of the ridge, chasing rock piles to scramble over. The trail repeatedly passes over a much easier route of old trail and forest road, so it is a trail builder's choice. It seems each trail builder wants a trail with challenges in their stretch, and pick the most difficult routes. As a long distance hiker I find this frustrating, I long for some easier stretches where I can walk without constant attention to my actual foot placement, sections where I can walk beneath the trees and just enjoy being in the forest environment, and make some miles while doing so. The stretches of easy hiking are so very rare, even where they could be so easy to put in.

The trail takes Hakuna Matata, Bluebird and I through Harriman State Park. I came here a long time ago, when I was a Boy Scout. It is a wonderful place, like a fairy tale forest. Big trees are widely spaced, with grass and wildflowers growing beneath them. As we hike we come to periodic rock structures and water features that add variety and an element of fantasy and wonder to our journey.

The Lemon Squeezer is here, a small but challenging rock structure the trail easily could have gone right by. It is a fun little obstacle, a narrow pinch climbing up a twenty foot channel between rocks. I am occasionally giving Bluebird a little boost to get over some of the rocks. It is a comfort to my ego, because she is liable to hike away from me on other stretches of the trail. She is a seventy year old woman who humbles me every time I hike with her. Her daughter Hakuna is a much quieter hiking companion, but equally amazing, with a life story of interesting adventures.

The section is challenging, and I feel slackpacking lets me get some extra miles under my belt. My only regret is that we are moving so fast and with so little in the way of rest stops that I don't see as much of the area as I might have on a slower day. We had a deadline today, a designated pick up point and time at the other end of the slackpack.

We pass Rain, Wobbles, and No Filter, I am glad to see them moving forward. We talk a bit about the water scarcity issues and they tell us a trail angel has left a water cache near a road crossing ahead.

Trail angels are very active on the New York sections of trail. They leave caches of gallon jugs of water where they will do the most good, and refill them periodically. I would have run dry several times on this section of trail, and gone very thirsty without them. I give silent thanks for the local angel's dedication to hikers, hikers they likely will never meet.

We get to the garden road where we are expecting our pick up. It is a New York State beach and recreation area on a large lake. Boston Ryan is there, and he happily tosses sass back and forth with Bluebird. They obviously are not strangers. Trisha from Anton's picks us up and drives us back to the hotel.

Anton's on the Lake is a lovely place to return to. I relax for a while and enjoy watching activities on the waterfront.

I want to go back to the Italian restaurant where I ate yesterday. I left my half of a Tom Clancy novel there last night, and I am hoping to pick it up and resume it. I like to read at night as a way to clear my mind of whatever is on it, and redirect it. It helps me to fall asleep. On the trail I usually read books I have downloaded onto the computer tablet I use for note taking, but I have been toting around this giant brick of a hard copy paperback.

I will tote the extra weight no longer. The restaurant staff found the tattered remnant I was reading, but they assumed it was an odd piece of trash and they tossed it into the garbage. I do not regret the loss much, as it was not a book to treasure, just an amusing read. I am a little bothered by how smoothly technology and spycraft work to fix all of our international problems in Clancy novels.

Day 125, August 8th
West Mountain Ridge, Trail Mile 1397.3

Daily Distance Mile 8.1 miles

TRAILTALK:

BSP (Baxter State Park): The final northern terminus of the trail in Maine, the centerpiece is Mount Katahdin.

Our shuttle out of town takes a little coordination to get all of us going back out to Harriman Gardens State Park in one trip. We don't get to the trail until a little after noon. Bluebird and Hakuna have a destination, a shelter that overlooks the Hudson River where they want to stay at tonight for sentimental reasons. The shelter is nearly a mile off of the main trail, and I want to try and make more miles today. We cordially part company.

I don't hike that far today. The Appalachian Trail here is what I am thinking of as typical New York trail, little climbs and rock scrambles with few water sources between. I have to leapfrog between speeding cars to cross the six lanes of the Palisades Parkway.

A creek just past the highway is the water source I have to rely on for resupply for the rest of the night's hiking and camping. It is a distinctly unappealing body of water. The water has a slow flow and a yellowish cast. There are some small fish and frogs living in it, so it can't be immediately lethal. I take a full load of 4 liters of water away and up the next hill to my resting place for the night.

I didn't want to stop with so few miles hiked for the day, but I prefer stopping with some daylight left. The October 15th Katahdin closure and the need to make miles are haunting me. There is a spiritual center ahead that offers camping and I would like to see and experience it, but my mileage goals put it in an awkward place. The relentless pressure of the miles means I miss a number of experiences and sights along the way I really would have enjoyed. If I had started in mid March it would all have been a lot more relaxed. I am playing the hand I am dealt though, and I am fortunate to have a real possibility of completing the entire trail despite the later start.

It is a good thing I stop when I do, I need the extra time. I manage to get my bear line tangled up in a tree branch trying to get a good toss, and spend thirty minutes getting it back down again. I curse the tree, my line, and the rapidly fleeing sun as I make multiple attempts from different angles to pull the line down. I finally find a 10 foot long fallen stick and use it to manipulate the line tangled high above me. After a number of experiments I find the right little twist and push to free my line. I like to get my camp set before cooking, eating and relaxing. Day fades to night as I get my bear bag hang established. I make my dinner and eat it in darkness.

I read the Appalachian Trials book (that is *trials*, not trails), in my hammock on my tablet as I relax and wait for sleep. The book focuses on the psychological preparation for the trail and how important attitude is towards shaping your journey.

Even today, when I finish my day with the frustration of the bear bag tug of war, I can reflect back to a time earlier during the day when I took a break and watched hawks coasting along above me and the Hudson River valley from one of the many views on the ridgeline I was hiking. It was a great moment of peace, and one to remember and carry forward.

Day 126, August 9th
Graymoor Spiritual Center, Trail Mile 1410.0
Daily Distance Mile 12.7 miles

I cross over Bear Mountain State Park today; it is the low point of the trail, literally. The lowest point of elevation anywhere on the trail is at the base of the mountain besides the Hudson River, a mere 124 feet above sea level. The low point is located in the state park's zoo, not far from the bear cage.

There are a number of people hiking and trail running as I climb up Bear Mountain, enough for me to feel a little uncomfortable. A swarm of trail runners coming down the trail in a group expect me to step aside for them, but I am unwilling to give up the trail, and they have to jump off the trail into the underbrush to avoid a collision.

Trail etiquette is downhill yields to uphill; the uphill hiker has the harder task, and gives up momentum in the fight against gravity if they stop and step aside. I am not always so stubborn, but the trail runners' expectation that the trail was theirs annoys me,

I am wholly unprepared for the swarms of humanity at Bear Mountain's peak. There are several structures on the summit, including a stone tower several stories high, and there is a road to the top and parking areas. Buses are pulling up every couple of minutes and disgorging crowds of day trippers up from New York City into the park. Several auto and motorcycle clubs are parked or cruising through.

Bear Mountain is near enough to be nature that is accessible from New York City. In fact, the park was conceived and implemented to be just that, and has remained true to the concept. It is a place for urban dwellers to meet the wild. Unfortunately the urban dwellers are present in such numbers the park feels far more urban than wilderness.

I join the line to go up in the Bear Mountain tower, and I look to the south and see the New York City skyline tiny in the distance. I follow the line back out of the tower. There are exhibits on each level going up and down the stairs on the history of the tower, and of the park. I pause and read each one. I have difficulty passing any historical placard.

The Appalachian Trail goes down the other side of the mountain. It is very crowded, many people who have bussed in for the day climb up from the zoo to see the tower. Some have no shame, and are sporting fancy, tight fitting athletic apparel on decidedly soft and lumpy bodies. They huff and puff going past me on their quest to reach the summit. I am reaching a level of fitness where Bear Mountain seems like a small bit of work, and I find I am bothered by the mobs.

My personal observations in my notes are condescending, a negative look at people who are just out for a nice day of fresh air and exercise. Four months ago I probably would have been huffing and puffing right along with them.

The base of Bear Mountain is madness. There is a pond with a beach and paddle boats, and there are hundreds of families picnicking nearby. There is a huge stone lodge, the Bear Mountain Inn, and they serve a buffet brunch. It is $36.00, before the tax and tip, but it is fabulous. Sublime, the crazy French Canadian whom I have not seen since Virginia shows up to indulge himself as well, and we sit together.

While we are eating an elderly lady falls to the ground at the buffet line and doesn't get up. Apparently she has tripped over a chair leg and banged her head. I get up, and figure I might be using my Army first aid training, but the crowd is well heeled and several doctors step forward and cluster around the victim offering assistance until a stretcher arrives. She is wheeled out, followed by her concerned family, and the bustle around the serving tables and the clink of cutlery resumes, albeit in a more subdued fashion.

Sublime and I linger and fill our plates several times, because a buffet this good and this expensive deserves serious attention, but I feel a little callused going back through the serving line while a casualty is being wheeled out.

Back out on the trail I skirt the mobs around the pond. The trail passes directly through the zoo. There is a small entrance fee but thru-hikers are exempt, and we are pretty easy to pick out of the crowd with our worn, dirty clothes, bulging packs, and battered hiking poles.

In the zoo I pass animals in cages that I have been seeing out in the wild, which is a little sad. Most of the animals are rescues or removals of one sort or another that can't be released back into the forest.

There is a statue of Walt Whitman with some inspiring quotes, and there, in the zoo, is the lowest elevation point on the trail, right by the bear exhibit.

Once through the park there is a bridge crossing the Hudson River. It has the usual suicide warning signs posted with the hotline numbers. There is steady stream of day hikers crossing the pedestrian walkway of the bridge. The views up and down the Hudson River valley from the bridge are spectacular. A large ship is moving down the river beneath my feet as I cross.

Boston Ryan had to get into the main town by Bear Mountain Park for a mail drop, and had some difficulties. There is a separate bridge into the town from the park, crossing an estuary, and they are doing construction on it. The sidewalk is closed, and the road work narrowed the lanes.

Crossing the bridge required Boston to walk in the street with cars following right behind him, honking at his walking pace in the lane.

On the far side of the Hudson River the sides of the road are lined with parked cars, and on the hiking trail up out of the river valley I pass a number of day hikers coming and going. At the top of the climb there is a forest road, and I get turned around at the top. There isn't a white blaze in sight and I follow the general flow of hikers to an overlook of the river. It is a wonderful view, but I am a good mile away from the Appalachian Trail when I realize I went the wrong direction, turn and retrace my steps.

I stop at the Appalachian Trails Market for dinner. New York's trail nickname is 'The Deli State'. There are many road crossings while hiking through the state, and on the roads there are many delis and sandwich shops within a half mile of the trail. It is possible to eat store bought food every day.

It is a hot day, and I have run out of water in the six miles (plus the two additional miles of wandering) hiking through a series of small climbs since leaving the Bear Mountain Park, so I feel obligated to stop for a little reward. At least that is what I tell myself as I munch down a sandwich.

The stops slow me enough so the day's hike ends at the Graymoor Spiritual Life Center. I wanted to visit here anyway, but it is a short day in miles. I thought somehow I would participate in some sort of spiritual activity, but the center is for Catholics, run by Franciscan Priests and Sisters. We don't get any spirituality besides what we bring with us.

We are allowed to camp on the baseball field. There is running water and a concrete structure serving as a shelter that looks like an abandoned concession stand. There are some symbols of Catholicism around, a few crosses and statues, but it is still recognizably a baseball field. A set of large fieldstone structures are visible on the walk in, which are the conference center and housing, but the ball field is isolated from the main center.

The thru and section hikers present are an easy group for me to get along with. Most have more than the usual ramen bombs to eat; hikers stocked up at delis coming in as I did, and we can do cold showers of sorts from the water hose.

It is festive. Some hikers set up inside the structure, and some set up tents in the field. There are a couple of porta-potties in place on the far side of the ball field. I put my sleeping mat atop of a collapsed table top inside the stand and call it home.

Day 127, August 10th
Near Long Hill Road, Trail Mile 1426.4
Daily Distance Mile 16.4 miles

The trail continues to chase rock piles across the ridgeline, with the occasional up and down. I hope every day is going to be a twenty mile day, but I never seem to get them done. Today is no different. I still consider a day with over sixteen miles as more than respectable. The idea of anywhere having easy miles is a myth. All trail miles are hard; some are just harder than others.

Most of the thru-hikers at Graymoor last night were solos, all of us making our way north on our own. It was a little different from a usual crowd of thru-hikers with their various trail pairings and families, with the odd solo (me).

I have lunch today with Yahtzee, and we talk a little about solo hiking. He says his biggest lesson is that you have to be your own best friend out here; otherwise you are going to be hiking all day with someone you don't like. So, you either like yourself, learn to like yourself, or you are going to be miserable. It is a good thought.

"The Trail will provide" is a thru-hiker saying. The Appalachian Trail is an entity, not just a line of dirt and rocks through the woods. It is a community as well as a place, and it is focused on getting people further along. The trail does provide. Angels appear when they are most needed, bringing food, water, rides, shelter, and companionship. Budget hikers are successful because so many other people give into the trail community. Usually it is not a lot, but a little *is* a lot for a person living out of a backpack.

Yahtzee's conversation sticks with me. The trail presented emotional challenges as well as physical ones for me. I spend a lot of time alone in the Mid Atlantic states and New England, and I remember this conversation: 'Be my own best friend'.

I wallow in misery more than a few times along the way. Being my own best friend meant realizing that when I was down and out that I was still out doing things that others only dreamed of, and that I had made this happen. I would catch myself dwelling in an unhappy closed circuit loop, then tell myself I was a decent guy, and doing an amazing thing, surrounded by beauty, and wake up. I would keep telling myself that all the way to the end.

The trail provided.

There is another New York state park centered on a lake with a beach and concession stand today. This area of the state seems to have many of them. The Fahnestock State Park attractions are half of a mile off-trail. It has an activity center, but the concessions stand and beach have closed by the time I get there. There are still free showers, and an opportunity to cool off and get clean is irresistible. Camping is another half a mile away, and the word is there is a trail angel camping in a trailer there who has a sandwich and a cold soda for thru-hikers. I want to make more distance for the day and head back out to the Appalachian Trail. Most of the thru-hikers I see are opting for the camping, and the sandwich and soda.

I load up on fresh water at the park and carry it with me for another two and a half miles to the expected dry camp.

I am alone tonight. It rains, hard, and water comes in under my rain fly.

Day 128, August 11th
Near NY Route 55, Trail Mile 1441.4,
Daily Distance Mile 15.0 miles

I think I would make more progress if I did not stop every day to eat in the great Deli State. I put in an extra mile going on and off-trail to another deli, and spend an hour sitting outside at a picnic table. Eating unrestrained without concern for weight gain is a joy, something I have not experienced since I was a teenager. Not only can I get away with it, I need it.

I don't see any other hikers today and spend the day alone with my thoughts. I have had another set of texts and a call from my wife. It is contentious, demoralizing, and adds to my general feeling of exhaustion.

I am sweating profusely. It is very hot, and has been since Pennsylvania. Water goes in and sweat comes out, until I walk coated in my own slime. My clothes are soaking wet within the first hour of hiking. I rinse off at every opportunity, but water sources are scarce and scary looking and I am resigned to being really nasty most of time. I have a second t-shirt and a pair of lightweight running shorts I can change into at night, and hang the nasty stuff up on my hammock ropes to dry out as well as it can overnight.

I still hike in long pants. They are lightweight breathable hiker pants, and I learned back in Georgia I do not want to give up the protection they are providing against ticks, poison ivy, and other trail hazards.

My sweat has an acrid ammonia like smell which hiker lore says is a sign the body is short on protein, and is breaking down muscle mass to get it. It would explain why I am so tired; I struggle to keep putting one foot in front of the other. What I don't understand is why. I have been eating very well over the past few days. I am getting lots of food, including fruit juices and vegetables, at my daily deli stops. It isn't stopping me from hiking, but I would be happier if I knew what was going on, and how to address it. I want a better energy level.

I have definitely lost a lot of weight now, I am looking gaunt. Somehow, I am still sporting a little jelly roll. My body just won't give up that last reserve despite my hunger.

I hike until near dark aiming to hitch out and stay at a motel near Route 55. I call the motel listed in the AWOL Guide and tell them I am thru-hiker, and the front desk gets evasive. They refuse to rent me a room. Much chagrinned, I backtrack to the last water source, a suspicious looking stream flowing from a swamp with a lot of dead trees and vegetation standing in it. I fill up my bottles, and I look for the first likely spot to set up camp. I am exhausted, and find something that will work. It is close to Route 55, near enough I can see into a nearby backyard. Bugs are swarming as I set up my hammock.

My gear is still wet from the previous night's rain, and I have an uncomfortable night. It is really not a suitable spot to camp. It is a poor choice driven by exhaustion. I have picked the two best trees in the vicinity. There is no good bear hang, so my food bag is on the end of my hammock. The area has been used for a lot of parties, and there is broken glass and other trash underfoot.

Day 129, August 12th
Wiley Shelter, Trail Mile 1454.4
Daily Distance 13.0 Miles

I sleep in. My hammock hangs awkwardly and I sag uncomfortably, tossing and turning in the night. It is damp, and nothing dries in the humidity.

Once I decide to face the day and get out of my hammock I realize I have set up in a local dumping ground. The area is littered with old appliances, trash, and the remains of parties. It sets my mood starting the day; I have another unresolved argument with my wife at home on the phone as I slowly get my breakfast ready and put gear away into my pack. I do not have enough water, and I am dehydrated, which probably contributed to my restless night.

The trail is improving, and under other circumstances I could really move. There is no more chasing rock piles.

I pass Nuclear Lake. Fifty years ago there was a discharge of nuclear material into the lake, and the AWOL Guide warns against swimming in it or drinking from it. It is sad, because the lake is absolutely beautiful, and very inviting, a pristine lake surrounded by forest untainted (except for radioactive waste) by humans. There are no signs posted, and I don't know if this is because the lake has been declared safe, or if the radioactive signs were taken as souvenirs.

I meet a steady flow of SoBos passing me heading towards Springer Mountain. I see at least ten today. Even though the NoBos have been on the Appalachian Trail two or three months longer, and have twice the distance under their belts, the SoBos radiate confidence, and a little superiority. The attitude does not go down easy with NoBos. The SoBos believe that they are the hardier hikers, and they tell us just how difficult the trail in New Hampshire and Maine is going to be. They have caught us in an easy stretch, and they may underestimate our accomplishments in the Smokes. It is good natured, competitive story telling, and there is real respect on both sides. We have all gone through a lot to be this far along.

A huge oak tree stands near the County Road 20 crossing. It is the Dover Oak, one of two oak trees touted as the largest oak tree on the Appalachian Trail. I take a break here to admire the gigantic tree, and I take some pictures of it with my pack standing next to it for perspective.

When I take my pack off of my shoulders it drops to the ground with a weighty and an audible thud. I name my pack after the sound, and from here onward my pack will be called 'Thud'.

The trail crosses a railroad track that is on a commuter line going into New York City near the Route 22 road crossing. The metro station is right on the trail. Hikers less pressed for time than I am will sometimes take a break to go to Manhattan for a day or two.

The Native Landscapes and Garden Center is very close to the trail crossing. They host daytime hikers in a gazebo outside in the garden displays, and there are treats and resupply for sale inside. There is a fancy hot dog cart across the road. I buy some freeze dried meals for the trail, and I get some hot dogs from the cart.

There is a fair sized group of thru-hikers gathered at the gazebo chilling out and waiting for the train into New York City. The garden center used to allow thru-hikers to camp on the grounds, but the yellow blazer party bubble preceded me by a couple of days, and a couple of them tried to break into the building during the night to get snacks. Presumably they were drinking. Now no one is allowed on the garden center grounds after dark. I wasn't planning on camping here, but the disrespect of my fellow hikers upsets me.

This is a surprisingly marshy section of the trail seeing how little there is in the way of actual water sources for drinking in the area. The intermittent rains have left a lot of standing water. It may not be potable water, but it does provide a wonderful environment for the breeding of mosquitoes and other pests, and it is a buggy day and night. I sleep in my hammock at Wiley Shelter, hiding inside my bug net.

Day 128, August 13th
Mt. Algo Shelter, Connecticut, Trail Mile 1466.6
Daily Distance 12.2 Miles

I have deliberately slowed my pace. I want to go into Cornwall Bridge tomorrow. There is an outfitter listed in the AWOL Guide, and as always I have equipment wearing out. I especially need a replacement gasket for my Sawyer water filter. Water is spraying out at the join when I am filtering or drinking my water. It is a huge annoyance; it slows the filtering process, and poses a risk of dirty water contaminating the filtered water. I have popped my last bladder bag and I am now using a used plastic ice tea bottle to serve as my bladder. My dry bags are all torn, no longer seal correctly, and need replacements as well.

I still want a Jetbboil stove. I have my Snow Peak stove, which is much faster than my original alcohol burner set up, but hikers with Jetboils are done eating before I am done cooking.

I have been considering altering my hammock hang and I want mountain climbing rope to do so. Climbing rope is very light and very strong, but considerably more expensive than ordinary rope or clothes line. Since it will be holding me suspended in the air, it is worth the expense.

I am in no hurry to arise in the morning. There are three SOBOs in camp, and one of them is carrying a plastic trumpet, it is not a toy, but a proper instrument made out of lightweight, durable plastic. He blows reveille at 6:00 AM. It is startling. I would have yelled at him, or maybe even choked him to death, but he knew how to play that horn, and it is a nice jazzy rendition. I fall back to sleep and I don't get going until 9:30 AM.

I plan on a short hike into town tomorrow. I have chores to do, and I have friends living in Connecticut I am hoping to see. They are some distance away, so it is a toss up whether we will connect. I am hoping to have breakfast with them before getting back on trail.

I am in Connecticut, a new state, and the trail is showing signs of hills again. Despite the additional undulations it seems an easier trail than New York. The trail runs along the Housatonic River for a distance. There is plenty of water to drink and to soak in. It is very pretty day, with occasional views of well kept farmland from the ridge tops.

It is the first day in a while I haven't had some sort of commercial food or deli stop. I eat a freeze dried meal instead, and it is a welcome break from the usual ramen bomb or Knorr Side. Some people buy cases of freeze dried meals to get the price down, and put them into mail drops. I am thinking about it.

Day 130, August 13th
Cornwall Bridge, CT, Trail Mile 1478.2
Daily Distance 11.6 Miles

The trail is kind today and I like what I see of Connecticut. Most of it is well built trail. There was an unexpected rock scramble down from Caleb's Peak, a surprise after a couple of days of tame terrain. It wasn't a big descent, but it requires some thinking and effort to get down safely.

The top of the descent looks as though the builders tried to put in steps. I can visualize it. Moving the big, awkward, heavy rocks must have been a lot of work, and the distance between each step increases, as I imagine they tried to speed the building process. After a few steps the trail builders must have been exhausted, and I suspect that when they looked down and realized how much farther they had to go down the mountain, they said, "well, to heck with it", and just started painting blazes on the rocks. Let the hikers figure out how to get down on their own. It is fun.

Six miles of forest road walking along the Housatonic River follow the scramble from Caleb's Peak. It is very pleasant strolling through the woods on an easy trail, the river on the left, and meadows and farmers' fields on the right. I pass Redlocks and Snack Time cleaning up and bathing in the river. I am not pushing all that hard either, even though I could have made quick miles. I am enjoying myself

I meet a couple of trail maintainers along this stretch, Richard and Tom, who are checking over their section of trail. I take a break to talk, and I learn a little bit about the commitment it takes to 'own' a section of trail. It is like owning a pet, a constant responsibility, with the occasional need to respond to unexpected disasters.

We talk about the partying bubble that is always ahead of me. There was a large drinking party recently at Wiley Shelter, where I spent the night two nights ago, a mix of locals and hikers, and the maintainers had had to call in the authorities to break it up. Then the maintainers had to clean it up. There is a church in the town of Kent that had a trial run allowing thru-hikers to camp on the grounds. The church decided to no longer support hikers as a campsite just the day before I came through, after a particularly loud party on the grounds disrupted the neighborhood.

Richard calls the party bubble 'trail anarchists'. He thought their definition of wild was as a place without law, not as a natural place to respect, and where man is an outsider. There are both NoBo and SoBo fringe groups riding the backs of their respective hiker bubbles, and they collided at Kent. Richard says he has been a maintainer for ten years, but it is only the last couple of years that the trail partiers have started getting out of hand.

The idea of escaping into the 'wild' has other manifestations. Richard ran into another hiker on the trail, he described as a "kid". He tried talking to the hiker, who was very evasive, shy about answering even basic questions, until he realized Richard was not law enforcement. Richard reckons him a trail hobo, someone who lives out on the trail. There were always a few shadowy characters living on the trail, avoiding people and evading the world.

I think about the whole problem of enforcing consideration of others and respect for the trail, while still allowing people the freedom to escape the world. Freedom is one of the primary reasons people come to the trail in the first place, and nobody wants a lot of oversight. I have my own stroke of brilliance.

The AT Passport is a souvenir passport you can buy from ATC. Many of the business along the trail, including the hostels, stamp the passport if you visit them. It wouldn't take too much more to make the passport a voluntary tracking system. A person would buy the passport (it isn't free) and it would identify the person as a thru-hiker and allow the use of all of the discounts and freebies already offered to thru-hikers. If someone creates problems they could be reported to a website, and if they were a consistent problem, say three complaints from businesses, they would lose the passport, and the assistance and freebies along with it. Since purchasing the passport would be voluntary, there would be no coercion. It would help protect those business and organizations trying to help hikers, and also help the ATC with population and trail use tracking.

I reach my goal for the day in mid-afternoon. The town of Cornwall Bridge is below the ridgeline the trail follows, a mile of walking downhill on hard, hot asphalt road from the trail crossing. I stick out my thumb but I do not get a ride as I walk down the road. There is a gas station at the bottom and I see Dixie on her way out. She is doing a nearo, in and out in the same day with a little break to get resupply.

The town of Cornwall Bridge is a small village with a couple of shops. The outfitter is really a fly fishing shop, and has almost nothing for hikers except a small rack of Coleman gear. None of the things I am looking for are there. There is a hardware store next door, and they have garden hose gaskets I can use as replacements in my Sawyer filter. There are no replacement bladders in town, and I will be squeezing from a Smartwater bottle.

I had hoped to see my friends Brad and Eileen, and their children and spouses, but it is a distance from where they live, and they are only able to organize one potential ride, on the back of a motorcycle. The idea of riding pillion with my backpack on freeways with an unknown driver really doesn't appeal to me, and I regretfully pass on seeing them at this juncture. I am staying in town.

There is a hostel BnB, but they are full up. I end up at the other lodging option in town, a pricey motor lodge called the Hitching Post. The room is clean, but small enough to be a little awkward, and it costs $80.00 after I bargain with the desk clerk.

The Cornwall General Store has a deli, and I get some serious sandwiches there, and a pint of ice cream. The deli is very good, and allows hikers to sit in booths inside or tables outside and use their wireless. There is a liquor store in town, and I pick up a couple of cans of beer for an evening treat.

It turns out the liquor store gives thru-hikers a free can of beer. The store clerk looks over the counter, looks at my battered hiking shoes, and asks me a couple of questions before letting me know about this largess. He is checking to make sure I am a real thru-hiker. I pass muster.

I retire for the evening into my motel room. The hot shower feels good, and I feast. The town as a whole is a little disappointing. At least I found a water filter gasket. It was the single item I couldn't do without. Otherwise, I could have kept going and made more miles on this day, and used a more convenient stop to get resupply.

Day 131 to Day 133, August 14th to August 16th
Cornwall Bridge, CT, to Laurel Ridge Campsite, MA.
Trail Mile 1478.2 to 1508.1, 29.9 miles
AVG 9.96 Daily Miles

Day 131, August 14th
Caesar Brook Campsite, CT, Trail Mile 1480.8
Daily Distance 2.8 Miles

I do not make much progress today. I sleep late, and then laze away the better part of the day sitting out on the deck at the Cornwall General Store, eating, reading a book on my tablet, and eating some more. It is a very heated and humid day, and I feel sluggish. It is difficult to leave the shade under the deck roof, and my comfortable chair. I don't move out of town until late afternoon.

It is a mile long slog up the hill on the hot blacktop road out of town. It is one of the very few times I am unable to get a ride hitching either to or from the trail. Many cars pass me and my outstretched thumb. None stop.

I enter the coolness of the woods, and hike in as far as the first water source and campsite. I stop and make camp just before 6:00 PM. Despite my lazy day in town, and my last couple of days of low miles, I am worn out.

I drank a lot of fluids while I was in town. I think the heat and the water shortages in New York have slowly sapped my energy day after day. I have talked to other hikers, and they are having the same sort of lethargy, and a lot of people are not making the miles they want.

Rain was predicted for this evening, and I use it to justify an early stop. It proves wise, at 8:00 PM a heavy rainstorm comes through, but I am already safely sheltered under the rain fly of my hammock.

I sleep poorly. I drank enough water and juice in town that I have to get up several times in the night.

Day 132, August 15th
Near Grands View, CT, Trail Mile 1495.6
Daily Distance 14.8 Miles

Several times during the night there are horrible, inhuman screeching noises; loud animal screams calling back and forth in the darkness. One is somewhere within a hundred feet of me, and it is answered by another frightful cry out in the meadow ahead somewhere. I am told later it is likely porcupines. In the middle of the night, all alone in the woods, the reasoning part of my brain is sure it is some sort of nocturnal mammal or possibly an owl, but the unreasoning part of my mind is finding it hard to sleep with some dark forest, soul stealing, man eating spirits lurking about.

There is a brief windstorm with some spatters of rain that wake me again later in the night. My hammock sways in the gusts, and a heavy limb comes crashing down to earth from a nearby tree. The forest is filled with hazards.

I play catch up sleeping a little long in the morning, and don't get out of camp until 9:30 AM. The area is rolling hills, and the trail wanders between the hills and the flat lands near the Housatonic River.

The trail has construction blocking it, and there is a detour down a road. I stop at Trinity Episcopal Church. They have an invitation posted out along the road inviting hikers to use their water spigot, outdoor electrical outlets, and wireless internet connection. Boston Ryan is there as well, and we compare notes as we take a short break on the cool shaded benches and use the free services.

I pass Housatonic Falls. The falls are big enough to have driven an old industrial site with a water wheel. It is quite a sight, masses of water thundering down a series of falls before hitting a final big drop of sixty feet. There are white water kayakers unloading their boats upstream.

The trail is still easy going, and if I can overcome the heat I should make some good miles through this stretch. I am still hoping I can make Katahdin before October 15th. The hikers in my bubble are pretty comfortable with the timeline they are on, but I have the wedding I am going to have to leave trail for yet ahead of me.

I camp solo again, and I scare the hell out of myself tossing up my bear bag. I find a suitable tree, and I am just about to throw my line up and over the branch when I notice a big bulbous object hanging down from the tree limb, and I pull my toss up short. I peer up at the object, and realize I am looking at a huge paper wasp nest. I am not sure exactly what would have happened if I caught on that thing with my bear bag toss and gave it a few tugs, but I can in no way imagine any sort of good outcome, except getting a lot of additional evening aerobic exercise.

I take a risk and hang my food bag from my hammock strap. I pee on the base of the tree below, which is supposed to let bears know the food is mine, and I will defend it. I have seen bear droppings on today's hike. New York did not appear to be bear country, but signs of their presence are coming back. The bears seem a lot shyer in areas where bear hunting is allowed, and Connecticut is one of those places.

I see a lot of other wildlife; much of it is small. A tree frog visits my pack as I set up my camp. I see many of the little toads I call scooters hopping off the trail. I see a garter snake, and another snake with a bright green head. The little Red Spotted Newts are appearing again; they like the wet, buggy areas. There are a few deer about, and many birds and hawks in the air and among the tree branches.

The mosquitoes are ferocious. Baltimore Jack warned us back in Virginia that Massachusetts would be a tunnel of insects, and it is looking like he was right. I should enter Massachusetts tomorrow. Of all of Jack's predictions, this is the one I like least, so it must be true. He was very optimistic about every other aspect of thru-hiking. I wear my raincoat with its hood up and long sleeves just to keep the biting insects at bay as I do camp chores, despite the heat. I hear insects buzzing all around my hammock as I fall off to sleep.

I sleep fitfully. I am very conscious of the food bag swaying from my hammock strap a few feet away from my head, and every time a squirrel dislodges a nut and it falls near me, I become alert, listening for mice or other food raiders out by my bag.

Day 133, August 16th
Laurel Ridge Campsite, Massachusetts, Trail Mile 1508.1
Daily Distance 12.5 Miles

My daily goal is 15 miles a day. I figure if I can complete ten 15 mile days between now and September 1st, when I have to go off-trail for my

254

sister's wedding, I will still have a chance of making Katahdin by October 15th. Today I come up short, a disappointment. Fifteen miles isn't far in theory, but in practice it is proves difficult to consistently make those miles.

I have to go back into a town. I lost another water filter gasket, a critical item. I hitch into Salisbury looking for a new one, but the outfitter listed in the AWOL Guide has gone out of business, and I cannot find a hardware store either. I will make do. I can suck a drink through the filter, but it leaks and sprays when I squeeze water out for cooking.

I still eat a nice lunch and resupply at the little supermarket in town. There are a couple of other thru-hikers taking a break. We talk about the heat. It is 103 degrees today, and humid. The air is thick, sucking energy out of you with every breath. The mosquitoes are keeping up their attacks as well. It would be wonderful hiking without those two factors.

The Appalachian Trail is making more climbs again and I am scrambling over the occasional rock formation. We are going to rise out of the Mid-Atlantic saddle and back into the real mountains in New England. There is plenty of water. I follow one stream for nearly a mile as it chuckles and gurgles down a mountain ravine beside the trail.

I meet Bookworm today, and we hike together for a while, and camp together. He offers me the use of his filter to purify water for dinner and morning coffee. Bookworm is another one of the remarkable people that seem to be the rule rather than exceptions in the thru-hiking community.

He is legally blind, and is going to follow me until he catches his friend Bison. He can see, but I think it is a very blurry world, and he wants someone to track on while he hikes, just in case. He is one of the High Flyers, but like most of that group he is a pretty amicable and pleasant person. He is also a collegiate forensic champion from an Ivy League school. What I get from his descriptions is that college Forensics is a debate forum, not a type of criminal investigation.

Today I enter a new state, and I have 681 miles left to reach the trail's end.

Day 134 to Day 139, August 17th to August 22nd
Laurel Ridge Campsite, MA, to Mt. Greylock, MA.
Trail Mile 1508.1 to 1586.3 Miles, 77.5 Miles, AVG 12.91 Daily Miles

Day 134, August 17th
Past Boardman Street, Massachusetts, Trail Mile 1522.3
Daily Distance 14.2 Miles

I am out early today, in part because Bookworm is motivating me, and we are on the trail at 7:30 AM. We encounter a series of short but hard climbs of 800 to 1000 feet. Combined with the heat and humidity it slows our pace.

We decide to hitchhike into nearby South Egremont for an in and out resupply and meal. I am still hoping for a new filter gasket, and we are going to pick up enough food to get us into Dalton, four days ahead. Hitching into town is slow; the road is not well traveled. The sixth car that comes by picks us up, after a half an hour of waiting.

There are no filter gaskets available in the hamlet, but the sandwiches are good and the trail resupply is sufficient. The very first car to see us with our thumbs out picks us up on the return trip, and we gladly cram ourselves and our packs into a little hatchback. The woman driving is a descendant of the owners of the dairy farm right where the Appalachian Trail crosses the road.

Our town trip costs us 3 hours of daylight. Bookworm and I might have pushed another mile today, but I am worn out by the heat. This trail section is in a swampy area with bad water and lots of mosquitoes. We carry full loads of water to ensure we have what we need, and our packs are heavy. I have found that it is possible to hike fast enough that the mosquito swarms cannot keep up. It is when I pause or stop that they become unbearable.

Day 135, August 18th
Wilcox North Shelter, MA, Trail Mile 1534.5
Daily Distance 12.2 Miles

Bookworm and I are up and moving on the trail at 6:15 AM. The effects of the heat are cumulative, draining our energy day by day, and we get fewer miles for more effort. The area is speckled with mosquito breeding marshes, ponds and small lakes.

It is all very pretty to look at. I am pleased to see a beaver finally, after seeing numerous dams all along the trail. He is sitting on a floating log out in a pond, chewing on a stick.

The water at the Wilcox North Shelter is a muddy puddle and I make a mess of filtering using my leaky gasket, but I am still able to get water. There is a large crowd of thru-hikers here. Steady Eddie, whom I saw last at the Graymoor Spiritual Life Center, Rocking Ronnie, Stormchaser, Turtle, and Waldo all put in appearances. The trail is crowded with familiar faces today.

I am still wrestling with my own attitudes towards pot smoking on the trail. It is a bigger internal issue now, since Bookworm likes a toke here and there. In fact, many of the people I like most on the trail are pot smokers, and I enjoy their company.

I sleep in my hammock near the shelter, not within it. None of the thru-hikers actually sleep in the shelter, pitching tents and hammocks to avoid the mice and mosquitoes. The shelter structure still serves as a gathering place, a little community center in the woods.

I am part of a discussion about the big party in Kent, Connecticut, where the yellow blazers from the northbound and southbound bubbles collided. The party closed the free campsite, which ATC had worked for years to get opened. The town's benevolence did not last the season.

There are rangers and ridge runners on trail looking for various suspects from the event. Redlocks is one of those sought, even though he wasn't there at all. One of the big troublemakers had dreadlocks, so there has been a case of mistaken identity.

The fuss about the Kent party and closure of the camping area is having an impact on the backpacking community. Angry thru-hikers are filling the trail registers with vitriol toward the people responsible for creating issues in general, and closing Kent specifically. I am hoping it cools down the yellow blazing party enough so they do not have a further negative impact on the trail community.

Day 136, August 19th
Upper Goose Pond Cabin, MA, Trail Mile 1548.5
Daily Distance 14.0 Miles

Massachusetts is another northeastern state that, like New Jersey, is unexpectedly beautiful and wild. It is easy to see why writers like Thoreau, Emerson, and Melville found inspiration here. The little forested lakes nestled into rolling mountains make an idyllic landscape.

Bookworm and I aim to get to Upper Goose Pond Cabin today. It is a sweet spot on the trail, a hostel in a lakeside cabin, part of what used to be some wealthy gentlemen's fish and game club. Getting there isn't too difficult.

The heat backs off a little, a relief. Climbs are gradually increasing to about 1000 feet of up and down, which is just stretching the legs at this point in the hike. The trail is very well maintained, and it reminds me of walking through the Shenandoah somehow, even though the terrain and vegetation are very different.

We are late getting out of camp. I felt a little ill last night, a little feverish from a passing cold or flu, but a good night of sleep seems to have laid it to rest. It may have been cumulative heat and dehydration getting me down. Once I get going I am full of energy today. Many factors work together: the diminished heat, a positive phone call from home, and a double ramen bomb the night before. I am a good hiker today.

I see Grip and Notes at a road crossing. I haven't seen Grip in a long time, maybe since Virginia. He injured his knee, but is still hiking as much as he can. He is one of those people who push themselves as hard as they can, for the sheer joy of going full tilt. The trail is hard on such people; day after day of relentless effort can cost them. He was doing 20 mile days. He is section hiking now, picking up the trail highlights and then taking rests for his knee.

Grip is supporting Notes when he isn't hiking. He has a van he uses to shuttle her about. He takes his sidelining pretty hard; I can hear it when I talk to him. He eventually will end up on a print in a book by Sketch holding the Katahdin sign.

The cabin at Upper Goose Pond is a half mile off-trail on a blue blaze, a mile of extra hiking there and back.

The cabin is awesome, and definitely worth the detour. It is also packed, there are twenty or more backpackers staying the night. The cabin has caretakers, volunteers who in this instance are taking a week of vacation to host hikers while staying at the cabin. An overnight stay is donation based, and includes a pancake breakfast.

Bookworm and I have arrived early enough that we secure bunks despite the steady flow of hikers arriving, and I go to the lake for a swim before cooking my dinner.

The water is cool, but not shockingly cold. I jump in off a dock with all of my clothes on as an expedient way to wash both my clothes and body at the same time, and I strip down in the water. The pond is really a small lake. There is an island visible a half mile away, and a couple of canoes are available to explore the lake.

It is a pleasant evening, and even the bugs seem less aggressive. It may just be they have so many hikers to choose from at the cabin they are spread out. A little after darkness there is a downpour, and more hikers show up in the thick of it. The bunks are full, and they have to set up camp in the rain.

Rocking Ronnie is one of the late arrivals. He is doing the trail in fits and starts. I am not sure he even thinks of himself as a thru-hiker, and I am pretty sure he has yellow blazed parts. He stops to work along the way to help support his hike, and he carries a full sized guitar. He picks up some free meals and a little cash busking at pubs and trail hangouts along the trail. He is a very talented guitar player and musician. He has taught me some here and there when we meet, just a little at a time, mostly on his guitar.

I have heard that Highlighter, whom I last saw at the motorcycle accident in Maryland, is off the trail. She took a little time to heal and then tried to flip-flop. She re-injured herself on Katahdin, the first day of her flip.

I am getting the idea. Maine is hard.

Dalton is 20 miles away. I am considering doing a twenty mile day and then taking my first zero since New Jersey. I will have to stop at the Cookie Lady's on the way.

Day 137, August 20th
3 miles past the Cookie Lady, MA, Trail Mile 1562.5
Daily Distance 14 Miles

I enjoy the pancake breakfast and hot coffee prepared by our Upper Goose Cabin hosts. There are so many hikers present that we have to eat in shifts. Passing SoBos who went through earlier told us about 'all you can eat' pancakes, but there are simply too many people. I still eat five pancakes, and have two cups of Joe.

The Cookie Lady, to the north of Upper Goose Pond on the trail, also sells 'you pick em' blueberries and SoBo's will often bring a pint down with them for the pancakes. We are almost all NoBos, and one pint of blueberries has to serve us all. There are a few fat blueberries in the pancakes, not many. It makes a nice tart surprise when I bite into one. They are delicious.

The hike today is a 1000 foot climb, followed a few smaller climbs before fading into flats approaching the Cookie Lady's house. There are some muddy patches, foreshadowing Vermont. Vermont is famous for its trail mud, and is often referred to as 'Vermud'.

I see a lot of SoBos passing me as they hike towards Springer Mountain. They all love the easier terrain in Massachusetts after coming through Maine and New Hampshire.

We come across a young female thru-hiker I have not seen before, sitting on a log just off the trail. She appears to be crying. Bookworm and I stop, but she will not tell us what is wrong. We make sure she is physically OK, and move along.

We stop for a while to talk to another NoBo thru-hiker, and he and Bookworm have a smoke break. The other NoBo is new to me, although I have heard a little about him. He is one of the hikers who is doing various sections of the trail rather than doing the entire thing. He is a yellow blazer, but not one of the troublemakers that I have heard about. Although he is friendly enough, he seems a bit sketchy to me. He asks about his female partner, the crying girl we just passed.

It turns out the male hiker is trying to figure out a trail lifestyle financed by selling pot, and by making pornographic videos with his partner on some kind of pay site. I think I know why the girl was crying, after hearing how she is financing her trail experience. I would be crying too. Bookworm is fascinated by it, and is young enough to view it as an outlaw lifestyle. I find it depressing, and sad.

The Cookie Lady has a house a quarter mile off of the trail at a road crossing. It is hard to tell which house it is without the AWOL Guide's description. There are a couple of abandoned older buildings on a lot with blueberry bushes visible growing in the back. The Cookie Lady's house is hidden behind the older buildings.

The Cookie Lady is in fact an older couple. It takes a while between the doorbell ring and someone coming to the front porch door. The constant stream of hikers showing up on their doorstep must wear on them, and I hear later that this may be their last year of supporting the trail. They have the free home baked cookies they are famous for, and a small list of other items available for sale at break even prices, including Klondike bars and hard boiled eggs. We get a couple of cookies each, some other snacks and drinks, and a hurried smile. The couple is on their way out, but they tell us where the water hose is, and allow me to access the power outlet in the garage to charge my phone and one-shot power supply.

We sit and have lunch at a picnic table under a shade tree. The Cookie Lady couple leaves, and when I get ready to go I find the doors to the garage have all been locked. My phone is still inside, perfectly visible through the window. I am stuck.

It is mid-afternoon, and Bookworm wants to the make miles towards Dalton, where he hopes to catch his friend Bison, and we part company. I sit at the picnic bench enjoying the sun, and resting as only a person given an unexpected break from continuous hard labor can rest. I cook a ramen bomb dinner and feed my crumbs to the chickens wandering around. A SoBo is also stuck with me in the same predicament, his phone also charging in the garage. He picks a pint of blueberries and sticks the money for them under the front door.

It is late afternoon when the owners come back. As soon as the garage door is opened we rush in and get our phones, and make hurried departures in our respective directions. The day is pretty much spent.

I call ahead and find there are no lodging rooms in Dalton, and so I only hike another 3 miles before I stop and camp trailside with an older NoBo named Boogie Pilgrim.

Boogie is definitely a budget hiker, and has last generation's gear to show it. His equipment is quite serviceable, but his pack and gear are a good five pounds heavier than equivalent modern gear.

Dalton is a bust, and I am going to try and get to Cheshire for a motel room stay. I need internet to take care of some business. I have seven miles to hike before Dalton tomorrow, and I will have to stop for resupply, even if I don't plan on staying. I am running low on necessities, and I am still slowed at each water resupply by my missing filter gasket. I was lucky today with water, being able to fill up at Goose Pond Cabin and again at the Cookie Lady's.

Day 138, August 21st
Past Dalton MA, Trail Mile 1572.0
Daily Distance 9.5 Miles

It was a chilly night and it is a cool morning, the first sign that summer is not endless on the Appalachian Trail. Boogie Pilgrim is already up and gone. I break the cold camp quickly and I am on the trail before 8:00 AM. There are no big climbs, just a series of hundred foot ups and downs into town. I compete the 7 miles into Dalton before noon. The AT goes right through town.

There is a hardware and feed store within the first quarter mile of entering town and I am finally able to find hose gaskets for my water filter. I have a couple of options to choose from. I buy several, they only cost $1.00 for a half dozen, and after losing two I am carrying spares. Every little item adds up in pack weight and I have gotten into the practice of carrying only what I immediately need, but the gaskets are light, and are vital. I only carry a couple of spare items of any kind; extra batteries for my headlamp and an extra mini Bic lighter. I have come a long way from the shakedown at Neel's Gap.

The Appalachian Trail passes through several blocks of older houses before reaching the business district on the main boulevard. The houses along the way have occasional AT emblems on them, and one, the house of Thomas Levardi, is a hiker landmark. Mr. Levardi has an impromptu hostel of sorts. He allows hikers to set up tents in his yard and use his hose, porch, and outdoor electrical outlets. He has old bikes that hikers can sign out to get around town.

It may be Tom Levardi's last year hosting thru-hikers. The large numbers of hikers coming through have turned maintaining his casual oasis into a full time job. His yard and porch are crowded. He has put rules in place to protect his home, his neighbors, and his privacy, which a few hikers resent and ignore. His neighbors have grown less and less pleased with the seasonal Woodstock in his yard. There have been incidents with people who are loud and boisterous, hiker's dogs attacking neighbors and their dogs, and hikers wandering around neighboring yards late at night. There have been even been incidents with hikers using neighboring yards as bathroom facilities

I check the single motel in the town of Dalton, the Shamrock, and it is full. There is a beer festival happening nearby, and the town is bursting at the seams. I go to the town library and get on the internet for an hour before they close, and eat at a small diner. There is no grocery store within reasonable walking distance, and I get an expensive and minimal resupply at a convenience store. I get hiking again. Since I will not be taking a zero here I am going to try to resupply again in Cheshire, just 8 miles further along the AT.

I only get a couple of miles down the trail before the day is spent. I set up my solo camp and try to sleep. I am still near enough to civilization that I can hear a lot of human background noise; some of the festival goers have set up encampments in the woods.

What I find more disturbing are the coyotes. The coyotes of the East are not the song dogs of the West. They are snarling, growling, screaming, fighting, and somewhere nearby. They give voice at unpredictable intervals, and I feel very vulnerable in my hammock.

Day 139, August 22nd
Mount Greylock, Bascom Lodge, Trail Mile 1586.3
Daily Distance 14.3 Miles

It is a good morning of hiking. I begin crossing a ridgeline that is higher than the thick bank of clouds obscuring the valleys below me. I hike on a long, thin, causeway surrounded by a sea of grey and white mist. My world narrows to the wooded ridgeline and the swirling clouds.

It is easy to forget the difficulties of hiking when I am walking in such a beautiful isolation. Thru-hiking hurts. It is an endurance contest, day after day of facing the weather, the bugs, the terrain, and my own physical weaknesses of discomfort and pain. Every day I still get up and move forward. It is a mental challenge to keep walking, more than any other. Any given day has its difficulties, but there is a sameness, a monotony to walking long miles each day.

I believe the monotony ends more hikes than any other factor. When it sinks in that this is it, that this hiking is every day for months, it is easy to just not get back on the trail one day on a town stop, Maybe something happens that requires a few days off the trail, and a few days of normal life turns into a week, and then you just never go back.

Moments like this morning offset the monotony. It is early in the day and the pain I know is coming is still ahead of me. The clouds hide the world while I hike across my little slice of trail in sunshine, content to just walk, enjoy serenity, and see beauty.

I complete the six and a half miles into Cheshire before noon. Cheshire is a hamlet rather than a town. The bed and breakfast I was looking forward to for a night of comfort is closed, permanently. There is no other lodging option. It is Sunday, and everything is closed, including the local library and general store. One of the local churches allows hikers to stay on the grounds, but as it is Sunday the priest is occupied with matters other than tending to thru-hikers.

I have a sandwich and an ice cream at the only available shop, positioned at the junction of a road with the Appalachian Trail and a rails-to-trails bike path. A veteran thru-hiker, Marshmallow (2012), and his girlfriend show up, and hand out bottles of cold beer as trail magic.

There is a park service lodge listed in the AWOL Guide on top of Mt. Greylock, the tallest mountain in Massachusetts, just ahead of me. I still need internet, and I am down to a few energy bars for food. I have been sustaining myself on the daily meals in towns, and on trail magic. Bascom Lodge is now my goal for the day.

I come across another spot of trail magic while leaving Cheshire, a few cans of beer and some chips stashed with a trail magic note near a road crossing. I eat a small meal of chips and have a beer, and leave a couple of beers behind. I meet three SoBos coming the other way another half mile down trail, and tell them of the two beers remaining. They do the math. Three hikers, two beers, and they go charging down the hill, packs bouncing on their backs. The race is on.

Mt. Greylock is the tallest mountain in Massachusetts, and the first real mountain I have climbed since Virginia. It is famous for other reasons beyond its height. It has a lighthouse on top of it, a war monument that is quite impressive, and the lodge. It was also America's first downhill ski resort. The ski resort is gone, but some of the trails and the old cabins remain. The mountain is visible from Herman Melville's historical home, and it is said that the vaguely whale-like shape of the mountain inspired him to write Moby Dick.

The climb is noticeable for its length, but is not particularly difficult. I arrive at the summit in fog and light rain. The views are supposed to be spectacular, so I hope for sunshine tomorrow morning.

The Bascom Lodge is expensive, and in the state I am in it is worth every penny. I have been looking for a break in town for several days now, and have been thwarted by circumstances every time. I get a single room rather than staying in the bunkroom. I do not want a crowded noisy room.

I find on later inspection that there is only one other person in the spacious and comfortable bunkroom. I believe it is the third time I have paid for an expensive single room when the bunkroom was more than suitable.

I have a hot shower, and a hot prepared dinner. The lodge has snacks but does not have any real trail resupply, so I still need a supermarket stop, but I am content, and relieved to have comforts for the night.

VERMONT AND NEW HAMPSHIRE

Day 140 to Day 168, August 23rd to September 28th
Mt. Greylock, MA, to Gorham NH, Trail Mile 1586.3 to 1890.9
304.6 miles, 28 Days (1 week off-trail)
AVG 10.87 Daily Miles

Day 140 to Day 144, August 23rd to August 27th
Mt. Greylock, MA to Green Mountain Hostel, Manchester VT,
Trail Mile 1586.3 to 1651.1. 64.8 miles,
AVG 12.96 Daily Miles

Day 140, August 23rd
Sherman Brook Campsite, Trail Mile 1594.2
Daily Distance 7.9 Miles

I sleep in at Bascom Lodge in my comfy bed, order a large leisurely breakfast, eat it, and take another hot shower before hitting the trail. There is wireless, and I have started shopping for items online that I want or will need for colder weather that I have not been able to find along the trail. I buy a Jetboil stove from Amazon, and have it shipped to my mother's house. I have to leave the Appalachian Trail for my sister's wedding in a week, and I will have time to reconstruct my pack load and prepare myself for the colder weather ahead while I visit.

I am looking at underquilts for my hammock. An underquilt is a blanket that suspends beneath the hammock to insulate the bottom. Regular sleeping bags don't work well in hammocks. The weight of the sleeper's body in the hammock compresses the stuffing against the fabric and takes away the material's insulating qualities. Air circulation under a hammock can quickly steal a body's heat. Even in summer I have been sleeping on a mat inside the hammock, and I am occasionally chilled.

Underquilts are expensive, and one will add additional weight and volume to my pack load, so I am taking time making my decision. I have solicited advice from other hammockers along the way, especially Redlocks. He was one of the very first hammockers I met, and survived some very cold weather at the very beginning of the journey,

The weather is still cloudy with an occasional drizzle. The lighthouse memorial to Massachusetts' war dead is impressive. There are recent entries on the wall for Iraq and Afghanistan, and they left plenty of room for future conflicts. The acceptance of the sacrifice of the state's sons and daughters, and the expectation that it will continue is a sad but realistic comment on man as an individual, nation, and species, and food for thought for the next mile or two of the Appalachian Trail.

I finally arrive in a town with a supermarket, and I hike the non-trail miles into and out of North Adams to get my shopping done, at the price of making less daily distance on the trail. The cost of food in Massachusetts is high; I am paying maybe a third more for resupply than I did in the South. Instead of spending $45.00 dollars for four to six days worth of food, I am paying more than $60.00 on the exact same items.

I have six days of food now, and it is difficult getting it all to fit inside my food bag. I have to carry a few items in a separate waterproof bag. I have been so light on food for so long the weight of a full load is a little bit of a shock.

I get out of town and stop at the first campsite I come to, a couple miles further along the trail. There is a ridge runner present, and a group of college freshman. Local colleges have pre-orientation events for groups of new students, coming out onto to the Appalachian Trail for a few days of backpacking and bonding. This is the first of many such groups I will encounter over the next couple of weeks.

I am only two miles away from the Vermont border. Vermont and the Long Trail are considered the training ground for the White Mountains and Maine. The Mid-Atlantic States diminished climbs and descents are behind me. The hills have slowly been getting taller as I move north, and now I am going to be in real mountains again, the Green Mountains of Vermont.

Day 141, August 24th
Compton Shelter, VT, Trail Mile 1606.7
Daily Distance 12.5 Miles

It is raining when I awake, and I lie in my hammock waiting until it changes from regular beats to an occasional pitter patter on my rain fly before getting out. I talk to Sawdog, a ridge runner, for a good half hour after getting my camp packed away. The ridge runners are usually past thru-hikers themselves, have lived interesting lives, and are well worth any time spent talking and listening to them.

I get on with my hiking at 11:00 AM. I soon enter Vermont, my 12th state, and I get my first taste of the Vermud. The rain has turned the trail to slop.

I continue to pass groups of college freshman on their pre-orientation trips, and they are camping at every shelter. While they are noisy, they maintain a certain distance, and don't camp inside the shelters.

Getting to play old man hiker and laugh at their naive antics is fun. The groups only manage five miles or so a day, as their experience is about bonding in the wilderness, not on hiking per se. They are quite hapless looking with their ill fitting, overloaded, unbalanced packs and gear.

My wife is talking about divorce during a phone call, again, so I have a big distraction and emotional issue to compete with the Zen of being on the trail, and I spend some part of my hike today zoned out in a misery within, muttering to myself as I move north. I expect to see my wife at my sister's wedding a week from now, but she goes back and forth on whether she will attend. She is bringing my daughter, who I very much want to see, with her.

I hear a rumor, later confirmed, that Tom Levardi, under pressure from his neighbors in Dalton, the trail town back in Massachusetts, went ahead and threw in the towel. He closed his yard to camping and ended his hospitality to hikers. Someone caught peeing on a neighbor's lawn seems to be the final straw.

Tonight, I am at Compton Shelter. I hang my hammock, and have another collegiate group for company nearby.

Day 142, August 25th
Goddard Shelter, VT, Trail Mile 1621.1
Daily Distance 14.4 Miles

TRAILTALK:

MINI TRIPLE CROWN: Completing the Long Trail, the Colorado Trail, and the John Muir Trail, each a segment of the 3 continental trails that make up the triple crown of long distance hiking (The AT, CDT, and PCT)

LT (The Long Trail): The Long Trail goes north to south the length of Vermont, traveling through the Green Mountains. It is older than the Appalachian Trail, which follows the Long Trail for much of its passage through Vermont.

The Appalachian Trail in Vermont follows the southern part of the Long Trail, a hiking path even older than the AT. When the Appalachian Trail was created it was linked together using a number of other pre-existing trail systems. These trails all have their own individual names and histories. The Long Trail (LT) runs north to south, border to border, through the Green Mountains of Vermont. The AT follows it for about half of the LT's length before turning east towards New Hampshire. There are plenty of Long Trail thru-hikers, and the hiking organizations here that maintain the trail identify themselves with the Long Trail, not the AT.

There is a mini triple crown that gives a hiker a taste of the three continental trails in the United States; the AT, PCT and CDT. The mini trails are the Long Trail (AT), the Colorado Trail (CDT) and John Muir Trail (PCT). If you can only spare a few weeks a year, and want to have a long distance hiking experience completing a trail, these are very good options.

The Green Mountains are a real mountain range, rather than the hills and ridgelines of the Mid Atlantic states. Today there is a significant climb near Bennington after the trail drops down into a valley and crosses a state road. There is a 1000 foot steep climb out of the valley, and then 1500 more feet of gradual ascent. I look forward to climbs in the morning as temperatures are cooling. It is a way to quickly warm up.

It is getting colder, and I feel it in my hammock. I am sleeping in through the chilly first part of the morning. Sometimes I am awake, but lie there shivering in my bag, unwilling to emerge fully into the cold day. My colder weather hiking gear awaits me at my sister's wedding.

I opt to stay inside Goddard Shelter itself tonight; I may be able to sleep a little warmer. There are four other hikers at the shelter with me; a group of LT section hikers about my own age. Someone left a battery powered, working keyboard in the shelter. I can't imagine why it is here, but it is a fun toy to play with.

Day 143, August 26th
Near a logging road north of Stratton Mountain, VT, Trail Mile 1639.1
Daily Distance 18.0 Miles

Stratton Mountain is a tough nut. Climbing up and over it is the major event of the day. The climbs are coming back, and this is reminiscent of the Smoky Mountains. I end up with a big mile day simply because the last seven miles over Stratton Mountain have no good campsites.

Stratton Mountain, besides being a popular east coast ski resort, also boasts an historical fire tower, and is reputed to be the place where Benton MacKaye had the first inspiration to combine the eastern trail systems into a single connected trail system, the Appalachian Trail.

I run into Boogie Pilgrim under the fire tower on the Stratton summit, and we both consider going up for a look. It is already 7:30 PM, and near sunset, the long days of summer are passing. We both go up for a hurried look, but darkness is coming, and we need to press on.

Neither of us really likes camping alone, and we hike down the mountain together looking for camping sites large enough for both a tent and a hammock. We hike nearly to the bottom of the mountain before finding a workable space. It is dark and we are wearing our headlamps by then. The mountain is thickly forested and there are not many open, flat spaces. We stop and look at a couple of places on our way down, peering about in the darkness by the beams of our lamps, but each proves unsuitable. We don't get settled until after 9:00 PM, in full darkness.

Day 144, August 27th
Green Mountain Hostel, Manchester VT, Trail Mile 1651.1
Daily Distance 12 Miles

It takes a long time to make my first five miles today. Boogie Pilgrim is awake, packed, and on the trail before I even get out of my hammock. I start hiking at 8:15 AM, and hitch into town at 5:00 PM. The trail is rugged, and very wet. Parts of the trail are deep in mud or are under two to six inches of water. Trail maintenance is haphazard. Some sections have rotting boards to cross the wettest, muddiest patches, and in some areas there is nothing. There are climbs again, although Stratton was the big ascent for this particular stretch of trail.

I go into Manchester, a little tourist town filled with high end clothing retailers and knick knack shops. There is, finally, a real outfitter, and a decent hardware store. The outfitter is Eastern Mountain Sports. EMS

267

does not have hammock or climbing equipment. They have lots of trendy clothing, and a reasonable assortment of outdoor and backpacking gear.

I find a long handled titanium spoon. I have been using a short handled one, but trade it out. Long handled spoons make it easier to scrape out the bottom of a pot or a dehydrated meal bag. I replace all of my dry bags, which are worn and torn, especially the fold over handles where I have been using the smaller ones as the weight on my bear bag toss.

The hardware store renews my supply of water filter gaskets, and the Price Chopper lets me complete a full resupply. My only disappointment is the only available instant coffee tubes are Nescafe, and I prefer the little Starbucks Vias. In a trendy little town like Manchester I am surprised they don't have Starbucks. My morning coffee on the trail is instant coffee shaken up in cold water using an old PowerAde bottle, with a hot chocolate packet to add cream and sugar, so I am not exactly enjoying a gourmet cup anyway.

I call the Green Mountain Hostel, and they agree to pick me up after I eat. I am a veteran and member of the Veterans of Foreign Wars, and have been in Afghanistan and Iraq three times. I have earned my Combat Infantry Badge. I belong.

I know VFWs often do a Friday or Saturday night dinner, and there is a VFW right there across from the EMS strip mall. I decide to check it out.

I walk into the VFW toting my trusty pack Thud, with a good coating of trail funk on us both. I am met by the hostile stares of the people sitting around the bar. They are an older group of barflies, Cold War and Vietnam era veterans I expect, not part of this last generation of vets.

I think about making a quick retreat, but I am a member, and I have earned a right to be here, so I advance to the bar. I ask about dinner, and I am met by contemptuous laughter. There is no dinner.

I have a momentary urge to sit up at the bar and order a drink just to see what would happen, but decide I have had enough humiliation for a day and withdraw from the smirks and looks.

There is a veterans' hiking group on the trail this year, and I know many VFWs have provided logistical support to it, feeding, housing, and transporting them to and from town. The Manchester VFW seems to be an exception to the hospitality VFWs usually provide, and an unsettling and upsetting experience.

I get a much better reception at the gourmet pizza place across the way. I have a post-hike feast and a beer, and my ride to the hostel picks me up there.

Green Mountain Hostel is a nice late 19th or early 20th century farmhouse that has been fully renovated and modernized. It is very comfortable. There are a couple of twin beds in each bedroom, and it is far more like a college dormitory than a bunkhouse. There is a nice kitchen, a living room, and a computer business center for use by guests

The hostel sells the inevitable pints of Ben and Jerry's Ice Cream. I have a pint for dessert while I do my laundry. I am sitting in the common room talking with the other hiking guests, and we talk about the issues of conflicts between the hiker community and trail towns. I present my idea of using the AT Passport as a voluntary control measure, and I think it gets a good reception,

I settle in, shower, and go to sleep.

Day 145 to Day 148 August 28 to August 31
Manchester VT to The Long Trail Inn, Rutland, VT,
Trail Mile 1651.1 to 1702.0. 50.9 miles
AVG 12.72 Daily Miles

Day 145, August 28th
Peru Peak Shelter, VT, Trail Mile 1661.2
Daily Distance 10.1 Miles

I spend the best part of the morning working at the computer center at the Green Mountain Hostel. I make arrangements to rent a car for a week to travel to my sister's wedding in North Carolina. The car awaits me in Rutland, VT, the next significant town on the trail, on September 2nd. Rutland is at trail mile 1701, so I have four days to hike 51 miles.

I make final gear decisions and order winter equipment online. I polled other hammockers about their set ups, and every one of them has different ideas and favors different equipment. I end up buying an over and underquilt system from Jacks R Better. They are highly regarded, and I spoke to the proprietors at the big equipment display and sales area at Trail Days back in Damascus, Virginia. I have it all sent to my mother's house to pick up at the wedding.

The Green Mountain Hostel owner will give me a ride back to Manchester. I missed the shuttle out to the trailhead first thing in the morning, so I have to hitch out the rest of the way. I quickly get a ride from a man named Mark.

Mark has his own connections to the Appalachian Trail community. He was the ferryman for the AT canoe crossing on the Kennebec River up in Maine. He asked me to leave a stone on a riverbank cairn he started in honor of Steve Longley, a friend of his who did much for the ferry, and the trail.

Mark is a craftsman working in birch bark, mostly making baskets, but taking into account his past, it is natural we talk about the old birch bark canoes and how they were constructed. He would like to embark on such a project (em-bark, get it?), but birch trees of a sufficient size to provide large enough pieces of bark for the construction are very rare now, and it is rarer still one is cut down.

Once on the trail I make 10 miles in 6 hours and 15 minutes, including a couple of moderately difficult ascents and descents of about 2500 feet.

The hiking in Vermont is different from the south and the Mid Atlantic States. The trail is poorly marked; white blazes are rare. It travels through designated Wilderness areas, and they are definitely are less touched by the hand of man. The trail maintainers have posted signs stating they are not performing trail maintenance in the Wilderness areas. Boardwalks are rotted, bridges are down, and the trail is covered with fallen trees, rocks, and the Vermud.

The same trail also wanders up and down ski slopes past snow blowing machines and chair lifts.

Some of the shelters have a fee to use them. The trail is in good condition within a mile of the fee shelters. The areas close to the fee sites are no camping zones, and you must use the fee site.

The fees are a nominal five dollars, but to thru-hikers it is out of character with the rest of the trail to have to pay to hike it, and fees are resented. The fee sites sit at the water sources on stretches where there is no water for miles before or after. They have a monopoly of sorts on critical sections of trail, like a highway motel in a town 45 miles from the next exit. You can pay what they ask, or you can keep going. In my case, I hang my hammock, not at the shelter, but nearby, and pay the caretaker as I pass in the morning.

My understanding is that there are just not enough volunteers to properly maintain the entire length of the Long Trail, and that the volunteer population they do have is aging retirees, not the fittest of workers for the grueling, physical tasks of working on trails. Compromises have been made to keep the trail viable.

White blazes marking the way in Vermont are infrequent, and their absence can lead to some scary periods of uncertainty, especially when the trail is not a clear path itself. I hiked a mile and more worrying about whether I missed a critical turn while I wasn't paying attention on several occasions. After getting lost for several miles on my very first day on trail, I can get pretty worked up internally, wondering if I am on the right trail when I don't see a white blaze for a while.

Day 146, August 29th
Greenwall Shelter, VT, Trail Mile 1675.7
Daily Distance 14.5 Miles

It is an unexceptional day of hiking, except that every day on the Appalachian Trail is an exceptional day. Today the climbs and descents continue and I am definitely feeling the mountains. There are some big views from the tops, one of which I sit on to eat lunch. A college orientation group out bonding before school begins comes by and my solitude is interrupted by the chattering, happy group as they scamper about the peak taking pictures and eating snacks.

I had a conversation about the trail conditions with the caretaker at Peru Peak Shelter before I left. He tells me that the average age of a Green Mountain Hiking Club member, the volunteer organization keeping up the trail in Vermont, is 67 years old. It is not a great age for hiking deep into the woods and performing the hard graft of working on the trail. There is an additional factor, which is that in Wilderness areas only hand tools are permitted, and have to be carried in and out on the workers' backs. So compromises are made.

There are many brooks and ponds along this section. Most of the water is as clear as glass, the bottom easily visible. In some areas the tannins from the trees and leaves have made the water a little brown, but it is still clean water. I filter it all, but it is starting to look drinkably pure.

It is a good thing water was plentiful along the trail, because when I arrive at Greenwall Shelter a female thru-hiker I will not name is already there, and she tells the other thru-hikers here for the night that there is no water at the spring. We take her word for it and don't check it ourselves. Later hikers tell me there was a perfectly good water point about 100 yards away, if we had just looked for it.

The female hiker does not prove to be a good shelter companion. She has an unleashed dog that barks and growls at anyone who comes near her, and it bites the sleeve of another hiker who tries to pet it at the picnic table while we are all cooking dinner.

"It's ok, he's just protective", the girl tells us. She brings her dog into the shelter to sleep that night without asking anyone if they have issues with it. She also smokes pot inside, again without asking if it bothers anyone else.

She tells us how she called a hostel for a shuttle that clearly was posted as 'no dogs' in the AWOL Guide. When the driver arrived she tried to get in with her dog, and when the driver balked, she browbeat him into taking her, claiming her dog was a service dog, which clearly it is not.

She tells the story with pride.

I occasionally run into a hiker like this on the trail, someone utterly unconscious or uncaring about how their actions affect the people around them. She is a poster child for the inconsiderate and entitled behaviors that turn people off about thru-hikers. There are not many hikers who are like her, but her actions are distinctive in a negative way, and the people she encounters are likely to remember her. The great majority of thrus, who consider it a privilege to be able to hike the trail, and are respectful and even awed by the hospitality and support found on and near the trail, are forgotten after an encounter with someone like her.

Day 147, August 30th
Governor Clement Shelter, VT, Trail Mile 1690.3
Daily Distance 14.6 Miles

I wake up late and thirsty after rationing water last night. The female thru-hiker with her dog are already gone. I am still on the trail by 8:00 AM. There is a good water point 2 miles up the trail after the shelter. I take a long break there to eat, get water, clean up, and generally refresh myself.

I hike a half mile off-trail at a road crossing to go to Qu's Whistle-stop Cafe. It is built in an old train station, a small one, and it has beautiful

Victorian features like paneled wooden walls and crown moldings. It is decorated with train and local history memorabilia. I have a nice lunch followed by a Vermont maple syrup flavored ice cream cone for dessert, and wrap up a club sandwich for dinner. Sublime is here, and we eat together. The owner gives us a ride back up to the trailhead after we eat, a nice little bit of trail magic.

An article has come out in the New York Times today discussing Appalachian Trail issues. It is centered on Scott Jurek's record setting 44 day supported hike he completed a month ago. There was a celebration and media event at the summit of Katahdin, his finish line. They left some trash up there, and Scott himself was photographed with a small celebratory bottle of champagne.

Baxter State Park, where Katahdin is located, has strict rules about Katahdin. It is a unique and fragile alpine ecological zone. There are a lot of hikers traversing this zone to reach the summit, and a number of those hikers are thru-hikers. Baxter is concerned with the pressure on the environment, and the increased traffic of thru-hikers contributes to the popularity of the peak as a hiking site.

The open flaunting of the rules by some thru-hikers is of particular concern to BSP, and there is discussion of rerouting the trail so Katahdin is no longer a part of the Appalachian Trail. The Appalachian Trail Conservancy is working to inform thru-hikers of the situation, and is asking for proper respect to be paid to Baxter State Park and adherence to the park's rules. From this point of the trail forward there will not be a trailhead or a hostel without notices posted from ATC on the issues, and it is a general topic of trail conversation. A lot of thru-hikers are rethinking their own little celebratory gestures for the summit and planning to have them in the nearby trail town of Millinocket instead.

I see plenty of mountains, views, and fresh, clean water as I hike through Vermont, but for whatever reason I have not seen much in the way of the larger mammals. No raccoons, porcupines, groundhogs, deer, moose, or bear. I hadn't really thought about it until I cross over Bear Mountain (our 7th one of that name on the trail) without seeing a bear. There is abundant sign; tracks, scat, and claw marks in trees, but I see none of the animals themselves. Squirrels, chipmunks and birds are still about, I hear grouse and turkeys on and near the ground, and see hawks, vultures and eagles above. At night the owls still hoot and cry. I still have not actually seen an owl, although I have heard them almost every night in the woods since leaving Springer.

I have 10 miles to go before I take my one week break for my sister's wedding. I look forward to civilization and seeing friends and family, while dreading the long drive and the return to the various frustrations of life dealing with rental cars and motels and store clerks. I am worried about losing my fitness edge and conditioning during a week off, with the White Mountains looming just ahead.

At Governor Clement Shelter I sleep in the shelter. There are six other people in there, LT and AT thru-hikers. One of them is an old hippie guy I met a Green Mountain Hostel who fancies himself a poet, and leaves verse in the trail logs in the shelters.

Day 148, August 31st
The Long Trail Inn, Rutland, VT, Trail Mile 1702.0
Daily Distance 11.7 Miles

I am woken in the shelter by two of the residents who are up early to smoke pot. One of them is the poet from Green Mountain Hostel. While they smoke pot in the shelter he presents the AT Passport idea for getting voluntary behavioral compliance to the other hiker that I introduced at the hostel as his own. I am a little upset about this piece of plagiarism, but I keep quiet. There is no personal profit for me in the idea, and if enough people think it is a good idea it might get traction.

The poet also wants to open a hostel where he will give away hand made pot pipes as souvenirs. I don't think he has a very firm grip on reality. My irritation is wasted.

I hike over Killington Mountain today. There is a large Vermont ski resort on the eastern side, but the trail stays to the west, away from the ski runs. It is a long climb and descent. The trail has a shelter just below the summit at 4281 feet, the highest point on the Appalachian Trail in Vermont. A trail leads to the true summit and the resort. The ski lifts are running; Killington operates the year round as a tourist destination even when there is no snow on the ground, and there is lodge a short walk down from the summit on the east side that serves food.

Cooper Lodge Shelter on Killington is graffitied, dirty, hard used, and trash is strewn about the place. It is close enough to the ski lift that it attracts less desirable visitors.

The idea of a hot lunch just a three hundred foot climb away is very appealing. What I don't know until I get started is that the three hundred feet is nearly straight up, a handhold and foothold struggle up a vertical ravine, and I have to stop and take a couple of breathers on my way.

When I get to the summit, I find a small hiking trail, radio towers, and Redlocks, Snack Time, and Disconnect. They are already staying in Rutland and have come back to Killington to play tourist for a day. The ski lift is free for thru-hikers, and they have ridden back up to the summit. They are staying at the Yellow Deli in Rutland.

The Yellow Deli is a deli with a hostel, and it is run by an obscure religious sect called the 12th Tribe. One of the charitable functions of the sect is hiker outreach. They are donation based, and so it is a give what you can afford operation. It is very appealing to budget hikers, especially since a stay includes a hot breakfast.

There are some peculiarities about the 12th Tribe. It is a small group scattered through Appalachia, and they hold on to some very traditional values in behavior and attire, including dietary restrictions and not working on their Sabbath. To the joy of budget hikers, they feed a sumptuous dinner to guests, including hikers, for free on that day. For various reasons they are considered a cult by the U.S. government. I do not stay there in Rutland, but they also have opened a hostel in New Hampshire I will visit later on and learn more about their ways.

I find the most expensive cheeseburger anywhere on trail awaiting me at the upper lodge cafeteria on Killington. It is $17.00, just for the cheeseburger. They also have some sandwiches at the same price. Since I have already come off-trail to get here, and I really have psyched myself up for the meal, I get a hot Cuban sandwich and a beer, and I pay more than $25.00 for my treat. The sandwich is good, not $17.00 good, but good.

After my meal I slide back down the vertical ravine from the summit and return to the trail, hiking down the back slope of Killington Mountain. It is easy hiking, the trail is in reasonable condition; the area is maintained because of its proximity to the resorts. There is signage posted indicating some of it is maintained by a group sponsored by the ski resort, so some of the profits from my excessively expensive sandwich are going to a good cause.

I arrive at the US Route 4 road crossing, and walk the mile uphill along the highway to the Long Trail Inn. There is a bus that will take travelers into Rutland from the parking lot for $2.00. I stick out my thumb at the beginning of my walk up the highway, but there is little traffic and what there is passes me by. After trying for a little while, considering the distance, I decide I might as well just walk it.

I go into the inn to inquire about the bus and I am charmed by the atmosphere. There is a big common room with comfortable furniture, and games and musical instruments are available. An Irish pub is attached to the inn. I decide to take the bus tomorrow morning, and stay at the Long Trail Inn instead. It is $57.00 for the night. After enjoying the seventeen dollar cheeseburger experience at Killington, it is a very attractive price.

I have Shepherd's pie and Guinness for dinner, and I buy a round of drinks for the rather thin crowd of day hikers and thru-hikers at the bar. Some of the hikers are camped out in a free camping area across the street and using facilities at the Long Trail Inn for a nominal fee. I raise a toast to my old dog, Clyde. My wife had to put him down during these past days due to various conditions that were crippling him, a factor of his advanced age.

To Clyde, the Wonder Dog, who drove off a home invasion one night when a burglar tried to force the door, and was a loyal companion and family member. Rest in Peace.

Day 0 / 0 September 1st to 8th
The Long Trail Inn, Rutland, VT, (Off-trail) Trail Mile 1702.0
8 Zero Days

Getting on and off the Appalachian Trail can be a difficult logistic venture. There are few airports near the trail; the nearest one to me in Vermont is Logan Airport, all the way down in Boston. There is a mass transit bus system that can get you there, but it is slow, and plane tickets are expensive. A week ago, when I was making my travel plans to go to my sister's wedding while I stayed in Manchester; I opted to get a rental car and drive. It is difficult to plan very far into the future when you are hiking the trail. There are so many variables that it is hard to pin a date to and a time when you will be near transportation until you are just a few days away.

There are only a couple of towns near the trail in Vermont that have rental cars available. Rutland works just fine, and I use Enterprise. They would have picked me up, but for two dollars the bus drops me on the doorstep of the rental agency. Everyone at the car rental place is cheerful and helpful, and I am driving south to North Carolina long before the day ends.

My trip includes visits to friends as well as the wedding. It is an enjoyable interlude, although driving takes a bit of getting used to after spending months going at walking speed. I change out my gear at my mother's, picking up my new Jetboil stove and hammock quilt system, and leave the old equipment behind in a box to ship home. I hit the Wal-Mart and arrange for four drop boxes of food to support the rest of my journey. I have been told that the areas of Maine I will hike through are so remote there is little in the way of big supermarkets, and the general stores I will have to rely on are both limited and expensive resupply points.

I find a new pair of hiking shoes at a local discount shoe shop near my mother's. They are Skechers, a reinforced walking shoe with memory foam insoles, in a wide size. They feel more comfortable than my worn out old Keens when I try them on at the store, and the discounted price is very nice. I am giving them a try.

My wife comes, bringing my daughter. Things remain uncomfortable between me and my spouse. There is no resolution, but I am happy and grateful she brought my daughter to see me, and participate in my family's event.

I reverse my steps to get back to the trail; Enterprise does drive me from my turn in back up to the Long Trail Inn fifteen miles out of town, and I am ready to start hiking the Appalachian Trail again on September 9th.

Day 149 to Day 152 September 9 to September 12
Rutland, VT to Hanover, NH, Trail Mile 1702.0 to 1747.8, 45.8 miles
AVG 11.45 Daily Miles

Day 149, September 9th
Stony Brook Shelter, VT, Trail Mile 1710.9

Daily Distance 8.9 Mile

My first day back on the Appalachian Trail has a slow start. I eat a big breakfast at the Long Trail Inn, and I raid the hiker box. The hiker box is actually 3 hiker boxes full of goodies. A lot of section and day hikers use the inn as a base of operations, and when they leave they put their unused and uneaten goods into the hiker box. Since most of the budget hikers making resupply stops in the area are going down to the Yellow Deli in Rutland, they miss out on the cornucopia.

I don't start hiking until after 11:00 AM, and I have to walk a mile back down to the trailhead before I am truly back on the Appalachian Trail. The trail winds back up the hill paralleling the road and passes within a couple of hundred yards of the Long Trail Inn. I knew the trail was near the inn, but as a purist I will not bypass any white blazes, and I walk the extra two miles.

I have lost some of my trail legs. There are two climbs, 1200 and 1300 feet, and my pack is heavily laden with food, and heavier still with my new cold weather gear. Fully laden I am over 36 pounds.

I don't think developing trail legs is about strength. Trail legs are really about pain tolerance and how well I adapt to the ongoing lactic burn in my legs, the pains in my feet, ankles and knees, and the twisting and pulling on my back by the load. Everything seems to hurt more starting out anew. The new discount Skechers are working well though.

There are numerous camping options along the way. The trail passes by a house with a big lawn fronting on a pond. The AWOL Guide says they allow camping on the grounds. Less than a mile further along there a state park with pull in campsites and public restrooms. It is nice and well maintained. I find a small shop, where I buy an ice cream. I think you have to pay a fee for the campsites. I keep moving towards the shelter.

I psych myself out approaching Stony Brook Shelter. I always worry about shelter camping, since I am forced into proximity with an unpredictable assortment of other hikers. I hike until near dark to get here, and I count on sleeping in the shelter rather than trying to set up camp with my new equipment in the dark.

The shelter only has two people in it when I arrive. They are younger section hikers who are far more interested in playing with their personal electronics than talking or fussing. It does strike me as a little odd. I go out into the woods to enjoy nature and the peace of the outdoors, and find youth ignoring it hunched over their smartphones and tablets for entertainment.

There are a couple of hammocks hanging nearby, a pair of packs that smell strongly of patchouli, and a conical hat sitting in the shelter. I know it is Jumanji when I hear his distinctive laugh out in the darkness. He is hiking with a girl named Pinecone.

I visit with them, and Jumanji tells me there is a big bubble of thru-hikers just a couple of days ahead of me. I am encouraged; I can still potentially make Katahdin by October 15th if I can reel in the bubble. I have fallen back into trail routine quickly after my week of civilization.

The trail feels like home.

Day 150, September 10th
Woodstock Stage Road, VT, Trail Mile 1726.1
Daily Distance 15.2 Miles

The trail goes continually up and down today, crossing just one short flat stretch. It is time to work at hiking, and getting my trail legs back. I am moving at 8:00 AM, but stop almost immediately at a nearby stream to fill water and clean up, there not being water right at Stony Brook Shelter itself.

At the Lookout there is a cabin with a viewing platform built on top, off of a short side trail that has a great Green Mountain view. There are several other thru-hikers on top. It is a private cabin, but the owners allow thru-hikers to use it. There is no water nearby, so I don't expect it gets too many overnight stays, but it is an outstanding place to eat lunch.

The downhills make the new shoes painful. My toes are sliding forward and jamming into the front end of the shoe, making a painful pinch. Another ache and pain to absorb.

I planned for a fifteen mile day today, and I do it, hiking until near dark to accomplish it. I put up my hammock using my new over and underquilt system for the first time. It starts raining while I am putting it up and I rush getting it set, and it ends up being a lousy hang.

I huddle beneath my rain fly and cook my dinner. While I prepare my meal and eat it, the bugs have their own dinner, me. I am too tired and it is too dark for me to make a proper bear hang, and my food bag goes onto the hammock rope, adding to its saggy quality. It is a hard night's camp, alone in the rain.

Day 151, September 11th
By a stream near Quechee West Hartford, VT, Trail Mile 1736.7
Daily Distance 10.6 Miles

It is not a heroic day. I sleep poorly, my saggy hang was not comfortable, the rain fly was not taut enough, and rain leaked in. I got out of the hammock a couple of times during the night trying to reset it, but I just got wetter. It was an awkward little campsite, on a slope with dense vegetation. Jumanji and Pinecone are camped nearby, and we trade hellos.

My wife texted me photos of herself and my daughter weeping and holding Clyde, our dog, when he was put down. I have sunk to another physical and emotional low just 3 days back onto the trail. The lack of human contact for long periods of time while hiking and the relationship issues from home are tearing me up. Appropriately, the sky is grey and weeps on me as I get going.

A place called the Cloudland Market is indicated in the AWOL guide as a place to get an ice cream, and I hike the half mile off-trail up a gravel road to get there. I want to brighten my day. The market turns out to be a restaurant that is only open a few evenings a week, and a butcher shop. They are out of ice cream and there are just a few oddities in their coolers. I try a maple syrup flavored organic soda. It is interesting but it fails to hit the spot.

I stop early enough to get a proper camp set up. I find a nice little glade at a point where a stream splits into two and makes a little island. Unfortunately the mosquitoes like it as much as I do; in fact they like it more now that dinner has arrived in the form of my humble self. I got rid of the citronella DEET mixture I was using, mostly ineffectively, to try and keep the bugs away. It was part of my constant efforts to lighten my load. Now I don't even have the psychological comfort of its protection. I still have my raincoat and head net to cover my exposed skin.

My shoes are feeling a little better. Either they, or my feet, are adapting.

Day 152, September 12th
Past Hanover, New Hampshire, Trail Mile 1747.8
Daily Distance 11.1 Miles

Hooray, another state! Hanover, New Hampshire is the home of Dartmouth College, and is the home of author Bill Bryson. He hiked parts of the trail and wrote a book about his experiences. A movie is opening this weekend made from the book, 'A Walk in the Woods'. The book is very entertaining; the movie is not.

My hike today is pleasant. The trail is a nice soft duff, easy on the feet, with graded ups and downs. I move easily and eat up the miles.

The trail passes through a village on the way to Hanover, crossing Patriot's Bridge over the White River and entering the little New England town of West Hartford. Directly after the bridge there is a house with a barn that has a huge AT emblem painted on it. There is a man on the porch of the house and he invites me in for a cup of coffee.

His name is Curtis, and he is an ex-Army Cavalry Scout like me. Coffee turns into breakfast as we exchange stories. He is an in-law of the family that owns the house, and they are long time trail angels. The barn with the AT symbol is being converted into an informal hostel. We sit on the front porch overlooking the river, and as we chat a pair of bald eagles soars down the river looking for fish.

There are three miles of road walking on the way into Hanover, first through Norwich on the east side of the Connecticut River, and then crossing a highway bridge into and through Hanover on the west side. The road bound trail passes directly by the Dartmouth College campus. Normally there is lodging to be had, and the Dartmouth Outing Club on campus provides support for thru-hikers, but it is freshman orientation week and the town is bursting at the seams with students and parents. There is no lodging and no support this week.

I thought I sent one of my mail drops from North Carolina here, to a small motel located five miles out of town, and I hitch hike out there to retrieve it and stay the night, only to find that it is NOT one of my mail drops. The crowds for Dartmouth extend out this far, and there is no vacancy at the motel. I review the notes I scribbled in the margins of my AWOL Guide and realize I changed this mail drop to a town further on. My trip is wasted. I hitch back into town.

The main street of Hanover has a lot of very trendy, very expensive stores, including a North Face outfitter that has a wide selection of sporting clothes, some packs, and some equipment. There is very little real hiking equipment of interest to me since I am on the very back end of wave after wave of thru-hikers who bought up the most useful items. I am pretty set on my gear now, so I am really passing time.

Back on the street the sidewalks are flooded with well dressed, affluent parents and students. I am obviously not part of the mix in my filthy hiking clothes and grimy pack, The people of Dartmouth all give me a lot of space and either stare, or avoid meeting my eyes altogether. Again, I know how the homeless feel, and I do not like it.

I pick up a new portable power charger for my phone and tablet at the Verizon store in town; my old one has given out. The new one is smaller and lighter, and holds four full charges. The one I got at the Pilot truck stop in Pennsylvania only had one recharge.

There is a co-op food store on the edge of town, just where the Appalachian Trail re-enters the woods from the road. I set up my camp near the wood line and go back to the co-op and feast. I plan a return for breakfast and resupply the next morning.

I am getting better at setting up my new hammock arrangement with the under and over quilt. I can't quite figure out the right way to hang the underquilt. I used the wireless at the co-op to research it, but I think I am still missing some key piece of knowledge in how to correctly hang it. It doesn't seem that efficient.

Day 153 to Day 157, September 13 to September 17
Hanover, NH, to North Woodstock, NH, Trail Mile 1747.8 to 1799.8, 52 miles
AVG 10.4 Daily Miles

Day 153 September 13th
Mink Brook, NH, Trail Mile 1755.6
Daily Distance 7.8 Miles

It is a wet, drab morning, and I am feeling it. I did not have my rain fly set up well, and suffered some leaks as it rained through the night. The wireless connection at the co-op put me into contact with home, and there is emotional turmoil as well.

I pack up my camp and return to the Co-op for a hot breakfast, and use the outside outlets to recharge my electronics. I eat, and sit under the overhang reading a book on my tablet while waiting for my power supply and phone to get a good charge, and watch the rain coming down. I talk for a good half hour to a SoBo coming down off the White Mountains, trading experiences, and also chat with some of the locals coming through. It is very hard to motivate myself this morning, and I end up eating lunch outside the co-op as well, before finally mentally kicking myself in the butt and getting a move on sometime after noon.

The trail on this stretch is maintained by the Dartmouth Outing Club, and it is in good condition. It is a welcome change after Vermont's haphazard and hazardous trails. My legs are tired from lack of sleep, and perhaps from moving so quickly yesterday. I not only hiked miles on the Appalachian Trail, I walked all over town adding extra miles doing errands.

I quit hiking early today, before 6:00 PM. I am avoiding the two and a half mile climb up to a waterless shelter at Moose Mountain, and camp by a stream instead. It stops raining, and I let my hammock hang for a while to dry it out before I crawl in to sleep.

I do not see any other NoBos today; I fear I am falling behind the critical mass. I take heart knowing a lot of thru-hikers stall out in the rain, and are more likely to remain in camp or in town when the weather is poor. Rain is forecast for the next couple of days, so I may yet catch the last bubble.

I am in my hammock before it is dark, and I fall into an exhausted sleep.

Day 154, September 14th
Lamberts Ridge, NH, Trail Mile 1767.6
Daily Distance 12.0 Miles

Yet another rainy night and morning, and another late start. I feel nothing like yesterday's reluctance to get on the trail. It is usually easier getting going after I have been out away from town for a day or two.

I meet another SoBo and spend another half hour talking, too much time, but I have not seen many people and I am a little hungry for human contact. I might still have gotten farther today, except a famous trail angel's house is along the way.

The trail dips down off of the hills onto a small hollow with a few houses, a pond, and a meadow. Bill Ackerly's home is 50 yards away from the trail in the little hamlet. He is famous as the Ice Cream Man, and has a sign up pointing the way to his house.

There is a freezer full of free ice cream bars and sodas. The house is a charming cottage with big porches festooned with Tibetan prayer flags and hiking memorabilia and there is a freezer full of free ice cream bars and sodas. The porch has comfortable furniture where a tired hiker can sit and rest a while. Birdhouses are everywhere, and a croquet game is set up in the yard. Bill allows hikers to overnight on his porch

Bill is here. He is an older gentleman, closer to ninety than eighty (He passes in May of 2016, Happy Trails, Bill) and he tells fascinating stories. He has counted 1900 thru-hikers coming by this year, the largest number ever. Last year his total was only 1300.

The Bionic Woman is also here. She has flip-flopped; she was moving too slowly to make Katahdin by October 15th, and went up to Katahdin from Harpers Ferry and started heading south. She had to go off-trail because of a leg infection.

The Bionic Woman was born German and is a naturalized American citizen, and is another one of the remarkable individuals on the Appalachian Trail. She is a leg amputee; she lost one leg below the knee in a motorcycle accident. Her challenges are my challenges, multiplied. She has completed the hardest sections of the trail now, and just has to get down through the middle states. It is still a long distance. (She finishes the trail in late November, becoming the first person with a leg amputation to complete the trail. Go, Go, gadget leg!).

Listening to the stories of Bill and the Bionic Woman, I spend a couple of hours on Bill's porch before getting underway again. I camp up on a ridge near a broad vista of the mountains and countryside. I only get the view in glimpses through clouds,

I am sleeping colder than I like; I have not quite figured out the right way to hang my underquilt, and my body heat is escaping during the night. I am concerned; it is still summer and I am moving north into fall.

Day 155, September 15th
By a stream near NH State Road 25H, Trail Mile 1779.9
Daily Distance 12.3 Miles

My planning during the hike was based around consistently hiking 15 miles a day. Looking back at the actual miles I achieved, I deluded myself; I so rarely made that many miles for any number of reasons. I was certainly physically capable of doing fifteen miles on any given day, but the trail makes its own plans.

Today I have two climbs, and there are elements of rock scramble in them. Smarts Mountain has so much water on it the trail is a stream, a briskly flowing current I wade through. In some places there are planks and boardwalks, but the water is overwhelming them. On one boardwalk I step onto the planks and they sink 6 inches under water. There is no keeping my feet dry. It is like Georgia and North Carolina all over again.

Where there isn't water there is a mud. The mud here is deep, at one place my hiking pole sank 2 feet into the muck and I had a tug of war with the earth to get it back. The worst patches are usually boardwalked in these stretches, but there are shorter patches that are quite treacherous. My usual strategy is to try and cross the mud at a brisk walk, or even a run, so I am moving my feet faster than they are sinking in. I don't dare stop. People lose shoes in this stuff.

Imagine lying flat on your belly, fishing around with your arm plunged shoulder deep into mud, looking for a missing shoe somewhere down in the muck. It happens.

A fire tower is perched atop Smarts Mountain, and I challenge my fear of heights to ascend it and get my first view of the White Mountains ahead. It could be argued that I am already in the Whites, although Mount Moosilauke is generally considered the first true White Mountain on the Appalachian Trail.

The view from the tower is awesome. I have a break in the weather, and I can see mountains ahead. There are patches of cloud hovering around and above the peaks. The wind blows hard, and the gusts howl around the cabin atop the tower. They tug and tear at me on the metal stairway and I clutch at the rails going up and down.

When I return to the safety of the ground I see a small sign posted on one of the uprights that says the fire tower is closed. I missed seeing it before hazarding the climb. A chain across the stairwell would have served as fair warning, but robbed me of a little adventure.

I see no NoBos today. I have definitely fallen behind. Other hikers are coming the other way, flip-floppers Twixless and Whisper, and a SoBo who calls herself Bear Bells.

Bear bells are small bells a hiker attaches to their pack or clothing that tinkle away with the rhythm of walking, warning bears of your approach. Bears generally do not want to interact with humans, but sometimes they are absorbed in their bear activities and hikers can be very quiet. Catching a bear unaware puts them in a fight or flight situation. Sometimes they choose to fight, and humans match up poorly versus a bear one on one.

Bear Bell's name takes some explaining, since she isn't actually wearing bear bells. She is hiking the extended version of the Appalachian Trail, a route that starts in Nova Scotia and ends in Florida. She obsessed about polar bear encounters in the far North, and wore bear bells through Nova Scotia, but took them off when she entered the more civilized wilds of the United States.

I meet another SoBo displaying the somewhat cliché attitude of superiority to a NoBo, because they have completed Maine and the Whites. I am not sure, but perhaps SoBos feel NoBos display the same sense of superiority. Maybe it is just confidence.

I am pretty sure that my 1800 miles of hiking stack up pretty well against this guy's 400, but I haven't quite gotten there yet. I do know what tough looks like though, and I am certain I am equal to it.

Wildlife is becoming common again. I flush two grouse as I hike, and I see a couple of ribbon snakes. There are plenty of moose and elk droppings along the trail, but don't see any mammals besides the usual chipmunks and squirrels.

Day 156, September 16th
NH Route 25 road crossing, (Hikers Welcome Hostel), NH, Trail Mile 1790.5
Daily Distance 10.6 Miles

I am on the doorstep of the White Mountains at the Hikers Welcome Hostel. Tomorrow I assault Mount Moosilauke.

I hike quickly today, after a late start at 8:30 AM, and I arrive at the crossing of NH Route 25 at 3:00 PM. There are small ups and downs, but the trail is in good condition and I move right along.

I know I am coming into a hostel tonight, and I have nearly a full charge of carefully hoarded power on my iPhone, so I use some of it to play some motivational music. I don't usually hike to music, and not just because it wastes power. I find it removes my connection with the world around me, and hiking becomes an exercise routine rather than an immersion in the natural environment.

Today music does not isolate me from the natural world. Today my music stirs nature into action. I am on the down slope of Mount Mist with my little iPhone speaker rocking me down the trail, when I hear a noise above me loud enough to break through my musical trance.

I look up at a tree 10 feet from me on the side of the trail, and I see an enormous set of paws sliding down the tree. I have disturbed a black bear from its siesta. The bear's body is hidden on the far side of the tree, and all I can see are the 4 to 6 inch long claws digging into the wood and coming down towards me, fast.

I have just enough time to get my hiking poles up in front of me before the bear hits the ground. I don't know what its intentions are, but I intend to give a good account of myself if it wants to mix it up. Fortunately, it does not. Mr. Bear wants no part of me today, I have scared him almost as much as he has scared me, and he scampers away from me and the trail. It is a good sized bear, over 200 pounds, bigger than the largest dog, and I am both awed and relieved to see his big hairy rump disappearing into the brush downhill from me.

I have a recovery moment, taking in what occurred in a period of less than 15 seconds. I am rejoicing inside. I have seen another bear, after not seeing any large mammals for weeks. I knew they were around because I have seen the scat and claw marks in the trees. I am trembling with an adrenal surge after the encounter, and it helps to speed me down the trail, now with my music off, and a smile on my face.

The Hikers Welcome Hostel is a half mile walk down a rural road from the trail. It is one of the more rustic hostels. The shower and toilets are outside in a screened enclosure, where there is plenty of hot running water, and a washing machine and dryer. There is a bunkroom upstairs and a common room downstairs, built as an addition to a larger house that is off limits to hikers. The common room has a TV, movies, and books, and a large table to sit around with the other hikers in residence. I find a loaner guitar for me to play on. Life is good.

A man named Legion runs the place, and shuttles everyone to a small local convenience store and deli for basic resupply and dinner. There are no fuel canisters, but my Jetboil uses very little fuel and I will be OK for another couple of days.

I meet a few new NoBos here, including Secret Squirrel. Some of the NoBos left at the back of the pack are starting to bounce around a little and doing slacks. They are younger, stronger hikers than I am, and are a little less worried about the Katahdin closing date. I am still a purist, determined to see the entire Appalachian Trail from Springer to Katahdin.

The partying bubble is affecting the businesses supporting the trail community. Legion is unhappy with the disrespect shown to the trail and trail community by those hikers who are on the trail to have their good time on someone else's dime. The closure of the camping area at Kent, in Connecticut, is particularly bothersome to him.

The Appalachian Trail Conservancy had been trying for years to get a town in that area of the state to become a trail town and support hikers. In Kent, a church finally opened up its grounds to hikers as an overnight camping area. There were numerous problems with drinking and disruptions, culminating with a hiker defecating in a neighboring back yard. The camping area is now closed to hikers, and again Kent is hostile to hikers.

Chef went into Kent for resupply, and a local lunatic actually shot him with an air rifle as he walked down the sidewalk, hitting him in the knee and putting him off the trail for a couple of weeks to heal.

Legion feels that the trail community is partly to blame for the lack of respect shown to the trail towns by some thru-hikers , for failing to police itself, and even supporting troublesome hikers as they continue to create problems as they move north on the trail.

There is a bookshelf in the common room, and I find a 1950s field guide to the animals of the Appalachian Mountains. In an odd way it is a book of hope. It shows very limited ranges and small populations for animals like black bears, moose, and wild cats. Black bears are only listed as living in two states, New York and Maine, and moose are only listed in Maine. The numbers and range of large mammal populations are considerably larger now; protection, conservation and wildlife management are paying dividends.

In some ways I wonder if increased human population is actually helping. Hunting is limited by residences, and animals are learning to coexist with humans in suburban environments.

Day 157, September 17th

Kinsman Notch, North Woodstock, NH, (The Notch Hostel), Trail Mile 1799.8
Daily Distance 9.3 Miles

TRAILTALK:

CAIRNS: Piles of rocks 3 to 8 feet high used to mark the trail on rocky ground where there are no trees to place white blazes upon.
NOTCH: The low elevation separation between two mountains. Similar to the usage of 'gap' down South, except the character of the northern Appalachian Mountains creates steeper cuts between the mountains.

I have conquered the first big mountain of the White Mountains. I have taken its measure and found it well within my abilities. Mount Moosilauke is just under 5000 feet high, more than 3500 feet of elevation gain from the NH Route 25 trailhead up to the summit. In the Whites, like the Smokies, the whole height of the graph in the trail guides is needed to show elevation gain and loss. The climb is steep, but fairly consistent, and the trail is pretty good, it is just long, nearly five miles of steep, laboring upness.

I get moving out of the hostel fairly early, and I am on the trail at 9:00 AM. There is another stretch of state road on the far side of the mountain, and I have a mail drop waiting for me at the Notch Hostel there. I am doing this single mountain today, less than a ten mile hike.

The climb up Mt. Moosilauke is forested with pine, until the last half mile when the trail emerges out from the forest through a scrub of bushes and peters out onto lichen covered rocks for the last couple of hundred yards. The summit view is unobstructed, and a visual treat. Like so many of the greater heights on the trail, the top of the world feeling is physical and emotional as well as visual. Franconia Ridge, one of the White Mountains' major landmarks is clearly visible to the east.

I sit up on high for a while and have a snack. There are several trails up to the Moosilauke summit, and they are marked with cairns. I follow the most distinct trail down, it is a stony groove beaten into the lichen and mosses. Small signs ask hikers to stay on the eroded area to preserve the delicate and invitingly soft looking alpine growth of mosses on either side of the rocky channel. I am respectful of the environment, and stay on the harder path walking on the stones. I envision myself as the fool who inadvertently steps on the last breeding flower holding the secret of faster than light travel or the cure for cancer within its genetic structure.

Four hundred yards down the trail I come across a sign informing thru-hikers that this path is not the Appalachian Trail. I need to retrace my steps. I am one of many who have come this way, judging by the fact that the maintainers felt the need to put up the sign. I wish they had put it much closer to the summit, and I grumble to myself about it most of the climb back up the rocks to the summit, until I reconnect with the correct line of cairns.

A short distance further down the correct trail, back into the treeline, is Beaver Brook Shelter. It is a little ways off on a side trail, and marks the beginning of Beaver Brook. The brook is a racing, tumbling stream the trail handrails for most of the two mile descent down the north side of Moosilauke. It is beautiful; the falling water is a constant moving presence alongside of me, but it is a treacherous companion. Spray and mist wet the rocks making them slippery and unpredictable. The trail down is very steep and quite challenging. There are a number of places requiring some technical climbing and iron handholds are set into the rocks to help the hiker along and down past the most dangerous sections. It is slow going burdened with my pack and poles.

The section of trail up and over Moosilauke can easily be slackpacked, since there are roads and hostels on either side of the mountain. I am traveling lightweight. I have my full pack but I have only a single day's snacks in it, and water is right here beside me so I carry very little on my person. My pack weight is less than 25 pounds.

I get to NH Route 112 on the far side of the mountain at 5:30 PM. My pace is barely a mile an hour between the climb, the break at the top, the detour and return where I got lost, and the careful climb down. I am tired. The trail provides, and I thumb a ride to the hostel very quickly.

The Notch Hostel is a very nice place, elegant even. It feels more like a bed and breakfast than a hostel. There is a shed outside with places to hang my pack and poles. The proprietors do not want hikers and other outdoor enthusiasts bringing their funk and trash inside with them. The big porch is furnished and is a comfortable place to organize, maintain, and repack gear without dragging its soiled presence indoors. There is a SoBo inside, and a couple of married touring bicyclists who are nearing the end of a cross continent ride. It is an interesting mixture of experiences.

A preplanned mail drop awaits me, and gives me between four and six more days before I will need to resupply again. I want to beef up my load with a couple more snacks. The SoBo tells me there is little resupply in the Whites themselves; the Appalachian Mountain Club huts don't carry much, so I plan to run into town tomorrow before heading out and buy a few Cliff Bars, just in case.

Day 158 to Day 162, September 18th to September 22
Kinsman Notch to Crawford Notch, Trail Mile 1799.8 to 1843.8, 44 miles
AVG 11.0 Daily Miles

Day 158, September 18th
Eliza Brook Shelter, NH, Trail Mile 1807.3
Distance 7.5 Miles

The cycling couple at The Notch hostel make a nice breakfast in the hostel kitchen and share it with me: a perfect portion of scrambled eggs with spinach, pasta, and fruit to get the day started.

I spend most of the morning getting back to the trail. I hitch into the little town of North Woodstock and get what I need at Fadden's General Store and a fat sandwich as well. Then I have to hitch back out to the hostel before hitting the trail when I discover I left my AWOL Guide behind. It is far too important to leave behind. At this point, everything in my pack is essential. AWOL is more than a map, it tells me all of the information essential to survive each leg of my journey. I hitch again to the Appalachian Trail.

I get to work just before noon, and work it is. The trail is difficult; there are many gradually ascending and descending stretches, with lots of rocks big and little, and deep muddy patches between. I was warned my pace would have to slow in the Whites, and I am working hard to make a mile an hour. My newly laden pack is an uncomfortable burden, and I am quite worn out by the day's efforts.

The next big mountain is Mt. Kinsman, and it has a fearsome reputation. The climb is a two and a half mile rock scramble, and is supposed to be one of the hardest sections of the entire trail. I am still hoping to make what normally would be an easy eleven miles tomorrow, but it is looking ambitious now.

Day 159, September 19th
Near the Flume Side Trail, NH, 1816.8
Daily Distance 9.5 Miles

TRAILTALK:

AMC (Appalachian Mountain Club): One of the oldest trail clubs, and one of the most influential. It predates the Appalachian Trail.
STEALTH CAMP: Making a low profile campsite, with the smallest footprint, to avoid damaging the environment and to avoid notice by passersby, sometimes because it is a questionable area to camp.

Mount Kinsman is two separate peaks, a South Kinsman and a North Kinsman, and the Appalachian Trail goes over both. The anticipated great and terrible climb up North Kinsman is as steep as advertised. Keeping up a steady pace making one small step after another gets me there. The mountainsides are pleasantly forested, and the mountaintops are bald.

It is a bright, clear day, and from the tops I can see forever. Mt. Moosilauke now is behind me, and the Franconia Ridge looms ahead. There is a stone throne atop South Kinsman, built into a large cairn. It is a wonderful photo opportunity, and a day hiker is already sitting in regal splendor when I get up there. We trade phones and take pictures.

The beautiful day has brought out crowds of day hikers and weekenders. I see at least fifty other people on the trail. They are coming up from the North Kinsman side, and I don't start encountering them until I leave the South Kinsman summit.

There is a shelter at Kinsman Pond, just into the woods after the North summit, but with so many hikers about I don't look for spaces, and it is too early to stop anyway. A little further along is Lonesome Lake Hut.

Lonesome Lake Hut is the first of the Appalachian Mountain Club (AMC) Huts I will pass in the White Mountains. The AMC huts are essentially hostels, with bunkrooms where the beds are stacked three high. There is no electric power, the huts are off the grid, but they are pretty comfortable places. A stay includes dinner and breakfast cooked over gas ranges, served family style in the common room. The huts fit a lot of people into a small space; there is room for 50 or 60 people to stay in the bunkrooms, even more in the larger huts. AMC huts are manned by a 'Croo' who maintain the hut, cook meals, and serve as human pack mules hauling the daily supplies a few steep miles up onto the ridgelines from nearby forest roads.

The AMC huts are the only shelters available through most of the Whites. AMC is resented by thru-hikers; the club has a monopoly on places to stay for the night. Much of the trail is above treeline going through the Whites, especially going through the Presidential Range, and there are not many alternative camping sites. You are not supposed to camp within a half mile of an AMC hut.

The major reason for thru-hiker resentment is that the huts are not free. There is a substantial cost incurred by AMC to maintain the hut system, and the trail network through the Whites. Thru-hikers are generally less than happy at having to pay to camp, especially when they are so self-sufficient everywhere else on the trail. The pay-to-stay shelters in Vermont and the fee for the National Park permit in the Smokies were both sources of discontent for a number of thru-hikers, especially the budget hikers. The Great Smoky Mountains National Park permit was $20.00; the shelters in Vermont were $5.00 a night.

A night at Lonesome Lake Hut is a staggering $127.00 a night, which includes dinner and breakfast. This is for a bunkroom where hikers are packed in like sardines, in a building without electrical power. The $127.00 is outside just about every thru-hiker's budget, and it is not a single night's situation. Thru-hikers are at the mercy of the AMC Hut system for nearly seventy miles of high mountain trail. The initials AMC are often referred to by thru-hikers as the Appalachian Money Club.

The White Mountains have a very sensitive alpine environment above the treeline. The natural and spectacular beauty makes the Whites a huge draw for hikers from Boston and New York City, and human pressure on the environment is intense.

USFS ridge runners are patrolling and strictly enforce regulations and camping exclusion zones. There are only a very few spots below treeline along the trail suitable for camping, and most of the time it requires hiking a mile or more down slope to actually get into the trees. There are a few areas along the trail an overnighter can actually stealth camp, but those places can usually only fit a single tent or two. They are not posted on the trail, but there are websites where you can find those few isolated places and plan your hike.

The AMC Huts do offer a work-for-stay option, but it is for the first two thru-hikers who present themselves to the Croo at 4:00 PM for the available positions. WFS is exchanged for sleeping on the floor of the common room, meals included, for an hour of work. When big bubbles come through there simply isn't enough work to take care of them all. I was trailing the last big bubble and was in sparse company, and I still was unable to secure a single night of WFS during my journey through the Whites.

The Croo is lenient about common room floor accommodations when the weather gets really bad. People die from exposure in the White Mountains every year.

I stop for a break and a snack at the Lonesome Lake Hut. They have a bowl of macaroni and cheese, a cup of juice, and a brownie on sale for $5.00, and I indulge myself in a prepared lunch. The hut is a very pleasant stop during the day when the crowds of hikers are out in the mountains.

I find a stealth campsite further along the path below the treeline at a trail junction. It is a dry camp. I have carried 3 liters of water a mile up from a creek anticipating the lack of water. My legs are aching after my first three days in the Whites, and even on the easiest sections I am trudging along under my fully loaded pack. The biggest mountains are still ahead.

Mosquitoes are still a bother. They pierce the thin fabric of my hammock, and I am getting bit on the butt while I sleep.

Day 160, September 20th
Gordon's Pond, NH, Trail Mile 1825.6
Daily Distance 8.8 Miles

It rained hard and was windy last night, interrupting my sleep. I slept in for an extra hour, and had to wipe down my hammock rain fly with my little Lightload pack towel before putting it away. Things will still be damp tonight, but better damp than wet.

I hike the Franconia Ridge today, a series of small knobs up on a 5000 foot high ridge. There is a climb of 3500 feet in a mile and a half just to get up on the ridge, trudging up a stairway of rocks and logs through a pine forest. I thought it was more taxing than the climb up South Kinsman. It is also beautiful, a single thin corridor of human movement through an ageless green wood.

The Franconia Ridge is one of the glory spots of the Appalachian Trail, a narrow, high ridgeline with steep sides and phenomenal views. It is a rainy day, and I am immersed in clouds for much of my time here, but the high winds are shifting the clouds around. Sometimes the wind tugs and tears away parts of the thick bank of moisture I am in, and I get spectacular glimpses of the world far below me.

The ridge is not easy hiking. It is open, rocky terrain, and the 60 MPH+ gale force winds push against me in unbalancing fits and starts. Visibility is poor enough that at times I am going from one cairn to the next barely visible cairn, twenty or thirty yards ahead in the mist making my way forward. It is hard to get a real sense of how far I have come, or how far I have to go. The ridge is narrow, a flat band only 10 or 20 yards wide, with the land dropping away on either side. It would be a real triumph of poor navigation to get lost.

I think each successive knob is Mount Lafayette, the high point of the ridge, but I go by several knobs in a misty succession before finally finding the one with the Lafayette plaque. There are the ruins of a few old structures even on this isolated ridge, an old remnant of a historic hiker's lodge. Hiking in this area reminds me that people have been escaping from the urban centers into the mountains for a century and a half.

The clouds start breaking up as I start my descent back down the ridge, and I am treated to the sight of a glider riding the air currents below me, appearing and disappearing into banks of clouds as it soars on the winds created along the ridge. The hike down the ridge is wet and cold, and the trail is rocky and uneven, demanding my attention and careful foot placement as I descend.

My daily mileage is down below ten miles a day. I was hoping to get further, but I knew that the White Mountains were going to be slower. I am putting forth a lot of effort each day, and I feel I should be doing still more, making greater efforts, and going greater distances.

It is cold tonight, getting down into the 30's. Gordon's Pond is in a notch between the Franconia Ridge and Mount Garfield. There is a very good campsite 50 yards off of the trail that I discover by accident. I put my gear down closer to the trail at a much less satisfying place, and I take a look around to see if there is something better. I get lucky and find this open area in a grove of widely spaced trees. There are a couple of fire rings in the area, so it was used before.

The trees are fir, narrow straight poles with few big branches. None are suitable for a bear hang, so my bag goes on the end of my hammock. I never like doing this, but I hope my presence will deter wildlife, and if it does not I can defend my food supply with my hiking poles. I lay them out right beneath my hammock ready for action. I can always retreat if I have to. I could put my bag away from me and I might be safer, but my food would be far more vulnerable.

These low wet areas are usually home to swarms of mosquitoes. A blessing of the cold is that the mosquitoes are gone. I may shiver tonight, but I will not be annoyed by the whine of little wings and proboscises seeking my blood through the hammock fabric.

Day 161, September 21st
Near mile 1833, NH, Trail Mile 1833.0
Daily Distance 7.4 Miles

It was cold last night, very, very cold. There was always some part of me I could not insulate and I spent most of the early morning awake and shivering. I don't actually rouse myself out of the hammock and start moving until 9:00 AM, still grasping for sleep, a cold weather syndrome.

While I break camp a pair of grey jays visit and search my area for crumbs. I break a few little morsels off of my breakfast granola bar and leave them on the ground when I depart.

The steep hike up Mount Garfield is a nice warm up, and the sun shows itself. Mt. Garfield is not a particularly large mountain in the White Mountains. It is a thousand feet lower than the other surrounding features, but it is situated so it has a great view from a rock ledge up on top of the surrounding peaks. Franconia Ridge dominates the area behind to the southwest while ahead the Presidential Range and Mount Washington are in sight.

Right off of the summit there is a small clearing in the low pine forest, and I run into a hiker who has another pair of grey jays fluttering about him. The birds scatter into nearby trees when I approach.

The man tells me to be very still, and to hold out my hand. I do so, and he puts a sprinkle of trail mix in my palm and steps away. I stand there for a minute and the grey jays return, flying around me, until one lands on my hand and eats the trail mix.

The jay is so light on my hand I can barely feel its weight; the sensations of its feet gripping are a delicate prickling. I know it is not good for the wildlife to become too accustomed to man, and see us as a food source, but it is a remarkable moment.

There is an AMC Hut on the eastern side of Mt. Garfield. It is 0.2 miles off-trail, and I stop in to see what they have for snacks and use the privy. I talk to the Croo, and get some idea of the costs of operating the huts. They carry a lot in on their backs, but some of their larger logistics are done by helicopter. I don't know if the expense of a couple of helicopter flights justifies the price of $140.00 a night for the bunkroom here. What is really telling is that the huts are full, with 50-80 people staying in each hut on a weekend night.

Benton MacKaye was the visionary who conceived of the Appalachian Trail, and Myron Avery was the mover and shaker who actually got it built. The original vision was of an easy and affordable escape into nature for the American working family. I even saw some of this in play back at Bear Mountain in New York, families coming out in buses from the city to spend the day outside.

The Appalachian Mountain Club predates the Appalachian Trail by a good 50 years. It was founded in 1876, and the Appalachian Trail follows a route already laid down by the AMC.

The AMC used to be a standard bearer for the vision promoted by MacKaye. The huts were absurdly inexpensive. A couple of decades ago the organization was operating in the red, and raised the overnight price of a hut stay with meals from $5.00 to $8.00 a night, and there was a huge outcry from the membership. The increased price was still too low to balance the books and AMC was soon operating in the red again. New management came on board to financially rescue the non-profit organization. Prices were raised to the current amounts, and now the AMC is the richest trail club.

I think about the math as I walk today. Even lowballing the estimate, I figure in 20 weekends, with an average of 50 people per hut, multiplied by $100.00, for 2 days, equaling $10,000 a hut over 14 huts, equals $140,000 a weekend, and 2.8 million dollars for the summer weekends alone. Some of the money goes back into operations, and into trail maintenance. I make that as a real lowball estimate: people are up at the huts the other 5 days of the week, there are more than 50 bunks in some of the huts, they charge considerably more than $100.00 for a night's stay, and the season begins in the spring and stretches into fall.

A family of four will be out nearly a thousand dollars for a weekend of hiking in the White Mountains, an amount I don't think the average working family can easily afford. The AMC is a profitable non-profit now, but the original vision is gone.

I looked up the 2015 Annual Report for the Appalachian Mountain Club after the trail as I wrote this, and my figures stand some correction. The AMC brings in 28 million dollars a year from operating revenues and funding sources. A whopping 10 million a year is generated from the huts. The money is spent on good causes; the money is put back into Appalachian recreation, conservation and protection. The AMC, together with other conservation organizations, is buying up the lands of the Appalachians to protect them, over 70,000 acres to date, including the lands of the 100 Mile Wilderness in Maine.

The AMC is generating funds to protect the Appalachians. This is a very good thing, but it still is at the cost of making part of the Appalachians a pay to play proposition. People without money are excluded from spending nights in the Presidential Range. Thru-hikers manage it, but we have a lot of experience making the woods and trail systems work for us; the expense of the AMC area of control is just another obstacle.

The climb down from Mt. Garfield is a shock. The trail turns into a stream of falling water. It is not runoff, it is an actual stream and waterfall, and the trail runs straight down through it. I thought I made a wrong turn somewhere and I backtrack just to make sure I was still on the trail.

I work my way down the section, expecting better trail to return, but the trail proves very hard, all day. Based on the profile I expected a second steep climb up the South Twin and Mount Guyot, but the profile is level between, and I expected it to be easier hiking.

The whole day is a challenge. I want to stride out, but I am confronted by a series of boulder scrambles and little ups and downs, insignificant in the profile but slowing my pace and throwing off my rhythm.

Particular care has to be given to descents. My pole can get trapped in the small gaps between rocks, and I don't realize it is stuck until I take another step forward and find myself making an unexpected pivot on the trapped pole. On a steep downhill it is unbalancing and dangerous. I have had a few small falls and a couple of big scares as a result. The bottom section of my pole is starting to come loose and stay stuck in the rocks, leaving me with half a pole in my hand. I have to stop and repair it each time it occurs.

An injury at this point in my journey is unthinkable, I am too far along to break a bone or suffer another catastrophe that would prevent me from finishing my journey. I have less than 350 miles to go, the end is in sight.

The thru-hikers left on the trail now are a hardened, determined bunch. They are going to make it. Except that a few don't. A few are going to have an injury now, late in the game, which stops their progress. Most of those will appear back on the trail next year to finish what they missed, but it will not be the same. I am going to be one of the ones who make it. I cannot see it otherwise. My name is Possible! Still, there are those moments after a fall or mishap, when the specter of injury and failure is there to haunt me.

Galehead Hut is at the base of the South Twin and I stop in for soup before beginning my second climb of the day. The AMC huts all have some sort of hot food available throughout the day, usually soup or a pasta dish. They don't charge much for these treats and they are an extremely welcome break. The Croo members at Galehead do not appear to like thru-hikers much; they are polite and correct, but reserved.

A weekender has left his extra food at the hut, and I get a free two day resupply of ramen, cheese and oatmeal. I feel the extra weight climbing South Twin, as well as the 3 liters of water I carry in anticipation of a dry camp ahead. I am certain I will not get seven more miles to the next water source.

The trail dips into a hollow on the ridge between South Twin and Mount Guyot, and there is supposed to be stealth camping in the wooded area. There is a shelter nearly a mile downslope on a side trail, and the stealth area is at the trail branch. I do not find the trail branch. I start climbing up the side of Mt. Guyot back out of the treeline and I realize I have missed the campsite. It is dusk, and it is getting darker with each step I take.

I stop, assess, and decide to backtrack to a very small opening in the trees I already passed, where I make a very rough and uncomfortable hang of my hammock by headlamp. The trees are small, and there is no suitable bear hang, so my food again goes on the end of my tree strap. My hammock pulls on the tree and bends it as I move around inside, and I worry about it holding through the night.

Day 162, September 22nd
Crawford Notch (the Yellow Deli), NH, Trail Mile 1843.8
Daily Distance 10.8 Miles

Eleven miles doesn't seem like much distance, again, compared to my pace just a couple of weeks ago, but in the White Mountains this counts as a big day.

I hike by Zeeland Falls Hut, which has a large number of visitors. I talk with one of the Croo who is a former thru-hiker, and he tells me I am probably not going to make Mt. Katahdin in time, and I should flip-flop soon. It is a hard nugget to digest, and I resent it just a little.

I have a little over three weeks, exactly 23 days of hiking to get to Katahdin by October 15th, and I still have over 300 hard miles to go. The truth is that the best I can hope for is a finish around the beginning of November. I am still focused on a one way trip, and I am still pushing aside the idea of a flip-flop.

From the hut down to the road at Crawford Notch the trail is a well-graded, long stretch of gradual downslope. I get to US Route 302 mid-afternoon. I am tempted to push on, but in the AWOL guide it says the AMC has a large lodge and conference area called the Highlands Center just down the road, and it has bunkrooms at a reasonable rate. There is also a shop and a restaurant. The lure of a little civilization is too great, and I am able to yogi a ride right in the trailhead parking lot.

I am dropped off at the Highlands Center. It is a big place, in a luxurious, rustic style, if you can forgive the oxymoronic turn of phrase. Amelia Earhart is loafing outside on the grass verge of the parking area next to a couple of backpacks. I pass on by with a greeting and head into the lobby. There is a big conference going on and there is no space available, not even in the expensive single rooms.

I find a Yellow Deli flyer at the front desk. The Yellow Deli is located some distance away in Lancaster, NH, but they shuttle to and from trailheads in the Whites. The local Yellow Deli is a new branch of the one in Rutland, Vermont. It is run by a religious group called the 12th Tribe, for donations, and has a good reputation as a hostel.

I call up the Yellow Deli and they will pick me up in an hour and a half, they make a big circle shuttle route in the Whites in the evening, and I am told they already have a couple at the Highlands Center already waiting. I go outside and sit by Amelia Earhart and Pockets, who has appeared. He had been down at the trailhead and hitched in to meet up with Earhart. She is his girlfriend in some undefined trail relationship pink blazing kind of way.

I am pretty jealous, not of their relationship, but of the fact that Pockets startled a moose along the road as he was trying to hitch up to the Highlands Center. I so want to see a moose. My nickname in my Army unit was Moose, a reference to strength, determination, and unfortunately, also to a certain lack of grace and a tendency to charge into things headlong without consideration of the consequences. I rather cherish that nickname, and I want to see my token animal. There has been moose sign, but Pockets is the first person I have talked to who has recently seen a moose, in his case less than an hour before.

The shuttle comes around. It is a big passenger van driven by an older bearded man in jeans and a flannel shirt. We drive to a series of trailheads over a period of an hour and a half, picking up Secret Squirrel and four other hikers. There are already a few hikers at the hostel from all over the White Mountains. Ramblur is in; I last saw him staying in New Jersey in the company of my favorite mother and daughter hiking team, Bluebird and Hakuna Matata.

The Yellow Deli hostel is in a Victorian era, red brick townhouse, with storefronts at street level and a cupola atop it, in the old town center of Lancaster. The 12th Tribe recently purchased the entire building, and they are slowly converting it to support various commercial ventures. The hostel is modernized on the inside, and a lot of detail work is still underway. There is an Italian food place next door and a bar across the street. I opt for Italian and an earlier night.

I will get up early and make my resupply at the Rite Aid a half of a mile up the road. The shuttle won't leave until 9:00 AM, and I won't get back to the trail until 10:30 or 11:00 AM. I am planning on completing the 25 miles across the Presidential Range in three days, but I will get four to five days of resupply. My pace has been slow, and the Presidential Range is a long, high series of mountains with only huts for sustenance. They have some of the worst and most unpredictable weather in the world. I am preparing for adversity.

Our 12th Tribe hosts wear conservative attire. The men are in jeans and flannel shirts, like many of the other men in New Hampshire, and have long beards. The women are in long, plain dresses and bonnets, reminiscent of the Pennsylvania Dutch. The 12th Tribe operates small farms and sells the produce through their delis. Members renounce all personal belongings when they join, everything is owned communally. Aspects of living simply and off of the product of your own hands are very appealing.

The U.S. government considers them a cult. Because there is no private property or funds in the 12th Tribe it is difficult to leave the community once you have joined. There is no communication with your former life, except with people who already belong to the 12th Tribe. If you are a mother with a child, you are also essentially a captive. The organization is male dominated, and marriages are often arranged. You can see where abuse can occur.

I only meet one 12th Tribe woman, Elizabeth. Whatever their beliefs and practices, Elizabeth seems very much in charge of the hostel, and appears to be the shaker and mover of the whole operation in Lancaster.

I am catching up to the party bubble again. The Yellow Deli had to ask a group of hikers to leave the hostel just a couple of days prior for getting drunk at the bar and coming in late, loud, and argumentative.

Day 163 to Day 166, September 23 to September 25
Crawford Notch to Pinkham Notch NH, Trail Mile 1843.8 to 1869.8
AVG 8.66 Daily Miles

Day 163, September 23rd
Lakes of the Clouds Hut, NH, Trail Mile 1855.0
Daily Distance 11.2 Miles

Today is one of the most breathtakingly spectacular days on the trail, and also one of the most taxing.

The late start on trail after the long shuttle ride is relaxing. I had a great night of sleep, rose early and walked through the still sleeping town of Lancaster to the Rite Aid at dawn. The town is a curious mix of architecture spanning the history of the United States. Stately Gregorian, early Greek Revival, and Victorian structures have 1940s cubes and 1950s motor lodges mixed in among them, along with recent construction.

I return to the Yellow Deli in time for breakfast: scrambled eggs and cheese mixed into white rice, with English muffins and coffee. There is some sort of meat restriction in the 12th Tribe dietary guidelines. It is a good, filling breakfast, and the meal, sleeping quarters, shower, and trailhead shuttle are a lot of services provided by a donation based enterprise. I have to ask where to make my donation, and I give a couple of twenties, more than I usually would for a hostel, but I feel a little bad about how much they do, and how many of the hikers they serve are utterly broke at this point and are only able to donate a couple of dollars.

Hiking today starts at Webster Cliffs. The cliffs are a series of steep climbs and knife-edge rock scrambles coming up out of Crawford Notch. There are many false summits, each with a successively bigger and more amazing view back down into the notch. It is a challenge for my fear of heights, and an awesome experience.

The 3 mile climb takes me four hours. The most intense section is 1500 feet of elevation in a space of a mile, with climbs along rock ledges jutting out into space, and some nearly vertical sections. My pack is loaded down and is working with gravity and against my forward momentum, creating a battle to remain stable and upright rather than testing my ability to fly dropping down into the notch.

Mt. Webster is the lowest of a chain of high peaks, but the initial climb out of a notch is usually the hardest part. It is 2500 feet of elevation gain to Webster peak, which is around 4000 feet high. After Webster the Presidential Range marches higher and higher until it reaches Mount Washington at 6280 feet, the highest mountain in the northeastern United States, and the second highest mountain on the trail.

It is a sunny day, warm but with a hint of autumn chill in the air, perfect weather for hiking. There are many hikers out, and I see people all along the way on Mt. Webster and Mt. Jackson until I get to Mizpah Spring Hut.

I stop in at the hut for a snack and information. The soup is a vegetable soup, a potato dill. I talk to a pair of doctors I meet who are long time White Mountain hikers. They say that the food quality at the AMC huts used to be much better. Twenty years ago when a hut stay was five dollars a night, not over a hundred, the food included more proteins. They just couldn't afford to stay operational at those rates. I have noticed that the midday the food offerings are all vegetable soups or in one case, macaroni and cheese. I am still grateful for the hot midday meal at a reasonable price.

A normal AMC Hut Croo is 3 or 4 people, but they are cooking, cleaning, making resupply runs, or getting in short hikes of their own during the day, and the huts have a deserted feel. There is always one Croo in residence to keep an eye on the place, and I ask the Croo member present at Mizpah about trail conditions ahead. I am trying to figure out how far I can get today.

The Croo member tells me two important things. The first is that water is scarce; there are no marked springs between the Mizpah Hut and Lakes of the Clouds Hut, four miles ahead. The second is that Lakes of the Clouds Hut has just closed for the season.

There is the dungeon, a small basement shelter, in the Lakes of the Clouds hut, and it has a couple of bunks that can be used as shelter for the night. The Croo member thinks I should be able to make it that far, and since it is all exposed high alpine ridgeline between here and there, I really don't have too many choices.

The Croo also tells me of a couple of possible stealth sites down side trails, but Lakes of the Clouds really seems to be the best bet. It is only four miles ahead. I have found covering that distance can take a lot of time in the Whites. I have three and half hours of daylight left, and I think I can make it. I have the headlamp if I must use it.

I set out, and pass Mounts Pierce, Monroe, and Franklin. The trail skirts along the edge of each peak; the summits are 200 to 400 feet higher up above the Appalachian Trail trace. Each mountain has a side trail up to the peak, but I do not want to waste time climbing the half mile up and down. The views from the edges are already like an out of body experience, soaring high above the world like a hawk.

I have packed out 3 liters of water from Mizpah because of the predicted lack of water. It may have been some time since the Croo member last hiked this way. The all too common rainfalls of the last couple of weeks have left plenty of water on the mountains, and I step over three or four flowing streams on my way to Lakes of the Clouds.

I make it to Lakes of the Clouds hut near darkness. The clear sky holds no heat, and it is rapidly getting colder. The wind is picking up as well, and it is blowing and gusting with vigor. Two backpackers are trying to make a shelter between the hut building and some benches in front of the structure, looking for some shelter from the winds.

I walk around the hut looking for the dungeon the Mizpah hut Croo member told me about. Around in the back there is a heavy steel door set into the hut foundation with a notice announcing it is an emergency shelter. I need to grab hold of the handle with both hands and pull hard to get the door open.

Dungeon is an apt description of what I find inside. There is a very small space, ten feet by ten feet, with six narrow bunks built into the walls. The room is already full, but a hiking couple consolidates onto a single bunk so I will have a space. The walls and floor are old, cold, damp concrete. There is a very small window, and a small drain in the center of the floor.

The hut charges ten dollars per thru-hiker for the privilege of staying here when it is open. Lakes of the Clouds is a renowned beauty spot, but it is also very exposed to the weather, and I am sure I would have been happy to pay the ten dollars. Since the hut is closed, I am staying for free.

The wind moans and howls outside, but inside seven hikers make merry little camp stove fires to cook our meals, and we tell each other tales. Our collective body heat helps keep the air from being more than chilled.

Sublime is one of my fellow inmates, and we exchange stories about our adventures since our last meeting at Bear Mountain in New York.

Day 164, September 24th
Madison Hut, NH, Trail Mile 1862.0
Daily Distance 7.0 Miles

I wake up to see the glories of Lakes of the Clouds. It is a very cold, still morning. The hut sits in the saddle between Mt. Monroe and Mt. Washington, and there is a spring that feeds two small bodies of water; the Lakes of the Clouds. Mt. Washington is tall even from this height up on top of the ridgeline, another 1700 feet of elevation and a mile of climbing to the final peak at 6288 feet. Mt. Washington is visible from all along the ridgeline approach, but the final look is breathtaking. Clouds are forming and breaking around the peak.

Mt. Washington makes its own weather. It is positioned where it presents a physical barrier at the point where the warm moist airs of the Atlantic meet the cold arctic airs coming down from Canada after sweeping across the Great Lakes and picking up a load of their own moisture.

Just getting out of the hut's Dungeon in the morning is a challenge. With seven hikers crammed into the cold, dank, tiny space only one hiker can get packed up at time.

I poke around the area just a little bit before leaving. There is a trail myth about seven mystical bongs of the White Mountains, and one is supposed to be located at the Lakes of the Clouds.

The story is that there are seven marijuana water pipes secreted within this stretch of mountains, the fabled Seven Bongs of the White Mountains. By asking the right people along the way through the Whites you can discover clues to their whereabouts. If a hiker finds one they can use it, and are then supposed to return it to its hiding place for the next smoker to find.

I am not a pot smoker, as I have discussed probably too much already, but I am teased by the idea of a hidden treasure, and want to find it just for the sake of finding it. I poke around prominent rocks and features near the water, but find nothing. I don't actually start climbing Mt. Washington until 9:00 AM.

The Mt. Washington summit is a major tourist destination. There is a road to the top, much like on Pikes Peak in the Rockies. 'This car climbed Mt, Washington' bumper stickers can be seen all over the Northeast. There is a cluster of buildings housing a museum, an information center, a theater, a weather station, a store, and a restaurant. There is even a post office.

Mt. Washington has been a tourist destination for many years, predating the automobile. There was a lodge that opened in the mid 19th century that is now preserved as a museum. A cog railroad built to the top of the mountain is still operational, although most of the locomotives are now electric rather than coal powered. The train starts up the mountain not terribly far from the AMC Highlands center, at an old resort called Breton Woods.

Breton Woods is a huge Victorian structure, of the type that used to populate sections of the Northern Appalachians and Catskill Mountains as summer getaways for the rich and powerful. Most of them faded away and are nothing more than foundations now, but the Breton Woods is still a grand structure and an active resort. It became historically significant back in 1944 when representatives from 44 nations gathered to set a series of rules governing the international monetary system as a precursor for the United Nations. It is formally known as the United Nations Monetary and Financial Conference.

The circus-like tourist atmosphere on the summit of Mt. Washington galls many thru-hikers. After slogging your way heroically up the hard miles along the Presidential peaks it is more than a little disheartening to see the train and vans disgorging loads of pudgy middle-aged gawkers at your goal, especially when you are one of the things gawked at. For many years the traditional thru-hiker response to this was to moon the cog railroad as it passed by the trail. The constabulary cracked down on the practice a few years ago by mounting cameras on the train, and started making arrests and writing tickets. A few thru-hikers do try to carry on the on the tradition. I am not one of them.

I find all of the tourists a bit annoying myself. I am not used to being pushed and jostled, especially after months in the woods, and I fiercely resent a couple that steps directly in front of me while I am studying a wall map. I want to say something, but I am still practicing being non-confrontational, and I let it go. It shapes my attitude and emotional state for more than a few minutes before I get past it.

I spend an hour and a half among the crowds on the summit. I eat, see the old lodge museum, send out postcards from the post office, and wash and shave with the hot water in the bathrooms. There is a big flat screen display showing a film of winter on Mount Washington, and there is a large board listing all of the recorded deaths on the mountain since 1869. There have been 155 fatalities thus far, with two added this year alone. Three causes repeat themselves; exposure, fell to death 1000 feet, and cardiac arrest.

I have seen many of the drop-offs, and I think 'fell 1000 feet' is just a way of saying they fell a very long way. There are winter hikers in the Whites, but some of the exposure deaths happen in mid-summer, when the weather suddenly turns brutal. There was a blizzard just last July that claimed the life of a young woman. I would not have wanted to be caught outside unprotected last night; it was certainly cold enough to kill.

Looking at the out of shape tourists crawling like ants all over the mountaintop it is easy to see where the majority of the heart attacks come from. They have ridden up on a train, and they have no comprehension of how hard or dangerous the mountain really is. Walking down to Lakes of the Clouds looks pretty easy from the top, but coming back is some real work. Occasionally it is even a seemingly fit person who dies. Of course, I can think of a lot worse ways to die than suddenly having my heart stop while I am already so close to heaven.

The worst recorded weather anywhere on the planet happens on top of Mount Washington. The highest wind speed ever recorded was up here, far in excess of 200 miles an hour. The anemometer broke during the storm, and there is no real way to know exactly how hard it was blowing, because at 231 miles an hour the wind took the instrument away.

The winter video on the visitor center's big screen display bears testament to the ferocious conditions. Long icicles stand out horizontally from manmade structures in a world of ice and snow. Parts of the film show men tethered together fighting against the wind just trying to cross the few yards from one building to the next.

I only hike seven miles today, and it is a long day's effort. The trail follows a chain of mountains reaching away to the north. Mounts Clay, Jefferson and Adams must all be conquered before getting to the Madison Hut. The trail climbs the shoulder of each one, but again shies away from the last couple of hundred feet to the summit, and again I pass side trails that go all the way to the tops.

The climbs on the main Appalachian Trail along this section are not big, perhaps 500 feet up and down. The trail stays on the high saddles between each peak. The trail is extremely rocky, a stretch of blazes following a worn groove through rocks up, across, and down each mountain. It is exposed; vegetation is a good 1000 feet and more below the trail. Views are tremendous and I make myself stop and look around every half hour. On the trail, the rocks are uneven and jagged, and movement is often a lateral rock climb. I do not arrive at Madison Hut until about 5:30PM, and it is a very welcome sight for this worn and bruised hiker.

Pockets and Amelia Earhart have beaten me to the hut and are the two Work-For-Stay thru-hikers for the evening. They are budget hikers, and I don't begrudge them the opportunity. Sublime is here as well, and he bargains for both of us with the Croo for bunks for the night. There are not many people at the hut tonight and there is a lot of space. Sublime gets us the AMC club rate of $105.00 each for the night.

I had planned all along to spend one night in a hut, even knowing the cost, just to have the experience. I was hoping for WFS, but even at the tail end of the thru-hiking season there are many more hikers than opportunities.

Dinner is served family style at common tables. There are several long tables and benches lined up in the common room, but there are so few hikers tonight that all of the guests and Croo sit at a single table. The Croo keeps conversation going with practiced ease while bringing out courses of food. There is soup, bread, quinoa salad and chicken fajitas, and a lemon poppyseed cake for dessert. The food is all made from scratch by the Croo, and it is simple, filling, and good. All of it has been carried 3500 feet up the mountain in 50 pound packs on four mile trips from the nearest road by the Croo.

Pockets and Amelia Earhart must wait for the leftovers, but there will be plenty for them. They will be washing dishes tonight, and have already set up sleeping arrangements on the far end of the common room.

The huts do not have showers or heat. I have lots of wool blankets on my bunk, and I have a large window looking out at Mount Adams filling one entire wall of my cubby. With only four guests occupying the 35 bed bunkroom I am in, one of two at the hut, there is lots of space. Filled, it would be a claustrophobic mess. I have looked in bunkrooms at other huts at busier times and there was gear and people everywhere.

Day 165, September 25th
Pinkham Notch (White Mountain Hostel), NH, Trail Mile 1869.8
Daily Distance 7.8 Miles

I eat the hut's breakfast and get back onto the trail. Mount Madison is the last peak of the Presidential Range, and the Appalachian Trail goes all the way to the summit, rather than skirting around it as it has the other Presidential peaks besides Mt. Washington. It is a steep, rocky climb, not quite the rock scrambles elsewhere, but a long and hard endeavor to start to the day. The peak is a narrow point; the land slopes away from it on all sides, and I stand atop a spike thrusting high into the sky.

The rest of the hike is downhill, a lot of downhill, and the first miles of it are as rocky, open, and slow as the climb up was. I can see the small figure of Sublime a couple of hundred yards ahead of me working his way down as well.

The trail eventually drops into the treeline, traveling first through a stunted growth of pine, which grows into larger, taller trees, and then the hardwoods like maples reappear. The trail becomes wider, better graded, and has a number of well marked side trails. Nearing the Pinkham Notch I see the marks of bears. There is bear poop, and big claw scars in the trees.

Pinkham Notch has another Appalachian Mountain Club operation, with lodging, a restaurant, an outfitter, and a hiker day room with pay showers. I get there at 4:30 PM and have another disappointing encounter with the AMC.

There are no rooms available at the lodge. It is shaping up to be a gorgeous weekend and many people have come out to enjoy it. There is a magnificent topographical relief map of the White Mountains set up as a table display, and I can trace my steps back and see where I will be going forward. I sense occasional looks of disdain from the outfitter staff but I ignore them.

I see the outfitter carries Leki poles, for sale and for rent. My Leki poles are coming apart, and I have been looking for an outfitter to restore them. I was told when I purchased them that Leki had an amazing lifetime warranty, and they would replace any broken parts. The outfitter in Waynesboro went so far as to show me the stock of shafts and parts Leki sent him each year as part of his dealer agreement, parts to be used to repair any poles brought in with damage.

My poles have seen hard usage, and I have wrapped duct tape around the shafts at the telescoping joins because they are slipping so much. I also need new tips, not covered by the warranty since they are made to slowly wear away with use, and replacement is a maintenance item, not warranty. My tips are nearly gone after over 1000 miles over rough terrain.

I ask one of the clerks at AMC Pinkham Notch outfitters for assistance. I understand that I am grubby, smelly, and tattered looking, as most thru-hikers are. The clerk must have seen thru-hikers before; somewhere around a thousand of them have passed through Pinkham Notch this year. Many other nearly as dirty section hikers also will have passed through.

She acts like I am dirt.

I can barely get a response out of her. When I persist in asking her for help, and show her my poles, she tells me that she cannot help me. I point to the racks of Leki poles, not just the ones for sale, but also the forty pairs or more they have in racks for rental use by day hikers.

The clerk tells me. "We do not have the technical expertise to help fix poles".

I am obviously being brushed off, the poles may be made of space age materials, but mechanically they are simple enough for a four year old child to disassemble and put them back together again. The pole is three telescoping shafts with a lever lock at each join. The AMC outfitter rents the poles and must be able to demonstrate their use to renters, as well as maintain their stock.

There is nothing I can do about her obvious lie. I am glad I am not committed to staying here though.

I briefly thought about pushing ahead into the Wildcat range and continuing a 21 mile hike to the next road. I already had set my mind to having a night in town, and I don't want to spend my money for resupply at the Notch. Prices are high, selection is limited, and after being treated so miserably I don't want to give them any of my money.

I call ahead to the White Mountain Hostel, which is on the far side of the Wildcats in Gorham NH, and they, much to my surprise, agree to pick me up. I am already planning to stay there at the end of the Wildcat hike in two days. The hostel is right on the trail at the road crossing, and I have one of my mail drops from North Carolina waiting in Gorham for me.

I hang around outside the AMC building until my ride comes, watching the bustle of people coming and going. There are crowds; this is a jump off point for all kinds of White Mountain adventures and people are enjoying the last days of the season. I do not wait long; the driver was nearby on an errand.

The White Mountain Hostel is a wonderful place. It is in an old, beautifully restored building. The bunkrooms are spacious and it one of the hostels that is more of a bed and breakfast operation than a flophouse. A woman named Marnie is the owner and operator.

Hakuna Matata and Bluebird, two of my favorite hikers, are at the hostel and we catch up on experiences, Bluebird is starting to look gaunt, as we all do at this point in the hike, but it is a little frightening to see on a 70 year old woman. She and Hakuna are setting up a series of slackpacks through the southern section of Maine; the border is only a couple of miles from White Mountain Hostel. Maine has a lot of hostels with slackpacking options, and while expensive it will save some wear and tear on the couple as they try to finish their hike.

I consider a slack back through the Wildcats, but 21 miles would leave me beat the next day and I would probably want a zero, which would defeat the purpose I was spending money to achieve. I don't think I have the legs for it.

Day 166 to Day 167, September 26 to September 27
Pinkham Notch to NH Route 2, Gorham, NH, Trail Mile 1869.8 to 1890.9
AVG 10.55 Daily Miles

Day 166, September 26th
Zeta Pass, NH, Trail Mile 1878.3
Daily Distance 8.5 Miles

Today I lack energy. Even after the rest at White Mountain Hostel I am worn out. The Presidential Range stole away some of my mojo.

I drag myself up another steep set of cliffs rising up on the east side of Pinkham Notch. The rises and falls of the Wildcat Range will mean that even though I don't hike ten miles today I will make over 5000 feet in elevation gains. Much of that happens in the initial climb out of the Pinkham Notch, over granite slabs and steep cliffs, where I use both my hands and feet to cling to the mountain. It is a little disheartening to find a ski lift in operation at the top of my first climb bringing a steady stream of families up for picnics at the top.

I meet a family at a viewpoint on a summit outcropping along the way, and Dad has brought along couple of craft beers in cans up with him. He shares one, a nice little bit of trail magic and a boost to both my morale and metabolism.

Carter Dome is the high point of this range, and is not as bad as the initial assault, but it is hard graft. On Mount Hight I find three men camped out on the summit, in the alpine zone. It is a bad place for them to camp. It is in a very sensitive ecosystem, and they are making things worse by trying to build a fire. The wind is doing its best to teach them the error of their ways. It is going to be a cold night, and I think a bitter cold night on an exposed mountaintop may make them pay for their sins.

The weather has been clear and views are amazing. A stretch of fine weather like this in the fall in the White Mountains is rare, and I have been very lucky. The men camped out on Mount Hight are there to see the stars and full moon, which will be spectacular. Tomorrow there will be a lunar eclipse on another predicted clear night, and people are starting to stake out choice viewing points along the ridge.

The AMC Carter Hut is down in a notch. There is a second, much easier trail coming into it through the valley from a trailhead down a forest road. The hut is officially closed, but it still has a single caretaker in residence so people can use the bunkhouse, common room, privy, and water sources. It is considered self-service, and it is only a $10.00 fee. There are no meals, and campers are expected to clean up after themselves. By AMC standards this is a bargain. All 40 bunks are occupied.

The caretaker finished his own thru-hike last year. By his telling he was a power hiker, completing several 100 mile weeks, including racing through the 100 Mile Wilderness in four days. He notes my slow pace (which bothers me, inside) and urges me to flip-flop. I am going to call ahead to Baxter State Park at Katahdin and get the real low down on actual closing dates. There is a persistent rumor about an extended season this year. I will continue to push forward as far as I can but I am slowly resigning myself to making the jump up to Katahdin at some point soon and working my way back to complete the entire Appalachian Trail.

I see Sublime several times during the day. He is hiking just ahead or just behind me at different times. He likes exposing his skin to the sun, as much of it as he can, and on a fine day like today he hikes with his shirt off and his shorts rolled up his thighs like a banana hammock. It is a little startling at times, and feels just a little creepy. He is totally unselfconscious about it. It is the trail, and this is his freedom. Clothing mores may be a little more relaxed in French Canada, or perhaps he thinks they are in the United States.

Sublime camps near where I set up my hammock at a trail intersection, and he shares some of his stories as we eat dinner together. He has had a very interesting life, including previous AT and PCT thru-hikes. I like not camping alone all the time, and I kind of have been trying to keep an eye out on him anyway. He is a type 1 diabetic, and he had a moment on the trail in the Whites where he felt himself slipping out of reality. He has to constantly monitor his sugar levels against his activity levels, and carries a pack filled with shots and insulin boosters.

Sublime is older than I am, I would guess in his early sixties. He is a true free spirit; he is hiking on the AT to enjoy being out on the trail. He doesn't really care if he finishes. He has already done that, and he goes as far and as fast as he wants, and he will get wherever he gets. He also doesn't let diabetes dictate his life to him; it is just something he has to take care of along the way.

Day 167, September 27th
NH RTE 2, Gorham, NH, (White Mountain Hostel), Trail Mile 1890.9
Daily Distance 12.6 Miles

Most of today is downhill hiking, and I find I am still able to hike at a decent pace if the terrain is favorable. I get to the front door of the White Mountain Hostel before 5:30 PM. I am racing against the clock for the last couple of miles. The hostel is quite a ways from town, and they have an evening shuttle into the town that leaves each evening at 6:00 PM. My mail drop in Gorham is at a different hostel, and I need the shuttle to get to it, as well as pick up other items at Wal-Mart, and eat, of course.

Early in the day I pass three female thru-hikers; Rock Ocean, Storybook and Kim Chi. They are hiking backwards from White Mountain Hostel in order to get on top of the Wildcats and see the lunar eclipse tonight. Their original plan was a slack of one day across the Wildcats, but now that they are up here they want to stay and see the eclipse. They have the basics to cowboy camp for the night in their slackpacks, but they are short on food. I am happy to lighten my pack a little more, I have a package waiting for me in Gorham after all, and I give Storybook my excess, more than a day's worth of food, and they are set.

While we stop and talk I mention Sublime is coming up behind me, I don't realize that they have not met him, and are unfamiliar with his desire to expose his skin to the sun while he is hiking. They are caught by surprise when he pops into view wearing little besides his pack, boots and a thong. Fortunately, they react with humor. He stops and chats for a minute, then passes me by.

On the descent I catch and pass Sublime, who is normally the better hiker, and I let the hostel know he is coming up behind me; he needs the shuttle as well. The van waits, and he shows up right at 6:00 PM.

The shuttle brings us into town. I get my package and my resupply. There are other thru-hikers in town staying at other places. It is the end of the hiking season, the last big weekend, and some of the hiker support places like hostels and bunkrooms in town will be closing very soon.

It is another indicator I am falling behind and should be thinking about a flip-flop. I still have 300 miles of hiking ahead, and Maine is supposed to be a very difficult state, on par with New Hampshire. I can't see making Mt. Katahdin in the 18 days before Baxter closes to overnight camping and begins restricting access to the mountain.

Peaches is an older hiker staying at the White Mountain Hostel, a big bearded man in a hiker kilt. He has had some injuries and started bypassing some Appalachian Trail sections while still trying to take in as much of the experience as he can. He has arranged for Trail Angel Miss Janet to come to the hostel and transport him north to Monson, Maine, at the beginning of the 100 Mile Wilderness, 112 miles from Mount Katahdin.

It is a golden opportunity for me to flip-flop, and meet Miss Janet again as well. I decide to ride up with him. She will be coming tomorrow or possibly the day after. I will have to take some zero days to travel. My weary body can use the rest.

The hostel is crowded, despite the lateness of the season. The owner, Marnie, checks to see if I will change form the bunkroom I was originally put in so she can keep a group together. Thru-hikers define portable, and I agree to change. I am rewarded with a better room, and a much more interesting one.

I am placed in the "Hoff" room, which is decorated with life sized advertising cardboard cutouts of David Hasselhoff selling products, and one of him in his Baywatch glory running across the beach.

Day 168, September 28th
NH Route 2, Gorham, NH, (White Mountain Hostel), Trail Mile 1890.9
Daily Distance 0.0 Miles, ZERO DAY

I am waiting for Miss Janet today. She is driving all the way down from Mount Katahdin. The towns and roads along the length of the Appalachian Trail are far away from main transportation corridors, and it takes many miles and hours of driving along winding two lane roads to get from point to point.

Miss Janet arrives late in the evening, and we plan on setting out for Monson the next day. My pack is hugely and heavily loaded with my mail drop and extras in anticipation of traversing the 100 Mile Wilderness.

Maine awaits.

MAINE

Days 169 to 208, September 30th to November 7th
Monson, ME, to Katahdin, ME, and Monson, ME, to Gorham, NH
TRAIL MILES 1890.9 to 2189.2
299.7 Miles 38 Days, AVG 7.88 Daily Miles

(I take 9 zero days between travel needs and weather in Maine, AVG without zeros is 10.88 Daily Miles)

Day 169 - 181, September 30 to October 30th
Monson, ME, to Mt. Katahdin, ME, Trail Mile 2074.7.to 2189.2
AVG 11.45 Daily Miles

Day 169 to 170, September 29th and 30th
Monson, Maine (Shaw's Hostel), Trail Mile 2074.7
Daily Distance 0.0 Miles (2 ZERO DAYS)

It takes an entire day for Miss Janet to drive us up from Gorham to Monson on wandering little state and county roads. I am jumping forward 184.7 trail miles. My flip-flop plan is to hike north 114.5 miles from Monson to Mt. Katahdin, then come back down to Monson by road and hike south back down the trail from there to Gorham to complete the Appalachian Trail.

Monson is a little town at the edge of civilization on a lakeside in the middle of Maine's backcountry forests and mountains. It was once a timber town, but the consolidation of mills and EPA and conservation pressures on the industry has left many of the little Maine towns that relied on the forest resources of wood economically abandoned.

Tourism has made up some of the loss. Monson now makes its living off of weekend travelers from the more urban parts of New England: hunters, canoers, cyclists, and hikers. The town has wonderful old 19th century buildings and storefronts, some of which are quite empty. There are two hostels and a couple of bars and restaurants still alive in town. The people are friendly and helpful, and the place in general has a comfortable, laid back feeling. It is a place where no one is in too much of a hurry.

The locals all know each other, and trail regulars like Miss Janet and Baltimore Jack are also well known and greeted like old friends.

I spend two days just sitting tight at Shaw's Hostel for a couple of reasons. It is raining. Not the usual rainfall, but great monsoons of water thundering down from the sky all day long.

The weather is the news. Western Maine is getting somewhere between 3 1/2 and 6 inches of rain in a single day. The rivers and creeks are overflowing, and we are hearing stories and rumors about hikers trapped on the trail between raging floods of water. A father at Shaw's is waiting for his thru-hiker son who is out on the trail, and is trying to arrange a helicopter rescue.

The second reason for staying put is more joyful. Miss Janet is gathering thru-hikers for a documentary film by REI and Outside Magazine on trail angels, specifically about Pony Tail Paul. She wants a group of us to hit the trail together so we meet him on the next section. In addition to Peaches and me, she has assembled Phyzzy, Tumbles, Scout and Waldo. In return for waiting a day at the hostel, which was kind of a given anyway with the weather, she will provide us with some support at some point in the 100 mile wilderness.

The details are a little fuzzy, but it is going to be an adventure, and around Miss Janet things seem to come together for thru-hikers. She doesn't leave anyone hanging.

I haven't seen Phyzzy since Virginia; he has gotten way ahead of me. He was a little plump down south, but now he is lean, and wears a great, big, curly, physicist beard like a mad doctor.

Tumbles and Scout are new to me; they are a young brother and sister from Tennessee. Tumbles is the sister and she turned seventeen on the AT. She is energetic and endlessly cheerful. Scout is the older brother, an Eagle Scout. He is a confident and capable hiker, and you can see he takes responsibility seriously watching over his rather more free-spirited sister. The two of them rescued another pair of hikers who were injured and stranded down by Mahoosuc Notch.

Waldo is a little bit of an enigma. He is a young man who is definitely a solo hiker, and a budget hiker. I think he is down to his last couple of dollars and he is moving forward now on a hope and a prayer. He is rather quiet but good company. He has adopted his trail persona and wears a red striped Waldo hat.

We are all sitting and waiting out the storm at Shaw's. Shaw's is a nice little hostel, run by a couple named Poet and Hippie Chick, recent Appalachian Trail thru-hikers themselves. They know exactly what we need. They make hikers a good breakfast in the morning served around a big kitchen table, and the common room is small but equipped with a TV, movies, books and guitars.

Shaw's maintains a nice little outfitter shop out back with choice hiker foods, and they have a very selective assortment of gear. There is not a lot of variety, but all of the critical items are there and are high quality. Prices are surprisingly good for a place in the middle of nowhere.

We resupply for the 100 miles ahead. In my case it is refinements; my pack is already the heaviest it has been since Georgia. I have another mail drop waiting in Monson. I have jumped ahead to it, but I am going to leave it where it is to await my return trip heading south.

There is a way to lighten your load in the 100 Mile Wilderness, but it is pricey. A backpacker can arrange for one of several places in Monson, including Shaw's, to place a part of your food and resupply load for the 100 miles in a 5 gallon bucket, seal it, and hang from a tree branch out of the reach of bears, at a predetermined location near a forest road 4 or 5 days into the Wilderness. The service is $50.00 or $60.00.

We sit, and wait, and listen to the rain drumming against the roof.

THE HUNDRED MILE WILDERNESS

Day 171-179 October 1 to October 9th
Monson ME to Abol Bridge ME, Trail Mile 2074.7.to 2174.1
AVG 11.04 Daily Miles

Day 171, October 1st
Little Wilson Creek Falls, ME, (Shaw's Hostel), Trail Mile 2081.3
Daily Distance 6.6 Miles

The sign posted at the beginning of the 100 Mile Wilderness, erected by the Maine Appalachian Trail Club (MATC):

Appalachian Trail

Caution

There are no places to obtain supplies or get help until Abol Bridge 100 Miles North. Do not attempt this section unless you have a minimum of 10 days supplies and are fully equipped. This is the longest Wilderness Section on the entire A.T. and its difficulty should not be underestimated.
Good Hiking!

M.A.T.C

We are slacking the first short section of the 100 Mile Wilderness with the intention of following Pony Tail Paul out off the trail for the first night. The rivers we are going to have to ford are just about impassable, and we are happy to have one more day letting water levels drop while making some forward progress.

The forest is dripping, some little wet still comes from the grey sky, but mostly it is just saturation. The two small creeks we have to ford today are normally a rock hopping exercise or maybe a foot wetting under normal conditions. Today they are carefully navigated, waist deep, yards wide endeavors, with everyone watching out for each other's safety. Scout and Phyzzy lead the way across for the rest of us to follow.

The water is cold enough to make my feet numb and my ankles ache for miles afterward. One of the creeks we manage to cross on a series of fallen trees and logs with just a splash or two into the water. The balancing on trees that are swaying above the powerful current takes concentration and a certain amount of devil may care to make it across.

Film crews chase us into the first section of the woods and film us hiking before breaking away and jumping ahead of us. They miss the fords, but they are there waiting for us when we get to Little Wilson Creek.

Little Wilson Creek Falls are a tremendous, powerful backdrop for Paul's trail magic. Other hikers have set out today, and a fair number gather to enjoy the feast of grilled hot dogs, potato salad, cookies and doughnuts.

Paul's tale as a trail angel, the subject of the video, is pretty moving, and the video tells it far better than I can. It can be seen online on YouTube if you search for 'REI presents: Trail Angel', or look up Ponytail Paul online.

Afterwards we hike over a mile off of the trail to get to the unimproved forest road from which Paul hauled in his trail magic, where Miss Janet is waiting to whisk us back to Shaw's. Our group enjoyed each other's company during the day's hiking challenges, and we are going to try and stick together through the Wilderness. With the water levels as high as they are, the river crossings are going to be difficult, and we all feel better approaching them as a team rather than as individuals.

Baltimore Jack is in residence at Shaw's when we return. Our AT experience is about over, and there is little left for him to tell us, but he is still quite charming when he gets going. It is the last time I will see him. (Baltimore Jack dies the next spring. Happy Trails, Jack).

Day 172, October 2nd
Near Wilbur Brook, ME, Trail Mile 2088.1
Daily Distance 6.8 Miles

We have the usual delays getting back out to the trail. We have our big breakfast, finish last minute errands, and then we all pile into Miss Janet's big brown van with the trail angel wings painted across the front.

Our connection back to the Appalachian Trail is a rutted dirt track loosely covered with gravel, and it is more than a couple of miles from the nearest paved road. We have to hike another mile back into the woods from our drop-off point to reconnect with the place we left the AT yesterday.

There are two major fords to cross today, one through Little Wilson Creek, followed three miles later by Big Wilson Creek. The terrain is relatively flat and while the trail has lots of roots and rocks to look out for as they grab at and turn our feet, it is relatively low effort. It is the fords that pose the main challenges.

Little Wilson Creek is tearing and roaring through a rock channel. It is not wide, maybe 15 or 20 feet across, but the water is a white torrent over stone, and we are hesitant to wade in. A tree has fallen across the river a little distance upstream at a point where there is a narrows. We cling to the face of a ravine and inch our way along just to get to the tree, and then shimmy across the log with the white froth racing by a couple of feet beneath us. We hand each other on and off the log. We are pretty unbalanced by the weight of our overloaded packs, and the crossing works better as a cooperative venture.

Peaches leaves us between the fords. There is a side trail back out to an unimproved road, and his ankle injury is flaring up again after the acrobatics of our first crossing. He is limping, and afraid that as we go deeper into the Wilderness it will get worse. The farther we go, the harder it will be for him to get back out. He resignedly accepts the inevitable, takes his leave of our group, and we are now five.

Big Wilson Creek is a good 20 yards wide, a river rather than a creek. It has a reasonably flat, gradually sloping bottom. The current is strong, but there is a rope tied from one large tree to another at head height across the river. We don't have to search out a place to cross; we cling to the rope and go. The water is very cold, and I cannot see my feet beneath me in the water. We slowly push forward a few inches at a time, feeling our way across the bottom, keeping our footing secure. The current is a constant pressure pushing at us relentlessly

Water that is waist deep on me and Phyzzy, who are both six feet tall, comes up close to Tumble's armpits. Phyzzy and I drop our packs on the far side and go back for her pack, and when she crosses Scout is right behind her, ready to make a grab for her if she is swept off her feet. We all make it across without any undue upset, but making the two crossings uses up most of the day.

We stop to camp next to Wilbur Brook. Just ahead of us there is another ford. It is taking us somewhere between one and two hours to execute each crossing, and we do not want to risk getting caught trying to cross in the dark. It makes this a short day.

It has not rained today, but clouds have hung low and grey overhead. A pervasive dampness haunts the forest following the downpours of a couple of days ago. Scout takes pride in his ability to start a fire every night, and is more than up to the difficulties getting a fire going in the sodden environment. He gets a small fire circle built and a cheering little blaze going shortly after arriving in camp.

I have gone without fire on the trail. Where someone has already built fire at shelters, usually weekenders and short section hikers, I have sat around the fire, but I usually avoid the crowds that bother to start one. With my new trail family we gather around the flames as a focal point while we cook our dinners and socialize. It provides light, some heat, and a place to attempt to dry out some of our clothing.

Sometimes campfires are called 'Hiker TV' because people sit around and stare at the flames at night. There is something mesmerizing about watching licks of fire slowly consuming each stick and log.

Our fires do not last long. When we are done eating Scout puts the fire out, dumps water and earth on it and scatters the ashes when the embers are dead and cool to the touch.

Waldo camps a little separate from the rest of us. He is like a stray dog, which comes in warily to socialize and eat, but goes back to his own little place at night. We are beginning to identify ourselves as a trail family, and he is a valued member. We are finding our own places in the family as we go along.

The next ten days of hiking with this group of hikers will be the longest period of happiness I will experience on the trail. I am sharing my adventure with people who make it greater as a shared experience.

Day 173, October 3rd
Mountain Bog, ME, Trail Mile 2096.0
Daily Distance 7.9 Miles

The ford at Long Pond Creek turns into a long reconnaissance along the river's edge looking for the safest place to cross. One of Phyzzy's observations is that every other state along the Appalachian Trail provides some kind of bridge over river crossings, however rough. Many of the bridges are prebuilt somewhere else and hauled into wilderness area and assembled with hand tools, or are made rough hewn with the natural materials at hand.

Ghost told me that Wilderness areas do not allow the use of power tools without special permits. Even after Hurricane Sandy in 2012, when the storm did massive damage to the trail, a request to use power tools on a repair permit was granted for a single weekend for the length of the AT, and it had to go all the way to the top of the Department of Agriculture to be approved. Power tools are a fairly new development to humans, and we still possess the knowledge and skills to build these structures using manpower alone. For whatever reason, Maine does not bother to provide bridges. It is part of what makes the state so challenging.

At Long Pond Creek ford, we find a rope leading across a section of river to a mid-creek island, and from that island another rope crosses to the far side. Phyzzy leaves us his pack to send across after him slung from the rope on carabiners, and manages to cross. He gets armpit deep in the water in the center, and then his feet are swept out beneath him by the fierce current. He clings desperately to the rope above, going forward hand over hand until he regains his footing in shallower water near the far bank.

The rest of us look on with apprehension until Phyzzy stands safe on the other side. We do not all want to take that same chance. Scout and I both venture out on the rope, but retreat in the face of the high pressure current. Tumbles will be at the most risk, being the smallest, but it is a dangerous crossing for anyone.

We consider rigging a second safety line to attach to each person as they cross, but our lines are meant for hanging ten pound bear bags from trees, not keeping two hundred pounds of hiker and pack from being carried away downstream.

Another thru-hiker, Moloch, comes up behind us, looks at the situation, and goes upstream looking for a better way across. He shows up on the far bank across from us in about half an hour, and tells us there is a difficult but practicable fording place upstream.

Waldo heads upstream and also finds the way across the river to the far bank. The rest of us follow up to where he and Moloch made their successful crossings. There are a number of large rocks in the river, and there is an eddy behind each rock where a hiker can get a break from fighting the current. Where the water is channeled between the rocks it is a waist deep gush of fire hose pressure water. It is just possible, using the rocks as piers, to cross the gaps and get across.

I follow Waldo, and Phyzzy wades in from the far side to help people across. It takes me three or four different attempts before I find a route all the way across, I enter the icy cold water each time, work my way out into the stream until I get trapped by a deep hole or a current too wide and swift to challenge, and back out of the stream. I thaw for a few minutes, and then go back in trying slightly different paths, until I finally find a way all the way across.

Tumbles crosses with Scout behind her, and her smaller frame is overwhelmed by the water. She loses her footing and starts to get carried away downstream, but Scout lunges, gets a hold of her, and helps right her. Phyzzy wades in deeper from the far bank in order to meet them halfway and together they all get across to the far side. I take pictures of the crossing, and catch the moment Scout snatches his sister away from the clutches of the river.

It takes us a good two hours to cross this single ford. Afterwards we stop at the first practical spot, Long Pond Shelter, a mile from the river crossing. Scout builds a fire so we can dry some things out, eat, and generally recover. The water was very cold, and we were all immersed in it for more than an hour.

Crossing the Long Pond Creek ford and taking the break eat up a lot of daylight. We don't get moving again until 1:30 PM. We have rocky climbs up 2000 feet over Barren, Fourth and Third Mountains, before camping at the base of Chairback Ridge. The trail is still covered with rocks and roots, and there are deep muddy patches. We have not been making very good miles, and we need to step up our pace or we will run out of food before we get out of the Wilderness.

Up on the ledges atop Mount Barren we find a falconer in his blind, with a fake pigeon set out to try and trap a hawk for him to train. As each of us comes up the trail in succession and find the bait pigeon sitting out on the rock the falconer's vigil is interrupted, and he finally stops trying to remain hidden and talks to us for a while, probably hoping we will soon all go away so he can go back to catching his hawk.

It can take days, or even weeks for a falconer to catch a hawk, even without thru-hikers interrupting the ambush. There is no captivity breeding of raptors, so the only way to acquire a hunting bird is to catch one and train it. It is a sport that takes an extraordinary amount of patience.

We still have the fords of the two branches of the Pleasant River ahead of us, and the fords are killing our time. Phyzzy is a daybreak riser, and he advocates a plan for us all to get up and get moving earlier so we can get more miles out of the day. He presents it to me first, since I am the latest riser and laziest person first thing in the morning. His logic, as can be expected from a scientist, is inescapable. He will wake us all at dawn, around 6:30 in the morning. I am down with it.

We are hearing rumors that Hurricane Joaquin is headed north, and we may get another deluge. It may be a category 5 storm, and out here that could be deadly. We send some text messages from a mountaintop where we get signal to Miss Janet, and set up some contingency plans for evacuation if the storm looks like it is going to hit us in force.

Day 174, October 4th
Carl A. Newhall Lean-to, ME, Trail Mile 2110.6
Daily Distance 14.6 Miles

Phyzzy's planned early wake-up gets the desired results, and we get in a solid day of hiking. There are a lot of ups and downs and we have around 3500 total feet in elevation gains and losses during the day, over demanding terrain. There are rock scrambles, roots and rocks on the path, and the mud.

The descent from Chairback Mountain is of particular note. There is a 200 yard long section where a steep drop over big rocks and cliff faces requires careful movement. After three days out in the Wilderness we have each eaten our way through 6 pounds of food. There is so much water about we don't carry more than a liter or two each. Our pack weights are coming down, making hiking a little easier.

Ravens live on the mountain and we look down on them soaring on the currents from our view along the edges on the ridge top. As we descend the big, black birds swoop and circle overhead as we make our way down the rocks.

A few miles from the base of Chairback Mountain is the West Branch of the Pleasant River. We have lost a lot of time fording watercourses over the last three days due to the high waters, but we catch a break. The river is wide, but it is only knee deep and has a pebbled bottom. We are all across in twenty minutes.

Our trail family splits up while we hike. I am the slowest, so I am usually at the rear, and catch everyone else at rest stops. I stop long enough to check in, and then keep going. The others all pass me again in the next half hour, and then I catch them again at the next break. It is a continuous game of leapfrog.

On the far side of the Pleasant River a ridge runner is waiting. We are entering an area called the Hermitage, a protected area of old growth white pine. The ridge runner is checking up on it and making sure no one lights warming fires on the far side of the river.

The ridge runner is very familiar with the area, and she tells us that we should be able to make the next shelter, five and a half miles ahead, before darkness. She is partially correct. It is 5:00 o'clock in the evening, and darkness will fall around 7:00 PM. Days are shorter in Maine, where we are farther north than anywhere in the United States south of Alaska,

We all start hiking like bats out of hell, and as the oldest bat I quickly fall behind. Through the Hermitage the trail is great, flat, smooth and wide. We walk through the forest of immense, ancient pines for two miles. Afterwards the trail follows a ravine created by a small watercourse. The trail starts bumping along through the ravine, and there are lots of rocks and little ups and downs.

I am still on the trail at 7:00 PM, and I have to take out my headlamp. The forest becomes shadowy and threatening outside my little tunnel of light, and I have to move slowly over the uneven path. I am overjoyed to see another headlamp bobbing along up ahead. I have caught Waldo.

I don't have to hike too much further before I see the welcome flicker of a campfire. I have found Scout and the rest of the trail family. I set up in darkness, but I am not alone, I am sleeping near my family.

Tonight, this Wilderness is home.

Day 175, October 5th
Past the 2nd Pleasant River Ford, ME, Trail Mile 2121.7
Daily Distance 11.1 Miles

Whitecap Mountain is our last big climb before Mount Katahdin. It is a staggered climb of 3 stairs, each section 800 to 1000 feet of elevation gain. The climbs are steep, but there is a break of easy terrain on each section. After the mountain there is a wide, flat piece of forested terrain between us and the final peak.

I am again reminded of the Hobbit, and the view of the Lonely Mountain. From the top of Whitecap Mountain, Mt. Katahdin is clearly visible, a single, great, inspiring mountain rising out of the woods against a clear blue sky. It looks like it is much closer than the 70 miles that still remain ahead.

The ford over the main branch of the Pleasant River proves the easiest one thus far. Water levels have dropped and it is a gradually sloped, pebbled bottom. We walk right across without any difficulty. The only delay is the time it takes to take our hiking shoes off and swap them with our camp or water shoes for the crossing, and change back.

The trail is leveling out. It is crisscrossed with the roots of thick growths of pine trees, and there are rocks and muddy spots still, but it is flat, and we expect to make better time.

We have arranged to meet Miss Janet tomorrow. It is Waldo's birthday, and I work out a plan with her to provide a special treat for him. I have to do a lot of texting from the top of Whitecap, which is the only place I have gotten any cell phone signal for the past couple of days. We will also get some resupply. Our packs are getting pretty light and we still have three or four days before we get to Baxter State Park, even if we can start pulling sixteen mile days. I am looking forward to a little change of diet and some security in our supplies. Our packs are starting to feel a little too light.

I talk out the rest of my journey returning to finish my flip-flop heading south with the rest of the trail family. Based on their progress when they came north, even though I am the weakest hiker of our lot, I think I can finish by the end of October. I will still have around 180 miles to go hiking back to Gorham from Monson, and they are among the hardest miles of the entire trail. I am planning on using the hostels to slack several legs of the more difficult stretches and make better time.

As we sit around the fire tonight we assign Lord of the Rings characters to each member of our trail family, Scout is Master Samwise, utterly brave and reliable. Tumbles is the lighthearted Pippin. Phyzzy is Treebeard the Ent, and he wonders, "Where are the Ent wives?" Waldo is Rufus the Brown, because he travels his own unpredictable path and you never know where and when he will turn up. I am Gandalf. Miss Janet is Tom Bombadil, a merry guide who appears at times of greatest need.

Day 176, October 6th
Jo Mary Road, ME, Trail Mile 2133.2
Daily Distance 11.5 Miles

It is a grey day, and there is a good chill in the air, but it is not the sort of bitter cold that makes it hard to leave the comforts of the hammock. There are a lot of squirrels and chipmunks active in the area, gathering and storing the pinecone cores and nuts that will sustain them through the rapidly approaching winter.

Squirrels can be possessive about 'their' trees. I secured my hammock to a couple of trees they claimed as their own, and the squirrels scold me from above. I am pretty sure the rain of little twigs and bits of pinecones upon my rain fly this morning is intentional.

The landscape has leveled out. We had a few, last small bumps to go over, and now we are on the final stretch across 50 miles of valley floor to Katahdin. We could have made serious miles today, but we have a meet up with Miss Janet at Kokodjo-B road. The trail is easy, and we get there much earlier than expected. We sit idle for a while, an amazing pleasure while thru-hiking. We have a Frisbee and toss it about.

The 100 Mile Wilderness is not entirely inaccessible. There are a few dirt roads built by old timber operations and USFS, and occasional little cabins and camps as well. Miss Janet somehow nurses her big trail angel van down rutted strips of mud to bring us a feast for Waldo's birthday.

It is a picnic of epic proportions deep in the forest. There are loaves of bread with meats and veggies and all kinds of fixings. There are sodas, and chips, and more vegetables. There are also some resupply items, so we can finish out our trek with a comfortable surplus of food. For Waldo there is a birthday cake, with candles. He is just 21 years old, and already an accomplished hiker and adventurer.

When we are done eating Miss Janet does us one more solid, and carries our packs ahead to Jo Mary road, so we can slackpack for 7 miles. I am the last to arrive there, even unburdened and on good trail it takes me 2 hours and 45 minutes to finish a stroll through the woods. I am a slow hiker.

Miss Janet is heading home to Tennessee now, and Peaches is riding shotgun with her. We are her last hurrah for this year's hiking season. She starts her year in February down on the Florida Trail, which a few hikers use as a preliminary for the Appalachian Trail. She spends 8 or 9 months of each year immersed in trail support.

We have much to celebrate and enjoy today. Tumbles and Scout get a cell phone signal at Jo Mary Road, call home, and find out their new baby sister is ready to be born. Their parents are working plans to expedite their trip home once they are done on Katahdin so they can be on hand to greet the newest member of their family.

Wildlife is abundant. There are a lot of moose droppings on the trail, but I have not seen a moose. All the other members of the trail family have, further south. I am hoping I will see one after I make my flip-flop. The smaller ponds we pass have beaver dams, and Tumbles saw a snake yesterday. It might be the last snake of the season; it is getting far too cold for them. Maine has no venomous snakes.

We have a great campsite tonight near a big brook. It is warm enough this evening that we are not hurrying through dinner and quickly retreating into the warmth of our sleeping bags. We relax together.

Tomorrow we will start pushing the big miles. Phyzzy and Scout are pushing for a heroic marathon and finishing the next 48 miles to Abol Bridge in 2 days. I am thinking 3 is more in range of my abilities. I may be discounting myself; I will have to see what the trail holds.

We are looking at summiting Katahdin in four or five days, and then everyone starts heading home except me. I will head south to finish my hike at a less dramatic endpoint.

Day 177, October 7th
Wadleigh Stream Lean-to, ME, Trail Mile 2151.0
Daily Distance 17.8 Miles

We are done with leisurely days of hiking. Scout and Tumbles got to another point on the trail with cell signal and things are not well at home. Their mother is in the hospital with pre-delivery issues and they have to get home as soon as possible. Their baby sister is now due in a week. We all still want to summit together, so we are death marching towards Katahdin.

We came up with a group plan so we can all summit on Saturday. It is a simple plan. We get up at dawn and hike all the hours of daylight. Today is no fun at all; I have to push myself hard just to keep up, and don't have a break that is more than five minutes long. I catch up with the others making camp after dark.

The trail is level, but rooty and rocky. It follows the Nahmakanta River and lakeshore. The fords we meet are easy, but there is a constant concern that we will have to ford the big river on our left. It is a good 30 yards wide and 8 feet deep. That ford never comes; we do not cross the river.

The weather stays fine, crisp and cool rather than bitter. We get another glimpse of Katahdin growing ahead of us, its top wreathed in forbidding looking clouds.

I startle three snakes and two grouse as I push myself along the trail. One grouse broke cover and flew away, but the other struts down the trail, as pretty as you please.

We aim for nineteen miles tomorrow, to a shelter just a couple of miles short of Abol Bridge. That will give is one more day to get to the base of Katahdin at Baxter State Park, and then summit the following day. Tumbles and Scout will start their journey home as soon as they come off the mountain. It is feeling very rushed, but it is necessary.

Day 178, October 8th
Little Beaver Pond Side Trail, ME, Trail Mile 2166.3
Daily Distance 15.3 Miles

We rise early, pack and go. We fall short of our nineteen mile goal. At any other time fifteen miles would be a good day, but we are under pressure. The trail defies us with roots, rocks, and more roots and rocks. Many seasoned hikers are able to cover this level stretch of trail doing twenty mile days. Not us, and not me. We are seventeen miles from the base of Katahdin tonight.

The trail stays by water the entire day, a succession of streams and rapids, lakes and ponds. I push myself hard enough that I hit a wall just half a mile from our final campsite. I stop hiking and stare mindlessly at a lake for five minutes before I realize I am out of it. We have been going hard and strong for seven days since entering the Wilderness on limited diets. The essential energy to keep going is just gone. My stomach is growling; I need calories.

I store my food in plastic bags sorted by meal. I take a bag and put the day's snacks into it each morning before setting out, and eat them at short breaks through the day. I shared out some of my food back when we saw Miss Janet, so we all had enough to make Katahdin without privation, and to drop a little more weight out of my pack. I thought I had it planned out well, and had just enough. I am going to have to be more careful and eat my last snack of the day later so I have the sustained energy to finish the day.

Expendable resources are generally low for all of us. Our headlamps are getting dim as the batteries run out, toilet paper and hand sanitizer are rationed, but mostly it is food we are running short of. We should all have enough left for two more days, but that is it. On the positive side, our packs are very light.

We camp by Rainbow Lake. Out here, where man's touch is so gentle, the water is crystal clear, and I can see the rocks and stones on the bottom of the lake far out from the shoreline, and I see fish and crawfish moving about beneath the water.

I am still looking to see moose. The sign is everywhere. Moose like to go in the water in the evening and early morning to eat aquatic plant growth. I stare along the lake edges as I get water and clean up hoping to see their big forms moving into the lake.

It is a cloudless night. When the sky is clear, the temperature drops at night. There is nothing to trap the day's warmth close to the earth. The waters of the lake are cold, but they are warmer than the surrounding air. There is a lot of fog rising off of water in the mornings, a beautiful sight.

Day 179, October 9th
Abol Bridge, ME, Trail Mile 2174.1
Daily Distance 7.8 Miles

It is a cold, weary, dreary day. We are all sapped of energy. We only get as far as Abol Bridge, at the end of the 100 Mile Wilderness and the beginning of Baxter State Park. We are still a day's hike from the base of Mt. Katahdin.

I see a strange creature on the trail near the Rainbow Ledges, an area of small rock topped hills. The animal is standing on the trail looking at me 100 feet away, on the top of a small rise. I stop and we stare at each other for a few seconds, then it breaks off and runs into the underbrush. It is good sized animal, the size of a large dog, and has a thick, fluffy looking coat and a big bushy tail. It has russet fur, with a black section on the tip of its tail. I think it might be a cat, but it doesn't really look like any cat I know of. It is too big to be a bobcat, and it really doesn't look like a cougar.

Abol Bridge has a small store, and a camping area. It is a small island of civilization to us, but it is still 15 miles down a dirt road to the nearest town, Millinocket. Millinocket is itself a small, isolated town, even by Maine standards. We buy and eat a bunch of junk food and drinks at the store, loading up on calories. I ask about my cat, and the store manager tells me it was probably a coyote, or it might have been a wolf.

I have seen lots of coyotes, I have lived out West for twenty years and they are as common as dirt. This looked like no coyote I have ever seen. I express doubt, and the manger tells me that the coyotes out here in the East have interbred with feral dogs, and possibly wolves, so they are larger and have more variation than western coyotes. I am still not sure of this, although I tell my story to several people in the area and they all come back to coyote.

I am the last person across the bridge and into the store. There are a couple of other hikers there, and before I can get into the store, Phyzzy grabs me and tells me "Kamikaze is here!"

I have mixed feelings about a meeting. My last interactions with Kami were all the way back in New Jersey when I was in an emotional funk, and I still feel a little abandoned by the weird behavior at Kittatinny Lake. Phyzzy looks around for her, and then spots her walking away 50 yards down the dirt road leading to the trail into Baxter towards Katahdin s base.

"Kamikaze, wait, Possible is here!" He shouts. I am standing next to him. Kami turns, waves, turns away, and keeps hiking. I feel a momentary urge to chase after her, to explain where I was at in those grim days back in New Jersey, and make some kind of amends. Our journeys are nearing an end, and finishing with closure would be good. The moment passes quickly as I look at Kamikaze's back moving away.

It looks like she met her health goals; she is a much thinner version of the Kamikaze than I knew. She is hiking alone though; I guess she never found her trail family. Her death march has put her a couple of weeks ahead of me in real miles. I hear more about her in town.

My trail family decides our own death march is over. We are all low on supplies, and the weather is supposed to be bad over next two days, followed by a day of sunshine. What is a cold, wet day down at Abol Bridge is deadly weather up on the high exposed peak of Mount Katahdin. There is some kind of hiker feed being set up at the campground, but the idea of a hot shower, a bunk, and hot food off a menu is irresistible. One day is not going to figure much into Scout and Tumble's plans to get home for their sister's birth. We will slack the miles between Abol Bridge and the Baxter State Park Birches campground at the base of Katahdin tomorrow, and then wait and see. We may hold off another day to summit and catch that day of glorious sunshine.

Arranging a ride into Millinocket takes some time. I walk around the area to find a cell phone signal and call to get the shuttle to come out. It will be an hour or so before the driver can make it. There are five of us to split costs. Waldo is on his last dollar so the rest of us agree to split his costs to get him into town and a hostel. We do not want to lose our quirky trail companion, and dividing costs so many ways the cost is negligible.

The shuttle shows up, and it is a little PT Cruiser hatchback. The five of us cram in with our gear, sitting on each other's laps with packs and hiking poles wedged into all the intervening spaces. The road is a bumpy graveled forest road, and each pothole and trench jars and pains us. We are in a happy mood anyway. We have conquered the 100 Mile Wilderness, the last great summit lies before us, and showers, hot food, and warm beds await us.

Millinocket is a town with little to sustain it, Timber used to be big business, but it is gone. Now the only outside income appears to be hikers and hunters. The town looks like it is barely hanging on; most of the storefronts we pass have an abandoned look. There are a lot of thrift stores but little in the way of thriving retail establishments.

The main hostel in town, The Appalachian Trail Lodge, is cheery enough, and there are a couple of bars and restaurants sharing the same street, including a café run by Ole Man and Navigator, the hostel owners. It is a friendly place for thru-hikers and as the last hostel on the Appalachian Trail (or first, for SoBos), it is a busy place

Doing laundry requires clothes to wear as the dirty items are going through the cycles, and there is a closet with random clothes for hikers to don while their trail clothes are in the machines. The closet yields some strange attire, including a couple of 1970s prom tuxedos. Waldo looks awesome in sky blue tails with a white ruffled shirt. It adds to the festive atmosphere.

We are surrounded by hikers this evening, all in celebratory moods, either approaching Katahdin or just having finished their thru-hike. We go to the Appalachian Trail Café for dinner and it is a party. The Café is a little rustic, and it is filled with trail and wilderness memorabilia. There is plenty of food and beer. It is a comfortable place for thru-hikers to let their hair down.

MT KATAHDIN APPROACH AND SUMMIT

Day 180 to 181 October 10 to October 11
Abol Bridge to Mount Katahdin, Trail Mile 2174.1 to 2189.2, 15.1 miles
AVG 7.5 Daily Miles

Day 180, October 10th
Mt. Katahdin Ranger Station, Baxter State Park, ME, Trail Mile 2184.0
Daily Distance 9.9 Miles

One of the services offered by the Appalachian Trail Hostel for paid guests is a five dollar shuttle out and back from Mount Katahdin and Abol Bridge. The shuttle leaves at a set time in the morning, and makes one evening trip back from the Birches Campground, at the base of Katahdin. The distance between Abol Bridge and the Birches is just under ten miles. Baxter Peak, the summit of Katahdin, is only another 5.2 miles from the Birches, but it is 5.2 miles of some of the hardest trail anywhere on the AT, and once you have summitted and finished your official AT hike, you still have to make the 5.2 mile descent back down the same hard trail, making a 10.4 mile day of hiking. Like Springer Mountain in Georgia, there is no road to the end of the Appalachian Trail.

Logistically this makes Katahdin a full day adventure. We will slack to the Birches and spend another night shuttling back and forth to Millinocket, before climbing Katahdin. We are still debating whether we will summit tomorrow, since the weather is supposed to be bad.

Ole Man drives us out on the shuttle. I ask him about moose. I am incredibly eager to see one. He says the moose population in Maine, after years of recovery, is declining again. Last year there were an estimated 76,000 moose in the state, this year numbers are down to 60,000. Tick borne diseases are believed to be the cause, weakening moose so they are more susceptible to other natural causes of death.

Ole Man tells me moose stories. The big animals are not an uncommon sight in the area, and they are a positive hazard to automobiles. When a vehicle collides with an animal weighing 1500 pounds, no one wins. Male moose are so aggressive during the mating season that they charge any perceived hazard, including moving cars (and hikers).

Incidentally, it is moose mating season. I have been warned.

The day's hike is easy. The trail is a park. I even see deer frolicking Bambi-like next to the path as I enter the woods. The Appalachian Trail follows the Penobscot River for a distance, and then travels alongside several ponds and streams. There are a couple of knee deep fords in very cold water, but other than the small challenges they present it is a stroll today. Baxter State Park is a popular day hiking area and the trail is well groomed, flat and easy.

I dither a bit in one of the fords seeking the best way across. I have chosen to cross barefoot, and by the time I get across my feet have turned an angry red color from exposure to the cold.

The whole hike takes me five hours at a pleasant walking pace. The Baxter State Park rangers are pleasant and helpful. After all of the stories I have heard about BSP's resistance to thru-hikers it is an unexpected welcome. There are a number of rules, no littering, no alcohol, and no dogs. They are Leave No Trace rules to protect the environment, and they are both reasonable and enforced. If you need have to have your dog, or a drink, it may seem oppressive I suppose.

We ride back in a full shuttle van to Millinocket. The weather tomorrow is not supposed to be good, and the following day is predicted to be beautiful. Scout is worried about his mother back home, and wants to get the thru-hike finished.

Waldo is uncomfortable having his hostel night paid for, although it is no burden to us. He chooses to stay at a lean-to in the Birches instead of coming into town tonight. We all want to summit together, and so we commit to Katahdin tomorrow, unless the weather is so awful the rangers close the mountain.

Day 181, October 11th
Mount Katahdin, ME, Trail Mile 2189.2
Daily Distance 5.2 Miles

Mount Katahdin is awesome, in the fullest meaning of the word. Some geographical places seem to announce their significance to the world. They are in some way different, and special compared to all the other space around them. Man is compelled to mark them in some way, and acknowledge their presence. Katahdin is one of these places that inspire awe.

The mountain stands a little distance separate from the many other peaks and ranges in northern and western Maine. It is the tallest mountain in Maine, 5,267 feet tall. The Indian tribes of Maine hold it as a holy place. Katahdin itself is an Abenaki word meaning 'greatest mountain'. Henry David Thoreau immortalized the peak to European man, writing an essay on his hike into the wild and his attempt to conquer the mountain in 1846. Now it is the end of the Appalachian Trail for NoBos. SoBo's begin here, of course, and have the far less imposing Springer Mountain in Georgia as their destination.

Hikers are required to sign in at the Baxter State Park ranger station. It is a safety protocol so the rangers know who is up on the mountain, and more importantly, if everyone has come back.

The rangers provide a lecture at the sign-in about the dangers of the mountain. Rescue parties can take several hours to climb up the mountain and retrieve an injured hiker. They have had people in the past get tired or scared on the way up or down, and try to call for a helicopter to give them a ride back down. You are advised to bring crampons and an ice axe.

The rangers lay it on pretty thick, but NoBo thru-hikers are as experienced as a hiker can get at this point, and they speed up the standard lecture for us. They tell us it normally takes between 8 to 12 hours to complete a round trip.

Katahdin has several different landscapes to hike through. The first mile is a gentle forested slope and a nice walking path. It follows a stream as it comes down from the mountain, and there are scenic little waterfalls and viewpoints along the way. The trail gradually increases its grade until I am working my way up through rocks as steep as a flight of stairs.

I emerge from out of the treeline, and a mile of rock towers above me. There are many small vertical sections, and the face of the mountain narrows as it rises. And this is the easy way up.

The weather starts taking its first bites as I ascend. Our trail family has spread out based on our different hiking and climbing speeds. I actually catch and pass Tumbles, Scout, and Waldo on this section. My legs may be slow, but my upper body strength, even diminished after six months of hiking, is still strong. This part of the trail is more arm work hauling myself up over rocks and crevices than strolling along on legs.

There are several places where steel rebar handholds are mounted into the rock at particularly hard areas to navigate. Arms are much slower than legs, and the area requires a lot of care and forward planning for movement. It is slow. Even against my fear of heights, the obstacles are enjoyable challenges. The trail is crowded with day hikers in groups, and at some points I have to wait in line to get over a particular obstacle as each individual tackles it in turn.

The rock face narrows into a passage no more than 20 or 30 feet wide at the top of the climb, and the world drops away on both sides. The views are fantastic. Within that fantastic view are storm clouds gusting in and accumulating around the peak.

The trail levels out after the big workout of coming up the long steep face. There is more than a mile yet to the summit, but Katahdin is flat up on top. Only lichens and very low bits of shrubbery adapted to an artic environment survive up here. The wind has an unimpeded runway all the way down from Canada to build up and batter me as I follow the worn way through the lichen across the scrabble of breadbox sized rocks on the path.

There is a spring up here, named after Henry David Thoreau, and the trail runs directly up the mountain on top of its frozen stream. It is a way of protecting the fragile life on the rocks on either side that is trying to hang on up here. The stream is still trickling beneath the covering of ice, and the ice is not strong enough in many places to support a man's weight. Regular immersions of my feet in the freezing water are part of the walk.

The clouds I could see approaching on my ascent arrive, and my hike turns into a world of rock, mist, and occasional flurries of snow. Visibility drops until I can only see twenty feet ahead of me. On the flatter stretch my companions are more than my equals, and each one catches and passes me with shared words of encouragement and joy.

There is no real way to know how far the peak is ahead of me. The trail is marked by cairns, and each mound of rock is a barely visible structure standing against a backdrop of swirling mist. I see fewer hikers; the weather is turning many of the day hikers back on the climb up the rock face.

The path rises after passing the spring. It is not the technical rock face of before, just a steady little climb over rocks. It seems a great distance. It is cold and wet, and our plan to get a group photo at the peak is not going to happen. Phyzzy and Waldo both pass me on their way back down, apologizing for not waiting. They tell me the conditions are too miserably wet and cold to wait at the top for us all to gather. They have summitted, and we will share experiences at the bottom. They assure me I don't have far to go.

I keep climbing. The rocks are coated with ice, making any misstep a potential disaster. I plant my hiking poles and put each foot down carefully, but I still have a couple of nasty falls. I finally see a cluster of shadowy figures appearing ghostlike ahead of me in the swirling clouds. It is the summit.

The summit sign requires a photo; it will go in the Hiker Yearbook. The sign is a wooden structure taller than man, built like a sawhorse. It has to be replaced every so often, and the old signs become museum pieces. The summit photo is a big deal; it goes on the postcards people send out as thank-you notes commemorating their hike, and in the Hiker Yearbook. Many people bring up special mementos or dress up just for the picture.

Today no one wants to linger more than a minute or two at the top, and Scout and Tumbles wait for me just long enough to take my picture before they head down. I want to savor my peak experience, but I am quickly driven off the peak by the wind chill myself, and I follow my trail family back down the trail after a couple of minutes.

I have made it to the northern terminus of the Appalachian Trail.

The hike back down is just as challenging as coming up, but the additional 5.2 miles are not a part of counted trail miles. It doesn't make them any easier.

I am hunched and cold crossing the frosted flat plateau of the peak, again passing Thoreau Spring and its iced over stream of water.

The mile high rock face is possibly even more daunting going down than coming up. My handholds and footholds are not always visible below, and out in front of me it is a long way down through empty space to rocks below.

As I descend I get underneath the clouds, and visibility improves. It is still windy and cold until I get down into the treeline. I am again delayed several times waiting for groups of day hikers slowly crossing chokepoint obstacles.

I hurry to get down. We started hiking at 8:30 AM, and the shuttle is supposed to leave at 5:00 PM. As I come down the mountain and into the trees five o'clock comes and goes, and I am still over a mile away from the BSP base and parking area. The last mile is an easy one, and my pace is brisk. I am the last hiker to arrive at the shuttle at 5:30 PM, but it is there waiting for me.

More than a dozen thru-hikers summit today; besides our family there is Wisconsin and High Life, Toasty, Peach, and Downhill. Many more are waiting out the weather in Millinocket and will try the climb tomorrow. There is a register at the Ranger Station, and I am the 984th thru-hiker to summit Mt. Katahdin in 2015.

We are all exhilarated as we drive back to Millinocket. The thru-hikers finishing here have accomplished a great and amazing feat, completing the Appalachian Trail. Of the more than 6000 estimated people who even dare to try a thru-hike, less than 15% make it.

I am not yet one of them and it tempers my joy. I still have nearly 200 miles of trail ahead of me, and the weather is getting worse.

Day 182, October 12th
Monson, ME, (Shaw's Hostel), Trail Mile 2074.7
Daily Distance 0 Miles, ZERO DAY

I enjoy a final breakfast with my companions. The main focus now for most of the thru-hikers is getting home. The hostel runs a shuttle down to Bangor, the largest population center in northern Maine. I hesitate to call

Bangor a city; a very large town is probably more accurate. It does have an airport, a bus station, and car rentals, and it is the way home for most hikers.

The shuttle leaves early, so after our last breakfast together as a trail family there is a flurry of activity as people get packed up and make final travel arrangements. I watch as they go, and the hostel is very quiet afterwards.

Tumbles and Scout were originally planning to rent a car with Phyzzy and drive south to Ohio, and then get picked up and driven the rest of the way to Tennessee. Phyzzy had to be a part of the plan since Scout is too young to rent a car. Phyzzy was lukewarm on the plan; he had some visits he wanted to make on the way home, but Tumbles and Scout are in a hurry to get home, and he will support them.

It works out in the end. Scout and Tumble's parents have a friend with a small plane who will be in the area, and they will fly home from Maine instead of drive. Tumbles is very excited, she has never flown in any kind of an airplane before.

My own plans require a shuttle back to Monson. Ole Man works on it, but the priority is getting the greater number of hikers to Bangor, and there is a single van. Shaw's, where I stayed in Monson, is owned by Ole Man and Navigator's daughter Hippie Chick, and son in law, Poet. They are as neighborly as can be for places 100 miles apart on winding roads and a van shows up in the early afternoon for a visit with kinfolk. I get a ride back with them to Monson.

Shuttle costs are by charged by the mile, pricey, but still cheaper than a local cab would cost. A local cab would charge me per mile for a round trip, since they would need to return to Millinocket after dropping me off.

I retrieve my mail drop in Monson, originally intended for the 100 Mile Wilderness. It is a big package, and with some staples added in from the resupply shop at Shaw's my pack is very heavy. I am planning on slacking tomorrow, and will leave all the food and extras behind, just carrying survival essentials in my pack, with a day's worth of snacks.

I was hoping to find a package from Leki as well, with repair parts for my hiking poles, but it is nowhere to be found. I will have to continue making do with duct tape holding my poles together, with the occasional pole collapses when the repairs are too stressed.

FINISHING
Day 183 to Day 208, October 13 to November 7th
Monson ME to Gorham NH, Trail Mile 2074.1 to 1890.9, 183.2 miles
AVG 7.63 Daily Miles

Day 183 to Day 187, October 13 to October 17
Monson ME to East Flagstaff Road, ME, (Stratton Hotel), 2074.1 to 2017.7
AVG 11.3 Daily Miles

Day 183, October 13th
Near the West Branch of the Piscataquis River, Trail Mile 2060.0
Daily Distance 14.7 Miles (Slackpack)

I am the only guest at Shaw's. The last wave of thru-hikers going north passed through just ahead of my arrival. I arrange a slackpack for my first day of southbound hiking. The shuttle costs are expensive, but it is a way to get some easy miles.

I have two fords of the Piscataquis River to cross in this section. It is the same stretch of land where hikers were stranded during the monsoon in Monson a week ago. There is neither road access nor bridges accessing the peninsula formed between the East and West branches of the river. The fords are the only way across.

A few trapped hikers were helicoptered out during the monsoon, and one hiker showed me a selfie video on his cell phone of a National Guard helicopter lowering a cable so he could be lifted up out through the treetops.

I am worried about going through the fords alone. The river proves tamer now, though, and the fords are just a little over knee deep, with a slow, gentle current. The river is wide, and very cold, but an easy passage.

The trail itself is flat, following the course of the West Branch of the Piscataquis River for much of the way. It is drizzling, and the rocks on the trail are slick.

I get back to the road into Monson in the late afternoon. I welcome finishing the day's hike with a ride back to a warm bed and a hot meal. Slackpacking is expensive, especially with no one to split costs. Some stretches are worth it, but for others it is easier to just keep moving forward. On a wet day like today I feel the cost is justified.

My whole bill for the trip down from Monson, two nights in the hostel, meals, resupply, and the two shuttles out to the AT access at trail mile 2060 come to about $300.00. My long stretch of limited town stops and overnight stays going through the Mid-Atlantic States and lower New England are now working in my favor, I am under budget, and I have the money to spend at hostels and on slackpacking for this final stretch of the trail.

I will need it.

Day 184, October 14th
Past the south end of Moxie Pond, Trail Mile 2049.9
Daily Distance 10.1 Miles

I am shuttled back to the West Branch of the Piscataquis River to start my next leg. I don't get out onto the trail until after 11:00 AM. It is a chilly day, and while I am in the hostel getting ready to go in the morning I cannot find my gloves. I unpack my entire pack and go through it looking for them, but it slowly dawns on me that I left them behind, either at one of the fords or at a break during yesterday's hike.

My gloves were a thin, lightweight fleece, and very warm for their weight. Like almost all good lightweight hiking gear they were expensive. I tend to become attached to certain pieces of equipment, and these gloves had served me well for many miles. I mourn their loss. I buy a set of fingerless lightweight woolen gloves at Shaw's resupply shop to replace them.

The trail continues to follow the river and is flat until it finally climbs up and away over Moxie Bald Mountain, a mellow 1500 foot bump. The middle section of Maine is rather benign hiking. The challenges of the 100 mile Wilderness are behind me, and the Maine section of the White Mountains still lies fifty miles ahead.

The trail challenges are the rocks and roots, the rain, and the lack of grading and trail maintenance through this section. The trail is very muddy, and there are copious amounts of standing water. My shoes, socks and feet are soaked through. Like the beginning of the trail in Georgia, there doesn't really seem to be anytime when the land (and the passing hiker) has a chance to dry out.

I cross two small fords. At the first one I change into my Crocs for the crossing to try and preserve my socks and shoes, but at the second my feet are already so sodden there isn't any point in trying to keep them dry, and I just wade on in and across in my hiking shoes and socks.

Fall has arrived, and the leaves blaze with color. Greens, browns, oranges, yellows, and reds are the colors reflecting in the surfaces of lakes and ponds that freckle the land up here. Often the land is shrouded in mist. It is a damp season, but when a clear break comes the land is vibrant under breathtaking blue skies. I get a fine view from the top of Moxie Bald.

Fall also brings cooler weather, and in Maine it can quickly turn rain into snow and ice, especially on the mountaintops. I should be in the Bigelow range in four days, and I will be arriving at the same time there is a predicted cold front coming through.

I have called ahead to the Sterling Inn, my next hostel stop in the town of Caratunk. It is a day ahead, and just before the Kennebec River crossing. There is a ferry across the Kennebec, a river too wide and deep to ford. A dam upstream periodically releases stored water for white water rafting, and to be caught mid-river during a water release could easily mean death. Signs are posted along this section of the trail warning hikers of the dangers of attempting a ford of the river ahead.

The ferry across the river is a canoe, and it is a free service of the Appalachian Trail Conservancy during the season. I am hiking late in the year, late enough I am now out of season. The person contracted to provide the service is supposed to continue to provide ferry trips for $50.00 a trip if you make prior arrangements. According to the host at the Sterling Inn, the contract ferryman and the ATC are having a disagreement, and he is now refusing to ferry anyone across.

I am left in a predicament. There is no other practical way to get across the river. I can get a shuttle to drive me down to the nearest bridge crossing and back up the other side for about the same cost, but the nearest road access to the Appalachian Trail on the far side is five miles in, so I will spend a day hiking back north to the river and then turning around and retracing my steps south if I am still intent on hiking the entire trail, which I am. It is not a pleasing thought.

The host at the Sterling Inn is going to ask around locally to see if he can help me. There are many boat and river guides in the area. White water rafting trips down the Kennebec are the primary business activity in the area.

I see two other hikers today, a newly married young couple spending their honeymoon in the Maine woods. They are staying at Harrison's Pierce Pond Camp, a rustic cabin resort that will provide pancake breakfasts for thru-hikers. It is only mid-afternoon when I pass. I could have a dry night here, but I am back on track hiking south and don't want to interrupt my flow.

I have not seen my moose yet. There are big piles of moose droppings all along the way, so the moose are definitely out here. I see a lot of grouse, each one a small heart attack when it explodes out of the brush and flies away. Frogs are also out in force, enjoying the wet weather.

Day 185, October 15th
Caratunk, ME, Trail Mile 2038.0
Daily Distance 11.9 Miles

I feel very tired hiking today and I am not sure why.

It is cool during the day, and cold enough to be uncomfortable at night. I am waking up early, feeling chilled, and reluctant to face the world outside my hammock until the morning sun has a chance to warm up the air. Dawn is coming later, both from the sun's retreat for winter and the northern latitude. I have less than 12 hours of sunlight a day now.

I am out of camp by 8:30 AM, once a sluggish time but now pretty reasonable; the sun has not been up for all that long. It is still hard for me to get my head around the later start; I feel I should be moving earlier and hiking later.

There is a long, gradual grade up Pleasant Pond Mountain. It is almost five miles of gentle uphill, only rising about 1500 feet, but it saps my little remaining energy. I take nearly five hours to go up, as long as my ascent of Mt. Katahdin.

The trail down is also gentle, but I can't get myself moving at any kind of pace and I trudge my way into town. I don't know if I am using more calories, even over shorter times and distances, because of the cold, or whether I have a dietary deficiency of some kind. It may just be the constant effort of hiking over roots, rocks and mud rather than on a cleaner trail. Whatever the issue is, it is frustrating to feel so weak.

There is a spooky quality to hiking today as well. The sun is making some appearances, and casting long shadows through the woods. There are large birds flying somewhere overhead, and shadows appear suddenly on the ground before me and sweep away as I hike. I cannot identify the birds; are they hawks, ravens, vultures, or something else?

A couple of times while I am hiking I hear a noise like blocks of wood being hit together, a toc, toc, toc noise, quite loud and echoing off the rocks. I have no idea what is causing it, and it repeats several times as I am hiking.

I see three NoBos today, the very last of them I believe I will meet on the journey. Poseidon is on the top of Pleasant Pond Mountain, and he is having a rough day, although he is in good spirits. The trail is very poorly marked on the mountaintop, and there are a number of little branch paths away from the main trail among the cairns in the open spaces and the small stands of pine. He followed one of the side trails thinking it was the Appalachian Trail, and it circled the peak and brought him back to where he started an hour earlier.

From the top of the mountain the landscape is a sea of scarlet and gold with blue lakes and ponds sitting jewel-like among the splendor. I pause to take it in, but I do not sit long to enjoy it. I have to maintain my slow movement forward,

Jumanji and the Pinecone are the other two NoBos I meet. We chat for a bit, but we are both in a hurry to move in our own directions. We are about equidistant from our ultimate goals. As they move north I hear Jumanji's jolly laugh for my last time on the trail.

There is a hardball road next to the Kennebec River, and I hike down it a half mile to a small village. Cell service is somewhere between spotty and non-existent out in this area of the world, but another communication arrangement is available in the village of Caratunk. Outside the village post office a free payphone stands that provides contact to the local hostel. I find it, make the call, and wait for my ride.

The Sterling Inn is run by an older man named Eric, with some help from his adult son. I have my own room. No other guests are here tonight, so again I probably should have taken the cheaper bunkroom option. The building is an historical inn, and is well laid out for the purpose of providing lodging. It is very comfortable and there is a large common room with the usual TV, movies, games, and a guitar.

There are no supermarkets nearby, but the inn has a well stocked resupply room, and the prices are quite reasonable. I worried while planning the Maine section of my trip about the lack of significant towns and the impact it would have on trying to find resupply, but the hostels recognize and meet this need. Some of the hostels in states further south on the trail charged a lot of money for necessities and convenience, but the hostels in Maine have not taken advantage of the situation.

Room prices are quite inexpensive at the Sterling, and on top of it all the inn offers a continental breakfast. Also included in the price is a shuttle a few miles up the road to a brewpub for dinner, and Eric offers to take me into the local hardware store in the morning to see if I can't find another pair of gloves. My fingerless gloves are good while hiking and gripping rocks while climbing, and I find out during a stream crossing mishap that they float. However, when I am still for a few moments my exposed fingers start getting cold and numb, making it hard for me to the perform fine motor skill functions of setting up camp. I want another pair like my lost fleece gloves.

Eric has made the arrangements with a local river guide to get me across the Kennebec River the following morning.

Day 186, October 16th
Past Scott Road, ME, Trail Mile 2029.3
Daily Distance 8.7 Miles

I make another slow roll out of town. I am the only person at breakfast besides my host Eric. The Sterling Inn offers a pretty basic continental breakfast; coffee, juice, cereal, muffins and fruit. It is filling and free.

I get my ride to the hardware store to look for a better pair of gloves. There is a very limited selection of clothing, mostly geared towards hunting. I find a cheap pair of blaze orange fleece gloves. It is moose hunting season, and I have heard occasional gunshots in the distance as I hike. Wearing some blaze orange will help me from being mistaken for a moose. I am going to carry 2 pairs of gloves now, my fingerless pair will be for hiking, and I will double up and wear the orange fleeces under them in camp. My hands have been cramping up in the cold making it hard to complete my chores.

My ferry ride across the Kennebec River is delayed. My river guide is running errands, and we meet up on the Kennebec riverbank at noon for my trip across. She tells me a little about the river as she paddles me across in her canoe. The river has a channel in it that can be as deep as 60 feet when the dam releases water. There are a few places were the river might be fordable during low water, but the Appalachian Trail crossing point isn't one of them. The river is more than 50 yards wide at this point, and supports light motorized boat traffic. The water looks dark, cold, and bottomless flowing beside the canoe as we cross.

It is supposed to be cold and wet today. There is a damp chill, but it is nowhere as bad as I feared it might be, and once I am moving the coolness in the air is welcome.

My tired spell of yesterday has passed. My own mental state is better. When I am tired it can bring out a self-pitying attitude in me that I dislike enormously, and engage in anyway. When I recognize it happening I give myself a mental kick in the butt to break free, but sometimes I wallow a bit,

The trail is flat in this area near the river. There are a lot of leaves on the trail, and they hide the puddles and rocks beneath them. I have a number of slips, and my feet get wet and stay wet. The coating of leaves obscures the beaten path, and I have to guess at times where the actual Appalachian Trail leads.

I have to call ahead to the next hostel, the Stratton Motel, to see if they are still open at the end of the season. They are, and I make arrangements with the host, Shane, for lodging, and to slackpack in the Bigelows, the next mountain range up ahead.

I end up speaking to Hakuna Matata on the phone for a while. She and Bluebird are at the Stratton. They jumped ahead to summit Katahdin before the mountain closure, and are now back picking up pieces of the trail they missed, much like I am, except they are heading north. We talk for a bit, and I think they have their thru-hike in the bag. All they have left to finish are the easy sections I have just completed through to Monson.

Hakuna warns me that the section I have left ahead is as hard, or harder than any other section of the trail. I hear a certain relief in her voice that what is left for them is easy, and their hike is almost over. It has been very hard on the 70 year old Bluebird, but she is going to finish.

I am still seeing lots of moose sign, but seeing no moose themselves. The trail passes many ponds and lakes of the sort they prefer. Moose like to wade in and eat aquatic vegetation near the shoreline, particularly at dawn and dusk.

I hear shouting and gunshots near the gravel Scott Road after I cross. Hunters like to be fairly close to a road. After they shoot a moose they have to pack it out, and a 1500 pound animal takes a lot of packing. I hike about a half mile away from the road before looking for a campsite for the night. I want to create a zone of separation between me and the hunters. I stop at several likely spots before I find one with trees a suitable distance apart for my hammock hang.

There are big piles of moose droppings everywhere. Moose droppings are similar to rabbit or deer droppings, piles of little balls, except that for moose the little balls are huge mounds of Swedish meatballs rather than chocolate covered peanuts.

I hear the cries of a barred owl as I am falling to sleep, and I am woken again in the middle of the night by coyotes snarling and crying from several different directions. If they are talking to each other it does not sound like a pleasant conversation. The coyotes make me a little nervous; I am sleeping alone trussed up in my hammock, right in the middle of a territorial dispute.

Day 187, October 17th
At East Flagstaff Road, ME, (Stratton Hotel), Trail Mile 2017.7
Daily Distance 11.6 Miles

I SEE MOOSE TODAY!

I wake up slowly, it is very cold and rain has been coming down steadily all night long. Wetness has seeped into my hammock along the edges and

I am pretty uncomfortable. I roll around a few times inside my cocoon trying to recapture sleep, but it eludes me. I peer out from beneath my rain fly to see the day, and not twenty feet away from my hang an enormous lady moose stands staring back at me.

I am very excited, but also a little fearful. Moose are nearsighted, and have a reputation for charging if they are startled. I am strung up between two trees, and there is no way for me to dodge if the moose gets the urge to have a nice trample.

I ease my phone out and start taking pictures. Lady Moose peers at me but shows no signs of alarm. I watch her for nearly a half hour as she wanders around my campsite before she finally disappears into the woods. Everything about the moment seems magical; the giant creature walking around unconcerned as I watch from a few feet away, Even the light leaking down from a misty sky enhances the natural colors of the foliage so my Lady is backdropped by kaleidoscopic fall colors.

The morning moose sighting sets a fine tone for the day. One moose was a great reward.

As I am crossing Long Falls Dam road, another graveled forest road, I see a pickup truck coming. I stop to wait for it to pass. It slows down and stops right in front of me instead. The driver is waving at me and pointing ahead on the road.

I look where the apparently crazy man is pointing, just in time to see a big male moose with a giant rack and a female companion trotting across the road together. The driver stopped so I would see the moose. I have spent all my time in New England hoping to get a glimpse of a single moose, and I get to see three in one day!

The trail today has a few, small rolling hills. The trail is obscured beneath its coating of wet leaves and I roll both of my ankles on hidden rocks. This has become a commonplace occurrence; I whimper a bit and keep marching. It is impossible to limp with both feet. I have tried many times.

It starts snowing as I am going over one of the hills. It isn't much, just enough to create a frosting on the plants and rocks. I am moving pretty quickly despite my sore ankles and the slippery conditions. I have arranged a ride into the Stratton Motel hostel from Shane on a road ahead, and we have a set meeting time. I can't rely on cell service, so it is an old school protocol of meeting at a specific time and place. I do not want to keep my host waiting.

I make good time despite the conditions, and arrive at East Flagstaff road, my goal, early. I sit and wait for a little while.

It is a welcome break. I am so driven to make miles I don't get many opportunities to take a long rest in the forest and just take in the sounds. I am actually disappointed when my ride shows up on time and interrupts my moment of peace.

The ride into and out of the town of Stratton to the hostel is expensive; the trail is a forty five minute drive from the remote town. I have plans for a two day slackpack across the Bigelows working out of the hostel.

I have been feeling a lot of tired days of late. I am moving slowly. I think it is the cold. I am walking all day and sleeping chilled most nights. I am burning calories and not getting the kind of deep, restorative sleep I need for recovery. I believe day after day of exercise and exposure is slowly wearing me down. I am willing to spend some money for a little bit of comfort.

Stratton is bigger than the last couple of towns I have been through, which is in no way the same as being a large, or even a middle sized town. There is a small center with a cluster of businesses around it, including my hotel. There are a couple of restaurants, one being a café and the other is more of a bar. There is another small motel, and a secondhand store.

My resupply will be a general store, a small place crammed with groceries, hunting supplies, and small bits of hardware. Prices are high. The hotel itself isn't bad; it is $50.00 for a private room, and $25.00 for a bed in the bunkroom.

I take a single room for the first night, but move into the unoccupied bunkroom the next morning. I have again found I prefer the bunkrooms to the private rooms if there are not a lot of hikers crammed into the space. The bunkroom has a common area with places to sit and relax, a small kitchen, and a dining table and chairs.

I make my arrangements to start my slackpack of the Bigelows tomorrow. I eat a good meal, and get a solid night of sleep.

Day 188 and 189, October 18th and 19th
At East Flagstaff Road, ME, Trail Mile 2017.7,
Daily Distance 0.0 Miles (2 ZERO DAYS)

A cold front has moved in, the weather driven by a freezing wind. Everything is iced over and it is snowing to boot. I see this down in town; up on the exposed ridges it must be brutal. I am advised against attempting the Bigelow Range in the ice and snow by Shane, my host at the Stratton Hotel. I spend the first day in my private room and watch Sunday football. I move into the hostel bunkroom afterwards.

I am not alone in the bunkroom. Tarzan, another flip-flopping thru-hiker, shows up heading south, and is holing up just like I am. He has to get all the way to Hanover, New Hampshire, and will have to cross the Presidential Range in some dicey weather. He is a strong hiker, but is concerned about what he is going to face up ahead. He chafes at the delay imposed by our current weather.

Tarzan appears as worn down mentally and physically as I am. The rest is very welcome for my body and soul, even as I look at the calendar and try to calculate how many days I have left. It will take me somewhere around 2 weeks to finish, if I can pick up my pace a little. I feel the end coming, and I am ready to finish my thru-hike.

Day 190 to Day 196, October 20th to October 25th
East Flagstaff Road, ME, to ME Route 4, Trail Mile 2017.7 to 1968.8
AVG 8.31 Daily Miles

Day 190, October 20th
Safford Brook, ME, Trail Mile 2011.3
Daily Distance 6.4 Miles (SLACKPACK)

My actual hiking distance today is 8.6 miles. Shane drives me to a trailhead, and I need to climb up 2.2 additional miles on a blue blaze before I can rejoin the Appalachian Trail near Safford Brook. I then hike north over Little Bigelow and back down to Little Flagstaff Road where I was originally picked up two days ago.

Weather conditions are uncertain, and I opt for this smaller hike instead of trying to knock out the Bigelow Mountains in a single day. There are some rather steep climbs and descents, and a lot of exposed ridgeline. I most emphatically do not want to get caught up there in the dark. It is seventeen miles of trail if I attempted to hike this all in a single day.

Tarzan, younger and stronger than I am, will be making a single day of it. He has a set of micro spikes for his shoes. Micro spikes are small steel cleats on a rubber overshoe worn over your regular shoes. The spikes allow a hiker to get traction on ice covered slabs of rock, which are going to be pretty common now. The spikes weigh almost a pound, but I definitely want a pair. There are none available in the town's general store, our single point of supply in Stratton. I will do without until the next town.

It turns out to be a pleasant day's hike. Most of the trail is below treeline and unexposed. The weather has warmed up to normal fall coolness. The hardest part of the day turns out to be the initial blue blazed side path getting back up onto the Appalachian Trail. There are nice views from up on top. I get a good look at Avery Peak and Big Bigelow, my hike for tomorrow, and they are intimidating. They are steep and rocky, and there is snow and ice glistening on the exposed peaks. I am glad I am not trying to do it all today

It would have been more economical if I continued my SoBo hiking until I had finished the Bigelows and then gone into town for a single night, but I have reached a point where I need rest. Fate spoke as well, I would have been up here in the terrible weather of the last two days if I had skipped town, and might have been forced to come down off the mountains anyway.

I am trying a new technique today, suggested in a book on ultralight backpacking I read on my tablet while lying in my hammock waiting for sleep to come. It recommends the use of plastic shopping bags for various purposes, one of which is to wrap around your feet and socks inside your shoes to keep them dry.

I try out the technique. It looks a little strange walking with shopping bags on my feet, and they feel very odd, making my feet slippery inside my shoes. I also sweat inside the bags, and my feet get slimy. I don't get to give them a real test: there is not much standing water on the trail today. What water there is has frozen solid. The bags are so light and take up no room in my pack, so I can easily afford to bear the weight of two bags until the day comes when they are useful

I finish sooner than I expected. I gave myself extra time, counting on my pace being slow. I don't mind sitting, leaning against a tree in the sunshine to wait for my pick up. I take notes and read a book on my tablet while I relax. Shane picks me up at Little Flagstaff Road at our prearranged time.

Day 191, October 21st
Hwy 27 crossing, Stratton, ME, Trail Mile 2001.0
Daily Distance 10.3 Miles (SLACKPACK)

Again I am dropped off in the notch at Safford Brook and have to climb 2.2 miles up the blue blaze side path to get to the junction with Appalachian Trail, making my total mileage for the day 12.5 miles. Today I change directions and head back south.

I summit three peaks today, Avery, West Bigelow, and South Horn. Two of the peaks are over 4000 feet high, and there are serious ups and downs. The two high peaks are at the front end of the day's hike, within the first five miles of trail. It is scary hiking. Much of the climb and the peaks themselves are knife edge ridges. They are exposed to the weather, and despite a warming trend in the weather there is still ice coating some of the rocks.

I am awestruck by the views, but they also induce a sense of vertigo as I slowly make my way along the narrow path between the long drops on either side of Avery summit. I want to get down on my knees and crawl over some of the sections closest to the peak. No one would know, but pride is strong, even when no one is looking. I end up adopting a wide legged stance, for an added sense of stability, and waddle across the final section of ridge like a sumo wrestler advancing across a ring. Crawling might have been more dignified.

Avery peak is named in honor of Myron Avery, the great builder of the Appalachian Trail. Benton MacKaye was the dreamer who conceived of the trail, but Avery was the man who made it happen, actually getting out and planning the route and organizing groups to build it. He walked the entire route rolling a measuring wheel ahead of him between 1930 and 1937.

The ground at lower elevations is covered with layers of leaves up to four inches deep. The leaves are nearly as treacherous as the ice on the peaks. I only hit my stride on the saddle between the West Peak and the South Horn.

There is a lovely little high lake in the saddle, with views of the Bigelows surrounding it. A campsite is here, the Horn's Pond Lean-tos (shelters), and a spring. There were a campsite and a spring on the smaller saddle between Avery Peak and West Bigelow as well, but it was high enough I think it would have been hard to survive a night up there in this season; it would be fearsomely cold. The spring for the site is frozen solid, a crystal cascade of ice hard on the rocks.

The hike is laborious, the long ascents and descents and difficult trail make me sweat. I can smell ammonia in it, a sign I am again sabotaging my muscle mass to supply my metabolism with protein. I have been eating in a café each night I stay in Stafford, getting a good meal, but it is not enough. I will have to manage my diet carefully to keep myself going,

Much to my surprise I meet seven other hikers heading north in the opposite direction on my trek today. Several of them are NoBos, still intent on completing an uninterrupted hike to Katahdin. They are still almost 200 miles away, and will need to do some power hiking to get to the end in two weeks. Gimli shows me a picture a friend sent from Katahdin taken two days ago. Katahdin is still a going concern, even without overnight camping. The photo shows the summit as bright and clear.

Word is it may rain tomorrow, which translates to snow and ice up on the ridges. I am going to be back up on exposed areas for much of the rest of the thru-hike. I may end up with another zero tomorrow, although I really want to get going,

Day 192, October 22nd
Near Caribou Valley Road, ME, Trail Mile 1993.1
Daily Distance 8.1 Miles

I have enjoyed my stay in Stratton very much, but it is feeling a little too much like purgatory. I get back on the trail today despite some questionable weather. It rains a light drizzle for most of the day.

Hikers discuss the Bigelows with respect; they have a reputation for toughness, but somehow the Crockers, the range I am in today, are never mentioned. They should be.

I don't break free from the suction of town until 11:00 AM. I am faced with a long slow grind up North Crocker Mountain. My pack is heavy with a full load out.

I get cell phone signal. I stop frequently because my spouse has initiated another argument by text and I am unable to let it go and just put the phone away. I stop every time I hear a chime, irresistibly, to read a new comment and reply. I finally force myself to shut it off and walk uninterrupted

The trail on the North Crocker summit travels through stunted pine trees, and it is absolutely covered in piles of moose droppings. This trail

337

must be the easiest way through the woods for man and moose alike. I would like to see moose again, but not head on in the confines of the trail.

I have no idea what the moose are doing up here, perhaps they have moonlight moose rituals in the dark of the night on the mountaintop. I am seeing evidence of the midnight march of the moose.

It may be that the lack of views on the Crockers is why they escape commentary. The tops are forested, a blessing in this weather. After North Crocker I go down and up a saddle to South Crocker. The hike down from South Crocker is a tough nut. It is steep, and there are lots of big rocks and trees jumbled together to make a rough kind of stairway. It takes me an hour to get down the last half a mile. I fall several times on rain slicked rocks and leaves.

I am in a vee notch, so I will face the same terrain going back up the far side tomorrow. I was hoping to ford the Carrabassett River today on the floodplain between South Crocker and Sugarloaf Mountain. The floodplain has the same big rocks as the slopes, and I am unable to get to the river before darkness. I camp by a spring along the trail instead.

There is a new reason for me to try and stay in sight of the trail when I am camping. A thru-hiker named Inchworm disappeared in this area a couple of years ago. She was an older woman with some heart issues, so it may or may not have been foul play. She was hiking alone, but there are rumors in the cafes in Stratton about various scenarios. The family posted a significant reward for anyone able to determine her fate; there are posters in the hostels.

A contractor working for the Navy, which has some training land up here, has just claimed the reward. Inchworm's body was found within her tent, several miles off of the trail, with no signs of foul play in evidence. It is hard to determine the actual cause of her demise; she was out there for a couple of years before the contractor stumbled across her tent

Inchworm was caught up on the ridges in bad weather, and it looked as if she tried to make her way down to lower elevations, either for better shelter, or to try and find a way to civilization. Investigators are unsure if she died of exposure, or if her heart issues caught up with her.

She is not the only thru-hiker to die in this vicinity. Another family has posters up about their young son, a fast mover going through Maine in the heat of August. The posters are warnings to other hikers about the dangers of swimming. Their son drowned in one of the ponds along the trail. He jumped in for a cooling dip after a long day of hiking, and his muscles, worn and heated after his efforts, cramped uncontrollably in the cold water. He died a few feet from shore.

I make camp in a cold, wet mist. The air temperature drops ten or fifteen degrees each night at sunset, so I try to be set up and bundled in my hammock before the onset of full darkness. Hiking in 30 degree weather is comfortable, but as soon as I stop I feel chills.

It is cold enough at night to make sleeping difficult. I am bringing my water bottles into my hammock at night because they freeze solid when I leave them outside. The bottles are not the most comfortable of bedmates.

Day 193, October 23rd
Sluice Brook, ME, Trail Mile 1983.0
Daily Distance 10.1 Miles

I am, as ever, falling short of my mileage expectations. Seasoned hikers and hostel operators were warning thru-hikers since the Mid-Atlantic States that the White Mountains and Maine would halve our daily mileage. Baltimore Jack was saying it all the way back down in Georgia, and he was definitely an optimist in estimating expectations.

I am doing fairly well, except for the accumulation of zero days, but it is hard for me to see it. The few other people I am on the trail with seem to be gobbling up 15 or 20 miles a day. Some of it may be wishful thinking and exaggerations on their part. I will see Tarzan again, and he is a power hiker, but he is not so strong he gets more than a day or two ahead of me during my last two weeks of hiking.

I get back on the trail a little after 9:00 AM. My first obstacle is the Carrabassett River. The river is 40 to 60 feet wide and it is strewn with boulders the size of refrigerators, with maybe a couple the size of small cars. The water pours between the rocks with a lot of force, but with some scouting and a couple of false starts I find a way across jumping from boulder to boulder without even getting my feet wet.

The other side of the notch between South Crocker and Sugarloaf Mountain is next. It is as difficult as I expected, and between the river and the climb I only complete 2.5 miles of hiking by noon.

I stay up on a ridge, crossing Sugarloaf Mountain without seeing the ski area, followed by Mt. Spaulding, Mt. Abraham, and Lone Peak. I call it a day at 5:15 PM, with dusk coming on. The ridgeline isn't too difficult; I play the usual game of foot Tetris across the rocks. I don't take any long breaks, but I stop for a renewed flurry of accusatory texts with the estranged wife.

I stop short of Sluice Brook. It is cold, freezing cold, and I do not want to risk falling in and getting wet with night coming on. It has been a chilly day of hiking, the water in my bottles froze as they sat in my side backpack pockets. There is plenty of running water about and I do not go thirsty.

The cold doesn't just affect my water supply. I burn more calories, and shiver though the nights with very little sleep. I cannot generate enough body heat to keep myself warm inside my hammock's quilt system, which is survival rated at 20 degrees.

A survival rating for a sleeping bag or quilt is just that; you will live through the night. It is not a comfortable rest rating. I have my Thermarest sleeping pad under me as an additional layer, and I am trying different techniques with my clothes. Slipping the bottom of my sleeping bag inside my zipped up raincoat seems to help some. Putting on my few layers of clothes at night, or taking them off, seems to make little difference in combating the cold.

I hope to make the town of Rangeley tomorrow, but it will take a very good day of hiking to make it happen. Saddleback Mountain is on tomorrow's agenda, and it has a reputation as a tough mountain. A town stop would revive my spirits, but it is probably farther than I can hike tomorrow.

I did not see a single other person today. Between the cold and the text battle with the wife I can't seem to find a way to right, I feel very alone tonight. I am out in the wilderness, and I am giving myself the creeps. The sounds of animals, the wind, and creaking branches all sound ominous, especially when the chill makes sleeping so hard to begin with.

Day 194, October 24th
Piazza Rock Lean-to, ME, Trail Mile 1970.6
Daily Distance 12.4 Miles

It is another morning of waking up late and getting out of camp slowly. It takes longer to get everything done when it is cold. I move sluggishly. Taking off my gloves to do detail work like lighting my stove and undoing my hammock ropes leaves my fingers numb and pained, and I spend minutes after each task warming them up. Again, I don't get out of camp until after 9:00 AM.

Hiking the Appalachian Trail becomes a déjà vu experience. Some of it is the result of accumulated experience, such as knowing fording a river is best done first thing in the morning. Thus I often camp on the near side of rivers, and I start many days' hikes with a water crossing. Today I cross the Obreton. I get across feet dry. There is a lot of ice on the rocks and I very carefully step from stone to stone over the water.

I conquer Saddleback Ridge today. There are four separate peaks on the agenda, and Saddleback is above treeline. Two of the peaks are exposed with a high, bald saddle stretching between them. It is a clear day, and the three miles up high also offer unparalleled views of the surrounding mountains. It is a beautiful hike.

With the clear weather comes more cold, and ice coats the rocks. Sometimes it is no more than a thin, almost invisible, glassy sheen on the stone faces. I have to watch every step, and in places where I have to scramble it can take a couple of tries sliding back down a rock before I get up and over. Sometimes I have to break up the ice on the steeper faces with a rock or my hiking poles and create spaces where my shoes and hands can grip

I push further and harder today and end up night hiking the last hour. I want to get down off the heights. I aim for Piazza Rock Lean-to. It is supposed to rain tonight and I want to stay dry.

The shelters in Maine are rough, even for shelters. Maybe that is why they call them lean-tos instead of shelters. They are small, and they use round six inch logs for flooring rather than planks, making for uneven, uncomfortable bedding. I am not especially looking forward to sleeping in one, but it beats being out under freezing rain.

I have a poor sense of what day it is once I am out on the trail, and I am surprised to find it is the weekend. I am a little disturbed to find the shelter occupied in force. While I have missed contact with other people hiking solo, I find I really am not ready for time spent with a crowd who have walked up here from a parking lot a couple of miles away. My attitude approaching the shelter is not real sociable. Events do nothing to cheer me up.

When I arrive at Piazza Rock I pass through a number of set up tents, and ten yards from the shelter a person stands directly in front of me, deliberately blocking my path, with his headlamp shining directly on my face. We stand there for a few seconds with him an unmoving silhouette, the bright flare of his light blinding me, until I say 'excuse me'.

The man stands aside, with a rather insincere sounding apology. He then tells me I am being too loud, his scouts are sleeping. It is only 7:15 PM. I must be a really loud walker. His scouts are up and moving about for at least another hour, so I don't know why he is seeking confrontation.

I find room in the shelter. The Scouts are following group protocol and are camped around the shelter rather than inside it. The shelter is still pretty full; the adults have stored a lot of gear inside, which they move aside for me. The main reason the shelter is full is two Québécois women are present and have erected their tent inside the shelter.

The women ask me if it is OK. After the Scouts rearranged their gear there is ample space for me to lay out my mat and bag, and I let the breach of shelter etiquette slide. I can understand how two attractive young women might want some kind of visual barrier between them and the troop of adolescent males as they sleep and change.

The man who initially stopped me is an ass, and unfortunately he seems intent on hanging around the shelter. He is trying to impress the women, and manages to mention his yacht and his fortune pretty quickly, and is trying to present himself as an expert outdoorsman.

I would like to ignore them all, get my dinner and go to sleep, but the inevitable questions about why I am out here reveal I am a thru-hiker. The women have a lot of questions for me. They are experienced backpackers, and have hiked the Presidential Range and done other excursions. I am too polite to just ignore them, plus, I do like to talk and I have missed people.

The man I now label the Yachtsman in my head does not like the conversational shift of focus away from his sailing stories, and his other sources of greatness. It is obvious he is unhappy with my presence. I crawl into my quilts, the women get in their tent, and he finally leaves us.

The two French Canadians talk and giggle for a while in their tent. I can hear the Yachtsman loudly lecturing some of the Scouts soon thereafter, and it is the last thing I hear as I fall to sleep.

Day 195, October 25th
ME Route 4, ME, Rangeley, (The Farmhouse Inn), Trail Mile 1968.8
Daily Distance 1.8 Miles

I could have finished this short distance last night, slept in town, and avoided the whole episode with the Scout leader and the French Canadians. It is an easy hike in the morning, and the predicted rain has yet to fall, although the skies look ready to let go.

I really don't like night hiking, and I find I hike at about a mile an hour when I am walking with my headlamp on. My other night hikes have not been enjoyable, and I just didn't want to push my luck with the weather being so cold and damp. I have the example of Inchworm getting lost on the trail to consider, as well as my own night of misery going to Greasy Creek way back down in Tennessee.

The morning brings on more shenanigans by my camp mates. There are two Scout leaders, the Yachtsman and another, older, and obviously more proficient outdoorsman. They have a fire going, and are boiling copious amounts of water. The young Scouts come and go on various camp errands. The older leader offers me some of the boiling water, which I gladly accept. I get a free hot oatmeal breakfast.

While I am eating the Yachtsman is fooling around with his cookware and fuel for some time. He has a pump style Whisperlite stove, and he spills fuel all over the place. He finally does something that sets his entire pot and the wood beneath it on fire. Then he walks away from it, leaving the pot and the wooden rail it sits upon wreathed in flames.

I see his lid and put it on the pot, and douse the fire surrounding his pot. The unattended stove fire gutters after a bit, and goes out. The Yachtsman returns and is angry with me because he meant to leave the fire burning, and blames my interference for spoiling his breakfast. He walks off in a huff, but doesn't try to relight his little inferno. When I leave he is hectoring the Scouts, yelling at them to get their tents packed up faster.

I am at the road trailhead in less than an hour. On Route 4 the first car heading towards Rangeley stops to pick me up. It is a man in his 60s driving a pickup truck, and he is in no hurry today. I miss my destination, the Farmhouse Inn, and we drive past. My angel turns right around and gives me a ride back.

There is no one at the inn when I get there, but the door is open and the place is warm and inviting. The owners have an artistic flair, and have incorporated repurposed materials from an old barn into a reconstruction of the inn. There are two sections, the main house with a spacious common room and large industrial sized kitchen layout, and a wing with its own smaller, but just as functional common room and kitchen.

The hostel caretaker, Marching Band, shows up. I am presently his only guest. He gives me a ride into downtown Rangeley for dinner and resupply. There are a couple of bars and restaurants, and a supermarket. The town center is only a half mile from the Inn, and it is not much of a walk, but it has turned very, bitterly cold, and the ride and return pick up are both very much appreciated

Day 196, October 26th
ME Route 4, ME, Rangeley (The Farmhouse Inn), Trail Mile 1968.8
Daily Distance 0.0 Miles (ZERO DAY)

I enjoy another day lounging about the Farmhouse Inn, waiting out a spell of bad weather. It is brutally cold, and combined with the wet there is definitely ice on the heights, and everywhere else for that matter, including here in town. Temperatures are closer to zero than freezing.

Another flip-flopper has appeared, a man named Smokey. He started his thru-hike much later in the year than I did, and like Tarzan decided to jump north from Hanover on the New Hampshire – Vermont border.

Smokey has 162.3 miles still ahead of him. He has the yet unseen difficulties of the last section of Maine, which includes Mahoosuc Notch, judged the most difficult mile on the trail. He also has the White Mountains of New Hampshire, and will be crossing exposed tops and ridgelines. He will go over Franconia Ridge and the Presidential Range, including Mount Washington, the deadliest mountain on the trail.

Smokey is a younger, stronger hiker than I am, and has been making much better time. He is very concerned about being able to finish his last miles and is especially worried about the Presidential Range. He will have to plan out his hiking against weather reports, and is working on a safety plan. We exchange phone numbers so we can text support and information back and forth. As far as I know, we are the only two thru-hikers left in proximity on this part of the trail.

I spend a very nice day in Rangeley. I have a leisurely wake up and cook breakfast and drink hot coffee, catch up on email and social media, read a bit, and go into town and get a massage. Relaxing while someone works away at my long abused muscles is bliss. I have spent so much time alone lately, and sometimes I feel removed from the rest of mankind up on my mountain peaks while the rest of the world scurries about below. Having someone care for a little bit, even a paid someone, is almost emotionally overwhelming.

My last mail drop is at the Farmhouse, and I load up my pack with my extra supplies and luxuries. There is enough to see me clear to the end of the trail, which I calculate to be seven hiking days away.

I get dinner in a local pub, and watch an NFL game with a bar full of Patriots fans. The Patriots win, which is a good thing, because I think the crowd would have taken the loss very hard. Maybe they would have gone out and tipped some frozen cows, or whatever else constitutes a riot in rural Maine.

Day 197 to 201, October 27th to October 31st
Rangeley, Trail Mile to East B Hill Road to Andover, ME,
Trail Mile 1968.8 to 1932.3, 36.5 miles
Daily Distance 7.3 Miles

Day 197, October 27th
Sabbath Day Pond Lean-to, ME, Trail Mile 1959.4
Daily Distance 9.4 Miles

I make a deliberate decision to slow my pace over the section between Rangeley and Andover. It is 26.4 miles, and I would have to push very hard indeed to make it in two days. In Virginia I did it in one, once, and in Tennessee, again, once, under duress, and over much kinder trail. Thirteen mile days are now too much for the terrain and my abilities. I plan for three easier days instead, and I can space out my hike to take advantage of shelters for stopping points. I don't think I am going to see any more Boy Scout troops during the week, especially in weather this cold.

Sleeping in a shelter is warmer. The three walls provide wind protection and a roof means fewer worries about wet gear in the morning. I should have two clear, dry days, and then on day three the weather is supposed to warm up, but it will rain. Day three looks like an excellent night to spend in a hostel.

It is easy hiking today. It is warmer than yesterday, below freezing still, but comfortable to a hiker working his muscles and metabolism all day. It is a sunny day and beautiful. The mud on the trail is frozen, and makes a solid, sometimes crunchy surface to walk upon.

My pack is heavy from resupply, and it feels unbalanced. I am carrying extra water since many of the sources are frozen. The massage and rest I received yesterday may be working against me. Physically I am tired and my muscles are knotting up.

Sabbath Day Pond Lean-to sits next to a serene pond. I have passed many piles of moose droppings and a few signs of bear as well. I am hoping to see moose in the evening or morning when they normally go into the ponds to feed. I have arrived with some time before dusk and I don't have to spend half an hour setting up my hammock since I am using the shelter. There is no one else out here foolish enough to be spending nights in the cold and I have the place to myself. I can enjoy the site, and chill, literally as well as figuratively.

I cook two dinners and eat them in succession. The Jetboil is a wonderful stove but only makes one meal at a time. I want the energy, and more significantly, the warmth of hot food in my system.

I gaze out across the stillness of Sabbath Pond as I eat. No moose appear, but I am content.

Day 198, October 28th
Beamis Mountain Lean-to, ME, Trail Mile 1951.1
Daily Distance 8.3 Miles

It is so very cold this morning.

I wake early. I want to stay wrapped up in the questionable comfort of my sleeping quilt but I cannot stop shivering, and I give up and get up. Despite not having a hammock to take down and put away it takes me nearly an hour and a half just to get out of camp. Getting water out of the pond is the hardest part. The water is so cold my hands are in pain afterwards and I have to walk around with them under my armpits until they are warmed enough to be functional again.

It is a good thing I get the icy cold but still liquid water at Sabbath Pond, because the next two ponds I pass, Long and Moxie Ponds, are completely iced over. I have a single 1700 foot climb in and out of the Height of Land notch, crossing Beamis Stream. I approach every ford with trepidation, especially in this weather, but I get across Beamis feet dry, hopping across on rocks.

The ridgeline afterwards is level, and I make my moderate planned goal for the day with ease, arriving at Beamis Mountain Lean-to at 4:00 PM. My shelter to shelter hop for this section is making a lot of sense. The weather steadily deteriorates as the day progresses, and while I didn't get wet from the stream, the sky soon remedies that. It goes to grey, then windy grey, then wind and rain, and then to wind and rain mixed with snow. I am glad of a fixed structure to protect me from the wind, wet and cold. I am again alone for the night.

I worry if the snow will obscure the trail tomorrow. The blazes are often painted on rocks rather than up on trees in Maine, and if the ground is covered, so are the trail markers. Five miles of trail will be across a ridgeline above the treeline. The way the weather is turning I fear tomorrow may prove a miserable slog.

Tonight I listen to the wind howl around the shelter, and watch the snow swirling around outside. The wind is blowing at an angle to the open shelter face and snow is accumulating across one half of the structure. I am tucked into the other corner. A blessing of the cold is I no longer have to worry about mice or other critters crawling over me or nibbling holes in my equipment looking for food during the night. I assume they are all sensibly tucked away in cozier little dens than mine.

Day 199, October 29th
South Arm Road, Andover (Pine Ellis Hostel), ME, Trail Mile 1942.4
Daily Distance 8.7 Miles

I have difficulty staying warm during the night. The wind, snow and hail continue until about midnight, and the inside of the shelter and the top of my quilt build a coating of frost.

A warmer front comes in around midnight, and I can feel the temperature rising minute by minute. It changes back to rain from snow, the frost coating melts, and I am sufficiently warm enough to get a few hours of sleep.

The trail in this section is a rocky trench worn into the duff and roots in a dense, low forest. The wet has filled the trench with water, and the vegetation on either side is too thick for me to go anywhere but straight down the middle of it, splashing through the cold water.

I try the trick of putting shopping bags on my feet again. Initially they help, although I do not like the slippery feel of them between my socks and the inside of my shoe. The trail is rough beneath the gushing water, and the bags are not strong enough to withstand the shifting and battering of my feet between rocks and mud. I quickly develop rips and tears in the bags, my feet get wet, and the plastic grocery sacks gather uncomfortably under my feet. I stop at a wide spot and get rid of the shreds, sticking them in my garbage bag.

It is a difficult day of hiking. The trail is not well maintained in this area, or for that matter, in most of Maine. The Appalachian Trail is far from population centers out here, and it is difficult to access for MATC maintainers and work crews. As a result, the bog bridges are either rotting or nonexistent, and fallen timber regularly blocks the trail. Most maintenance is done in the spring, so I am experiencing the result of a half a year of erosion, entropy, and windfalls.

It is a reasonably flat stretch of the AT, but the water is knee deep in places. There are still some rock scrambles between sections of trenched trail, and water is sluicing down the granite faces. I slip, slide, and more than once fall as I cross them.

On a particularly memorable fall I grab a tree for support as I feel myself losing my footing. The water has soaked and weakened the tree's root ball enough that it gives way while I am holding it, and as I fall into the cold water filling the trail the tree follows and comes down on top of me. It takes me more than a minute to extricate myself and my pack from the resulting tangle halfway under the water.

I am checking my phone as I come across high ridges, and I call Pine Ellis Hostel in Andover as soon as I find signal to arrange a pick up on South Arm Road. I am fortunate I do so, because it is the only place on the day's hike where signal is available. The hostel is 12 miles from the trailhead down an infrequently traveled dirt road.

The descent off of the Beamis ridgeline and Old Blue Mountain down to the road is steep and slick. I am late for my rendezvous and I move with as much haste as I can muster, falling some more on the way down. The Pine Ellis operator is waiting for me with a big white van at a parking pull out by the trailhead. He has been waiting for more than hour.

I am so tired and hurting coming off the trail that my communication with the host is little more than a series of grunts. He long wait did not make him happy, and he is further disgruntled by my lack of communication. I just climb into the van and wait for him to start driving.

He lectures me a bit, telling me it is not wise to be out hiking in this season during this weather. There is no one out there to find me or rescue me if I take a header out there. He seems to lack enthusiasm for hiking in general and for me in particular. We have caught each other at our worst it seems, and it is a strained ride to Andover.

Pine Ellis Hostel is an older house on a small town neighborhood street. It has a makeshift conversion feel to it, although it has all of the basic hostel amenities. The operators are Native Americans, and the decorations are thematic. I am not the only hiker in the hostel tonight. Smokey came in the night before and took a zero in the face of the bad weather.

Smokey is having a trail crisis. The weather has turned aggressive, and he still has to get all the way through the Whites in New Hampshire. He is tired, and worried, and it is affecting his attitude about finishing his thru-hike. He has less than 200 miles left, not a vast distance compared to the scope of all he has already accomplished, but what is left include mountains with reputations as killers, in the most literal sense. I share some of his attitude after my trials over the last couple of days, but there is no way I will quit now, with only 53.4 miles left.

Smokey had a rough time just getting to Pine Ellis from the trailhead at South Arm Road. He completed the same stretch from Rangeley I finished in three days in just two, and came down to the road after dark. He was unable to get a phone signal and set up a pick up as I did, and was hoping to hitchhike into Andover. There was no passing traffic at all on the dirt road. The area is an Indian reservation, and there are very few reasons for anyone to be out there. Smokey started walking.

He walked four or five miles down the road until he came to a house. He had not seen a car the entire time he had been walking, and this was on the same bitter, snowy night I spent covered in frost up at Beamis Mountain Lean-to. He was exhausted and cold, and faced another five or six miles of road walking to get into town. His phone still had no signal. He decided to take a chance and went up to the house and knocked on the door,

The man who opened the door was not pleased to find a dirty, smelly hiker on his doorstep asking to use his telephone. After all, he probably chose to live out in the woods on the reservation just to avoid having strange white men ask him for things, and here was one on his front porch doing the very thing.

Initially he refused, but Smokey was persuasive in his desperation, obviously in need, and it was dark with the wind driving an icy rain. The man relented, allowing Smokey to call Pine Ellis and arrange a pick up. He let Smokey stay in the warmth of the house until the shuttle arrived to pick him up about half an hour later.

Smokey and I exchange stories in the bunkroom, and talk about what lies ahead. The weather is not expected to improve and we debate taking zeros tomorrow.

Day 200, October 30th
South Arm Road, Andover (Pine Ellis Hostel), ME, Trail Mile 1942.4
Daily Distance 0.0 Miles (ZERO DAY)

It is another day of freezing rain, and I take the zero along with Smokey. I am experiencing conflicting desires, one to get the Appalachian Trail finished and over with, against a certain dread of leaving it.

The trail is now my home and my space, and going back to my house in New Mexico means confronting a number of difficult situations, including my collapsing marriage, finding a job and reintegrating back into normal life.

There are many thru-hikers that have difficulty with the transition back to civilization. There are a small percentage of hikers who reach Katahdin, turn around, and start hiking back south, remaining on the trail for a year or two. Others figure out winter arrangements and jobs, and then head to the PCT or the CDT or other trails, or hike the AT again the following season. Some find jobs related to hiking or the trail; it is where many hostel and other support businesses get their employees. The trail is not just a hike, it is a culture, a linear community to call home, and it is hard to leave.

A zero day means one more day on the trail, one more day to call it my home, and I have no regrets. The town of Andover has a couple of general stores and places to eat. A diner called the Red Hen has a wonderful country atmosphere; it is open 6 days and 2 nights a week. Friday night is a prime rib special, and it is Friday night!

I have a day of indulgences. There is a masseuse in town who advertises at the hostel. I am a little dubious; we are on the middle of nowhere so how good can she be? Nonetheless, I am pampering myself today after the last three days of suffering. I make an appointment. She comes, picks me up, and takes me to her house.

The masseuse is named Donna Gifford, and she is amazing. She has a room outfitted especially for her business. Her table is hydraulic, and can be raised and lowered during the massage with a switch, Wooden bars are mounted above the massage table, and Donna climbs up onto the table and uses her feet, elbows and hands on me, holding onto the bars overhead as she exerts pressure in all of the right places. She pulls and kneads me like a Stretch Armstrong doll.

When Donna is done she drives me back to the hostel and drops me back at Pine Ellis feeling wonderfully limp, a nice, relaxed glow suffusing my whole body.

I make a shopping trip for resupply to one of the convenience stores, and I go to the local hardware store and find a set of micro spikes to wear over my hiking shoes on the icy patches. They weigh close to a pound, but based on what I have already experienced they are needed, and might save me a nasty fall or two on this last hard bit of trail.

The town itself is eclectic; much of it is late 19th and early 20th century structures, with a few split level ranch houses thrown in for dissonance. There is a beautiful, prairie style Craftsman house across the street from the hostel that is beautifully restored, and I slow and admire it each time I walk by.

I make plans for a slackpack tomorrow with our host, and I will get to spend another night here in town. The weather predictions for the next couple of days are not good, but it is supposed to clear up and be fine for a week after that, so I am stalling the end of my thru-hike just a little.

Day 201, October 31st
East B Hill Road, Andover (Pine Ellis Hostel), ME, Trail Mile 1932.3
Daily Distance 10.1 Miles (SLACKPACK)

Our host has warmed up to me and Smokey. We are not demanding guests, I have made an effort to be pleasant, and he has become helpful and informative. I am going to hike up and over Moody Mountain today and come back to Andover to wait out the bad weather predicted for the next two days.

Smokey wants to try and get to the Presidential Range and past them in the good weather predicted to follow, but he needs to get a move on to position himself strategically. We exchange phone numbers for mutual support, for me to get advance trail conditions, and for him, if he gets hurt and stranded he knows I am coming up behind him.

Mahoosuc Notch lies in this last stretch of Maine, and is reputed to be the single hardest mile of the Appalachian Trail, and there is no easy way out to a road from it

Today's hike is an easy climb up and over some humps. Hall, Wyman and Moody Mountains are pretty happy places today. There are a couple of fords but I rock hop across, feet dry. I climb up for four miles going over the three peaks, and then descend for six. The weather is fair and the trail is drying out in some spots. There is still some ice in patches, but it is a pleasant day on the trail.

I call for a pick up from where my host told me to. I only wait ten minutes at the trailhead before he picks me up.

While the weather is sunny it is in no wise warm, it is just warmer than it has been. In Andover the kids are trick or treating, and their costumes are hidden beneath coats, warm hats and gloves.

Day 202-203, November 1st and 2nd
East B Hill Road, Andover (Pine Ellis Hostel), ME, Trail Mile 1932.3
Daily Distance 0.0 Miles (2 ZERO DAYS)

The weather is cold and wet. I hole up at Pine Ellis and take the zeros. Smokey is on the trail and texts me. There are 3 inches of ice and snow on top of Baldpate Mountain.

After the couple of days of miserable weather pass, four days of good weather are expected. It will be enough for me to finish my thru-hike. I have already experienced all the excitement Andover has to offer and I laze away these two days sitting in my bunk and reading. I am ready to finish the Appalachian Trail.

Day 204-208, November 3rd to November 7th
Andover, ME, to Gorham, NH (End of Trail), Trail Mile 1932.3 -1890.9
AVG 8.28 Daily Miles

Day 204, November 3rd
Grafton Notch, Trail Mile 1922.0
Daily Distance 10.3 miles (SLACKPACK)

I slackpack from Grafton Notch back north to East B Hill Road.

During the drive in the van out to the trailhead we startle a moose along the side of the road. It runs alongside us for a hundred yards before turning away into the woods. I stare at it out the window. It has a huge, awkward gallop, keeping pace with the van, smashing through tree branches as it flees.

The primary climb of the day is a steep ascent 2500 feet up Baldpate Mountain. The weather has warmed up to above freezing, warm enough to melt the ice and snow Smokey texted me about. The climb is not too bad, but the descent crosses over a number of granite rock slabs, and there is still some ice on them. I inevitably roll my ankles a couple of times, stretching and pulling on the tendons tightened by two days of inactivity in Andover.

I see a barred owl. Although I have heard owls nearly every single night I have spent out on the Appalachian Trail, this is the first and only time I will see one. It perches on a branch right over the trail and preens for me. I stand and watch it silently for ten minutes before something else stirs it and the owl flies away.

I meet a SoBo today. Not a flip-flopper like me or Smokey, but an actual southbound hiker who started his thru-hike at Katahdin a month ago and is headed for Springer Mountain in Georgia. He is a Québécois, and has adopted the trail name Quebec. There seems to be a lack of imagination working there, but there is no crowd of fellow hikers getting to know him and trying names out on him, so Quebec he is.

Quebec is going to get as far south as he can, then take a break for the holidays. He intends to get back on the trail afterwards. There are hikers who make it through winter on the trail, but they are very rare. The hike is already a challenge without making freezing to death a daily possibility. I wish him luck.

I have one more night in Andover, my sixth and last. I am thirty two miles from the end of my Appalachian Trail thru-hike.

Day 205, November 4th
North end of Mahoosuc Notch, Trail Mile 1915.0
Daily Distance 7.0 miles

The weather is as good as November gets in Maine, sunny with temperatures rising into the 50s during the day. I climb over Old Spec today; it is the last time I will ascend to over 4000 feet on the hike. It is a long, gradual ascent. Going down the other side is another story. The mountains of the Northern Appalachians have been shaped and carved by glacial action, and are often carved and steep on one side and gently eroded on the other.

The descent is known as the Mahoosuc Arm, and it is stone hopping and steep rock slabs. I have a few hard falls on the way down.

One fall is terrifying; I lose my grip on a rock slab and start sliding down the mountain, shouting in a release of surprise and fear as I drop. No one is around to hear my yells as they echo off the mountainsides. I fall ten or fifteen feet before getting a hand on a protruding tree root to slow and stop my plummet. I leave some skin on the rocks.

The trail is not well marked and the traveled path is covered with leaves, so I am guessing where the actual trace of trail is located. Near the entry to Mahoosuc Notch there are a lot of divergent ways; a braided trail. Many people either camp here before entering or after leaving Mahoosuc Notch. I have to retrace my steps several times to find just where the trail enters the notch proper.

It is still early, a little before 4:00 PM, but I give Mahoosuc Notch's reputation its due, and choose to stop early. Darkness comes quickly down in the shadows of the mountains, and sunset is just after 5:00 PM. I will use one of the camping areas rather than get caught in the notch in darkness.

Water is down fifty yards of hillside covered with slippery leaves and mud, and my falls are not over for the day. Down is a little hazardous, but coming back up is the real challenge. I slip and slide in the leaves and mud, and end up on my belly a few times when my footing just gives away. I get back to my camp and I have to scrape the cold mud and leaves off of my clothes and hands. I am a grubby mess turning in for the night.

Day 206, November 5th
North side of Carlos Mountain, Trail Mile 1909.0
Daily Distance 6.0 miles

It is a very long day. I am excited at the beginning of the day, even waking up with the dried mud from my falls last night caked onto my clothing, on my hammock, and my sleeping quilt.

Today I meet Mahoosuc Notch, the most difficult mile on the trail. The notch is deeply shaded between the mountains, and it takes a while to warm up in the morning. I can see blue skies and fleecy white clouds in between the mountains overhead, but the sun isn't reaching down into the narrow slot.

Mahoosuc Notch is 1.2 miles of hard stone trouble. The notch is between two steep mountainsides, and millennia of rock falls have piled boulders up to the size of school buses in the narrow gap. The gap is only yards wide, and the trail has to work its way over, around, and sometimes under the great rocks. Trail marking heading south is sporadic, occasional blazes or arrows indicate the best routes through the stones. You can't get really get lost, as there is only one way through the gap.

I have to take my pack off and push it ahead or drag it behind me in order to squeeze through some of the tighter passages. It takes me nearly three hours to get to the southern end of the notch.

Hikers all talk about Mahoosuc Notch, and the challenge of that single mile between the mountains. What is left out of the discussion is just how hard it is getting into and out of the notch in the first place. I was already tired before I started the notch from my previous day's adventures descending the Mahoosuc Arm. I rest at the end of the notch and then I have a long, steep slog up the opposing mountainside.

I rise from the damp, shaded notch into sunshine. The view from Goose Eye Mountain gives me a vista of the Presidential Range in the distance. The weather looks good over there, and I hope Smokey, Quebec, and Tarzan are making progress. A beautiful sunset paints the mountains and clouds in gold, pink and purple against a fading sapphire backdrop of sky as I traverse the peaks.

I am moving very slowly, a combination of tough terrain and physical exhaustion. My mileage is so poor, even after Mahoosuc, that I only make a total of six miles for the day. In order to get even that meager distance I end up hiking for 45 minutes into the evening by the light of my headlamp.

From the heights I can see the twinkling lights of Gorham down in a valley 18 miles ahead of me. I had entertained hopes of finishing tomorrow, but after today's difficulties I expect it will take two more days to reach my end of trail. I am just a mile or two now from the New Hampshire state line.

I am off the spacing rhythm to use the shelters, and I am going to end up in my hammock for these last two nights on the trail. If the weather stays above freezing, as it has today, I should be OK.

Day 207, November 6th
Near Wocket Ledge, NH, Trail Mile 1899.7
Daily Distance 9.3 miles

The clouds are a low, solid sheet across the sky. There are occasional spritzes and spatters of rain, but nothing sustained. Temperatures remain above freezing, at least at the elevations I am working. Up on the

Presidential Range I imagine Smokey and Quebec are probably having a hard time of it.

Mount Carlo and Mount Success are two peaks of no particular significance, except that I am exhausted and the effort of going up and across their rocks and ledges is slow work. After them I pass Gentian Pond, and the trail becomes more mannerly; it is graded and maintained. I cross the state line into New Hampshire, and someone is now looking after the Appalachian Trail with a different set of standards.

Even on the more walkable path I am so worn I cannot push my pace. I only have nine or ten hours of daylight, and I use a couple to take camp down and to set it up again, so I am down to seven or eight hours of actual hiking time a day.

It is warm enough today that I see a large, rather sluggish newt on the trail near Dream Lake. It is over 6 inches long, and black with bright yellow spots. I look at it for a couple of minutes, and nudge it over to the side of the trail with the tip of my hiking pole after I take a photo, lest someone or something hazard it in its exposed location.

I set up camp at 4:00 PM. Tomorrow, barring any unexpected disasters, I will end my thru-hike. I feel less excitement at the prospect than I would have thought. My timing has been irregular enough that my mother has not been able to set up plans to meet me, and it will be a solitary end.

I am tired.

END OF TRAIL

Day 208, November 7th
Gorham, NH, Trail Mile 1890.9
Daily Distance 8.8 miles

It is done, 2189.2 miles of the Appalachian Trail. There is no feeling of excitement or joy. Katahdin was those things, hikers finishing after climbing the final summit, and coming back down to celebrations and telling their tales in town.

I walk out of the woods on another grey day. It is a ridgeline, generally sloping down to the finish, passing over the slightly higher Mount Success (Yeah!) and Mount Hayes. I see a single other person, a trail maintainer all the way from Portland, Maine, checking his section. It is the first person I have seen in four days. I talk for a few minutes, but move along quickly. The road is three miles ahead at that point, and I am ready to see the end.

Near Mount Hayes I hear a crazy howling and barking. It starts down in a valley and slowly gets closer and louder to me on the trail. A pair of dogs finally appears from the undergrowth. One is the howler, his nose to the ground, a sort of a Lab mix looking dog. The other, a smaller nondescript mutt, is the barker, trailing along in the howler's wake. They are on to something, and cross the trail just a few yards from me. They take absolutely no notice of my presence but continue on up and over the mountain. I can hear them for another half an hour carrying on, their cacophony slowing fading away with distance. There is no sign of an owner.

The Appalachian Trail comes out of the woods and joins with a forest road that I follow for a mile until the dirt road intersects with a paved road. I follow the paved road until I find myself looking at the White Mountain Hostel across from me at the head of a T-intersection. This is where I left for Maine on my flip-flop.

I am done.

The hostel has closed for the season. I feel I should be dancing, or there should be a parade, a crowd of cheering onlookers, or something, but it is just me, a very tired and dirty man with a backpack on the side of a busy State Highway.

I pause for a moment, check signal, and find my phone is connected. I send out a text:

Finished it, every single one of 2189.2 rocky, muddy, rooty, ice coated, wind swept, sweltering, sweaty, soaking wet, waterless; tick, spider, black fly, rattlesnake and copperhead infested; black bear, moose and coyote patrolled; hawk, eagle, owl, and raven watched; forested, boggy, meadow, cornfield, exposed ridge line, cliff, ledge, and mountaintop crossed, miserable, painful, awesome, breathtaking, joyful miles.

I stick my thumb out so I can get a ride for the 3.6 miles into the town center of Gorham. Many cars pass me by, and I start walking, still sticking my thumb out when a car passes. It feels like the longest road stretch I have had to hitchhike before getting a ride. Eventually a man pulls over in a rattletrap van filled with every kind of outdoor gear imaginable, a hiker kind of person.

My destination is the Royalty Inn, where my mother booked a room for me as a gift. It is rated as the best motel in town. It has a hot tub and a sauna, and is located next to a decent Italian restaurant. It also has a nice gym, which I really don't need. My mother is trying to celebrate my feat from afar, and it is greatly appreciated.

First, of course, I have to get there.

My ride takes me all the way past the motel to the other side of town and the Wal-Mart, at my request, and drops me off. I force some money on him for gas against his protests, mostly for appreciation, since a hundred cars passed me walking weary before he picked me up, and I am profoundly grateful for the ride.

At the Wal-Mart I buy myself food treats, a pair of khakis, and a shirt. I want something other than my hiking rags to wear on my flight home.

Gorham is a linear town, stretched out along a main road following the course of a river between the mountains. The road is four lanes of busy traffic going through town, No one stops for my thumb on the way back, and I walk the two miles back to the motel.

My room is a fine thing, as is the hot tub, the sauna, and the Italian dinner. Football is on the television, and I begin my reintegration back into the world of comforts and containment.

AFTERWARDS

Hiking the entire Appalachian Trial is a great feat. It takes a while for the accomplishment to sink in. It is now a part of me, an achievement at my center, and a solid core of emotional strength. It is part of my self-identity. I am a Thru-hiker. No one can take it away.

The physical change wrought by the trail didn't last. The forty plus pounds I lost while hiking came back, mostly. I was a physical wreck at the end of my journey, gaunt and exhausted. The binge eating of staying in towns came back to haunt me. It is not uncommon for thru-hikers to get very fat afterwards. The calorie burn is gone, the appetite remains.

There is a sense I should be saying something profound after such a great event. So much happened, but I lack that final statement. Unlike the trail there is no end statement to life, it just continues.

Adjusting back to normal life is difficult. I have found my way back into the tedium of a 40 hour plus a week job and the small freedoms of occasional weekends and vacations. After the individual freedom of the trail a secure job seems less necessary, a construct that imprisons me with middle class living.

After the hiking the trail I learned something I already knew, something we all know, really. I value experience more than money, and cherish the love of family and friends above all. It was always there, but now it is more real somehow.

I am looking to find my way to a better life now by living with less, and finding a skill set that will support a smaller cost of living with fewer restrictions on my time. I will readily trade the relative affluence of a life of wage slavery for freedom. It is out there, I am sure. I am looking for it, and like the end of the trail, it will come, eventually.

My wife sent me a Hallmark card early on during my hike, in the first mail drop. It said:

"'You'll be Missed,
Remember that the road you're taking also leads back here…
…and it will always be wonderful to see you."

As bad as things were between us, I hung onto the card the entire hike, carrying the precious couple of ounces in my protected dry bag. I read it nearly every night. It was one of the things that sustained me on the long journey. When it came time to return home though, it wasn't home anymore.

I realized it was a place more achingly lonely than any mountaintop, and had been for years. I carried the pain and sorrow of the end of my marriage across every mile of the trail, a background noise to my experience. I had hoped to hike away from it. Instead, ultimately, it was not I who was freed, but my wife. When I came home she was ready to move on, and despite a few tries at reconciliation it was over. I was out and living on my own in a couple of months, and writing this book.

I still have the card, tucked away in a drawer with other trail memorabilia.

I considered not including the parts of my journal where my troubles with my wife intruded onto the trail, but it seems more real to leave it in, with a lot of editing. The trail is not one long joyful vacation; it is a journey of self as well as miles. The walk takes you to Katahdin, but the self goes where it will.

My ex-wife, and many people I think, do not understand the trail at all. It is a place outside their experience, one they do not wish to understand. Perhaps it is a form of self preservation. So many of us are trapped in soulless jobs, and looking out the window to another way, a riskier way, is painful. Man is meant to walk the world, not cower in a cave. The security of the cave beckons. It is necessary to raise our young ones safely, but I do not think I am alone in struggling to find joy there.

I think only someone who has been on a long backpacking trip or expedition will ever know why the trail is my home, and they are all, good, bad and ugly, my brothers and sisters in an extended family. It is one that may not get along so well or agree on much of anything off of the trail, but all of us share a common bond forged across the backbone of a continent.

I get out into the forest, desert and mountains often now. I have been on several short backpacking trips, I have found peace and experienced much joy. I have seen wonders; I have lived life. There is much out there still to see.

The trail will always be my place. It is not my only place, but I know it is out there, an idea as well as a construct, the white blaze marking something that is a permanent part of me. And I know there is a world of other trails out there, waiting for me.

I long to return to the trail. I still want to go home.

IF YOU GO

I wrote this section for those preparing themselves for a long expedition. My way is not the only way, but a way that worked for me. I hope that my knowledge and experience is beneficial to others.

A DAILY TIMELINE

My daily routine while hiking was fairly simple and I have laid it out in a timeline. Wake up time and make camp times are varied, since sunrise and sunset changed, as did other factors like the weather. In June I could hike until nearly nine o'clock at night, and I would wake up at 6:00 AM to daylight. In November the days were short, and daylight only lasted from 7:30 AM to 5:00 PM.

This is a routine day:

0700 AM	Wake Up
0700-0710	Dress, stretch, pee, drink water
0710-0720	Take down and pack hammock or tent
0720-0735	Breakfast
0735-0745	Personal Hygiene
0745-0755	Load rest of pack
0755-0800	Look through area for forgotten items, pick up trash
0800-1730	Hike; take occasional short breaks
1730-1800	Look for and select a camping site
1800-1815	Hang hammock / set up tent. Eat protein as a snack.
1815-1825 dinner	Fill and filter water, some filtering done while cooking
1825-1845	Make and eat dinner
1845-1855	Clean up dinner, personal hygiene
1855-1900	Strip down for sleep, retire.

In my hammock I wrote down some notes for the day and usually read an e-book on my tablet until I fell asleep. Most of the time I was asleep within an hour or so from the time darkness fell.

FOOD

In my regular day to day existence before I went on the trail, I didn't think too hard about what I was eating. I tried to eat relatively healthily, but mostly I ate when I was hungry, or ate when something looked appealing, or at a social event or celebration. I tried to keep on eye on calories and not overeat, more or less (less) successfully. The trail taught me lessons about fueling my body that have permanently changed my eating habits

On the trail meal planning is important. It is not only having food to eat, but also having the foods that will allow you to progress. Your food weight has to be minimal, and so a backpacker must be selective. I learned important lessons about nutrition while I was hiking, as certain deficiencies made themselves known. Foods that kept me going for a week or two were not sufficient for prolonged endurance exercise.

There was not a tremendous variety in my trail meals. This was my choice; other people had a lot more differentiation based on food availability and their individual preferences. I followed a 'keep it simple' philosophy. Sticking to eating patterns allowed me to monitor my diet and its effect on my performance. It also made shopping less of an ordeal. I knew exactly what I needed for my basic foods at each town stop.

While I was hiking I was fully conscious of how much food I had in my pack and how far it would get me. If nothing else, the heft of my food bag in my pack was a constant reminder. I carried four to six days worth of food after each resupply stop. I expected four or five days of hiking, and carried an extra day's food just in case. Just in case proved fortuitous on a number of occasions, either to keep myself going or to help out another hiker.

My overall financial outlay for five days' worth of food and other expendables, such as batteries and hygiene items, was between $40.00 and $80.00 per resupply stop. I generally bought the same items over and over, so it was a question of how much of a price markup there was at different trail towns.

I would often carry treats out for my first day back on the trail. A nice sandwich for lunch or dinner, or a couple of cans of beer would help me ease back into trail routine. When there were prepared foods available at road crossings I often indulged and would gorge myself.

I ate large meals and constantly snacked when I was in town to make up for the lack of calories and taste on the trail. I ate on impulse, and loaded up on fats, sugars and proteins. I craved fresh fruits and vegetables, as they were too heavy, too fragile, and too quick to spoil to carry in my backpack.

I am providing a sample of my daily food plan. It is by no means comprehensive, but it served as my guideline when I went into a store to fill my pack for the next leg of my journey.

BREAKFAST

(2-3) Mini-Bagels
(2-3) Tablespoon of Peanut Butter
(2-3) Instant Coffee,
(1) Hot chocolate,
(1) Emergen–C packet.

Most mornings I woke up thirsty. Even when I did not I followed the same routine, because routine allowed me to get out of camp in a timely manner without forgetting anything important.

I drank a liter of water with an Emergen-C vitamin packet in it first thing upon getting out of my hammock in the morning. I wanted to hydrate and rebalance the chemical composition of my body after recovering through the night.

I kept my breakfasts simple. My standard breakfast was two or three mini-bagels with peanut butter smeared on them. I had a good dose of fat, protein and carbohydrates to start the day. No cooking was required.

I experimented with my breakfasts as time passed. Many hikers, especially the budget hikers, ate Little Debbie's Honey Buns. They have over 500 calories each, and cost a dollar apiece. Honey Buns can be eaten as you walk; the ultimate breakfast efficiency. I tried them, but found they were getting smooshed in my pack, and I didn't like eating sugary goo for breakfast. I also tried mixing peanut butter and trail mix together and eating that. It worked pretty well, and it had a lot of protein, but came up a little short on carbs. Some hikers just ate an energy or protein bar.

I tried making oatmeal in my early days on the trail, but I found it wasn't worth the time to cook it and clean up. Breakfasts became a meal I would eat right after I had taken down my hammock, with minimal fuss and bother. The meal was a little ritual, a 15 minute break in the morning when I sat and got my head together.

I like coffee, and like a little caffeine boost in the morning. Coffee served as an additional round of hydration before facing the trail. I didn't want to spend the time to heat water though. I found that if I put one or two packets of Starbucks Café Via instant coffee together with a packet of hot chocolate in a half full 1 liter water bottle and shook it vigorously I had a cold mocha. It was not my favorite, but it served my need.

I preferred the Starbucks Café Vias; they are small tubes of finely ground coffee, almost a powder. Other companies make similar products for a lot less money. Bustelo and Folgers were often all that was available.

I like cream and sugar in coffee, and hot chocolate packets provided both. I had to make sure the hot chocolate I purchased was the type that had powdered milk as part of its composition rather than requiring milk to be added. Usually I got a Swiss Miss product, but if it was available, and I felt like splurging, I occasionally bought the Starbucks fru-fru drink products.

SNACKS (4-5 per day)

Protein bars (15 grams or more) (1-2)
Cliff Bars (1-2)
Other Snack or Breakfast Bars (1-2)
Trail Mix
Beef Jerky
Candy Bar or M&Ms. Peanut Butter and Cheese Crackers, Peanuts, Oreos, Emergen-C, water flavor packets, preferably with Taurine

I did not eat a lunch while I was hiking. Some hikers ate lunch as a meal every day, bringing hard cheese and dried meat and wrapping them in a tortilla, or even cooking a hot meal. They had a nice little break somewhere and relaxed for a little while.

I am a slow enough hiker that I didn't want to stop for long, and I wanted to spread out my food intake. I could take shorter breaks and enjoy views while I ate my snacks, or eat them on the go as I wished on any given day. Everyone's body chemistry and needs are a bit different, and personal dietary choices and patterns reflect it. I know what worked for me.

I ate three to five snacks a day, and I packed for five. The body needs constant nutritional intake to fuel the continuing output of energy required from a thru-hiker. Even if you are overweight starting off you need to eat frequent snacks. The body slows down if it has to entirely rely on breaking down fat reserves for fuel. If there is some primer in the system it works a lot better.

The body also looks for protein, and if it isn't supplied from food protein reserves are in the muscles. A hiker needs muscles, so making sure you are getting protein in your snacks is very important. A body can only break down so much protein from food per hour, so you need a steady supply, you can't just load up on it for breakfast and call it good.

When I began my thru-hike I wasn't really aware of just how much protein I needed, and I fed on a protein deficient diet. I had focused my snack supply on quick energy, and since I have a sweet tooth anyway, I indulged it and I ate candy bars and Little Debbie's snack cakes. I carried a bit of jerky and trail mix for variety.

Three things happened to make me change my snacks. The first was the result of experimentation. I tried to minimize snacks, and carried a single baggie with a little bit of trail mix, a strip of beef jerky, and a few bite size candy bar miniatures for each day.

My idea was that I could keep myself going by just taking a small bite of something every half hour to an hour and that would be just enough fuel in an even flow to keep me moving forward. Minimizing snacks would lighten my load and reduce my food costs. I envisioned myself a lean, mean hiking machine.

Instead, after a couple of days of hiking my energy started to wane, and then on day four I just quit going. I had no energy. I found myself stopping frequently and just staring off into space for several minutes at a time before rousing myself and trudging forward again. I could feel the lack of energy, and one day I was so spent I ended up sitting down at lunch time and cooking a meal, and spent the rest of the day in camp, eating whatever food reserves I had.

I carried more snacks thereafter. I would still occasionally find myself stopping and staring away, and it was a wakeup call to eat another snack.

My second change occurred when the weather started to get warmer. Certain foods do not handle heat well. Chocolate in particular would become a gooey mess. I like chocolate, and chocolate bars were a staple of my snack routine. I would have some kind of chocolate bar every day. I saved it for just before a tough climb as an incentive and energy boost. I usually went with Snickers, since they have one of the highest protein amounts per bar, 6 grams.

Backpacking is a messy enough endeavor, and when my snack was a melty blob that ended up on my hands and equipment while I was trying to eat it, I ditched chocolate. Well, mostly. Peanut M&Ms also have 6 grams of protein per serving, and did melt in my mouth, not in my hands. Payday bars also soothed my sweet tooth and provided some protein.

The biggest change in my snacks was when I realized just how protein deficient my diet was. I limited my candy intake, and got rid of the Little Debbie snack cakes and sleeves of Oreo cookies, which had no protein at all, and started carrying protein supplement bars instead. Protein supplement bars are not especially tasty, and are expensive; usually a couple of dollars each, but I needed them.

I started paying close attention to nutritional labels. Snacks without protein were not worth carrying. I wanted at least six grams of protein per snack. If I had 4 to 5 snacks, that was 24-30 grams of protein during the day. If one was a protein bar with 20 grams or more, I was getting close to 40 grams. Combined with the snacks, eating peanut butter for breakfast and some sort of protein when I got into camp gave me close to the 73 grams a day I needed.

I ate a Cliff Bar every day. Cliff Bars have a good balance of protein and carbs, and also have vitamin and mineral supplements, so they are good trail snacks. I did not enjoy them much; all Cliff Bars kind of taste the same to me, boring variations on paste. I carried two a day after doing protein calculations. They are pricier than candy bars, and my food costs went up.

The up side of my dietary change was bars are very easy to carry. I ate a bar every two hours or so, sometime I would sit and eat half, and eat the other half in bites as I went along, to keep hunger pangs at bay and sustain the energy. I picked up other sorts of snack and granola bars as well.

Trail mix is a hiker staple. I was lazy, and would buy the pre-made snack bags at stores. The nuts and dried fruits were a healthy and nutritious addition to my diet, and provided some variety from a steady diet of bars. Little packets of peanuts were also good, and are inexpensive.

Many hikers made their own trail mix. Phyzzy would mix nuts and dried fruits with Cheerios, giving him a lot of bulk that was still lightweight and had a nice crunch to it. Gorp, Good Old Raisins and Peanuts, is easy to make as well, and a lot cheaper than fancier pre-packaged trail mixes.

I still carried some sort of treat for each day, to create an incentive snack for myself. Most often this was peanut M&Ms, or a candy bar.

I used a water flavor packet each day. I was drinking a lot of water, and flavoring helped to make it a little treat as well. I used an Emergen-C or one of the little sport drink tubes of flavoring. I liked the ones with Taurine, which gave a caffeine boost. The flavor packets helped to restore electrolytes as well, and electrolytes are another dietary need. Low electrolytes cause exhaustion.

DINNER

Tuna packet (or peanut butter) (1)
Dried fruit,
Ramen noodles with Instant Mashed Potato Flakes (1) or Knorr's noodle or rice side (1), mixed with Dried Ground Beef and Vegetables,
Hot Chocolate Packet (1)

Dinner was a focal point of each day. As routine as it became, it still was a time to sit back and relax, and enjoy eating something hot.

Various other hikers suggested that when I was done hiking for the day I should immediately eat some protein to help my body start recovering. I started eating a tuna packet as soon as I put my pack down in camp. There are a variety of flavored single serving tuna packets available, selling for about a dollar apiece. I tried to mix up the tastes, buying some flavors and spice combinations that didn't have as much appeal to me, just to have something different.

When I didn't have a tuna packet for protein, I would eat a couple of spoonfuls of peanut butter. To be truthful, I didn't particularly care for peanut butter before I started hiking the Appalachian Trail. Some foods you will come to hate on the trail, just because you eat them so much. Peanut butter had an opposite effect, coming to grow on me. All the fat and oil and protein was something my body craved. Like the tuna, I changed up varieties frequently, not always getting my favorites.

I hydrated as soon as I got into camp, slowly drinking a full liter of water before dinner, sometimes with an Emergen-C vitamin packet. I would also nibble on some dried fruit such as pineapple or apple rings.

When I heated my water for dinner I would pour off some of the first boil to make a cup of hot chocolate, which warmed me up in cold weather, and provided some carbs and more hydration. Dinner itself was typically a ramen bomb.

Ramen bombs are a food no one not on a long backpacking trip would ever eat. I boiled a ramen packet, added the flavor packet, and then mixed in flavored instant potato flakes to the liquid to make it a semi solid, starchy mass. Then I added in some kind of protein; tuna, Spam, or Parmesan cheese were common additions. My wife sent me a couple of large shipments of dehydrated beef or bison granules she figured out how to process researching online, and I broke these up into packets at my mail drops.

Ramen was cheap, quick to cook, and available everywhere. It is also nutritionally suspect. At the end of the trail, when I had lost 40 pounds, I still was sporting a slight jelly roll, I was gaunt, but still had the band of fat on my stomach. I am not any kind of biochemist, but my interests in improving my diet led me to a little online research once I got home

I believe my jelly roll was from my regular diet of ramen. Much of cheap ramen is made of artificial things the body doesn't recognize, and automatically stores as fat. I have been looking at substitutes.

An alternative is Knorr's pasta and rice side dishes and their equivalents. Knorr's took longer to prepare, requiring 7-11 minutes of cooking time. Based on one of Phyzzy's comments that there is no specific magic for cooking other foods using boiling water, and just using really hot water, I would save fuel by bringing my water to a boil, adding the side, turning off the stove, and relighting it and bringing it back to a boil two more times at 3 minute intervals.

Dinners cooked well that way. After the side was done I usually treated the Knorr's with potatoes and protein, ramen bomb style. Little dried tortellini also worked well in a bomb.

My dinner, which in any other context was questionable nutritionally and absolutely disgusting, hit the spot night after night. It filled me up, warmed me up, provided needed salts and carbs, and also put a slow block of hydration into my system for my body to feed on through the night as I slept. Much of the hydration a person normally gets comes through food, and the foods I ate on the trail, such as protein bars, contained less water than in a regular diet. The ramen bomb helped balance that out.

There are any number of little additions you can make to provide variety to your trail meals, and some people make much more elaborate dinner preparations. I was lazy in camp, and just wanted to cook, eat, and get into my hammock on most nights.

Some backpackers really like the freeze dried meals such as Mountain House products. I thought they all kind of ended up as mush (not unlike ramen bombs) and they are individually quite expensive, costing $5.00 and more per meal. You can get the price down by buying in bulk case lots and dividing them into mail drops, but I didn't like them enough to bother. When I found one in a hiker box I would sometimes grab it for variety.

I divided my food into gallon Ziploc bags, each one with a day's worth of food, and I had another bag with extras or bulk items. There was always a jar of peanut butter in my food bag too.

A LOOK INSIDE MY FOOD BAG:

1 Day of Food (X5)

1 packet ramen noodles or Knorr's Sides
1 Tuna packet
1 or 2 tubes of Coffee Vias
2 packets hot chocolate
1 or 2 packets Emergen-C
1 or two packets drink mix
2 Cliff Bars
1 protein bar
Package of trail mix
Package of MnM's (sometimes I would buy in bulk and separate into baggies)
Dried fruit in Ziploc bag

Bulk bag (X1)

Bag of bagels/mini bagels
Jar peanut butter
Dehydrated ground beef in gallon Ziploc
Extra snacks, coffee, seasoning packets
2 Family sized packages of flavored potato flakes
Parmesan cheese (in a Ziploc)

COMMON FOOD ITEMS USED BY OTHER HIKERS

Blocks of cheese or cheese sticks
Hard Salami or Summer Sausage
Tortillas
Hazelnut Spread
Triscuits or other crackers
Gatorade packets
Pop Tarts
Dehydrated Meals
Apples or other hard fruit
Fruit Roll Ups
Pasta
Beans
Lentils
Oatmeal
Mountain House and other brands of freeze dried meals
Little Debbie's Snack Cakes
Hard candies
Electrolyte tablets
Beef Jerky
Trail Mix and nut packets
Oreo, Fig Newton, and other sleeves of cookies

GEARING UP

Getting the proper gear together for an expedition is a big task for most people. There are a few hikers that already have backpacking gear, throw some of it in a pack and go, but most thru-hikers spend time researching each piece of equipment they bring along, and agonizing over each decision.

I am a little OCD, and I went pretty deep into the decision making process, reading a lot of books and doing online research, making various spreadsheets of equipment lists, weights, and costs. Ultimately, most of my research was wasted effort, and I switched out most of the major pieces of gear I started out with.

There are many different ways to equip yourself for backpacking. Each piece of gear that you use will be an individual choice based on what suits your personal needs, level of comfort desired, and financial situation. There is a rarely a single right answer. Some people preach a particular way, their way as it so happens, as the 'right' way. The only 'right' way is what works best for you.

There are also any number of wrong choices. Some are individually wrong, and some are probably just wrong. No one carrying a cast iron Dutch oven or a chainsaw on a long backpacking trip has really thought things through.

Just about everyone who starts the trail at Springer is carrying too much equipment. My pack was 51 pounds, which was ridiculously heavy compared to what I would carry as I gained experience. Some purported backpacking equipment is designed for camping within a few feet of a vehicle, and not for carrying on long treks, as many people discover in the first few days of their hike. I saw any number of iron skillets, hatchets and saws, cabin style tents, flannel lined sleeping bags, and a bewildering variety of camp life gadgets and tools sitting in nearly new condition in the shelters of Georgia. More to the point, they stayed in the shelters, no one passing picked them up.

You could start an outdoor outfitter shop with the equipment cast aside on the trail in the first 100 miles. Some people just up and quit, leaving their full packs behind, sitting on the trail or in a shelter. I saw a couple of tents standing empty by the trail, where someone woke up after another rainy, cold morning and just couldn't summon the energy to take down and pack out their shelter. The would be thru-hikers walked back to a world of electric power and hot showers abandoning their fully erected tent in the forest.

Everyone brings extra gear starting out, a sop to our insecurities. An extra lighter, a second knife, extra tent stakes, another bottle of hand sanitizer, little multifunction gadgets that duplicated purposes, a backup spork for if the first one breaks or is lost; all of these things will find the way into your pack while you are loading it up in your living room.

I was particularly bad in this respect, a habit I developed as a leader in the Army, where I occasionally made up for someone else's deficiencies. I would be a little bit of a hero, pulling the needed item out of my pack and presenting it to a soldier who desperately needed it, if only to keep the First Sergeant off of his back.

Extra items for a thru-hiker are just that, extra items. It is needless weight you are toting around, and all of those little redundant items add up to a significant weight. During the first couple of months on the trail there will always be other hikers around, and they are happy to let you use their knife or lighter if you have misplaced yours. During the first weeks, as hikers came to understand what the weight of extras cost them in effort, and how useless they were, the items were left in hiker boxes and shelters along the way.

Everybody makes a few foolish personal choices. I had a backpacker guitar strapped on the back of my pack, and it, along with extra strings, sheet music, picks and a tuner, added 4.5 pounds to my overall weight. It was not the only instrument on the trail, and some people carried their instruments and enjoyed them all the way through to Mt. Katahdin, but for me it was a liability.

I found my focus on hiking left me little time for developing my musical talent. The guitar itself constantly reminded me of its presence. The extra weight was significant, and no matter how well I lashed it to the back of my pack it would perversely wander around back there, pulling me left and right and back and forth as I hiked, inducing an odd stagger to my gait.

I wasn't carrying the heaviest pack heading north from Springer Mountain by any means; in fact I was probably close to the average. There were a few packs close to 100 pounds starting out up there, some of them with some unusual or patently impractical items. There was a man taking his six year old son with him who had brought a Tonka truck and action figures along for his child to play with in camp.

Hiker boxes were full of an item called a GoGirl, a funnel that ostensibly allowed women to pee standing up. I don't know how effective it was, but I saw a lot of them, and I always felt the need to use hand sanitizer after finding one in a hiker box. Ladies, please test those things out a few times before coming onto the trail, and please don't abandon them in a hiker box; it really isn't something I want touching other things that I might be interested in. Ditto that on poop trowels, another common hiker box item.

After the first day's struggle up and down the trail carrying a massive pack most hikers were already assessing what items they could get rid of without creating problems. Some of it gets left right along the trail, but most backpackers have the decency to wait until they get to Neel's Gap and the Mountain Crossings outfitters 32 miles up the trail, where they can either put items in the hiker box for others to use, or ship them back home.

Mountain Crossings provides a shakedown service, where experienced thru-hikers go through all of the items in your pack and help you assess their true value to you. Mountain Crossings also has some very good replacement equipment, lighter, more durable, and more functional than the equipment in your own pack. It is also at the high side of retail pricing, and you will pay for your lighter pack load. Fixing problems early is worth the cost.

Picking out equipment is a challenge. If you don't already have extensive backpacking experience you really are taking some chances and may end up spending money down the trail to fix or change some of your choices. Most thru-hikers do not have enough experience starting out. What you are about to undertake is not the same as the short weekend trips you may already have under your belt.

I thought of myself as an experienced backpacker when I started my thru-hike. I had been on backpacking trips up to a week long, including AT and PCT sections, I been a Boy Scout, and in the Army I was in different positions including straight up, rucksack hauling leg Infantry, and as a Quartermaster. I will say that I was used to certain aspects of backpacking, and had some familiarity with gear. However, I was hiking then to a different purpose than a thru-hiker. I had experience, but it wasn't valid experience, and it led me down the wrong path when I made my first load out.

I had in all previous cases simply carried too much equipment. One of the primary concepts that you have to get into your mind, one that I didn't have fully mentally articulated until I was in the Smokies, but what I was already realizing on a subconscious level, was laid out for me by Burglar. He was an experienced thru-hiker on the Appalachian Trail finishing his triple crown of long distance hiking, having already completed the PCT and CDT. He shared a lot of wisdom on the single night I was camped near him. He said what I had been thinking, but hadn't quite clearly defined.

"We are on a hiking trip, not a camping trip." is what Burglar said. It is true, words have power, and his simple statement clarified my idea of what thru-hiking was about.

I made a list of the items I had in my pack when I walked out of the woods on my last day of hiking the Appalachian Trail. With 4-5 days of food and a couple of liters of water my pack weighed around 35 pounds. It is a cold weather load out, and several pounds of gear were taken out in Virginia for the summer heat and put back in when I was in Vermont. After getting everything home and washing it, I found that a couple of pounds of my load were plain old dirt.

I have divided my Gear List into two sections. First is a basic list of the items, followed by a detailed item by item explanation and describing why I chose it, how it was used and where it was carried. The list does not include food and water.

EQUIPMENT LIST:

(1) An ultralight Elemental Horizons Backpack
(2) A contractor strength large plastic garbage bag

SHELTER AND SLEEP SYSTEM:
(3) Hennessey Hammock with bug screen, rain fly, tree straps, 2 carabiners, and Vargo titanium stakes
(4) Over and under Jack's 'R' Better sleeping quilts (2 quilts equal one system)
(5) Thermarest ¾ sleeping pad

COOKSET:
(6) Jetboil camp stove with built in pot and cup
(7) 1 five-ounce fuel canister
(8) Long handled Vargo titanium spoon
(9) 1.5 inch blade Gerber folding knife
(10) Bic Mini Lighter

(11) Leki hiking poles (carried, not packed)

WATER FILTER AND HYDRATION:
(12) Sawyer Squeeze water filter, full size
(13) 3 water bottles (one 1 liter PowerAde, two 1.5 liter Lipton ice tea bottles)

(14) Black Diamond headlamp with 3 spare AAA batteries

PERSONAL HYGIENE:
(15) Paper towel squares (for toilet paper)
(16) 3 ounce bottle of hand sanitizer
(17) 3 ounce travel sized toothpaste
(18) Travel sized toothbrush
(19) 2.5 ounce Dr, Bronner's ecologically friendly soap
(20) Disposable Razor

CLOTHING:
(Clothing includes the items I was wearing)
(21) 1 pair Skechers Memory Foam trail shoes
(22) 1 pair full length hiking pants, with web belt.
(23) 2 ultralight wicking Outdoor Research t-shirts
(24) 3 pairs Darn Tough socks
(25) 1 Smartwool long sleeve pullover
(26) 1 Adidas runner's pullover
(27) 1 Marmot down coat with hood

(28) 1 Mountain Hardware ultralight raincoat with hood
(29) 1 pair of lightweight running shorts
(30) 1 balaclava
(31) 1 pair wool fingerless gloves
(32) 1 pair blaze orange fleece gloves
(33) 1 Green bandana with chili peppers on it
(34) 1 Lightload towel
(35) 1 pair of Crocs

ELECTRONICS:
(36) Samsung Galaxy Tab 4 tablet in a Survivor case
(37) IPhone 5s in a LifeProof case
(38) Ear buds
(39) Charging cords for each device
(40) Portable Power Supply 4 charge

STORAGE:
(41) 3 large dry bags (one food, one sleeping bag, one clothes)
(42) 1 medium dry bag (electronics and paper items)
(43) 2 small dry bags (one first aid and other small items, one for phone)
(44) 6-8 gallon Ziploc bags
(45) 6-8 sandwich sized Ziploc bags

MISCELLANEOUS:
(46) AWOL AT Guide
(47) Several pieces of paper and a pen
(48) First Aid kit: a couple of band aids, tube of Neosporin, a piece of moleskin, small medic's scissors, bag of pills (aspirin, Benedryl, Tylenol PM, Imodium). Duct tape (wrapped around hiking pole handles). I also had a pair of foam ear plugs in here.
(49) Fix it kit: Small sewing kit, extra pack buckles, duct tape, garden hose gaskets for water filter
(50) 30 foot paracord bear line with carabiner attached
(51) Bug defense: In the heat I carried various things for bugs, including essential oils and DEET, and a head net for bugs. Only the head net actually worked.
(52) A pair of reading glasses
(53) A Hohner harmonica
(54) 1 pair of overshoe ice spikes

The list is everything that I carried at the end of my thru-hike. It is not what I began the hike with; I discarded or mailed home a lot of gear. Much of my equipment was swapped out for lighter or more efficient versions as I traveled. The only original pieces of gear I had remaining from my start at Springer Mountain were the Samsung tablet, the down coat, the raincoat, the balaclava, the bandana, and the AWOL guide.

I changed out most of my major pieces of equipment on my journey, and trimmed down on nonessentials. I had a smaller knife and no spare, I ditched a solar panel early, and the guitar and its accessories. I had no ball cap (although I wore one until I got to Gorham), no sunglasses, no compass, no spare lighter or matches, no extra spork, no camp towel, no poop trowel, no sleeping bag liner, no sunscreen. All of those items were sent home or left in hiker boxes along the way; they just were not worth the weight they represented.

I explained much of the how and why in my trail narrative, but I am going to break it down piece by piece right here, so you have a consolidated thought process, and can see how one thru-hiker arrived at their pack load.

I also note how I packed and carried each item. I had a system so I knew where every item was in my pack, and could load and unload them quickly. I was more methodical than some hikers, and some disorganized people certainly made it to Katahdin, but it helped me day by day, and helped me finish my hike.

Piece by Piece

(1) An ultralight Elemental Horizons Backpack

I tried a number of different backpacks before getting on the trail. I was smart enough to limit myself to a 70 liter pack, knowing that if I got a larger pack I would just carry more equipment. 70 liters was a great size for me, and I didn't see any larger ones carried by thru-hikers after the first week. The larger sort of pack is called an expedition pack, and is really designed for Sherpas to haul the gentleman's silver place settings into the jungle, not for real long distance movement.

I didn't really like any of the backpacks I tried initially, an assortment I picked up online. You really do need to try packs on for fit and comfort. I went to my local Albuquerque REI for equipment advice. I told them I was going to thru-hike. I don't think many people in New Mexico walk into the REI and announce they need equipment for thru-hiking. The store is more mentally geared to the weekend explorer, and the equipment they set me up with showed it down the trail.

The sales person I talked to led me to an REI brand backpack. It had all kinds of bells and whistles, and I was comfortable walking around the store with it on my back loaded with sandbags, so I bought it. What I failed to account for was that it weighed six and a half pounds.

Ospreys were the most common pack on the trail, and I own a couple of them now. They are a well-made, sturdy product, and only weigh four and a half pounds. They have most of the same bells and whistles as the REI backpack, but are two precious pounds lighter. They are also sold at REI, and are even about the same price, a little under $300.00.

The incredible thing about Osprey is they guarantee any backpack they make for life, for any pack they have made since 1974, and they mean it. I sent them an Osprey pack I bought used, online, that had multiple holes in it (the previous owner had spent a summer schlepping it across Europe), and they replaced it. The only question asked was what color I would prefer.

Osprey provides excellent support for their products on the trail, and will work out repair schemes at mail drops for thru-hikers. At Trail Days in Damascus, they set up a couple of enormous circus tents filled with sewing machines and they fixed thru-hiker packs right there. It was amazing.

So the Osprey was the pack I didn't get, and they were right there at REI. The pack I started out carrying, the REI Crestrail 70, turned out to be a heavy, awkward beast. The 15 extra pounds I was carrying, including the guitar, contributed to this, but the pack itself was a factor. The worst problem I had with it, besides the weight, was the waist belt. It was a wide, soft, foam support that was supposed to make carrying big loads more comfortable. I found that it would not ride my hips correctly. It slipped down over my hips as I moved, allowing my pack to slowly creep down my back with it, dropping the weight onto my shoulders. Worse, the wide belt chafed, and in the heat I developed a terrible rash on both hips and on the top of my butt cheeks. It was an effect from how my body is shaped as much as the pack's design.

I went to Trail Days in Damascus about a month into my hike specifically looking to replace equipment that would save me weight, and I was hoping to drop 4 or 5 pounds overall. I was looking for an Osprey or a ULA (Ultra Light Adventures) pack, but the Ospreys were sold out, and ULA didn't show up.

ULA packs are extremely lightweight, at three to three and half pounds. The company started in someone's garage and became the most popular mass produced ultralight pack company. They provide some customer service and hiker support on the trail; I heard both praise and complaints.

While ULA wasn't at Trail Days, a man named Matthew was starting his own company making a similar product. The company is called Elemental Horizons. Matthew only had display models at Damascus; he made packs to custom order. The packs were a little over three pounds in weight and made of Cuben Fiber, the latest wonder cloth; a waterproof, tear proof, ultralight material popular enough there was a manufacturing shortage of it at Trail Days (which was relevant for other choices I made).

I wasn't interested in waiting a month or two for a custom made pack, but I liked what Matthew had on display. He put a lot of thought into his designs and had some innovative features. I convinced him to sell me one of his display models.

The next morning I unloaded my old pack and carried it and other items to the post office to send home, while wearing my new pack. It was a major improvement. It didn't have all of the (unneeded) frills, straps and zippers of my REI pack, but it was half the weight, a full 3 pounds less.

The Elemental Horizons pack made it all the way to the end of the Appalachian Trail with me. Matthew sent me replacements for a couple of buckles that broke (he sent several extra as well, which were ultimately unneeded, but it was a great comfort to me knowing I had them). Otherwise the pack survived. The Cuben fiber eventually started to wear through in a few places where I repeatedly dragged it through and across rocks. The shoulder straps, designed for lightweight loads, slipped a little towards the end if I had a load of over 32 pounds, so sometimes on the first day out I would have to tighten the straps a time or two during the day. This is not uncommon for any pack, and overall I was very pleased with my Elemental Horizons. Because of the burden it represented on the trail, and the feeling I got when I took it off and put it down, I named it Thud. Thud is still in my closet at home, loaded up and ready to go

(2) A contractor strength large plastic garbage bag

A durable garbage bag, contractor strength or a trash compactor bag, was what I used as a pack liner. I started out with regular garbage bags lining my pack and wrapped around my guitar. They did not hold up, but the trash compactor bags did.

You can buy commercially made pack covers at outdoor outfitters. They weigh 6-8 ounces, twice the weight of the heavyweight trash bags. If you buy one made by the same company as produced your pack, it will fit nicely. Some packs come with a pack cover already built in, but most charge extra for it, as much as $100.00.

I found an Etowah pack cover in a shelter on my third day on the trail. It was also the third continuous day of rain, and my regular kitchen garbage bags were already ripping. The Etowah was big, built for a 90 liter pack, so it fit nicely over my pack and the guitar I had strapped on the back. It kept things dry, and hung on a cord on the outside of the pack in a little compression bag. I used it through the next month or so, which saw copious amounts of rainfall, and it worked well. One of the best things about it was I didn't need to figure out how to protect my pack at night if I didn't bring it into my tent, the pack cover protected everything. The only thing I didn't care for was the inconvenience of taking it off and putting it back on any time I stopped for a break and wanted something out of my pack.

After I gave my guitar away the pack cover no longer fit so snugly, and during some powerful storms it was loose enough that it started collecting water in its bottom as I hiked in the rain. I had a couple of extra liters of water accumulated in it when I realized what that heavy blob was bouncing against my butt, and emptied it out.

I put the pack cover in the next hiker box.

Using the heavy duty trash bags worked well for me afterwards. Everything in my pack was already in a dry bag, so I was doubling my protection. Plenty of thru-hikers used pack covers all the way to the ends of the hike, and were happy with them. An argument for the pack cover is they prevent the backpack itself from absorbing water and adding weight to the load. I thought it was balanced out by the lesser weight of the trash bags. It is a matter of personal preference.

(3) Hennessey Hammock with bug screen, rain fly, tree straps, 2 carabiners, and Vargo titanium stakes

The Big Three in backpacking refers to the three largest, heaviest items you carry; the shelter, the sleeping bag, and the backpack itself. They are critical items, and it is where a lot of money gets spent trying to get the most efficiency and least weight from each piece.

I used a hammock as my shelter for three quarters of my thru-hike. I hadn't planned on a hammock, and began my hike with a tent, and most people prefer them.

There was a bewildering array of tents set up at early encampments. The REI Quarter Dome tent seemed to be the most popular. It is a tent that weighs less than three pounds complete, is self-supporting, double walled, and well made for under $250.00. It is rather small, but tall enough to sit up in. I saw plenty of other options, and there are tarp tents that weigh less than 2 pounds, but they can cost upwards of $600.00.

I envied the lightweight tarp tents, as expensive as they were. A tarp tent is a single wall tent. It has no rain fly and relies on the waterproof material of the single wall to protect you and keep you dry. They are usually made of Cuben fiber. It does away with the weight of a rain fly, and the additional time added to tent set up, and the space it took up as part of the load. Tarp tents are designed to use your hiking poles as tent poles, getting rid of more additional weight by making tent poles redundant. The biggest drawback I saw of tarp tents, besides their high cost, was that they could build up a lot of condensation on the inside of the tent. On double wall tents the condensation builds up on the inside of the rain fly instead on the interior tent wall. Tarp tents are also not free standing; they require stakes to keep them upright. On rocky ground it can be a challenge. You can usually cobble something together placing stones at the corners if need be. It is not a frequent issue on the Appalachian Trail.

I started the trail with a Eureka Spitfire two person tent. I am a bigger man, over six feet tall, and many one person tents are too narrow or too short for me to sleep in comfortably, much less move around changing clothes and performing small maintenance chores out of the rain. I also had my guitar to take care of, and I had room inside my Eureka for it and me. I got into the habit of bringing my pack into my tent and placing it under my feet to get them off the cold ground while I slept, something a smaller tent would not have allowed.

The rain fly of my Eureka extended out from the entrance far enough to allow me to put my shoes there, under cover but still outside of my tent, to give them some chance of drying out over the night. The rain fly also helped keep me warm, the second wall created an additional layer of air as insulation, and if I kicked leaves up around the gap at the base it kept some of my body heat inside. The venting system worked well, and I had little trouble with condensation inside the tent.

I liked my Eureka, but it was heavy. I swapped out the original steel stakes to lighter aluminum stakes, which saved some ounces. I used a piece of Tyvek I cut to size as a ground cloth, a lighter and considerably cheaper option than getting the custom made item from the company. Ground cloths are not a necessity, strictly speaking, but they do protect the bottom of your tent from wear, and create another layer between you and the cold wet ground at night.

All told, with the ground cloth, my tent was another 4 pounds attached to the back of my pack.

When I arrived at Trail Days I went looking for a lighter tent. There were some wonderful tents there, lightweight and roomy, weighing less than 3 pounds, double wall, made out of silnylon (Silicone-Nylon), for $300.00-$400.00. Some companies had Cuben fiber tarp tents on display, and I was seriously thinking about dropping $500.00 dollars to get a 2 pound tent, and halving my shelter weight. Fortunately for my wallet there was a nationwide shortage of Cuben fiber; the manufacturer could not keep up with demand. I could look at Cuben fiber tents at Trail Days, but I couldn't buy one.

I walked around the sales and exhibition area in Damascus looking for other things, and contemplating tents. I came across three hammock manufacturers with their wares on display, and available for sale. Several thru-hikers were already using hammocks as their shelters, and I had talked to them about their shelter selection. I was a little dubious, but they all seemed to think they had made good choices.

Backpacking hammocks are not the old sailor's cloth sheet, but sophisticated, high tech constructions. The bed you sleep in is suspended by a ridgeline from which hangs a bug mesh to keep the pests out, and over the top of that goes a rain fly much like a tent's in purpose, creating a layer between you and precipitation, and giving you a little privacy.

I looked at the three manufacturers at Trail Days, each one with very different approaches to hanging a hammock. Hennessey, one of the bigger manufacturers, had 3 or 4 different hammocks set up, and their most popular model for backpackers was half price for thru-hikers at Trail Days, just $160.00. I bought one.

It was an asymmetrical model, so it used less material and took up less space and weight. The hiker positioned themselves in it at an angle, that when done correctly, allowed you a very comfortable night of sleep. I am a side sleeper, but the asymmetrical design allowed me to sleep facing whatever direction I pleased. It was a lot easier on my old back than sleeping on the ground,

I kept telling myself I needed to open myself more to new things and new approaches, and hammocking fit the bill. I mailed my tent home with my REI backpack, and henceforth, I hammocked.

My hammock took some getting used to. Just learning how to hang it properly so I wasn't bent into a U shape took practice, as did learning to select trees and tie the knots on the tree straps. I ended up tying a series of trucker's hitches (loops) in the hang line and snapping carabiners in at the appropriate length to the tree straps. It saved time tying and untying knots, a difficult task when it was cold, and the carabiners were useful in other ways. My carabiners were titanium climbing gear, expensive, but extremely lightweight and strong.

Stakes were still needed to stretch out the rain fly, and I used lightweight Vargo titanium stakes. The weight savings were small, and the cost high, but the steel and aluminum stakes I experimented with bent over time, hammering them with a rock into a rock had that effect. The titanium stakes were stronger.

It was cooler sleeping in a hammock than on the ground, which was great in the summer, but something to be overcome in fall. I developed techniques for keeping warm. I slept on top of my air mattress, and added one of the cheap windshield reflectors people stick in their cars when they are parked. The reflector weighed little, cost almost nothing, and did a pretty good job of keeping in my body heat in the hammock. I threw it away as unneeded weight when summer hit, which brings us to our next item.

(4) Over and under Jack's 'R' Better sleeping quilts (Sleeping Bag)

I started my journey with an inexpensive Teton sleeping bag I purchased online for less than $100.00. It weighed less than 3 pounds, had a synthetic filling, and was rated at 20 degrees.

Sleeping bags are rated to a temperature, but that rating is a survival rating, not a comfort rating. My Teton kept me warm down to about freezing, and then I started shivering. The synthetic filling was heavier than a down bag, but much cheaper. More importantly, down loses some of its insulating qualities when it gets wet, and we were hiking through a lot of rain.

Down in general just doesn't mix well with water; it clumps up as well as being less efficient. Down bags require more care, are harder to wash, and to me were just not worth the additional expense. Good down bags can cost upwards of five or six hundred dollars.

I went a little too cheaply with the Teton. Teton is a low end manufacturer. They make good, usable products, but they have to make sacrifices in quality to keep prices down. You probably wouldn't notice over a weekend, or even a week of backpacking, but the continual hard use of the Appalachian Trail was more than my sleeping bag could handle. The zipper on my bag was cheap plastic, and it wore out after a month; the teeth would not stay interlocked.

I bought a new sleeping bag in Franklin, NC. There are two outfitters in the town and I had a pretty good selection. I chose a Marmot bag with the same temperature rating, again with an artificial fill, but it was 6 ounces lighter at two and a half pounds in total weight. It also cost $200.00, not terrifically expensive as sleeping bags went, but a lot more than the Teton.

I mailed the compression and storage bags it came with home. These are useless items on the trail. Some people still used compression bags, but I found sticking my sleeping bag in a dry bag at the bottom of my pack was sufficient, as the weight of all my other belongings on top of my bag compressed it just fine, and it adapted to whatever shape it needed to be, rather than sitting in the pack as a defined, solid lump.

Snoozing in my hammock the sleeping bag didn't trap any warmth beneath me. The hammock pressing against my body compressed all the insulation in the bottom of the bag, making it ineffective. I knew this wasn't going to work in the fall, and I spent a considerable amount of time looking at other hammock users' set ups seeking ideas to improve mine, and examining quilt systems.

A hammock quilt system is two separate sleeping blankets. One goes over you inside the hammock, while the second one hangs outside the hammock as an envelope to trap in body heat. I finally settled on an over and under set made by Jacks 'R' Better. I stored them loose in a dry bag at the bottom of my pack, the same as I had my sleeping bag.

Hanging an underquilt requires a certain amount of tension, and it took a lot of trial and error to get the best effect. The quilt system was rated at 20 degrees, like my sleeping bag, and like my sleeping bag I started shivering whenever the temperature got below freezing.

I tossed my windshield reflector out when summer came and it started getting hot, figuring that I would just get another one when fall arrived. I hadn't considered that people in New England apparently don't use them; it just doesn't get that hot. Trying to describe what I was looking for to store clerks was a bafflement to them. So I had my air mattress and my quilts, and I was cold on many nights.

But I survived.

(5) Thermarest ¾ Sleeping Pad (and one foot square foam pad)

A sleeping pad is an essential part of the sleep system. Its primary purpose is not comfort, but insulation. When it is cold, the ground vacuums all of the heat from your body. Even in tents the bottom of a sleeping bag is compressed and a lot of insulating quality is lost where it is smooshed against the ground. The sleeping pad creates warming layer of insulation between you and the ground.

Sleeping pads also serve a comfort purpose in tents and shelters, giving the hiker a bit of softness between the rocks, twigs, and hard wood floors lying between you and a good night's sleep.

There are two basic types of sleeping pad. There are foam pads, and air mattresses. The foam pads can be as simple as a yoga mat or be a complex, high tech, honeycomb construction. Foam pads are cheaper than inflatable models; a good one can be had for $30.00. They are infallible; they always work. Drawbacks are they are bulky and heavy, taking up more room on the outside of the pack. They are not quite as efficient or comfortable as a good air mattress, at least by my reckoning.

Air mattress pads take up a lot less room, and expand into a bigger, warmer, and much cushier rest. The good ones are half the weight of foam pads, but are also upwards of $100.00. The biggest issue I had with inflatable mattresses is they develop leaks.

Another air mattress drawback is the noises some of them produce. An air mattress can make weird rubber balloon squeaky noises as the people sleeping on them shift about in the night, and it is irritating as hell to a light sleeper sharing a shelter with them. The squeakers are generally are the bigger mattresses, the ones that inflate into a four to six inch high bed. I saw (and heard) a number of them at the beginning of the hike, but they all but disappeared among thru-hikers within the first 500 miles. They must have developed leaks easily, or been extra heavy, or maybe just ticked off enough people sharing spaces with them.

I started the trail with a Klymit V mattress. I tested it at home, and I still have one I use on short trips today. It only weighs 6 ounces and has an inflation pattern that makes for a very nice supported night of sleep.

Unfortunately, the Klymit I started the trail with was also an utter failure. The very first night on the Appalachian Trail a splinter or nail in the shelter floor punctured the mattress. I woke up cold and sore about an hour after going to sleep, hard up against the floor of the shelter. The chill of the wooden floor was leaching the warmth from my body. I re-inflated my mattress, but half an hour later I was shivering on the planks again. I repeated this through the entire night. Needless to say, I did not wake rested.

I hiked for the next three days going into Neel's Gap without an air mattress to insulate or cushion me. I had three more very poor nights of sleep. It was a rough start on the trail. At Mountain Outfitters in Neel's Gap there is a washtub a hiker can use to submerge a mattress. You look for a tiny stream of bubbles to indicate the source of the air leak.

I was already frustrated with my Klymit, and I was in no mood to spend a lot of time repairing a mattress that very well might develop new leaks. I started looking at the accordion style foam mattresses at the outfitter, but didn't think they were comfortable enough, and at the time I still had a guitar and tent taking up a lot of room on the outside of my pack.

Squarl, the experienced thru-hiker who took me through my pack shakedown and dropped many pearls of wisdom on me, showed me a

Thermarest air mattress. The Thermarest is a composite mattress; it is an air mattress with a honeycombed interior, so even if it springs a leak it retains some of its padding and insulating qualities. It was heavier than the Klymit, but more durable. I cut the weight (and cost) down a little bit by getting a 3/4 sized mattress, which left my feet hanging out (I put them up on my pack in my tent, and covered them with my rain jacket in the hammock).

The Thermarest worked very well, and was a popular choice on the trail. The Thermarest is one of the more expensive pads, but mine lasted the entire hike, and was well worth the cost. Eventually it developed a pinhole leak somewhere, but it still gave me enough padding so I made it through the night. I usually woke to go the bathroom at once or twice a night, and I would blow another puff or two of air into the pad to make up for the small air loss.

My pad served an important secondary purpose. When I switched to an ultralight pack one of the weight cuts in the pack design was the removal of the padding between the pack and the back. The technique to provide padding is to fold your deflated sleeping pad into a pocket in the pack against your back, and it provides the padding needed without a weight penalty.

I ended up carrying a small piece of foam pad with me as well. It was a piece about a foot square and I used it for a seating pad to soften my rest in camp, and keep my butt off of the cold wet ground. I also used it as a hitchhiking sign, with the words 'Hiker to Town' written in Sharpie on one side, and 'Hiker to Trail' on the other.

(6) Jetboil camp stove with built in pot and cup
(7) 5 Ounce Fuel Canister

The cooking set is an item that deserves a lot of consideration. I carried mine in the main compartment of my pack on top of my food bag. I didn't cook while hiking, just when I was in camp, so I didn't need access to it during the day on the trail.

There are many different styles of cook sets and stoves. A few hikers, generally the ultralight crowd, didn't cook at all while they were on the trail, living entirely on energy bars and other foods that did not require preparation. It saved them two pounds of weight, the expense of a stove and fuel, and the time needed in camp to prepare meals. Some budget hikers cooked over campfires to save the same expenses, but still carried a pot and an eating utensil. They spent a lot of time building their fire and cooking over the open flame.

Camp stoves are efficient ways to cook a quick, hot meal. Trail food gets to be boring and routine, and a stove provided a hot meal at the end of the day to look forward to. I used three different stoves while I was on the trail.

I started out as an alcohol burner. Alcohol burners use a small, cheap stove with some sort of a stand for the pot, and a windshield. They are super simple and super light. The stove is basically just a cut off tin can with holes punched into it. A wind shield can be made out of a folded over piece of tinfoil, and pot stands are available in stores or online for a couple of bucks, or can be made by bending a coat hanger into a tripod. I bought my first stove, made from the bottom of an aluminum soda can, online for under $2.00 from a man who machined them in his garage. I bought a fancier Vargo titanium model later on, but it didn't prove any better than the soda can model, and in fact may have been a little less efficient. You can make your own stove pretty easily if you are so inclined. Instructions can be found on the internet.

Denatured alcohol is the fuel and it is marketed in different ways commercially. It is easy to find when you know what you are looking for.

Rubbing alcohol is a common form. I started out using rubbing alcohol but found some additive in it creates a sooty residue that coats the cooking pot and transfers onto your other belongings and yourself. It is very hard to get off.

A product called Heet is sold in most dollar stores, gas stations, Wal-Marts, and thru-hiker pit stops for a couple of dollars per 16-ounce bottle. Heet is sold as an automotive fuel additive, a drying agent and antifreeze). There are two different types; the stuff sold in the yellow bottle is pure denatured alcohol, and what you want. The kind in the red bottle has additives that again leave soot behind, and the vapors probably are not very good for your health.

Alcohol stoves are light, but carrying the fuel adds some weight. The alcohol stove can be a temperamental creature to light. I usually ended up slopping a bit of fuel everywhere, and I set fire to a number of logs, benches, picnic tables, and the like which I quickly put out. I also burned some holes in my clothing and set myself on fire a few times. These events were alarming moments. The sight of a hiker jumping up and down waving a flaming sleeve in the air does create entertainment for other hikers at the shelter.

The biggest drawback of the alcohol stove is the time it takes to heat water to boiling. It could take 15 minutes of tending my stove to get a liter of water to boil. In that time hikers with more efficient stoves were already done eating and cleaning up. When you are constantly hungry and cold, and watching other people eating their hot meals and drinking their hot beverages while you fiddle with your stove, you start thinking about getting a new stove. By the time NoBo thru-hikers reach Virginia, almost no one is an alcohol burner.

So I looked to upgrade. Canister stoves are the most common stove on the trail, and the Jetboil is the most popular model. Most canister stoves have a little lightweight burner you screw into the top of a 3 or 5 ounce fuel can. The cook pot balances on top, and a windshield wraps around the base, Turn a knob, light it, and five minutes later there is a pint of boiling water. The canisters are small, and lighter than carrying a supply of alcohol. A single canister can last a week or two, and they are sold everywhere along the trail. Budget hikers could scavenge cans out of hiker boxes, since people like me would get down to about a quarter of a canister and buy a new one, leaving the 3 or 4 burns left in the old can behind in a hiker box.

I wanted a Jetboil, but their popularity was such that every outfitter I came to along the trail was sold out. I eventually gave in and bought something else in Daleville, Virginia, a Snow Peak. The Snow Peak was a good stove, far faster than my alcohol burner, but hikers with Jetboils were still eating before I was, and using less fuel.

The Snow Peak and other stoves like it have an advantage over the Jetboil system. The Jetboil boils water. You can't control the heat so you can't really cook in it. The Snow Peak type of canister stove, in comparison, allows you to control the heat and use a variety of pots and pans on it, allowing more elaborate meal preparation. Some people enjoy cooking on the trail, and found this type of stove to be wonderful. I was still eating foods I added to boiling water, so the advantage was lost on me, and I still looked for a Jetboil.

I kept looking. I was at the back of the last big wave of northbound thru-hikers for the season, and the bubbles ahead of us had scoured the countryside clean of equipment like a swarm of hungry locusts. I finally stopped looking in stores and went online. I had a Jetboil mailed to my mother's along with a number of other pieces of gear I was switching out for colder weather when I left the trail to go to my sister's wedding.

My Jetboil was the basic model. It is a complete cooking system, including a stand, the burner, an insulated 1 Liter pot and lid, and a small plastic cup and storage compartment. The whole assembly stores together as a single unit, and the pot had space inside for a 3 ounce fuel canister, my lighter, and my little pocket knife, The pot design has heat exchangers built into the bottom and it slots onto the burner. The fit is tight enough no heat shield is needed, and the stove is so efficient it boils water in two minutes.

I loved my Jetboil. It cost me $70.00 online, and replaced not just my stove but my pot and cup, and was cheaper as a unit than all the assembled parts of my initial cooking arrangements, and it was lighter to boot.

There is another cooking option out there now, stove assemblies similar to a Jetboil that burn twigs to provide cooking heat. They are the best environmentally, but they are slow. The more popular campsites on the trail have been scoured of dry wood, and burnable twigs can be hard to find, as difficult as that might be to believe in a forest. If it is raining, (and it rains a lot) getting wet wood to burn can be a challenge. I saw a few of these stoves in the first week of hiking, and then they all disappeared.

(8) Bic Mini Lighter

A lighter is needed to fire up the cook stove. Some stoves come with some sort of automatic lighter, but none of them work very well, and are not worth the additional cost.

I also carried a box of waterproof matches most of the way, just in case, but never needed them. The Bic was enough. In fact, the sparks from the flint were usually enough to light my stove without there being an actual flame. I still replaced my lighters as they were depleted, just in case I needed a fire for something else.

I never did.

(9) Long handled Vargo titanium spoon

An eating utensil is essential if you are going to eat prepared foods. I started with lightweight and cheap plastic sporks. I lost, melted or broke several, and at one point I was without an eating utensil entirely. I carved out a forked stick each night to eat with. The stick was not ideal.

I ended up buying a long handled titanium spoon and wrapping a little orange tape around the handle for visibility. The titanium spoons are pricey, $20.00 or so apiece, but they are durable and the long handle allows you to reach deep into a pot or a dehydrated meal bag to get food out without smearing food all over your hands..

The low budget hiker can stick with sporks. Plastic spoons can be picked up for free at fast food places, for the ultimate low cost. You really just need something to eat with. Bright colors are helpful to avoid leaving your utensil behind or tossing it into a garbage can by accident, as I know from personal experience,

(10) One and a half inch blade Gerber folding knife

I started the trail with a Buck folding knife that had a 3 inch blade, and I also carried a Gerber multi-tool. In my relentless quest to shave ounces from my load (ounces add up to pounds) I discarded the multi-tool early, and ended up sending my Buck knife home and buying a smaller, lighter knife.

Knives are so associated with outdoor survival that hikers first coming into the trail carry multiple blades. What I discovered is that you really don't need much knife. You aren't going to be hunting for moose, fighting off vicious carnivores, or hollowing logs into canoes. All that is needed is a bit of sharp on hand to slice open food packages, cut string, and help with minor repairs and first aid. Some ultralight backpackers carry only an old fashioned razor blade protected by a fold of cardboard. It works, but I liked having a handle.

(11) Leki hiking poles

I consider hiking poles an essential piece of backpacking equipment. Poles help a hiker keep their balance on slippery or uneven surfaces, and they also allow you to use more of your upper body strength to help propel you up and down the trail.

Poles serve a number of other functions as well. They may serve as tent poles, they give the hiker something to brandish at bears, rattlesnakes, dogs and mean humans, and they serve as a tool to help bury poop. There are hikers who hike without poles, but the majority does use a pair

There are many variations on hiking poles. Manufactured poles run from cheap, basic steel poles to space age materials. I know at least one hiker who found a pair of straight tree branches in the woods.

Redlocks had a black stick and a white stick which he named Ebony and Ivory. Ivory broke and was easily replaced by a new found stick. He took some time trying out new sticks until he found one that suited him just right. I believe the selection process was also a form of entertainment.

My friend McGyver carried two rather mismatched poles. One was a staff, he received on his first backpacking trip on the AT way back in the 1965 and he had carved the date into it then.

He topped one that staff with a tennis ball. That stick was called 'Wilson'. His other pole was a modern hiking pole.

Manufactured trekking poles have a lot of advantages over those found in the woods. They are stronger, lighter, and are telescoping, allowing the hiker to collapse them and stick them in their pack at times they are not really needed, or when traveling in a car. Some poles come with little springs in the shafts to help absorb some of the shock of walking.

I went through 3 sets of poles on my thru-hike, beginning with a set of REI poles. The REI poles had twist locks, and I got them on sale for $80.00. They were made of steel, and did not hold up to the rigors of the trail. The twist locks broke, all of them (there are two on each pole), and tended to collapse when too much pressure was put on them. Usually this was when I was trying to save myself from a fall, when I needed them most. The collapse resulted in a new kind of fall, with an unexpected catch and change of direction in it. The metal didn't stand up well to these sudden changes of direction, and the shafts ended up with little bends in them which prevented their collapse when I wanted to store them. I tried using duct tape to reinforce them, but at Trail Days in Damascus I gave up and mailed them home for return.

REI says they guarantee their products for a year from purchase, if you are dissatisfied for any reason. When the clerk at the REI in Albuquerque was presented with my poles he refused to accept them. He said they weren't used for their designed purpose. I am pretty sure that dissatisfied for 'any reason' covered that, and I damaged the trekking poles while trekking, so I think this clerk was just being a jack ass, but the poles ended up in the garbage, and I am still poorer by $80.00, and rather put out by the experience.

I replaced the REI poles with a beefier set of Kelty poles. The Kelty poles lasted until Waynesboro in Virginia, just before Shenandoah National Park. The poles were still in pretty good shape, but there was one odd bend in one so I couldn't collapse it, and I had worn down the tips constantly clackity-clacking along across rocks and other rough surfaces. Rockfish Gap Outfitters in Waynesboro didn't carry Kelty, but the proprietor would try and jury rig new tips for me on my poles and make other repairs (like straightening the bends) for $40.00.

He also had a sale on Leki trekking poles, and I could get a much lighter set of new aluminum poles for $80.00. He sold me particularly on Leki's guarantee; a lifetime warranty on everything except the straps and tips, which are designed to wear out over time. Leki supplies its dealers with parts to quickly effect repairs when needed. I went ahead and bought the Lekis, and the Keltys went into a hiker box.

The Lekis finished the hike with me. They were falling apart and bent as much as the REI and Kelty poles that preceded them by the end of the trail. Just like other popular items, pole parts had been cleaned out by the waves of thru-hikers ahead of me, and I was not able to get repairs on the trail.

I tried once by phone, but was unable to get a mail drop coordinated. When I got home and called, Leki sent me a full set of replacement parts, and I now have a brand new set of poles, with just enough of the old remaining for nostalgia.

12) Sawyer Squeeze water filter, full size

Water purification is a must on the trail. There are a few thru-hikers who scoff at the idea, but the hikers I know who tried going all the way without water treatment eventually got very sick at some point from drinking questionable water. The culprits are various microorganisms.

A lot of animals, wild and domestic, poop in or near the water they are drinking from, and the feces generate things that do not mix well with human digestive systems. Going through the Smokies pure water was gushing right out of mountainsides. In Virginia and farther north the water source was more likely to be a creek or a stream, and the water might have looked clear, but it was not.

There are four ways to treat water. It can be boiled, treated chemically, or filtered. There are also light pens out there that use ultraviolet light to kill the microorganisms.

I preferred filtering, as boiling takes forever; chemical treatments leave a taste and all of the sedimentary muck in the water, as do the UV light pens.

Filters are the most common method in use currently on the Appalachian Trail, and the Sawyer Squeeze filter is the most common filter used by thru-hikers. The Sawyers are simple, lightweight and inexpensive.

I preferred the full sized filter; the Mini is lighter weight and smaller, but it also has a slower flow rate, and I was wasting hiking time when I was sitting next to a water source squeezing out clean water.

The Sawyer comes with squeeze bladders, but the bladders break after a while, and cost about $10.00 to replace. The Sawyer screw threads also fit various types of water bottles and drink bottles, and you can squeeze through those rather than a bladder. Replacement bottles are easily found for a dollar at any convenience store. Many hikers just filled up their water bottles, screwed on the Sawyer, and squeezed water directly from the bottle when they wanted a drink.

Every couple of days the Sawyer filter needs to be flushed out to wash out built up sediment. A Sawyer filter comes with a big syringe for that purpose, but the 700 ml size Smartwater bottle comes with a nozzle top that works well too.

My biggest issue with the Sawyer was the internal gasket in the threaded top. It fell out after long use, and without it my Sawyer became a spray bottle rather than a filter. There is a cheap and easy repair. Garden hose gaskets fit perfectly and can be found for pennies at any hardware store. I ended up carrying a couple as spares after losing my first gasket.

My Sawyer was always screwed onto the top of one of my water bottles sitting on the side of my pack.

(13) 3 water bottles (one 1 liter PowerAde, two 1 liter Lipton ice tea bottles)

I began my thru-hike with a lot more water capacity than I carried at the end. I started with a two and a half liter Platypus bladder along with 2 one liter bottles. The bladder was great when I was strolling down the trail. I sipped water out of the hose as I walked along with no need to stop and get out a bottle. I always had a continuous flow of hydration.

The bladder had some drawbacks. It was a chore to refill it with water. I had to dig it out of my pack, fill it up, and stick it back into my pack against the resistance of all the other items wedged inside. The bladder's lack of rigidity caused problems as it flopped around while I was trying to fill it with water from the filter. My biggest concern was it was hidden in my pack, and I never knew how much water I had unless I stopped and took the bladder out. On a couple of occasions, I hiked past water sources thinking I had more water in my bladder than I thought only to run dry another mile up the trail.

I sprang two bladder leaks during my journey. Both were my fault, not the manufacturer's, as I failed to tighten the hose properly and water seeped out of the joint. On one occasion this was at night in my tent, and I woke up in a puddle of water and a soaked sleeping bag. The other leak was in my pack. Fortunately, I had everything in the pack stored inside separate dry bags.

I finally got tired of working with the bladder while thru-hiking (I still use one on short backpacking trips and day trips). I ended up carrying three bottles full of water instead, each one a drink bottle acquired at a convenience store. I would rotate the bottles out when they got manky. I carried 2 one and a half liter bottles that had threading that fit my water filter. I generally used ice tea bottles or Smartwater bottles. The plastic walls are thin, and could be squeezed to push water through the filter.

I also carried a sturdy, wide mouthed PowerAde or Gatorade bottle, which I used for mixing drinks. I don't really care for either drink. I find them too sweet, but I particularly liked the shape of the PowerAde bottle. I could put powdered coffee and hot chocolate mix in the bottle, shake it vigorously with water, and have cold mochas in the morning,

I could see how much water was in each clear bottle and I could control how much I drank, rationing out my water on drier sections of the hike. The bottles rode in the lower side pockets of my pack. I had to take off my pack or ask for someone to hand one to me in order to have a drink, which was a nuisance.

I learned to drink an entire liter of water every time I stopped at a water source, once or twice a day, and at camp. I forced myself to drink even if I wasn't thirsty, to extend the supply of water I carried. I drank four to eight liters of water a day while hiking, depending on the heat and how long I hiked. I went through another 2-3 liters of water cooking and hydrating myself in camp.

(14) Black Diamond headlamp with 3 spare AAA batteries

A headlamp is a must for thru-hikers. Headlamps allow a hiker to keep their hands free and still direct a beam of light, allowing hiking into the night when needed, setting up camp in darkness, as well as not tripping over things during bathroom trips in the dark. I started with a spare light, a hand crank flashlight that I got rid of early in my hike as impractical additional weight. I had an iPhone that had a small flashlight on it to serve as a backup, and on the few occasions my headlamp failed I was able to make do using the little light on the phone. Most hiking and setting up of camp occurs during daylight hours, and when my light failed I made sure I made camp early enough to get set up in daylight.

The Black Diamond I used is a popular headlamp choice. It is an LED light, the light could be brightened or dimmed, and there is a red light option, so I wasn't blinding others in the camp when I staggered to the bathroom at midnight. It was one of the less expensive models; I think mine was $25.00.

The Black Diamond headlamp had a critical flaw, a tendency to switch itself on as it jostled around inside the pack while hiking. It ran down the batteries, leaving me a few days out from resupply with a dead light source. There was a lock on the switch but it didn't work very well.

The fix is to take a battery out when it is stored. I carried at least one or two spare batteries (it used three). Batteries are heavy and expensive, and no one liked carrying spares. Most of the time I didn't use the lamp for more than an hour or so each day, but if I had to night hike I wore down the batteries pretty quickly and having spares was a necessity.

(15) Paper towel squares (for toilet paper)

The next six items were items in my personal hygiene kit. It was very minimal, but kept me clean enough on the trail. On town stops I took very long showers and was very particular, but on the trail I was a lot less concerned with appearance and odor, I just didn't want to get sick.

I originally carried a partial roll of toilet paper and a pack of baby wipes, along with a poop trowel, to take care of business. The baby wipes are nice, but heavy, and are not biodegradable, even the ones labeled as being so. Instead of carrying a dedicated poop trowel, there was always a stick around or one of my hiking poles to scratch out a cat hole and cover it again.

I switched to paper towels from toilet paper. While not as soft as toilet paper, paper towels did not disintegrate and turn to mush when they got wet. Toilet paper is fragile, and even a little moisture getting into their storage Ziploc ruined it. Instead, I would take 10 or 15 squares of paper towel with me and get the same functionality as the TP. I would fold the sheets up and stick them into a Ziploc. McGyver, who first taught me the trick, would cut down a paper towel roll into 3 TP sized rolls, keep one and put the other two in a hiker box. A dab of water on a sheet helped with the cleaning functions provided by baby wipes, so I was able to do without that heavy package, and be more environmentally friendly.

I carried my pooping supplies in a Ziploc bag on the lower side pocket that only had one water bottle in it.

(16) 3 ounce bottle of hand sanitizer

Hand sanitizer is must have item for thru-hikers. Hikers do some unsanitary things, such as going to the bathroom in the woods. Usually there will be a water source nearby, and you can rinse off your hands, but a dab of hand sanitizer will ensure you will not get sick. I also put dabs of sanitizer on open cuts as a disinfectant. As a bonus, hand sanitizer is an alcohol gel, and a little dab will serve to get a fire started at need,

I used the little travel sized squeeze bottles. There were often larger sized partially used bottles in hiker boxes, and I would just refill my little bottle from those if they were available. If not, I would buy a regular sized one, refill my bottle, and contribute the rest to the hiker box myself.

I carried my sanitizer in the waist belt pocket of my backpack, so it was always right to hand.

(17) 3 ounce travel sized toothpaste

I bought little travel sized toothpaste tubes and replenished them as needed. I brushed my teeth at night before going to bed, and in the morning after breakfast before setting out. It was the single area of my body I could keep minty fresh on the trail.

I carried a small mesh bag with my personal hygiene items for camp in a larger dry bag in the top of my backpack main compartment.

(18) Travel sized toothbrush

I like little folding toothbrushes. My little hygiene bag was too small to put a full length toothbrush in it, and the bigger ones also needed a case. The little travel toothbrushes folded the brush onto the handle. Some people bought full length toothbrushes and cut down the handle to save a couple of grams, but I liked having a handle,

(19) 2.5 ounce Dr. Bronner's ecologically friendly soap

Dr. Bronner's makes a liquid soap from some kind of root extract or herbal something and is environmentally friendly and biodegradable. It is labeled as organic and Fair Trade. Sometimes I just wanted some soap, and Dr. Bronner's let me clean up (or my cookware) and shave in a stream without worrying about the effects I was having downstream.

Dr. Bronners comes in a little squeeze bottle, so you can use a few drops at a time. It is not particularly foamy or even that great at getting out the dirt or removing strong odors, but it was better than nothing, and there certainly is a psychological effect to using soap.

I was warned by a friend that the peppermint and lavender scented versions of Dr. Bronner's soap are very attractive to bears, and these items must be hung in your bear bag at night. There is an unscented version of the soap available if you wish not to smell like a treat to the ursine community.

(20) Disposable razor

Most people don't bother shaving, men or women, while hiking. I think some women use town stops for maintenance, but I also saw a lot of hairy legs out there. Nobody particularly cares; we were all a bit grimy and gamey anyway.

It is very rare for a man to shave on the trail. Letting hair and beards go has a ritualistic quality, like sporting playoffs. I personally couldn't do it. I tried growing a beard but it really bothered me. It might have been all those years of military time shaving, but it just felt really uncomfortable and unclean to me.

I didn't shave every day, but I did shave every couple of days, especially if I knew I was going into town. I thought showing I took care of myself might help me get rides hitchhiking. It probably didn't matter.

I used Dr. Bronner's as my lubricating shave cream; it was made with some sort of oil so it worked pretty well.

CLOTHING:

Clothing includes what I was wearing. When I was wearing my base layer I would have eight articles of clothing, excluding gloves and whatnot, inside my pack. When it got cold I would have a lot less.

(21) 1 pair Skechers Memory Foam trail shoes

Hiking shoes are a highly individual choice. Whatever shoes a thru-hiker starts with will not last the entire Appalachian Trail. A thru-hiker can reasonably expect to go through three to five sets of shoes on the journey.

Many people have shoe and boot problems the first weeks of thru-hiking. Feet change and swell as they have the hell beat out of them day after day on the trail. Thru-hikers experiment with types of shoes until they find something that works for them. Some hikers never find that perfect shoe, and fight with blisters and foot pain all the way to Maine. I saw some very elaborate morning foot preparation rituals as people prepared their feet for the ordeal of the day.

I used four different pairs of shoes completing the hike. I used low cut shoes the entire hike to reduce weight and to give me more freedom of movement, taking the occasional rolled ankle as the cost of greater maneuverability.

I started out with a pair of Merrill trail shoes; they felt comfortable in the store and on practice hikes. The Merrills fit tighter on the trail as my feet swelled, and I developed small, permanent blisters and lost the feeling in my small toes. I still went nearly 800 miles in this first pair, until the soles began to part company with the uppers.

I was worried about the rocks of Pennsylvania, and bought a wider and much sturdier shoe approaching the state, a pair of extra wide Keens. I switched away from the extra cost of Gore-Tex shoes since there really wasn't any way to keep shoes from periodic total immersions, defeating the waterproofing. Gore-Tex takes longer to dry out once it gets soaked,

The Keens were sturdy enough to protect my feet from banging into rocks, and proved quite durable. I went another 800 miles in them. They were still intact when I swapped them out. They were a heavy shoe, and the extra width meant the fit was a little sloppy, and caused its own kind of blistering.

I went off-trail for my sister's wedding, and I used the break as a shopping opportunity. I found a pair of Skechers trail shoes in a discount shop. They were the flimsiest shoes I tried, they were a lot more like sneakers than trail shoes, but they came in a wide fit, and they had a memory foam sole insert that was very comfortable. They were also only $60.00, half to a third of the cost of my other shoes. I threw away the

Keens, which were still serviceable but very, very smelly, and tried the cheaper shoes.

I absolutely loved the Skechers. They were light, comfortable, and had enough grip in the soles for most of the surfaces I crossed. They only lasted about 300 miles, but they were also sold on Amazon and I was able to have a replacement pair sent to a mail drop in Monson for the last 300 miles of trail. I still wear Skechers for backpacking today.

(22) 1 pair full length hiking pants, with web belt.

I was advised to hike in shorts during my gear shakedown at the outfitters in Neel's Gap a few days into the trail. I discarded the long hiker pants I was wearing at the time. I also discarded underwear (they were making me rashy). I didn't like the change; I felt more comfortable wearing long pants. They were a little warmer, and provided protection against sunburn, poison ivy, sticker bushes, and insects. Even through the summer I continued to wear long pants. Most hikers did go with shorts, and had the scratches and bug bites to prove it.

I went through three pairs of hiking pants during my time on the Appalachian Trail. My pants were designed for hiking. I could zip the bottoms off if I actually wanted shorts, and the material dried quickly, was lightweight, and still provided protection. I had a cheap, web belt, but even using it my shrinking waistline required adjustments and I had to buy trousers with smaller waistlines as I moved north.

(23) 2 ultralight wicking Outdoor Research t-shirts

Cotton is not the best material for hiking. It loses its insulating qualities when it is wet and dries slowly. My t-shirts were synthetic. My starters were Adidas products, and weighed 7 ounces, which is lightweight, but I found an Outdoor Research hiking t-shirt in an outfitter in Damascus that only weighed 2.6 ounces, and I replaced both shirts, saving me almost three quarters of a pound. The OR shirts were expensive at $40.00 apiece.

The two new shirts made it all the way to the end, without any issues. One was blaze orange, and I wore it for hiking; I thought the blaze orange might help keep me from being targeted by overzealous hunters. It is stained beyond recovery. The neon green shirt I wore in town is still a part of my wardrobe.

(24) 3 pairs Darn Tough socks

Socks, like shoes, are a very individualized choice. Cotton is not a good material for socks for the same reasons it is poor for t-shirts; it gets wet, stays wet, and loses its insulating qualities when it is wet. Most thru-hikers wear some kind of Smartwool variant. Some also wear a silk sock liner to try and reduce friction and prevent blisters. I just wore a single pair of socks.

I wore holes in one of my pairs of Smartwool socks. I replaced them at Harpers Ferry with a pair of Darn Tough socks, made from a Smartwool blend. Smartwool is some sort of Merino wool blend, and is expensive, between $20.00 and $30.00 a pair. Smartwool socks breathe nicely, dry quickly, and help warm your feet in the cold without being overly sweaty and nasty in the heat.

Darn Tough has a lifetime guarantee on their product and will replace any damaged socks. I liked the warranty, and I liked the ATC logo they had on the socks (They have many designs). I ended up replacing all three pairs of my socks with the Darn Tough brand. I found them very comfortable.

I ended up testing the warranty. I burned a hole in a sock trying to dry it by a fire. I didn't expect them to replace it, but I mailed it home just in case, and when I had leisure I sent in the sock with the downloaded warranty form, dutifully writing 'burnt by campfire' as the damage cause. I had a new pair of socks in a week.

I carried three pairs of socks. One was to wear, one to change into if a pair became too wet or disgusting, and a third emergency pair. I only needed the third pair once. Socks can serve as emergency mittens, as an oven mitt, or even as little bags at need.

(25) 1 Smartwool long sleeve pullover

My intermediate cool weather layer was another Smartwool product. It was a thin, long sleeved garment and did a good job of taking the edge off of cooler weather. It was only 8 ounces, and was my favorite REI product on the hike.

(26) 1 Adidas runner's pullover

As it turned from summer into fall up in Maine, ice and snow appeared up on the higher elevations, and I added another pullover layer for the cold. Runners use a lot of products suitable for hiking, and these items are often cheaper than the hiking specific ones. My Adidas pullover was an extra pound, and I didn't carry it through the summer. I realized I needed another layer when the temperature consistently stayed below 40 degrees, I don't like being cold.

The pullover was bright red, to let hunters know I was not a game animal. I would have bought blaze orange, but I couldn't find a good, lightweight, quick drying pullover in that color.

(27) 1 Mountain Hardware ultralight raincoat with hood

My raincoat was my most versatile item of clothing. It was my only waterproof garment. In the spring rains I learned that I was going to be wet, regardless, as the raincoat trapped sweat inside. It did keep the colder rain out. It also was a good warming layer. The hood was important both in keeping rain off of my face and in trapping body heat.

I used it as a waterproof cover over my pack when I was in camp. When it was really cold I would zip it up and slip my feet and legs into it when I slept, and it would help keep my lower body warm. During the bug seasons and at night, when the bugs were at their worst, I would put on the raincoat to cover my arms and head, and wear a bug net over the top to protect my face. It meant I was hotter, but I personally preferred heat to bugs.

(28) 1 Marmot down coat with hood

I called this turquoise blue coat my 'puffy coat'. Every thru-hiker had something similar. The good ones cost $200.00 and more, but it is money well spent. I think the hood is an important element, keeping your head warm and your ears from being frostbitten are key to comfort.

Because my puffy coat was insulated with a down stuffing, I couldn't get it wet, and I usually wore it beneath my raincoat. I only wore my puffy coat in camp. I protected it while I was hiking, and it was in a dry bag as a pillow when I slept, unless it was extremely cold.

(29) 1 pair of lightweight running shorts

I had a pair of shorts as backup pants and for town wear. I needed a second pair of pants.

I bought mine at Wal-Mart for six dollars. They were some kind of nylon and weighed 6 ounces.

(30) 1 balaclava

A balaclava is a head garment similar to a ski mask. It covers the head and neck and leaves an opening for the nose and eyes. It can be rolled up over your face to be just a warm cap. Mine was something I had from my days in the Army, and I wore it a lot in cold weather.

(31) 1 pair wool fingerless gloves

I started the trail with a good pair of Smartwool gloves. They were an REI product designed for runners, and cost around $60.00. The REI gloves were great, and had some kind of finger pad built in so I could operate my smartphone without taking them off. They were not really warm, but they kept the wind chill off of my hands, and were nimble enough so I didn't have to take them off every time I had a task that requited dexterity.

I bought a warmer pair of fleece gloves when I got into wintry weather in the Smokeys. They were great gloves, warm without being bulky. They were grey, and not especially noticeable; I took them off at a break and left them on a rock somewhere in Maine. They may still be there, blended in with the landscape.

I replaced them with a thicker pair of fingerless wool gloves. The woolen gloves were a beige color, bright enough to notice lying on the ground. I found out on a river ford that they floated as well. My fingertips still became very cold and numb in these gloves, especially when I was working around camp.

(32) 1 pair blaze orange fleece gloves

I bought my fleece gloves in a hardware store in Maine. There was not a lot of selection. I wanted to keep my fingertips warm. I went with blaze orange to help make hunters aware I was not edible, and I really only had two color choices, orange or camouflage green. The fleece gloves helped keep my hands warm, but I was still chilled in really cold weather. I had to take them off anytime I needed to use my fingers for finicky work.

(33) 1 Green bandana with chili peppers on it

I used my bandana as a washcloth, and usually wore it rolled up around my neck. When the bugs came out I sprayed it with different repellents and oils to try and keep the bugs away from my face and neck without having to actually apply chemical things to my skin. Sweat would clear away any bug repellent on my skin in 15 minutes anyway.

The bandana ended up with a lot of uses, but was primarily a sentimental item. My daughter gave it to me as a reminder of home. Green chili peppers are a symbol of New Mexico, and when I looked at it I thought of her.

(34) 1 Lightload towel

The Lightload towel was a super absorbent rectangle that was like an incredibly resilient paper towel. It was small, only 12 by 24 inches, and it weighed less than an ounce, but it sucked up water like nobody's business. It was easy to wring the soaked up water out, so I could wipe until it was full, wring it out, and start sucking up water again. I primarily used it to wipe off my rain fly before packing it in the morning. The rain fly would still be damp afterwards, but it wouldn't be soaked, and water is weight. A rain fly that is a little damp is better than a wet one in the bag. It will not get everything else wet.

I could use the towel to strip water off of my body after a dip in a stream. It lacked the comfort and softness of a cloth towel. I would tie the towel to one of the loops on the back of my pack so it would dry out during the day.

I had a micro fleece towel in my pack initially, but got rid of it early. It was nearly a pound of weight, more when wet, and didn't dry as quickly. I received my first Lightload towel in Damascus as a give away item at Trail Days. The towels didn't last forever; I used two or three during the rest of my hike. They only cost a couple of dollars, and were available at most outfitters.

(35) 1 pair of Crocs

Camp shoes are not an absolute necessity for a thru-hiker, but they are a nice transition to change into in camp. I had a bright neon green pair of Crocs. Everything I could get in a bright color I did. All the wonderful earth toned sporting items blended right into the ground making them difficult to locate in the dark, and possibly overlooked and forgotten when packing up camp.

The crocs weighed less than a pound, even the big size 11s that fit my feet. They were just about indestructible, and mine lasted the entire trip. They provided an emergency set of footwear if something catastrophic had happened to my regular hiking shoes. High Life hiked for a week in a pair when his boots blew out.

My Crocs also became my river fording shoes. I attempted to keep my feet drier by switching into the Crocs at fords where I knew I was going into the water. They were rugged enough to protect my feet as they banged into the rocks beneath the surface of the water, and I had dry shoes and socks to change back into after I crossed.

My Crocs hung from a carabiner on the outside of my pack.

ELECTRONICS:

(36) Samsung Galaxy Tab 4 tablet in a Survivor case

My tablet would be a luxury item for most backpackers, but I considered it a necessity. I knew I wanted to take daily notes on the trip for this book. I am also a reader; I read myself to bed each night, and I needed books. I was not the only reading hiker, there were a number of Kindles and tablets on the trail.

Prior to the hike I went down to my local Best Buy looking at options. I have a Kindle (or two) at home, but I was looking for something with a little more function as a computer. I didn't want to spend more than $200.00. The Samsung Galaxy Tab 4 was a model that was being superseded by the next best thing, so I picked it up with a waterproof, shock absorbing Survivor case, on sale, within my target price range.

The office and word processing programs it came with were kind of awkward, but were serviceable for taking notes. At hostels I could get on the internet with it and do business. I could download books onto it and make other purchases from Amazon.

Tablet, case, and charging cord were over a pound of extra weight. I stored it in a Ziploc bag inside a dry bag with my other electronic items inside the main compartment of my pack. I only used it in camp.

(37) iPhone 5s in a LifeProof case

A smartphone is a highly recommended hiking item. Besides providing a way to talk to home, post pictures on Facebook, play music, and serve all of the other functions of being connected in the modern world it is your safety line. If something happens to you, or if you come across an emergency, there is a way to call for help.

The trail guides, like AWOL, are downloadable, and if you don't mind looking at a small screen you can dispense with the hard copy of a guidebook. A trail guide and a smartphone weigh about the same, so you are trading weights.

There is a downloadable application called Guthook that has trail maps and the most up to date information on sites along the Appalachian Trail, including recent pictures. It synchs in on GPS so you can accurately tell where you are on the trail when you have signal. The program is a little pricey, $70.00 dollars for the entire trail, but it can be a great resource. It is better to download it before getting on the trail, I tried to pick it up on trail but couldn't get a complete download due to poor signal, and I was having other phone issues that complicated it.

Cell phone signal is dicey on most of the trail. You are traveling through rural areas. If you have a carrier that is focused on urban areas, you may not get much connectivity. I had Verizon, and I thought I had better service than hikers using other carriers.

I had three different phones during the hike due to the failure of the OtterBox protective case I had on my first iPhone. The OtterBox was supposed to be weatherproof and shockproof, but in the continual wet conditions I was in, water slowly seeped inside the box and got into the phone. I was caught in a downpour with my phone out, and the phone shut off. I tried emergency measures to get it going again, but the water seeping inside the case over time had corroded the inner workings of the phone

I sent the phone home to a trusted repair shop to see what they could salvage, and while I waited for results I bought a cheap monthly rate burner phone from a Kroger supermarket. It was supposed to be a smartphone, but I thought of it as a phone of lower intelligence. It had all the basic functions, and cost less than $100.00 to purchase the phone and cover the first month's fees.

My burner phone was kind of lame. The photo resolution was weak, it was tough getting signal, and internet access was really slow. It didn't have the moxie to run complex downloaded applications and programs but it still served the basic functions I needed from it.

When word came from home that they could rescue my photos and such from my old iPhone, but it would never work again, I bit the bullet and bought a new one. After OtterBox failed me, I got different case, a LifeProof. It cost more, but came with its own phone insurance policy. It protected my phone for the rest of the trip, including a couple of total immersions in ponds and fords. Ultimately, after I was long done with the trail, the case developed a crack. LifeProof sent me a new case after a short phone call.

I carried my iPhone on a Ziploc sandwich bag in my waist belt pocket, always accessible; I took a lot of amazing photos on the trail.

(38) Ear buds

I occasionally listened to music on the trail. I rarely used the ear buds, but they also served as earplugs when there was a loud snorer in a shelter or hostel bunkroom.

(39) Charging cords for each device

My Samsung and iPhone used different power cords. I carried them, and my ear buds in another Ziploc bag, inside my electronics dry bag,

(40) Portable Power Supply, 4 charges

My sister gave me a solar panel that mounted to the top of a backpack as a Christmas gift to keep me powered up in the woods. It, with its attachments and such, weighed a pound.

I didn't use it during the first four days in Georgia, and when I did my shakedown at Neel's Gap it was one of the first things set aside. There were no leaves on the trees yet, but I was told that as soon as the canopy came in I would be under it most of time, and a solar panel wouldn't be effective. I sent it home.

Keeping my phone and tablet charged proved to be a challenge. Power would last two or three days before the low battery light started flashing. I either put my phone in airplane mode or powered it down when I didn't need it.

I used my phone to contact home, check the weather, look at emails, and take pictures. I didn't use it very often for music or any of its other functions to conserve the battery life. I tried to keep enough of a charge on the phone to let me make calls for reservations and other arrangements as I was approaching a town.

I also had to be conservative using my tablet. I would read books on it at night, but once the power dropped below about a third of its battery I would reserve it for its primary purpose, taking notes.

I still ran out of juice regularly. I ended up buying a cheap portable power supply at a Pilot truck stop for $20.00. It provided a single full recharge for my phone, and it had a LED flashlight built into it as well. I was able to use my phone more, and would start conservation measures once I had used the initial charge from the power supply. I was able to use more of my phone's functions, even listening to music once in a while as I hiked.

The cheap truck stop portable power supply didn't survive long. It lasted a couple of months and then quit on me. I stepped up my game, and bought a 4 charge portable power supply at a Verizon store. It was a lot more expensive, costing me $100.00, but it was very much worth it. It weighed about the same as the first one, around 6 ounces, but carrying 4 charges meant I never ran out of juice on the trail for either my phone or my tablet. As I moved north and nights got longer this was an enormous benefit.

I carried my power supply in its own Ziploc bag in the electronics dry bag. I was very careful with it in wet weather. It was not waterproof, and I believe the repeated exposures to damp helped kill the first, cheaper model I bought at the truck stop.

STORAGE

These items were what I used to carry, organize and protect my belongings.

(41) 3 large dry bags (one for food, one for my sleeping system, one for my clothes)

I bought cheap dry bags online before I set out on the trail. They all gave out on me and I spent a lot more money ($20.00-$40.00 each) on quality replacement bags at outfitters along the way. I ended up with a variety of different brands. There are different sorts of dry bags, and I picked up the lightweight versions made for backpacking. There are heavier, more durable versions made for kayaking and other water sports, but I did not think they were worth the extra weight. The ones I purchased while on the trail all worked well.

The most expensive and most durable bag was my Sea to Summit food bag. I was hanging it and 10-14 pounds of food, cooking gear, and personal hygiene items from a tree branch most nights to get those items away from bears, so it took a lot of abuse. I still have the same bag now in my current backpack.

(42) 1 medium dry bag (electronics and paper items)

This bag started out cheap, and was soon replaced with the best bag I could find. The value of the items inside represented a considerable monetary investment, and irreplaceable notes and photographs. They were items worth protecting with a quality product.

(43) 2 small dry bags (one first aid and other small items, one for phone)

I went through a lot of small bags. It was not because the small bags were defective but because I would empty one, put a rock in it, and use it as the weight to throw my bear line over tree branches in camp. This was very abusive, and the buckles and straps did not withstand the torture well, until I bought the toughest little dry bags I could find.

(44) 6-8 Gallon Ziploc bags

I used gallon Ziploc bags for a variety of purposes. I had each day's worth of food separated into a bag, and kept other items I particularly wanted to protect in a Ziploc. I replaced Ziplocs every other town stop or so. I would buy a box of the best quality bags, change out all of my bags, and leave the rest of the box in a hiker box.

(45) 6-8 sandwich sized Ziploc bags

Sandwich bags protected my smaller items, and I would use them to break down bulk food items in to daily portions. Like the gallon bags, I changed them out regularly and used better quality products. It was worth a little extra cash to protect my belongings.

MISCELLANEOUS

(46) AWOL AT Guide

There are several guides to hiking the Appalachian Trail. The two most common are the ATC Thru-Hikers Companion, and David "AWOL" Miller's AT Guide. I looked at both, and found I preferred the AWOL guide. I liked how it was laid out a little better; I thought information was more accessible in AWOL's format. The difference between the two is not that great. The Thru-Hikers Companion is the official' guide put out by the Appalachian Trail Conservancy, and your purchase helps to support the trail (AWOL also makes a contribution for each book sold).

I debated which one I should bring, finally weighed the two guides and found the AWOL Guide was an ounce lighter, and went with it.

You can also purchase a download of the AWOL Guide to put on your smartphone, to get rid of the weight altogether. I am a bit myopic, and I preferred larger print in a hard copy.

I kept the AWOL guide in a separate gallon Ziploc bag in my electronics dry bag,

(47) Several pieces of paper and a pen

I carried a couple of pieces of paper and a pen or two. I sometimes left a pen at registers that had lost theirs, and I could leave notes on the trail at need; 'Watch out, rattlesnake 20 feet ahead!' I kept them with my AWOL guide in its gallon Ziploc bag.

(48) First Aid kit:

My first aid kit was minimal. I had a couple of band aids, a two ounce tube of Neosporin, a piece of moleskin, and small medic's scissors. It had been larger to start with, but I just didn't use any of it. I picked up any number of contusions and scrapes, but never had any large open wounds. I had duct tape if I needed it for cuts and blister covering wrap. The tiny pair of plastic handled medic scissors got a lot of use.

I used a sandwich sized Ziploc bag to keep some pills on hand. Mostly this was aspirin, but I also carried a few tablets each of Benadryl, Imodium and Tylenol PM. I carried a pair of foam ear plugs in my kit as well; I considered blocking out powerful snores while sleeping in a shelter a health issue.

My first aid kit went into a Ziploc in a small dry bag that also included my repair kit and my bear line. I usually used this bag as my bear line toss weight.

(49) Fix-it kit

My fix it bag was very small. I had a small sewing kit consisting of a couple of types of thread wrapped around a piece of cardboard with two needles stuck in the cardboard. I had a couple of extra pack buckles, and garden hose gaskets for my water filter. The sewing needles got most of their use popping blisters.

Duct tape is versatile; I used it for first aid and repairs, including patching holes on my tent and my hammock bug net. Carrying a whole roll is overkill, and most hikers just peel off a couple of long strips and wrap them around the handles of their hiking poles. My tape took a beating there, and needed to be stripped off and replenished several times during the hike. I used pink tape, as an identifying mark.

(50) 30 foot paracord bear line with carabiner attached

Thru-hikers need a bear line to hang their food at night. Paracord is very strong and lightweight. I started the trail with a 50 foot cord that I cut down to about 30 feet. The extra wasn't needed, and I had occasion to use the cord for repairs and other tasks, so it naturally shrank to that length over time.

There are always uses for a piece of paracord. In a camp with an established bear box or hang system the cord became a clothesline. I had a very light carabiner tied on to clip my food bag into. It was a duplicate, I also had a carabiner I used to hold my camp shoes on the back of my pack that I could have used, but I didn't like tying and untying it every night, sometimes in dim light. My farsightedness could make this a chore, and the weight of the extra carabiner was a single ounce.

(51) Bug defense

In the heat I carried various things for bugs, including essential oils and DEET, and a head net. I mixed all the different oils together; citronella, lemongrass, tea tree oil, and commercial product, in a 3 ounce bottle. I was hoping for a combined effect after the different things failed individually. Only the head net actually worked. I sweated off the repellent quickly, and bugs are almost as annoying buzzing in clouds around you as they are when they are actually landing and biting. I still slathered the stuff on, if only for psychological effect.

I carried my insect repellent and bug net in one of the two pouches on my waist belt during the bug season. When it cooled off I stuck it in my pack.

(52) A pair of reading glasses in a cardboard case

Yep, I don't see well. I didn't wear them often, but sometimes I needed to see little things up close. My glasses went into a sandwich Ziploc in my clothing bag, to buffer them from falls and knocks.

(53) A Hohner harmonica

I gave away my guitar, which I seldom had time to play, and picked up a harmonica instead. I also seldom played it, but psychologically I wanted to have a musical instrument. It also went in a waist belt pouch. I played the blues a few times when I was alone on mountaintops.

It was definitely an unneeded luxury item.

(54) 1 pair of overshoe ice spikes

I picked up the micro spikes during my last couple of weeks on the trail, when ice and snow became common at the higher elevations. I only donned them a couple of times when I was hiking over icy granite slabs. They worked well.

The ice spikes were inexpensive, I paid less than $20.00 for them in a hardware store in Maine, but they weighed nearly a pound. Even though I didn't wear them much I considered them a necessary safety item.

That is everything I brought home from the Appalachian Trail. I survived for seven months of backpacking with these items, and the combined weight of what was actually in my pack was right around 22 pounds. Food and water weight varied, but I was usually around 35 pounds fully loaded on my way out from a resupply. When I came into town I was carrying considerably less than 30 pounds on my back.

LOADING THE PACK

When I loaded my pack, my sleep system and hammock went in the bottom. I wanted the heaviest item, my food bag, in the center to balance my load. Remaining large items were stuffed in atop the food bag in the main pack compartment.

Various small items I wanted access to while I was hiking went into my waist pouches and my pockets. My raincoat was rolled up and strapped on top of the outside of my pack. The rest of my smaller items of snivel gear like my gloves and balaclava were in the top pouch of my pack, along with my hygiene kit. Water bottles, one with the filter attached, went into the backpack's side pockets.

10 LESSONS LEARNED

BE YOUR OWN BEST FRIEND

The trail is a physical and emotional challenge. It will beat you down day after day if you let it. Each day can also become a victory, another success to celebrate in your mind, another affirmation of your personal ability.

I was a solo hiker most of the time I was on the Appalachian Trail. I spent many of my days hiking and my nights camping either alone or with strangers. I had to stand outside myself sometimes and have an inner monologue (Sometimes, not so inner, I talked to myself aloud like a crazy man) reminding myself why I was out there, being encouraging, and realizing I was a good person doing a great thing.

A thru-hiker is doing something admirable, and you can be positive about yourself. Like yourself even. At the very least you have to believe in yourself, or you are not going to make it. Think 'I can' instead of 'I can't' and you are already halfway to success. You have every reason to admire, and respect yourself as a person.

The trail provides continuous moments of wonder and beauty to balance the struggles. Some you know are coming, celebrated views and locations, but many will appear unexpectedly. Each event is a time to celebrate the trail, and yourself.

While you are on the Appalachian Trail you are as free to control your destiny as you will ever be in your life. No one will tell you to go out in the rain, or climb the next hill, or keep going, or quit. You shed most belongings, and you have little in the way of obligations; I consider good stewardship of the trail and the wilderness a responsibility, but beyond that, you only take care of yourself, and such companions as you choose along the way. Use your freedom, explore yourself, and love yourself.

There is a book called Appalachian Trials (not trails) focused on psychological preparation for a thru-hike. It is thought provoking, and makes a number of good points. I highly recommend it as pre-journey reading,

THE KISS PRINCIPLE

KISS means Keep It Simple Stupid. Your basic tasks are walk and camp. Everything else on the trail is extraneous clutter. Everything you plan or do should be basic and robust. Murphy is working hard out on the trail, so anything that can go wrong, will go wrong. Stay focused, walk, camp, and take in the world.

PACK LIGHT

You are on a hiking trip, not a camp out. You won't need nearly as much stuff as you think you need. You will feel every additional pound of weight as you hike.

There are all kinds of elaborate gadgets made for camping and hiking. Leave them at home. You will not have time to cook elaborate meals or develop new hobbies on the trail either. It is extra stuff you have to carry that you likely will never use. The simplest, lightest, and least expensive solutions to your basic needs are what you need, nothing more.

Pay attention to ounces, and the pounds will take care of themselves.

LISTEN TO EXPERIENCED THRU-HIKERS

No two thru-hikers will entirely agree on anything. That being said, they completed the hike, and know in their bones what you may have only read about. Listen, learn, and take the benefit of experience. Do it right and one day you will be the one telling tales.

YOU DON'T NEED FIRE

Everyone's picture of camp life includes sitting around a fire. In reality fire is more or less a waste of time, Building and maintaining a fire is a chore without a practical use while thru-hiking, besides providing a social focal point. If it is raining you are not going to get dry, you live in the woods now. Unless you plan to keep a fire watch through the night wild animals will only stay away until the fire goes out. Animals are not stupid; they don't usually approach camping areas on the prowl until people are asleep. You have a headlamp to see in the dark with, and thru-hikers don't stay up much past sundown anyway. They need rest.

You have a camp stove for cooking, and it is far more efficient than a fire. It also will not blacken your pots and throw up embers to burn holes in your clothing. You can even hike without cooked foods altogether, and save the weight of a cook set and the time for cooking,

The Forest and Park services are not big fans of campfires. Too many of them are not put out completely, and pose a great risk for starting forest fires. If you must have a fire they want you to use established fire rings to contain the flames. These are not uncommon along the way.

My attitude towards campfires is a personal bias. If you like fires and are willing to do the work, and are safe, by all means have a fire. Just remember, you don't *need* one.

TAKE CARE OF YOUR FEET

Your feet are about to take an enormous amount of daily abuse. Make a daily ritual of foot care. Inspect them, keep them clean, and tend to your blisters. Get good socks, sock liners, foot powder, moleskin, and bandages, whatever works for your feet.

You will spend all day pounding on your feet in the same pair of shoes, so make sure they are the most comfortable trail shoes you can find. Wear them before starting the trail. If they are at all uncomfortable after starting, do not hesitate to change them out. This is an area where cutting costs will come back and cripple you, literally.

DO NOT DIET

If you are on the trail to lose weight, do not try to short change yourself on food to promote weight loss. You are going to lose a lot of weight regardless. Not eating enough will cause you to run out of energy and stall on the hike. In colder weather not having enough calories can make you weaker faster, and make you susceptible to hypothermia,

Keep fueling the furnace.

This is not to say you should not be conscious of the food you are eating, You will want to eat lots of protein, and should pay attention to make sure you are eating the kinds of foods that will help sustain muscle mass.

Pay attention to how much protein is in your food and make a point of getting foods high in protein. Long term, your body will eat muscle mass to provide for itself. You want 60-90 grams (and aim high) a day.

TAKE A BREAK

The concern with miles will make you want to push past the wonders. There are many little side trails along the way, blue blazes that lead to little scenic viewpoints, waterfalls, swimming holes, and historical sites. They are worth visiting. You will probably only be able to hike the Appalachian Trail one time, and hiking the whole trail without really seeing any of it is a possibility if you get to focused on making forward progress.

Take days off periodically. Your body needs the rest more than you need one more day of miles. Some of the best days on the trail will actually happen off the trail, where you spend a day in town relaxing and socializing with other hikers.

Some people can do twenty miles a day, every day. Most people's bodies just can't sustain that kind of pounding day after day. If you are older, or just not in tiptop shape getting on the trail, you are just not going to be able to keep up with a young athlete's pace. Hikers who try are inviting trouble.

I am in no way a medical professional, so what I am writing about here is based on personal experience, observation and internet research. That doesn't make it any less valid. Most thru-hikers are not experienced endurance athletes. One thing any book or article on the subject of endurance sports such as running and cycling will offer as advice is to start slowly.

Mentally we want to push ourselves. The mind has power over the body, and you can in fact push it faster and further than it wants to go, in the short run. This is great for a race or a single day or weekend's effort. The Appalachian Trail is on a different scale. You are going to be pushing yourself day after day, week after week, month after month, and if you don't pace yourself, and take periodic down times for recovery, you will break down.

Your body will eventually fail you. A tired, worn out body is prone to injury. Without recovery time even small injuries can take a long time to heal. They are more likely to get worse rather than better. Repetitive use injuries are common on the trail, and it is very hard to recover from a repetitive use injury on the trail once you have developed one. Rest is generally the only way to heal, and it will be more than a day. Trying to push it will make it worse.

It sucks watching all your friends hike away from you as you sit idling in a motel waiting to heal. The urge is that as soon as you feel some recovery you get right back on the trail, and since you have fallen a little behind, you now have to make up the time to catch up. On day one this seems feasible, but soon enough the muscles that were injured are stressed again and the pain returns. It may even be worse.

You have to read your body. When your body is aching and sore take a break. Pain is a warning system telling you something is wrong. There is the normal lactic acid build up muscular ache, which you will feel a lot of, especially at first, and then there is the pain that comes from damaging yourself. You should be able to tell the difference.

A thru-hiker has to keep going for months, and damage is going to get worse, not better, if you don't take care of it.

I know I am beating a dead horse on this topic. I watched a number of hikers fall into the cycle of trying to push themselves through injuries. None of them completed the trail. Take the rest you need, force yourself if you have to. Exert the same will you have to push yourself to hike with the injury to show the discipline needed to prevent the injuries in the first place.

START EARLY

I started my hike on the 6th of April. Baxter State Park, at the end of the trail, closes for overnight camping on the 15th of October. I counted forward 6 months to the 6th of October, and thought I would make it easily. I was wrong.

I finished my hike on the 7th of November, a full seven months after I began. I had to flip-flop the end of my hike. As a result I experienced some bitterly cold days and nights, I was in the forest at the beginning of hunting season, and spent my last 3-4 weeks on trail almost entirely alone. I finished alone, and rather than having a celebration with fellow hikers, I was just at an end.

One of the biggest regrets of my hike was that I did not start earlier, so as to finish when others were finishing. If I had started in mid March, even at my pace, I would have finished with plenty of time. I would have been able to take more zeros, and more to the point, I would have enjoyed myself far more without the constant driven worry of making enough miles always hovering over my head. An extra 3 weeks of hiking time at the front end would have set me up for a comfortable finish.

I lost a lot of days at the end of my hike traveling forward and back for my flip-flop. I also took a lot of extra zeros because the weather was so bad in Maine in the fall. In total, I added a couple of weeks of extra days that I did not hike, all of which could have been avoided with an earlier start.

Starting early means more than showing up on the trail in March. Each day has a finite amount of daylight to get down the trail, and you should use all of it. I was hard on myself mentally for not getting out of camp until 8:00 AM most mornings. The majority of thru-hikers are moving earlier, getting miles. Getting out of camp at 10:00 AM would have been unthinkable.

Getting up and getting going in the morning was a trial to me. I wanted to rest, my body wanted to recover, and it was especially difficult after nights where I hadn't gotten a good night of sleep. Peering out of my shelter and seeing rain or snow falling out of the sky also made for a slow rising. I really just wanted to sleep until the bad weather passed. Since at times it lasted for days, or weeks, this was not an option.

I got up and hiked.

KEEP IT CLEAN

You are going to be living in dirt, exercising hard all day, and will have no hot shower or closet full of clothes to refresh yourself at night.

A hiker can still take basic steps to keep themselves clean. It may not keep the funk away entirely, but at some point dirt is going to become a health hazard. Brush your teeth each day, wipe yourself off with a cloth, especially those areas that get stinkiest, use hand sanitizer, and jump into a creek or pond once a day when the opportunity presents itself. Have something to wear at night so you can rinse out hiking clothes and hang them out to dry while you sleep. These are basic acts that will keep you healthier, and make you a little more bearable as company to others. It will make you more comfortable, and help keep down infections and rashes.

Most hikers give up on haircuts and shaving. It is a form of freedom, and shaving is a needless chore. Cleaning the hair and beard are still a necessity. I continued to shave and kept my hair short as a convenience, I didn't want to take care of long hair and a beard. I found them a distraction and rather uncomfortable. I was very much a minority in this practice.

Some through hikers revel in their filth. They take pride in their stench, and retain it when they enter civilization as part of their identity. They take a perverse joy in inflicting their reeking selves on others. It does not take many exposures to stinky thru-hikers for townspeople to view all thru-hikers with distaste.

Body funk is not the smell of freedom.

TRAIL TRADITIONS

There are a number of trail traditions that are passed forward from year to year by each succeeding generation of thru-hikers. Some of these traditions are parts of trail books, some of them are passed on by word of mouth. There are always people who have already completed thru-hikes on the trail, passing on the wisdom and traditions of the trail to the latest group of hopefuls.

I missed a few traditions. As a solo hiker I was a little less plugged into the community, and I found out about the traditions after the fact. I also passed on one or two because they didn't suit me. I made a list of the traditions I know about. It is not comprehensive, what a thru-hiker might consider a tradition is as varied as thru-hikers themselves.

Pack Weigh In at Amicalola Falls State Park

I missed Amicalola Falls State Park in Georgia. It isn't actually on the Appalachian Trail. It is seven miles from the official start point for NoBos on the Approach Trail. There is a lodge with a bunkroom, and a scale. Since so many thru-hikers start their journeys here, there is a festive atmosphere, as thru-hikers meet each other and their friends and families see them off.

Hikers weigh their packs at the start point to see just how much weight they are lugging up Springer Mountain. The weight becomes a reference point, and most backpacks get a lot lighter as a thru-hiker progresses north.

Picture on Springer Mountain

Most hikers get a picture of themselves at the plaque marking the start point on Springer Mountain, and make an entry in the register. Many of the entries are long, philosophical dissertations. When I was at Springer there was a line of fifteen people waiting to take their summit picture, and then to make the register entry. I was too eager to get going, and I took the photo but did not take the time to make the register entry.

Shakedown at Neel's Gap

Mountain Crossings outfitters at Neel's Gap is the first resupply point on the Appalachian Trail for NoBos. Thru-hikers have now had a few days of hauling their overloaded packs up and down mountains and are ready to lighten their loads. Mountain Crossings hires experienced thru-hikers to go through hikers' backpacks, item by item, making recommendations on what can be sent home. There are a lot of gear exchanges for better, lighter versions. Mountain Crossings makes a lot of sales, and thru-hikers leave with smaller burdens.

Many thru-hikers have also discovered their footgear is not appropriate at this point, and try something new. There is a tree outside the outfitter with hundreds of pairs of discarded footwear hanging in the branches.

The Damascathon

The distance from Iron Mountain Shelter to the trail town of Damascus in Virginia is 26.2 miles, the distance of a marathon. The trail is gentle at this point, and thru-hikers have started building their trail legs. Thru-hikers will attempt to hike into Damascus from Iron Mountain in a single day.

Trail Days at Damascus

There are a number of towns along the trail that have weekend celebrations to lure in thru-hikers. The largest of these is Trail Days in Damascus, Virginia. Just about every AT thru-hiker will find their way to the town for the four day event. It is also a popular reunion event for past generations of hikers, and the little town is packed with people.

Every hostel and bed and breakfast is full, and most celebrants camp in the town's playing fields and nearby woods. At night there are bonfires and drum circles. Law enforcement is present but are discreet and tolerant, they provide for safety.

There are huge lines everywhere to eat and shop. Gear manufacturers show up and set up display tents. Some companies, like Osprey, are there to support their equipment with repair facilities. There are gear raffles and other promotional activities to draw in the crowds.

There are many events, including a hiker parade where townspeople give thru-hikers 'showers' with hoses, water balloons and buckets as they pass. There is a hiker talent show, and a hiker prom. The thrift stores are swamped with thru-hikers seeking something festive to wear for the dance.

Roan Mountain Shelter, highest and coldest on trail

A number of shelters have special significance on the Appalachian Trail for one reason or another. Roan Mountain Shelter is the highest shelter, and the coldest shelter on the AT. It is an old ranger station, a small, fully enclosed structure. I didn't stay here, but I took the short side trail to it just to see it, as did many other hikers.

Picture at McAfee Knob

McAfee Knob is a ledge that projects out over the surrounding landscape. You can sit on the ledge and dangle your feet out over empty space. It is the single most photographed point on the trail, even more so than Springer or Katahdin.

Hike Naked Day

The summer solstice, the longest day of the year, is sometimes celebrated by thru-hikers by hiking in the buff. I did not take part, and I only saw a few hikers who did. They usually had a few strategic drapes of cloth somewhere to hide those parts of their anatomy that might most offend any parties of day hiking nuns or schoolchildren they might encounter.

Confessions at The Priest

The Priest Shelter sits on top of a difficult climb in Virginia, and is the best water source for many miles, so it is much visited. A tradition has developed where people write trail confessions in the register. This allows hikers to unburden themselves, and provides entertainment for anyone staying at the shelter. A lot of trail gossip is generated from the register. I stopped at the shelter for water, but it was very crowded and I was unaware of the significance of the register here. I moved on, and missed out on a key trail social event.

Jumping off the James River Bridge

The longest pedestrian bridge crosses the James River near Glasgow, Virginia. Despite prominently posted signs prohibiting the practice, it is a tradition to jump off the bridge into the river. I was unaware of the tradition until I was already further up the trail. As a solo hiker, I would not have hazarded a jump anyway as there would have been no one to help me if I encountered troubles. Just two years prior a hiker drowned just a few feet from the shore of a lake in Maine, his muscles cramping up uncontrollably in the cool water from the abuse of hiking all day.

Signing in and photo at the ATC Headquarters, Harpers Ferry

The Appalachian Trail Conservancy is the non-profit organization with oversight over the entire Appalachian Trail. They have a couple of other offices along the trail, but the big headquarters is located in Harpers Ferry, West Virginia. Harpers Ferry is also considered the spiritual halfway point of the trail. Thru-hikers log in at the ATC HQ, a picture is taken, and they are put in a log with their number for that year (I was number 1200) and contact information, if the hiker wants to provide it. Less than half, perhaps even as few as a quarter of the hikers who started at Springer Mountain and Katahdin remain on the trail at this point.

The Four State Challenge

Maryland and West Virginia have very small sections of the trail. It is 42 miles from the Virginia state line, across West Virginia and Maryland, into Pennsylvania. Some hikers will attempt to hike this in a single 24 hour period.

The Half Gallon Challenge in Pine Grove Furnace State Park, PA

In Pennsylvania, at one of many former half way points of the trail, there is a hostel, a cafe and grill, and the Appalachian Trail Museum. To celebrate the halfway point and the area's dairy heritage (and to sell ice cream) the grill offers the Half Gallon Challenge. The goal is to eat a half gallon of ice cream in less than an hour. A half gallon of ice cream is now a box and a pint. The prize is a little wooden ice cream spoon, the little paddle type, with the words 'Half Gallon Challenge' stamped on it with ink. My spoon is one of my most cherished possessions. I also had a hamburger afterwards.

Mooning the Mt. Washington Cog Railroad

There is a certain amount of resentment from thru-hikers who are slogging their way up the slopes of Mt. Washington in New Hampshire, the highest mountain in the Northeast, to being passed by tourists on an old cog railroad. In the past, thru-hikers would express this resentment by turning and dropping trousers, presenting a view of their posteriors for the tourists to enjoy.

Mt. Washington State Park finally decided to put an end to the practice by mounting cameras on the train to catch these evil hikers and present them with a ticket. The word is out, but there are still some brave, tradition bound thru-hikers saluting the cog railroad as it passes.

Picture at Katahdin (Summit photo)

You have to have that final photo on top of Katahdin, at the end if the Appalachian Trail (or the beginning, if you are a SoBo)

Postcards

When the hike is over a number of hikers make up postcards with photos from their journey on it. They send the postcards to family and friends, but also to trail angels, hostels and businesses that helped along the way. Many trail businesses have a bulletin board displaying the postcards they have received.

GLOSSARY

AMC (Appalachian Mountain Club): One of the oldest trail clubs, and one of the most influential. It predates the Appalachian Trail by over 50 years.

AQUA BLAZE: The Shenandoah River parallels the AT as it passes through Shenandoah National Park, and it is a common adventure for Thru-hikers to raft down from Waynesboro to Harpers Ferry, taking a break on their feet and missing a section of trail.

AT (Appalachian Trail): The 2189.2 mile (2015 mileage) continuous hiking trail traveling the length of the Appalachian Mountains, stretching from Springer Mountain in Georgia to Mount Katahdin in Maine.

AT PASSPORT: A passport that gets stamped at various places along the hike route as a memento of the trip. Collecting stamps becomes a bit of a scavenger hunt for those who purchase one.

ATC (Appalachian Trail Conservancy): The non-profit organization maintaining oversight of the Appalachian Trail.

ATKO: The Appalachian Trail Kick Off, a preparatory event for thru-hiking the AT held in Amicalola Falls State Park in Georgia every year at the beginning of hiking season. It is a seminar, a gear exhibition, and all things Appalachian Trail

AWOL GUIDE: David Miller's mile by mile guide to the trail, mapped by elevation profile and distance.

AYCE (All You Can Eat): A buffet restaurant. Hikers love AYCE buffets. AYCE establishments do not generally return that love to hikers. Besides eating them out of a profit, hikers sometimes eat first when they get to town, before cleaning up, bringing their unwashed trail funk in with them.

BALD: An open pasture or meadow on the top of a mountain. The term and terrain feature are particular to the southern Appalachians. The balds provide a unique ecological niche as well as spectacular views.

BASHER: A Bad Assed Section Hiker. A section hiker doing a long stretch of the Appalachian Trail. Also see LASHER.

BEAR BAG: A bag in which food and scented items are placed and hung from a branch to protect it from bears and other creatures getting into them during the night.

BLUE BLAZE: Trails marked with blue blazes (as opposed to the white blazes of the main Appalachian Trail) are side trails, bypasses, cut offs and short cuts that avoid some of the more difficult sections of trail

BLUE BLAZER: A person who habitually uses bypasses and shortcuts rather than facing every challenge of the trail is called a 'blue blazer'. Sometimes this practice is a response to physical limitations, or weather, but it can be attributed to laziness and used as a derogatory term.

BnB: A Bed and Breakfast, a lodging option providing a bedroom and a meal in a house for about the same price as a decent hotel. It is an expensive option compared to a hostel, and like a hostel you can never be quite sure what you are going to get.

BOUNCE BOX: A supply maildrop prepared on the trail and sent on ahead. If a hiker does not open the box they can continue to keep sending it forward through the postal system for free. Hikers who have things like medicines that are cheaper to keep in bulk, that they need a continual supply on hand but do not want to carry will often keep a bounce box going.

BRP (Blue Ridge Parkway): A two lane highway running up the spine of the Blue Ridge Mountains of Virginia. The Appalachian Trail parallels it for much of Virginia.

BSP (Baxter State Park): The final northern terminus of the trail in Maine; the centerpiece is Mount Katahdin.

BUBBLE: A group of people hiking in rough proximity to each other as they move up the trail. As the hike progresses hikers maintaining the same rate of progress will see each other often. Each bubble forms its own community and identity.

CAIRNS: Piles of rocks 3 to 8 feet high used to mark the trail on rocky ground where there are no trees to place blazes upon.

CCC (Civilian Conservation Corps): During the 1930s Great Depression, one of President Franklin Delano Roosevelt's back to work programs employing people and teaching them marketable work skills doing construction projects in National Forests and Parks.

COWBOY CAMP: Sleeping in the open without erecting a tent or having a fire. Just roll out the sleeping bag and look at the stars above. Romantic, but risky, since weather can change rapidly.

EYE BOMBER: A pesky sort of gnat that looks for moisture. They make suicidal dives into your eyes while you are walking.

FIRE TOWER: The United States Forest Service used to have watchers who sat up in little cabins mounted on top of steel framework towers on mountaintops, where they would scan the forest for the smoke of forest fires. Detecting fires is now mostly done by aircraft, but the old towers remain scattered throughout the National Forests.

FLIP-FLOP: An alternative to the standard NoBo or SoBo hike. Instead of starting from one of the endpoints a hiker can start out somewhere in the middle of the trail, hike either North or South to Springer Mountain or Mt. Katahdin, then go back to the start point and go the other way to complete the thru-hike. It avoids crowds and can work better with the seasons if you cannot start at one of the traditional times.

FOUR STATE CHALLENGE: From the northern border of Virginia it is 42 miles through West Virginia and Maryland to the Pennsylvania border. Hikers can attempt to hike the distance in a single 24 hour period in an unofficial personal endurance event called the Four State Challenge.

GAP: A common term in Southern Appalachia for a terrain feature consisting of a saddle or low spot between two hills or mountains.

GREAT SMOKIE MOUNTAINS NATIONAL PARK (GSMNP): A stretch of the Appalachian Mountains in western North Carolina and eastern Tennessee. It is the heart of the southern Appalachians, and has the highest mountain peaks east of the Mississippi River.

GO OFF-TRAIL Leave the trail, either for an extended period of time or permanently.

HIKER BOX: Hostels and other places where hikers stay often keep a box or two filled with of food and equipment left behind by hikers who ended up with more than they wanted to carry. Because many hikers set up mail drops far in advance of starting the trail their packages can be overloaded with more than they want to use. Many hikers also purchase boxes of items rather than individual sets, take what they need for their next leg, and leave the rest in the hiker box. The hiker boxes in the South are usually so full you can do a full resupply out of one if you are not too particular about what you eat.

HIKER HOBBLE: The cramped, limping gait brought on by stiffening muscles and small injuries at the end of a day of hiking, or immediately after a break before a hiker's legs have warmed back up.

HIKER HUNGER: Thru-hikers cannot carry enough food to sustain themselves for the 4000-5000 calories or more they burn each day. Thus, thru-hikers are always hungry, and eat massive quantities of food whenever they get the opportunity. Most hikers loose a lot of weight even with the binge eating.

HIKER MIDNIGHT: A reference to how early thru-hikers go to bed. When the sun goes down, thru-hikers go to sleep. Hiker midnight is about a half hour after sunset.

HYOH: (Hike Your Own Hike): a trail philosophy that recognizes and embraces the many different ways and reasons to hike the Appalachian Trail. Sometimes it is used as an admonishment, as in mind your own business.

LASHER: A Long Assed Section Hiker. Some hikers are knocking the AT off in long sections over a couple of years, or are just out on an extended hike and are going hundreds of miles. Many of them are experienced hikers with a broad background of experience, and are generally held in high regard by Thru-hikers.

LEAVE NO TRACE (LNT): A philosophy, and often a policy, wherein hikers endeavor to make the smallest possible impact on the wilderness, ideally as if man had never been there. "Take only pictures; leave only footsteps".

LEDGES: Long flat stones on a ridge, generally alongside a steep drop or on a summit, the exposed rock underlying a mountain.

MAYFLIES: Hikers who start in May, generally when college gets out of session. They must hike quickly as they have four and a half months or less to get to Katahdin before Baxter State Park closes for overnight camping.

MAIL DROP: A supply box filled with goodies mailed forward or from home to provide logistical support along the trail

MINI TRIPLE CROWN: Completing the Long Trail in Vermont, the Colorado Trail, and the John Muir Trail in California, each a segment of the 3 continental trails that make up the triple crown of long distance hiking (The AT, CDT, and PCT).

NEARO: A day with very little hiking, nearly a zero, where you only go a couple of miles down the trail. These are often days where a hiker runs into and out of town on a same day resupply, but a particularly fine spot on trail such as a waterfall or a view might inspire a short day of hiking, spending the rest of the day enjoying the location.

NoBo: North bounder, a thru-hiker starting at Springer heading to Maine.

NOC (The Nantahala Outdoor Center): A tourist destination along the Nantahala River in North Carolina for outdoor sports near the Smoky Mountains, with river rafting, kayaking, bike touring, mountain biking, and hiking all supported. There are restaurants, an outfitter, a resupply grocery shop, lodging, and a hiker hostel.

NP: Abbreviation, National Park

NOTCH: The low elevation separation between two mountains. Similar to the usage of 'gap' down South, except the character of the Northern Appalachian Mountains creates steeper cuts between the mountains.

PACK WEIGHT: The weight of your pack on your back. This can be fully loaded, wet (with water), dry (without water) or base (without food or water).

PATC (Potomac Appalachian Trail Club): One of 22 non-profit trail organizations that maintain the Appalachian Trail. PATC has a long stretch of trail reaching from the middle of Virginia up into Pennsylvania, and has a large and active membership.

PCT (Pacific Crest Trail): A trail similar to the AT on the west coast running from Mexico to Canada through the Sierra Nevada and Cascades of California, Oregon and Washington.

PINK BLAZING: Thru-hikers engaging in romance on the trail, or at least chasing it.

PRIVY: A trail outhouse, without running water.

PUDS: Pointless ups and downs. The trail often seems to take the most difficult route for no other reason than it is there. Sometimes there are geographic or engineering reasons, but sometimes it seems to be just plain orneriness. Each little section is built and maintained by another club or individual trying to put their own stamp or memorable bit on the section. Most thru-hikers wish they wouldn't indulge themselves.

PURIST: A thru-hiker determined to follow the trail past every single white blaze on the trail, avoiding any shortcuts.

RAMEN BOMB: A meal made by mixing ramen, instant mashed potatoes and meat or vegetables in a single pot, It makes a gelatinous but filling carbohydrate mass for dinner.

RIDGE RUNNER: A person hired by the USFS, or in some cases a hiking club, to hike and watch over the trail, seeing to the safety and welfare of hikers, cleaning up sites and informally watching for adherence to local and federal rules. They are not law enforcement personnel but carry radios to call in enforcement if needed.

ROCKSTACKING: Placing rocks on top of each other in aesthetically pleasing stacks. It is an art form that conforms to 'Leave No Trace' concepts, since the rocks are picked up from the ground and the stacks eventually fall and redistribute the rocks. There is a popular book on the subject.

SECTION HIKER: A hiker doing a section of the Appalachian Trail.

SHAKEDOWN: Going through a pack and assessing each piece of equipment, getting rid of excess items to reduce weight.

SLACKPACK: Hiking a section of the trail as a supported hiker, with just some basic needs for a day in your pack. You are slacking off, and also carrying a nearly empty, or 'slack' pack.

SNP (Shenandoah National Park): National Park in Northern Virginia. Much of the infrastructure was built by the Civilian Conservation Corps (CCC) during the Great Depression.

SoBo: South bounder, a thru-hiker starting in Maine and heading towards Springer Mountain in Georgia.

SOLO: A solitary hiker not associated with the trail families, groups and couples that form and hike together on the trail

SPRINGER: Springer Mountain, the start of the Appalachian Trail for North Bound hikers.

STEALTH CAMP: Making a low profile campsite, with the smallest footprint, to avoid damaging the environment and to avoid notice by passersby, sometimes because it is a questionable area to camp.

STILE: A small set of steps or a ladder over a livestock fence. They are common on the trail since hikers can't be trusted to close gates behind them.

SUPPORTED HIKE: Hiking sections of the trail with someone else providing logistical support. Usually it involves someone with a vehicle waiting at road crossings and other vantage points to provide either camping support or trips to town each night. It is hiking the trail without the need to carry all of the camping gear with you.

TARP TENT: A small lightweight tent that is erected on hiker poles. It is essentially just a waterproof cover. They provide a level of protection from the weather but since they are not fully enclosed, there is no protection from insects.

THRU-HIKER: A hiker attempting to hike the entire distance of the Appalachian Trail. They are going all the way through. This is normally completed in a single season.

TICK CHECK: Examining every inch of your body for ticks, paying special attention to the cracks, crevices and hot spots they prefer. Deer ticks are very small, and can easily be overlooked, especially on a dirty body. Ticks carry a number of diseases, including Lyme Disease.

TRAIL ANGEL: A provider of trail magic; a person who provides assistance to a needy hiker.

TRAIL DAYS: Various towns along the Appalachian Trail in the South celebrate the flood of hikers coming through with festivals called Trail Days. There are often gear representatives and people marketing other things to hikers present, and there is usually some kind of free food and camping involved. The largest of these events, the Trail Days, is a 4 day event in Damascus, Virginia.

TRAIL FAMILY: A group of hikers that form a lasting social bond on the trail, usually hiking and or camping together.

TRAIL LEGS: A level of fitness developed on the trail where every step is not a struggle, ideally a state where striding along the trail seems effortless.

TRAIL MAGIC: Assistance or comforts provided free along the trail. Trail magic takes many forms. Sometimes it is just serendipitous, like a ride into town on a rainy night, but it also takes the form of organized events supporting the hike.

TRAIL MAINTAINER: A person who works on building and repairing the trail. Most of the maintainers are part of trail organizations, and are volunteers. Many of them receive support from USFS.

TRAIL REGISTER: A book and a pen are kept in each shelter and many hostels along the Appalachian Trail. Hikers will provide information about trail conditions and write their thoughts and reflections down. By making entries a hiker also establishes a last known point if they disappear. Also called a trail log.

TRAIL TOWN: A town on or near the Appalachian Trail that supports backpacking and trail activities. Some receive an official designation by the ATC by meeting certain requirements.

TRIPLE CROWN: The triple crown of long distance thru-hiking in America consists of completing the three trails that span the United States from South to North; the Pacific Crest Trail (PCT), the Continental Divide Trail (CDT), and the Appalachian Trail. The AT is the shortest but also the most physically demanding of the trails. Each trail has its own particular challenges.

USFS (United States Forest Service): The primary federal organization on the Appalachian Trail. The USFS is separate from ATC, the National Park service, and the various state lands that create the land mosaic the AT crosses.

VIRGINIA BLUES: Virginia is the longest single state on the trail, over 500 miles long. Virginia is often where the novelty of backpacking and camp life can fade away into a tiresome repetitive blur, and a number of hikers get burned out on the trail experience and quit.

WAYSIDE: A roadside restaurant along the Blue Ridge Parkway in the Shenandoah National Park. Famous for their blackberry milkshakes.

WIDOWMAKER: A dead tree branch caught up high in a tree, a deadly gravity powered missile waiting for a gust of wind to release it.

WORK-FOR-STAY (WFS): Trading work for a space in a bunkroom and a meal at a hostel.

YELLOW BLAZE: To skip sections of trail by hitching rides on the road. To purists, people who make a habit of yellow blazing the difficult or boring sections are cheating.

YOGI: Begging for food or other services, like Yogi Bear; "Hey Boo Boo, I think I smell a Pic-a-nic"

ZERO DAY: A day without any hiking, usually a full rest day in town.

RESOURCES

In no particular order, take it as it comes.

The Appalachian Trail Conservancy. The non-profit agency dedicated to maintaining and preserving the Appalachian Trail. All things Appalachian Trail!
www.appalachiantrail.org/

REI: If there is an REI near you it can be an invaluable resource, both for equipment and for knowledge. My experience with the Albuquerque store is a little mixed, I would not rely solely on them, but they have the gear you need. By buying a membership (it is a co-operative) you can defray a little of the retail costs, and they have a scratch and dent garage sale every few months that can provide all kinds of bargains.
https://www.rei.com

How to set up a Bear Hang
PCT Method bear hang
https://www.backpacker.com/skills/how-to-hang-a-bear-bag-pct-style
Bear Hang YouTube
https://www.youtube.com/watch?v=aKPmwfHxRsc

Building an alcohol stove from a soda can
https://www.thesodacanstove.com/alcohol-stove/how-to-build.html

Making a Tyvek Ground Cloth, more advice from Backpacking Light
https://www.backpacker.com/skills/make-a-tyvek-groundcloth-for-your-tent

The A.T Guide by David 'AWOL' Miller, published by Jerelyn Press. What I and most thru-hikers refer to as the 'AWOL' guide, after the author. I preferred it to the Companion, and carried it on my thru-hike. I thought the layout was better and more understandable, but it was a personal preference. Available on Amazon and at: *www.theATguide.com*

DIXIE: A female thru-hiker who wrote a nice book about her experiences and a lot of Video Logs on different aspects of long distance backpacking. She is particularly informative for women on long distance trails.
Vlog: www.Homemadewanderlust.com

Her book: *Take a Thru-Hike: Dixie's How-To Guide for Hiking the Appalachian Trail* by Jessica 'Dixie' Mills is available on Amazon

Appalachian Trials: a Psychological and Emotional Guide to successfully thru-hiking the Appalachian Trail by Zach Davis, available on Amazon. The challenge of completing the Appalachian Trail is mental more than physical. Davis' book helps you understand what you are really getting into. The author maintains a website: www.theGoodBadger.com

The (annual) Appalachian Trail Thru-hikers Companion Produced by the Appalachian Long Distance Hikers Association and published by the Appalachian Trail Conservancy. The Companion is a yearly production that lays out the trail in an elevation profile for hikers, providing maps, resources, lists of resupply points, and other badly needed information. It has a downloadable version, so you can save the weight of the book on trail if you are carrying a phone or tablet.

Grizzle Gear: Both a series of gear reviews on You Tube and a Facebook long distance hikers group:
https://www.youtube.com/channel/UC6W68V4z7O5uxjEt9MXAHaA
https://www.facebook.com/groups/181564135627922

Trail Angel is a short video about Pony Tale Paul, professionally produced as a joint venture by REI and Outside magazine. It is a moving piece, and it also features the author and his trail family in Maine.
https://www.youtube.com/watch?v=-l1AZA5mWeo

Stumbling Thru, by A. Digger Stoltz, published by Follyworks Publishing LLC. is a two book novel about Thru-Hiking the Appalachian Trail. I read it before my hike, and again after. It is a very good representation of a thru-hike, and a good, entertaining read. Highly Recommended. Available on Amazon

GutHook is an online mapping service that is available as an application downloadable onto your portable electronic device or cell phone. It has pictures of the sites, recently taken. Its best feature is that users can upload photos and commentary on sites along the trail, giving follow-on users real time data on conditions at campsites, water sources, and other areas of interest. The downside is there are areas without wireless service along the trail, creating blind spots. GutHook is best downloaded before starting the trail, since the same unreliable wireless can make it difficult to install once you are underway.
www.guthookhikes.com/2013/03/guthooks-guide-to-appalachian-trail.html

As Far As the Eye Can See: Reflections of an Appalachian Trail Hiker by David Brill, published by the University of Tennessee Press. Written in the 1970s and now on its 4th edition, Brill's tales of his experiences helped kindle my own dreams when I read his book in the 1980s.

Walking with Spring, by Earl V. Shaffer, published by the first person to thru-hike the Appalachian Trail in a single sustained journey of less than a year. Trail founder Myron Avery also walked the entire distance while mapping out the initial route, but over a period of 10 years, making him the first Section Hiker and 2000 Miler.

A Walk in the Woods; Rediscovering America on the Appalachian Trail, by Bill Bryson, published by Anchor Books recounts Bryson's experiences on the AT. He did not hike nearly the entire trail, but his book is a humorous and informative account of his travels. It was made into a rather lackluster film release in 2015

A Sketch and a Prayer, by Michael 'Sketch' Wurman. Sketch is section hiking the Appalachian Trail, and is a good writer and an inspiring artist. His book is filled with experiences and advice, and is illustrated with photos and his drawings. Prints are also available. I have given copies of his book as a gift to people who are interested in a thru-hike. Available on Amazon.

Backpacking Light A website locating non-AMC backcountry camping sites in the White Mountains, and other valuable information on lightening your pack load: *https://backpackinglight.com/forums/topic/86526/*

Hiker Yearbook, produced by Odie Norman
hikeryearbook.com

63580992R00250

Made in the USA
Middletown, DE
07 February 2018